Directors' Duties in Canada

CCH
a Wolters Kluwer business

3rd Edition

Barry Reiter
Corporate Governance Group
Bennett Jones LLP

CCH Canadian Limited
300-90 Sheppard Avenue East
Toronto Ontario
M2N 6X1
1 800 268 4522
www.cch.ca

Published by CCH Canadian Limited

Edited by:

Kathleen Jones-Lepidas, B.A.

Library and Archives Canada Cataloguing in Publication

Reiter, Barry J., 1948–
Directors' duties in Canada/Barry Reiter. — 3rd ed.

Previous ed. published as Directors' duties in Canada: managing risk/
Margo Priest, Hartley R. Nathan.
Includes bibliographical references and index.
ISBN 1-55367-693-9

1. Directors of corporations — Legal status, laws, etc. — Canada. I. Title.

KE1402.R45 2006 346.71'06642 C2006-905659-5 KF1423.R45 2006

ISBN 1-55367-693-9

Typeset by CCH Canadian Limited.
Printed in the United States of America.

ABOUT THE AUTHOR

Barry Reiter

Barry Reiter is a senior partner in the Toronto office of Bennett Jones LLP. Barry's practice focuses on corporate governance, development, and finance.

Barry regularly advises boards, directors, directors' committees, and management on corporate governance issues. He is an experienced director and has chaired boards and served as a director on, or the chair of, a variety of board committees.

As Chair of the Bennett Jones LLP New Economy Practice, Barry has extensive experience in all aspects of technology law, including the protection of intellectual property rights, representation of start-up, growth and mature companies and private equity sources, international distribution arrangements, strategic alliances, partnerships and joint ventures, licensing, private and public financings, stock exchange listings, and mergers and acquisitions.

Formerly a law professor at the Faculty of Law, University of Toronto (1974–1982), Barry has published numerous books on a variety of legal topics (joint ventures, contracts, the legal process, and real estate) and many articles on corporate governance, boards of directors, and advisory boards. As a recognized expert in the field, Barry writes a monthly column on corporate governance in *Lexpert Magazine* and is a member of the ICD Blue Ribbon Commission on Governance of Executive Compensation. Barry is recognized in many peer-rating listings, including the 2006 LEXPERT® *Guide to the 100 Most Creative Lawyers in Canada.*

The Bennett Jones LLP Corporate Governance Group includes many partners and associates, several of whom have been contributors to this book, as noted in the Acknowledgements. The diversity of their interests and expertise reflects the breadth of the issues that are part of, and can affect, "corporate governance".

ACKNOWLEDGEMENTS

This book is the product of a real team effort. The individual chapters were written by the following members of the Corporate Governance Group at Bennett Jones LLP:

Chapter 1:	Barry Reiter
Chapter 2:	Art Peltomaa and Maria Sountas-Argiropoulos (articling student)
Chapter 3:	Bryan Haynes and David Spencer
Chapter 4:	Gary Solway and Khalil Haji (summer student)
Chapter 5:	John MacNeil, Shawn Lynn (articling student), Andrea MacDonald (articling student), Andrea Gede-Lange (articling student), and Khalil Haji (summer student)
Chapter 6:	Nick Fader and Steven Tanner (articling student)
Chapter 7:	Grant Haynen
Chapter 8:	Jeff Kerbel
Chapter 9:	Mary Beth Currie and Kristopher Hanc (articling student)
Chapter 10:	Deron Waldock
Chapter 11:	Heather Forester, Adrienne Moore (articling student), Aaron Hirschorn (summer student), Olivia Dixon (summer student), and David McKinnon (summer student)
Chapter 12:	Art Peltomaa, Duncan Card, Roch Beharry (articling student), William Vass, Leonard Griffiths, Hilary Stedwill (associate), Preet Gill (summer student), Adrienne Moore (articling student), Raj Sahni, and Lee Cassey (articling student)
Chapter 13:	Steve Sibold and J. Brindle (associate), John MacNeil, Rob Staley, Lee Cassey (articling student), and Nicholas Crosbie (articling student)

Chapter 14: Jim Patterson, Lincoln Caylor, Linda Visser (articling student), Adrienne Moore (articling student), and Nathaniel Brand (summer student)

Chapter 15: Marty Kay, Khalil Haji (summer student), and Lee Cassey (articling student)

Chapter 16: Rose M. Carter, Carole L. Hunt, Stephanie A. Wanke, Laura Inglis-Chubb (summer student), Lisa Millman (articling student), Lee Cassey (articling student), Nathaniel Brand (summer student), Khalil Haji (summer student), and Mike Kershaw (summer student)

Chapter 17: Barry Reiter and Lee Cassey (articling student)

Chapter 18: Barry Reiter, Lee Cassey (articling student), and Andrea Gede-Lange (articling student)

Two Bennett Jones LLP summer students, Melissa Robins and Melanie Baird, cheerfully and enthusiastically spent most of the summer of 2006 supporting the lead authors with research, editing, and supplemental writing. Two articling students, Adrienne Moore and Lee Cassey, also picked up this role and the role of indexing when Melissa and Melanie had to return to their final year of law school.

Heather Forester acted as editor of the book, attempting to ensure consistency in style, presentation, and references.

Debra Forman, Director of Professional Development at Bennett Jones LLP, played a hugely important role in assembling and organizing the large team and in managing administrative arrangements with CCH.

My assistant, Karen Harvey, was, as always, most helpful both in producing my material and in internal team administrative matters.

Hugh MacKinnon, National Managing Partner of Bennett Jones LLP, was immensely encouraging of this project, and both he and Jim Smeltzer, Managing Partner of the Calgary Office, assisted in identifying and supporting the team throughout.

I also acknowledge Margot Priest and Hartley R. Nathan, Q.C., co-authors of the second edition of this book. This third edition builds on the organizational and substantive foundations that they provided.

It was a pleasure to deal with Simon Bossick and his team at CCH.

To all of these people, I am most grateful. Thank you.

INTRODUCTION

Since the second edition of this book was published in 2002, there has been an enormous focus on corporate governance. The corporate failings and scandals that occurred in the United States and Canada produced a veritable landslide of views, writings, legislation, regulation, guidelines, measurement scorecards, and shareholder and media interest. The volume of this material has created great difficulty for those on the front lines. As a director or as someone who may be called upon to advise directors, it is difficult to keep up with so much new and relevant information. More importantly, it is becoming increasingly difficult to know and to advise upon what to do in particular situations.

This book attempts to respond to these challenges. It is a snapshot (as of the summer of 2006) of a great deal of the material that bears upon corporate governance today. In many cases, the actual material is presented in the book; in others, we offer specific references so that the material may be accessed conveniently. The book attempts to provide practical guidance about what to do in a variety of situations in which directors and their advisors may find themselves. The book includes actionable precedents with respect to many of the important current corporate governance topics.

The precedents and other actionable materials are drawn from products that we have created, or with which we have been involved. While we believe that these materials were useful and appropriate to the companies and boards that adopted them, they may not be appropriate in other circumstances. One of the themes of this book is that each board and each director must consider what is right for that board and that director in the context of particular and individual circumstances. Accordingly, none of the materials should be regarded as suitable for adoption without further consideration.

While the authors believe that what we say is legally correct and that we are offering sound advice, the material does not constitute legal opinions and it is not intended to be a comprehensive treatise. We have provided supporting references where we feel that they will be helpful to the reader, and we have included a bibliography that can take the reader to more detailed sources as desired.

In order to make this a practical and advisory book, we have attempted to make our material accessible in two ways. The book may be read cover to cover to provide an overview of currently relevant corporate governance information. We have also attempted to make each chapter relatively self-contained so that the reader can go to a specific chapter to obtain information relevant to a particular matter of immediate interest. The result is that some topics are addressed in more than one place since they bear on a variety of issues.

We hope that you will find the book useful.

Barry Reiter
Corporate Governance Group
Bennett Jones LLP
Toronto

September 2006

TABLE OF CONTENTS

CHAPTER 1

CORPORATE GOVERNANCE: BASIC PRINCIPLES AND CURRENT ENVIRONMENT

There has never been a more exciting time to be a director of a corporation. There has never been a more challenging time to be a director of a corporation. Directors operate in a new and very changed environment. Expectations are high, and directors' actions (and inaction) are subject to observation and comment from a wide variety of interested constituencies.

This book attempts to provide guidance to directors, and to those who advise them, about the expectations that exist and the requirements and best practices that will help meet such expectations.

In general, the phrases "corporate governance" and "corporate accountability" refer to the broad functions of those who oversee a corporation's affairs and the means by which they are held to account for their stewardship.[1]

"Corporate governance" refers to the overseeing and directing of a corporation, as distinguished from the day-to-day managing of one. It entails supervising and contributing to the executive functions of management.

Corporate governance obliges directors to:

- ensure the development and implementation of strategic direction for the corporation's survival and prosperity;
- select the CEO and, possibly, other principal executives, supervise the performance of these executives, and ensure adequate succession planning;
- evaluate risks and ensure that appropriate control mechanisms are in place;
- monitor the corporation's business results;
- ensure that the corporation has met appropriate standards of financial and ethical behaviour;
- be accountable to shareholders, employees, customers, suppliers, regulators, and the community in which the corporation functions;
- ensure that they have adequate information and support to enable them to discharge their responsibilities;
- monitor and ensure the satisfactory and appropriate reporting of business results; and
- discharge specific duties that are imposed on directors by legislators, regulators, stock exchanges, and observers of corporate affairs.

At its most basic level, the duty of a director is established under the governing legislation of the corporation and, in common law jurisdictions, in a very lengthy history of judicial decisions. The legislative regime of the *Canada Business Corporations Act* is typical.[2] Under s. 102(1) of the CBCA, "[s]ubject to any unanimous shareholder agreement, the directors shall manage, or supervise the management of, the business and affairs of a corporation." The directors function by enacting by-laws (which ultimately must be confirmed by shareholders) or by passing resolutions that are signed by all directors or enacted by a majority of the directors at meetings.

---

[1] See the Selected Bibliography, which contains a sample of some of the many articles, books, law firm publications, and regulatory and legislative materials produced in the past three years on the subject of corporate governance.

[2] *Canada Business Corporations Act*, R.S.C. 1985, c. C-44, as amended ("CBCA").

Each jurisdiction's business corporation legislation specifies the qualifications for directors. The legislation also specifies residency requirements for directors.[3] Directors may, subject to specific exceptions, delegate many of their activities to executives, a managing director who is a resident Canadian, or a committee of directors.[4]

Directors must disclose the nature and extent of any interest they may have in a material contract or material transaction, whether made or proposed, with the corporation if a director (1) is a party to the contract or transaction; (2) is a director, officer, or individual acting in a similar capacity of a party to the contract or transaction; or (3) has a material interest in a party to the contract or transaction.[5] In general, a director who is required to disclose a conflict may not vote on any resolution to approve the contract or transaction.[6]

Directors, in exercising their powers and discharging their duties, are required to (a) act honestly and in good faith with a view to the best interests of the corporation, and (b) exercise the care, diligence, and skill that a reasonably prudent person would exercise in comparable circumstances.[7]

Layered on top of the statutory obligations are the results of centuries of judicial decisions about the responsibilities of directors. Courts have expanded greatly on the obligations to act honestly and in good faith with a view to the best interests of the corporation and to exercise the care, diligence, and skill that a reasonably prudent person would exercise in comparable circumstances. Directors are fiduciaries who are subject to obligations to meet stringent standards of ethical and altruistic behaviour. Directors must follow the high standard that is set for a trustee with respect to dealing honestly, in good faith, and without conflict of interest. A great many cases have elaborated on the implications of these principles.

---

[3] For a more detailed discussion of director qualifications and residency requirements, see section II of Chapter 3, "Constituting the Board".

[4] CBCA, s. 121 and ss. 115(1) and (3); see also the Ontario *Business Corporations Act*, R.S.O. 1990, c. B.16 ("OBCA"), s. 133 and ss. 127(1), (2), and (3). But where directors delegate to a committee, a majority of the members of the committee must be resident Canadians; see also Alberta *Business Corporations Act*, R.S.A. 2000, c. B-9 ("ABCA"), s. 121 and ss. 115(1), (2) and (3). Where the directors delegate to a committee, 25 percent of the members of the committee must be resident Canadians.

[5] CBCA, s. 120(1).

[6] CBCA, s. 120(5) creates an exception to this rule where the contract or transaction is (a) connected mainly to a director's remuneration as a director; (b) for indemnity or insurance under CBCA, s. 124; or (c) with an affiliate. ABCA, s. 120(6) and OBCA, s. 132(5) create an additional exception where the contract or transaction is by way of security for money lent to or obligations undertaken by the director for the benefit of the corporation or an affiliate. The British Columbia *Business Corporations Act*, S.B.C. 2002, c. 57 ("BCBCA") contains no such exceptions.

[7] CBCA, s. 122(1).

The second element of a director's duty to the corporation is the prescribed duty of care. This duty obliges directors to spend the time and pay the attention that is appropriate to someone who is charged with such responsibilities.[8]

These legislative and common law principles have been in place for some time and remain largely unchanged. What has changed, however, is the environment of corporate governance and the response of a plethora of interested constituencies as a consequence of that change. Corporate governance has received more attention as the power and significance of corporations have increased over the past one hundred years. Interest in corporate governance jumped sharply following a number of high profile, and in some cases, spectacular corporate failures. Reports asking such things as "Where were the directors?" were produced as long as a dozen years ago.[9] But interest in corporate governance grew dramatically following the reporting of a number of colossal corporate failures whose names have now become synonymous with the view that there must have been massive dereliction of duty by the directors. In each of these cases, the state of health of the business appears to have been misrepresented to financial stakeholders, employees, and regulators. Although inept or criminal managers may have been the root cause, attention was also focused on the failure of the directors to identify and address the risks involved.

The response to this problem has been broad. In the United States, the most significant initiative has been the *Sarbanes-Oxley* legislation that imposes specific obligations on directors, prohibits certain behaviours, and requires regulators and stock exchanges to enact supplemental regulations.[10] These matters have direct relevance to Canadian corporations that offer securities (or whose shares trade on stock exchanges) in the United States, and to Canadian professionals who advise companies that file materials with the Securities and Exchange Commission (the "SEC").[11] They have also served as a model against which the responses of comparable Canadian regulators might be contemplated and judged.

---

[8] The matters addressed in this brief overview are dealt with in more detail in Chapter 2.

[9] Report of the Toronto Stock Exchange Committee on Corporate Governance in Canada. *Where Were the Directors? Guidelines for Improved Corporate Governance in Canada* (the "Dey Report") (December 1994).

[10] *Sarbanes-Oxley Act of 2002*, Pub. L. No. 107-204, 116 Stat. 745.

[11] *Ibid.* at s. 307. The SEC has the authority to issue rules in the public interest that set standards of professional conduct for lawyers "appearing and practicing before the Commission". This phrase is defined broadly by the SEC and includes transacting any business with the SEC, representing an issuer in an administrative proceeding or in connection with an SEC investigation, providing advice in respect of United States securities law or the SEC's rules or regulations regarding any document that will be filed with or submitted to the SEC, and advising an issuer as to whether information or writings are required to be filed or submitted to the SEC.

Accordingly, four years after the passage of the *Sarbanes-Oxley Act*, the corporate governance responsibilities of directors are affected not just by basic corporate legislation and fiduciary duty law, but also by the following factors.

I. Regulation

Regulators have focused on the qualifications of directors, the process and substance of what directors do, and the visibility of these matters to interested constituencies. Since many of the first corporate disasters involved a lack of financial integrity, the initial focus was on financial reports and audit committees.

The rules in place across most of Canada require that public companies have audit committees and that these committees be entirely made up of directors who are "independent" of management.[12]

While the question of who is "independent" is, in general, left to the discretion of the directors, in the case of audit committees, very specific rules define independence. (For instance, the rules deny the status of independence to a director who has been a former employee within the past three years, to a member of a professional firm whose firm has any dealings with the corporation, or to a director who received any compensation whatsoever for services other than as a director.)[13] Audit committee members must meet the qualification of "financial literacy", defined as "the ability to read and understand a set of financial statements that present a breadth and level of complexity of accounting issues that are generally comparable to the breadth and complexity of the issues that can reasonably be expected to be raised by the issuer's financial statements".[14] Audit committees must operate under a mandate that is made public by the company[15] and are required by the rule to deal with a number of specific matters, including the following: making recommendations to the board of directors regarding the selection and compensation of auditors; reviewing financial information before it is published; approving non-audit services to be performed by the auditors in respect of matters where these services are not prohibited; establishing procedures for the receipt, retention, and treatment of complaints received regarding accounting, internal accounting controls, or auditing

[12] Multilateral Instrument 52-110, *Audit Committees*, ss. 2.1(1) and 3.1(3) ("MI 52-110"). This Instrument has been adopted in all jurisdictions except British Columbia.

[13] *Ibid.* at ss. 1.4–1.5. See Chapter 6, "The Use of Committees", for further discussion on audit committees.

[14] *Ibid.* at s. 1.6.

[15] *Ibid.* at s. 5.1, which requires every issuer to include Form 52-110F1 in its Annual Information Form. Form 52-110F1 requires the inclusion of the text of the audit committee's mandate.

matters; establishing procedures for the confidential, anonymous submission by employees of concerns regarding questionable accounting or auditing matters (so-called "whistleblower procedures"); and approving the company's policies regarding the hiring of present and former members of the auditor.[16] What all of this regulation represents is a statement that audit committee members cannot be trusted to develop and meet a satisfactory standard of care on their own, and therefore, their duties should be specified by regulators.

The current focus of regulatory direction is on compensation matters. Compensation issues have been identified in current materials and in speeches published by securities regulators in the United States and Canada. The first step actually occurred some time ago with the requirements for individualized disclosure of the compensation of the most highly paid executives and for transparency (in the form of a detailed report by the board committee charged with the management of executive compensation matters, which is, typically, the human resources or compensation committee).[17] Regulators on both sides of the border have been increasing the pressure on such committees to provide more detailed, comprehensive, accessible, and entirely accurate disclosure of executive compensation and of the principles and mechanics used to determine that compensation.

Regulators have strongly encouraged the existence of mandates specifying the responsibilities of the board (rather than those of management), of committees, and of those in certain positions (such as the chair, lead director, or CEO).[18] Typically, where mandates exist, they must be made public.[19] The most significant step has been the promulgation of National Policy 58-201, which is discussed in detail below. All of the Canadian Securities Administrators ("CSA") have agreed upon a set of duties, qualifications, processes, and substantive matters that they believe are appropriate for the operation of effective boards. Where the obligations are not mandatory (as they are, for instance, with respect to audit committees), the CSA have encouraged compliance with the guidelines and disclosure of the manner in which each particular concern is being addressed. In a far less than subtle way, public companies are strongly encouraged, by the trans-

---

[16] *Ibid.* at s. 2.3.

[17] See, for example, the Ontario *Securities Act*, R.S.O. 1990, c. S.5, Form 40, *Statement of Executive Compensation* ("OSA"). This form was revoked by O. Reg. 56/04, s. 14(4), effective June 1, 2004. The disclosure of executive compensation is now required by National Instrument 51-102, *Continuous Disclosure Obligations*, Form 51-102F6 ("NI 51-102").

[18] National Policy 58-201, *Corporate Governance Guidelines*, ss. 3.4-3.5 ("NP 58-201").

[19] National Instrument 58-101, *Disclosure of Corporate Governance Practices*, Form 58-101F1 ("NI 58-101").

parency of their reporting, to be able to say that they have addressed a particular concern in a satisfactory manner.

Chapter 6, "The Use of Committees", discusses board committees in more detail and provides sample committee mandates.

II. Stock Exchanges

Under the *Sarbanes-Oxley* legislation in the United States, stock exchanges were assigned a major role in developing and implementing regulations.[20] While this situation has not been the case in Canada, the Toronto Stock Exchange ("TSX") has had a lengthy history of interest in corporate governance, dating back at least to the Dey Report in 1994.[21] Its recent interest was expressed through the promulgation of disclosure guidelines against which listed companies were required to report. These guidelines have now been surpassed by NP 58-201, although many companies continue, on at least a transitional basis, to also provide disclosure against the TSX guidelines.

III. Consequences

The legal environment provides for severe and direct consequences to directors who are derelict in their duties. Chapter 11 includes a catalogue of legislation and regulations that attach personal liability to directors. In general, the only escape from the various liabilities is on the basis of a "due diligence defence", meaning proof (with the burden being on the director) that the director took the appropriate steps to ensure that the particular requirement was complied with. Civil, criminal, or regulatory penalties against the director personally are used as indirect means of ensuring compliance by management, who typically have responsibility for the particular matter in the first instance.

This approach was given a significant boost with the enactment into law (on December 9, 2002) in Ontario of Bill 198, which added ss. 138.1–138.14 to the OSA.[22] This legislation provides for director responsibility to those who buy or sell securities on the secondary market (for instance, through trading on a stock exchange) during a period when there is a "disclosure violation". A disclosure violation occurs when a company has failed to disclose material information when it should have or when it has disclosed

[20] *Supra* note 10, s. 3.

[21] The Dey Report, *supra* note 9.

[22] See OSA, Part XXIII.1, *Civil Liability for Secondary Market Disclosure*, in force as of December 31, 2005.

erroneous information.[23] Directors have a due diligence defence. Boards are currently working with their legal advisors to understand what due diligence means in the various contexts in which disclosure violation issues can arise. Bill 198 makes class actions far more likely by eliminating the need to prove reliance on inaccurate disclosure by a person who traded during the relevant period and by establishing the damages of each person who traded during that period on a formulaic basis (so that anyone buying or selling securities during that period will have damages that are assessed on a comparable basis). Legislation similar to Ontario's Bill 198 has been enacted in Alberta and British Columbia and will come into force on proclamation.[24]

The regulatory initiatives described above (for instance, the specified skills required of audit committee members and the duties that they must undertake) have had an additional consequence. For centuries, the view adopted with respect to determining a director's duty of care was on an objective standard, a comparison to what was to be expected of a hypothetical director, without reference to the director's particular skills or background. A variety of more recent cases in litigation and in regulatory proceedings have suggested that the standard now includes a subjective element[25] so that, for instance, an audit committee member might be held to a higher standard than another director with respect to a financial issue, a highly experienced financial expert on an audit committee might be held to a higher standard than another member of the audit committee, a lawyer serving on a board might be held to a higher standard than a non-lawyer with respect to corporate governance matters, and the like.[26] There is also a widespread view that the bar has been raised for directors generally. While at some time in the past it might have been regarded as acceptable to review material briefly before a board meeting and then to politely attend a management presentation that constituted the meeting, all of those involved in the regulation of corporate governance have made it clear that diligent effort and a significant commitment of time are now required and expected.

---

[23] See a more detailed discussion of this matter in Chapter 7.

[24] In Alberta, Bill 25, the *Securities Amendment Act, 2006*, 2d Sess., 26th Leg., Alberta, 2006, s. 52, creates civil liability for secondary market disclosure under Part 17.01 of the Alberta *Securities Act*. In British Columbia, Bill 38, the *Securities Act*, 5th Sess., 37th Leg., British Columbia, 2004, provides for a new *Securities Act* that includes civil liability for secondary market disclosure.

[25] For discussion, see Barry J. Reiter, "Risky Business", *Lexpert* (October 2005). See also *Peoples Department Stores Inc. (Trustee of) v. Wise*, [2004] 3 S.C.R. 461 at paras. 63-64; *YBM Magnex International Inc., Re* (2003), 26 O.S.C.B. 5285; and Vern Krishna, "Liability of Professionals in Business Decisions" (2004) 23 *The Lawyers Weekly* 41.

[26] In *YBM Magnex International Inc., Re* (2003), 26 O.S.C.B. 5285, the Ontario Securities Commission considered the skill set and background of each individual director in determining culpability. See also OSA, s. 138.4(7)(*b*), which explains that in determining director liability, the court must consider all relevant circumstances, including the knowledge, experience, and function of a director.

These higher standards are backed by the transparency requirements described previously and by the existence of a significant number of constituencies paying attention to governance issues. Institutional investors have promulgated their own codes of good governance or have banded together as groups to do so.[27] They observe corporate governance behaviours and rank companies against the standards they have set. Some of the organizations have voting guidelines that require them to withhold votes on matters that do not meet their guidelines.[28] Some organizations are active in speaking to influencers of corporate governance behaviours with a view to encouraging compliance with guidelines; some go even further by introducing and supporting shareholder proposals that are introduced and required to be debated and voted upon at annual shareholder meetings.[29] Corporations sometimes require the votes of these powerful influencers and will comply with their guidelines in aid of (for instance) passing a particular compensation regimen or obtaining approval for an additional allocation of stock options.

Beyond this, media interest in corporate governance is now intense. *The Globe and Mail's Report on Business* conducts an annual survey of corporate governance practices and ranks companies on a points system against its own questions and standards.[30] While many take issue with the *Globe's* standards and weightings, there is no doubt that corporations and directors pay attention to the rankings and are pleased with, or concerned and embarrassed by, the performances of their companies. Transparency in corporate governance reporting has facilitated these sorts of surveys and rankings, since information in regards to compensation, director shareholdings, director meeting attendance records, the number of meetings held, the basis of compensation decisions, and other such matters are now public information and readily accessible. The views of the media, as expressed in surveys of this sort, and those of institutional shareholders, as expressed in guidelines and public statements, are significant factors influencing corporate governance behaviours.

---

[27] See Canadian Coalition for Good Governance. *Corporate Governance Guidelines for Building High Performance Boards* (November 2005), online at: www.ccgg.ca.

[28] Ontario Municipal Employees Retirement System ("OMERS"). *Proxy Voting Guidelines* (April 2005), online at: www.omers.com. For an example, see the section on "Independence of Board of Directors".

[29] Teachers' Pension Plan. *Good Governance Is Good Business: Corporate Governance Polices and Proxy Voting Guidelines* (2006). See, for example, Guideline 1.1, where the Teachers' Pension Plan encourages companies to permit shareholders to vote for or against each individual board nominee, instead of for an entire slate of board nominees. Teachers' Pension Plan has been proactive in contacting companies (by a senior Teachers' Pension Plan official to a senior corporate executive) and encouraging them to follow this Guideline.

[30] *Corporate Governance Rankings, 2005*, published by the *Globe and Mail's Report on Business*, is available online at http://www.theglobeandmail.com/servlet/Page/document/special/robmagazine/boardgames/2005/2005-sub2.

So, what are the practical implications of saying that standards and expectations of directors are now at a higher level? This question focuses attention on a series of issues that arise about what directors should do and how they can do their jobs.

IV. Management and the Board

While management, through the CEO, executive team, and others, is responsible for managing the corporation, the board's role (except in a time of crisis) is limited to oversight and supervision. Difficulties arise when boards and management teams are unable to establish clarity about what fits into each of these essential elements of corporate life. Unless there is an agreement on what is and is not management business or board business, board time may be wasted on minor administrative trivia and important decisions may be made by management without the board's knowledge or approval. Matters of this sort are best resolved, in the first instance, through the existence of a board of directors' mandate and by delegating authority to management. Virtually every corporate governance initiative of the past few years has either required a mandate of this sort or strongly recommended one.[31]

Boards should not adopt an "off the shelf" mandate. While it is certainly useful to consider what other companies have done, it is important for boards and management teams to work together to determine what is right for their corporation. The exercise of creating a mandate suited to a particular company is valuable in building the relationship between the board and the management and in enhancing the relationships between board members and among them.

The types of issues that should be addressed in a board mandate are:

- the corporation's strategic business goals and objectives and how they are to be achieved;
- the corporation's responsibility for ensuring the integrity of the CEO and other executive officers;
- the corporation's policy on communication;
- the corporation's means of receiving feedback from stakeholders;
- the corporation's policies and processes for the appointment, training, evaluation, and succession of management;

[31] NI 58-101, *Disclosure of Corporate Governance Practices*, Form 58-101F1; NP 58-201, *Corporate Governance Guidelines*, Part 3.

- the corporation's strategic and operational policies within which management will operate;
- the corporation's annual targets against which corporate and executive performance will be measured;
- the corporation's approach to appointing directors to the board committees;
- the corporation's executive compensation policies;
- the corporation's approach to identifying and monitoring the risks of the business in which the corporation is engaged; and
- the corporation's approach to corporate governance.

A sample board mandate is found in Appendix I at the end of this Chapter. A sample Delegation of Authority, in partial implementation of a board mandate, can be found in Appendix II at the end of this Chapter.

Board mandates should be reviewed regularly. The circumstances of the corporation, the governance environment, and the composition of the board and the executive team change so that minor refinements or even significant revisions in the relationship between the board and management may be appropriate. It is typical for board mandates to be reviewed at least once a year. The usual process is that the review is initiated by the corporate governance committee, working with the general counsel or secretary in consultation with the CEO and other appropriate board members, before being approved by the corporate governance committee for recommendation to and approval by the board.

V. Board, Committees, and Individual Directors

Once a mandate has indicated what the board believes its responsibilities encompass, the board must get on with doing the job.[32] While much of what boards do occurs at meetings of the entire board, focused and detailed work is often undertaken by board committees. While audit committees are required, and some of their duties are specified with respect to public companies, boards usually create compensation committees (sometimes called human resources committees) and corporate governance committees. Depending on the size and nature of the responsibilities of the business and the board, other committees, such as environmental committees, risk committees, finance committees, executive committees, or other commit-

[32] This is particularly the case because any mandate will be viewed as the "bar" that has been set by a board and committee, and it specifies the minimum requirements of the job.

tees may be created to ensure that important matters are considered on an ongoing and timely basis. Such matters are considered by a group that is smaller than the entire board and is usually made up of board members who have a distinctive expertise and a particular interest in the committee's business.

It is important that boards and committees come to a clear understanding about which responsibilities are those of the committee (many matters could be assigned to more than one committee) and which are those of the entire board. In the past, the division of authority may have been decided by a loose agreement, but today, such a division is usually expressed and achieved through the adoption of committee mandates. Such mandates are required for audit committees and strongly recommended for other committees.[33] The use of committees and matters related to their mandates are addressed in detail in Chapter 6.

At a more basic level, individual directors must determine for themselves the nature of their role and responsibilities. Within the broad rubric of their role in overseeing and directing a corporation, directors must ascertain for themselves which matters, of a great many possibilities, they must pay careful attention to, they can defer to the careful work of others (such as a committee or a director who is an expert in a certain area), or they should provide personal leadership on.

Boards are collective and dynamic organizations. In general, directors must work well together, and they must be respectful of each other if their business is to get done. It is not the role of a board member to take an adversarial position at all times in order to challenge or assess the competence or good faith of other board members or management. On the other hand, a director should be expected, by both the board and by regulators and others involved in corporate governance, to become more actively involved in, and to take a leadership role in, situations requiring that director's particular expertise, experience, or interests.[34] During the recruitment process, directors should begin the task of understanding their role within a board by reading available information about the corporation and its current board, by speaking with the CEO and other corporate executives, and by learning about current directors and speaking with them. An individual director's roles and responsibilities vary with a particular board and with the circumstances and dynamics of that board over time. There is no substitute for experience when understanding what a director's responsibili-

---

[33] MI 52-110, s. 2.3. Note also that NP 58-201 requires both the nominating and the compensation committees to create a written charter (see Part 3).

[34] Barry J. Reiter, "When Directors Should Get Worried", *Corporate Governance Review* (August/September 2004).

ties may be in any particular case. Directors can rely on their own advice or they should feel free to seek advice from fellow board members or from other advisors.

VI. Leadership

An examination of any board mandate reveals that the board has its own business that is distinct and separate from that of management. Corporate governance reformers of the past decade have recognized an inherent conflict in combining these roles, since the role of the chair is ultimately to lead the supervision of the CEO. Accordingly, the separation of these roles has been consistently recommended,[35] and the implementation of these changes has occurred to a very large extent in Canada (but at a slower pace in the United States).[36] The most relevant current reform initiative strongly supports the separation of these roles and requires that the leader of the board's business, the lead director, be in place if the roles of the chair and the CEO are otherwise combined.[37] The CSA guidelines also recommend clarity in understanding the nature of the board leader's role, and therefore, the development of a position description for that leader. Examples of position descriptions for the chair of the board and for the lead director are found in Appendices III and IV, respectively, at the end of this Chapter.

There is much to be said beyond the words used in these position descriptions. Board leadership is an art in the field of interpersonal relations. The chair or lead director must be effective in being tactful, forceful, deferential, insistent, inclusive, and determined, as required by the circumstances, while remaining respectful of fellow directors and seeking to build and maintain a consensus and alignment between, and among, directors and management.

VII. Director Recruitment

Historically, directors were proposed by management, frequently from a small network of close business associates and friends of the CEO. Requirements for distinctive skill sets (for example, financial acumen, legal knowl-

[35] The Dey Report, *supra* note 9; Report of the Toronto Stock Exchange, Report on Corporate Governance, *Five Years to the Dey*, (1999); Final Report of the Joint Committee on Corporate Governance. *Beyond Compliance: Building a Governance Culture* (the "Saucier Report") (November 2001); NP 58-201, *Corporate Governance Guidelines*.

[36] See Spencer Stuart. *The 2005 Canadian Board Index* (January 2006), available online at: www.spenserstuart.com. Spencer Stuart's analysis of the 100 largest publicly held Canadian companies revealed that the boards of 80 percent of these companies split the roles of chair and CEO. In the U.S., however, such a split is only made by 31 percent of comparable boards.

[37] NP 58-201, *Corporate Governance Guidelines*, s. 3.2.

edge of corporate governance, human resources, and compensation) or simply for more independent directors have led searches further afield. This process has been accelerated by the recognition that the board's business is its own, and that an effective board must be comprised of compatible directors who will be respectful of, and work well with, each other and management, while bringing a suitable range of skills and experience to ensure that the various jobs required at the board and committee levels are performed well.

The process of building a board should be a continuous one, one in which the skill sets and contributions of existing directors are assessed on a regular basis against those of others and against the evolving needs of the corporation. While the invitation to become a director was once thought to be a great privilege, and prospective directors usually accepted, without hesitation, offers to join boards, most individuals now think carefully about such an offer and assess it against their personal interests, the considerable time required, the nature of the responsibility involved, and their view of what it will be like to work with the other directors and the current management team. Accordingly, the best boards are constantly in board-building mode, preparing lists of skill sets that might be useful to the board in the future, and considering and meeting on a preliminary basis with individuals who might possess those skill sets. Decisions are made carefully and incrementally, rather than being undertaken on a wholesale basis, only under the pressure of a massive change in board composition induced by a crisis or a fundamental disagreement.[38] Boards now work hard at expanding the range of networks from which future directors might be drawn, and it is now common for boards to use professional executive recruitment services to aid the process.

VIII. Making Directors Effective

It is not easy to be a director. A good director must learn enough about the business to be able to offer his or her views in a supervisory capacity to those who are expert in managing the corporation on a day-to-day basis. Directors must also know enough about their board and its processes, as well as enough about governance generally, to be able to make an effective contribution as a board member and to comply with applicable policies and rules. The process of becoming an effective director begins before the director is recruited, with the director's due diligence in considering a board position. In a good board, this process continues with a director orientation

[38] Barry J. Reiter, "Building a Great Board of Directors — a Committed and Sustained Process", *Corporate Governance Journal* (2003).

program that is designed to move the director as far up the learning curve as quickly as possible. Such an orientation might include meetings with the CEO and with various members of operating management who can describe elements of the business, tours of the facilities, meetings with other directors, meetings with the general counsel and corporate secretary, one-on-one meetings with the chairman or lead director, and supplying the director with the appropriate materials presented in an organized form.

When supplying directors with materials, it is often helpful, both to a new recruit and to existing directors, to create and maintain an up-to-date "Directors' Binder" that is a comprehensive, current repository of relevant legal and constitutional material relating to the company. The table of contents of a typical board of Directors' Binder is reproduced in Appendix V at the end of this Chapter.

Directors require considerable ongoing support.[39] While they should be interested in the company's affairs at all times, they should also be intensely focused on board or committee meetings and should not be engaged in the corporation's business on a day-to-day basis.[40] As members of a collectivity, they are also not, generally, responsible for the leadership of the various tasks that must be undertaken. While board or committee chairs have a greater leadership role, they require professional support and ongoing attention. Such help is usually supplied through the management liaison to the board, usually the corporate secretary and/or the general counsel who have responsibility for implementing the board's legal obligations. In practice, significant reliance is placed on these individuals to organize the business of the board and its committees to establish an annual agenda that will permit matters to be addressed in a timely way and to recommend to appropriate members of the board initiatives that may be required by new legislation, best practices, or the evolving corporate governance environment. These individuals, who are employees of the corporation, have line responsibilities and report directly or indirectly to the CEO. They often find themselves in a difficult position because they are given competing responsibilities to management and the board, and often, to professional regulators, accountants or lawyers, and securities regulators, who may

[39] The costs of a public company, in particular, are substantial. Directors' compensation (see below) and support costs factor into the overall costs, and they have led to a rash of privatizations of smaller public companies, for which the costs do not justify the benefits of continuing to be public.

[40] There is often a two-way benefit to involving directors on an informal, and more frequent basis. Directors have their reputations on the line for (typically) little compensation. They are therefore interested in the affairs of the company (why they serve), knowledgeable (by nature of their formal responsibilities), and (typically) expert in some specific aspect of the company's or board's operations (why they were recruited). They are, therefore, often excellent sounding boards for management and help to keep the directors up to date by testing their thoughts on them.

see them as gatekeepers responsible for the overall administration of securities regulation.[41]

The board process needs to continually improve. Directors need to focus on how they can do their collective job better and on the nature of the contribution of particular directors. The existence of board and director evaluation processes is rated highly by governance observers, and it is recommended strongly by regulators. A well-run process can allow the board to identify which areas it wants to spend more of its time on (typically, strategy) and which areas it may be able to spend less time on. (For instance, it could reduce time spent on administrative matters through the use of well-constructed materials that are delivered on time, a consent agenda, or pre-framed resolutions.)[42] The process may also identify constructive counselling that should be provided to particular directors or to directors in respect of whom succession is warranted. These are delicate matters, but the legal and interpersonal issues involved can be addressed by a careful and committed board.[43]

IX. Director Compensation

Traditionally, directors were paid reasonably nominal compensation. Such compensation coincided with the apparent view that being a director was mostly an honourary position that required formal attendance at meetings four times a year and limited practical responsibility or liability. This view has changed dramatically over time with the fall-out from the corporate scandals discussed above.

As a consequence, compensation levels for directors have been rising. The issue now is to strike a correct balance on a number of points. First, directors must be compensated adequately for the time and effort they are expected to dedicate to their jobs and for the very significant liability risks that they assume. Directors do not expect to be paid at a rate similar to that charged for their services as executives, but most of them now expect meaningful compensation for meaningful input and exposure. However, directors and companies are aware of the need to keep remuneration in line so that directors retain their independence (in the sense of not becoming unduly dependent on their directors' compensation).

---

[41] Barry J. Reiter, "Counsel in the Crosshairs: Creativity in the Boardroom", *The 2006 Lexpert Guide* (April 2006).

[42] See Chapter 6, "The Use of Committees", for a fuller discussion of director evaluation processes.

[43] Jim Turner and Barry J. Reiter, "Board Evaluations: Establishing an Effective Process", *Lexpert* (March 2006).

Secondly, boards and shareholders have attempted to compensate directors so that the interests of the directors are aligned with those of the shareholders. Such compensation was initially attempted through the granting to directors of stock options, which were believed to be a (cash) costless incentive for directors to improve shareholder value. Lately, some individuals have been questioning the wisdom of using stock options for this purpose. In general, stock options must now be expensed when granted as part of employment (including the employment of directors) remuneration. Of course, stock options also have an upside. Some observers believe that options create incentives for short-term, stock-enhancing behaviours, rather than a long-term view of what is ultimately in the best interests of shareholders. Accordingly, there has been some experimentation with a variety of long-term, director incentive arrangements, including the direct granting of shares and variations on that theme that either produce perceived better tax results or that tie the value of these incentives more to corporate performance, longer-term tenure, or the maintenance of stock positions by directors.[44]

Traditionally, directors' compensation consisted of an annual cash retainer, meeting fees, and some type of long-term incentive. In cases where this pattern is still maintained, all elements of the compensation package have increased significantly over the past few years. A number of studies track director compensation, and they can be used, along with executive compensation consultants, if required, to establish suitable compensation levels for particular boards. More recently, it is becoming an increasingly common practice to eliminate the meeting fee element of compensation. The theory behind this practice is that directors contribute at board and committee meetings but are also available to management between meetings and contribute in other important ways; therefore, they should be paid a single fee for their roles. Companies that adopt this compensation model tend to pay additional fees for committee service (although participation as a member of one committee may be considered to be part of the base retainer), and an additional retainer to the chairs of each of the standing committees. Payment for chairs tends to be graded, with a non-executive chair or lead director receiving the greatest amount, the chair of the audit committee receiving a substantial premium over committee members, and the chairs of corporate governance and human resources/compensation committees receiving lower amounts. Such a pay structure reflects the expected time commitment and responsibility involved.

---

[44] Examples include deferred share units that produce tax benefits but require equity to be held through a director's entire tenure; restricted stock units that may "vest" on the basis of corporate performance, either in absolute terms or against a peer group; requirements to own stock in some multiple (typically three to five times) of the annual base director's retainer; and direct cash payments that are tied to corporate performance (as defined in various ways).

An express provision of the CBCA permits directors to vote on their own remuneration in their capacity as directors, despite the apparent conflict of interest.[45] While the compensation of directors is usually a matter for the corporate governance or human resources/compensation committee in the first instance and ultimately, for the board, management tends to provide significant input into the process.

X. Self-Protection

Service on a board carries a significant risk. Directors' service carries risks of personal and collective criminal, regulatory, and civil liability, and a reputational risk (in the context of directors who, for whatever reason, are perceived to have failed in their duties). Chapter 18, in particular, deals at length with the various means by which directors can manage these risks. However, it bears noting here that part of a director's duty is to manage personal risk and the risk to the other directors, officers, and the corporation. While management, the general counsel or the corporate secretary, the corporate governance committee, the audit committee, or the human resources/compensation committee might take charge of certain elements of risk management, it is important that a director address his or her own mind to this issue.

A most significant matter for public companies is NP 58-201, which was approved by the CSA on April 15, 2005 and became effective on June 30, 2005. The policy, which is reproduced in Appendix VI at the end of this Chapter, reflects the considered view of securities regulators in the provinces of Alberta, British Columbia, and Ontario. In general, it is in keeping with the spirit and substance of corporate governance reform thinking over the past decade. This policy, combined with Form 58-101F1, which is reproduced as Appendix VII at the end of this Chapter, deals with corporate governance disclosure requirements, in effect, compliance with the best practices guidelines, or an explanation for how each matter recommended by the guideline is otherwise being addressed. These provisions, taken together, reflect the approach that has been taken generally in Canada to date, which is to rely on education and disclosure rather than on expressly required practices and procedures (other than those related to audit committees).

As will be apparent, the general obligations to manage or supervise the management of the business and affairs of the corporation, to act honestly and in good faith with a view to the best interests of the corporation, and to exercise the care, diligence, and skill that a reasonably prudent person

[45] CBCA, s. 120(5)(*a*).

would exercise in comparable circumstances, become complex when they are executed. The remainder of this book will attempt to address those complexities.

APPENDIX I

Board Mandate[1]

The directors' primary responsibility is to act in good faith and to exercise their business judgment in what they reasonably believe to be the best interests of the Corporation. In fulfilling its responsibilities, the Board is, among other matters, responsible for the following:

- Appointing the CEO and other corporate officers; On an ongoing basis, satisfying itself as to the integrity of the CEO and other executive officers and that the CEO and the other senior management create a culture of integrity throughout the Corporation;
- Monitoring and evaluating the performance of the CEO and the other senior management against the approved corporate goals and objectives;
- Succession planning (including the training of senior management);
- Adopting a strategic planning process;
- Approving an annual strategic plan which takes into account, among other things, the opportunities and risks of the business;
- Approving, on an annual basis, the corporate goals and objectives;
- Satisfying itself that the Corporation is pursuing a sound strategic direction in accordance with the approved corporate goals and objectives;
- Review with management, the Corporation's financial plans;

[1] Used by permission of Alliance Atlantis Communications Inc. and its general counsel, Andrea Wood, who was primarily responsible for management of the process by which it was developed.

- Reviewing operating and financial performance results relative to established corporate goals and objectives;
- Ensuring that it understands the principal risks of the Corporation's business, and that appropriate systems to manage these risks are implemented;
- Ensuring that the materials and information provided by the Corporation to the Board and its committees are sufficient in their scope and content and in their timing to allow the Board and its committees to satisfy their duties and obligations;
- Reviewing and approving the Corporation's annual and interim financial statements and related management's discussion and analysis, annual information form, annual report and management proxy circular;
- Approving material acquisitions and divestitures;
- Overseeing the integrity of the Corporation's internal control and management information systems;
- Approving any securities issuances and repurchases by the Corporation;
- Declaring dividends;
- Approving the nomination of directors;
- Approving the charters of the Board committees and approving the appointment of directors to Board committees and the appointment of the Chairs of those committees;
- Adopting a communications policy for the Corporation (including ensuring the timeliness and integrity of communications to shareholders and establishing suitable mechanisms to receive shareholder views); and
- Developing the Corporation's approach to corporate governance, including developing a set of corporate governance principles and guidelines that are specifically applicable to the Corporation, or delegating these issues to a committee composed of a majority of independent directors and the balance being non-management directors.

APPENDIX II

Delegation of Authority[1]

The purpose of this document is to articulate the delegation of decision making and operating authority within 724 Solutions Inc. between the Board of Directors and management.

Matters Requiring the Approval of The Board of Directors and/or Duly Authorized Committees of The Board of Directors:

1. Governance:

(a) the setting of strategic corporate direction, the establishment of corporate performance objectives;

(b) the approval of operational policies regarding the conduct of the business, including, but not limited to: acquisitions, research and development, sales and marketing, finance and investment, risk management, human resources, codes of conduct for employees, customer relationships, relationships with significant shareholders, and management and reporting information;

(c) any decision that will result in a material deviation from Board approved strategic, business or operational plans or policies;

(d) the establishment of effective procedures for monitoring corporate performance;

[1] Used by permission of 724 Solutions Inc. and Ian Giffen, Chairman of the Board of 724 Solutions Inc.

(e) on the recommendation of the Governance Committee, the establishment of effective procedures for reviewing the performance of the Chief Executive Officer and senior management;

(f) on the recommendation of the Governance Committee, the development of effective Board governance processes and procedures, including the establishment of Board Committees;

(g) any matter that requires the review and approval of any Committee of the Board of Directors under the terms of the respective Committee mandates, as may be amended from time-to-time, and appended to this delegation;

(h) the enactment, amendment, restatement or repeal of any By-laws;

(i) the approval of policies governing related party transactions;

(j) the Corporation's investor and public relations policies;

(k) except pursuant to explicit delegated authority by the Board in accordance with the *Ontario Business Corporations Act*, the making of, directly or indirectly, loans or advances to, or the giving of security for or the guaranteeing of the debts of, or otherwise the giving of financial assistance to, any Person;

(l) except pursuant to explicit delegated authority by the Board in accordance with the *Ontario Business Corporations Act*, mortgage, hypothecate, pledge or otherwise create a security interest in all or any currently owned or subsequently acquired property, real or personal, movable or immovable of the Corporation, including book debts, rights, powers, franchises and undertakings, to secure any present or future indebtedness, liability or obligation of the Corporation;

(m) any decisions required to be made by the Board of Directors under the terms of the applicable legislation and regulations governing the Corporation, including the declaration and payment of dividends;

(n) fundamental changes in the way in which the Corporation is governed, including, but not limited to, structural changes in the organization of the Corporation;

(o) matters which may involve personal legal liability of individual directors;

(p) on the recommendation of the Corporate Governance Committee, the appointment and compensation of directors; and

(q) any other matter that in the opinion of the Chief Executive Officer, or the Chair of the Governance Committee, on the advice of external counsel to the Corporation, should be determined by the Board of Directors.

2. Finance and Operations:

(a) the approval of any multi-year or annual business, capital or operating plans or budgets for the Corporation, or any amendment thereto;

(b) any material deviation from the approved business, capital or operating plans or budgets;

(c) the terms and conditions of any public or private distribution of securities of the Corporation (except pursuant to any Board-approved stock option, share purchase or dividend re-investment plans);

(d) the purchase or redemption or issuance of any shares in the capital of the Corporation;

(e) the purchase, sale, mortgage or lease by the Corporation of any material real property; except for those involving commercial leases for office space and other real property transactions of a minor nature;

(f) on the recommendation of the Audit Committee, any change in the accounting policies or practices of the Corporation;

(g) the Corporation's investment and treasury management policies; (on an interim basis, the following delegation regarding strategic investments shall prevail):

(i) for investments under U.S. $1 million, provided the investee company will yield a relationship to be expected to have measurable benefit to the Company's core business (i.e., perhaps assist in the speed of roll-out of licenses or installation), management would have an independent ability to pursue these transactions;

(ii) for investments in excess of U.S. $1 million to and including U.S. $5 million, approval of the Corporate Governance Committee is required; and

(iii) for investments in excess of U.S. $5 million, there shall first be a detailed review of the proposed investment by the Corporate Governance Committee, prior to the matter going to the Board for its approval. The Corporate Governance Committee may then decide whether such approval can be obtained by written resolution accompanied by written material, or whether the formality of a Board meeting will be required.

(h) on the recommendation of the Audit Committee, the approval of any annual or interim quarterly financial statements of the Corporation;

(i) any purchase, commitment, lease or expenditure which, if completed, would raise the total of capital expenditures of the Corporation in any fiscal year to more than the dollar amount authorized pursuant to an approved business plan for any fiscal year;

(j) the authorization, execution or entering into by the Corporation of any contract or transaction (or series of related contracts or transactions), the performance of which will require the expenditure or result in an actual or contingent liability of the Corporation for an amount exceeding $________;

(k) the entry by the Corporation into any line of business outside of the ordinary business as specified in the Board defined corporate policies; except for circumstances relating to a Board approved acquisition;

(l) any material contracts out of the ordinary course of business;

(m) any matter that presents a real or perceived material risk to the financial position of the Corporation; and

(n) acquisitions or divestitures that are:

- of strategic significance to the Corporation; or
- represent a material deviation from the ordinary course of business; or
- have the potential for jeopardizing the Corporation's ability to meet its ongoing service commitments; or
- the performance of which will require the expenditure or result in actual or contingent liability of the Corporation for an amount exceeding $__________.

The Chief Executive Officer:

The Chief Executive Officer is delegated the authority to supervise the business and affairs of the Corporation, subject to the direction of the Board of Directors and the execution limitations established by the Board. This delegation shall include the authority to make all decisions on behalf of the Corporation that do not require shareholder approval, or have not been reserved by the Board of Directors to itself or to a Committee of the Board, under the terms of this Delegation of Authority.

All Board authority delegated to management is delegated through the Chief Executive Officer, so that all authority and accountability of management, unless otherwise stated in this Delegation of Authority, is considered to be the authority and accountability of the Chief Executive Officer. This shall not be interpreted as precluding interaction between the members of the Board and senior management, and relates solely to the accountability link between the Board and the Chief Executive Officer.

The Chief Executive Officer shall have the authority to sub-delegate operational decision making as he or she may determine as necessary and appropriate for the effective operation of the business. In this regard, the Chief Executive Officer shall put in place a delegation of operational authority policy within the organization.

APPENDIX III

The Chair Of The Board[1]

Accountability:

The Chair of the Board is accountable to the Board of Directors for the fulfillment of the responsibilities of the office of Chair as outlined in the Corporation's by-laws and will lead the Board in establishing effective corporate governance processes and practices.

Role/Responsibilities:

The role and responsibilities of the Chair of the Board will include:

- To assume principal responsibility for the operation and functioning of the Board of Directors
- To provide overall leadership to the Board without limiting the principle of collective responsibility and the ability of the Board to function as a unit
- Fulfilling his or her Board leadership responsibilities in a manner that will ensure that the Board is able to function independently of management. This should include ensuring that the appropriate procedures are in place for the Board to meet regularly without management present, and to allow for Directors to engage outside advisors at the expense of the Company in appropriate circumstances, subject to the approval of the Governance Committee

[1] Used by permission of 724 Solutions Inc. and Ian Giffen, Chairman of the Board of 724 Solutions Inc.

- Consulting with the Board and the Corporate Secretary to set board agendas that are based on the responsibilities of the Board and reflect current priorities
- Chairing Board meetings effectively, including ensuring that appropriate briefing materials are delivered in a timely fashion, encouraging full participation and discussion by individual Directors, stimulating debate, facilitating consensus, and ensuring that clarity regarding decisions is reached and duly recorded
- Ensuring compliance with the governance policies of the Board regarding conduct of board meetings, managing and reporting information and other policies related to the conduct of the Board's business
- Taking a leadership role in ensuring effective communication and relationships between the Corporation, shareholders, stakeholders and the general public

APPENDIX IV

Lead Director[1]

There will be a Lead Director as long as the Chairman is a member of management.

1. Provide Leadership to Enhance Board Effectiveness

- The Lead Director shall be elected by the entire Board and shall be fully independent of management.
- The Lead Director shall be entitled to request materials and receive notice of and attend all meetings of Committees.
- The Lead Director shall have primary responsibility for:
    - Ensuring that the responsibilities of the Board are well understood by both the Board and management and the boundaries between the Board and management are clearly understood and respected;
    - Providing leadership to ensure the Board works in an independent, cohesive fashion;
    - Ensuring the Board has the requisite resources to support its work effectively;
    - Ensuring a process is in place to regularly assess the effectiveness of the Board, its committees and individual directors; and
    - Ensuring that a process is in place to monitor legislation and best practices which relate to the responsibilities of the Board.

[1] Used by permission of Alliance Atlantis Communications Inc. and its general counsel, Andrea Wood.

2. The Lead Director Shall be Responsible for:

- Consulting with the Chairman to set the agenda for Board meetings;
- Ensuring Board leadership in times of crisis;
- Where functions are delegated to Board committees, ensuring the functions are carried out as represented and results are reported to the Board;
- Chairing regular meetings of independent Board members without management present; and acting as liaison between the independent directors and the Chairman on sensitive issues; and
- Chairing Board meetings when the Chairman is not in attendance.

3. Acting as Liaison Between Board and Management

- The Lead Director shall work to ensure that the relationship between the Board and management is conducted in a professional and constructive manner. The Lead Director will work with the Chairman to ensure the conduct of Board meetings provides adequate time for serious discussion of appropriate issues and that appropriate information is made available to Board members on a timely basis.

This description will be revised from time to time.

A P P E N D I X V

Directors' Binder[1]

I. Corporate Information

(1) 2005 Annual Information Form

(2) 2005 Annual Report and MD&A

(3) 2005 Management Information Circular

(4) Articles & By-Laws

(5) Corporate Chart

(6) Executive Management Chart

(7) Business Plan – 2005 – 2009

II. Board Policies

(8) Charter of Expectations

(9) Disclosure Policy and Disclosure Committee Terms of Reference

(10) Confidentiality and Insider Trading Policy

(11) Insider Trading Report and Memo Regarding New Procedures

(12) Insider Reports filed on your behalf (to be inserted as filed)

(13) Whistleblower Policy

(14) Code of Conduct

[1] Used by permission of Alliance Atlantis Communications Inc. and its general counsel, Andrea Wood.

III. Corporate Policies

(15) Corporate Commitment Policy

(16) Payment Approval Policy

(17) Privacy Code

(18) Other Policies (to be inserted as approved)

- Workplace Harassment Policy

IV. Board and Committee Information

(19) Directors' Contact List

(20) Directors' Bios

(21) Senior Management Contact List

(22) Board/Committee 2006 Meeting Schedule

(23) Board of Directors

I. List of Directors

II. Board Mandate

III. Lead Director Mandate

IV. 2006 Minutes

(24) Executive Committee

I. Chair and Member List

II. Terms of Reference

III. Chair Description

IV. 2006 Agenda Outline

(25) Audit Committee

I. Chair and Member List

II. Terms of Reference

III. Chair Description

IV. 2006 Agenda Outline

V. 2006 Minutes

(26) Human Resources and Compensation Committee

I. Chair and Member List

II. Terms of Reference

III. Chair Description

IV. 2006 Agenda Outline

V. 2006 Minutes

(27) Corporate Governance and Nominating Committee

I. Chair and Member List

II. Terms of Reference

III. Chair Description

IV. 2006 Agenda Outline

V. 2006 Minutes

NOTE: (28) and (29) do not appear related to IV Board and Committee Information

(28) Directors' and Officers' Insurance

I. Policy

II. Extension

(29) Directors Indemnification Agreement

V. Compensation Information

(30) Directors' Share Ownership Memo

(31) Share Compensation Plan

(32) Deferred Share Units

I. DSU Plan

II. Notice of Redemption

III. Election Form

IV. Your 2006 Election Form

(33) Restricted Share Unit Plan

(34) PSAP

(35) 2006 Compensation Statements (to be inserted as received)

VI. Other

(36) Analyst Contact List

APPENDIX VI

National Policy 58-201
Corporate Governance Guidelines

Part 1 — Purpose and Application

1.1 Purpose of this Policy — This Policy provides guidance on corporate governance practices which have been formulated to:

- achieve a balance between providing protection to investors and fostering fair and efficient capital markets and confidence in capital markets;
- be sensitive to the realities of the greater numbers of small companies and controlled companies in the Canadian corporate landscape;
- take into account the impact of corporate governance developments in the U.S. and around the world; and
- recognize that corporate governance is evolving.

The guidelines in this Policy are not intended to be prescriptive. We encourage issuers to consider the guidelines in developing their own corporate governance practices.

We do, however, understand that some parties have concerns about how this Policy and National Instrument 58-101 *Disclosure of Corporate Governance Practices* affect controlled companies. Accordingly, we intend, over the next year, to carefully consider these concerns in the context of a study to examine the governance of controlled companies. We will consult market participants in conducting the study. After completing the study, we will consider whether to change how this Policy and National Instrument 58-101 treat controlled companies.

1.2 Application — This Policy applies to all reporting issuers, other than investment funds. Consequently, it applies to both corporate and non-corporate entities. Reference to a particular corporate characteristic, such as a board of directors (the board), includes any equivalent characteristic of a non-corporate entity. For example, in the case of a limited partnership, we recommend that a majority of the directors of the general partner should be independent of the limited partnership (including the general partner).

Income trust issuers should, in applying these guidelines, recognize that certain functions of a corporate issuer, its board and its management may be performed by any or all of the trustees, the board or management of a subsidiary of the trust, or the board, management or employees of a management company. For this purpose, references to "the issuer" refer to both the trust and any underlying entities, including the operating entity.

Part 2 — Meaning of Independence

2.1 Meaning of Independence — For the purposes of this Policy, a director is independent if he or she would be independent for the purposes of National Instrument 58-101 *Disclosure of Corporate Governance Practices.*

Part 3 — Corporate Governance Guidelines

Composition of the Board

3.1 The board should have a majority of independent directors.

3.2 The chair of the board should be an independent director. Where this is not appropriate, an independent director should be appointed to act as "lead director". However, either an independent chair or an independent lead director should act as the effective leader of the board and ensure that the board's agenda will enable it to successfully carry out its duties.

Meetings of Independent Directors

3.3 The independent directors should hold regularly scheduled meetings at which non-independent directors and members of management are not in attendance.

Board Mandate

3.4 The board should adopt a written mandate in which it explicitly acknowledges responsibility for the stewardship of the issuer, including responsibility for:

(a) to the extent feasible, satisfying itself as to the integrity of the chief executive officer (the CEO) and other executive officers and that the CEO and other executive officers create a culture of integrity throughout the organization;

(b) adopting a strategic planning process and approving, on at least an annual basis, a strategic plan which takes into account, among other things, the opportunities and risks of the business;

(c) the identification of the principal risks of the issuer's business, and ensuring the implementation of appropriate systems to manage these risks;

(d) succession planning (including appointing, training and monitoring senior management);

(e) adopting a communication policy for the issuer;

(f) the issuer's internal control and management information systems; and

(g) developing the issuer's approach to corporate governance, including developing a set of corporate governance principles and guidelines that are specifically applicable to the issuer.[1]

The written mandate of the board should also set out:

(i) measures for receiving feedback from stakeholders (e.g., the board may wish to establish a process to permit stakeholders to directly contact the independent directors), and

(ii) expectations and responsibilities of directors, including basic duties and responsibilities with respect to attendance at board meetings and advance review of meeting materials.

In developing an effective communication policy for the issuer, issuers should refer to the guidance set out in National Policy 51-201 *Disclosure Standards*.

---

[1] Issuers may consider appointing a corporate governance committee to consider these issues. A corporate governance committee should have a majority of independent directors, with the remaining members being "non-management" directors.

For purposes of this Policy, "executive officer" has the same meaning as in National Instrument 51-102 *Continuous Disclosure Obligations.*

Position Descriptions

3.5 The board should develop clear position descriptions for the chair of the board and the chair of each board committee. In addition, the board, together with the CEO, should develop a clear position description for the CEO, which includes delineating management's responsibilities. The board should also develop or approve the corporate goals and objectives that the CEO is responsible for meeting.

Orientation and Continuing Education

3.6 The board should ensure that all new directors receive a comprehensive orientation. All new directors should fully understand the role of the board and its committees, as well as the contribution individual directors are expected to make (including, in particular, the commitment of time and resources that the issuer expects from its directors). All new directors should also understand the nature and operation of the issuer's business.

3.7 The board should provide continuing education opportunities for all directors, so that individuals may maintain or enhance their skills and abilities as directors, as well as to ensure their knowledge and understanding of the issuer's business remains current.

Code of Business Conduct and Ethics

3.8 The board should adopt a written code of business conduct and ethics (a code). The code should be applicable to directors, officers and employees of the issuer. The code should constitute written standards that are reasonably designed to promote integrity and to deter wrongdoing. In particular, it should address the following issues:

(a) conflicts of interest, including transactions and agreements in respect of which a director or executive officer has a material interest;

(b) protection and proper use of corporate assets and opportunities;

(c) confidentiality of corporate information;

(d) fair dealing with the issuer's security holders, customers, suppliers, competitors and employees;

(e) compliance with laws, rules and regulations; and

(f) reporting of any illegal or unethical behaviour.

3.9 The board should be responsible for monitoring compliance with the code. Any waivers from the code that are granted for the benefit of the issuer's directors or executive officers should be granted by the board (or a board committee) only.

Although issuers must exercise their own judgement in making materiality determinations, the Canadian securities regulatory authorities consider that conduct by a director or executive officer which constitutes a material departure from the code will likely constitute a "material change" within the meaning of National Instrument 51-102 *Continuous Disclosure Obligations*. National Instrument 51-102 requires every material change report to include a full description of the material change. Where a material departure from the code constitutes a material change to the issuer, we expect that the material change report will disclose, among other things:

- the date of the departure(s),
- the party(ies) involved in the departure(s),
- the reason why the board has or has not sanctioned the departure(s), and
- any measures the board has taken to address or remedy the departure(s).

Nomination of Directors

3.10 The board should appoint a nominating committee composed entirely of independent directors.

3.11 The nominating committee should have a written charter that clearly establishes the committee's purpose, responsibilities, member qualifications, member appointment and removal, structure and operations (including any authority to delegate to individual members and subcommittees), and manner of reporting to the board. In addition, the nominating committee should be given authority to engage and compensate any outside advisor that it determines to be necessary to permit it to carry out its duties. If an issuer is legally required by contract or otherwise to provide third parties with the right to nominate directors, the selection and nomination of those directors need not involve the approval of an independent nominating committee.

3.12 Prior to nominating or appointing individuals as directors, the board should adopt a process involving the following steps:

(A) Consider what competencies and skills the board, as a whole, should possess. In doing so, the board should recognize that the particular competencies and skills required for one issuer may not be the same as those required for another.

(B) Assess what competencies and skills each existing director possesses. It is unlikely that any one director will have all the competencies and skills required by the board. Instead, the board should be considered as a group, with each individual making his or her own contribution. Attention should also be paid to the personality and other qualities of each director, as these may ultimately determine the boardroom dynamic.

The board should also consider the appropriate size of the board, with a view to facilitating effective decision-making.

In carrying out each of these functions, the board should consider the advice and input of the nominating committee.

3.13 The nominating committee should be responsible for identifying individuals qualified to become new board members and recommending to the board the new director nominees for the next annual meeting of shareholders.

3.14 In making its recommendations, the nominating committee should consider:

(a) the competencies and skills that the board considers to be necessary for the board, as a whole, to possess;

(b) the competencies and skills that the board considers each existing director to possess; and

(c) the competencies and skills each new nominee will bring to the boardroom.

The nominating committee should also consider whether or not each new nominee can devote sufficient time and resources to his or her duties as a board member.

Compensation

3.15 The board should appoint a compensation committee composed entirely of independent directors.

3.16 The compensation committee should have a written charter that establishes the committee's purpose, responsibilities, member qualifications, member appointment and removal, structure and operations (including any authority to delegate to individual members or subcommittees), and the manner of reporting to the board. In addition, the compensation committee should be given authority to engage and compensate any outside advisor that it determines to be necessary to permit it to carry out its duties.

3.17 The compensation committee should be responsible for:

(a) reviewing and approving corporate goals and objectives relevant to CEO compensation, evaluating the CEO's performance in light of those corporate goals and objectives, and determining (or making recommendations to the board with respect to) the CEO's compensation level based on this evaluation;

(b) making recommendations to the board with respect to non-CEO officer and director compensation, incentive-compensation plans and equity-based plans; and

(c) reviewing executive compensation disclosure before the issuer publicly discloses this information.

Regular Board Assessments

3.18 The board, its committees and each individual director should be regularly assessed regarding his, her or its effectiveness and contribution. An assessment should consider

(a) in the case of the board or a board committee, its mandate or charter, and

(b) in the case of an individual director, the applicable position description(s), as well as the competencies and skills each individual director is expected to bring to the board.

APPENDIX VII

Form 58-101F1 (National Instrument 58-101) Corporate Governance Disclosure

1. Board of Directors

(a) Disclose the identity of directors who are independent.

(b) Disclose the identity of directors who are not independent, and describe the basis for that determination.

(c) Disclose whether or not a majority of directors are independent. If a majority of directors are not independent, describe what the board of directors (the **board**) does to facilitate its exercise of independent judgement in carrying out its responsibilities.

(d) If a director is presently a director of any other issuer that is a reporting issuer (or the equivalent) in a jurisdiction or a foreign jurisdiction, identify both the director and the other issuer.

(e) Disclose whether or not the independent directors hold regularly scheduled meetings at which non-independent directors and members of management are not in attendance. If the independent directors hold such meetings, disclose the number of meetings held since the beginning of the issuer's most recently completed financial year. If the independent directors do not hold such meetings, describe what the board does to facilitate open and candid discussion among its independent directors.

(f) Disclose whether or not the chair of the board is an independent director. If the board has a chair or lead director who is an independent director, disclose the identity of the independent chair or lead director, and describe his or her role and responsibilities. If the board has neither a chair that is independent nor a lead director that is independent, describe what the board does to provide leadership for its independent directors.

(g) Disclose the attendance record of each director for all board meetings held since the beginning of the issuer's most recently completed financial year.

2. Board Mandate

Disclose the text of the board's written mandate. If the board does not have a written mandate, describe how the board delineates its role and responsibilities.

3. Position Descriptions

(a) Disclose whether or not the board has developed written position descriptions for the chair and the chair of each board committee. If the board has not developed written position descriptions for the chair and/or the chair of each board committee, briefly describe how the board delineates the role and responsibilities of each such position.

(b) Disclose whether or not the board and CEO have developed a written position description for the CEO. If the board and CEO have not developed such a position description, briefly describe how the board delineates the role and responsibilities of the CEO.

4. Orientation and Continuing Education

(a) Briefly describe what measures the board takes to orient new directors regarding

(i) the role of the board, its committees and its directors, and

(ii) the nature and operation of the issuer's business.

(b) Briefly describe what measures, if any, the board takes to provide continuing education for its directors. If the board does not provide continuing education, describe how the board ensures that its directors maintain the skill and knowledge necessary to meet their obligations as directors.

5. Ethical Business Conduct

(a) Disclose whether or not the board has adopted a written code for the directors, officers and employees. If the board has adopted a written code:

(i) disclose how a person or company may obtain a copy of the code;

(ii) describe how the board monitors compliance with its code, or if the board does not monitor compliance, explain whether and how the board satisfies itself regarding compliance with its code; and

(iii) provide a cross-reference to any material change report filed since the beginning of the issuer's most recently completed financial year that pertains to any conduct of a director or executive officer that constitutes a departure from the code.

(b) Describe any steps the board takes to ensure directors exercise independent judgement in considering transactions and agreements in respect of which a director or executive officer has a material interest.

(c) Describe any other steps the board takes to encourage and promote a culture of ethical business conduct.

6. Nomination of Directors

(a) Describe the process by which the board identifies new candidates for board nomination.

(b) Disclose whether or not the board has a nominating committee composed entirely of independent directors. If the board does not have a nominating committee composed entirely of independent directors, describe what steps the board takes to encourage an objective nomination process.

(c) If the board has a nominating committee, describe the responsibilities, powers and operation of the nominating committee.

7. Compensation

(a) Describe the process by which the board determines the compensation for the issuer's directors and officers.

(b) Disclose whether or not the board has a compensation committee composed entirely of independent directors. If the board does not have a compensation committee composed entirely of independent directors, describe what steps the board takes to ensure an objective process for determining such compensation.

(c) If the board has a compensation committee, describe the responsibilities, powers and operation of the compensation committee.

(d) If a compensation consultant or advisor has, at any time since the beginning of the issuer's most recently completed financial year, been retained to assist in determining compensation for any of the issuer's directors and officers, disclose the identity of the consultant or advisor and briefly summarize the mandate for which they have been retained. If the consultant or advisor has been retained to perform any other work for the issuer, state that fact and briefly describe the nature of the work.

8. Other Board Committees

If the board has standing committees other than the audit, compensation and nominating committees, identify the committees and describe their function.

9. Assessments

Disclose whether or not the board, its committees and individual directors are regularly assessed with respect to their effectiveness and contribution. If assessments are regularly conducted, describe the process used for the assessments. If assessments are not regularly conducted, describe how the board satisfies itself that the board, its committees, and its individual directors are performing effectively.

Instruction:

(1) *This Form applies to both corporate and non-corporate entities. Reference to a particular corporate characteristic, such as a board, includes any equivalent characteristic of a non-corporate entity.*

Income trust issuers must provide disclosure in a manner which recognizes that certain functions of a corporate issuer, its board and its management may be performed by any or all of the trustees, the board or management of a subsidiary of the trust, or the board, management or employees of a management company. In the case of an income trust, references to "the issuer" refer to both the trust and any underlying entities, including the operating entity.

(2) *If the disclosure required by Item 1 is included in a management information circular distributed to security holders of the issuer for the purpose of electing directors to the issuer's board of directors, provide disclosure regarding the existing directors and any proposed directors.*

(3) *Disclosure regarding board committees made under Item 8 of this Form may include the existence and summary content of any committee charter.*

CHAPTER 2

THE DUTIES OF DIRECTORS

Directors' duties under Canadian law arise from three principal sources: (1) the common law applicable to persons exercising powers of a fiduciary nature, (2) the governing business corporations statute, and (3) other statutes that impose duties on directors with respect to specific subjects (e.g., securities regulation, environmental protection, taxation, and employment standards).

This Chapter deals with the general duties of directors under the common law (as codified in the relevant governing business corporations statute) and with other specific duties imposed upon directors under the terms of the governing business corporations statute. The duties imposed upon directors under other statutes and regulations are referred to in Chapter 11, "Regulatory Liabilities", and elsewhere in connection with a consideration of particular subject areas, for example, in Chapter 9, "Duties and Liabilities of Directors Under Employment Laws".

I. Overview of Directors' Duties

Directors are charged by statute with the fundamental obligation to manage, or supervise the management of, the business and affairs of the corporation.[1] As the size and complexity of corporations and their operations have grown, directors, particularly outside directors, have increasingly been expected to focus on monitoring the activities of management, as opposed to being actively involved in the management of the corporation's business and affairs. Directors are required to assume responsibility for overall stewardship of the corporation. With the exception of directors who are also members of management, directors are not expected to devote themselves full-time to the corporation. They are entitled, in the exercise of their business judgment, to delegate to management the powers to manage the business and affairs of the corporation, except for certain specific powers, which only the full board of directors may exercise.[2]

Directors should not be expected to engage in a detailed review of management's day-to-day activities. Especially with respect to very large corporations, it is not realistic to expect the board to be involved in anything other than the most significant decisions. Generally, it will be sufficient for the board to make sure adequate and appropriate systems are in place to ensure the timely and effective monitoring and review of operational matters. However, boards are ultimately accountable for how delegated powers are exercised, and they should not proceed on the basis that once a power or duty has been delegated, they no longer have any responsibility over the matter. While directors are entitled to regard management as capable and

---

[1] *Canada Business Corporations Act*, R.S.C. 1985, c. C-44, as amended, s. 102(1) ("CBCA").

[2] CBCA, ss. 115(1) and (3); note that the British Columbia *Business Corporations Act*, S.B.C. 2002, C-57, as amended, ("BCBCA") does not have an equivalent provision to s. 115(3) of the CBCA, which limits the delegation of specific powers.

honest unless shown otherwise, they must be alert to warning signs that might suggest problems.

In carrying out their mandate, directors are subject to two overriding duties, both of which were first developed by the courts at common law and are now codified in the statutes governing all corporations incorporated in Canada, either federally or provincially. As stated in s. 122(1) of the CBCA, directors are required:

(a) to act honestly and in good faith with a view to the best interests of the corporation; and

(b) to exercise the care, diligence, and skill that a reasonably prudent person would exercise in comparable circumstances.

The first of these duties, commonly referred to as the fiduciary duty or duty of loyalty, requires directors to give the corporation's best interests unqualified priority over their personal interests or other competing claims. The director's fiduciary duty is closely akin to the duty owed by a trustee to trust beneficiaries. In general terms, this means that actual or apparent conflicts of interest or self-dealings must be avoided and that confidentiality must be maintained. Furthermore, directors must exercise their powers only for a proper purpose, i.e., a purpose relating to the honest pursuit of the best interests of the corporation and not to the director's own purposes or to other collateral or improper purposes.

The second branch of a director's duties involves the duty of care. This duty requires a director to act carefully and on an informed basis and to exhibit the diligence and skill that a reasonably prudent person would exercise in comparable circumstances. The duty of care encompasses an objective standard of what a reasonably prudent person would be expected to do in comparable circumstances.

Except by way of a unanimous shareholder agreement, directors cannot contract out of these duties. Accordingly, any contract or undertaking by which the director agrees to fetter his or her discretion with respect to future decisions and actions as a director will be illegal and unenforceable.

While, properly speaking, the fiduciary duty concerns the duty of honesty and loyalty and is distinct from the duty of care, the term "fiduciary duties" is sometimes used to describe both the duty of care and the duty of loyalty. In order to avoid the confusion that can arise from imprecise terminology, references throughout this Chapter will be either to the fiduciary duty or the duty of loyalty or to the duty of care. Collectively, they will be referred to as the duties of directors.

II. Duty of Loyalty

The director's duty to act honestly and in good faith with a view to the best interests of the corporation involves several related concepts, including:

- the duty to avoid conflicts of interest;
- the duty not to use his or her position for personal gain;
- the duty to maintain the confidentiality of the corporation's information;
- the duty to serve the corporation selflessly, honestly, and loyally; and
- the duty to exercise independent judgment.

In the leading Canadian case on the subject of directors' duties and liabilities, *Peoples v. Wise*,[3] the Supreme Court of Canada described this duty as follows:

> The statutory fiduciary duty requires directors and officers to act honestly and in good faith *vis-à-vis* the corporation. They must respect the trust and confidence that have been reposed in them to manage the assets of the corporation in pursuit of the realization of the objects of the corporation. They must avoid conflicts of interest with the corporation. They must avoid abusing their position to gain personal benefit. They must maintain the confidentiality of information they acquire by virtue of their position. Directors and officers must serve the corporation selflessly, honestly and loyally: see K.P. McGuinness, *The Law and Practice of Canadian Business Corporations* (1999), at p. 715.[4]

However, the duty to avoid conflicting interests and to eschew personal profit is not absolute. As will be explained below under section III, "Interested Director Contracts", subject to compliance with the procedures set out in the business corporations statutes, directors may, in certain situations, function notwithstanding an actual or potential conflict of interest, and they may, within prescribed parameters, realize a profit or gain from dealings with the corporation.

Four key components of a director's discharge of his or her fiduciary duty are that the director must:

- act honestly and openly;

[3] [2004] 3 S.C.R. 461 ("*Peoples*").

[4] *Ibid.* at para. 35.

- maintain confidences;
- act independently; and
- avoid conflicts of interest and the appropriation of corporate opportunities.

A. Act Honestly and Openly

The fiduciary duty requires a director to be honest in dealing with other directors and with the corporation. A director must not actively mislead them. In fact, a director must disclose all relevant information that he or she has to the board.[5] The collegial structure of the board and the practical delegation of responsibilities to committees will suffer if directors deprive their fellow directors of important information needed to carry out responsibilities and to practise due diligence. Since individuals with different types of expertise are appointed to boards because of their expertise, it is expected that all members of a board or a committee will have the benefit of that expertise. The more relevant or critical a piece of information is, the more likely it is that the board of the corporation will expect to receive that information. However, directors cannot be expected to disclose information that they are required to hold in confidence by virtue of fiduciary duties owed to third parties. As discussed below, this situation can give rise to difficulties when a person serves on multiple boards, especially as a director of competing corporations.

B. Maintain Confidences

The fiduciary duty requires a duty of confidentiality. Directors must not reveal information that they learned in their capacity as directors. In general, this is a wise practice, particularly because the repetition of boardroom discussions can have other consequences. For example, a conversation may be construed as "tipping", contrary to s. 132(4) of the Ontario *Securities Act* ("OSA").[6] The disclosure of confidential information may lead to the loss of an opportunity or competitive advantage for the corporation and consequent liability of the director for any foregone profits.

All information about the board's or the corporation's activities should be presumed to be confidential. Only matters that have clearly become public knowledge (because announcements have been made or because the situation is obvious in the circumstances) should be discussed by directors outside of the boardroom.

---

[5] *Colborne Capital Corp. v. 542775 Alberta Ltd.* (1999), 45 B.L.R. (2d) 21 at 62 (Alta. C.A.).

[6] R.S.O. 1990, c. S.5, as amended.

C. Act Independently

Closely tied to the requirement that directors avoid conflicts of interest is the requirement that they must, at all times, fearlessly promote the best interests of the corporation through the exercise of their independent judgment. If this duty requires them, following careful review and consultation, to disagree with the views of management, other directors, or a majority of the shareholders, then so be it. As will be discussed further under section IV.C., "Nominee Directors", directors are elected to exercise their independent judgment and, while they will want to know the views of shareholders, they should not simply follow a controlling shareholder's marching orders. This idea was expressed in *Teck Corporation Ltd. v. Millar*,[7] a decision of the British Columbia Supreme Court, which was referred to with approval by the Supreme Court of Canada in *Peoples*,[8]

> The defendant directors were elected to exercise their best judgment. They were not agents bound to accede to the directions of the majority of the shareholders. Their mandate continued so long as they remained in office. They were in no sense a lame duck board. So they acted in what they conceived to be the best interests of the shareholders, and signed a contract which they knew the largest shareholder, holding a majority of the shares, did not want them to sign. They had the right in law to do that. When a company elects its board of directors and entrusts them with the power to manage the company, the directors are entitled to manage it. But they must not exercise their powers for an extraneous purpose. That is a breach of their duty. At the same time, the shareholders have no right to alter the terms of the directors' mandate except by amendment of the articles or by replacing the directors themselves.[9]

D. Avoid Conflicts of Interest and the Appropriation of Corporate Opportunities

Directors cannot profit at the expense of the corporation. They cannot divert opportunities or benefits from the corporation to themselves or put themselves in a position of conflict. They must disclose their interests in a

---

7 (1972), 33 D.L.R. (3d) 288 (B.C.S.C.).

8 *Supra* note 3.

9 *Ibid.* at p. 330.

timely manner, and they must refrain from voting on matters in which they have an interest.[10]

Directors are usually compensated for their work on boards and committees. They cannot use their position to acquire other benefits for themselves. Any other benefits, such as contracts or property that directors receive through their position as directors, belong to the corporation. The directors are accountable for such benefits. The profit (or possibly, the contract or property itself) belongs to the corporation, even if the directors believed that they were acting in good faith or acting to the corporation's advantage.

As part of their duty to maintain the confidentiality of corporate information, directors are prohibited from appropriating opportunities that belong to the corporation. Directors who take advantage of opportunities that they became aware of as a result of their position with the corporation (which the corporation might conceivably have had an interest in pursuing) are in breach of their fiduciary duties, and they may be required to account to the corporation for any profits or gains realized from such activities.

In the leading case of *Canadian Aero Service Ltd. v. O'Malley*,[11] the Supreme Court of Canada found two senior officers breached their fiduciary duty by taking advantage of an opportunity they learned about as a result of their positions with the corporation. It did not matter that they had left the corporation prior to taking up the opportunity or that the corporation itself was not at that time in a position to take up the opportunity. In some situations, it may be legitimate for a director to pursue an opportunity that came to his or her attention through his or her role in the corporation, but only after the director has made full disclosure and an uninterested majority of the directors or a committee of directors has rejected the opportunity on behalf of the corporation and voiced no objection to the director pursuing it independently. However, if the opportunity will result in the director becoming a competitor of the corporation, there is a high likelihood that the director's fiduciary duty to the corporation would preclude the director from pursuing it.

In determining whether a business opportunity belongs to the corporation and is not available to the director for exploitation, several factors should be considered. Relevant factors include the nature of the opportunity (e.g., how it relates to the corporation's business; its potential importance to the corporation), and the "ripeness" of the transaction (e.g., whether it is a hypothetical possibility or is close to consummation). The relationship

---

[10] See also section III, "Interested Director Contracts".

[11] [1974] S.C.R. 592.

of the director to the transaction in question (e.g., involvement in negotiations or the development of the terms of a contract or proposal) is also an important factor.

III. Interested Director Contracts

If an existing or proposed contract or transaction of the corporation is material from the perspective of either the director or the corporation, and if the director is a party to, or has an interest in a party to, that contract or transaction, then s. 120 of the CBCA provides that the director is required to disclose, in a timely manner, his or her interest in the contract or transaction.[12] In addition, except for contracts or transactions relating to the director's remuneration, indemnification, or insurance, or contracts with affiliates of the corporation, directors are required to abstain from voting on any resolution to approve contracts or transactions in which they have a material interest.[13] While the CBCA does not expressly require a director who is required to abstain from voting on the resolution to also refrain from any direct or indirect participation in the decision-making process, it is suggested that such a director should not have any involvement in the process other than to respond to requests for information that the uninterested directors may make.

At common law, a contract in which a director was interested was voidable at the instance of the corporation, and the interested director could be made to account to the corporation for any profits made from such a contract. However, under s. 120(7) of the CBCA, if the statutory requirements for disclosure and abstention from voting are met, and if the contract or transaction, as approved by the uninterested directors, was reasonable and fair to the corporation, the contract or transaction will not be invalid, and the interested director will not be required to account for profits made from it. However, if the CBCA is not complied with, the court may set aside the contract on such terms as it sees fit and/or require the interested director to account to the corporation for any profits made from that contract.[14]

In addition, an interested director contract that was made contrary to the CBCA may, in any event, be confirmed by a special resolution of the

[12] BCBCA, s. 153(2) covers timely disclosure for both directors and officers.

[13] CBCA, s. 120(5); note that the Ontario *Business Corporations Act*, R.S.O. 1990, c. B.16, ("OBCA"), s. 132(5) and the Alberta *Business Corporations Act*, R.S.A. 2000, c. B-9, ("ABCA"), s. 120(6), contain an additional exception for an arrangement by way of security for money lent to or obligations undertaken by the director for the benefit of the corporation or an affiliate. Note that the BCBCA does not contain this additional exception.

[14] CBCA, s. 120(8).

shareholders, provided that adequate disclosure is made to the shareholders and that the contract is reasonable and fair to the corporation at the time shareholder confirmation is obtained.[15]

While the types of contracts or transactions to which s. 120 of the CBCA applies are relatively narrow (for example, the interest must be material and it would appear that it does not extend to decisions such as whether to initiate litigation or to discontinue it), a director's overriding fiduciary duty of loyalty may preclude participation in a decision or require the disclosure of an interest in a matter, even though the decision or matter is not caught by the statute. Accordingly, good practice is to apply s. 120 of the CBCA broadly and to follow its procedures whenever there appears to be an actual or reasonable perception of a conflict between the director's direct or indirect interests and those of the corporation.

IV. To Whom Do Directors Owe Their Duty of Loyalty? The Position of Creditors and Other Non-Shareholder Interests

A. General

Directors owe their fiduciary duty of loyalty exclusively to the corporation, not to its shareholders nor its creditors, even where the corporation is in financial distress. Whereas there was at one time uncertainty as to whether directors' fiduciary duties shifted to the corporation's creditors when the corporation approached insolvency or became insolvent, the Supreme Court of Canada rejected such a notion in *Peoples*:

> At all times, directors and officers owe their fiduciary obligation to the corporation. The interests of the corporation are not to be confused with the interests of the creditors or those of any other stakeholders.
>
> . . .
>
> The directors' fiduciary duty does not change when a corporation is in the nebulous "vicinity of insolvency".[16]

However, as will be explained below, in *Peoples*, the Supreme Court of Canada left open the possibility that directors might nonetheless be held

---

[15] CBCA, s. 120(7.1); note that the BCBCA does not contain such a provision for confirmation by shareholders where the statutory disclosure requirements have not been met.

[16] *Peoples*, *supra* note 3 at paras. 43 and 46.

liable to creditors on the basis of a breach of their duty of care or the statutory oppression remedy.

The CBCA requires directors to act in "the best interests of the corporation" but it does not define that phrase.[17] With respect to the interests of shareholders, while it is true that directors owe their fiduciary duties to the corporation and not to its shareholders, the practical reality is that in most situations, it will be appropriate for the directors to equate the "best interests of the corporation" with the best interests of "all of the shareholders, taking no one sectional interest to prevail over the others".[18]

This does not mean that it will never be appropriate for directors to have regard for the interests of non-shareholder constituencies. In *Peoples*, the Supreme Court of Canada held that directors, in appropriate circumstances, may consider broader community interests, such as those of employees, suppliers, consumers, governments, and the environment:

> We accept as an accurate statement of law that in determining whether they are acting with a view to the best interests of the corporation it may be legitimate, given all the circumstances of a given case, for the board of directors to consider, *inter alia*, the interests of shareholders, employees, suppliers, creditors, consumers, governments and the environment.[19]

However, to the extent that directors do take non-shareholder interests into consideration, they should only do so with an eye to the "best interests of the corporation" in the sense that they believe that a "better corporation" will thereby be created. In other words, directors are not required to focus exclusively on short-term profit and shareholder value maximization, but they may chart a course that they honestly and reasonably believe will result in the corporation, and ultimately its shareholders, growing and prospering in the long-term, having regard for the social, political, and economic environment in which the corporation operates.

In this regard, a corporation may make charitable donations, provide benefits to its employees (such as educational leave, daycare, or exercise facilities), endow scholarships, and sponsor community activities. Directors can take a reasonably broad view of what uses they will authorize for the corporation's assets. It is inappropriate, however, for directors to advance particular interests at the expense of the corporation, and to advance the

---

[17] CBCA, s. 122(1)(*a*).

[18] *Palmer v. Carling O'Keefe Breweries of Canada Ltd.* (1989), 67 O.R. (2d) 161 at 168 (Ont. Div. Ct.).

[19] *Peoples, supra* note 3 at para. 42.

interests of one stakeholder at the expense of another, such as by favouring a particular class of shareholders.

The ABCA expressly provides that, in determining what is in the best interests of the corporation, if a director is elected or appointed by holders of a class or series of shares or by employees or creditors, the director may give special, but not exclusive, consideration to the interests of those who elected or appointed the director.[20] There is little judicial or academic discussion of the subsection, and it is likely to be viewed as an interpretive provision that codifies current Canadian law rather than one that modifies it. The primary duty of a director to advance the interests of the corporation remains untouched. The focus of the entire provision is defined through the lens of the "interests of the corporation".

On the other hand, the director's duty of care is not necessarily owed just to the corporation. Indeed, in *Peoples,* the Supreme Court of Canada expressly recognized that creditors could be the beneficiaries of the director's statutory duty of care:

> [T]he statement of the duty of care in s. 122(1)(*b*) of the CBCA does not specifically refer to an identifiable party as the beneficiary of the duty.... Thus, the identity of the beneficiary of the duty of care is much more open-ended, and it appears obvious that it must include creditors.[21]

In addition to the potential for an action based on a breach of the duty of care, the court recognized the possibility of creditors securing recourse under the statutory oppression remedy. The availability of these other remedies strongly influenced the court's decision not to extend the director's statutory fiduciary duty to creditors:

> Section 241 of the CBCA provides a possible mechanism for creditors to protect their interests from the prejudicial conduct of directors. In our view, the availability of such a broad oppression remedy undermines any perceived need to extend the fiduciary duty imposed on directors by s. 122(1)(*a*) of the CBCA to include creditors.
>
> . . .
>
> In light of the availability both of the oppression remedy and of an action based on the duty of care, which will be discussed below, stakeholders have viable remedies at their

---

[20] ABCA, s. 122(4); the CBCA, OBCA, and BCBCA do not contain a similar provision.

[21] *Peoples, supra* note 3 at para. 57.

> disposal. There is no need to read the interests of creditors into the duty set out in s. 122(1)(*a*) of the CBCA.[22]

To sum up, while directors do not have a fiduciary duty to creditors (which means that they are never required to place the interests of creditors ahead of the interests of the corporation), they may be held liable if they act carelessly (with resulting damage to creditors) or oppressively or unfairly prejudice or unfairly disregard the interests of creditors. Accordingly, when the corporation is on the verge of insolvency, directors should be careful not to take undue risks, with the knowledge that it is the creditors who will suffer if all is lost. This is not to say that the directors thereby become subject to the fiduciary duties towards creditors; their duties continue to be owed to the corporation. However, in determining the best interests of the corporation, the directors must recognize that in insolvency situations, the persons with the greatest stake in how the corporation is managed are the corporation's creditors. In addition, when a corporation is insolvent or on the verge of insolvency, the potential for unfair prejudice to the interests of creditors is enhanced, making it necessary, in light of the oppression remedy, for directors to consider with particular care the potential impact of their decisions on the reasonable expectations of creditors.

However, as will be discussed below, the business judgment rule will ordinarily be available to protect directors from liability, provided they were acting in good faith and on an informed basis. The bottom line would appear to be that directors will not be held liable to creditors, provided that the directors were honestly pursuing a business plan that they had reasonable grounds to believe might have resulted in the rescue or survival of a financially distressed corporation.

B. Resignation of Directors

An issue that often arises in the context of financially troubled corporations is whether directors, faced with potential personal liability for the liabilities of the corporation relating to such things as unpaid taxes, wages, and employee source deductions, may resign *en masse* in order to avoid such liabilities. The one Canadian case on point indicates that directors have an unfettered right to resign if they become legitimately concerned about their potential personal liabilities.[23] However, it is suggested that a more conservative approach will usually be appropriate. The fiduciary duty of the directors would presumably require them to take reasonable steps to avoid the corporation being left in a state of chaos. Such steps might include

---

[22] *Ibid.* at paras. 51 and 53.

[23] *Brown v. Shearer* (1995), 102 Man. R. (2d) 76 (C.A.).

giving major creditors sufficient advance notice of the directors' intended resignations to allow new directors to be appointed; placing the corporation under the protection of a receiver or monitor; or offering the directors adequate indemnities or insurance coverage to persuade them to remain on board.

C. Nominee Directors

Directors owe their duties to the corporation and to the corporation alone, subject, of course, to the broad range of interests that can be considered under the statutory duty of care. They are required to exercise judgment that is independent of the wishes of management and, in the case of nominee directors, independent of the wishes of those responsible for their election or appointment to the board.[24] A frequently quoted statement of the relevant principles governing the conduct of nominee directors is found in the trial court decision in *PWA Corp. v. Gemini Group Automated Distribution Systems Inc.*:[25]

> A director nominated by a particular shareholder of the corporation is not in any sense relieved of his or her fiduciary duties to the corporation. A nominee director is not accorded an attenuated standard of loyalty to the corporation. The director must exercise his or her judgment in the interests of the corporation and comply with his duties of disclosure, and must not subordinate the interests of the corporation to those of the director's patron.[26]

According to Justice Farley in *820099 Ontario Inc. v. Harold E. Ballard Ltd.*,[27] a nominee director must have sufficient courage of conviction to act contrary to the wishes of his or her appointer if this is what the best interests of the corporation call for:

> It may well be that the corporate life of a nominee director who votes against the interest of his "appointing" shareholder will be neither happy nor long. However, the role that any director must play (whether or not a nominee director) is that he must act in the best interests of the corporation. If the interests of the corporation (and indirectly the

[24] As discussed earlier, ABCA, s. 122(4) provides that in determining what is in the best interests of the corporation, directors may give special, but not exclusive, consideration to the interests of those who appointed or elected them.

[25] (1993), 8 B.L.R. (2d) 221 at para. 176 (Ont. Gen. Div.), aff'd (1993), 10 B.L.R. (2d) 109 (Ont. C.A.)

[26] *Ibid.* at p. 265.

[27] (1991), 3 B.L.R. (2d) 113 at para. 106 (Ont. Gen. Div.).

> interests of the shareholders as a whole) require that the director vote in a certain way, it must be the way that he conscientiously believes after a reasonable review is the best for the corporation. The nominee director's obligation to his "appointing" shareholder would seem to me to include the duty to tell the appointer that his requested course of action is wrong if the director in fact feels this way. Such advice, although likely initially unwelcome, may well be valuable to the appointer in the long run. The nominee director cannot be a "Yes man"; he must be an analytical person who can say "Yes" or "No" as the occasion requires (or to put it another way, as the corporation requires).[28]

The principle that directors owe their duties to the corporation and not to individual shareholders or other stakeholders is rooted in the fundamental notion that fiduciaries must avoid putting themselves in positions of conflict, either of interest or of duty. In other words, a fiduciary must not only avoid conflicts between his or her own personal interests and the interests of those to whom a fiduciary duty is owed, but he or she must also avoid a situation where duties are owed to act in the best interests of two or more persons whose interests may be divergent. In such a case, the fiduciary will not be able to serve the interests of one person without breaching a duty owed to the other. As one writer put it: "In such cases the ancient Biblical admonition will be appreciated — indeed, no man can serve two masters".[29]

The difficulty nominee directors may encounter in attempting to serve "two masters" often arises where there are contractual dealings between a parent corporation and a subsidiary that has minority shareholders (for example, with respect to transfer pricing issues).[30] To address the concerns relating to conflicting interests in these types of situations, the usual practice is to assign responsibility for consideration of the transaction to a committee of independent directors.[31] However, in order for this solution to be effective, it is essential that the members of the independent committee be effective and truly independent.[32]

---

[28] *Ibid.* at pp. 171-172.

[29] James A. Millard, *The Responsible Director* (Toronto: Carswell, 1989).

[30] See *Ford v. OMERS*, 79 O.R. (3d) 81 (C.A.).

[31] See *Brant Investments Ltd. v. Keep Rite Inc.* (1987), 60 O.R. (2d) 737 (H.C.J.), aff'd (1991), 3 O.R. (3d) 289 at 301 and *Maple Leaf Foods Inc. v. Schneider Corp.* (1998), 42 O.R. (3d) 177 at 192 ("*Maple Leaf Foods*").

[32] See further Chapter 6, "The Use of Committees".

D. Service As Directors of Competing Corporations

Canadian corporate law does not establish an absolute prohibition on persons serving at the same time on boards of corporations that compete with each other. However, in such situations, the directors in question must be careful to avoid favouring the interests of one corporation over those of another. Although it may be possible to mitigate the risk by establishing internal walls and procedures to exclude the director from situations where conflicts may arise, this solution will not always be practicable. There will often be cases where such dual service will simply be untenable.

As noted above, an important aspect of a director's fiduciary duty is the duty to maintain the confidentiality of non-public information acquired in the course of serving as a director of the corporation. Where a person is a director of both Corporation A and Corporation B, which compete with each other, an apparent tension may arise between the director's duty to maintain the confidentiality of information respecting the business and affairs of Corporation A and the duty to protect and advance the interests of Corporation B. Corporation B could gain an advantage if it acquires Corporation A's confidential information, or *vice versa*. Canadian corporate law resolves this apparent tension by providing that directors are not, as a general rule, required (or allowed) to advance the interests of one corporation to which they owe duties by disclosing confidential information pertaining to the business or affairs of another corporation to which they also owe fiduciary duties.

However, an exception to this general rule is recognized where the directors of Corporation A possess information relating to the business or affairs of Corporation B that is of such fundamental importance that it can be said to affect Corporation A in "a vital aspect of its business".[33] In such circumstances, the director in question will be in a position of irreconcilable conflict, which will necessitate the director's resignation from at least one board and possibly both of them. In summary, while serving on boards of competing corporations may not be strictly prohibited in all situations, it is fraught with potential risk and difficulty, and it should, as a matter of good practice, be avoided.

E. Unanimous Shareholder Agreements

It is possible for directors to be relieved of the duties and liabilities arising under the business corporations statutes or otherwise by means of a unanimous shareholder agreement or a sole shareholder declaration. A

---

[33] *PWA Corp. v. Gemini Group* (1993), 10 B.L.R. (2d) 109 at 149 (Ont. C.A.).

unanimous shareholder agreement is defined in s. 146(1) of the CBCA as a "written agreement among all the shareholders of a corporation ... that restricts, in whole or in part, the powers of the directors to manage, or service the management of, the business and affairs of the corporation".[34]

Subsection 146(5) of the CBCA provides that to the extent the powers of the directors are restricted by a unanimous shareholder agreement, those powers, and the rights, duties, and liabilities of directors relating thereto, are assumed by the shareholders, and the directors are relieved of those powers, rights, duties, and liabilities to the same extent.[35]

V. Duty of Care

The second branch of a director's duty to the corporation involves the requisite duty of care. This duty may be paraphrased as requiring a director to act carefully, on an informed basis, exhibiting the diligence and skill that a reasonably prudent person would exercise in comparable circumstances. As discussed below under the heading, "A. Standard of Care", the duty of care contains an objective standard to measure a director's care, diligence, and skill against. However, it is emphasized that any assessment of the actions of a director must be made in the context of "comparable circumstances". Thus, a decision that must be taken within a short period of time due to market forces beyond the corporation's control should be reviewed in that context and not in isolation.

Given the possibility that the decisions and actions of the board may be the subjects of subsequent examination, it is essential that an adequate record be kept of the deliberative process followed by the board, including the alternatives and issues considered; information, advice, and analyses prepared for the board and made available to it; and decisions taken by the directors (including the reasons for such decisions). This record will ordinarily take the form of written reports and other material furnished to the directors prior to meetings at which the proposed business will be considered, together with minutes of such meetings, which reflect the directors' decisions and the nature and extent of the directors' consideration and debate of the issues.

---

[34] Note that the ABCA does not contain a provision with respect to relieving directors of duties and liabilities under the statute by means of a sole shareholder declaration. The BCBCA does not contain any provisions with respect to relieving directors of duties and liabilities under the statute by means of a unanimous shareholder agreement or a sole shareholder declaration.

[35] There is no such provision in the BCBCA.

A. Standard of Care

The common law imposed a relatively relaxed and subjective standard of care on directors. Directors were merely required to avoid being grossly negligent, and they were judged according to their own personal skills, knowledge, and abilities. However, amendments to the CBCA in the 1970s sought to upgrade this standard to one of simple, rather than gross, negligence and to require that directors be judged by the objective standard of a reasonably prudent person rather than by a subjective standard related to their personal attributes. While previous case law had suggested that the test was a combined objective/subjective one, in *Peoples,* the Supreme Court of Canada held it to be a purely objective one.[36] However, as a practical matter, it is reasonable to expect that courts will not be oblivious to the fact that particular directors may have been appointed to the board because of their particular areas of special expertise, and they will judge their conduct against the backdrop of that expectation. In other words, while directors will not be allowed to escape liability on the grounds that their levels of skill, knowledge and ability fell below the norm, they may be at a higher risk of being held liable if it can be shown that they failed to identify and act upon problems that ought to have been readily apparent to a person possessing their particular set of skills, training, or professional accreditation.

B. Due Diligence and the Business Judgment Rule

Subsection 123(5) of the CBCA provides a due diligence defence to directors. Directors will be found to have complied with their fiduciary duties and duties of care if they have relied in good faith on:

- financial statements of the corporation represented by an officer or auditor of the corporation to fairly reflect the financial condition of the corporation; or
- a report of a person (such as a lawyer or a financial advisor) whose profession lends credibility to a statement made in such a report.[37]

This defence makes clear the value to directors of relevant expert opinions and advice in the course of their review and consideration of the issues.

Another source of protection from personal liability for directors is the "business judgment rule", originally developed by U.S. courts and, in recent years, adopted in revised form by courts in Canada. In a nutshell, this rule protects directors from second guessing by the courts and recognizes that

[36] *Peoples, supra* note 3 at para. 63.

[37] See the heading below, "VII. Due Diligence", for a discussion of other due diligence defences.

directors should not be held to a standard of perfection. Mere errors in judgment will not give rise to liability, provided that the directors acted on an informed basis and within a range of reasonableness. The rule is intended to provide directors with reasonable assurance that they will not be exposed to personal liability merely because their business decisions and strategies do not work out as anticipated. In the absence of such a rule, risk-taking and creativity within the boardroom — the very hallmarks of successful entrepreneurship — could be seriously stifled.

This is what the Ontario Court of Appeal wrote in *Maple Leaf Foods*:

> The law as it has evolved in Ontario and Delaware has the common requirements that the court must be satisfied that the directors have acted reasonably and fairly. The court looks to see that the directors made a *reasonable* decision *not a perfect* decision. Provided the decision taken is within a range of reasonableness, the court ought not to substitute its opinion for that of the board even though subsequent events may have cast doubt on the board's determination. As long as the directors have selected one of several reasonable alternatives, deference is accorded to the board's decision: *Paramount, supra,* at 45; *Brant Investments, supra,* at 320; *Themadel Foundation v. Third Canadian Investment Trust Ltd.* (1998), 38 O.R. (3d) 749 (C.A.) at 754. This formulation of deference to the decision of the Board is known as the "business judgment rule".[38]

In *Peoples*, the Supreme Court of Canada referred with approval to *Maple Leaf Foods* and described the business judgment rule as follows:

> Directors and officers will not be held to be in breach of the duty of care under s. 122(1)(*b*) of the CBCA if they act prudently and on a reasonably informed basis. The decisions they make must be reasonable business decisions in light of all the circumstances about which the directors or officers knew or ought to have known. In determining whether directors have acted in a manner that breached the duty of care, it is worth repeating that perfection is not demanded. Courts are ill-suited and should be reluctant to second-guess the application of business expertise to the considerations that are involved in corporate decision making, but they are capable, on the facts of any case, of determining whether an appropriate degree of prudence and diligence was brought to bear

[38] *Maple Leaf Foods, supra* note 31 at 192.

in reaching what is claimed to be a reasonable business decision at the time it was made.[39]

In summary, courts will defer to the decisions of directors that were taken in good faith and in the absence of conflicts of interest, provided that the directors undertook a reasonable investigation and consideration of the alternatives and acted fairly. Courts will not subject the directors' business judgment to microscopic examination and will not substitute their view of what should have been done for the business judgment of the directors, even if subsequent developments show that the directors did not make the best decisions. In order to avail themselves of the full protection of the business judgment rule, the directors should, where appropriate, seek the guidance and advice of expert advisors, who can assist in determining processes and maintaining evidence that may be helpful.

In light of the foregoing, directors should:

- attend all board meetings, or, if they are unable to attend them, inform themselves about what took place at the meetings; and
- ensure that they follow appropriate steps and procedures, including making the appropriate inquiries, obtaining the appropriate expert and independent advice, establishing appropriate committees when necessary, reviewing the documentation that is provided to them, giving due consideration to issues that may arise, and ensuring that such proceedings are properly recorded.

Directors are reminded that if they disagree with a decision of a board, they should ensure that their dissent is recorded. Section 123 of the CBCA provides that directors are deemed to have consented to any resolution passed or action taken at a meeting of the board or a committee, including meetings at which they were not present, unless they formally dissent in the manner and within the time periods set out in that section.

VI. Other Duties Under the Business Corporations Statutes

In addition to the codification of the directors' fiduciary duty and duty of care in s. 122(1), the CBCA contains a number of other provisions that impose specific duties on directors and liabilities for the breach of those duties.

---

[39] *Peoples, supra* note 3 at para. 67.

Subsection 122(2) of the CBCA imposes a general duty on directors and officers to "comply with this Act, the regulations, articles, by-laws and any unanimous shareholder agreement".[40]

A person who contravenes the CBCA or the regulations without reasonable cause may be found guilty of an offence under s. 251 of the CBCA. In addition, such a contravention may be the subject of a compliance order under s. 247 of the CBCA, and it may give an aggrieved party the grounds for maintaining a complaint for oppression under s. 241.

Various provisions of the CBCA are designed to protect the interests of creditors by preventing steps or transactions that would result in shareholders obtaining a return of their capital whilst the corporation is of dubious solvency. Other provisions are designed to protect shareholders from the unfair dilution of their shares by preventing steps that favour certain shareholders or insiders over others. For example, s. 118 of the CBCA imposes personal liability on directors who vote for, or consent to, a resolution authorizing:

- the issuance of shares for inadequate consideration;
- a purchase, redemption, or other acquisition of shares by an insolvent corporation, contrary to ss. 34, 35, or 36;
- the payment of unreasonable commissions relating to the purchase of the corporation's shares, contrary to s. 41;
- the payment of a dividend by an insolvent corporation, contrary to s. 42;
- the payment of an indemnity to an officer or director of the corporation, contrary to s. 124; or
- the payment of amounts by an insolvent corporation to shareholders under either the dissent and appraisal provision (s. 190) or the oppression provision (s. 241).

In addition, s. 119 imposes upon directors potential personal liability for up to six months of unpaid wages.[41]

Various other provisions of the CBCA impose on directors duties relating to the governance of the corporation. For example:

---

[40] BCBCA, s. 142(1) provides that a director or officer must act in accordance with the Act and the regulations and act in accordance with the memorandum and articles of the company.

[41] Note that the BCBCA does not contain any provision for directors' liabilities for unpaid wages.

- subsection 133(1) imposes a duty upon the directors to call an annual meeting of shareholders by no later than the date set out therein;
- upon receipt of a valid requisition for a shareholders' meeting, the directors have a duty to call such a shareholders' meeting in accordance with s. 143;
- section 155 requires the directors to place certain financial statements before the shareholders at every annual meeting, and s. 158 requires the directors to approve such financial statements;
- under s. 170, the directors are placed under a duty to provide information and/or access to books and records of the corporation to the auditor of the corporation for purposes of the auditor's examination and report; and
- section 171 requires the directors to establish an audit committee.

VII. Due Diligence

The business corporations statutes each create a due diligence defence for directors; however, each statute's defence may differ somewhat, both in respect of its requirements for application of the defence and in respect of the liabilities the defence covers.

Subsection 123(4) of the CBCA creates a due diligence defence for directors for liabilities referred to in s. 118 (unauthorized return of capital and unfair dilution of shares), s. 119 (unpaid wages), and s. 122(2) (non-compliance with the Act, the regulations, articles, by-laws, and any unanimous shareholder agreement) if the director exercised the care, diligence, and skill that a reasonably prudent person would have exercised in comparable circumstances, including reliance on specific financial statements or reports of professionals.[42] Subsection 123(4) provides as follows:

---

[42] ABCA, s. 123(3) also creates a due diligence defence for directors for liabilities referred to in s. 118 (unauthorized return of capital and unfair dilution of shares) and s. 122(2) (failure to comply with the ABCA, regulations, articles, by-laws, or any unanimous shareholder agreement), as well as for liabilities referred to in s. 122(1) (breach of fiduciary duty and duty of care), but it does not create a due diligence defence for liabilities referred to in s. 119 (unpaid wages). OBCA, s. 135(4) also creates a due diligence defence for directors for liabilities referred to in s. 130 (unauthorized return of capital and unfair dilution of shares) and s. 134(2) (failure to comply with the Act, regulations, articles, by-laws, or any unanimous shareholder agreement), as well as for liabilities referred to in s. 134(1) (breach of fiduciary duty and duty of care), but it does not create a due diligence defence for liabilities referred to in s. 131 (unpaid wages). BCBCA, s. 157(1) also creates a due diligence defence for directors for liabilities referred to in s. 154 (unauthorized return of capital and unfair dilution of shares) and s. 142 (failure to comply with the Act, regulations, corporate memorandum, and articles and breach of fiduciary duty and duty of care), but the BCBCA does not impose liability on directors for unpaid wages.

> (4) A director is not liable under section 118 or 119, and has complied with his or her duties under subsection 122(2), if the director exercised the care, diligence and skill that a reasonably prudent person would have exercised in comparable circumstances, including reliance in good faith on
>
> (*a*) financial statements of the corporation represented to the director by an officer of the corporation or in a written report of the auditor of the corporation fairly to reflect the financial condition of the corporation; or
>
> (*b*) a report of a person whose profession lends credibility to a statement made by the professional person.

As noted above under the heading, "V. B. Due Diligence and the Business Judgment Rule", s. 123(5) of the CBCA also provides a due diligence defence to directors for liability for the breach of fiduciary duty and duty of care if the director relied in good faith on specific financial statements or reports of professionals.[43] Subsection 123(5) of the CBCA states:

> (5) A director has complied with his or her duties under subsection 122(1) if the director relied in good faith on
>
> (*a*) financial statements of the corporation represented to the director by an officer of the corporation or in a written report of the auditor of the corporation fairly to reflect the financial condition of the corporation; or
>
> (*b*) a report of a person whose profession lends credibility to a statement made by the professional person.

---

[43] As noted, ABCA, s. 123(3) also creates a due diligence defence for directors for liabilities referred to in s. 122(1) (breach of fiduciary duty and duty of care); however, while the CBCA due diligence defence for breaches of such duties requires only that the director relied in good faith on the said financial statements and reports of professionals, ABCA, s. 123(3) also requires that the director exercised the care, diligence, and skill that a reasonably prudent person would have exercised in comparable circumstances, including reliance in good faith on such statements and reports. OBCA, s. 135(4) is similar to the CBCA defence in requiring only that the director relied in good faith on the said financial statements and reports of professionals in order to receive the protection of the due diligence defence for breaches of fiduciary duty and duty of care. BCBCA, s. 157 requires only that the director relied in good faith on the said financial statements and reports of professionals (or statements of fact represented as correct by an officer, or any record, information, or representation that the court considers provides reasonable grounds for the actions of the director, whether or not it was forged, fraudulently made, or inaccurate) in order to receive the protection of the due diligence defence for liabilities imposed under BCBCA, s. 154 or s. 142.

VIII. Conclusion

In earlier times, before such high-profile corporate scandals as Enron, Worldcom, and Hollinger, service on corporate boards was regarded by many people as more of a symbol of honour and prestige than a commitment to diligent oversight and the advancement of the corporation's interests. A private club mentality often prevailed. Of course, all that has changed. At the same time, while the need for care, diligence, and skill and the risk of liability for those who fall below the bar have become more pronounced, legislators and the courts have sought to avoid imposing unreasonable or unrealistic demands on directors. Accordingly, directors are entitled to rely on the advice of experts and, in general, on representations made to them by management. They are given various statutory due diligence defences and the protection of the business judgment rule. They are permitted, within reasonable limits, to protect themselves from personal liability through indemnification and insurance arrangements. Therefore, it is suggested that the greatest risk that directors face today arises not from honest errors in judgment, but from inattentiveness or indifference to the interests they were elected to serve and protect.

CHAPTER 3

THE ROLE OF THE DIRECTORS

This Chapter addresses the role of the directors, rather than their actual duties, beginning in section I with a discussion of the principal functions and responsibilities of the board. Section II describes the requirements for constituting the board of directors, including general requirements under the business corporations statutes; the number of directors, executive, and non-executive directors; and the relationship of the directors to management, controlling shareholders, and other shareholders. Section III examines the directors' powers, including their powers to delegate, to establish compensation, to borrow on the credit of the corporation, to issue and redeem shares and declare dividends, and to fill vacancies on the board. Finally, there is a brief discussion of the effect of unanimous shareholder agreements.

I. The Role of the Board

Directors are legally obligated to manage, or supervise the management of, the business and affairs of a corporation. In all but the smallest enterprises, the supervision of management is the only practical option. Business corporations statutes do not detail what this oversight role specifically involves. National Policy 58-201, *Corporate Governance Guidelines* ("NP 58-201"),[1] recommends that boards of public corporations adopt a written mandate in which the corporation explicitly acknowledges the board's responsibility for the stewardship of the corporation. The types of issues that should be addressed in a board mandate are summarized in section IV of Chapter 1, "Management and the Board", and the full text of NP 58-201 can be found in Chapter 1, Appendix VI.[2]

While all of the listed aspects of stewardship are important, the adoption of a strategic planning process and the approval of a strategic plan are critical. The process of taking opportunities and risks into account begins with a thorough understanding of the business. The strategic plan should be reviewed and approved annually, as opportunities and risks can change. While it is management's role to develop the strategic plan, the board's role is to consider whether the plan is the right one and whether the plan has the right vision and mission. A strategic plan should contain specific objectives against which progress can be measured. As noted, risks must be taken into account. The board must understand those risks and determine whether they are acceptable in the circumstances. The board should also consider management's proposals for mitigating risk. Finally, a strategic plan is not an operating plan, and directors should avoid becoming inappropriately involved in management's task of designing and implementing an operating plan.

---

[1] NP 58-201, s. 3.4.

[2] See a sample of a Board Mandate in Chapter 1, Appendix I.

II. Constituting the Board

A. General

The business corporations statutes set out the general requirements for constituting the board of directors.[3] Private corporations are generally required to have only one director, while distributing corporations[4] are generally required to have at least three directors, at least two of whom must not be officers or employees of the corporation or one of its affiliates.[5] It is common for a corporation's articles to provide for a range in the number of directors the corporation's board is required to have. Such a range permits the board to be expanded or reduced as circumstances warrant without having to amend the articles.[6]

Only individuals can be directors of a corporation. Under the CBCA, an individual is disqualified from serving as a director of a corporation if he or she is less than 18 years old, is of unsound mind (and has been so found by a court in Canada or elsewhere), or has the status of a bankrupt.[7]

The business corporations statutes also impose residency requirements on directors. Subject to certain exceptions, at least 25 percent of the directors of a CBCA corporation must be resident Canadians. With the excep-

---

[3] See *Canada Business Corporations Act*, R.S.C. 1985, c. C-44, as amended ("CBCA"), Part X.

[4] Canada Business Corporations Regulations, 2001, S.O.R./2001-512, s. 2 defines a "distributing corporation" as a corporation that is a "reporting issuer" under any provincial *Securities Act*. Additionally, even if a corporation is not a "reporting issuer", it is a "distributing corporation" if: (a) it has filed a prospectus or registration statement inside or outside of Canada; (b) it has any securities listed for trading on a stock exchange inside or outside of Canada; or (c) it is a corporation involved in, formed for, resulting from, or continued after, an amalgamation, a reorganization, an arrangement, or a statutory procedure where one of the participating bodies corporate is a "distributing corporation".

[5] CBCA, s. 102(2); note that s. 115(3) of the Ontario *Business Corporations Act*, R.S.O. 1990, c. B.16, ("OBCA"), requires that at least one-third of the directors of an offering corporation not be officers or employees of the corporation or any of its affiliates; note that the British Columbia *Business Corporations Act*, S.B.C. 2002, c. 57 ("BCBCA") does not specify the number of independent directors required in a public corporation.

[6] OBCA, s. 125(3) provides that the shareholders may pass a special resolution fixing the number of directors and authorizing the directors thereafter, from time to time, to determine by resolution the number of directors to be elected at the next annual meeting. No other jurisdiction's business corporations statute has a similar provision.

[7] CBCA, s. 105(1); note that, in addition, BCBCA, s. 124(2)(*d*) disqualifies individuals from serving as directors if they have been convicted of an offence in connection with the promotion, formation, or management of an incorporated or unincorporated business, or of an offence involving fraud. Individuals will not be disqualified, however, where the court orders otherwise, a pardon was granted or issued under the *Criminal Records Act*, or five years have elapsed since the last to occur of (a) the expiration of the period set for suspension of the passing of a sentence without a sentence having been passed, (b) the imposition of a fine, (c) the conclusion of the term of any imprisonment, and (d) the conclusion of the term of any probation imposed. Note also that the Alberta *Business Corporations Act*, R.S.A. 2000, c. B-9, ("ABCA"), s. 105(1)(*b*) disqualifies anyone who: (i) is a dependent adult, as defined in the *Dependent Adults Act*, or is the subject of a certificate of incapacity under that Act, (ii) is a formal patient, as defined in the *Mental Health Act*, (iii) is the subject of an order under *The Mentally Incapacitated Persons Act*, appointing a committee of the person or estate, or both, or (iv) has been found to be a person of unsound mind by a court elsewhere than in Alberta.

tion of non-resident corporations, if a corporation has less than four directors, at least one of the directors must be a resident Canadian, and if a corporation has only one or two directors, that the one director, or one of the two directors, as the case may be, must be a resident Canadian. In cases where a corporation carries on business in a prescribed business sector or is subject to Canadian ownership requirements, the corporation may be required to have a board of directors in which resident Canadians make up the majority of the members.[8] In some jurisdictions in Canada, there are no Canadian residency requirements. This factor sometimes determines a Canadian subsidiary of a foreign corporation's choice of jurisdiction of incorporation in situations where it may not be possible or desirable for the foreign corporation to satisfy the Canadian residency requirements.

In most cases, directors are elected at the annual general meeting and serve until the next annual general meeting or until their successors are appointed or elected. However, directors may be elected to hold office until no longer than the third annual general meeting following their election, and not all directors of a corporation are required to hold office for the same term (i.e., longer and staggered terms are permissible but they are not commonly used in Canada).[9] Directors cease to hold office upon death, disqualification, resignation, or removal by a resolution of the shareholders.[10] As discussed in section III.F., below, a quorum of directors can fill vacancies on the board, subject to certain restrictions.

---

[8] CBCA, ss. 105(3), (3.1), and (3.2) and ABCA, s. 105(3). CBCA, s. 2, defines "resident Canadian" as an individual who is a Canadian citizen ordinarily resident in Canada. A Canadian citizen who is not ordinarily resident can still be considered a "resident Canadian" if the individual is a member of a class of persons listed in the Canada Business Corporations Regulations, 2001, SOR/2001-512, s. 13. The CBCA definition also includes individuals who are permanent residents according to the *Immigration and Refugee Protection Act* and ordinarily resident in Canada (except a permanent resident who has been ordinarily resident in Canada for more than one year after the time at which he or she first became eligible to apply for Canadian citizenship). Note that OBCA, s. 118(3) requires the majority of directors to be resident Canadians; there are no Canadian residency requirements under the BCBCA.

[9] CBCA, ss. 106(3), (4), and (5) provides that if no term is specified in the election of a director, such a director ceases to hold office after the annual general meeting following his or her election. ABCA, s. 106(9) provides that in order for the directors to be elected to hold office for a term expiring later than the close of the next annual meeting following their election, the articles of the corporation or a unanimous shareholder agreement must so provide that in such cases, directors may not be elected for terms expiring later than the close of the third annual meeting of shareholders following their election.

[10] CBCA, s. 108(1). OBCA, s. 121(2) provides that a resignation is effective at the time a written resignation is received by the corporation or at the time specified in the resignation, whichever is later. This provision is intended to prevent the backdating of resignations. CBCA, s. 108(2) and ABCA, s. 108(2) both refer to the time the resignation is sent to the corporation as opposed to being received by the corporation. BCBCA, s. 128(2) provides that the resignation of a director takes effect only when the written resignation is provided to the corporation or to a lawyer for the corporation.

The directors may, if the articles of the corporation so provide, appoint one or more additional directors between annual general meetings, provided, however, that such directors hold office only until the next annual general meeting of shareholders and the total number of directors at any one time so appointed must not exceed one-third of the number of directors elected at the previous annual general meeting of shareholders.[11]

Ultimately, subject to complying with the applicable statutory requirements discussed above, the number of directors a corporation has should be determined by the near to medium term needs of the corporation and, to a lesser extent, by accepted best practices in corporate governance and by any norms developed in the industry in which the corporation carries on business. In order to be effective as a board of directors and be in a position to effectively fulfill its role and duties and to provide sound and objective judgment, a board should have enough directors to serve on various committees, and the directors comprising a board should represent a variety of skills, experience, and perspectives.[12] Most corporations will be well served if the board possesses some level of expertise in each of the areas of marketing, finance, accounting, human resources, and corporate governance. Depending upon the corporation's business, other specific areas of expertise, such as reserves evaluation for a natural resources company or computer technology for a software company, will be helpful.

Boards ought to consider which specific skill sets are most relevant to the corporation's business and which of those skill sets are missing from the board, as it is presently constituted. New directors who have the missing skill sets should be sought, whether they are added to increase the size of the board or to replace existing directors. In order to effectively build the board, it is advisable to maintain a list of potential candidates so that approaches may be made, on a timely basis, to those best qualified to sit on the board. Normally, a committee of the board handles this task, increasingly with assistance from an executive search firm.[13]

---

[11] CBCA, s. 106(8). OBCA, s. 124(2) provides that the total number of additional directors appointed may not exceed one and one-third times the number of directors required to have been elected at the last annual meeting of shareholders.

[12] For example, Multilateral Instrument 52-110, *Audit Committees,* s. 3.1(4) ("MI 52-110"), requires audit committee members to be financially literate; they must have "the ability to read and understand a set of financial statements that present a breadth and level of complexity of accounting issues that are generally comparable to the breadth and complexity of the issues that can reasonably be expected to be raised by the issuer's financial statements".

[13] Barry J. Reiter, "Building a Great Board of Directors — a Committed and Sustained Process", *Corporate Governance Journal* (2003).

B. Board Independence

Most private corporations are controlled by one shareholder or by a small group of shareholders whose role in the management of the corporation (particularly, their ability to nominate directors) will be set out in a unanimous shareholder agreement. However, as noted above, in the case of a public corporation, the business corporations statutes generally require that at least two directors not be officers or employees of the corporation or its affiliates.[14] These directors are sometimes referred to as "outside", "independent", "unrelated", or "non-executive" directors.

Independent directors enable the board of directors to effectively discharge one of its principal functions: the supervision of the management of the corporation. Independent directors can provide an objective viewpoint in discussions of issues brought forward by directors who are also major shareholders (or their nominees), or members of senior management, or both. Independent directors are available to serve on committees, particularly committees that are required by law, or encouraged by regulators or institutional shareholder groups, to have independent directors serve as members.

The term "independent" has different meanings, depending on the context. Under the CBCA, a director is independent if he or she is not employed by the corporation or its affiliates.[15] NP 58-201 requires public corporations to disclose which directors are independent and which are not independent.[16] If a majority of the board is not independent, the corporation is required to disclose what the board does to facilitate its exercise of independent judgment in carrying out its responsibilities. Independence is defined as the lack of a "material relationship" with the corporation. A "material relationship" is one which could, in the view of the board, be reasonably expected to interfere with the exercise of independent judgment. Certain specific relationships are deemed to be material, such as being a current or recent employee or executive officer of the corporation or a current or recent partner or employee of the corporation's auditor.

The question of independence is also relevant to audit committees. MI 52-110 requires that all members of an audit committee be independent.[17] The definition of independence for the purposes of qualification for audit committee membership is more strict than for the purposes of the

---

[14] *Supra* note 5.

[15] CBCA, s. 171(1).

[16] *Supra* note 1.

[17] *Supra* note 12, s. 3.1(3). Note that this instrument has been adopted in all jurisdictions except British Columbia.

general test in National Instrument 58-101, *Corporate Governance.*[18] For the purpose of determining the independence of a member of the audit committee, the director must not have a material relationship with the corporation and must not have accepted any fee from the corporation other than board or committee fees. The acceptance of fees includes indirect receipt where the corporation pays a fee to an entity of which the director is an active member. Therefore, where a director is a partner of a firm providing services to the corporation, the director is not eligible to be a member of the audit committee, even if the amount of the fees received by the firm is so insignificant that the board concludes that a material relationship does not exist.

Ultimately, it is the board that determines whether a director is independent. A board's judgment on that question is not likely to be questioned by a court or a regulator if it was made following the proper consideration of all relevant circumstances. Corporations should develop questionnaires designed to bring to the surface all of the facts that are relevant to a determination of independence. Where the information provided suggests a potential material relationship, boards should make further inquiries. The board's deliberations in concluding whether or not a director is independent should be reflected in board minutes. Since circumstances change over time, directors should be required to disclose any changes in their circumstances, and the independence of directors should be reviewed at least annually.

C. Nominee Directors' Relationship to the Corporation

A director who is nominated by the majority shareholder, a special class of shareholders, debenture holders, or a holding corporation occupies a position of inherent tensions. He or she may even be an employee or a director of the nominating body. Nonetheless, the nominee director must reconcile the duty to act in the best interests of the corporation as a whole with a natural (and even encouraged) inclination to further the interests of the nominator. Where does such a director's loyalty lie if he or she becomes aware, through connections to the nominating party, of information that is important to the deliberations of the board on which that director sits as a nominee director? Recent case law indicates that a nominee director must disclose such information.[19]

---

[18] ("NI 58-101").

[19] *PWA Corp. v. Gemini Group Automated Distribution Systems Inc. et al.* (1993), 10 B.L.R. (2d) 109 (Ont. C.A.) at para. 140; leave to appeal to S.C.C. refused, (1993), 10 B.L.R. (2d) 244 (S.C.C.). For a further discussion of this decision, see section IV.C. of Chapter 2, "Nominee Directors".

The nominating party may also be held responsible for the actions of the nominee director.[20] Furthermore, the courts have clearly held that the nominee director's responsibilities to the corporation override any responsibilities to the nominator.[21] The directors' duty is to the corporation, and each director is required to exercise independent judgment, irrespective of their relationship(s) with the corporation.

III. The Powers of Directors

Directors are responsible for the management (or the supervision of the management) and governance of the corporation.[22] To enable them to carry out these duties, they are given specific powers in the business corporations statutes. These statutory provisions are sometimes repeated in the articles of incorporation or in the by-laws, which may also offer guidelines for the exercise of the directors' powers or, in some cases, may limit their powers. Directors should be familiar with the articles and the by-laws, and they should review them from time to time to refresh their memories.

Unless the by-laws, articles, or a unanimous shareholder agreement provide otherwise, directors may by resolution make, amend, or repeal any by-laws that regulate the business or affairs of the corporation. These changes must be submitted to the shareholders at their next meeting. The shareholders may confirm, reject, or amend the proposed changes.[23] A by-law is effective from the date of the resolution of the directors until the date it is confirmed, amended, or rejected by the shareholders. If a by-law is rejected by the shareholders or it is not submitted to the shareholders as required, it ceases to be effective.[24]

A. Delegation of Powers

The board of directors can delegate a number of their powers and responsibilities to a managing director or to a committee of directors[25] and to the corporation's officers.[26] Under the CBCA, the managing director, if

[20] *Ibid.*

[21] *Ibid.*; see also *Scottish Co-Operative Wholesale Society Ltd. v. Meyer*, [1959] A.C. 324 (H.L.).

[22] CBCA, s. 102.

[23] CBCA, ss. 103(1) and (2); the BCBCA does not contain provisions on the changing of by-laws by directors.

[24] CBCA, ss. 103(3) and (4).

[25] CBCA, s. 115(1). See Chapter 6, "The Use of Committees", for additional discussion.

[26] CBCA, s. 121.

there is one, must be a resident Canadian.[27] However, certain core responsibilities cannot be delegated: declaring dividends; approving disclosure documents; issuing securities; purchasing or redeeming shares issued by the corporation; the payment of certain commissions in connection with the sale of shares; approving annual financial statements of the corporation; adopting, amending, or repealing by-laws; submitting to the shareholders any questions or matters requiring the approval of the shareholders; filling a vacancy on the board or in the office of the auditor; or appointing additional directors. Matters that cannot be delegated require the exercise of powers for which directors must be personally responsible. In some cases, the directors will be held personally responsible for the misuse of these powers.

Even when decisions cannot be delegated, it is common to use committees, professional advisors and other outside consultants, and senior management to advise the entire board of directors. Since, in some circumstances, directors will be entitled to rely on written expert advice or financial statements to relieve themselves of personal liability, the board should expect to be provided with written reports, descriptions and analyses of alternative proposals, and enough information so that the board can effectively make the decisions it is required by statute to make.[28]

While the CBCA denies a managing director or committee of the board the authority to fill a vacancy on the board or in the office of auditor, the directors of CBCA companies can delegate the power to appoint or remove the chair, president or chief financial officer to a managing director, or a committee of the board (such as a hiring or compensation committee).[29]

How (and in what circumstances) the board chooses to delegate these powers will depend on the size of the corporation, the nature of its business, how often the powers will be exercised, and the expertise of board members and senior management. For example, a corporation that acquires and sells real property in the course of its business may delegate greater responsibility to a senior officer or a committee than a corporation whose real estate transaction experience is very limited and infrequent. Similarly, the delegation of a power to issue multi-million dollar guarantees is reasonable for a

---

[27] CBCA, s. 115(1). ABCA, s. 115(2) also requires that at least one-fourth of the members of a board committee be resident Canadians; OBCA, s. 127(2) requires that the majority of the members of a committee of directors be resident Canadians.

[28] See the discussion in section VII of Chapter 2, "The Duties of Directors".

[29] See Chapter 6, "The Use of Committees".

large corporation where the guarantee is small in proportion to the corporation's assets and revenues, but it is not reasonable for a small corporation.[30]

Notwithstanding that certain matters may fall within the mandate of a committee, it may be appropriate to refer such matters for consideration to the full board of directors in cases where, for example, the matters are extraordinary or affect the corporation's policies or strategic direction. As well, in practice, committees often refer matters within their mandate back to the full board of directors, often along with the committee's recommendations.

B. Establishing and Reporting Compensation

The directors may fix their own remuneration, as well as the remuneration of the officers and employees of the corporation. This authority may be exercised by the board as a whole, but the common practice is to establish a compensation committee.[31] While there is no requirement that members of a public corporation's compensation committee be independent, there is a requirement for the committee's members to disclose potential conflicts, such as being a current or recent employee or officer of the corporation or being indebted to the corporation. Best practices of public corporations and the guidelines of institutional shareholder groups require that all members of the compensation committee be independent.

The compensation committee must establish the compensation of directors and senior employees and ensure that such compensation is properly disclosed.

The establishment of compensation, like all acts of directors, must be done in the best interests of the corporation. Therefore, directors attempt to find a balance between attracting and retaining qualified directors and senior employees and not wasting the corporation's resources. Finding this balance requires directors to understand the key roles in their organization and the market for individuals who are able to fill those roles. In order to have accurate, relevant data, compensation committees usually engage experts who can provide information regarding peer companies' practices and other market data.[32]

---

[30] See Chapter 1, Appendix II for a sample Delegation of Authority in partial implementation of a board mandate.

[31] Sometimes the compensation committee will deal with the compensation of management, leaving directors' compensation matters to the Corporate Governance Committee.

[32] Barry J. Reiter, "The Role of Compensation Committees in Corporate Governance", *Corporate Governance Journal* (2004).

Directors must also consider the various methods of compensating employees. While salaries are an important element of compensation, other methods provide creative alternatives. Mechanisms such as long-term incentive programs, stock appreciation rights, share purchase programs, and performance options have evolved in the last several years. In essence, each of these mechanisms attempts to properly align the corporation's interests with the employees' interests. Favourable tax treatment of certain types of income to directors is also a significant motivating factor for directors.

When assessing a compensation proposal, directors should consider whether the proposal will foster the sort of behaviour from directors and employees that will further the corporation's best interests. A simple stock option plan might be found lacking because there is an insufficient link between an employee's individual performance and the price of the shares. Conversely, a system that allows an employee to prosper when his or her individual targets are met while shareholders suffer a decline in share price may not be appropriate. Most corporations seek a balance that aligns the interests of employees and shareholders while allowing employees to benefit from properly performing their specific roles in the corporation.

The reporting of compensation has become highly complex (and, based on recent announcements from each side of the Canada-US border, it is threatening to become even more complex), due to detailed securities regulations and the myriad of compensation plans in existence. Directors should be satisfied that qualified experts are assisting management in the preparation of this type of disclosure.[33]

C. Borrowing, Debt Obligations, and Mortgages

Directors are required to make certain decisions relating to the corporation's financial situation. Unless the articles, by-laws, or a unanimous shareholder agreement impose limits, directors have the power:

- to borrow on the credit of the corporation;
- to issue or pledge debt obligations of the corporation;
- to give guarantees on behalf of the corporation; and
- to mortgage the corporation's property,

all without the approval of shareholders.[34]

---

[33] See section IX of Chapter 1, "Director Compensation", and section VI of Chapter 6, "Nomination, Compensation, and Corporate Governance Committees", for a further discussion of this matter.

[34] CBCA, s. 189(1).

The directors can delegate these powers to a single director, a committee of the board, or an officer of the corporation, although an extraordinary sale, lease, or exchange of the corporation's property will require shareholder approval.[35]

D. Issuing and Redeeming Shares; Payment of Commissions

Directors, subject to the articles, by-laws, or a unanimous shareholder agreement, must determine when, and for how much, the securities of the corporation will be issued.[36] If the articles of incorporation authorize the issuing of shares in series, the directors may be authorized to determine the rights, privileges, restrictions, and conditions that are attached to a particular series of shares.[37]

While boards of directors generally have the exclusive authority to issue shares, in certain instances, this authority may be delegated. For example:

- if previously authorized by the board of directors, a managing director or a committee of directors has the power to issue shares of a series; and
- the board may delegate the authority to fix the price of a share issuance within a price range determined by the board.

There is a special liability provision dealing with directors who issue shares for consideration other than cash, such as property or past services. Such directors can be jointly and severally liable to the corporation to make good any difference between the value of the non-cash consideration and the amount that the corporation would have received if the shares had been issued for money.[38] Directors have a defence to this liability if they can show that they could not reasonably have known that the value of the consideration received was less than the value of the shares or that they relied on the written opinion of experts.[39]

---

[35] CBCA, ss. 189(2) and (3).

[36] CBCA, s. 25(1).

[37] CBCA, s. 25(1).

[38] CBCA, s. 118.

[39] CBCA, ss. 118(6) and 123(4). See section VII of Chapter 2, "Due Diligence", for a discussion of the directors' due diligence defence.

Shares cannot be issued in consideration for a promissory note.[40] Directors are also unable to delegate the decision to purchase, redeem or otherwise acquire the corporation's shares. In addition, prior to resolving to purchase, redeem, or otherwise acquire the corporation's shares, the directors, acting reasonably, must be satisfied that a such purchase, redemption, or acquisition will not be contrary to the financial solvency tests prescribed in the governing business corporations statute.[41] If the directors fail these tests, they will be jointly and severally liable to restore to the corporation any amounts so distributed or paid and not otherwise recovered by the corporation. Directors may be relieved of this liability if they rely in good faith on financial statements presented by an officer of the corporation, a written report of the auditor, or a report of an accountant or other expert.[42] Directors may demonstrate prudence and good management by ensuring that an adequate financial investigation is made and a written report on the advisability of the redemption is provided to the board.

The board of directors may also authorize the payment of a reasonable commission to any person for purchasing or finding purchasers of shares.[43] These commissions are a standard part of underwriting agreements or private placements. Directors who pay a commission contrary to the statute may be held personally liable for the amount of the payment, but they may also rely in good faith on reports of experts to relieve them of liability.[44]

---

[40] CBCA, s. 25(5).

[41] The solvency tests are found in CBCA, s. 34(2). The first test prohibits a corporation from making any payment to purchase or otherwise acquire its own shares where there are reasonable grounds for believing that the corporation will be unable to pay its liabilities as they become due or will be unable to pay them after the shares are paid for. The second test prevents a corporation from making any payment to purchase or otherwise acquire its own shares where there are reasonable grounds for believing that, as a result of the payment, the realizable value of the corporation's assets would be less than the aggregate of its liabilities and stated capital of all classes of shares. If either test is met, a corporation cannot make any payment to purchase or otherwise acquire its own shares. Under s. 35(1), however, a corporation may purchase or otherwise acquire its own shares, notwithstanding s. 34(2), where the purpose is to settle debts, eliminate fractional shares, or fulfill put and call options. Where a corporation makes a payment for its shares under this subsection, it is subject to s. 35(3), which prohibits a corporation from making such a payment where there are reasonable grounds for believing that the corporation will be unable to pay its liabilities as they become due or the realizable value of the corporation's assets would be less than the aggregate of its liabilities and the amount required for payment on a redemption or in a liquidation of all shares where the shareholders have the right to be paid before the holders of the shares to be purchased or acquired, to the extent that the amount has not been included in its liabilities. See CBCA, s. 36(3) for the solvency tests that will apply when a corporation redeems its shares. Under CBCA, s. 35(2), a corporation may, notwithstanding s. 34(2), buy shares to satisfy the claim of a dissenting shareholder or to comply with a court order. Note that the exceptions listed above are not found in the BCBCA.

[42] CBCA, ss. 123(4) and (5).

[43] CBCA, s. 41.

[44] CBCA, ss. 118(2), 123(4), and (5).

E. Declaring Dividends

Subject to a unanimous shareholder agreement, only the board of directors has the authority to declare a dividend.[45] The dividend may be in the form of cash, property, fully paid-up shares, or options or rights to acquire fully paid-up shares.[46] Although the board of directors cannot delegate the responsibility for a decision on dividends, it would be expected to receive expert advice on the financial situation of the corporation, its prospects, the appropriate size and form of the dividend, and any other implications for the market. Even for a small, closely held corporation, the directors should obtain the advice of an accountant or auditor.

The advice of the auditor or accountant is particularly important since directors can be held personally liable if a dividend is declared or paid when there are reasonable grounds for believing that:

- the corporation is, or after the payment of the dividend would be, unable to pay its liabilities as they become due; or
- the realizable value of the corporation's assets would thereby be less than the aggregate of its liabilities and stated capital of all classes.[47]

Directors who rely in good faith on the financial statements of the corporation or on the written report of the corporation's auditor or of another expert whose profession lends credibility to a statement made by such an expert will not be held liable under the business corporations statutes for the inappropriate declaration of a dividend.[48] Note, however, that the *Bankruptcy and Insolvency Act*[49] may also impose liability on directors if a corporation is insolvent when a dividend is paid. A director's reliance on financial statements or on an expert's reports is a matter that *may* be considered by a court in determining liability.[50]

F. Filling Vacancies

Ordinarily, the directors are elected by the shareholders at an annual general meeting. However, vacancies on the board occur from time to time. Although a board can function as long as it has enough members to form a quorum, it may be advisable for the directors to fill a vacancy prior to the

---

[45] CBCA, s. 115(3). The BCBCA does not address limitations on the authority of the managing director or of a committee of directors.

[46] CBCA, s. 43.

[47] CBCA, s. 42.

[48] CBCA, s. 123(4).

[49] R.S.C. 1985, c. B-3.

[50] *Ibid.* at ss. 101(2) and (2.1).

next shareholders' meeting in order to ensure that enough directors are always available to gather a quorum and validly constitute a meeting. It may also be advisable to fill vacancies to ensure that a range of expertise and experience is available.

A quorum of directors may fill a vacancy in the board of directors, except when the vacancy results from the failure to elect the required number of directors at the shareholders' meeting or from an unauthorized increase in the size of the board.[51] A new director who is appointed to fill a vacancy will hold office for the unexpired term of his or her predecessor.[52] If the remaining directors cannot form a quorum, they must call a special shareholders' meeting to elect new directors. If they fail to call a meeting or there are no directors in office, any shareholder can call the meeting.[53]

The articles of a corporation may provide that a vacancy among the directors be filled by a vote of the shareholders or by a vote of the holders of any class or series of shares having an exclusive right to elect one or more directors if the vacancy occurs among the directors elected by that class or series.[54]

Shareholders also appoint the auditor of the corporation.[55] If the auditor resigns, dies, or is removed, the directors must fill the vacancy forthwith.[56] An auditor who is appointed to fill a vacancy will hold office for the unexpired term of the auditor's predecessor.

The directors, or a managing director or committee of the board to whom such authority has been delegated, may appoint any person to fill a vacancy in an office of the corporation.

G. Approving Important Disclosure Documents

In response to the collapse of such corporations as Enron and Worldcom, legislators in the United States and Canada have strengthened existing laws and regulations that hold directors responsible for corporate disclosure. In the United States, the much publicized *Sarbanes-Oxley* legislation[57] includes provisions relating to certification of the accuracy of finan-

---

[51] CBCA, s. 111(1). A notice of change of directors must also be sent to the appropriate authorities within a prescribed period of time: CBCA, s. 113(1).

[52] CBCA, s. 111(5).

[53] CBCA, s. 111(2).

[54] CBCA, s. 111(4).

[55] CBCA, s. 162(1).

[56] CBCA, s. 166(1). The articles of incorporation may state that only the shareholders can appoint a new auditor.

[57] *Sarbanes-Oxley Act of 2002*, Pub. L. No. 107-204, 116 Stat. 745.

cial statements and certification of the integrity of internal control systems by chief executive officers and chief financial officers, the establishment of an auditor oversight board, and protection for those bringing corporate wrongdoing to the attention of boards and regulators. In Canada, our own version of *Sarbanes-Oxley* has developed with the adoption by securities regulators of various instruments and policies such as NP 58-201,[58] NI 58-101,[59] MI 52-110,[60] and Multilateral Instrument 52-109.[61]

The cornerstone of any system of securities legislation is a requirement that public companies make full and timely disclosure of all information required by investors. It is therefore appropriate to place responsibility for corporate disclosure with directors.

Securities legislation in Ontario and Alberta has recently been amended to provide for secondary market civil liability for misstatements in a corporation's public disclosure record.[62] Those who are potentially liable to secondary market purchasers of a corporation's securities include the corporation, its directors and other experts. Previously, corporations, directors, and experts were, in general, only liable for misstatements in a prospectus offering.

Securities legislation distinguishes between core documents, other documents, and oral statements. For core documents, directors are liable whether or not they had knowledge of the misrepresentation. For other documents and oral statements, a director is liable if he or she knew of the misrepresentation, deliberately avoided acquiring knowledge of the misrepresentation, or is found guilty of gross misconduct in connection with the circumstances surrounding the misrepresentation.

Core documents are usually documents that are brought to the board for approval. They include annual information forms, information circulars, management discussion and analysis, prospectuses, and take-over bid circulars.

Various defences to an action for misrepresentation exist. The most useful one for directors is the defence of due diligence, which is available to a director if the director can establish that he or she conducted a reasonable

---

58 *Supra* note 1.

59 *Supra* note 18.

60 *Supra* note 12.

61 Multilateral Instrument 52-109, *Certification of Disclosure in Issuers' Annual and Interim Filings*.

62 The Ontario *Securities Act*, R.S.O. 1990, c. S.5, Part XXIII.1, *Civil Liability for Secondary Market Disclosure*, in force as of December 31, 2005; Bill 25, *Securities Amendment Act, 2006*, 2d Sess., 26th Leg., Alberta, 2006, s. 52 (comes into force on proclamation).

investigation, and at the time of the disclosure violation, had no reasonable grounds for believing that a violation would occur.

Due diligence defences are based in part upon the principle of third party verification. It is not enough for directors to ask management to confirm that the disclosure is accurate. Directors are required to consider the disclosure carefully, question management regarding the facts, and seek third party verification where appropriate. Of course, directors are entitled to have the due diligence investigation conducted on their behalf by qualified experts such as counsel, auditors, and others. Directors should be sure that all such experts have been properly instructed to take steps and maintain files so that a successful due diligence defence can be put forth.

Another important step to minimize the risk of being liable for a disclosure violation is the adoption by the corporation of a disclosure policy setting forth the systems in place to ensure the corporation's public record is accurate. Typically, disclosure policies establish a disclosure committee that is charged with monitoring the corporation's disclosure practices, setting forth guidelines for determining what is material information, and detailing procedures for making news releases, conducting investor conference calls, and communicating with securities analysts. One purpose of a disclosure policy is to communicate to employees various rules and policies, such as the need to keep certain information confidential, the need to avoid selective disclosure, and the need to bring business developments to the attention of the proper individuals so that timely disclosure can be made of material changes in the affairs of the corporation.

H. Unanimous Shareholder Agreements

A written agreement among all of the shareholders can wholly or partly restrict the powers of the directors to manage, or supervise the management of, the business and the affairs of the corporation.[63] Such an agreement is referred to as a unanimous shareholder agreement. To the extent that a unanimous shareholder agreement restricts the powers of the directors to manage, or supervise the management of, the business and affairs of the corporation, the parties to the unanimous shareholder agreement who are given that power have all of the rights, powers, duties, and liabilities of the

[63] CBCA, s. 146 (1).

directors of the corporation, and the directors are relieved of their rights, powers, duties, and liabilities to the same extent.[64]

The implementation of a unanimous shareholder agreement is a practical way to reduce the potential liabilities of a director. Although unanimous shareholder agreements are commonplace in private corporations and are impractical to implement in the context of public corporations, some public corporations will implement a unanimous shareholder agreement for its subsidiaries. A written declaration made by an owner of all of the shares of a corporation that restricts, in whole or in part, the powers of the directors to manage or supervise the management of the business and affairs of the corporation is deemed to constitute a unanimous shareholder agreement.[65] In addition, certain shareholders of a public corporation may enter into various voting arrangements, such as voting trusts, pooling agreements,[66] or shareholder agreements, whereby they agree to vote their shares in a consistent manner. However, such voting arrangements (unlike unanimous shareholder agreements) do not have the effect of reducing the powers and liabilities of directors.

Unanimous shareholder agreements will not necessarily eliminate directors' liability under other statutes or other sources of liability.

IV. Conclusion

It is essential that the directors of a corporation fully comprehend their roles, functions, and responsibilities. Directors should not only be familiar with the technical requirements for constituting the board under applicable statutes and guidelines, but they must also develop an appreciation for their particular relationship to management and to controlling shareholders and other shareholders. These relationships will vary from one corporation to another and from time to time. Directors must be fully aware of their powers, including the extent of their power to delegate the duty to manage the business and affairs of the corporation. Above all, directors should recognize that they are legally bound to exercise independent judgment and that their duty lies to the corporation as a whole.

---

[64] CBCA, s. 146(5). The BCBCA does not address unanimous shareholder agreements that restrict the powers of directors. ABCA, s. 146 provides that all shareholders who are party to, or deemed to be party to, a unanimous shareholder agreement incur the liabilities of a director, as opposed to just those shareholders to whom the powers to manage are given. As well, under the ABCA, the terms of a unanimous shareholder agreement may exclude the application of s. 146 thereto, including s. 146(7), which relieves directors from liability.

[65] CBCA, s. 146(2); note that the ABCA and the BCBCA do not include comparable sections.

[66] CBCA, s. 145.1.

CHAPTER 4

BOARD MEETINGS

Much of a director's work is done at board meetings or in preparation for them. This Chapter reviews the statutory requirements for calling board meetings, starting with a general discussion in section I, then, in section II, dealing with what must and should be included in the notice of the meeting. Sections III and IV deal with the frequency of meetings and their location. Section V looks at the required quorum of directors, including the requirements for resident Canadians to be present.

Information about telephone meetings and written resolutions signed by the directors is found in sections VI and VII, while the benefits of holding directors' meetings in person are discussed in section VIII. Section IX sets out the requirements for dissenting to resolutions or actions taken at meetings, and section X discusses the procedures for directors to use when disclosing an interest in a material contract or a transaction. Section XI discusses some of the ways directors should conduct themselves during board meetings, while section XII outlines some best practices for conducting efficient meetings. The minutes of board or committee meetings and the need for directors to maintain their own notes of meetings are discussed in section XIII. Finally, Section XIV sets out some suggested best practices for diligent directors to observe.

I. Board Meetings

Subject to any unanimous shareholder agreement, directors are responsible for the control and management of the corporation. They operate collegially but must make their decisions personally. Unlike shareholders, they cannot give proxies to others for board decisions. Directors make decisions by resolution at properly constituted meetings of the board. In some cases, their decisions will be set out in the by-laws of the corporation, which must be confirmed at the next shareholders' meeting. The directors' meetings have a structure, and they should be conducted with sufficient formality to ensure that agenda items receive appropriate discussion and that decisions are properly recorded.

The business corporations statutes require that notice be given, that a quorum be present, and that a certain number of resident Canadian directors be present at the meeting. For some matters, the business corporations statutes provide guidance, but the corporate by-laws or a unanimous shareholder agreement can be tailored to the individual needs of the corporation.[1] In practice, most corporate by-laws authorize greater flexibility in the conduct of meetings than what is found in the statute. Therefore, directors can generally expect to find the requirements governing the meetings of their board in their corporation's by-laws or in a unanimous shareholder agreement.

While directors are not legally required to attend meetings, they should attend them as frequently as possible. They will be deemed to consent to business conducted at meetings when they are absent from them, unless they specifically dissent.[2] An absent director is more likely to be considered

[1] *Canada Business Corporations Act*, R.S.C. 1985, c. C-44, ("CBCA"), s. 6(2) provides that the articles may set out any provisions permitted by the CBCA or by-law to be set out in the by-laws of the corporation. The British Columbia *Business Corporations Act*, S.B.C. 2002, c. 57 ("BCBCA") does not have a similar section.

[2] See Section IX, below.

to have ignored his or her responsibilities than to be insulated from liability. Risk management involves care, attention, monitoring, reviewing documents, asking questions, and ensuring that the corporation's management and employees have put in place the appropriate systems to handle compliance and risk. Absent directors cannot fulfill these responsibilities.

II. Notice of the Meeting

The CBCA does not provide any time requirements for the giving of the notice of the meeting, nor does it require that the notice specify the purpose of the meeting or the business that is expected to be transacted. Certain matters, however, must be specified in the notice if they are going to be considered at the meeting. These are the items that are required by statute to be considered by the full board of directors and cannot be delegated to a committee. Such items include decisions to declare dividends, approve take-over-bid circulars or directors' circulars, approve financial statements, or adopt, amend, or repeal by-laws.[3] The by-laws or articles may also require that notice of the business to be conducted at the meeting be given, as well as the statutorily required notice of time and place.

Provincial business corporations statutes differ on these points. For example, the Ontario *Business Corporations Act* requires that, in the absence of other provisions in the by-laws or articles, notice of the time and place for the meeting be given to the directors ten days before the date of the meeting.[4] There is no requirement to provide an agenda of the business to be conducted at the meeting.

Directors may waive the requirement of notice of the meeting, and in most cases, attendance at the meeting is a waiver of notice. There is an exception to the waiver when the director attends the meeting for the express purpose of objecting to the transaction of business on the grounds that the meeting was not lawfully called.[5] If a meeting must be called without adequate notice because of an emergency, it is a good practice for the directors to sign written waivers at the time of the meeting to avoid later questions about whether the meeting was properly called. The board is not

---

[3] CBCA, s. 114(5) requires that notice be given to directors of matters that are referred to in s. 115(3).

[4] Ontario *Business Corporations Act*, R.S.O. 1990, c. B.16, s. 126(9) ("OBCA"); no time requirements for the giving of notice are found in the Alberta *Business Corporations Act*, R.S.A. 2000, c. B-9, ("ABCA"), or in the BCBCA.

[5] CBCA, s. 114(6); note that the British Columbia *Business Corporations Regulation*, B.C. Reg. 65/2004 ("BCBCA Regulations"), Table 1, s. 11.8 only provides for the waiver of notice by a signed document, and it makes no mention of waiver by attendance.

required to give notice of an adjourned meeting if the time and place of the continuation of the meeting are announced at the original meeting.[6]

The by-laws or articles generally provide more detail about who convenes the meeting and what the usual form of notice will be. For example, the by-laws may state that the chair, the secretary, or the president of the corporation (if a director) may call a meeting of the board. While the OBCA provides no statutory procedure for calling a directors' meeting, it provides that a quorum of the board may call a meeting at any time to transact business whose general nature is specified in the notice of the meeting.[7]

The statutory notice requirements are a minimum and do not necessarily represent good practice for modern boards. Directors must be given sufficient notice to allow them to prepare for board or committee meetings. Even the ten days' notice provided in the OBCA may not be adequate in many circumstances. Ideally, regular meetings should be set in advance so that directors can arrange their calendars to accommodate the meetings.

The notice should include a full agenda of the business to be transacted. The statutory minimum is not sufficient to allow board members to deal with business efficiently or thoughtfully. The members of the board should be invited to place items on the agenda for discussion or consideration. The notice and agenda should be accompanied by documents, briefing notes, draft resolutions, experts' reports, committee reports, or anything else that directors might require in order to participate fully in the meeting. In the ordinary course, they should be sent to directors well in advance of the meeting. Two weeks is usually a satisfactory time period.

III. Frequency of Meetings

How frequently a board meets will depend on the corporation: its size, its business, the size of the board, the number of committees, whether the business environment is calm or turbulent, and the personal preferences of the directors. Some boards prefer frequent short meetings, while others would rather devote one or two days to intensive discussions. What is important, however, is that the board meet often enough for the members to fulfill their responsibilities. The members must be able to discuss agenda items, ask questions, follow up on previous meetings and decisions, hear reports from committees, and participate actively in the meeting.

---

[6] CBCA, s. 114(7); note that the BCBCA does not contain a provision relating to notice of adjourned meetings.

[7] OBCA, s. 126(8); note that neither the ABCA nor the BCBCA have provisions allowing a quorum of the board to call a meeting.

Some boards schedule meeting dates (e.g., a date in the following year or regular dates, such as the first Wednesday of every month) so that directors can plan in advance to attend them. Regular meetings are often held quarterly so that the directors can consider dividends, quarterly financial statements, and housekeeping matters. Other meetings may be held for special purposes; they may be called to discuss particular subjects, like strategic planning or regulatory compliance reports, or to consider problems as they arise.

IV. Location of Meetings

Directors of federally incorporated companies can hold meetings at any place the by-laws permit.[8] The by-laws commonly state that the meetings can take place either within or outside of Canada.

Provincial business corporations statutes are not entirely consistent with the federal regime. For example, the OBCA states that the directors of Ontario corporations must hold the meetings at the place where the registered office of the corporation is located but that the by-laws can allow for the meetings to be held at any place within or outside of Ontario. The by-laws may also provide that most of the meetings in a financial year may be held outside of Canada.[9] In practice, the by-laws usually allow meetings to be held within or outside of a province or territory, and they relieve the directors from the requirement of holding the majority of the meetings in Canada. However, the majority of the meetings of non-resident Ontario corporations must be held in Canada.[10] When directors come from different regions or a corporation has several offices, the location of meetings is often rotated.

V. Quorum and Residency of Directors

A quorum of directors may exercise all of the powers of the directors. Subject to the articles and by-laws, a majority of the directors or the minimum number of directors specified in the articles constitutes a quorum.[11] Provincial legislation may differ on this point. For example, there is an

[8] CBCA, s. 114(1).

[9] OBCA, ss. 126(1) and (2). ABCA, s. 114(1) allows directors to hold meetings at any place the by-laws permit; note that the BCBCA Regulations, Table 1, s. 11.1 provide that meetings of the board may be held at any place determined by a resolution of the board.

[10] OBCA, s. 126(2); a non-resident corporation is defined in s. 1(1) as a "corporation incorporated in Canada before the 27th day of April, 1965, and that is not deemed to be resident in Canada for the purposes of the *Income Tax Act* (Canada) by s. 250(4) of that Act". No provisions are found in the ABCA or the BCBCA regarding the location of meetings of non-resident provincial corporations.

[11] CBCA, s. 114(2).

additional restriction under the OBCA: the quorum cannot be less than two-fifths of the total number of directors or, if the corporation has the minimum number of directors, then that minimum is the quorum.[12] A publicly-traded company must have at least three directors, while a private corporation must have at least one.[13] If an OBCA corporation has fewer than three directors, then all of them must be present at the meeting to constitute a quorum.[14]

Directors of a CBCA corporation shall not transact business at a meeting of directors unless at least 25 percent of the directors (or, if the corporation has less than four directors, at least one of the directors) present is a "resident Canadian", as that term is defined under the CBCA.[15] Provincial legislation may again differ. Under the OBCA, one of the directors present must be a resident Canadian if the corporation has fewer than three directors; otherwise, a majority of them must be resident Canadians.[16] The board will therefore have to consider both the number and the residency of directors in determining whether a proper quorum exists.

However, the board can act if a resident Canadian director approves in writing, by telephone, or by other communications facilities the business transacted at the meeting and if a majority of resident directors would have been present at the meeting if that director had attended it. This saving provision applies to only one director, whose presence would have resulted in satisfying the Canadian residency requirement for directors. It cannot be applied to more than one director at the same meeting.[17]

VI. Telephone Meetings

Directors may use the telephone or other communications facilities (such as video-conferencing) to hold a meeting of the board or a committee of the board. All of the directors of the corporation, not just those partici-

---

[12] OBCA, s. 126(3); note that ABCA, s. 114(2), and the BCBCA Regulations, Table 1, s. 11.10 do not contain this additional restriction.

[13] CBCA, s. 102(2).

[14] OBCA, s. 126(4); note that no such restriction is found in the ABCA or the BCBCA. CBCA, s. 114(8) states that: "where a corporation has only one director, that director may constitute a meeting"; OBCA, s. 126(5) provides that, in the event of vacancies on the board, the remaining members may conduct business as long as a quorum of the board remains in office.

[15] CBCA, s. 114(3).

[16] OBCA, s. 126(6); note that ABCA s. 114(3) requires that at least one-quarter of the directors present at a meeting to be resident Canadians. The BCBCA does not have a Canadian residency requirement for directors.

[17] CBCA, s. 114(4); note that the BCBCA does not have a Canadian residency requirement for directors. It is possible, however, for directors to hold their actual meetings by telephone (see the text in section VI below), so that the inability of resident Canadian directors to physically attend a meeting should not limit a board's capacity to act.

pating in the meeting, must consent to the use of the technology. This consent should be obtained in a form signed by the individual when he or she agrees to act as a director. The technology must permit all of the persons participating to hear each other or to communicate with each other simultaneously and instantaneously.[18] A director who participates in a meeting by means of telephone or video-conference is deemed to have attended the meeting. Under the OBCA, if a majority of the directors participating in the meeting by telephone are in Canada, the meeting will be considered to have been held in Canada.[19]

Telephone meetings allow boards to communicate quickly and frequently at a low cost. For committees in particular, it may be efficient to meet regularly by phone. The conduct of a telephone meeting may be different from that of a regular meeting. Directors should identify themselves when they begin to speak and votes may have to be taken orally so that the minutes can accurately reflect the discussion and resolutions. Directors should ensure that they have all of the necessary documents, including proposed resolutions, before the meeting begins, since copies may not be conveniently distributed. Although telephone meetings may appear to be less formal, greater care and attention may have to be given to the agenda and to the preparation for the meeting if the meeting is to be effective.

VII. Resolution in Lieu of Meeting

A written resolution that is signed by all of the directors who would have been able to vote on that resolution at a meeting of directors or a committee of directors is as valid as if it had been passed at a meeting.[20] While a simple majority of directors attending a meeting at which a quorum is present is sufficient to pass a resolution at a meeting, it is not sufficient to pass a written resolution. Nevertheless, the language of the section recognizes that, in some circumstances, directors cannot vote on a particular resolution (for example, where the director has an interest in the transaction that is the subject of the resolution). In such circumstances, that director is not required to sign the resolution. The section does not require directors who sign a resolution to consent to that resolution. Accordingly, it would appear open to a director to oppose, consent, or abstain by indicating one

[18] CBCA, s. 114(9); note that BCBCA, s. 140(1) does not require the consent of directors to use the technology. The requirement to hear each other (in the CBCA) would prevent the use of computer conferences. The OBCA is more likely to accept new technologies, although at the time of this writing, computer conferences are unlikely to meet the requirements of a simultaneous and instant transmission.

[19] OBCA, s. 126(14). See the text in section IV, above, "Location of Meetings". There is no provision relating to location of telephone meetings in the ABCA or the BCBCA.

[20] CBCA, s. 117.

of these choices when signing the resolution. As long as each eligible director signs the resolution, with a majority consenting to it, the resolution should pass, but it is not free from doubt. In practice, written resolutions are generally consented to by all directors. A copy of the resolution must be kept with the minutes of the proceedings of the board or the committee.[21]

VIII. Importance of Meeting in Person

While the business corporations statutes have been modified in recent years to permit boards to meet electronically or to pass resolutions in writing, face-to-face meetings are recommended as a best practice. Meeting face-to-face enables directors to build a better rapport, to see the facial reactions of the other directors and the management who are present, to better communicate (the disruption caused by imperfect telecommunications services can be avoided), to avoid distractions (such as other telephone calls), and to communicate informally with each other during the meeting. Attendance in person may also, but not necessarily, indicate a director's level of commitment to the corporation.

IX. Dissents

Directors who are present at a meeting of the board or of a committee are deemed to have consented to any resolutions passed or actions taken at the meeting unless they dissent from them.[22] Directors cannot dissent from a resolution or action if they have voted in favour of it at the meeting.[23] A director may express a dissent in several ways:

- the dissent may be entered in the minutes of the meeting;
- the director may send a written dissent to the board's secretary before the end of the meeting; or
- the director may send the dissent by registered mail or deliver it to the corporation's registered office immediately after the meeting has ended.

Directors who were not present at a meeting will be deemed to have consented to the resolutions that were passed, or to the actions that were taken, at the meeting unless they specifically dissent from them.[24] They must register their dissent within seven days of becoming aware of the resolution

---

[21] CBCA, s. 117(2); note that the BCBCA does not contain a similar filing requirement.

[22] CBCA, s. 123(1).

[23] CBCA, s. 123(2).

[24] CBCA, s. 123(3); note that there is no deemed consent for absent directors under the ABCA.

or action. A director may place a dissent on the minutes by communicating with the board's secretary, who prepares and distributes the minutes. The dissent will be appended to the minutes. The dissent is expressed two ways:

- the dissent is appended to the minutes of the meeting; and
- the director sends the dissent by registered mail or delivers it to the registered office of the corporation.

X. Limitations on Voting; Disclosure of Interest by a Director

Directors have a fiduciary duty to the corporation that requires them to put aside self-interest and be loyal to the interests of the corporation.[25] As a general rule, directors may not profit at the expense of the corporation: they may not divert opportunities or benefits from the corporation to themselves or put themselves in a position of conflict.

If a director discloses an interest in a material contract or transaction that receives independent ratification by the board or the shareholders, the corporation may enter into the contract, even though the director also benefits. With some exceptions, the interested director may not vote as a director on the proposed contract or transaction. However, the interested director may be counted to determine if a quorum exists for the board meeting.[26]

A director must disclose certain kinds of interests in writing to the corporation or have the nature and extent of the interest entered in the minutes of a board meeting or board committee meeting. If a director is a party to a material contract or transaction with the corporation, the interest must be disclosed. If the director has a material interest in a company, which, in turn, is a party to a material contract or transaction with the corporation, the director's interest must be disclosed. A "material contract" is usually interpreted as something significant and something that might benefit, or be perceived to benefit, the director in some way.[27] A "material interest" would certainly include any interest or relationship that makes the director an insider of the second company. In general, it is better for a

---

[25] CBCA, s. 122(1). See the discussion in Chapter 2, "The Duties of Directors".

[26] CBCA, s. 120(7). The spirit of the law would require the disclosure of all contracts, transactions, and arrangements in which a director might have an interest and benefit from the corporation entering into the contract. For a full discussion of CBCA, s. 120, see *UPM-Kymmene Corp. v. UPM-Kymmene Miramichi Inc.* (2002), 27 B.L.R. (3d) 53 (Ont. S.C.J.), aff'd (2004), 183 O.A.C. 310 (C.A.).

[27] *Dimo Holdings Ltd. v. H. Jager Developments Inc.* (1998), 43 B.L.R. (2d) 123 (Alta. Q.B.).

director to interpret these provisions generously and err on the side of too much disclosure to the board, rather than too little.

The director must make this disclosure at the board meeting or board committee meeting at which the proposed contract is first considered or at the first meeting after becoming interested in the contract. If the director has an earlier interest and then becomes a director, he or she must disclose that interest at the first meeting after becoming a director. If the contract or transaction is one that would not normally be brought to the attention of the board or the shareholders, the director must disclose the interest in writing or have it entered in the minutes of the board meeting or board committee meeting as soon as he or she becomes aware of the contract or proposed contract.[28] A general notice to the directors by the interested director that a material interest in a contract or transaction exists is considered sufficient.[29]

Non-compliance with the foregoing disclosure provisions does not invalidate the contract or make a director accountable for any profit realized from such a contract or transaction if the director acted honestly and in good faith and the contract or transaction was approved or confirmed by a special meeting of the shareholders, sufficient disclosure was made to the shareholders prior to the contract or transaction being approved or confirmed, and the contract or transaction was reasonable and fair to the corporation when it was approved or confirmed.[30]

If an interested director fails to disclose an interest in a material contract or transaction, a court, on application by the corporation or any shareholder, may: (a) set aside the contract or transaction; (b) require the director to account to the corporation for any profit or gain realized from the contract or transaction; or (c) do both (a) and (b).[31]

The shareholders of a CBCA corporation may examine the portions of any minutes of directors or committees of directors that contain the requisite disclosure and any other documents that contain those disclosures during the regular business hours of the corporation.[32]

---

[28] CBCA, ss. 120(2), (3), and (4).

[29] CBCA, s. 120(6).

[30] CBCA, s. 120(7.1).

[31] CBCA, s. 120(8).

[32] CBCA, s. 120(6.1); note that none of the provincial statutes contain similar provisions relating to access to disclosures.

XI. Conduct of Directors' Meetings

Directors can exercise their powers only at duly convened meetings of the board at which a quorum is present.[33] The shareholders expect the directors to engage in a meaningful exchange of ideas and views. The minority directors have a right to be heard at any meeting of directors,[34] and they certainly may not be excluded from a meeting.[35]

XII. Best Practices for Efficient Meetings

Experienced directors are often very busy people. Board meetings are relatively infrequent events. Accordingly, it is desirable to make the best use of the directors' time by running meetings as efficiently as possible. A number of procedures can be implemented to make board meetings more efficient without increasing risks to the directors.

In order to ensure that the directors' time is used wisely, materials should be distributed to the directors before the meeting. It is inefficient to spend time at board meetings dumping information that can be better delivered by other means or in advance. Since directors will have thoroughly reviewed the information found in the materials, that material should not be repeated at the meeting. Instead, the meeting should be directed toward a discussion that leads to the decisions that need to be taken.

Various types of agenda templates can be prepared in advance. A standing agenda should be prepared by listing items that should be considered at every meeting or on some other recurring basis, including, but not limited to, regulatory requirements. A meeting template is a slightly enhanced version of a standing agenda. It sets out the order in which the items are to be dealt with and the approximate time estimated to complete each item. Standing agendas and meeting templates help to plan meetings and to ensure that important matters do not get lost, forgotten, or overwhelmed by other matters. A form of meeting template for quarterly meetings is included as Appendix I at the end of this Chapter.

Several items that require approval on an annual basis should be added to the year-end meeting agenda as required. Year-end financial statements and the annual report and proxy circular must be approved annually. Also

---

[33] This provision is subject to written resolutions being signed by directors (or by shareholders, in the case of shareholder resolutions): CBCA, s. 117(1) and s. 142(1). Where articles required the corporation to have two directors and the corporation had only one director, a resolution signed by that director was not valid: see *Mega Blow Moulding Ltd. v. Sarantos* (2001), 16 B.L.R. (3d) 2 (Ont. Sup. Ct. Jus.).

[34] *Great Western Railway Co. v. Rushout* (1852), 64 E.R. 1121 (Ch. D).

[35] *Trounce v. NCF Kaiapoi Ltd.* (1985), 2 N.Z.C.L.C. 99, 422 (H.C.N.Z.).

annually, at the appropriate point at the beginning of management's annual planning cycle, the board should hold a "strategy session" to re-confirm long-term strategy, make adjustments for the upcoming year, review a "high-level" budget, and set the stage for the preparation of the annual business plan by management. The board's mandate and other mandates and policies should be included in the agenda for review on an annual basis, and they should receive input from the applicable board committees. The review and approval of the directors' and officers' insurance and indemnification policies are also required on an annual basis.

A consent agenda also improves the efficiency of board meetings. A consent agenda is a list of items which, under corporate, securities, or other areas of law or under a corporation's rules and procedures, require the approval of the board but are unlikely to require a discussion. A typical example of a consent agenda is the minutes of a prior board meeting. While there is no legal requirement for the minutes of a prior board meeting to be approved by the board, many boards approve them to encourage the minutes to be prepared promptly and to ensure that the directors agree with their content while their memories of the meeting are reasonably fresh. However, there are usually no comments on the minutes and the process of formally presenting them at the meeting and going through the process of moving, seconding, and passing a resolution to approve them is inefficient. A form of consent agenda is included as Appendix II at the end of this Chapter.

As noted elsewhere, directors are entitled to rely on others to do their jobs within the corporation. The job of the directors is to supervise others. However, in certain circumstances, directors must be able to establish that they have been duly diligent. One tool that can help directors establish a due diligence defence is the certificate from each officer of the corporation in which the officers certify certain types of information to the board. Such a certificate will help the board demonstrate that it addressed the issues involved with management, and management's responses will be formally recorded with the minutes of the meeting. Issues that are often addressed in certificates of this type include the following: all taxes, tax withholding, source deductions, and other government remittances have been made and paid; there is no material litigation pending by or against the corporation; and the financial statements or other disclosure documents that are presented to the board have been reviewed and approved by the certifying officer. In addition, the board may wish to receive a certificate on information that is specific to that corporation's business. For example, if the corporation is in a hazardous business, it may wish to receive at each board meeting a report on serious personal injuries or deaths on its sites. A form of chief executive officer's certificate is included as Appendix III at the end of this Chapter.

XIII. Minutes and Other Records

Corporations must maintain certain records and keep them either at the registered office or at another place designated by the directors.[36] These records must be kept in the jurisdiction of incorporation. A federally incorporated company must keep its records in Canada. Provincial business corporations statutes generally require a company to keep its records within the respective incorporating province.

The records include:

- the articles and by-laws, and the amendments to them;
- a unanimous shareholder agreement (if existing);
- the minutes of shareholders' meetings and their resolutions;
- a securities register; and
- information about the directors.

Corporations must also keep adequate accounting records and records containing the minutes of meetings and resolutions of the directors and committees of the board.[37]

Some records are kept permanently, but financial records are subject to various record-retention requirements. For example, an Ontario corporation does not have to keep accounting records longer than six years if all other record-retention requirements established by taxing authorities, such as the Canada Revenue Agency, have been satisfied. The directors are also responsible for amending financial statements if the auditor, or the former auditor, informs them of errors or misstatements in financial statements.[38]

The board and committee minutes are important records for the directors. While directors may keep their own notes of board and committee meetings, they should also review the formal minutes for accuracy and

---

[36] CBCA, s. 20(1). Each jurisdiction's business corporations statute requires that a corporation keep records containing the articles and by-laws as well as minutes of meetings and resolutions. In addition, each statute lists various additional records that must be kept.

[37] CBCA, ss. 20(2) and (4); the directors' records must be kept at the registered office or in such other place as the directors think fit; they must be available for inspection by the directors at all reasonable times.

[38] CBCA, s. 171(8). A director also has a responsibility to inform the audit committee and the auditor if he or she becomes aware of an error in a financial statement: CBCA, s. 171(6).

completeness.[39] The best practice likely dictates that directors' own notes should be destroyed once the formal minutes have been approved. The directors should particularly ensure that abstentions, dissents, and disclosures of interest are fully and accurately noted. The minutes should include information on who attended the meeting (including non-directors) and whether anyone attended by telephone. The level of detail to be included in the minutes is an issue of debate. Significant detail can be useful but it can also be harmful if something is inadvertently omitted. Significant detail can also be embarrassing if the minutes are read by others, such as prospective purchasers, lenders, auditors, or other employees. However, where there are significant issues or divergent opinions, consideration should be given to documenting the discussions in a summary fashion, including the identification of who spoke and the position that he or she took. In fact, the minutes can offer convincing evidence that the directors have put their minds to the issues. Proper documentation can be a critical means of proving due diligence.[40]

XIV. Best Practices for Diligent Directors

Some suggested best practices for the diligent director to observe in regard to board meetings are:

(i) attend meetings; be sure to bring critical judgment to bear on the matters brought forward at meetings;

(ii) prepare for each meeting by thoroughly reviewing the materials distributed;

(iii) take notes of any critical point, decision, or evidence of having directed careful attention to a matter at meetings of directors or committees; destroy notes once the formal minutes record the matter in a satisfactory manner;

---

[39] Advisors provide differing views on the wisdom of returning notes subsequently. The evolving best practice appears to be to destroy personal notes to avoid the risk of inconsistency with official meeting minutes and the risk of notes being misconstrued or taken out of context.

[40] *R. v. Bata Industries Ltd. et al.* (1992), 9 O.R. (3d) 329 (Prov. Div.); see also *Benson v. Third Canadian General Investment Trust Ltd.* (1993), 14 O.R. (3d) 493 (Gen. Div.), where the court found that frank minutes evidenced that the directors had independent minds and had thoroughly discussed the matter. See also *Re The Walt Disney Company Derivative Litigation*, 2006 WL 1562466 (Del. S.C.), released June 8, 2006, involving a dispute over whether the Disney board had breached its fiduciary duties by approving an employment contract for Michael Ovitz containing a $140 million dollar termination provision (ultimately paid after fourteen months' employment). In this case, the Delaware Supreme Court said that better procedures, including the provision to the board and the preparation of a detailed summary of Mr. Ovitz's contract and the appending of the contract to the minutes would have left no room for litigation over what information was provided about Mr. Ovitz's contract to the board for its consideration.

(iv) vote only after due deliberation; a vote should not be cast in favour of a resolution if the director does not understand it or is not satisfied that the issue has been given enough consideration;

(v) reserve a portion of each meeting for discussions without management or management directors present; and

(vi) file a formal dissent in respect of any board decision that is opposed.

XV. Conclusion

The business corporations statutes set out a framework for meetings of the board of directors. This framework is only a minimum, however. Directors should demand that they be given adequate notice and a full agenda for each meeting. For all but the most urgent meetings called on short notice, directors should be provided with documents and background briefings well in advance. How frequently directors meet depends on their personal preferences and on the type of business on the board's agenda. Occasionally, full boards or committees may meet by telephone or video-conference; directors may also transact business by written resolution in lieu of meetings. Directors should attend meetings regularly and should dissent from any decision or action with which they do not agree. The minutes of meetings are important records for the directors. Aside from documenting the business of the meeting, they can provide important evidence of the directors' due diligence.

APPENDIX I

Quarterly Meeting Agenda Template for a Public Company

(Agenda requires approximately 3–4 hours) (Generally: Board dinner the evening before, followed by an 8:00 a.m. start, with the meeting finishing with lunch; working lunch if necessary)

1. Minutes and Matters Arising (5–10 minutes)

- Review and approve previous meeting minutes.
- Speak to any matters arising out of the minutes.

2. Officers' Certificate (1 minute)

- Certificate from CEO/CFO/GC stating that all taxes have been paid and withholdings have been made and there is no material litigation. [Certificate may be expanded to include other matters of particular interest to the board, such as a report of any accidents causing serious personal injury or death to company personnel on company property, or a report on any regulatory issues.]

3. Consent Agenda Items (5–10 minutes)

- Include here any matters requiring the formal approval of the board by-law, or company or board policies and procedures; however, do not require a full board discussion (to be determined by the chair in consultation with the corporate secretary and/or legal counsel).

- Material would be included in the meeting materials sent to directors in advance of the meeting, and any director wishing to have a full discussion on the matter can request it.
- One resolution would normally carry all of the consent agenda items.

4. Committee Reports (10–20 minutes)

- Chairs of board committees report to the full board on the results of discussions/decisions made by a board committee since the last board meeting.

5. Chief Financial Officer's Report (approx. 1 hour)

- Review and approve quarter-end financials and MD&A.
- Review quarter-end press releases.
- Review year-end forecast.
- Review GAAP statements.
- Business cases requiring approval (for transactions/expenditures that require board approval).
- Dividend declaration (if applicable).

6. Chief Executive Officer's Report (approx. 1 hour, depending on whether there is a significant transaction on which to report)

- A "state of the nation" strategic level report
- Highlights over the last quarter
- Report on pending significant transactions (acquisitions, divestures, new business, etc.)
- Status reports on programs compared to strategic and business plans made during the quarter, setbacks, etc.
- Status report on business development
- Status report on operational performance

- Status report on customer satisfaction with respect to major customers
- Status report on any significant matters relating to the operation of the corporation (human resource/compensation issues, organizational structural changes, significant audit findings, etc.)

7. CEO/CFO Certificates (1 minute)

- Certificates from the CEO/CFO/GC regarding accuracy to the best of their knowledge of financial statements and other disclosure documents presented to the board, similar to the certificates required by securities law to be filed with securities regulators

8. Business Review (approx. 30 minutes)

- Quarterly presentation of key business executives, as determined by the board at its previous meeting

9. Risk Review (approx. 15 minutes)

- The CEO presents an assessment of the principal risks facing the business and how they are being addressed.

10. Meeting De-Brief (5–10 minutes)

- At the end of each meeting, the board will consider the effectiveness of the meeting just held and will provide feedback to management (whether the agenda focused on "board matters", quality of supporting material and presentations, the adequacy of time for full discussion, full participation by individual board members).

11. In Camera Meeting of the Board (approx. 10 minutes)

- Routine meeting in the absence of management (chaired by a non-executive chair, lead director, or chair of the corporate governance committee)
- If there are no issues to bring forward or the board has no matters it wishes to discuss in camera, then the meeting will terminate at this point.

APPENDIX II

Consent Agenda

[Name of Corporation]
Board of Directors' Meeting
[Date of Board Meeting]

Consent Agenda

Instructions and Procedures

The Consent Agenda items listed on the attached Consent Agenda form will require a resolution of the board but are not scheduled for a formal presentation and/or full discussion at the board meeting. If you agree with management's recommendation, as detailed on the Consent Agenda, the items listed will be adopted by a resolution of the board without a formal presentation or a full discussion at the board of directors' meeting. However, if you wish to have a full discussion at the board meeting with respect to any of the items listed, please **complete and sign the attached Consent Agenda form and fax it to the number indicated at the top of the form**. No cover page is necessary. Please note that **no action** is required if you agree with management's recommendation.

You will also have the opportunity to move items from the Consent Agenda to the Meeting Agenda for a full discussion by the board during the proceedings of the board meeting.

Should you require additional information or wish to discuss management's recommendations with respect to any of the items listed, please communicate directly with the contact person identified on the attached Consent Agenda form.

Fax to: **[fax number]**

Attention: Corporate Secretary's Department

[Name of Corporation]
Board of Directors' Meeting
[Date of Board Meeting]

Consent Agenda

Each item listed below will require a resolution of the board of directors and is not scheduled for a full discussion at the board meeting. However, if you wish to have any of the items listed below presented at the board meeting, please indicate accordingly.

Item Agenda	*Description*	*Recommendation*	*Contact Person*	*Telephone*	*Full discussion required (X)*
6	Minutes of Meeting — *[date of meeting]*	Resolution to approve minutes	•	(416) xxx-xxxx	

Director's signature: ____________________

Director's name: ____________________
(Please print name)

Date: ____________________

APPENDIX III

Officer's Certificate

[•]
(the "Corporation")

Officer's Certificate

To: The Directors of the Corporation

I, •, the [Chief Executive Officer] of the Corporation, hereby certify as an officer of, and on behalf of, the Corporation and not in my personal capacity, as follows:

1. The Corporation has paid all taxes, premiums, contributions, and payments required to be deducted at source, paid and/or remitted under the *Income Tax Act* (Canada), the *Excise Tax Act* (Canada), the *Canada Pension Plan*, the *Employment Insurance Act* (Canada), the *Income Tax Act* (Ontario), the *Workplace Safety and Insurance Act* (Ontario), the *Employment Standards Act, 2000* (Ontario), the *Retail Sales Tax Act* (Ontario), or any similar statute or legislation, applicable to the Corporation, together with the applicable regulations thereto.

2. There are no court, administrative, regulatory, or similar proceedings, arbitration or other dispute settlement procedures or investigations or inquiries by any governmental, administrative, regulatory, or

other similar body either pending or, to my knowledge, threatened against the Corporation.

Dated this ______ day of ____________________, 200●.

____

Name: ●

Title: [Chief Executive Officer]

CHAPTER 5

ANNUAL AND SPECIAL MEETINGS OF SHAREHOLDERS

The purpose of this Chapter is to familiarize directors with the procedures for calling a meeting, the requirements of shareholder communication, and regulatory disclosure. These provisions are meant to ensure that shareholders' meetings are called and conducted in a manner that maximizes the effectiveness of the proxy solicitation process and the meetings themselves.

I. Introduction

While directors are charged generally with the responsibility to manage the business and affairs of the corporation, shareholders enjoy limited management rights and privileges stemming from share ownership. Such rights and privileges include the right to elect directors, the right to appoint auditors, and the right to approve fundamental changes to the corporation's constitution and business. These rights and privileges come from, or are regulated by, the business corporations statutes, the corporation's articles, and the corporation's by-laws. In the case of a public corporation,[1] share-

[1] The term "public corporation" is used instead of the defined terms found in the following Acts: Canada *Business Corporations Act*, R.S.C. 1985, c. C-44, as amended ("CBCA"); the Ontario *Business Corporations Act*, R.S.O. 1990, c. B.16 ("OBCA"); the Alberta *Business Corporation Act*, R.S.A. 2000, c. B-9, as amended ("ABCA"); the British Columbia *Business Corporations Act*, S.B.C. 2002, c. 57, as amended ("BCBCA"); the Ontario *Securities Act*, R.S.O. 1990, c. S.5, as amended ("OSA"); the Alberta *Securities Act*, R.S.A. 2000, c. S-4, as amended ("ASA"); and the British Columbia *Securities Act*, R.S.B.C. 1996, c. 418, as amended ("BCSA"). The term refers generally to a corporation that files prospectus-like and continuous disclosure documents with a securities commission or whose shares are listed on a stock exchange. For the defined terms, see "distributing corporation", CBCA, s. 2(1) and ABCA, s. 1(*p*); "offering corporation", OBCA, s. 1(1); "public company", BCBCA, s. 1(1); and "reporting issuer", BCBCA, s. 1(1), OSA, s. 1(1), ASA, s. 1(*ccc*), and BCSA, s. 1(1).

holders will also derive rights and privileges from securities legislation, the decisions and policies of securities commissions, and stock exchange policy statements.[2]

The unanimous shareholder agreement is also a powerful tool used by the shareholders of private corporations to acquire additional management rights and responsibilities. By a written agreement among all of the shareholders of a corporation, the shareholders can restrict the powers of the directors to manage or supervise the management of the corporation. To the extent that shareholders restrict these powers, the directors are relieved of their duties and liabilities to the same extent.[3]

It is the board of directors or, by delegation, management,[4] that is responsible for proposing director and auditor nominees. The board is also responsible for proposing fundamental changes to the corporation's structure and business, such as the creation of new classes of shares or the sale of substantial assets. Shareholders' decisions with respect to these matters are typically taken at meetings, and it is the board of directors that controls the agendas for these meetings.

In the corporate democratic model, the ultimate control rests with the shareholder who owns or controls sufficient shares to elect the board of directors. Increased shareholder activism has, however, fostered the development of other, more informal, and consultative processes for shareholder input. Investor advisory committees and informal shareholder information sessions are becoming increasingly popular as informal methods of obtaining shareholder input. In addition, institutional investors have increased their participation in investor associations, such as the Pension Investment Association of Canada; their participation has provided a means of influencing corporate governance standards in general.

---

[2] See, for example, the following documents: (1) Ontario Securities Commission ("OSC") Rule 61-501, *Insider Bids, Issuer Bids, Business Combinations, and Related Party Transactions*, s. 5.6, which provides for minority approval of certain related party transactions; (2) Policy Statement 9.2, *Policy of the Director as to "Export" Transactions Under the CBCA*, Corporations Canada (May 29, 2002), Part II, s. 2.03 ("Corporations Canada Policy Statement 9.2"), which sets out the level of disclosure the Director appointed under the CBCA expects to find in meeting materials for any shareholders' meeting required to approve an export transaction; and (3) *Toronto Stock Exchange Company Manual*, Part VI, s. 613 ("TSX *Company Manual*"), which sets out the TSX's requirement for approval of stock option plans in certain circumstances.

[3] CBCA, s. 146; OBCA, s. 108, and ABCA, s. 146 contain similar provisions. The BCBCA does not contain an equivalent provision, but see BCBCA, s. 137(1), which permits a corporation's articles to specify that the directors' management powers may be transferred to one or more other persons.

[4] Under CBCA, s. 121, subject to the articles, the by-laws, or any unanimous shareholder agreement, the directors may delegate their powers to manage the business and affairs of the corporation to the officers of the corporation, except for powers specifically enumerated in CBCA, s. 115; BCBCA, s. 141 is similar, but it does not include a reference to a unanimous shareholder agreement, and the BCBCA does not contain an equivalent provision to CBCA, s. 115.

The procedures for calling and conducting shareholders' meetings are more or less regulated, depending on the nature of the corporation. For public corporations or large private corporations, the arrangements are complex and require detailed advance planning. Even for smaller corporations, care must be taken to ensure that the shareholders receive the necessary information and are prepared to vote at the meeting. Directors and officers are responsible for complying with shareholder communication rules. They must provide the corporate secretary with the necessary information and authority to organize the meeting. Also, they must consider and decide what business they want to accomplish at the meeting and how to effectively communicate this business to the shareholders.

Directors should be aware that the task of organizing a large shareholders' meeting is a complex and time-consuming one. While the organizational tasks are often delegated to management and the corporate secretary, the directors are responsible for reviewing and approving financial statements, annual reports, proxy circulars, and other information disclosure documents. The board members require a considerable amount of time and attention to carry out these duties responsibly, and board meetings must be planned in order to accommodate this requirement.

II. Annual Meetings

The directors of a company organized under the CBCA must call the first annual meeting of shareholders not more than eighteen months after the corporation comes into existence. They must hold an annual meeting every year after that, never leaving more than fifteen months between meetings; however, the meeting must be held no later than six months after the end of the corporation's preceding year-end.[5] The OBCA and the ABCA provide for identical timing with respect to the requirement to call annual meetings, except that there is no requirement that meetings also be held no more than six months after the end of the corporation's preceding year-end.[6] The BCBCA's requirements for annual meetings are the same as the OBCA's and ABCA's requirements except that, by unanimous resolution, shareholders may defer, waive, or consent to the business of the annual general meeting. In such a case, they must select the company's annual

[5] CBCA, s. 133; CBCA, s. 142(1) provides that meetings are not required if a written resolution is signed by all of the shareholders entitled to vote, except where a written statement is submitted by a director relating to that director's resignation or removal (s. 110(2)), or where representations in writing that relate to the auditor's resignation or removal (s. 168(5)) are submitted by an auditor.

[6] OBCA, s. 94 sets out the directors' obligation to call the annual meeting within this time frame, and s. 104(1) allows written resolutions in lieu of a meeting; ABCA, s. 132(1) sets out the obligation to call the annual meeting, and s. 141 allows written resolutions in lieu of a meeting.

reference date that would be appropriate for holding the meetings.[7] The Toronto Stock Exchange ("TSX") requires that listed public corporations hold annual meetings within six months of the end of each financial year.[8] TSX-listed corporations should send a written request to the TSX's Listed Issuer Services well in advance of any deadline if the annual meeting will be delayed beyond the six-month period.[9]

Annual meetings are held for the shareholders to receive financial statements, elect directors, and appoint auditors. All of these matters are considered to be the ordinary business of the annual meeting.[10] Any additional matters dealt with at a meeting are considered to be "special business" that requires additional notice and disclosure.

III. Special Meetings

Directors are empowered to call a special meeting of shareholders at any time.[11] Directors might call special meetings to consider special business and to seek shareholder approval for various matters that cannot be delayed until the next annual meeting. Special business is basically all business other than the ordinary business of the annual meeting. It includes such matters as the passage of special resolutions, the confirmation of by-laws, removal of the auditor, or removal of a director.[12] With advance planning, most special business can be organized and dealt with at the annual meeting; this procedure will reduce the costs associated with transacting the special business. Particular circumstances and timing requirements may, and often do, dictate that a separate special meeting be held.

---

[7] BCBCA, s. 182.

[8] TSX *Company Manual*, s. 464.

[9] TSX *Company Manual*, s. 465. The TSX may permit postponement in justifiable circumstances, but it has no power to waive business corporations statute requirements.

[10] Presentation of financial statements: CBCA, s. 155(1); election of directors: CBCA, s. 106(3); and appointment of auditors: CBCA, s. 162, are all considered to be ordinary business under CBCA, s. 135(5). OBCA, s. 96(5) adds the consideration of minutes of an earlier meeting to the matters listed in the CBCA; ABCA, s. 134(6) adds the fixing of the number of directors for the following year to the matters listed in the CBCA. The BCBCA does not include an equivalent to CBCA, s. 135(5).

[11] CBCA, s. 133(2). The BCBCA does not contain an equivalent provision to s. 133(2). See BCBCA, Part 5, Division 6 for provisions related to shareholders' meetings under that statute.

[12] CBCA, s. 135(5). For corporations organized under the BCBCA, see British Columbia *Business Corporations Regulation*, B.C. Reg. 65/2004, Table 1, s. 8.1 ("BCBCA Reg".). Special resolutions must be passed by two-thirds of the votes cast (CBCA, s. 2; under BCBCA, s. 1(1), a company may specify in its articles that a special resolution be passed by some other number of votes, provided that the specified majority is no less than two-thirds and no more than three-quarters of the votes cast). Special resolutions may be required for such matters as voluntary dissolution (CBCA, s. 211) or amending the articles (CBCA, s. 173; the BCBCA does not include an equivalent to CBCA, s. 173, but it includes multiple sections addressing many of the same issues).

IV. Other Meetings

Holders of not less than 5 percent of a corporation's issued voting shares are permitted to require the directors to call a shareholders' meeting for the purposes stated in the requisition.[13] The directors must call a meeting within twenty-one days after receiving the requisition unless notice has already been given to the shareholders of a record date or of a shareholders' meeting.[14] Directors can decline to hold a requisitioned meeting if the purpose of the meeting includes the following:

- proposals intended to redress personal claims or grievances;
- a matter not related in a significant way to the business of the corporation (or, under the ABCA, if the primary purpose of the meeting is to promote general economic, political, racial, religious, social, or similar causes, or to obtain publicity); or
- to consider a matter that was considered within the previous two years (five years under the BCBCA) and defeated at a shareholders' meeting.[15]

Typically, shareholders requisition a meeting when the directors do not support the proposed business and will not bring it before a meeting of the shareholders. Often the board of directors will be reluctant to call a requisitioned meeting and will be predisposed to find a reason to refuse to call one. The directors are entitled to carefully scrutinize the requisition to ensure that it meets with statutory requirements and to refuse to hold the meeting if it does not. Directors should be careful, however, that the grounds for refusal are valid and provided for in the statutory scheme. Inconvenience or expense is not a sufficient reason to refuse to call a meeting.

An individual director or shareholder can also apply to the court to requisition a shareholders' meeting. The court may grant the application if it is impracticable either to call or to conduct a meeting of the shareholders in the manner prescribed by the by-laws, the articles, the business corporations statute, or, in the case of a company formed under the OBCA, for any other

---

[13] CBCA, s. 143(1).

[14] CBCA, ss. 143(3) and 143(4). If the directors do not call the meeting within the prescribed period, any shareholder who signed the requisition can call it. See *Paulson & Co. v. Algoma Steel Inc.* (2006), 79 O.R. (3d) 191 (S.C.J.), where the court considered the meaning of the word "call" in OBCA, ss. 105(3) and 105(4). The court concluded that publicly announcing the intent to hold a meeting satisfied the requirement to "call" the meeting within twenty-one days of receiving the application. The corporation did not need to provide notice within twenty-one days; notice is governed by OBCA, s. 96. Under BCBCA, s. 167(8), the directors must send a notice of meeting within twenty-one days. See also section VI, "Notice", below.

[15] CBCA, ss. 137(5) and 143(3); ABCA, s. 136(5). Note that BCBCA, s. 167(7) contains additional exceptions.

reason the court thinks fit.[16] The court-ordered meeting has been used effectively to deal with technical difficulties or with situations in which there are disputes among shareholders.[17]

V. Preparation for Calling a Meeting

The time limits established by the business corporations statutes and by the policies of the stock exchanges give the directors and responsible officers of public corporations a time frame within which meetings must be called and held. The corporation and the directors must further comply with the requirements for sending properly prepared notices and other shareholder meeting materials within this time frame.

Directors, especially directors of public corporations, should make sure that a timetable is set well in advance of any proposed meeting. This timetable should establish convenient dates for conducting business, and it should set out the necessary and realistic time commitments of those who will attend the meeting and of those who will prepare for it. With the many requirements that must be fulfilled before a meeting is held,[18] a timetable should set out the mandatory deadlines and the internal deadlines, and it should assign responsibilities for completing the necessary tasks. Such a timetable will permit the preparations for the meeting to be handled in the ordinary course of business and not as an exercise in crisis management.

While there is no requirement for directors to attend annual meetings, it is desirable for them to do so since the annual meeting is often the shareholders' only opportunity to meet them. (This is especially true for the shareholders of public corporations.) In addition, the first directors' meeting of the year is usually held immediately after the annual meeting, and it is at that meeting that officers are appointed for the following year.

Typically, the directors delegate the responsibility to call the meeting, prepare the meeting materials, and conduct the meeting to the officers of the corporation. The corporate secretary usually prepares and organizes the

---

[16] CBCA, s. 144(1). CBCA, s. 144(1) (but not the equivalent provisions of the OBCA, ABCA, and BCBCA) also permits the Director appointed under the CBCA to make the application, while ABCA, s. 143(1) permits the Executive Director of the Alberta Securities Commission to make the application.

[17] See, for example, the situation in which there is a problem to be rectified with the quorum for a meeting as in *Re Routley's Holdings Ltd.*, [1959] O.W.N. 89 (Ont. H.C.), aff'd O.W.N. 160, 22 D.L.R. (2d) 410 (Ont. C.A.); or a situation in which there is a shareholder dispute as in *Croatian Peasant Party of Ont. Can. v. Zorkin* (1981), 38 O.R. (2d) 659 (H.C.). See also the recent case of *Paulson & Co. Inc. v. Algoma Steel Inc.* (2006), 79 O.R. (3d) 191 (S.C.J.), which considers requisitioned meetings timing requirements.

[18] See, for example, the notice and proxy solicitation requirements discussed in sections VI and IX of this Chapter.

distribution of the meeting materials, arranges for a meeting room, and takes care of any follow-up matters after the meeting. Depending on the complexity of the matters to be dealt with in the meeting and how much preparation is needed, the corporate secretary may seek advice and assistance from legal counsel, the auditor, and the transfer agent.

Before any shareholders' meeting is called, the directors must hold a meeting to take any action that is required before the shareholders' meeting. Certain tasks, which may be required in order to prepare for a shareholders' meeting, cannot be delegated by the board. Such tasks include the following:

- the submission to shareholders of any question or matter requiring the approval of the shareholders;
- the approval of the financial statements;
- the approval of a management information circular; and
- the adoption, amendment, or repeal of by-laws.[19]

The financial statements should be considered and approved by the directors at their meeting. Directors must approve the financial statements (with prior consideration by the audit committee, if required),[20] and the statements are then "presented" to shareholders at the annual meeting. Shareholders receive financial statements for their information only. While financial statements are presented for the consideration of shareholders at annual general meetings, shareholders are not asked to approve or reject the financial statements.[21]

Draft meeting materials, including the texts of resolutions, are also usually considered at this directors' meeting. Professional advisors should have been involved in the preparation of these materials to this stage to ensure that they meet compliance requirements. The directors should be supplied with materials well in advance of this meeting so that they can be properly prepared to carry out their responsibilities. The directors will approve the shareholder meeting materials either in final form or in draft form, giving authority to a corporate officer to settle the final form. Ideally, by the time this meeting is held, the corporate secretary will have circulated

---

[19] CBCA, s. 115(3). The BCBCA does not include an equivalent to CBCA, s. 115(3).

[20] CBCA, s. 158(1). Under CBCA, s. 171(1), a public corporation is required to have an audit committee, and any other corporation may have an audit committee. The audit committee of a public corporation must have at least three directors, a majority of whom are outside directors; OBCA, s. 158 and ABCA, s. 171 contain similar provisions; BCBCA, ss. 223–224 only require public companies to have an audit committee but that audit committee must have at least three directors, a majority of whom are outside directors. See also Multilateral Instrument 52-110, *Audit Committees*; note that this instrument has not been adopted by the British Columbia Securities Commission. See also Chapter 6, "The Use of Committees".

[21] CBCA, ss. 158(1) and 155(1)(*a*).

a questionnaire or confirmation asking all directors to verify their personal information (which is required for the meeting materials) and taken care of the mechanics of the meeting, such as reserving the appropriate meeting room.

If the directors of a public corporation approve a material transaction that must go to the shareholders for approval, the corporation may be required to issue and file a press release and, possibly, a material change report immediately following the directors' meeting at which the approval has been given.[22] When a fundamental change is proposed for a listed public corporation, it may be necessary to comply with the exchanges' notice requirements and with other filing requirements before the meeting materials are finalized and distributed to the shareholders.[23] Certain proposed activities may require consultation and advance filings with the securities commissions and with the Director appointed under the CBCA.[24]

VI. Notice

A. Entitlement to Receive Notice

Subject to waiver rights,[25] notice must be given to all shareholders who are entitled to vote at the meeting (or, under the BCBCA, to all shareholders who are entitled to attend the meeting), to each director, and to the corporation's auditor (except under the BCBCA).[26] The articles of the corporation may require that notice be given to the holders of shares of classes that are not entitled to vote. In certain circumstances, the holders of shares of a class affected by a proposed course of action have a statutory right to vote

[22] See OSA, s. 75; ASA, s. 146; and BCSA, s. 85. See also the following documents: (1) National Instrument 51-102, *Continuous Disclosure Obligations*, Part 7, *Material Change Reports* ("NI 51-102"); (2) National Policy 51-201, *Disclosure Standards*, Part II, *Timely Disclosure* ("NP 51-201"); and (3) TSX *Company Manual*, Part IV, for the timing requirements and other requirements for the disclosure of material changes and material information.

[23] TSX *Company Manual*, Part VI.

[24] See, for example, Corporations Canada Policy Statement 9.2, *supra* note 2.

[25] CBCA, s. 136. Shareholders may waive notice for a shareholders' meeting in any manner and at any time. Attendance is deemed to be a waiver of notice unless the shareholder attends the meeting for the purpose of objecting to the transaction of the business at the meeting on the grounds that the meeting was not lawfully called.

[26] CBCA, s. 135(1). The BCBCA, s. 169(1) does not require that notice be sent to the corporation's auditor, though under BCBCA, s. 214, a shareholder may require that the auditor attend if financial statements are to be in place before the meeting. If notice is not sent to the persons entitled to receive it, subject to waivers, the meeting will not be properly constituted for the transaction of business. See *John v. Rees*, [1969] 2 W.L.R. 1294 ("John").

separately as a class, whether or not those shares are otherwise voting.[27] The holders of these shares would be entitled to receive notice of any meeting that is called to consider the proposed action.

In the absence of a provision in the articles or of a statutory right to vote, holders of shares in a private corporation that do not have the right to vote have no right to receive notice of the annual meeting or of a special meeting. However, OSC and TSX policies dictate that the holders of non-voting shares of a public corporation are entitled to receive notice of shareholders' meetings.[28]

B. The Record Date

The business corporations legislation permits, but does not require, directors to fix a record date for determining which shareholders are entitled to receive notice of a shareholders' meeting and to vote at one.[29] If a record date is not fixed, it is the close of business on the date immediately preceding the day on which the notice of the meeting is given, or, if no notice is given, the day on which the meeting is held.[30] If the record date is set, it cannot precede the particular action to be taken by less than twenty-one days or more than the following: sixty days under the CBCA; fifty days under the OBCA and ABCA; or two months under the BCBCA.[31] The record date for a public corporation shall be set not less than thirty days or more than sixty days prior to the date of the meeting.[32]

If a record date is fixed, notice must be given in a newspaper and to each stock exchange in Canada where the corporation's shares are listed not less than seven days before the record date, unless notice of the record date

---

[27] See, for example, CBCA, ss. 175–176, which provides that shareholders may have the right to vote separately as a class on certain proposals to amend the articles, including any proposals to (a) change the rights attaching to those shares; (b) create a new class of shares equal or superior to such a class; and (c) remove the restrictions on issue, transfer, or ownership of the shares of such a class. The shareholders may also have the right to dissent and to demand to have their shares purchased.

[28] TSX *Company Manual*, s. 624(h).

[29] CBCA, s. 134.

[30] CBCA, s. 134(3); BCBCA, s. 171(3) contains a similar provision.

[31] CBCA, s. 134(3) and Canada Business Corporations Regulations, 2001, SOR/2001-512, s. 43(2) ("CBCA Reg".); OBCA, s. 95(2); ABCA, s. 133(2); and BCBCA, s. 171(2) and BCBCA Reg., s. 3(1).

[32] National Instrument 54-101, *Communication with Beneficial Owners of Securities of a Reporting Issuer*, s. 2.1 ("NI 54-101").

is waived in writing by every affected shareholder.[33] This notice must also be sent to each stock exchange in Canada where the corporation's shares are listed for trading. Public corporations are also required to file, at least twenty-five days before the record date, notice of the record date and the meeting date with all depositories, including the Canadian Depository for Securities Limited, and with each exchange in Canada on which the securities of the corporation are listed.[34]

C. Timing of the Shareholders' Meeting Notice

The CBCA requires that notice of the shareholders' meeting be sent not more than sixty days but not less than twenty-one days before the meeting for all public corporations. For non-public corporations, the notice may be sent within a shorter period if such a period is specified in the by-laws or articles.[35] Other jurisdiction's business corporations statutes prescribe varying time limits.[36] NI 54-101 requires that proxy-related materials be sent to intermediaries at least four business days before the twenty-first day before the meeting date.[37]

D. Contents of the Notice

The notice for an annual shareholders' meeting must set out the time and the place of the meeting.[38] The business corporations statutes require that the notice state the nature of any special business in sufficient detail to

---

[33] CBCA, s. 134(3): The newspaper must be published or distributed where the corporation has its registered office, where it has a transfer agent, or where its shares may be recorded. The BCBCA does not include an equivalent to CBCA, s. 134(3). A list of shareholders who are entitled to receive notice is required to be prepared: CBCA, s. 138. Under the CBCA, a separate list setting out those entitled to vote must also be prepared. The persons whose names appear on the list are also entitled to vote at the meeting except in transfer situations where the procedure set out in the applicable section has been followed by the transferee; BCBCA, s. 112(1) requires any corporation with more than 100 shareholders to maintain an index of the corporation's shareholders.

[34] NI 54-101, s. 2.2. The Canadian Depository for Securities Limited provides a service to assist public corporations with the advertising requirements for notice.

[35] CBCA, s. 135(1) and CBCA Reg., s. 44.

[36] OBCA, s. 96 requires that notice be sent not more than fifty days, but not less than twenty-one days, before the meeting for a public corporation and not less than ten days before the meeting for a private corporation; ABCA, s. 134(1) requires that notice be sent not more than fifty days, but not less than twenty-one days, before the meeting for all corporations; BCBCA, s. 169(1) requires that notice be sent not more than two months before the meeting for all corporations, but the minimum notice period varies (see BCBCA Reg., s. 3(1)). For public corporations, notice must be sent not less than twenty-one days before the meeting. For non-public corporations, the minimum notice can be specified in the corporation's articles, provided that the period is at least ten days (if it is less than ten days, the prescribed period is twenty-one days).

[37] NI 54-101, s. 2.12. If the proxy materials are sent by first-class mail, the materials need to be sent to the intermediary at least three business days before the twenty-first day before the meeting. Note that NI 54-101 does not address the sending of the notice.

[38] CBCA, s. 135(1).

permit shareholders to form a reasoned judgment on it.[39] It is a common practice to also specifically refer to the ordinary business to be dealt with at the meeting.

The business corporations statutes also require that the text of any special resolution to be considered by shareholders be set out in the notice.[40] The OBCA further requires that the text of any by-law also be set out in the notice.[41] There should be no errors in the text of special resolutions or by-laws, not even grammatical or typographical errors, as the general rule is that special resolutions must be set out precisely. If the special business deals with a "fundamental change", such as amending the articles to change the nature of the business or creating new classes of shares, certain additional disclosure requirements must be satisfied.[42] Shareholders' dissent and appraisal rights must be described wherever it is appropriate.[43]

E. Method of Delivery of the Notice

Notice of the shareholders' meeting may be delivered personally or sent by prepaid mail to the shareholder's latest address that is shown in the records of the corporation or its transfer agent. The notice is deemed to be received under the CBCA and ABCA at the time it would ordinarily be delivered. Under the OBCA, the notice is deemed to be received on the fifth day after mailing, and under the BCBCA, the notice is deemed to be received the date after it is mailed unless the corporate charter provides for a later deemed receipt date.[44]

F. Consequences of Failure to Give Notice

Failure to give adequate notice will generally invalidate the proceedings unless the shareholders are present in person or by proxy and consent to the holding of the meeting.[45] The TSX may require the postponement of the

[39] CBCA, s. 135(6). The BCBCA does not contain an equivalent provision, but see BCBCA Reg., Table 1, s. 7.4, which sets out the notice requirements for special business under the BCBCA.

[40] CBCA, s. 135(6)(*b*); OBCA, s. 96(6)(*b*) also requires that the text of any by-law be set out in the notice. The BCBCA does not contain an equivalent provision, but see BCBCA Reg., Table 1, s. 7.4, which sets out the notice requirements for special business under the BCBCA.

[41] OBCA, s. 96(6)(*b*).

[42] See, for example, CBCA, s. 183(2) and BCBCA, s. 271(3) (amalgamation); OBCA, s. 169(2) and ABCA, s. 175(2) (amendment of articles).

[43] See, for example, CBCA, s. 189(4).

[44] CBCA, s. 253(3); OBCA, s. 262(2); ABCA, s. 255(3); BCBCA, s. 6(2). If the notice is sent in accordance with these sections and is returned on two consecutive occasions (three, under the OBCA) because the shareholder cannot be found, the corporation is not required to send any further notices or documents until the shareholder informs the corporation in writing of the shareholder's new address.

[45] CBCA, s. 136.

meeting of a listed public corporation where there is reason to believe that timely and adequate notice has not been given, and it may suspend trading in the corporation's securities if proper notice has not been given.[46]

VII. Place of Meeting

Directors generally have the right to decide where to hold the shareholders' meeting, subject to certain statutory restrictions, the corporation's articles or by-laws, and any unanimous shareholder agreement.[47] Under the CBCA, the meeting must be held in Canada unless all of the shareholders who are entitled to vote agree otherwise or if the meeting place is specified in the articles. As a practical matter, this provision means that only private CBCA corporations can hold shareholders' meetings outside of Canada.[48]

It is a common practice to hold shareholders' meetings in the place where the registered office or the principal place of business is located. Another common practice is to hold the meetings in the locale where a large portion of the shareholders reside so that they can attend the meeting with a minimum of inconvenience.

VIII. Information to be Provided or Made Available to Shareholders in Connection With Meetings[49]

A. Annual Financial Statements and the Auditor's Report

The CBCA requires that financial statements, any auditor's report, and, where applicable, further financial information be laid before the shareholders at an annual meeting.[50] Further information respecting the financial position of the corporation and the results of operations may be required in

[46] TSX *Company Manual*, s. 459.

[47] CBCA, s. 132(1). The BCBCA, s. 166 does not explicitly give this discretion to the directors.

[48] CBCA, s. 132(2). This right is subject to the requirement that shareholders' meetings are required to be held at the place within Canada provided in the by-laws, or failing such a provision, at the place within Canada determined by the directors; OBCA, s. 93(1) permits the directors to choose a location inside or outside of Ontario. The directors of OBCA corporations should determine the place of the meeting at the directors' meeting that is called to consider the meeting materials if the shareholders' meeting is to be held in a locale other than the registered office. ABCA, s. 131(3) permits meetings to be held outside of Alberta, provided all shareholders who are entitled to vote agree; the BCBCA permits meetings to be held outside of British Columbia, provided that the location is provided for in the articles or that the necessary approvals are obtained.

[49] Note that proxies and management information circulars are dealt with below under section IX, "Proxies and Proxy Solicitation", and they may be required to be provided to shareholders.

[50] CBCA, s. 155. It has been held that the board may not defer the holding of the annual meeting because the financial statements are not ready for presentation at the meeting. See *Canadian Javelin Ltd. v. Boon Strachan Coal Co.* (1976), 69 D.L.R. (3d) 439 (Que. S.C.).

the articles, by-laws, or any unanimous shareholder agreement. The financial statements presented at the annual meeting of a private corporation must be for the period commencing on the date the corporation came into existence or for the period immediately following the end of the corporation's last completed financial year. The financial period must end not more than six months before the annual meeting.

The financial statements presented to the annual meeting of a public corporation are those required to be filed under the jurisdiction's securities legislation. They relate separately to

(a) the period beginning on the date the corporation came into existence or the period immediately following the end of the last completed financial year and ending not more than six months before the annual meeting; and

(b) the immediately preceding financial year, if any.[51]

Public corporations must file these comparative financial statements with the securities commissions, and listed public corporations must file those statements with the stock exchanges on which their securities are listed.[52]

B. Annual Report

There is no requirement to provide an annual report to the shareholders of a private corporation, but management of large private corporations or private corporations with a broad shareholder base (including the employees or former employees) often do so as a method of communicating with shareholders. The TSX requires every listed public corporation that produces an annual report containing annual financial statements to file it electronically on SEDAR.[53] Typically, such a report will contain audited financial statements and a message from the chair, some promotional material, and the Management's Discussion and Analysis ("MD&A"), which is described below.

---

[51] The financial statements are required to be prepared in accordance with Part XIV of the CBCA, Part 13 of the ABCA, Part XII of the OBCA, Parts 5 (s. 185(1)) and 6 (s. 198(2)) of the BCBCA, and in accordance with Generally Accepted Accounting Principles ("GAAP"). CBCA Reg, Part 8, ABCA Reg. 118/2000 ("ABCA Reg".), s. 21(1), OBCA General Regulation, R.R.O. 1990, Reg. 62, as amended, ss. 38–42 ("OBCA Reg. 62"), and BCBCA Reg., Part 8. Financial statements for public corporations are required to be prepared in accordance with the requirements of NI 51-102.

[52] OBCA, s. 156; TSX *Company Manual*, Part IV, ss. 436; NI 51-102, Part 4; CBCA, s. 160(1) requires that the financial statements be sent to the Director; ABCA s. 160(1) requires that the financial statements be sent to the Executive Director; BCBCA Reg., Part 8 requires that comparative financial statements be sent to shareholders and on demand to debentureholders; OSA, s. 78.

[53] TSX *Company Manual*, s. 437.

C. The Annual Information Form and Management's Discussion and Analysis

NI 51-102 states that most public corporations[54] should prepare and file an Annual Information Form ("AIF"), which, among other things, includes the Management's Discussion and Analysis ("MD&A").[55] While the AIF need not be mailed to shareholders, it must be made available to any persons or companies upon request and it must be free of charge.[56] The corporate secretary or other officer organizing the annual meeting is usually responsible for preparing the AIF and the MD&A, in consultation with the corporation's professional advisors. These materials are used by securities analysts, dealers, and investors.

A narrative description of the business of the corporation must be disclosed in segments, in accordance with the *Handbook* of the Canadian Institute of Chartered Accountants.[57] Since such disclosure could be harmful from a competitive or market point of view, a discretionary exemption from the securities commissions is often applied for and obtained on the grounds of competitive confidentiality. The disclosure requirements of the AIF relate to material items that entail the application of reasoned judgment by management.

MD&A has been described as a painting that adds colour to the pencil sketch provided by a corporation's financial statements.[58] MD&A disclosure is intended to provide a narrative explanation of the issuer's current financial position and future prospects. Known trends, commitments, events, or uncertainties that are reasonably expected to have a material impact on the issuer's business, financial condition, or results of operations must be disclosed.[59] As with the AIF requirements, the MD&A disclosure requirements relate to material items upon which reasoned judgments must be based.

---

[54] NI 51-102, s. 6.1 states that a reporting issuer that is not a venture issuer must file an Annual Information Form.

[55] The Annual Information Form ("AIF") must be filed with the OSC on or before the ninetieth day after the end of the reporting issuer's most recently completed financial year (NI 51-102, s. 6.2(a)). See also Form 51-102F1, *Management's Discussion and Analysis* ("Form 51-102FI"), and Form 51-102F2, *Annual Information Form* ("Form 51-102F2"), to ensure compliance and avoid common errors.

[56] NI 51-102, Part 6.

[57] NI 51-102, Form 51-102F2, Item 5. For example, segmentation must be by principal products and services and by methods of product or service distribution.

[58] See introductory commentary, Office of the Chief Accountant, *1991 Report on Management Discussion and Analysis* (1991), 14 O.S.C.B. 5848. This report contains disclosure examples and comments on compliance with the disclosure policy, which management might find helpful in preparing the required discussion.

[59] Form 51-102FI, Part 2.

MD&A requires discussion on a segmented basis only if it is appropriate or necessary.

MD&A must accompany the annual audited financial statements of a public corporation, be mailed to all security holders, and be filed with the OSC.[60] If a public corporation files an annual report containing its annual financial statements, the MD&A may be included in the annual report and be incorporated by reference as part of the AIF.

IX. Proxies and Proxy Solicitation

A. Proxies

Every shareholder of a corporation who is entitled to vote at a shareholders' meeting is entitled to appoint a proxyholder, who need not be a shareholder.[61] The proxy authorizes its holder to attend and vote at a meeting on behalf of the shareholder. The management of all corporations are required to send a form of proxy, which is an uncompleted printed form, to all shareholders who are entitled to receive notice of the meeting, subject to certain exceptions.[62]

Forms of proxy may also be sent to shareholders by "dissidents", who are usually not part of management. Dissidents may be institutional shareholders, individuals, groups or committees, or even directors. They often wish to challenge a proposal put forward by the incumbent management. Dissidents soliciting proxies must use a prescribed proxy form, which must be sent not only to shareholders, but also to the corporation's auditor and directors and to the corporation itself. Under the CBCA, dissidents must send a copy of the dissident's proxy circular to the Director appointed under the Act. Similarly, under the ABCA, dissidents must send a copy to the Executive Director. Under the OBCA, they must send a copy to the OSC.[63]

---

[60] NI 51-102, s. 5.1.

[61] CBCA, s. 148(1) includes the right to name an alternate.

[62] CBCA, s. 149(2) stipulates that the management of the corporation is not required to send a form of proxy under subsection (1) if it (a) is not a distributing corporation, and (b) the corporation has fifty or fewer shareholders who are entitled to vote at a meeting, two or more joint holders being counted as one shareholder. Sending a form of proxy must be done concurrently with the sending of the notice of meeting. CBCA proxies must be sent to the Director under CBCA, s. 150(2). There are no exceptions in OBCA, s. 111; ABCA, s. 149(2) stipulates that the management of a corporation that is not a private issuer within the meaning of the *Securities Act* is not required to send a form of proxy under subsection (1) if all of the shareholders who are entitled to vote at a meeting of shareholders have agreed in writing to waive the application of subsection (1); BCBCA, s. 3.2 stipulates that this requirement is subject to any exemption granted under section 155 of the *Company Act*, 1996.

[63] CBCA, s. 150(2); ABCA, s. 150(3); OBCA, s. 112(2). There is no equivalent provision in the BCBCA.

The form of the proxy for both the management and a dissident is prescribed by statute.[64] A proxy solicited by management or by a dissident for a public corporation is required to identify the meeting at which it is to be used, whether it is solicited by or on behalf of management, and the name of the proxyholder, with an explanation of how to designate an alternate. It must provide a means of specifying a vote for or against[65] each matter identified in the notice, a provision conferring authority where no choice is specified, and a provision conferring discretionary authority. It should include a statement that the proxy will be voted on any ballot, according to instructions of the shareholder.

NI 54-101 requires that a reporting issuer sending security holder materials indirectly to beneficial owners shall send to each proximate intermediary that responded to the applicable request for beneficial ownership information the number of sets of those materials specified by that proximate intermediary at least four business days before the twenty-first day before the date fixed for the meeting, in the case of proxy-related materials that are to be sent on by the proximate intermediary by prepaid mail other than by first-class mail.[66] Listed public corporations are not generally required to file copies with the stock exchanges before sending them to shareholders.[67]

Companies sometimes retain proxy solicitation firms, who are paid to ensure that enough proxies are received so that a quorum is present or that enough supportive proxies are received to ensure that particular resolutions pass or pass by the required majorities at the meeting.

B. Information Circulars

The information circular, whether it be a management information circular,[68] proxy circular,[69] or dissident circular,[70] is the base document used by shareholders to obtain information that is relevant to the meeting. It

[64] CBCA Reg., Part 7, ss. 54–56; OBCA, s. 110(3) and OBCA Reg., s. 27; ABCA Reg., s. 19; BCBCA Reg., s. S3.6.

[65] Most proxy forms provide for an indication of voting for or withholding a vote on the particular matters specified in the form.

[66] NI 54-101, *Communication with Beneficial Owners of Securities*, s. 2.12.

[67] TSX *Company Manual*, ss. 460-461; NI 54-101.

[68] Under the CBCA, s. 150(1), the requirement to send circulars applies to all corporations; under the OBCA, s. 112(1), they apply to all "offering corporations"; and under the OSA, s. 86(1), they apply in all circumstances where a corporation solicits proxies from the holders of voting shares in Ontario.

[69] See CBCA Reg., Part 7, ss. 57–59; ABCA Reg., s. 19; OBCA Reg. 62, ss. 30 and 31; BCBCA Reg. s. S4.4.

[70] See CBCA Reg., Part 7, ss. 61–64; ABCA Reg., s. 19; OBCA Reg. 62, ss. 33–36. Note that dissident circulars are not discussed in the BCBCA regulations.

contains information on the nominees for directors and auditors, any special business, and other specific disclosure that is deemed of interest to the shareholders. For example, it may give information on executive compensation, the costs of purchasing directors' and officers' liability insurance, and whether or not the directors have been indemnified under any insurance policy.

If the corporation is subject to a mandatory proxy solicitation regime, the requirement and contents of an information circular are prescribed by statute, regulation, and policy statement.[71] Even if the corporation is not subject to a mandatory solicitation regime, the directors often provide a circular if there are complex matters to be considered by shareholders.

The information contained in an information circular must be current as of a specific date that is not more than thirty days prior to the date on which the circular is first sent to shareholders.[72] The business corporations statutes and securities statutes all contain other general provisions on the contents of information circulars.[73] These general guidelines must be followed in preparing the materials, and expert advice is usually required for the purpose of completing such materials.

Under the business corporations statutes, the person sending the management information circular on behalf of a public corporation must concurrently file a copy of the circular with the securities commissions, along with the notice, proxy form, and any other documents to be used in connection with the meeting.[74] For CBCA corporations, these documents must also be sent to the Director appointed under the CBCA, and they must be accompanied by the statement of a director or officer of the corporation that the documents have been sent to each director, to each shareholder who is entitled to receive notice, and to the auditor.[75]

---

[71] CBCA, s. 149; CBCA Reg., Part 7, ss. 61–64; ABCA, s. 149; ABCA Reg., s. 19; OBCA, s. 112(1); OBCA Reg. 62, ss. 30-36; BCBCA Reg., s. S4.4; OSA, ss. 85, 86, and 88; ASA s. 157.1.

[72] CBCA Reg., s. 65; ABCA Reg., s. 19. There is no equivalent provision in the BCBCA.

[73] See, for example, CBCA Reg., Part 7; ABCA Reg., s. 19; ASA, s. 157.1; OBCA Reg. 62, s. 37; BCBCA Reg., s. S4.3.

[74] CBCA, s. 150(2); ABCA, s. 150(3) requires the corporation to file with the Executive Director; OBCA, s. 112(2) must file with the Commission; there is no equivalent provision in the BCBCA.

[75] CBCA, s. 150(2); ABCA, s. 150(3) requires that a copy of the management proxy circular be sent to the Executive Director, together with a copy of the notice of the meeting, form of proxy, and any other documents for use in connection with the meeting; OBCA, s. 112(2) requires that a copy of the management information circular be filed with the OSC, together with a copy of the notice of meeting, form of proxy, and copies of any other documents for use in connection with the meeting. There is no equivalent provision in the BCBCA. If there is special business to be conducted at the meeting, management should review the financial and draft policy statements dealing with going private transactions, arrangements, and export transactions issued by the Director under the CBCA. Shareholder meeting materials in any of these areas may have to address certain matters or require prior review by the Director.

C. Contents of Information Circulars

Certain specific information must be included in an information circular.[76] The circular must tell the shareholder that he or she has the right to revoke a proxy. It must also provide information about the person who is making the solicitation, and it must state who is paying for it. Information about all of the matters to be acted upon at the meeting must be provided, including copies of any proposed resolutions and the percentage of votes that is required to enact the proposals. When directors are to be elected at the meeting, the circular must provide information about the individuals who are nominated by management and the terms of the existing directors.

The details of any arrangement between a management nominee and any other person to elect the nominee must be disclosed. Any remuneration, contract or arrangement, and pension plan participation for directors and officers must be disclosed, as well as the amount of officers' and directors' liability insurance purchased and any payouts that were made under the policy.

The circular must also provide information on the interests (if any) of directors, officers, and proposed management nominees in all matters to be acted upon at the meeting, except for the election of the directors and the appointment of the auditor. The indebtedness to the corporation of directors and senior officers must also be disclosed.

The circular must also contain a statement of the right of any class of shareholders to elect a specific number of directors or cumulate their votes. It must also state the number of shares and voting rights, shareholders' names, and the percentage of votes that are beneficially held by persons who are in a control position. If control has changed, the circular must state the name of the person who acquired control, the date and description of the transaction, and the percentage of shares that the new control person is entitled to vote.

X. Ratification by Shareholders of Directors' Actions

At the annual meeting, the directors sometimes ask shareholders to ratify all of the actions that were taken by the directors and officers during the preceding year, which the shareholders have complete information

[76] CBCA Reg., Part 7; ABCA Reg., s. 19; OBCA Reg 62., ss. 30–38; BCBCA Reg., Part S4. The circular should be set out with respect to any special business, and it should contain sufficient detail to enable shareholders to form a reasoned judgment. See *Pacifica Papers Inc. v. Johnstone* (2002), 17 B.L.R. (3d) 92 (B.C.S.C.).

about. The business corporations statutes provide a mechanism for the shareholders to ratify actions in situations in which the directors have a conflict of interest in a particular transaction.[77] The policies of the securities administrators and stock exchanges dictate additional disclosure and possibly, the approval of a majority of an affected minority of shareholders when conflicts of interest or other related-party transactions are proposed to be dealt with at a meeting of shareholders.[78] However, the directors cannot rely on ratification to absolve them of responsibility in areas of irregularity or mismanagement.

XI. Preparation for the Actual Meeting

The meeting room has been booked (and confirmed)[79] and the shareholder materials and other documents have been mailed and filed. Now, the organizers must attend to the details of the meeting. One of the key tools used to make sure that the meeting runs according to plan is the script that is prepared for the chair of the meeting. The chair and the corporate secretary usually annotate the script during the meeting so that it can be used to prepare the minutes of the shareholders' meeting, which will be retained for the corporation's records. Another item to prepare in advance is the chair's address to the shareholders. This speech should ensure a smooth presentation of all of the information that the board and management want to convey to the shareholders. It may be a good idea to attempt to anticipate shareholders' questions and to prepare adequate responses to them.

Those responsible for running the meeting should determine early which materials should be at the meeting and who will be responsible for providing them. Additional copies of the annual report, financial statements, the management information circular, and the annual information form should be on hand. The transfer agent should be contacted to provide the proof of mailing of the materials for the meeting.

Many corporations are, as outlined in their articles or by-laws, subject to the requirement that there be at least a certain number of shareholders represented at the meeting. Corporations, therefore, sometimes retain proxy

---

[77] CBCA, s. 120(7.1). Procedures referred to in these sections should be followed to ensure that the shareholder ratification is effective. See Chapter 2, "The Duties of Directors", for further discussion.

[78] See, for example, OSC Rule 61-501.

[79] *Byng v. London Life Association Ltd.*, [1989] 1 All E.R. 560 (C.A.) ("Byng") demonstrates that the poor planning of a locale for a meeting could result in the meeting being held to be invalidly constituted for the transaction of business. Here, the locale was too small to accommodate all of the shareholders who wished to attend it, and the audio-visual links did not work in the overflow facilities made available.

solicitation firms to ensure that a quorum is present or to get support for important initiatives.

XII. Practical Advice for Conducting the Meeting

A. Preparing for the Unexpected

Shareholders' meetings are technically a forum designed for a corporation to seek the approval of, or consideration by, its shareholders in connection with a number of fundamental matters: the annual appointment of directors; the annual appointment of auditors; changes to the articles and by-laws (the corporation's constating documents); the adoption or renewal of shareholders' rights plans; the approval of share compensation arrangements; significant acquisitions, dispositions, or merger transactions; financial statements; etc. These meetings have also evolved as a forum in which shareholders interact with the directors and management of the corporation, and they serve to permit shareholders, both through the provisions of the applicable business corporations legislation governing the corporation and from the floor of the meeting, to put forth personal agendas and to be heard by the corporation.

The directors and management of a corporation are well served by understanding the rights of the participants at shareholders' meetings and being prepared to deal with them accordingly. The following material addresses many of the questions that are frequently asked in connection with shareholders' meetings. It is only a summary and should not be relied upon as legal advice: each specific circumstance has unique facts that must be analyzed and considered when providing appropriate legal advice. The material assumes that some version of Robert's Rules is governing the procedure of matters at the meeting. While many corporations default to procedural rules of this sort, there is no requirement that they do so, and any fair procedures that are applied with consistency may be adopted.

B. The Chair

(a) *What is the role of the chair?*

- The chair must act impartially, in good faith, and with a view to the orderly conduct of the meeting.[80] In doing so, the chair must act in accordance with the will of the shareholders. [81]

---

[80] *National Dwelling Society v. Sykes*, [1894] 3 Ch. D. 159 at 162 ("National").

[81] *American Aberdeen-Angus Breeders Association v. Fullerton* (1927), 156 N.E. 314 at 316 (Ill. Sup. Ct.).

- Additionally, the chair should maintain the integrity and propriety of the voting system and must be honest and fair to all shareholder interests.

(b) *What are the duties of the chair?*

- *Opening the meeting*: The chair calls the meeting to order and determines that a quorum exists.[82] The chair will also appoint the secretary and scrutineers for the meetings.

- *Maintaining order and fairness*: The chair ensures that the shareholders have a reasonable chance to be heard; preserves the order of the meeting and decides incidental questions relating to the meeting.[83]

- *Settling points of contention*: The chair decides who is entitled to attend and vote at the meeting; declines to submit motions that infringe upon the rules of procedure; and gives a second or casting vote where authorized to do so.[84]

- *Procedural matters*: The chair calls for motions and nominations; calls for the questions and asks for discussion; calls for votes by a show of hands or by proxy where appropriate; and announces voting results.[85]

- *Closing the meeting*: The chair must be satisfied that all business before the meeting has been completed and adjourns or terminates the meeting accordingly.[86]

(c) *What are the rights of the chair?*

- The chair is entitled to seek, and to rely upon, independent advice in connection with the meeting or during the meeting in order to address any questions or concerns that he or she may have.[87]

- The chair may seek the advice of the registrar and transfer agent of the corporation and scrutineers for the meeting as to standard industry practices concerning proxy issues.

---

[82] H.R. Nathan and M.E. Voore, *Corporate Meetings: Law and Practice*, looseleaf (Scarborough, Ont.: Thomson Carswell, 1995) at 2-7.

[83] *Ibid.* at 2-7–2-8.

[84] *Ibid.* at 2-7.

[85] *Ibid.*

[86] *Ibid.*

[87] *Ibid.* at 2-17.

- The chair may adjourn the meeting as necessary to take the necessary time to hear both sides of any procedural issues and to come to a reasoned conclusion in respect thereof.

(d) *Does a conflict of interest taint the chair?*

- Unless the by-laws of the corporation require a wholly disinterested chair, the fact that the chair has an interest in the outcome of the meeting does not taint his or her ability to serve as chair.[88]

- The chair must comply with the responsibilities and duties set out above and should focus on the actual conduct of the meeting.

(e) *Can shareholders move to replace the chair of a meeting?*

- If the by-laws of the corporation are silent as to who is to serve as the chair for shareholders' meetings, which means that the chair is appointed by the meeting, that individual can be replaced by the meeting.

- If, however, the by-laws of the corporation designate who is to serve as chair for shareholders' meetings (which is most often the case), shareholders may not move to replace the chair unless he or she breaches his or her duty to conduct the meeting in a fair and impartial manner.[89]

- If, for example, the chair acts in an improper or malicious manner or wrongly tries to adjourn the meeting, then he or she may be disqualified from continuing to act as chair, and the shareholders may replace him or her at the meeting.[90]

C. Attendance at Shareholders' Meetings

(a) *Who can attend?*

- Attendance is governed by the by-laws of the corporation and by the applicable legislation governing the corporation.

- Generally, persons with the right to vote (which means shareholders and proxyholders who are duly appointed for purposes of the meeting), all directors, and the auditors of the corporation.[91]

---

[88] *Gray v. Yellowknife Mines Ltd.*, [1946] O.W.N. 938 at 942 (H.C.).

[89] *Ibid.*

[90] *National, supra* note 80.

[91] See, for example, CBCA, ss. 110(1) and 168(1).

- Others by invitation or with the consent of the meeting.[92]

- All other persons may be properly refused admission.

- It is an accepted practice to admit interested parties such as employees, advisors, the media, and analysts; however, a record should be kept of all attendees.[93] Such record keeping is generally the responsibility of the registrar and the transfer agent of the corporation and the scrutineers for the meeting.

D. Speaking at Shareholders' Meetings

(a) *Who may speak?*

- Essentially everyone having the right to vote (again, the shareholders in attendance and proxyholders who have been duly and properly appointed for purposes of the meeting), as well as the directors and auditors.

- Others may speak only with the consent of the meeting.

(b) *How long may a shareholder speak?*

- The chair has the ability to limit the time for discussion and the length of shareholders' speeches, but he or she must be mindful that by limiting a speaker's time, he or she does not impair the rights of the minority.

- Reasonable presentations and arguments should be heard for a reasonable period of time. The chair must strike a balance between the right of the minority to be heard with the right of the majority to transact business.[94]

(c) *Can restrictions be placed on speakers?*

- Yes, while every person with the right to vote has the right to speak once on each motion, comments must be relevant to the subject,[95] impersonal, and directed to the chair.

---

[92] Hartley R. Nathan, *Nathan's Company Meetings Including Rules of Order*, 6th ed. (Toronto: CCH Canadian, 2005), Rule 10 at 6.

[93] Nathan and Voore, *supra* note 82 at 16-3–16-4.

[94] *Wall v. London & Northern Assets Corp.*, [1898] 2 Ch. D. 469 (C.A.).

[95] Nathan and Voore, *supra* note 82 at 19-15.

(d) *How does the chair terminate a discussion?*

- The procedure used to terminate a discussion and put the matter of business to a vote is known as "calling the question", in essence, a motion to move to "vote immediately" on the matter of business.
- The chair has the discretion to call the question but must not exercise such discretion arbitrarily.
- If the question is called and the motion is carried, the matter of business that was the subject of discussion is then put to an immediate vote without further discussion. If the motion to call the question is defeated, discussion on the matter of business resumes.
- It is prudent for the chair to explain that a "yes" vote on a motion calling the question is not a vote in favour of the matter of business under discussion but is merely a vote to terminate the discussion, while a "no" vote on the motion calling the question will permit the discussion to continue.

E. Business of the Meeting

(a) *Can a shareholder introduce new business at a meeting?*

- Generally no, the chair should be hesitant to permit the introduction of new items because to do so gives rise to procedural unfairness to those shareholders who are not present at the meeting. Obviously, absent shareholders will not have had notice of the new item of business and, consequently, no opportunity to consider the matter, decide to attend the meeting in person, or otherwise direct their proxy to vote in respect of that matter.
- The only matters of new business that might be considered by the chair would be ones that are not substantive but rather are of a minor and routine nature that would qualify as "other business". Further, the chair should be satisfied that a shareholder, without notice of such an item, would not be in a position of claiming unfair treatment. Such circumstances are extremely rare.

(b) *How does one deal with shareholder proposals or motions at the meeting?*

- The situation we are addressing here is one where a shareholder puts forward at the meeting a proposal or a motion that essentially amounts to new business.

- In such cases, the chair should explain that the proposal or motion creates procedural unfairness to those who have not had notice of it and hence, it is viewed as out of order.
- The shareholder should be asked to submit the proposal or motion to the corporation for inclusion as a shareholder proposal in accordance with the governing corporate legislation for consideration at the next shareholders' meeting.
- If that doesn't work, the chair can point out that proxies in the name of management nominees will be voted against the matter in any event, given that it is procedurally unfair to those shareholders without notice of it.

(c) *What if a motion must be amended?*

- To the extent that a motion is amendable, it may be amended at any time after the chair has invited discussion on it.
- Typically, an amendment varies the terms of the main motion without effecting a material change in its principal intent.[96]
- Where a proposed amending motion has the effect of creating a new motion altogether or results in a material change to the terms of the main motion, the chair should rule it out of order, again, for the reason that all shareholders will not have had notice of such an amendment.[97]
- Amendments should be stated clearly and, if possible, in writing, in order to avoid any misunderstanding about their content and effect.[98]
- The amendment's effect must be such that the main motion remains grammatical and intelligible.

(d) *Can any shareholder move to amend a resolution?*

- Yes, although certain types of procedural motions are not amendable. Examples of such motions include motions to conclude or terminate a meeting; determine a quorum; withdraw a motion; vote immediately; amend an amendment to an amendment; and to make a resolution unanimous.[99]

---

96 Nathan and Voore, *supra* note 82 at 19-16.

97 *Ibid.*

98 *Ibid.*

99 *Ibid.* at 19-17.

- Certain other motions are amendable on a restrictive basis, such as motions to adjourn where amendments might relate to time, date, and place of continuance.

- However, if a motion is amendable, it may be amended any number of times, provided the amendment is relevant to the subject, proposed at the proper time, is within the power of the meeting, and is within the scope of the constitution and governing statute relating to the corporation.[100]

- An amendment may be moved at any time after the main motion has been placed before the meeting and before the question on such a motion has been put to a vote; however, it cannot be moved while another speaker has the floor.

- An amending motion can be moved by any person who is entitled to vote at the meeting, except the chair or the mover and seconder of the main motion, and, like the main motion, it requires seconding and may itself be amended.

- In terms of the procedure to be used by a shareholder to properly amend a motion, there are essentially seven steps:

  (i) the initial motion to be amended must be within the scope of the agenda and must have been moved and seconded;

  (ii) the chair must have called for a discussion on the initial motion;

  (iii) the motion to amend the initial motion under discussion must be made and seconded;

  (iv) the chair must consider the relevancy and the form of the amendment and, if satisfied that it is in order, he or she must call for discussion on the amendment. If there is any confusion in respect of the wording or meaning of the amendment, the chair may ask the mover to repeat or clarify the amendment;

  (v) when the discussion has ended, the chair should restate the motion to amend and call for a vote;

  (vi) the vote is taken; and

  (vii) the chair declares the result.

---

[100] Nathan, *supra* note 92, Rule 133 at 80.

- An amending motion must be passed by the same majority that is necessary to pass the initial motion and, if it is successful, the original motion will be re-worded to incorporate the amendment and to proceed with it. Otherwise, the amendment will be dropped and the motion, in its original form, will be proceeded with as if no amendment had been proposed.

(e) *When is a ballot required or recommended?*

- Technically, a ballot is the most accurate method of voting and, in a perfect world, should be used for all matters.
- The corporate legislation states that, unless the by-laws of the corporation otherwise provide, voting at a meeting of shareholders is to be conducted by a show of hands, except when a ballot is demanded by a shareholder or a proxyholder who is entitled to vote at the meeting.
- There is a provision in most corporate legislation providing discretion to the chair in connection with how proxyholders exercise the voting rights conveyed upon them.
- That provision allows the chair to conduct a vote on a particular matter by a show of hands, notwithstanding the fact that a proxyholder may have conflicting instructions from one or more shareholders, putting him or her in the position where a vote by way of ballot is technically required in order to have the shares he or she represents properly voted.
- The chair can only exercise this discretion (i) where a shareholder or proxyholder does not demand an actual ballot, (ii) where the chair is satisfied that the number of votes attaching to shares represented at the meeting by proxy that are required to vote against a particular matter is less than 5 percent of the votes attached to the shares that are entitled to vote at the meeting, and (iii) where the chair has knowledge that the decision of the meeting will be in favour of the matter of business.
- Where there is any question as to whether the shareholders are split on a particular issue and the outcome is of critical importance, the vote should always be taken by ballot.

(f) *Can a shareholder demand a show of hands?*

- The by-laws of most corporations, the common law, and corporate legislation provide shareholders with the right to demand that a vote be carried out by way of a ballot.

- Such a demand may be made either before or upon the declaration of the result of any vote by a show of hands.

- In terms of a shareholder demanding a show of hands, there is no parallel provision in the common law or corporate legislation that provides a shareholder (other than the chair) a right to demand that a vote be taken by a show of hands where a ballot would otherwise be appropriate.

- If a shareholder were to demand a vote be taken by a show of hands, a demand for a ballot by the chair or by any other shareholder or proxyholder would prevail.

(g) *Can a shareholder move to remove the board of directors or a particular director at the meeting?*

- No, in the context of removal as opposed to adding additional nominees to a slate of potential directors proposed by management. Shareholders are free to make nominations for directors from the floor.

- Corporate legislation requires that a notice be sent to shareholders specifying the nature of the business to be transacted, and the removal of the board or a particular director is not within the scope of the election of directors, which is what is usually contemplated in the notice for an annual meeting that is sent to shareholders.[101]

- A shareholder who wishes to remove the board or a particular director would need to provide a new notice proposing that change and to send it to all shareholders before such a motion could be considered at the meeting.

- Additionally, that process would need to comply with the proxy solicitation requirements in the applicable legislation.

- Typically, corporate legislation requires that the removal of directors be carried out by way of an ordinary resolution at a special meeting that is called for such a purpose.[102]

---

[101] CBCA, s. 135(6).

[102] CBCA, s. 109.

F. Proxy Matters

(a) *Under what circumstances may a proxy be rejected?*

- A shareholders' right to vote by or through a proxy is conferred under the legislation governing the corporation.[103]
- An individual who has been appointed as a proxyholder is entitled to be treated by the corporation in the same manner as the shareholder he or she represents.[104]
- To be valid, a proxy must comply with the statutory provisions, common law principles, and the by-laws of the company, notwithstanding that there is a general presumption in favour of the validity of the proxy.[105]
- Accordingly, if a proxy appears to be properly executed, it is inappropriate to reject it purely on the basis of assumed irregularities in its execution, such as an improper seal, lack of a corporate seal, lack of signing authority, etc.
- The ultimate decision as to whether to accept or reject the proxy lies with the chair,[106] notwithstanding that it is the scrutineer who is faced with the question of validity in the first instance.[107]
- Where the rejection of a proxy is considered, it is good practice to advise the shareholder and to allow the shareholder to remedy any defect in the proxy.
- The chair has a duty to examine the errant proxy and to make inquiries before deciding to reject it.[108]

(b) *Can a shareholder countermand a written proxy?*

- Yes, by complying with the provisions of the applicable corporate legislation.
- The ABCA, for example, permits a proxy to be revoked if an instrument executed by the shareholder or his or her attorney, authorized in writing, is deposited either (i) at the registered office of the corporation at any time up to and including the last business day preceding the meeting (or at any adjournment thereof), or

---

[103] CBCA, s. 148 (1).

[104] CBCA, s. 152 (2).

[105] Nathan and Voore, *supra* note 82 at 18-73.

[106] *Wall v. Exchange Investment Corporation Limited* (1926), Ch. D. 143 (C.A.).

[107] Nathan and Voore, *supra* note 82 at 18-73.

[108] *Johnson v. Hall* (1957), 10 D.L.R. 243 (B.C.S.C.).

(ii) with the chair of the meeting on the day of the meeting (or any adjournment thereof).[109]

- Corporate legislation typically makes reference to revoking a proxy in "any other manner permitted by law", which serves to include the common law position on revocation of proxies.[110]

- At common law, there have been instances where a proxy has been revoked either orally or by conduct[111] but, given the nature of modern business transactions and the way shareholders meetings are conducted (namely, with precise resolutions put forward to shareholders well in advance of the meeting and meetings that are based on clear agendas), these forms of revocation may not be valid.[112]

- It is clear that a proxy cannot be exercised, and it is considered to be impliedly revoked if the registered shareholder attends the meeting in person and votes.[113]

(c) *When must proxies, in respect of shares purchased after the record date, be accepted?*

- The chair is only obligated to recognize proxies for shares that were acquired after the record date when their holders have complied with the procedures under the applicable corporate legislation governing the corporation.

- No later than ten days before the meeting, a request must be made to have the new shareholder's name added to the shareholders' list. If such a demand is not made in a timely fashion, the chair is free to rule that proxies relating to such shares do not need to be recognized.

(d) *What if proxies are received after the cut-off time?*

- Proxies that are clearly received after the cut-off time may be rejected by the chair.

- Where there is a question as to whether or not proxies were received prior to the cut-off time, the chair may rely upon a statutory declaration to that effect from the proxy depositary.

---

[109] ABCA, s. 148(4)(*a*).

[110] CBCA, s. 148(4)(*b*).

[111] See, for example, *R. v. Wait* (1823), 147 E.R. 551 (Ex. Ch.).

[112] Nathan and Voore, *supra* note 82 at 18-66–18-67.

[113] *Cousins v. International Brick Co. Ltd.*, [1931] 2 Ch. D. 90 (C.A.); *Mercator Enterprises Ltd. v. Harris* (1978), 29 N.S.R. (3d) 691 (C.A.).

- Where the chair determines to accept a late proxy, he or she should be consistent and should accept all late proxies as a matter of procedural fairness.

(e) *What if a proxy is deposited to the wrong office of the proxy depositary?*

- Where a proxy depositary has multiple offices and proxies are received prior to the cut-off time at any of the offices, notwithstanding the fact that they were to be deposited to a particular office, the courts have ruled that it would be unduly technical to disenfranchise beneficial shareholders from their right to vote. The corporate legislation governing most corporations focuses on the time of the receipt of the proxy and on the identity of the agent who is designated to receive it. The place of deposit is not mentioned.

G. Adjournment and Termination

(a) *How can a meeting be adjourned?*

- A meeting may be adjourned in one of three ways:[114]
  - (i) by a resolution of the meeting;
  - (ii) by failing to obtain a quorum; or
  - (iii) by the action of the chair.
- Where a shareholder makes a motion to adjourn the meeting, the chair must be careful to ensure that such a motion is not made when someone has the floor, when a point of order is being considered, or when the meeting is engaged in voting. Such an adjournment motion would be out of order in those circumstances.
- The by-laws of the corporation may provide the chair with the express right to adjourn shareholders' meetings; however, if such a right does not exist, the chair may not adjourn meetings over the objections of the majority of the shareholders who are present in person or by proxy.[115]
- If the majority cannot be properly ascertained, the chair is permitted to adjourn the meeting on his or her own volition.

---

[114] Nathan and Voore, *supra* note 82 at 22-4.

[115] *Byng*, *supra* note 79.

- In summary, the chair does not have the power to adjourn a meeting without the consent of the meeting unless:

  (i) there is an express power to adjourn the meeting without the approval of the meeting granted in the by-laws;

  (ii) the circumstances are such that the chair is unable to ascertain the will of the majority; or

  (iii) the meeting is disturbed by a serious disorder, amounting to possible fear or violence among the shareholders.[116]

(b) *May a chair terminate a meeting to avoid an unexpected negative vote?*

- Not without the consent of the meeting unless, as indicated above, in connection with adjournments: (1) the chair has a specific power that is expressly granted in the by-laws of the corporation; (2) the will of the majority cannot be ascertained; or (3) there is a case of serious disorder.

H. The President's Address

(a) *What kind of information can be included in the president's address?*

- There are no formal requirements relating to content.
- The formal part of the meeting should be properly concluded and terminated before the representatives of the corporation provide a business address.
- The law is evolving in this area, and the dissemination of information to the public, in any form, is becoming seen as a representation of the corporation's performance.
- The safest and best practice is to restrict information in the president's business address to the public record.
- Some corporations are evolving the practice of issuing press releases that deal with new information first thing in the morning on the day of their shareholders' meeting so that the president may address that information specifically in his or her remarks.

---

[116] *John, supra* note 26.

- Projections and forecasts in the business address can create expectations and, ultimately, liability on the part of the corporation.[117]

XIII. Follow-up to the Meeting

The minutes of the shareholders' meeting should be prepared as soon as possible after the meeting to ensure the accuracy of the corporate records and to identify matters that need to be followed up on. If a public corporation transacts any special business at the meeting that constitutes a material change in the corporation's affairs (which requires disclosure under securities legislation), it must immediately issue a press release and file it with the securities commissions. The corporation must then file a material change report within ten days.[118] A listed public corporation must also comply with exchange requirements.[119]

If new directors are elected, notices of change must be filed under the relevant corporate information statutes,[120] confirmation must be given to the exchanges (in the case of listed public corporations),[121] and insider trading reports for new directors must be co-ordinated and filed.[122] If they have not already done so, directors should sign consents to act, which contain a declaration of Canadian residency, a consent to carry on business at directors' meetings by way of a telephone conference, and undertakings to advise the corporation of any change of status (e.g., residency, bankruptcy).

If any fundamental changes have been approved at the meeting, articles of amendment must be filed with the government authorities to fully implement the changes. If the directors are authorized to do so, they may reconsider proceeding with a corporate action that may have been approved by

---

[117] See OSA, Part XXIII.1, *Civil Liability for Secondary Market Disclosure*, in force as of December 31, 2005. In Alberta, Bill 25, the *Securities Amendment Act, 2006*, 2d Sess., 26th Leg., Alberta, 2006, s. 52, creates civil liability for secondary market disclosure under Part 17.01 of the Alberta *Securities Act* (Bill 25 comes into force on proclamation). In British Columbia, Bill 38, the *Securities Act*, 5th Sess., 37th Leg., British Columbia, 2004, provides for a new *Securities Act*, which includes civil liability for secondary market disclosure (Bill 38 comes into force on proclamation).

[118] OSA, s. 75; ASA, s. 146; and BCSA, s. 85. See also: NI 51-102, Part 7, *Material Change Reports*; and NP 51-201, Part II, *Timely Disclosure*.

[119] TSX *Company Manual*, Part IV.

[120] CBCA, s. 113(1) requires that notice be given within fifteen days to the Director appointed under that Act; ABCA, s. 133(1) and BCBCA, s. 127(1) require that notice be given within fifteen days to the Registrars appointed under those Acts; Ontario *Corporations Information Act*, R.S.O. 1990, c. C.39, s. 4, requires that notice be sent to the Minister of Consumer and Business Affairs within fifteen days of the changes to the directors.

[121] TSX *Company Manual*, Part IV, s. 424 and TSX *Company Manual*, Appendix H, Form 3.

[122] OSA, s. 107(1); ASA, s. 182(1); and BCSA, s. 87(2).

the requisite majority if a significant number of shareholders dissent to it and ask to have their shares bought out.[123]

XIV. Conclusion

As noted at the beginning of this Chapter, while directors have the responsibility to manage the affairs of the corporation, shareholders have limited management rights and responsibilities deriving from their share ownership. It is the directors who are responsible for the processes that permit the exercise of these rights and for the corporate disclosure that enables shareholders and the marketplace to make informed decisions about the corporation and its prospects. The disclosure requirements — including communications requirements — are increasingly specific and detailed, but they all have at their root the goal of delivering the meaningful information necessary for shareholders to play their part in corporate governance.

[123] Where they have been so authorized, directors can reconsider and revoke a special resolution: CBCA, s. 173(2); BCBCA, s. 139 contains a similar provision.

CHAPTER 6

THE USE OF COMMITTEES

With the increasing expectations of directors held by investors and others and the expanding universe of business matters requiring deliberation at the board level, boards of directors are placing more reliance on committees than ever before. Today, boards commonly use committees to more closely scrutinize a number of important areas, such as the quarterly and annual reporting of financial results, the appointment and compensation of senior executives, and the approval of significant business transactions. Sections I and II of this Chapter look at numerous circumstances that give rise to the appointment of committees and the general responsibilities of committee members. The Chapter then examines several specialized committees in greater detail. Audit committees, which are a fixture within publicly-traded corporations within and outside of Canada are examined in section III. Sections IV and V discuss the responsibilities of environment committees and pension committees, respectively. Nominating committees, compensation committees, and corporate governance committees (which have become increasingly important in light of the corporate governance guidelines that are applicable to public corporations) are addressed in section VI, together with various requirements relating to executive compensation disclosure for public corporations.

Corporations may also establish special committees to handle particular matters such as litigation or to allow groups of independent directors to deal with areas of perceived conflicts of interest. Special committees are discussed in section VII.

I. The Use of Committees

The directors of corporations often oversee organizations that have complex relationships with their employees, customers, the community, and other segments of society. To assist in the discharge of their responsibilities, many boards of directors establish committees to deal with particular aspects of the corporation's operations or governance. Although committee members take on additional duties, committees generally permit the time and energy of the full board to be used more effectively. The dynamics of the smaller group allow directors to actively question and explore issues. While the extent to which members of specialized committees will be held to a higher standard of care than the board as a whole is not yet settled, the members may be required to take advantage of their opportunity to ask more questions and to gather and analyze more detailed information.[1]

The benefits of enhanced committees include protection against potential liabilities, the increased accountability of management, enhancement of the independence and work quality of the auditor, and improved performance of the board.[2] Committees that are largely or entirely composed of outside directors provide independent advice and analysis in areas where the management and directors may have a real or perceived conflict of interest.[3]

Corporate legislation in Canada generally permits boards of directors to delegate many of the directors' powers to a managing director (who must

---

[1] *Re Standard Trustco Ltd.* (1992), 6 B.L.R. (2d) 241 (O.S.C.). See also *YBM Magnex International Inc., Re* (2003), 26 O.S.C.B. 5285 at para. 185; *Securities Act*, R.S.O. 1990, c. S. 5, s. 138.4(7) ("OSA"). For a fuller discussion of the standard of care, see Chapter 1, "Corporate Governance: Basic Principles and Current Environment", and Chapter 2, "The Duties of Directors".

[2] N. Campbell, "Holding Audit Committees Accountable" (1990), 16 C.B.L.J. 134 at 145. See also Lynne L. Dallas, "The Multiple Roles of Corporate Boards of Directors" (2003) 40 San Diego L. Rev. 781 at 789.

[3] Courts are more likely to accept that directors are acting in the best interests of the corporation rather than in their own personal interest when outside directors, particularly a committee of outside directors, advise the board. See *Pente Investment Management Ltd. v. Schneider Corp.* (1998), 44 B.L.R. (2d) 115 (Ont. C.A.).

be a resident Canadian) or to a committee of directors.[4] There are, however, limits on the authority to delegate powers, since public policy requires that the entire board of directors make certain decisions and exercise certain powers. Thus, committees do not have the authority to do the following:

- submit to shareholders any question or matter requiring their approval;
- fill a vacancy among the directors or in the office of auditor, or to appoint additional directors;
- issue securities, except when they are authorized by the directors;
- issue shares of a series except when they are authorized by the directors;
- declare dividends;
- purchase, redeem, or otherwise acquire the corporation's shares;
- pay a commission for the sale of shares;
- approve a management proxy circular;
- approve a take-over bid circular or a directors' circular;
- approve financial statements to be placed before shareholders; or
- adopt, amend, or repeal by-laws.[5]

Committees, however, can and do examine some of these matters. They then report the results of their examination, with recommendations, to the entire board. Committees provide a mechanism for in-depth examination of issues (often in consultation with independent advisors) and the acquisition of expertise. Indeed, committees often make their most valuable contributions in critical areas where the entire board must make the final decision.

Each corporation will have an individual mix of committees that reflects its business and the particular risks it faces. A publicly-traded corporation is required to have an audit committee.[6] Having regard to existing

---

[4] *Canada Business Corporations Act*, R.S.C. 1985, c. C-44, as amended, ("CBCA"), s. 115, general delegation powers, and s. 189(2), delegation of borrowing powers. Note that although the British Columbia *Business Corporations Act*, S.B.C. 2002, c. 57 ("BCBCA") allows directors to delegate their powers, it does not specifically address to whom they may be delegated.

[5] CBCA, s. 115(3); Ontario *Business Corporations Act*, R.S.O. 1990, c. B.16, ("OBCA"), s. 127(3) is similar, except that it also restricts a committee from appointing or removing any of the chief executive officers, the chief financial officer, the chair, or the president of the corporation and from amalgamating holding corporations; British Columbia *Business Corporations Regulation*, B.C. Reg. 65/2004, Table 1, s. 12.1 does not allow directors to delegate the following powers: (a) the power to fill vacancies in the board, (b) the power to change the membership of, or fill the vacancies in, any committee of the board, and (c) the power to appoint or remove officers appointed by the board.

[6] CBCA, s. 171.

corporate governance practices and guidelines, public corporations often also have a compensation committee and a governance and nominating committee. The establishment of committees to deal with environmental affairs and pensions or employee matters is also common. Committees need not be permanent; *ad hoc* committees are often formed to deal with special matters, such as a major acquisition or the consideration of strategic alternatives.

Committees are usually established by a resolution of the board or are authorized in the by-laws of a corporation. Written mandates should be developed for each committee, outlining its responsibilities and powers. Since, in some circumstances, the committee members will be asked to devote considerable time to committee business and deliberations (in addition to their ordinary duties as directors), it is important to address the issue of compensation at the outset. The issue of access to independent outside advisors should also be covered.

Committee members should be chosen for their relevant expertise, experience, and interest. Many of the Canadian corporate statutes require the members of board committees to meet minimum Canadian residency requirements.[7]

II. Responsibilities of Committee Members

Committees allow boards to delegate responsibility to a subset of members who can examine issues in greater depth and detail and make full use of their experience and expertise in a smaller forum. The board has a responsibility to assign the appropriate members to committees. The board must also ensure that the committees have the structure and resources they need to do their work. Some committees, such as audit committees, have specified duties, while others derive their responsibilities and powers from their mandates. Committee members may be at a higher risk of being held liable than other members of the board. They are expected to use their opportunities to acquire the information necessary to bring an informed view to their decisions.[8] Committee members must use their expertise, and if they lack expertise, they will be expected to acquire it or hire those with such expertise.[9]

---

[7] OBCA, s. 127(2); Alberta *Business Corporations Act*, R.S.A. 2000, c. B-9, ("ABCA"), s. 115(2). This requirement is no longer under the CBCA; however, there are some exceptions.

[8] *Re Standard Trustco Ltd.*, *supra* note 1; see Chapter 2, "The Duties of Directors", for a full discussion of the standard of care.

[9] See, for example, Multilateral Instrument 52-110, *Audit Committees*, ss. 3.1, 3.8 ("MI 52-110"). In order to sit on an audit committee, a member must be financially literate or be in the process of becoming financially literate.

Committees should follow certain procedures. Audit committees provide a useful example for discussion, since their procedures are well established. Like full boards, committees should meet regularly, provide adequate notice of the meetings, and have written agendas. Materials should be circulated to members before meetings to permit members to prepare for them. Every meeting should be held without the presence of management (in camera).[10] The members should make every effort to attend meetings, since each member is appointed because of the contribution he or she can make to them. Minutes of meetings should be kept. Members should take their own notes and review the minutes later to ensure that they are complete and accurate. Advisors provide differing views on the wisdom of retaining notes after meetings. The evolving best practice appears to be to destroy personal notes to avoid the risk of inconsistency with official meeting minutes and the risk of the notes being misconstrued or taken out of context.

If a member disagrees with a decision or a recommendation of the committee, a dissent should be recorded. A dissenting member should have an opportunity to discuss the dissent with the full board. The minutes of committees should be distributed to the full board.[11] Committees should make regular reports to the board of directors, and agendas for board meetings should be structured in order to provide an opportunity to discuss committee reports and question them.

The existence of committees does not relieve boards of their overall responsibility to manage or supervise the management of the corporation. In deciding whether board members have met the necessary standard of care in their decisions, including decisions to delegate matters to various committees, consideration may be given to the following items:

- the composition of the committee;
- the availability of expert and independent advice;
- the procedures of the committee; and
- the care and attention taken by the committee.

These factors may be particularly important, for example, in determining whether a special committee has exhibited the degree of independence that would allow a court to find that its deliberations were not

[10] Note that as a best practice, management should have no right to attend committee meetings but they should be required to attend them if they are asked.

[11] If sensitive information is contained in the minutes, committee members should ensure that the information has been excised before they are circulated to the entire board of directors. This is common practice for compensation committees, for example, as committee minutes often contain a discussion of management's performance.

impaired by a conflict of interest or by a similar concern.[12] Other committees, which devote board-level attention to the establishment of compliance policies (and monitor compliance with those programs), provide evidence of due diligence and the corporation's commitment to compliance.

As previously noted, some decisions cannot be delegated to committees. In such cases, committees can still play a useful role in gathering information and developing recommendations for consideration by the entire board. While it is legal for some decisions to be fully delegated to a committee, it may be inappropriate to leave matters of basic policy or strategic importance to a committee for a final determination.

Even when committees make final decisions, a board cannot divide its responsibilities among committees and neglect its obligations vis-à-vis the entire corporation. In general, where a committee has been authorized to make a final decision, it is advisable that members of the board be apprised of that decision at the next meeting of directors or sooner, depending upon the importance of the decision.

III. The Audit Committee

Public corporations must have audit committees. Under corporate legislation in Canada, the audit committee is responsible for reviewing the annual financial statements of the corporation before those statements are approved by the directors.[13] Corporations that have not sold securities to members of the public are not required to have an audit committee,[14] but a number of larger private corporations have established them to review their financial statements, deal with the external auditor, agree on the scope of the audit, and oversee the implementation of financial information and reporting systems. Under Canadian corporate legislation, an audit committee is required to consist of not fewer than three members, a majority of whom are not officers or employees of the corporation.[15]

For public corporations in Canada, the composition of the audit committee and the committee's responsibilities are largely dictated by

[12] *Maple Leaf Foods Inc. v. Schneider Corp.* (1998), 44 B.L.R. (2d) 115 (Ont. C.A.) at paras. 37, 46.

[13] CBCA, s. 171: "... a corporation described in subsection 102(2) shall, and any other corporation may, have an audit committee composed of not less than three directors of the corporation, a majority of whom are not officers or employees of the corporation or any of its affiliates". Subsection 158(1) of the OBCA states: "A corporation that is an offering corporation shall, and any other corporation may, have an audit committee composed of not fewer than three directors of the corporation, a majority of whom are not officers or employees of the corporation or any of its affiliates, to hold office until the next annual meeting of the shareholders". BCBCA, s. 224(1), also only allows audit committees "to hold office until the next annual meeting of shareholders".

[14] CBCA, s. 171(1).

[15] *Ibid.*

MI 52-110, which became effective in most Canadian provinces in March 2004.[16] The importance of the audit committee's role in public corporations has increased as securities regulatory authorities have placed more emphasis on intelligible financial statements and meaningful discussions of corporate performance.

MI 52-110, which applies to many reporting issuers in Canada,[17] requires that audit committees be composed of a minimum of three members and, subject to certain exceptions,[18] that each member be independent of the corporation. For the purposes of MI 52-110, a person is considered to be independent if he or she has no relationship with the corporation that could, in the view of the board of directors, reasonably interfere with the exercise of that person's independent judgment. Although the board of directors has the authority to determine whether a relationship that impairs independence exists in the case of particular members, MI 52-110 provides that persons are deemed to have their independence impaired in certain cases, including the following: (1) an individual who is, or who has been, an employee or executive officer of the corporation, unless three years have elapsed since the end of that person's service or employment with the corporation; and (2) an individual whose immediate family member is, or has been, an executive officer of the issuer, unless three years have elapsed since the end of that person's service or employment with the corporation. Under MI 52-110, lawyers whose firms provide legal services to a corporation are also deemed to be non-independent.[19]

Audit committees have a number of responsibilities under MI 52-110, including the following:

1. to recommend to the board of directors the external auditor who will be responsible for auditing the financial statements of the corporation;

---

[16] Amendments to MI 52-110 became effective on June 30, 2005. Note also that British Columbia has not adopted this instrument.

[17] See MI 52-110, s. 1.2. This instrument does not apply to the following reporting issuers: investment funds, issuers of asset-backed securities, designated foreign issuers, and SEC foreign issuers. Subject to exceptions, issuers that are subsidiary entities, exchangeable security issuers, and credit support issuers are also excluded from the application of this instrument.

[18] MI 52-110, s. 6.1 exempts venture exchange issuers from the independence requirements listed in Part 3. See also s. 3.1(3), which creates a number of independence exemptions for the following: initial public offerings; an audit committee member who is a director of an affiliated company; events that are outside of the audit committee member's control; vacancies in the audit committee due to death, disability, or resignation of an audit committee member; and other exceptional circumstances.

[19] MI 52-110, s. 1.4. Also note that an audit committee member is not independent if one of his or her relatives is either a current partner or employee of the corporation's auditor or was a partner or an employee of the auditor and worked on the corporation's audits within the last three years of service or employment.

2. to be directly responsible for overseeing the work of the external auditor (including the resolution of disagreements relating to financial reporting between management and the external auditor);

3. to pre-approve all non-audit services to be provided to the corporation or to any of its subsidiaries by the corporation's external auditor;

4. to review the corporation's financial statements, management's discussion and analysis, and news releases respecting annual and interim earnings before the corporation publicly discloses that information;

5. to be satisfied that adequate procedures are in place for the review of any public disclosure of financial information that was extracted or derived from the corporation's financial statements and to periodically assess the adequacy of those procedures;

6. to establish procedures for the receipt, retention, and treatment of complaints received by the corporation regarding accounting, internal accounting controls, or auditing matters, and the confidential anonymous submission by the corporation's employees of concerns regarding questionable accounting or auditing matters; and

7. to review and approve the corporation's hiring policies regarding partners, employees, and former partners and employees of the present and any former external auditor of the corporation.

In addition, the corporation must require its external auditors to report directly to the audit committee.

Generally, members of the audit committee have financial, legal, and managerial backgrounds. They must be prepared to fully understand the corporation's business and the requirements of financial reporting. Subject to certain exceptions, MI 52-110 requires members of the audit committee to be financially literate, meaning that the member has the ability to read and understand a set of financial statements that present a breadth and level of complexity of accounting issues that are generally comparable to the breadth and complexity of the issues that can reasonably be expected to be raised by the corporation's financial statements.

Audit committees provide continuity in dealing with the auditor and with the financial statements themselves. External auditors usually use the committee as an identified point of contact for communication with the board. The auditor may attend the committee's meetings and can call a meeting of the committee.[20] The committee can also provide a liaison with the internal controller or internal audit department, if there is one. Regular reporting by the internal controller to the committee is a valuable exercise. These reports should deal with the effectiveness and efficiency of the corporation's operations, information systems, and internal controls.[21]

As noted above, the audit committee should also review any problems that were encountered by the auditor when he or she performed the audit. Such problems might include restrictions on the scope of the audit that were imposed by management or areas of disagreement between the auditor and the management. The committee should review management's responses to recommendations made by the auditor.

The audit committee also plays a role in ensuring that errors in financial statements are corrected, if necessary. If a director or an officer of the corporation becomes aware of an error or misstatement in financial statements that the auditor or a former auditor has reported on, he or she must immediately notify the audit committee and the auditor. In turn, the auditor must report any material errors or misstatements to each director. Under applicable corporate legislation, the directors must then issue revised financial statements or otherwise inform the shareholders of the misstatement.[22] For public corporations, securities laws may also require action to be taken when an error is identified in previously issued financial statements.

In general, financial statements filed under securities laws in Canada are required to be prepared in accordance with Canadian generally accepted accounting principles ("GAAP"). This requirement will not be satisfied in cases where a corporation's financial statements contain an error that results in those statements not complying with Canadian GAAP. Accordingly, material errors will give rise to an obligation to file restated financial statements with securities regulatory authorities. Ontario Securities Commission ("OSC") Staff Notice 51-711 discusses the expectations of the OSC in cases where public corporations are required to file corrected materials (including financial statements) with the commission.

Depending on the type of business and the existence of other committees established by a corporation, an audit committee may also be asked to

---

[20] CBCA, ss. 171(4) and (5). The auditor is entitled to receive notice of every committee meeting and, if asked by the committee, he or she shall attend every meeting of the committee. Under the OBCA, s. 158(4), the auditor has the right to attend the board of directors' meetings at the corporation's expense and to be heard by the board on matters relating to the auditor's duties.

[21] Regular reports to the committee and to the full board of directors on the internal controls and internal audit system can provide, for example, the basis for a due diligence defence relating to liabilities under the *Income Tax Act*, R.S.C. 1985 (5th Supp.), c. 1, s. 227.1 and related statutes; see Chapter 9, "Duties and Liabilities of Directors Under Employment Laws".

[22] CBCA, ss. 171(6), (7), and (8).

monitor regulatory compliance, pension management, investment policies, risk management in general, whistleblower processes, the procurement and renewal of directors' and officers' insurance, and matters dealing with finance and compliance in general.

A sample audit committee mandate is found in Appendix I at the end of this Chapter.

IV. The Environmental Committee

Environmental legislation is one of the fastest growing sources of responsibilities and potential liabilities for corporations and directors. Directors can be found liable for directing, authorizing, assenting to, acquiescing, or participating in the commission of offences under a variety of environmental statutes,[23] and a number of Ontario statutes impose a positive duty of care on directors to take "all reasonable care" to prevent the corporation from not complying with the legislation.[24] Fines and penalties imposed for environmental contraventions may range into the hundreds of thousands of dollars to millions of dollars for each day an offence is committed or continued; in some instances, environmental statutes provide for terms of imprisonment.[25]

Corporations must establish compliance policies and programs in order to fulfill regulatory requirements. An effective step that directors and officers can take to reduce the risk of environmental liability is to appoint an environmental committee to deal with environmental matters. The directors must be actively involved in monitoring the effectiveness of the compliance programs and demanding changes when they are necessary. As an iterative process, this involves knowledge of the environmental requirements and the corporation's environmental risks, as well as the periodic review and adjustment of the compliance programs. An environmental committee can devote the attention needed to properly oversee the corporation's environmental compliance program.

Where the corporation's business involves particularly high or frequent risks of environmental damage, one or more board members, chosen for his or her technical expertise in environmental matters, may be assigned to the

[23] For example, see the *Canadian Environmental Protection Act, 1999*, S.C. 1999, c. 33, s. 280 and the *Fisheries Act*, R.S.C. 1985, c. F-14, s. 78.2.

[24] The Ontario *Environmental Protection Act*, R.S.O. 1990, c. E.19, s. 194; the *Ontario Water Resources Act*, R.S.O. 1990, c. O.40, s. 116(1); the *Mining Act*, R.S.O. 1990, c. M.4, s. 167(5); the *Pesticides Act*, R.S.O. 1990, c. P.11, s. 49. For further discussion, see Chapter 11, "Regulatory Liabilities".

[25] For example, *Canadian Environmental Protection Act, 1999*, S.C. 1999, c. 33, ss. 272–273; *Environmental Protection and Enhancement Act*, R.S.A. 2000, c. E-12, ss. 228 and 231.

environmental committee. The establishment of an active environmental committee will not relieve the other directors of liability for failure to take the appropriate care to prevent an offence. However, it can be an important factor in the corporation's and directors' favour if they are required to prove that due diligence was exercised.[26]

V. Pension Committee

As part of the general supervision and management of the corporation, the directors are responsible for dealing with employee pension arrangements. The directors will decide on the general structure and type of plan. In order to deal more carefully with this important area, some boards appoint a pension committee. For further discussion of pension committees, see Chapter 10, "The Duty of Directors in the Pension Context".

VI. Nomination, Compensation, and Corporate Governance Committees

Effective June 30, 2005, National Instrument 58-101, *Disclosure of Corporate Governance Practices* ("NI 58-101"), came into force, together with National Policy 58-201, *Corporate Governance Guidelines* ("NP 58-201"). NI 58-101 and NP 58-201 apply to public corporations in Canada, although a distinction is drawn between public corporations having shares listed on the Toronto Stock Exchange and public corporations whose securities are listed on the TSX Venture Exchange. TSX Venture Exchange listed corporations are subject to reduced expectations, given that they tend to have fewer resources available to them (and fewer directors).

Although the guidelines set out in NP 58-201 are not prescriptive (i.e., public corporations are free to structure their corporate governance arrangements in a manner that makes sense in their particular circumstances), NP 58-201 suggests that the boards of directors of public corporations appoint both a nominating committee and a compensation committee, with both committees composed entirely of independent directors.[27] In the case of the compensation committee, the guidelines set out in NP 58-201 indicate that the committee should be responsible for reviewing

---

[26] J. Swaigen, *Regulatory Offences in Canada: Liability and Defences* (Toronto: Carswell, 1992) at 75-139.

[27] Note that NI 58-101 and NP 58-201 adopt the general "independence" definition found in MI 52-110. This standard, however, does not include the additional independence requirement under MI 52-110, s. 1.5, which deems anyone who has received any fees from the corporation (other than board or committee fees) to be non-independent. See also Chapter 3, "The Role of the Directors", for a further discussion of board independence.

and approving corporate goals and objectives that are relevant to the compensation of the chief executive officer, evaluating the performance of the chief executive officer in light of those corporate goals and objectives, and determining (or making recommendations to the board with respect to) the compensation of the chief executive officer based on its evaluation. As well, the compensation committee should formulate recommendations to the board with respect to the compensation payable to directors and officers other than the chief executive officer.

The compensation committee should also be vested with the responsibility for reviewing executive compensation disclosure before that information is publicly disclosed by an issuer. Under securities legislation in Canada, public corporations must provide detailed disclosure of executive compensation in various disclosure documents, including prospectuses and management proxy circulars.[28] Subject to certain exceptions that apply to public corporations whose securities are listed on the TSX Venture Exchange, executive compensation disclosure must include information respecting the composition of the compensation committee and the policies it relies upon to establish the compensation of certain officers. The discussion must include the relative emphasis placed on different types of compensation by the corporation (base salary, bonuses, options or other non-cash compensation, for example), the relationship between corporate performance and compensation, and the basis on which the compensation of the chief executive officer is calculated.

The mandate of a compensation committee can be very broad, depending on the size of the company, the nature of its business, and the type of work force it employs. For example, the committee may be called upon to deal with labour issues, pay equity and employment equity policies, workplace discrimination, sexual harassment policies, stock option plans, share purchase plans, and the hiring and firing of senior executives.

In the case of the nominating committee, the guidelines set out in NP 58-201 indicate that the committee should be responsible for identifying individuals who are qualified to become new board members and recommend to the board new director nominees for election at the next annual meeting of shareholders. In formulating recommendations in that regard, NP 58-201 directs nominating committees to consider the competencies and skills that the board should possess as a whole, the competencies and skills that the board believes each existing director possesses, and the competencies and skills that each new nominee will bring to the board.

[28] National Instrument 51-102, *Continuous Disclosure Requirements*, Form 51-102F6.

Another relevant consideration is whether or not a new nominee can devote sufficient time to his or her duties as a member of the board.

The range of expertise and experience needed on modern boards is broad, and it may not be easily found among the acquaintances and business associates of current board members. A nominating committee of the board can identify the skills required by the board as a whole as well as the skills required by the various committees, taking into account the strategic direction and the specific business of the corporation. It may directly supervise the search for candidates or use a search firm. It may be responsible for the training and orientation of new directors. As well, nominating committees are often given the responsibility for conducting assessments of individual directors and of the whole board on a periodic basis.

The nomination or human resources committee may also be responsible for recommending the hiring (or firing) of senior executives. These decisions can be among the most important ones the board makes and, in some circumstances, they may require a committee of independent directors. Succession planning is also an important task for this type of committee. An orderly transition in management can be crucial to a corporation's continuing ability to succeed. This situation is particularly true in cases where an enterprise is founded upon the efforts, ideas, or discoveries of one or two people.

Apart from the need of having to make a plan to address the retirement of key people, it is necessary to be prepared for the possibility of the unexpected absence, incapacity, or death of retired people. Such preparations may entail "key person" insurance, a program of mentoring, guidelines for keeping other executives informed, designated substitutes, and so on.

Although corporate legislation does not require corporations to have corporate governance committees, almost all public corporations have them as a matter of best practice. The purpose of the corporate governance committee is to assist the board in developing the corporation's policies regarding corporate governance and to assist in making recommendations to the board in the areas of corporate governance, board practices, and the roles and responsibilities of directors. Like any committee, members should have relevant experience and interest. Corporate governance committee members are therefore often experienced board members and individuals such as lawyers who deal with corporate governance matters on a daily basis.

Corporations may decide how broad or narrow a focus the nominating, compensation and corporate governance committees should have. Sample committee mandates are found in the appendices at the end of this Chapter.

VII. Special Committees

Committees of independent directors are often established to deal with circumstances in which a real or perceived conflict of interest exists. For instance, they are used to develop responses to take-over bids, set the terms and conditions of issuer bids, and analyze or negotiate transactions in which one party has an interest in the corporation. Independent committees can also play a role when a lawsuit is brought against the corporation, management, or the directors themselves. The conduct of the case and questions of indemnification can require a disinterested viewpoint and a source from whom counsel can take instructions.

The OSC has indicated that it is good practice for boards of directors to establish special committees in certain circumstances, as noted in the Companion Policy to Ontario Securities Commission Rule 61-501:

> To safeguard against the potential for an unfair advantage for an interested party as a result of that party's conflict of interest or informational or other advantage in connection with the proposed transaction, it is good practice for negotiations for a transaction involving an interested party to be carried out by or reviewed and reported upon by a special committee of disinterested directors.[29]

Once a special committee has been established, a key first step is to give it an agreed upon mandate and to ensure that it acts on that mandate independently. Independent counsel is often retained by special committees, and it is important to how well they function.

The use of independent directors can reassure the courts that transactions are fair to the corporation and the shareholders[30] and that the directors did not breach their duty of care in approving a particular transaction. The failure to establish an independent committee of directors to consider the fairness of a proposed amalgamation on certain shareholders led on one

---

[29] Companion Policy 61-501CP, *To Ontario Securities Commission Rule 61-501, Insider Bids, Issuer Bids, Business Combination and Related Party Transactions*, s. 6.1(6). OSC Rule 61-501, *Insider Bids, Issuer Bids, Business Combination and Related Party Transactions*, s. 7.1(2) provides guidance as to who constitutes an "independent" director for purposes of the rule, that is, someone who is not an interested party in the take-over bid or special transaction. Additionally, a director is not independent if he or she is a current or recent employee, associated entity, or insider of a party interested in the transaction, is an advisor or an employee, associated entity or insider of an advisor to a party interested in the transaction, has a material financial interest in an interested party, or is expected to benefit as a result of the transaction.

[30] *Corporacion Americana de Equipamientos Urbanos S.L. v. Olifas Marketing Group Inc.* (2003), 38 B.L.R. (3d) 156 (Ont. Sup. Ct.); *CW Shareholdings Inc. v. WIC Western International Communications Ltd.* (1998), 39 O.R. (3d) 755 (Gen. Div.); *Brant Investments Ltd. et al. v. KeepRite Inc. et al.* (1991), 80 D.L.R. (4th) 161 (C.A.).

occasion to a successful oppression application under the *Ontario Business Corporations Act*.[31]

VIII. Conclusion

Committees allow directors to apply their individual expertise to particular areas. They also allow boards to deal with issues and make decisions on the basis of an in-depth examination and the recommendations of selected board members. It is important that boards and committees establish, understand, and adhere to their mandates. Boards have a responsibility to see that they use committees effectively and provide committee members with the resources they need to carry out their mandates. Large corporations and public corporations may be required to have at least an audit committee, and they are likely to have several other committees as well. All corporations, however, can benefit from a structure that requires identified members to pay particular attention to certain matters and to develop informed recommendations for the consideration of the full board.

[31] See *Palmer v. Carling O'Keefe Breweries of Canada* (1989), 67 O.R. (2d) 161 (Div. Ct.).

APPENDIX I

Audit Committee Mandate[1]

Statement of Purpose

1. The Audit Committee (the "Committee") will assist the Board of Directors (the "Board") of the Corporation in fulfilling its stewardship responsibilities through the oversight of:

(a) the accounting and financial reporting processes of the Corporation, its subsidiaries and any other business entity controlled in fact by the Corporation (each an "affiliate") and their appropriateness in view of the Corporation's operations and current GAAP in Canada and other applicable jurisdictions;

(b) the adequacy and effectiveness of management's system of internal controls and procedures in the Corporation, its subsidiaries and affiliates through the development and oversight of the internal audit function;

(c) the quality and integrity of the Corporation's, its subsidiaries and affiliates' financial reporting and disclosure;

[1] Used by permission of Alliance Atlantis Communications Inc. and its general counsel, Andrea Wood.

(d) the relationship with the external auditors (the "Auditors"), including the audit of the financial statements and any other audit and permitted non-audit services provided by the Auditors; and

(e) the compliance with laws, regulations and guidelines affecting the Corporation which relate to the duties and functions of the Audit Committee;

provided that with respect to the Corporation's subsidiary [Subsidiary Name], the Committee will be entitled to rely on [Subsidiary Name's] audit committee.

Membership

2. Number

The Board will appoint not fewer than three members to the Committee.

3. Composition

All members of the Committee must be members of the Board and "Independent" of management as that term is defined from time to time in relevant securities authorities governing the Corporation. The current independence definition for audit committee members is reproduced in Appendix I.

4. Qualifications

(a) All Committee members must be "Financially Literate" as that term is defined in Multilateral Instrument 52-110 (and reproduced in Appendix I); and

(b) The Committee will have at least one member whom the Board will deem an "Audit Committee Financial Expert" (as defined under the *Sarbanes-Oxley Act of 2002* ("S-Ox") and reproduced in Appendix I)).

In addition to the foregoing, the composition of the Committee, and qualifications of its members, will comply with such additional requirements as may be imposed by those regulating bodies having jurisdiction over the Corporation.

5. Chair

The Board will appoint the Chair of the Committee (the "Chair") annually, to be selected from the members of the Committee. The Chair must be an Audit Committee Financial Expert. If, in any year, the Board does not make an appointment of the Chair, the incumbent Chair will continue in office until that Chair's successor is appointed. In the Chair's absence, or if the position is vacant, the Committee may select another member as Chair.

6. Ex Officio Members and Management Attendance

The Lead Director is entitled to attend Committee meetings. The Committee may invite, at its discretion, non-Committee members to attend a meeting. Any member of management shall attend a Committee meeting if invited by the Chair.

7. Removal and Vacancies

Any member of the Committee may be removed and replaced at any time by the Board and will automatically cease to be a member of the Committee as soon as such member ceases to be a director. The Board may fill vacancies in the Committee by election from among the members of the Board. If and whenever a vacancy exists on the Committee, the remaining members may exercise all its powers so long as a quorum remains in office.

8. Tenure

The Board will appoint members of the Committee annually following the Corporation's annual general meeting. Each member of the Committee will hold office until the following annual general meeting or until his or her term as a member of the Board is terminated or until his or her successor is appointed.

Meetings

9. Notice of Meetings

(a) The Chair of the Committee may call meetings of the Committee periodically and will do so at the request of any member of the Committee, the Auditors, or at the request of any of the Lead Director, Executive Chairman, Chief Executive Officer, the Chief Financial Officer or the head of Internal Audit of the Corporation.

(b) The Auditors will be given notice of every meeting of the Committee and will be permitted to attend and be heard at such meeting on such matters relating to the Auditors' duties as Auditor.

(c) Notice of the time and place of each meeting of the Committee will be given to each member by telephone not less than 48 hours before the time of the meeting or by written notice not less than four days before the day of the meeting, and, subject to the requirements of any applicable law, need not specify the purpose of or the business to be transacted at the meeting. Meetings of the Committee may be held at any time without notice if all the members have waived or are deemed to have waived notice of the meeting.

10. Times and Places of Meetings

The Committee will ordinarily meet at least quarterly each fiscal year, and at other times as necessary, at times and places to be determined by the Committee.

11. Agenda

The Chair of the Committee will, in consultation with management and the Auditors, establish the agenda of the meetings and, where possible, circulate materials in advance to provide sufficient time for study prior to the meeting.

12. Quorum

A quorum at any meeting will be a simple majority and will require the attendance of an Audit Committee Financial Expert.

13. Procedure

The procedure at meetings will be determined by the Committee unless otherwise determined by the by-laws of the Corporation or by a resolution of the Board of the Corporation.

14. Secretary

The Secretary of the Corporation will, subject to any contrary direction of the Committee, act as secretary of the Committee.

15. Minutes of Meetings

The Committee will keep regular minutes of its proceedings and will report to the Board at each meeting of the Board. Minutes will be circulated to all directors on a timely basis.

16. Transaction of Business

The powers of the Committee may be exercised at a meeting where a quorum is present or by resolution in writing signed by all members of the Committee entitled to vote on that resolution at a meeting of the Committee.

17. Exercise of Power Between Meetings

Between meetings, the Chair of the Committee, or any member of the Committee designated for the purpose by the Chair, may exercise any power delegated by the Committee.

Duties and Responsibilities

18. Duties and Responsibilities

19. Relations With the Auditors

The Auditors will report directly to the Committee and the Committee will:

(a) recommend to the Board, the appointment, compensation and retention of the Auditors;

(b) recommend to shareholders the appointment of the Auditors;

(c) review the Auditors' engagement letter;

(d) review and take action to eliminate all factors that might impair, or be perceived to impair, the independence of the Auditor;

(e) review the audit plan of the Auditors to satisfy itself regarding appropriate coverage of risks, to understand the audit approach, including areas of reliance on internal controls, and to understand how changes in the accounting policies of the Corporation might impact the audit approach;

(f) oversee the work the Auditors perform quarterly (whether review or specified procedures, as determined by the Committee), including resolution of disagreements with the Corporation's management;

(g) pre-approve all audit review and attest services;

(h) approve on an annual basis, the pre-approval policy for audit, audit-related and non-audit services that are permitted to be provided by the Auditors and satisfy itself that the Committee receives regular updates of the services and fees being provided by the Auditors under this framework;

(i) pre-approve any non-audit services to be provided by the Auditors (including tax services, which are not in effect prohibited legal or expert services) that are not expressly forbidden by legislation ("Prohibited Non-Audit Services", as such term is defined in Appendix I), in accordance with applicable securities laws. Such pre-approval may be delegated to one or more members of the Committee who is an Audit Committee Financial Expert;

(j) review the basis and amount of the Auditors' fees in light of the number and nature of reports issued by the Auditors, the quality of the internal controls, the size, complexity and financial condition of the Corporation and the extent of internal audit and other non-prohibited support provided to the Corporation by the Auditors;

(k) review all other non-audit fees and services of the Auditors or other accounting firms;

(l) review post-audit or management letters, containing recommendations of the Auditors and management's response, and oversee their implementation or resolution;

(m) provide the Auditors with the opportunity to meet with the Committee or the Board without management present, at each quarterly meeting of the Committee, for the purpose of discussing any issues which have arisen during that fiscal quarter or any previous fiscal quarter;

(n) meet regularly with the Auditors without management present to receive reports of any significant disagreements between management and the Auditors regarding financial reporting, the resolution of any such disagreements and any restrictions imposed by management on the scope and extent of the audit examinations conducted by the Auditors;

(o) review and approve the Corporation's hiring policies regarding current and former partners and employees of the present and former Auditors;

(p) satisfy itself that the rotation of "lead", "concurring" and "audit partner" as those terms are used under S-Ox is in accordance with applicable laws and professional standards;

(q) annually review the expertise, resources and overall performance of the Auditors and, if necessary, recommend to the Board the termination of the Auditors or the rotation of the audit partner in charge. In the case of a recommendation to terminate the Auditors, the Committee will enquire as to the qualifications and independence of the newly proposed auditors before making its recommendations to the Board; and

(r) have authority to satisfy itself that adequate provisions are made to fund the compensation to be paid to the Auditors.

Audit and Financial Reporting

20. The Committee will be primarily responsible for satisfying itself and on behalf of the Board, that the Corporation (including its subsidiaries) fulfils all of its audit and financial reporting obligations, and will:

(a) review all financial statements and the related MD&A which require approval by the Board, including, without limitation, interim statements, year end audited statements, statements for use in prospectuses or other offering documents and statements required by regulatory authorities; determine whether the financial statements are complete, accurate and are in accordance with GAAP in all material respects; review all variances between comparative reporting periods; and recommend such financial statements and related MD&A for Board approval;

(b) review all annual and interim press releases relating to the Corporation's financial statements prior to their dissemination to the public;

(c) review all public disclosure documents containing audited or unaudited financial information before release including (without limitation) any: Prospectus, Annual Report, Form 40F, and/or any other documents extracted or derived from the Corporation's financial statements filed with regulatory agencies and satisfy itself that all information is consistent with the financial statements and that such document or statement does not contain any untrue statement of any material fact or omit to state a material fact that is required or necessary to make the document or statement not misleading, in light of the circumstances under which it was made;

(d) review the disclosure in the Annual Information Form regarding details of the Committee's membership; exemptions relied on, if any; instances of the Board not accepting the Committee's recommendations, if any; summary of Auditors' fees and services provided; and inclusion of the Audit Committee Terms of Reference;

(e) review the form of the audit report;

(f) review the audit results with the Auditors and management's proposed handling of audit adjustments;

(g) review and discuss the Auditor's report and the related MD&A for the audited annual financial statements with management and the Auditor;

(h) review any material changes in accounting practices or policies and the financial statement impact thereof;

(i) review any major areas of management judgment estimates that have a significant effect upon the financial statements;

(j) review with the Auditors, any disagreements with management over the application of accounting principles, the basis for management's accounting estimates, and the disclosures in the financial statements;

(k) review with the Auditors and management:

   (i) critical accounting policies and practices used by the Corporation, including critical accounting estimates, the selection of major accounting policies, reasons why certain policies are not considered critical and how current and future events affect that determination;

   (ii) all alternative material accounting treatments that have been discussed with management, the ramifications of these alternative treatments and the Auditor's preferred method; and

   (iii) all material written communications between the Auditors and management that would facilitate Auditor and management oversight by the audit committee such as management representation letters, reports on observations and internal control reports, schedules of material adjustments and proposed reclassifications, schedule of unadjusted audit differences and listings of adjustments and reclassifications not recorded, engagement letters and independence letters.

(l) discuss the effect of off-balance-sheet transactions, arrangements, obligations (including contingent liabilities) and other relationships with unconsolidated entities or other persons that may have a material current or future effect on the Corporation's financial condition, changes in financial condition, results of operations, liquidity, capital expenditures, capital resources, or significant components of revenues and expenses;

(m) review with the Auditors and management all material related party transactions and the development of policies and procedures related to those transactions;

(n) review with the Auditors and management the methods used to account for significant unusual transactions; and

(o) consider any other matter which in its judgment should be taken into account in reaching its recommendation to the Board concerning the approval of the financial statements.

Internal Controls and Internal Audit

21. The internal audit function will report directly to the Committee (with a dotted reporting line to the CFO and the CEO). The Committee will oversee management's design and implementation of an adequate and effective system of internal controls, and will:

(a) review the audit plan of the Auditors and consider the extent the planned audit scope can be relied upon to detect weakness in internal control or fraud or other illegal acts;

(b) review the plan of the internal audit function and consider the extent the planned audit scope can be relied upon to detect weakness in internal control or fraud or other illegal acts and any significant change in the execution of the internal audit plan;

(c) review with management the Corporation's financial policies and compliance with such policies;

(d) satisfy itself that the Corporation maintains an appropriate internal audit function, and approve the responsibilities, budget and staffing of the internal audit function, oversee the recruitment, operational independence, evaluation and termination of the head of Internal Audit and approve the objectives, plans and recommended changes made by internal audit;

(e) meet privately with the head of Internal Audit on a regular basis;

(f) satisfy itself that adequate and effective internal controls are in place including those covering accounting, financial reporting and disclosure, compliance and management information systems through oversight of management's design and implementation and through a review of significant recommendations made by the internal auditors, the Auditors, or other independent parties, for the strengthening of internal controls and/or the deficiencies identified by management and any follow-up corrective action;

(g) review the processes for complying with internal control reporting and certification requirements and for evaluating the adequacy and effectiveness of specified controls;

(h) approve or pre-approve the scope, mandate and compensation paid to third party internal control consultants, if any;

(i) review material changes to the Corporation's Commitment Policy and Payment Policy;

(j) review any major issues regarding the adequacy of the Corporation's internal controls and the actions being taken in light of any material control deficiencies identified by the Auditors, the internal auditors, third party consultants or management and management's response thereto;

(k) review internal certifications provided by the CEO and CFO to the Committee, from time to time, (as required under the Corporation's Disclosure Policy) regarding the adequacy of disclosure controls and the accuracy of publicly filed documents;

(l) review the disclosure regarding the disclosure controls and procedures and internal controls for financial reporting and understand the impact of any unremediated deficiencies on any periodic certifications or reports filed with regulators;

(m) satisfy itself that that all of the Corporation's material subsidiaries have adequate financial reporting controls, disclosure controls and internal control processes in place; and

(n) review and assess the adequacy of the Audit Committee Terms of Reference on an annual basis and the Committee's performance vis-à-vis its Terms of Reference.

Risk Management

22. The Committee will discuss the guidelines and policies to govern the process by which the Corporation undertakes risk assessment and management, and will:

(a) establish procedures for the receipt, retention and treatment of complaints received by the Corporation regarding accounting, internal accounting controls or auditing matters, including the confidential and anonymous submission of complaints by employees including reviewing on an annual basis, the Corporation's Whistleblower Policy;

(b) review with management and bring to the attention of the Auditors any correspondence with regulators or government agencies, employee complaints or published reports that raise material issues regarding the Corporation's financial statements or accounting policies;

(c) review with management any litigation, claim or other contingency, including tax assessments, that could have a material effect upon the financial position of operating results, and the manner in which these matters have been disclosed in the financial statements;

(d) identify, assess and monitor the risks inherent in the business of the Corporation and establish and monitor compliance with policies and procedures necessary to address, as much as is reasonably possible, those identified risks;

(e) in conjunction with management, review on an annual basis all aspects of the Corporation's risk management program, including insurance coverage, foreign exchange exposures, and investments (including its use of financial risk management instruments), disaster recovery and business continuity plans;

(f) review with management the presentation and impact of significant risks and uncertainties associated with the business of the Corporation;

(g) oversee the investigation of alleged fraud, illegal acts and conflicts of interest; and

(h) have the authority to engage and determine the funding for independent counsel and other advisors to carry out its duties.

Relations with Management

23. The Committee will coordinate with management on audit and financial matters, and will:

(a) review decisions of the Corporation's Disclosure Committee in which unanimity was not achieved and in instances where the Disclosure Committee deems appropriate;

(b) meet privately with senior management at least quarterly to discuss any areas of concern to the Committee or management;

(c) review with management and assess the results of instances, if any, where management seeks a second opinion on significant accounting or auditing matters;

(d) review the performances of the Chief Financial Officer and other senior executives involved in the financial reporting process, obtaining feedback from internal audit and the Auditors; provide results to the Human Resources and Compensation Committee; and, where possible, consult on the appointment of and departure of individuals occupying these positions; and

(e) have the Chair of the Committee review the expenses incurred by the Executive Chairman.

Access to Records

24. The Committee will be permitted access to all records and corporate information that it determines to be required in order to perform its duties.

APPENDIX II

Corporate Governance and Nominating Committee Mandate[1]

Statement of Purpose

1. The Corporate Governance and Nominating Committee (the "Committee") will act on behalf of and subject to the direction of the board of directors (the "Board") of the Corporation in all matters pertaining to the implementation of appropriate standards of corporate governance of the Corporation. The Committee is responsible for ensuring the Board is comprised of suitable directors, including director and Board review, director succession planning, proposing new director candidates to the Board and making recommendations with respect to the remuneration of the Board of the Corporation and its affiliates [other than Affiliate Name].

Membership

2. Number

The Board will appoint not fewer than three members to the Committee.

3. Composition

The Committee must consist of only directors who are "Independent" of management (as that term is defined, from time to time, in the relevant statutes that govern the Corporation, and reproduced in Exhibit I). Member

[1] Used by permission of Alliance Atlantis Communications Inc. and its general counsel, Andrea Wood.

qualifications include familiarity with corporate governance and previous relevant experience in assessing potential board nominees.

4. Chairperson

The Board will appoint the Chairperson of the Committee annually, to be selected from the members of the Committee. If, in any year, the Board does not make an appointment of the Chairperson, the incumbent Chairperson will continue in office until that Chairperson's successor is appointed.

5. Ex Officio Members and Management Attendance

The Committee may invite, at its discretion, non Committee members to attend a meeting. Any member of management shall attend a Committee meeting if invited by the Chairperson. The Lead Director, so long as one has been appointed, or failing that, an independent Chairperson of the Board, will be entitled to attend Committee meetings as an observer.

6. Removal and Vacancies

Any member of the Committee may be removed and replaced at any time by the Board and will automatically cease to be a member of the Committee as soon as such member ceases to be a director. The Board may fill vacancies in the Committee by election from among the members of the Board. If and whenever a vacancy exists on the Committee, the remaining members may exercise all its powers so long as a quorum remains in office.

7. Tenure

Each member of the Committee will hold office until his or her term as a member of the Board is terminated or until his or her successor is appointed.

Meetings

8. Notice of Meetings

(a) The Chairperson of the Committee may call meetings of the Committee periodically and will do so at the request of any member of the Committee or at the request of any of the Lead Director, Executive Chairman or Chief Executive Officer of the Corporation.

(b) The Committee will have the right to require the attendance of any member of management of the Corporation at meetings of the Committee.

(c) The Committee will have the right to invite any person to attend meetings of the Committee.

(d) Notice of the time and place of each meeting of the Committee will be given to each member by telephone not less than 48 hours before the time of the meeting or by written notice not less than four days before the day of the meeting, and, subject to the requirements of applicable law, need not specify the purpose of or the business to be transacted at the meeting. Meetings of the Committee may be held at any time without notice if all the members have waived or are deemed to have waived notice of the meeting.

9. Times and Places of Meetings

The Committee will ordinarily meet four times during each fiscal year at times and places to be determined by the Committee. Meetings of the Committee may be held at any place in or outside Canada.

10. Agenda

The Chairperson of the Committee will, in consultation with management, establish the agenda of the meetings and, where possible, circulate materials in advance to provide sufficient time for study prior to the meeting.

11. Quorum

A quorum at any meeting will be a simple majority.

12. Procedure

The procedure at meetings will be determined by the Committee unless otherwise determined by the by-laws of the Corporation or by resolution of the Board of the Corporation.

13. Secretary

The Secretary of the Corporation will, subject to any contrary direction of the Committee, act as secretary of the Committee.

14. Minutes of Meetings

The Committee will keep regular minutes of its proceedings and will report to the Board at each meeting of the Board. Minutes will be circulated to all directors on a timely basis.

15. Transaction of Business

The powers of the Committee may be exercised at a meeting where a quorum is present or by resolution in writing signed by all members of the Committee entitled to vote on that resolution at a meeting of the Committee.

16. Absence of Chair

In the absence of the Chairperson of the Committee at a meeting, the Committee may elect one of its members present to act as Chairperson of that meeting.

17. Exercise of Power Between Meetings

Between meetings, the Chairperson of the Committee, or any member of the Committee designated for the purpose by the Chairperson, may exercise any power delegated by the Committee.

Duties and Responsibilities

18. Duties and Responsibilities

19. Corporate Governance

The Committee will, in all cases in respect of the Corporation and its affiliates [other than Affiliate Name]:

(a) review and report to the Board on the organization and structure of the Corporation;

(b) review annually the mandate of the Board and the terms of references of the Board's committees and recommend the appointment of Directors to the various Board committees;

(c) develop, implement and review annually appropriate policies with respect to disclosure, confidentiality, insider trading, conflicts of interest, code of business conduct and ethics and other relevant policies;

(d) authorize any waiver of the Senior Management Group (as that term is defined in the Human Resources and Compensation Committee Terms of Reference) or Directors' compliance with the Corporation's Code of Business Conduct and Ethics and oversee the investigation of any alleged breach of the Code of Business Conduct and Ethics;

(e) monitor developments and make recommendations to the Board in the areas of corporate governance and board practices and the roles and responsibilities of Directors;

(f) monitor compliance with any rules, regulations or guidelines promulgated by regulatory authorities relating to corporate governance;

(g) satisfy itself that appropriate processes are established by the Board to fulfil its responsibility for: (i) oversight of strategic direction and development and review of ongoing results of operations; and (ii) oversight of investor relations and public relations activities and procedures for the effective monitoring of the shareholder base, receipt of shareholder feedback and response to shareholder concerns.

Director Selection, Compensation, Orientation and Evaluation

(h) establish a process for recruiting suitable candidates to the Board, including identifying the characteristics and skills required by the Board and those existing on the Board and reporting to the Board with respect to appropriate candidates for nomination to the Board;

(i) review management's recommendations regarding the Corporation's nominees on the board of Motion Picture Distribution LP;

(j) establish a process for determining the "Independence" of directors, the identification of a "financial expert" and the "financial literacy" of directors, as those terms are defined from time to time, under applicable securities laws;

(k) review the compensation of the Board and members of Board committees and provide recommendations to the Board;

(l) review recommendations concerning the operation of any compensation plan pertaining to directors, including recommendations as to entitlement, price and all matters related to the plan and liaise with the Corporation's Human Resources and Compensation Committee to the extent such plan is also for the benefit of officers;

(m) satisfy itself that a comprehensive orientation is in place for new directors, that directors understand the commitment expected in terms of time and resources and that continuing education opportunities are provided to all directors;

(n) satisfy itself that position descriptions are developed and reviewed annually for the Chair of the Board, the Lead Director, the Chair of each Board committee and the directors;

(o) conduct an evaluation of the performance of the Lead Director; and

(p) assist the Lead Director in carrying out an evaluation of the performance of the Board, the Board Committees and each individual director.

Other

(q) have the authority to engage and determine the funding for external advisers to carry out its duties;

(r) approve any reports required or recommended on corporate governance for inclusion in public disclosure documents;

(s) review directors' and officers' third party liability insurance proposals and coverage;

(t) review all material related-party transactions; and

(u) as required, report to the Board on the advisability of appointing an independent committee to evaluate and confirm to the Board, the fairness of any material transaction involving the Company and a significant shareholder.

20. Access to Records

The Committee will be permitted access to all records and corporate information that it determines to be required in order to perform its duties.

APPENDIX III

Human Resources and Compensation Committee Mandate[1]

Statement of Purpose

1. The Human Resources and Compensation Committee (the "Committee") will act on behalf of and subject to the direction of the board of directors (the "Board") of the Corporation in all matters pertaining to the appointment, compensation, benefits and termination of all senior executives of the Corporation and its subsidiaries (other than Motion Picture Distribution LP) including, without limitation, the Executive Chairman, the Chief Executive Officer and the Executive Vice-President and Chief Financial Officer.

Membership

2. Number

The Board will appoint not fewer than three members to the Committee.

3. Composition

The Committee must consist of only directors who are "Independent" of management (as that term is defined, from time to time, in the relevant statutes and guidelines that govern the composition of this Committee, and

[1] Used by permission of Alliance Atlantis Communications Inc. and its general counsel, Andrea Wood.

reproduced in Appendix I). Member qualifications include board experience and an understanding of compensation programs.

4. Chair

The Board will appoint the Chair of the Committee annually, to be selected from the members of the Committee. If, in any year, the Board does not make an appointment of the Chair, the incumbent Chair will continue in office until that Chair's successor is appointed.

5. Ex Officio, Members and Management Attendance

The Committee may invite, at its discretion, non Committee members to attend a meeting. Any member of management shall attend a Committee meeting if invited by the Chair. The Lead Director, so long as one has been appointed, or failing that, an independent chair of the Board, will be entitled to attend Committee meetings as an observer.

6. Removal and Vacancies

Any member of the Committee may be removed and replaced at any time by the Board and will automatically cease to be a member of the Committee as soon as such member ceases to be a director. The Board may fill vacancies in the Committee by election from among the members of the Board. If and whenever a vacancy exists on the Committee, the remaining members may exercise all its powers so long as a quorum remains in office.

7. Tenure

Each member of the Committee will hold office until his or her term as a member of the Board is terminated or until his or her successor is appointed.

Meetings

8. Notice of Meetings

(a) The Chair of the Committee may call meetings of the Committee periodically and will do so at the request of any member of the Committee or at the request of any of the Lead Director, Executive Chairman, Chief Executive Officer or the Senior Vice-President, Human Resources, of the Corporation.

(b) The Committee will have the right to require the attendance of any member of management of the Corporation at meetings of the Committee.

(c) The Committee will have the right to invite any person to attend meetings of the Committee.

(d) Notice of the time and place of each meeting of the Committee will be given to each member by telephone not less than 48 hours before the time of the meeting or by written notice not less than four days before the day of the meeting, and, subject to the requirements of applicable law, need not specify the purpose of or the business to be transacted at the meeting. Meetings of the Committee may be held at any time without notice if all the members have waived or are deemed to have waived notice of the meeting.

9. Times and Places of Meetings

The Committee will meet at least four times during each fiscal year at times and places to be determined by the Committee. Meetings of the Committee may be held at any place in or outside Canada.

10. Agenda

The Chair of the Committee will, in consultation with management, establish the agenda of the meetings and, where possible, circulate materials in advance to provide sufficient time for study prior to the meeting.

11. Quorum

A quorum at any meeting will be a simple majority.

12. Procedure

The procedure at meetings will be determined by the Committee unless otherwise determined by the by-laws of the Corporation or by resolution of the Board of the Corporation.

13. Secretary

The Secretary of the Corporation will, subject to any contrary direction of the Committee, act as secretary of the Committee.

14. Minutes of Meetings

The Committee will keep regular minutes of its proceedings and will report to the Board at each meeting of the Board. Minutes will be circulated to all directors on a timely basis.

15. Transaction of Business

The powers of the Committee may be exercised at a meeting where a quorum is present or by resolution in writing signed by all members of the Committee entitled to vote on that resolution at a meeting of the Committee.

16. Absence of Chair

In the absence of the Chair of the Committee at a meeting, the Committee may elect one of its members present to act as Chair of that meeting.

17. Exercise of Power Between Meetings

Between meetings, the Chair of the Committee, or any member of the Committee designated for the purpose by the Chair, may exercise any power delegated by the Committee.

Duties and Responsibilities

18. Duties and Responsibilities

The Committee will (in all cases in respect of the Corporation and its subsidiaries other than [Subsidiary Name]):

(a) review the recruitment, appointment and termination of senior executives of the Corporation which for the purposes hereof means the Executive Chairman, the Chief Executive Officer and the Executive Vice President and Chief Financial Officer, and such other senior employees as may be identified by the Committee from time to time, this group being referred to below as the "Senior Management Group";

(b) review management succession plans and processes of the Senior Management Group;

(c) review retention programs for the Corporation's Senior Management Group;

(d) review the training of the Corporation's Senior Management Group;

(e) review the Corporation's goals and objectives relevant to the Senior Management Group's compensation;

(f) review the annual salary, bonus, pension, severance and termination arrangements, and other benefits, direct and indirect, of the Senior Management Group;

(g) satisfy itself that procedures are in place so that (i) the Chair of the Audit Committee reviews all expenses of the Executive Chairman; (ii) the Executive Chairman reviews all expenses incurred by the Chief Executive Officer of the Corporation; and (iii) the Chief Executive Officer of the Corporation reviews all expenses incurred by the senior officers of the Corporation reporting directly to him or her;

(h) review the Senior Management Group's employment agreements;

(i) assist the Lead Director and the Board in carrying out performance evaluations of the Executive Chairman and Chief Executive Officer;

(j) review and approve recommendations concerning the operation of any employee compensation plans, including the terms, eligible participants, vesting, price, and incentive targets;

(k) grant options pursuant to any share option plan and approve any stock option grants outside such plan;

(l) review executive compensation disclosure in public disclosure documents and all executive compensation arrangements that in management's reasonable view, might be subject to disclosure requirements under securities or stock exchanges rules;

(m) review with management on a regular basis the Corporation's human resources policies, including, pay equity, employment equity, health and safety, travel and expenses, executive perquisites and other benefit policies to satisfy itself that they are acceptable to it and in compliance with applicable legislation and regulations;

(n) review all mandates for the negotiation of labour contracts (excluding production labour contracts);

(o) review annually this Committee's Terms of Reference; and

(p) have the authority to engage and determine the funding for external advisers to carry out its duties.

19. Access to Records

The Committee will be permitted access to all records and corporate information that it determines to be required in order to perform its duties.

CHAPTER 7

CORPORATE FINANCE

As outlined in Chapter 2, corporate directors have a statutory duty to manage or supervise the management of the corporation's business and affairs. A crucial aspect of the directors' management and supervisory responsibilities is their duty to ensure that the corporation has the adequate capital to carry on its business activities.

Every corporation that proposes to raise financing, regardless of its size and circumstances, should have a business plan that outlines the corporation's business objectives, prospects, and risks in the near-term, mid-term, and long-term future. The plan should describe how the corporation intends to finance itself in order to achieve its business objectives and to protect itself against the financial risks that are identified in the plan. Although the business plan will be prepared primarily by management, the directors should take an active role in reviewing and refining the plan. The directors should ensure that they understand and concur with the plan's analysis and objectives, including the means of financing the corporation's current and planned operations. For many corporations, the review and revision of the business plan by management and the directors are important elements of an annual strategic and business planning process.

The amount and nature of capital that the corporation requires, the potential sources of capital, and the means of raising capital will vary significantly, depending upon the size and nature of the corporation's business, the corporation's financial condition, and its business prospects and objectives. Is the corporation a small "private" company owned and managed by a family or by another small group of individuals, or is it a large "public" company with hundreds or thousands of shareholders? Is the corporation engaged in a single business that provides a steady operating cash flow and earnings but has no plans to grow, or does it have ambitions to expand its operations, possibly through acquisitions? Is the corporation financially robust or in financial difficulty? Does the corporation have a sufficient equity base and sustainable cash flow to be able to "leverage" its equity through debt financing, or does it have excessive debt and therefore have a need to raise equity capital despite the resulting "dilution" of its existing shareholders? The directors must consider all of these factors and other relevant factors when they are deciding on the optimum means of financing the corporation.

This Chapter outlines the legal framework within which corporations engage in capital raising activities. It then describes the more important matters that directors should consider as the corporation grows from a small "private" company into an enterprise that raises capital from the public through an initial public offering ("IPO") to become a "public" company with ongoing financing requirements.

I. The Legal Framework

Corporate legislation, such as the *Canada Business Corporations Act*, R.S.C. 1985, c. C-44, as amended ("CBCA") regulates certain aspects of corporate finance, particularly the issuance of shares or other securities by a corporation. The issuance of securities is also regulated under provincial securities laws such as the Ontario *Securities Act*, R.S.O. 1990, c. S.5 ("OSA") and its rules and regulations. "Public" companies with securities listed on a stock exchange must also comply with the exchange's rules whenever they issue new securities of the listed class or securities that are convertible into or exchangeable for shares of the listed class.

The legal landscape governing corporate finance is complex. Whenever the corporation considers issuing shares or other securities, the directors and management should obtain advice from experienced lawyers in order to ensure that all legal requirements are met. However, the directors should have a general knowledge of those requirements; the following list provides a broad overview of them.

A. Corporate Legislation

Corporate legislation gives directors the powers to authorize the corporation to borrow money and to issue shares and other securities. The corporation's articles must specify "the classes and any maximum number of shares that the corporation is authorized to issue".[1] The directors have the power to issue only those shares that are part of the corporation's "authorized capital", as set out in the articles. A corporation may amend its articles to create new classes of shares, but any such amendment must be approved by a special resolution of the corporation's shareholders.[2]

1. Directors' Powers

The directors have the power, without the authorization of the shareholders, to borrow money on the corporation's credit and to mortgage or otherwise encumber the corporation's assets to secure any of the corporation's obligations. Such powers may be limited by the corporation's articles or by-laws or by a unanimous shareholder agreement ("USA") between the corporation and all of its shareholders, and the directors collectively may delegate any of those powers to a director, a committee of directors, or an officer, subject to the same potential limitations.[3]

The directors have the power to issue shares of the corporation at such times, to such persons, and for such a consideration as the directors determine. Those directors' powers also may be limited by the corporation's articles or by-laws or by a USA.[4] Unlike the power to borrow money, the

---

[1] CBCA, s. 6(1)(*c*); note that the Ontario *Business Corporations Act*, R.S.O, 1990, c. B.16 ("OBCA") does not require the articles of incorporation to set out this information.

[2] CBCA, s. 173(1)(*e*). Note that the OBCA and the British Columbia *Business Corporations Act*, S.B.C. 2002, c. 57 ("BCBCA") do not require that this amendment be approved by a special resolution of the corporation's shareholders.

[3] CBCA, s. 189.

[4] CBCA, s. 25.

directors' powers to issue shares may not be delegated by the directors except on terms authorized by the directors.[5]

Shares cannot be issued until the consideration for the shares has been paid in full. The consideration paid for shares can be in the form of money, property, or past services. However, a consideration in the form of property or past services must have a value that is at least equal to the amount of money that the corporation would have received if the shares had been issued for money.[6] Under some statutes (for example, the OBCA), the directors are required to make specific determinations concerning the value of any non-cash consideration.[7] Furthermore, "property" does not include a person's promissory note or another promise to pay the share purchase consideration unless the promissor is a person who is at arm's length from the person to whom the shares are issued (for example, a bank).[8] Valid means of payment for shares include a bank draft, and possibly, a cheque certified by the bank on which it is drawn. However, an uncertified cheque is not a valid means of payment.

2. Classes of Shares

A corporation may have one or more classes of shares authorized in its articles. If only one class of shares is authorized, the rights of the shareholders are equal in all respects and include the rights to vote at shareholders' meetings, to receive dividends declared by the corporation, and to receive the remaining property of the corporation upon its dissolution after the payment of all of the corporation's indebtedness and other obligations.[9] If more than one class of shares is authorized, the articles must set out "the rights, privileges, restrictions and conditions attaching to the shares of each class".[10]

Many corporations have more than one class of shares authorized in their articles. One class, typically called "common shares", usually carries one vote per share, as well as the dividend and dissolution rights referred to above. One or more other classes, typically called "special", "preference", or "preferred" shares, may carry no votes, one vote, or multiple votes per share, and they often carry rights to receive fixed dividends and a fixed amount on

---

[5] CBCA, s. 115(3); note that the BCBCA does not include this limitation.

[6] CBCA, s. 25(3).

[7] OBCA, s. 23(4).

[8] CBCA, s. 25(5).

[9] CBCA, s. 24(3). Note that although the BCBCA, s. 59(3) requires every share to be equal to every other share; it does not include a list of specific rights that are attached to those shares.

[10] CBCA, s. 24(4)(a). Note that the BCBCA does not include such a requirement.

the dissolution of the corporation. Those dividend and dissolution rights usually rank ahead of the rights attached to the common shares.

B. Securities Laws

The OSA and the similar legislation of other provinces regulate every issuance of "securities" by a corporation, whether the corporation is small or large, "private" or "public". Every new issuance of securities by a corporation must be made under a prospectus that has been filed with and receipted by the securities commissions in the relevant jurisdictions, unless the corporation is able to rely on an exemption from the prospectus requirement. There are numerous prospectus exemptions that may be available to "private" companies as well as to "public" companies; the more significant ones are described below.

The term "security" is defined very broadly in securities legislation. The term is not restricted to shares and bonds; it also includes "any document commonly known as a security", "any document constituting evidence of an option, subscription or other interest in or to a security", "any profit-sharing agreement or certificate", any "investment contract", and numerous other instruments that a typical businessperson might not recognize as "securities".[11]

The failure to comply with securities laws may have serious repercussions for the corporation and for the directors personally. For example, the OSA authorizes the Ontario Securities Commission ("OSC") to make certain orders that it considers to be "in the public interest", including orders that (1) suspend a person's ability to trade in securities, (2) reprimand a person, (3) require a person to resign his or her position as a director or officer of an issuer, (4) prohibit a person from acting as a director or officer of any issuer, (5) require a person to disgorge any amounts obtained through non-compliance with securities laws, or (6) require a person to pay an administrative penalty of up to $1 million for each failure to comply with securities laws. More serious offences that are prosecuted in court are punishable on conviction by fines of up to $5 million or by imprisonment for up to five years less a day, or by both. The corporation and its directors should obtain competent legal advice in connection with any issuance of shares in order to ensure that all the requirements of securities laws and other legal requirements are met.

---

[11] Alberta *Securities Act*, R.S.A. 2000, c. S-4, s. 1 ("ASA"); British Columbia *Securities Act*, R.S.B.C. 1996, c. 418, s. 1(1) ("BCSA"); OSA, s. 1(1). For example, courts have held the following to be "securities": interests in mineral prospecting or drilling rights; "pyramid" contracts; profit sharing interests in apartment buildings and other managed real estate ventures and syndications; membership rights in a private social club; scotch whisky warehouse receipts; and interests in the profits derived from breeding a pair of chinchillas.

C. Stock Exchange Rules

"Public" corporations that have shares or other securities listed on a stock exchange must obtain the exchange's approval before issuing any additional securities of the listed class or any other securities that are convertible into or exchangeable for the securities of the listed class. A listed company must give the exchange prior notice of any proposed issuance of such shares, and it must request the exchange's approval to list the securities of the listed class that will be issued or potentially issued.

In certain cases, the exchange may require shareholder approval of the issuance: if a large number of securities (more than 20 percent of the number then outstanding in the case of securities listed on the Toronto Stock Exchange) is proposed to be issued to investors under private contracts rather than to the public under a prospectus, if the issuance is to "insiders" of the corporation, or if an issuance would have a material effect on the control of the corporation. The exchange may require that certain shareholders be excluded from voting to approve the transaction; for example, a significant shareholder may be excluded from voting to approve a private issuance of securities to himself or herself.

II. Raising Capital for "Private" Companies

Many corporations begin as small businesses that are owned and operated by an entrepreneur and his or her family. Typically, those individuals provide equity capital by purchasing common shares from the corporation for cash. Additional operating capital is raised through loans from the entrepreneurs or their relatives or from banks. Such capital is frequently secured by the corporation's assets or by the entrepreneur's guarantee, which is, in turn, secured by his or her home or by other assets. The entrepreneur is often the corporation's sole director, and compliance with the applicable legal requirements is relatively simple.

As the corporation grows, it may raise equity from other sources, often other relatives and friends. The corporation may also decide to issue shares to key employees in order to retain and motivate them. Customers, suppliers, and others who have business relationships with the corporation may invest in the corporation's shares. Shareholders beyond the circle of the founders and their relatives and close friends may have a heightened awareness of their legal rights as shareholders, including the right to vote on the annual election of directors. Such shareholders may be concerned about the founders' ability to exercise majority voting power and, conversely, the founders may be concerned about the potential "veto" voting power held by shareholders outside of the circle of founders, family, and friends. In such circumstances, a "private" corporation and its shareholders often consider it wise to enter into an agreement such as a USA to govern and regulate their ongoing relationships.

A. Unanimous Shareholders' Agreements

A USA is essentially a contractual code of conduct that governs the corporation's affairs. A USA can cover a broad range of topics, and it should be carefully drafted to suit the particular circumstances of the corporation and its shareholders. Matters frequently dealt with in a USA include the following:

- restrictions on the businesses that the corporation may carry on;
- restrictions on dividends and the uses of the company's earnings and cash flow;
- the rights of certain shareholders or groups of shareholders to elect or appoint directors and officers;
- limitations on the directors' and officers' powers to manage the corporation, such as a provision that certain actions cannot be taken unless they are approved by certain shareholders or by the holders of a specific percentage of shares;
- restrictions on the transfer, pledge, or other encumbrance of the corporation's shares;
- pre-emptive rights of the existing shareholders to subscribe for any shares that the corporation proposes to issue before the shares are made available to third parties;
- "rights of first refusal" providing that any shareholder who wishes to sell his or her shares to another shareholder or to a third party must first offer those shares to the existing shareholders *pro rata* or to the founders or other specified shareholders;
- "drag along rights" providing that if the holders of a specified majority of shares wish to sell their shares to a third party, they can compel the other shareholders to sell their shares to that party; and
- "come along rights" providing that if the holders of a specified majority of shares, after having complied with any rights of first refusal and other transfer restrictions in the USA, wish to sell their shares to a third party, the other shareholders have a right to include their shares in the sale.

It is important to note that the CBCA and other corporate legislation provide that, to the extent that the USA restricts the directors' powers to manage or supervise the management of the corporation's business and affairs, the parties to the agreement who are given those powers assume the rights, duties, and liabilities of the directors, and the directors are relieved of those rights, duties and liabilities.[12]

Given the breadth and complexity of the subject matter that is covered in it, a typical USA is often a lengthy, complicated document. The corporation and the principal shareholders who will be most affected by the USA (and possibly, other shareholders) should consider engaging experienced and knowledgeable legal counsel to prepare the USA in order to ensure that it adequately covers each subject without any "loopholes", particularly with regard to more complex matters such as rights of first refusal and "drag along rights".

B. Prospectus Exemptions Available to the "Private" Company

As previously noted, any issuance of shares by a corporation, even a small "private" company, is regulated by the securities laws of the relevant jurisdiction and requires that a prospectus be filed and "receipted" (that is, accepted for filing by the relevant securities commissions) unless an exemption is available. A brief description of the prospectus exemptions that are commonly relied upon by small "private" companies follows.

1. Issuances to Founders and Others

Shares issued to the founders of the corporation are exempt from the prospectus requirement. A founder is defined in the securities laws as someone who, alone or with others, takes the initiative in founding, organizing, or reorganizing the corporation's business and who, at the time the securities are issued, is actively involved in the corporation's business.[13]

Prospectus exemptions are also available for the issuance of securities to others who are closely connected to the corporation. In Ontario, the circle of permitted investors is limited to the following:

---

[12] CBCA, s. 146(5); note that the BCBCA does not address unanimous shareholder agreements that restrict the powers of directors. The Alberta *Business Corporations Act*, R.S.A. 2000, c. B-9 ("ABCA"), s. 146 provides that all shareholders who are party or deemed to be party to a unanimous shareholder agreement, not just those shareholders to whom the powers to manage are given, incur the liabilities of a director. As well, under the ABCA, the terms of a unanimous shareholder agreement may exclude the application of s. 146 thereto, including s. 146(7), which relieves directors from liability.

[13] National Instrument 45-106, *Prospectus and Registration Exemptions*, ss. 1.1, 2.5, 2.6, and 2.7 ("NI 45-106").

- corporations controlled by a founder;
- spouses and close relatives of a founder (i.e., parents, grandparents, brothers, sisters, and children);
- executive officers and directors of the corporation and their spouses and close relatives;
- significant shareholders of the corporation;
- employees and consultants of the corporation; and
- certain others described in the relevant securities law provisions.[14]

In provinces other than Ontario, the circle of permitted investors is considerably wider and includes many of the persons described below in connection with the "private issuer" prospectus exemption.[15]

2. Issuances by "Private Issuers"

The securities laws permit a corporation to expand its shareholder base beyond the circle of founders and family without the need for a prospectus if the corporation is a "private issuer" and if the investors fall within the categories prescribed in the securities laws.

In order to qualify as a "private issuer", a corporation must meet the following criteria:

- the right to transfer securities of the corporation must be restricted in the corporation's articles or by-laws or in a USA (for example, by prohibiting transfers of securities unless the approval of the directors or shareholders is obtained);
- there must be fewer than fifty security holders of the corporation, excluding employees and former employees, and
- the corporation must not be a "reporting issuer" (that is, the corporation must not be a "public" company).

In order to meet the prospectus exemption requirements, the securities of the private issuer must be issued to persons who have existing relationships with the issuer or who are sophisticated investors. Such persons include the following:

- directors, officers, employees, founders, or significant shareholders of the issuer;

---

[14] *Ibid.* at ss. 2.7 and 2.24.

[15] *Ibid.* at ss. 2.5 and 2.6.

- spouses, close relatives, close personal friends, and close business associates of the persons described in the first item above;
- close relatives of the spouses of the persons described in the first item above;
- persons who are already security holders of the issuer; and
- "accredited investors" (i.e., banks, trust companies and other financial institutions, securities dealers, pension and investment funds, individuals who meet certain prescribed net worth or net income criteria, and certain others).[16]

3. Resale Restrictions on Securities

The securities laws impose resale restrictions on securities issued under the prospectus exemptions described above. Generally speaking, those securities may be resold only within the circles of the permitted investors described above. The resale restrictions cease to apply four months after the corporation becomes a "reporting issuer" in the relevant jurisdiction (i.e., after the corporation becomes a "public" company).

III. Becoming a "Public" Company: The IPO

There are few events more momentous for a corporation and its shareholders and directors than an initial public offering ("IPO"), whereby the corporation "graduates" from its status of a "private" company and becomes a "public" company.

The management and directors of a corporation may decide to proceed with an IPO for a variety of reasons. For example, the corporation may have growth plans that require a level of equity financing that is available only in public markets, or the founders may plan to sell some or all of their investment in the corporation over time and may wish to have the liquidity, flexibility, and pricing advantages of selling some or all of their shares of a "public" company in the market instead of seeking private buyers for all of their "private" company shares. Shares of a "public" company for which there is a liquid market will almost always be preferred over "private" company shares in cases where the company is seeking to acquire a business or other assets by issuing shares rather than by paying cash to the vendor.

The advantages of being a "public" company ("reporting issuer" is the term used in securities laws to describe what is commonly referred to as a "public" company) are counterbalanced by serious obligations and potential

---

[16] *Ibid.* at ss. 1.1 and 2.4.

liabilities. Following the completion of the IPO, the corporation will have onerous ongoing obligations, including the following:

- The corporation must prepare and publicly disclose quarterly unaudited and annual audited financial statements. The financial statements must be accompanied by a management's discussion and analysis ("MD&A") of the corporation's financial results and forward-looking information about its future financial prospects.

- The corporation must make the prompt public disclosure of all material changes and developments in its business and affairs, whether such information is favourable or adverse. The corporation and its directors and management will be subject to penalties and civil liabilities if information that is published by the corporation is inaccurate or incomplete or is otherwise misleading in any material respect.[17]

- The corporation must hold annual meetings of its shareholders at which directors are elected and auditors are appointed by the shareholders. The management of the corporation must solicit proxies from shareholders for use at each shareholders' meeting by sending a management proxy or information circular to shareholders. The circular must contain detailed information about any business that is proposed to be dealt with at the meeting and, in the case of annual meetings, it must also contain specific detailed disclosure concerning management compensation and corporate governance policies and practices.

- The corporation and its directors and management must comply with mandatory standards of corporate governance, and they must also disclose any departure from non-mandatory governance guidelines. The board of directors must include directors who are independent of management. The board must appoint committees of directors who will take on important oversight responsibilities; the most important of these committees is an audit committee that is composed of directors who are independent of management and who are "financially literate" and able to supervise the preparation of the corporation's financial statements.

---

[17] Ontario's Bill 198, *Keeping the Promise for a Strong Economy Act (Budget Measures),* 3rd Sess., 37th Leg., Ontario, 2002, and similar legislation pending in other provinces, impose significant liabilities on a corporation if investors suffer damages due to the corporation's failure to make prompt, accurate disclosure about material changes in its business or affairs. For further discussion, see Chapter 1, "Corporate Governance: Basic Principles and Current Environment", and Chapter 3, "The Role of the Directors".

- The directors, senior officers, significant shareholders, and other "insiders" of the corporation must publicly disclose their ownership of the corporation's securities. The securities laws prohibit such persons from buying or selling the corporation's securities at any time when they have knowledge of any material information concerning the corporation that has not been publicly disclosed, and if they engage in improper trading, they will be subject to criminal and civil liabilities. The board of directors must establish policies for trading in securities by the corporation's directors, management, and employees that are designed to avoid any improper trading.

It is crucial that a corporation prepare itself thoroughly to address and manage its ongoing reporting issuer obligations before it proceeds with an IPO.

A. Preparing for the IPO

Preparing for an IPO is a daunting process for everyone involved. The corporation must ensure that it can accomplish the extensive work that needs to be done to prepare for and to execute the IPO efficiently and successfully and to manage its ongoing "public" company responsibilities.

1. Assembling the IPO Team

Preparing for and executing an IPO requires the extensive efforts of numerous people working as a team. Important elements of the team include the following:

Lead Underwriter. The securities offered under the IPO will be marketed to the public by one or more investment dealers acting as agents or underwriters. The careful selection of the right underwriter, or lead underwriter, by the corporation's management and directors is crucial to the success of the IPO. This subject is addressed in greater detail below.

Senior Management. The most important management team members are the chief executive officer ("CEO") and the chief financial officer ("CFO"). They must have the character and the ability to effectively manage the business operations and financial affairs of the corporation. They must also have, and be perceived to have, the integrity and credibility to instill confidence in the underwriters and in others in the investment community. Depending on the size of the business, they must also assemble and lead the other members of the corporation's operating and financial management team. The directors should ensure that the corporation has an effective senior management team that can accomplish those tasks.

Directors. Prior to an IPO, the members of the corporation's board are often limited to the controlling shareholders and senior management, and there is limited, if any, representation by persons who are independent of management. After an IPO, the corporation must comply with the applicable corporate governance requirements and guidelines by including on the board independent directors, including directors who have sufficient financial and accounting knowledge and expertise to act as members of the audit committee. The independent directors, and the board as a whole, should also be perceived by the underwriters and by others in the investment community as having the necessary experience and integrity to oversee the ongoing management of the corporation. The existing directors, senior management, and the lead underwriter should think carefully when they are making additions and changes that are necessary to create an effective board of directors.

Auditors. It is very important to the success of the IPO process that the corporation's auditors be well regarded by the underwriters and by others in the investment community. For that reason, prior to an IPO, the corporation and the underwriters often find it advisable to change the corporation's auditors to a national accounting firm or to a leading regional firm.

Lawyers. Whether or not the corporation has "in-house" legal counsel, it is almost always necessary for the corporation to engage a law firm to advise it prior to, during, and after the IPO process. The firm should have expertise in corporate and securities law, experience in handling IPOs, and the capacity to prepare the prospectus and all of the other documentation that is required to complete the IPO in a timely fashion. The underwriters will also engage a law firm to advise them in connection with the IPO. It is most often advisable for the corporation and its legal counsel to have some input in the selection of the underwriters' counsel to ensure that the process proceeds as smoothly and as efficiently as possible.

2. Selecting the Lead Underwriter

The directors and management of the corporation should consider a number of factors in selecting the lead underwriter for the IPO:

- *Size of the Issue and the Offering.* The corporation should select a lead underwriter that is well suited to the task of underwriting. If the corporation is of a significant size and needs to raise a substantial amount of money in the IPO, one of the bank-owned dealers or the larger independent dealers is likely to be best suited to lead the IPO process. If the issuer is a smaller company or if the project for which it is raising money is speculative, a smaller investment house may be more suitable.

- *Nature of the Issuer's Business.* The nature of the corporation's business may be an important factor in selecting an underwriter. For example, if the corporation is a technology company or a mining exploration company, certain investment dealers will have significantly more expertise than others in those industries, better access to investors who are interested in those industries, and specialized research analysts who are more likely to have a continuing interest in the corporation after the IPO is completed.

- *"Track Record".* The corporation should review other IPO transactions that a potential underwriter has recently completed and consider consulting the senior management or directors of those issuers about their experience with the underwriter. How did the underwriter perform during the IPO process? Were the members of the underwriter's team consistent and accessible during the process? Did the underwriter continue to be supportive after the IPO was completed, for example, by publishing analysts' reports about the company, helping to create an active trading market in the company's shares, and providing continuing value-added advice to senior management?

- *Enthusiasm.* The corporation should consider the potential underwriter's overall level of enthusiasm for the IPO transaction. Did the investment dealer initially approach the corporation with an IPO proposal? Has the firm continued to show strong interest in the transaction after several interactions with management and a review of the corporation's business plan? Does the firm clearly understand the corporation's business, plans, and prospects? What valuation metrics are the firm using to estimate the IPO share price, and how does that estimate compare to the market prices of comparable "public" companies?

3. Principal Pre-IPO Tasks

Once the IPO team has been assembled, there are numerous important tasks that must be completed before a preliminary prospectus can be filed.

Business Plan. The corporation's senior management and directors, with input and assistance from the lead underwriter, should ensure that the corporation has an up-to-date business plan that clearly outlines its business objectives and financing requirements in the near-, mid- and long-term future. The plan should indicate in detail how the proceeds from the IPO will be used by the corporation.

Financial Statements. The corporation and its auditors must prepare audited financial statements in accordance with Canadian generally accepted accounting principles ("GAAP") for inclusion in the prospectus. In most cases, the statements must cover the corporation's three most recently completed fiscal years. The prospectus may also need to include interim, unaudited financial statements for periods that ended after the end of the most recent fiscal year.

Description of the Business. The prospectus must contain a detailed description of the corporation's business history and its current business operations. That information, together with the financial statements, will form the "backbone" of the prospectus, and it will require a great deal of thought and effort by the corporation's management, the underwriters, and their respective legal counsel.

Books and Records. The corporation should ensure that all of its important books and records are up to date and well organized. Financial books and records are obviously very important, as are the corporation's material contracts with suppliers, customers, and key management. Title documents relating to the corporation's material properties, plant, equipment and intellectual property should also be assembled and organized for review by the underwriters, auditors, and lawyers.

The "Due Diligence" Process. The corporation's directors and senior managers and the underwriters will be able to avoid any statutory civil liability to purchasers of the corporation's IPO securities who suffer damages in circumstances where there has been a misrepresentation in the prospectus if the directors, senior managers, and underwriters conducted such reasonable investigation as to provide reasonable grounds for a belief that there had been no misrepresentation in the prospectus. This defence against liability is commonly referred to as the "due diligence" defence. In order to assist in establishing the defence, the underwriters and legal counsel to the corporation will thoroughly review the corporation's business operations, financial statements, and books and records to ensure that all material information is included in the prospectus. They will interview the corporation's senior management, other key employees, suppliers, customers, and auditors. They will also require senior management and the directors to complete and sign questionnaires in which they confirm that they have read the prospectus and that they believe the prospectus disclosure to be accurate and complete.

B. Completing the IPO

When the corporation and the underwriters are satisfied that the preliminary prospectus contains full, true and plain disclosure of all material facts relating to the offered securities, the preliminary prospectus is signed by the corporation and the underwriters, and it is filed with the securities commissions of the provinces in which the securities will be offered for sale.

The preliminary prospectus can be used by the underwriters "to solicit expressions of interest" from potential investors, but it cannot be used as the basis for the sale of the securities. Sales can be made after the (final) prospectus has been filed and accepted by the relevant securities commissions.

After the preliminary prospectus has been reviewed by the securities commissions and all of the commissions' comments have been resolved, the corporation and the underwriters will prepare to "go final". The size of the offering and the price per share will be negotiated and agreed upon. The terms of the offering will be set out in an agreement between the corporation and the underwriters. The agreement will also contain extensive representations and warranties by the corporation and, to a lesser extent, by the underwriters, covenants by each party, provisions allowing the underwriters to terminate the agreement in specified circumstances, provisions describing the documentation that must be delivered by each party at "closing" (i.e., at the completion of the IPO), and the other usual provisions. The (final) prospectus will then be signed and filed with the relevant securities commissions, and when the commissions have accepted ("receipted") the prospectus, the underwriters will commence the process of distributing the prospectus to potential investors and finalizing the sale of the securities to purchasers.

When the underwriters have completed the process of "contracting" with investors, the closing will occur. The corporation will then deliver to the underwriters a certificate representing the sold shares in exchange for payment of the purchase price by the underwriters, and all other "closing deliveries" will be made, including legal opinions and the corporation's written confirmation that the prospectus continues to be accurate and complete.

The IPO process typically requires a minimum period of ninety days from the time that a decision is made to proceed with the IPO until the closing of the IPO, and it can take significantly longer if the corporation has not completed considerable organizational work and other preparatory work beforehand. An IPO is expensive. Underwriting fees are typically 5 percent or more of the gross proceeds raised. Other IPO expenses, including auditor's fees and other accounting fees, fees of the corporation's and the underwriters' lawyers, printing costs, and costs of "road shows" (shows in which the underwriters and management travel to selected cities to present the corporation and the IPO opportunity to brokers who will market the IPO shares to their clients), can total hundreds of thousands of dollars and may exceed $1 million. It is not uncommon for the corporation's total expenses (underwriting commissions and other costs) to approach 10 percent of the gross proceeds. For a corporation that embarks on an IPO but fails to complete it successfully, the financial costs and the other costs can be considerable.

IV. Raising Capital for "Public" Companies

By becoming a reporting issuer, a corporation significantly increases the range of alternatives that are available to it in raising the capital it needs to finance its business. The corporation can issue securities by way of a "private placement" to institutions and to other sophisticated investors under available prospectus exemptions. The corporation and the investors typically enter into subscription agreements that contain detailed representations and warranties by the corporation concerning the state of its business and the accuracy and completeness of its public disclosure record. The costs associated with a private placement financing are typically lower than the costs of a prospectus financing. However, securities that are issued under a private placement are subject to resale restrictions that tend to reduce the issue price for the securities, compared to the price that the corporation could realize if it were to sell freely tradeable securities under a prospectus.

The corporation may also elect to raise capital by issuing securities under a prospectus. Reporting issuers that are relatively small or that have been reporting issuers for less than a year must use the normal "long form" prospectus system. However, if the corporation has been a reporting issuer for at least twelve months, has equity securities listed on a Canadian stock exchange, and has a market capitalization of at least $75 million, then the corporation is eligible to issue securities using a "short form" prospectus. One advantage of using a short form prospectus is that the issuer can eliminate much of the disclosure that would be required in a "long form" prospectus by incorporating by reference in the short form prospectus the principal documents that are contained in its public disclosure record (such as financial statements, annual information forms, etc.), thereby reducing costs. Another advantage is that the period between the filing of a preliminary prospectus and the filing and receipting of a (final) prospectus is significantly shorter in the short form system than in the regular "long form" system. As described below, that timing advantage makes the corporation eligible to receive "bought deal" proposals from underwriters that are not available to corporations that must use a "long form" prospectus.

A. Forms of Underwriting Commitments in Prospectus Offerings

Depending upon the corporation's circumstances and the state of the financial markets, underwriters may be more or less willing to take the financial risks that are inherent in underwriting an offering of the corporation's securities by prospectus. The following list briefly describes the variety of commitments that an investment dealer may be prepared to make in connection with a prospectus offering.

1. "Best Efforts" or "Agency" Offerings

In this form of financing, the investment dealers act as the "agents" of the corporation and not as its "underwriters". The dealers only commit to use their "best efforts" to market the securities to investors, and they make no commitment to purchase any of the offered securities.

2. "Fully Marketed" Underwritten Offerings

In a "fully marketed" underwriting, the underwriters use the preliminary prospectus to solicit interest in the offered securities from potential investors. At the time the (final) prospectus is filed, the underwriters commit to purchase the securities from the corporation at closing and to resell the securities to investors as principals for the underwriters' account. The underwriters have the right to terminate their purchase commitment in specific circumstances, including the right to exercise a "market out" if they conclude that market conditions are too weak to enable them to market the offering profitably.

3. "Bought Deal" Underwritten Offerings

In a "bought deal", the underwriters make a proposal to the corporation to purchase a specific number of securities from the corporation at a specific price before a preliminary prospectus has been filed. If the corporation accepts the proposal, a preliminary prospectus is filed as soon as possible (within two days), and the closing occurs reasonably shortly after the (final) prospectus has been filed and receipted. The underwriters' "market out" rights are more limited in a bought deal than they are in a fully marketed deal. Such rights can be exercised by the underwriters only if there are serious adverse developments in national or international markets or other similar serious adverse developments. For that reason, the right to terminate a bought deal is often referred to as a "disaster out" right. Because of the significant financial risks to the underwriters during the period between the time that the corporation accepts the bought deal proposal and the time that the underwriters are able to obtain firm purchase commitments from investors, a bought deal financing is feasible only if the corporation is to use a short form prospectus, which abbreviates the underwriters' at-risk period.

V. General Financing Considerations

The corporation's management and directors should continue to review and develop the corporation's business plan, including the amount and the nature of the capital it will need to finance its business operations and objectives. In considering how and when to finance the corporation, the directors and management should give thought to the following matters:

- *Timing*. When is the best time to raise funds, having regard to the corporation's business cycle, anticipated market conditions, and other considerations?
- *Purpose*. What is the optimum use of the proceeds from the financing? Capital expenditures? Repayment of indebtedness? Acquisitions?
- *Nature of Financing*. What is the optimum form of the financing? Bank borrowings or other forms of debt, such as bonds, debentures, or notes? Equity capital in the form of common shares or preferred shares? Does the corporation need the capital temporarily (short-term or mid-term borrowings) or for a longer term (long-term debt or permanent equity capital)?
- *Sources of Financing*. Should the corporation approach banks or other financial institutions for loans? Should it approach an investment dealer to raise debt or equity capital? Should it issue securities to the public under a prospectus or to institutional and other sophisticated investors under a private placement?

VI. Conclusion

Whether a corporation is large or small, "public" or "private", decisions concerning the financing of the corporation are among the most important ones that the directors are called upon to make in carrying out their duty to supervise the management of the corporation's business and affairs. The raising of capital has an impact on the corporation's balance sheet, its earnings, and its cash flow and, consequently, the value of the corporation's shares and other securities. An acquisition or other growth opportunity may succeed or fail, depending upon how well or how poorly the corporation finances that opportunity.

The directors are more likely to make wise decisions on financing matters if they ensure that the corporation prepares and regularly updates a business plan and if the directors continually ask themselves, management, and the corporation's financial advisors the right questions about when and how to finance the operations and objectives in such plan.

CHAPTER 8

TAKE-OVER BIDS

This Chapter addresses directors' conduct in the context of a "control transaction", which is defined herein as any transaction whereby *de facto* control of an entity is acquired. Such transactions can include take-over bids,[1] arrangements,[2] amalgamations,[3] or treasury issuances of securities. This Chapter reviews directors' conduct in the circumstances where the corporation acquires control of another entity, another entity acquires con-

[1] A take-over bid is defined in the Ontario *Securities Act*, R.S.O. 1990, c. S-5 ("OSA"), as an offer to acquire outstanding voting or equity securities of a class that is made to any person or company who is in Ontario or to any security holder of the offeree issuer whose last address as shown on the books of the offeree issuer is in Ontario, where the securities subject to the offer to acquire, together with the offeror's securities, constitute in the aggregate 20 percent or more of the outstanding securities of that class of securities at the date of the offer to acquire. As seen from the definition, securities legislation sets the take-over bid threshold at 20 percent.

[2] An arrangement is defined in s. 192 of the *Canada Business Corporations Act*, R.S.C., 1985, c. C-44 ("CBCA") as (a) an amendment to the articles of a corporation; (b) an amalgamation of two or more corporations; (c) an amalgamation of a body corporate with a corporation that results in an amalgamated corporation subject to the CBCA; (d) a division of the business carried on by a corporation; (e) a transfer of all or substantially all the property of a corporation to another body corporate in exchange for property, money, or securities of the body corporate; (f) an exchange of securities of a corporation for property, money, or other securities of the corporation or property, money, or securities of another body corporate; (f.1) a going-private transaction or a squeeze-out transaction in relation to a corporation; (g) a liquidation and dissolution of a corporation; and (h) any combination of the foregoing. The CBCA sets out certain prerequisites before the arrangement provisions can be used.

[3] Under s. 181 of the CBCA, an amalgamation can be used to acquire control of a corporation either through the issuance of redeemable preferred shares, which are then redeemed for cash, or through the issuance of participating securities to shareholders of the amalgamating entities.

trol of the corporation, or shareholders of another entity acquire control of the corporation.

I. Statutory Duties

Whether the corporation is the acquiror or is being acquired, directors must conduct themselves in accordance with the requirement in s. 122 of the CBCA that they act honestly and in good faith with a view to the best interests of the corporation, and exercise the care, diligence and skill that a reasonably prudent person would exercise in comparable circumstances. Directors' conduct in the context of a control transaction will be judged by a court in light of these requirements. These provisions essentially require directors to adhere to both process and substance in the circumstances of a control transaction.

II. Process and Substance

The term "process" relates to how directors evaluate a transaction. For example, have they set up an independent committee if some of the directors are in a conflict situation? Have they retained the necessary legal, accounting, and investment experts? Have they been duly diligent in evaluating the transaction? Have they met an appropriate number of times before approving the transaction and have they considered all of the relevant facts?[4]

The term "substance" means the nature of the transaction itself, and it effectively requires the directors to satisfy themselves that the transaction is an appropriate one for the corporation. Generally, the directors will obtain a fairness opinion from a financial advisor to back up their conclusion, although an investment banker's fairness opinion goes to the transaction's "fairness from a financial point of view", whereas the directors must consider the entire fairness of the transaction.

III. Preliminary Steps

When they are planning a control transaction or when they find themselves the subject of a control transaction, the directors of a public company should take some or all of the following steps:

[4] See *Re Peoples Department Stores Ltd. (1992) Inc.*, [2004] 3 S.C.R. 461 ("*Peoples*"); *Smith v. Van Gorkom*, 488 A.2d 858 (Del. S.C., 1985); *UPM-Kymmene Corp. v. UPM-Kymmene Miramichi Inc.* (2002), 214 D.L.R. (4th) 496 (Ont. S.C.J. [Commercial]), aff'd (2004), 250 D.L.R. (4th) 526 (Ont. C.A.).

- obtain market intelligence as to the composition of the shareholder base of the target;
- retain legal counsel;
- consider putting in place any available defensive measures that may buy time (e.g., so-called "poison pills");
- retain investment bankers to provide an opinion as to the fairness of the transaction, to provide advice on defensive tactics, and if the board so directs, to solicit other bids;
- retain other experts if required, such as geologists (for an oil and gas company) and economic consultants (if competition issues are relevant);
- consider retaining a public relations firm;
- if the corporation is the target, obtain advice as to whether the directors should constitute an independent committee of the board because of potential conflicts they may face in evaluating the transaction;
- review director indemnification provisions in place to ensure that they are appropriate;
- obtain advice on whether the nature of the offer or the type of transaction subjects the transaction to special rules such as Ontario Securities Commission ("OSC") Rule 61-501[5] and Quebec Securities Commission Policy Q-27;[6]
- obtain advice on the likelihood of the transaction being completed in light of any *Competition Act* (Canada) approvals, foreign anti-trust law approvals, or other regulatory approvals being required;
- obtain advice on whether any key contracts have change of control or key man provisions (terms that allow the other party out of the contract or involve special payments in the context of particular events);
- prepare a data room so that information about the company can be shared quickly, if appropriate;

---

[5] Ontario Securities Commission Rule 61-501, *Insider Bids, Issuer Bids, Business Combinations, and Related Party Transactions*.

[6] Quebec Securities Commission, Policy Statement Q-27, *Weekly Bulletin*, Volume XXXI, no. 6, February 11, 2000. These instruments require that in the case of an insider take-over bid, a valuation of the security that is the subject of the bid be prepared, and in the case of a business combination that involves the shareholders being squeezed out, a valuation be prepared and majority of the minority approval be obtained.

- if the corporation is the acquiror, determine how the transaction will be financed;
- if the corporation is the acquiror, determine how the market will perceive the transaction and what the effect will be on its stock price;
- determine the likely effect of the transaction on the corporation's credit rating;
- determine who the various relevant constituencies are. It is clear that the common shareholders are a constituency. However, directors also need to obtain advice on the effect of the transaction on other security holders, such as preferred shareholders, debt holders, option holders, warrant holders, and employees;[7]
- determine whether there are key employees whose retention is integral to the success of the combined entity;
- determine the implications of the change to customers, including the implications of any uncertainty that may persist through the actual deal process;
- if the corporation is the target, the acquiror is offering its own securities as consideration, and the transaction is friendly, arrange for due diligence on the target; and
- consider the "social issues": What will the combined corporation be named? Where will it be headquartered? Who will be on the board of directors? Who will make up the senior management? Will there be employee layoffs?

IV. The Corporation as Acquiror

If the corporation is acquiring another entity and the target entity is private, the corporation will enter into a share (or asset) purchase agreement with the target. If the target is public and the transaction is a "friendly" one, the acquiring corporation will want to enter into a support agreement with the target whereby the target's board of directors agrees to support the transaction. The corporation will also attempt to lock-up any significant shareholders so that they will agree to tender their shares to the transaction. If the transaction is structured as a take-over bid, the corporation will be required to prepare a take-over bid circular for the target.[8] In a transaction effected by way of an arrangement (a court approved acquisition procedure)

---

[7] See the discussion in *Peoples*, *supra* note 4.

[8] This is Form 32 to the Regulations to the Ontario *Securities Act*, R.R.O. 1990, Reg. 1015 (Ontario "Securities Act Regulations").

or an amalgamation, the corporation will enter into an arrangement agreement or amalgamation agreement with the target whereby the target agrees to complete the transaction and to call a meeting of its shareholders to approve the transaction. In such a situation, the acquiring corporation does not make its own offer to the shareholders of the target entity but relies on the vote of the shareholders of the target entity to acquire the corporation. So-called "friendly" acquisitions provide opportunities for co-operation in tax and business planning. Many hostile take-over bids become friendly take-overs for this purpose once it is clear which bidder (of a number of competing bidders) has won the contest.

If the transaction is "unfriendly", the corporation will have no choice but to proceed by way of a take-over bid. The directors of the acquiring corporation will have to decide whether they are prepared to go that route since, based on marketplace perception and other factors, it is often difficult to be the victor in a hostile situation.

In a situation where the corporation is the acquiror, the directors must satisfy their fiduciary duties by concluding that the transaction is beneficial to the corporation (e.g., it is accretive to earnings, or it is synergistic, or the corporation is acquiring key technology).

V. The Corporation as Target

If the corporation is a private company and it is prepared to be acquired, its shareholders will enter into a share (or asset) purchase agreement with the acquiror.

If the corporation is a public company and it is approached with a control transaction, the board first needs to determine whether it will negotiate with a potential acquiror. In the case of an unsolicited offer, the board also needs to determine whether it will negotiate that offer exclusively or attempt to widely market the corporation.

If the board is determined to negotiate with the acquiror, the target corporation will require the acquiror to enter into a confidentiality agreement with it before allowing the acquiring corporation to conduct due diligence. The entering into of such an agreement is important because the corporation is providing confidential information and because the process may devolve into an auction of the corporation. There is some question as to whether it is appropriate for directors of a targeted corporation to provide a real or potential business competitor of the acquiror or target with such information about the target company, even pursuant to an agreement, when the result may well be a better offer than what is presently on the table.

That is an issue which is often faced by directors, senior officers, and their advisors when they are seeking to find a superior alternative, and it clearly raises concerns about whether such persons are acting in the best interests of the corporation by doing so. Confidentiality agreements ordinarily have four principal elements to them:

First, the recipient of confidential information must agree to keep it confidential, unless such information is already public or becomes public through no fault of the potential offeror. Potential offerors are typically permitted to share this information only with those who "need to know" it (such as bankers, lawyers, investment advisors, and key employees), and they are prohibited from using such information for any purpose other than evaluating the control transaction or from divulging that discussions with the target are taking place. The potential offeror also agrees that information that is provided to it will be returned or destroyed if it decides not to pursue the acquisition or if the target requests that it be returned or destroyed.

Second, the potential offeror agrees not to acquire or offer to acquire any shares or assets of the target or to engage in any proxy solicitation with respect to the target for a specific period of time (usually six months to two years) without the consent of the target's board of directors.

Third, the potential offeror agrees to not have any contact with management or employees of the target except through designated representatives and to not solicit any employees of the target for a specific period of time.

Fourth, the agreement contains an express disclaimer on the part of the target with respect to any liability arising from the furnishing of confidential information to the potential offeror, unless provided otherwise in a definitive agreement.

The target corporation will also be asked to enter into a support agreement with the acquiring corporation whereby the board of directors of the target corporation agrees to support the transaction. Support agreements are very common, but the board of directors needs to ensure that such an agreement contains a "fiduciary out" clause whereby the board has the right to terminate the agreement and accept a "superior transaction". The *quid pro quo* for the fiduciary out is a break fee whereby if the board accepts another bid, it must pay a negotiated fee to the first acquiror both to reimburse expenses and to reflect the fact that the first acquiror's offer put the corporation in play, thereby resulting in a higher price for shareholders. In a support agreement, the directors should also ensure that the acquiror agrees to maintain directors' insurance for a specific period of time.

In terms of disclosure documents for the transaction, if the control transaction is a take-over bid, the board of directors of the target corporation is required to prepare a directors' circular for dissemination to the target corporation's shareholders within fifteen days after the offer.[9] The directors' circular outlines the board's recommendation to the target corporation's shareholders on the offer and discloses relationships between the offeror and the target's directors and officers, share ownership and trading history, material undisclosed changes since the last published financial statements, and other information that the directors feel is relevant to a shareholder's assessment of the offer.

The directors must make either a positive recommendation, a negative recommendation, or refrain from making any recommendation; in each case, they must give reasons. The directors of the target may defer the communication of their final views until seven days before the expiry of the offer. Directors are expressly required to disclose any proposed defences to be used against the offer.

If the transaction is an arrangement or amalgamation, the board must prepare a proxy circular in accordance with the CBCA[10] and Canadian securities legislation.[11]

VI. Defences Available to the Target

The defences available to the target of an unwelcome take-over bid are limited, which is perhaps the principal reason why a very high proportion of Canadian companies that are put "in play" are ultimately the subject of some type of transaction, although not necessarily with the initial offeror. Defences can be categorized into five types:

(a) Structural defences: such defences include the adoption of a shareholder rights plan or poison pill;[12] the provision of "golden parachutes" to senior officers and of "tin parachutes" to many or all

---

[9] This is Form 34 to the Ontario Securities Act Regulations.

[10] See Canada Business Corporations Regulations, 2001, SOR/2001-512, ss. 57–59.

[11] See Form 51-102F5 to National Instrument 51-102, *Continuous Disclosure Obligations* ("NI 51-102").

[12] Many Canadian companies now have some form of shareholder rights plan or poison pill ("SRP"). An SRP serves two purposes. It will prevent creeping acquisitions and will extend the period of time the bid remains open. All Toronto Stock Exchange listed companies are required to have the SRP approved by its shareholders usually within six months of adoption by the board of the target. SRPs in Canada typically include the concept of a "permitted offer", which would be an offer that would not trigger the SRP. While the precise terms of permitted offers differ from plan to plan, they most typically require the offer to be outstanding for longer than thirty-five days (ranges from 45 to 120 days). Generally speaking, hostile offerors have not attempted to conform their offers to permitted offer provisions. Instead, they have made their offers conditional on the SRP provisions being neutralized.

employees (thereby raising the acquisition cost and concurrently protecting employees from termination or dislocation); and adopting mutual protection stances through interlocking shareholdings.

(b) Regulatory defences: such defences include participation in a regulated industry or environment where governmental approval to a change of control is required, and reliance on the provisions of legislation such as the *Competition Act* (Canada)[13] or the *Investment Canada Act*.[14]

(c) Activity defences: such defences include a positive description of the target's future prospects; an increase in the dividend or the making of an extraordinary distribution of cash or securities; and a significant change of management or other efforts to persuade investors to hold their shares for future benefit. More effective and challengeable alternatives are the making of an issuer bid that effectively competes with the unwanted offer, making a concurrent major investment, and even. more effectively, making an investment financed through the issue of voting shares.

(d) Alternative investor strategies: such defences relate to finding a "white squire" (a significant investor whose position will block the hostile offer); enticing a "white knight" to make a superior offer; or identifying an attractive business combination with a willing partner, although this alternative can take so long to consummate that it is not often a useful approach.

(e) Contractual impediments: such defences can arise in contracts that are critical to the target's business and/or very significant financially. For example, a contract can contain change of control provisions that render the contract cancellable upon a change in control or otherwise impose a significant economic cost upon a change in control.

VII. Review of Defensive Tactics

Directors' defensive tactics are subject to review in two forums: before the Canadian Securities Administrators ("CSA") and before the courts. The efforts of directors and senior officers to defend against hostile take-over bids, and in particular, the lengths to which some boards have been prepared to go in mounting such a defense, have led to concerns on the part of

---

[13] R.S.C. 1985, c. C-34.

[14] R.S.C. 1985, c. 28.

the CSA about the degree to which directors should be able to deny shareholders the ability to participate in a take-over bid that is otherwise not clearly objectionable. In response, the CSA adopted National Policy 62-202,[15] which proceeds from the premise that the primary objective of take-over bid regulation is to protect the *bona fide* interests of the shareholders of the target, and the secondary objective is to create an environment that permits take-over bids to proceed in an open and even-handed manner. The policy applies notwithstanding the fact that the board of directors' actions may be in accordance with their corporate fiduciary duties. The policy declines to articulate a code of conduct, but it identifies three types of actions that may be scrutinized by the CSA if they are taken during the course of, or immediately prior to, a take-over bid. They are:

(a) issuing or granting an option over securities that represent a significant percentage of the outstanding securities;

(b) the sale, acquisition, or agreement to sell or acquire assets in a material amount; and

(c) entering into an agreement or taking a corporate action that is not in the ordinary course of business.

The policy notes that the directors of a target may take actions, including those set out in the list above, while making a genuine search for a better offer. As long as the intention is not to deny or severely limit the ability of target shareholders to respond to an offer, the CSA will not act to prevent such initiatives.

In recent decisions involving contests for control, the OSC has indicated that target boards could, within reason, use the provisions of an SRP to facilitate an active auctioning process; however, such a process must be *bona fide* and not indefinite in duration. Recent OSC rulings appear to support the target's use of SRP provisions to complete a thorough search for competitive offers once it has determined that the corporation is in play. However, the OSC will not support an indefinite time line, and the target must demonstrate that it is pursuing reasonable alternatives.

Canadian regulators have determined that a rights plan cannot be used to "just say no" to an offer, and their decisions on this matter demonstrate that it is not a question of "if" a rights plan should go, but rather "when" it should go. Regulators have made it clear that they will not necessarily require that an offer be made by way of a "permitted offer" under the terms of a plan.

---

[15] National Policy 62-202, *Take-Over Bids, Defensive Tactics.*

To date, the OSC has consistently intervened to terminate SRPs after the target has had sufficient time to find a better offer during the period the SRP will stay in place. Past experience indicates that it is likely that the regulators will find a period of forty-two to fifty days from the date that the offer is announced to be a reasonable one.

The other forum that reviews directors' actions is the courts. Courts will review directors' actions both by considering whether the directors' actions are in accordance with their fiduciary duties and their statutory duty of care and whether their actions can be seen to be oppressive of shareholders.

More specifically, courts will examine directors' actions to determine whether they acted in good faith, whether there were reasonable grounds for their belief in the fairness and reasonableness of their actions, and whether their conduct was actuated by a proper purpose.[16]

Ultimately, director's conduct will be accorded the deference of the business judgment rule.[17] The court must be satisfied that the directors have acted reasonably and fairly, and the court will look to see that the directors made a reasonable decision, not a perfect decision. As long as the decision taken is within a range of reasonableness, the court should not substitute its opinion for that of the board. The fact that the board rejected alternative transactions is irrelevant unless it can be demonstrated that a particular alternative was clearly beneficial and definitely available.[18]

---

[16] See *Teck Corp. Ltd. v. Millar* (1972), 33 D.L.R. (3d) 288 (B.C.S.C.), where the court held that if the directors decide, on reasonable grounds, that a take-over bid will cause substantial damage to the company's interests, they are entitled to use their powers to protect the company.

[17] The business judgment rule is discussed in more detail in Chapter 2.

[18] See *Pente Investment Management v. Schneider Corp.* (1998), 92 O.R. (3d) 177 (Ont. C.A.) and further discussion in Chapter 2.

CHAPTER 9

DUTIES AND LIABILITIES OF DIRECTORS UNDER EMPLOYMENT LAWS

I. Introduction

In this Chapter, we will deal with directors' liability for wage-related obligations and other obligations that are imposed by employment standards legislation and by corporate legislation such as the *Canada Business Corporations Act*[1] ("CBCA"). Directors' liability for tax remittances or liabilities relating to the insolvency of the corporation will be addressed in other Chapters. We will also identify personal liability that is imposed upon directors under regulatory statutes and the *Criminal Code*[2] to ensure a safe workplace.

Generally, directors' liability in the employment context arises primarily in relation to the following:

(a) Failure by the corporation to make monetary payments: Directors may face personal liability in the event that the corporation fails to make certain monetary payments that are required by legislation, such as payments to employees for wages, vacation pay, and other

[1] R.S.C. 1985, c. C-44 ("CBCA").
[2] R.S.C. 1985, c. C-46.

"debts owed for services rendered", and payments to taxing authorities in respect of required withholdings and source deductions.

(b) Participation by directors in the corporation's breach of a statute: Certain statutes impose personal liability in the form of fines and/or imprisonment on directors and officers who "authorize, permit or acquiesce in" the breach of a statute by the corporation.

(c) Regulatory offences: Certain regulatory statutes impose personal liability on directors as a means of ensuring effective corporate compliance in relation to health and safety, and environmental laws. Under these statutes, directors face liability where they fail to take reasonable care to ensure that the corporation complies with the applicable legislation.

(d) *Criminal Code* offences: Directors can be criminally liable if they commit a criminal negligence offence, or if they direct the corporation to commit a criminal offence. Now too, corporations can more easily be held liable for the acts of their directors.

II. Wage-Related Obligations

A. Basis of Liability

A cornerstone principle of company law is that a corporation is a separate legal entity from its shareholders and directors and is liable for its own debts. However, express legislative enactments have modified this principle to make corporate directors personally liable for debts that are owed to the employees of the corporation on whose board the director sits if the company fails to pay those debts (to certain defined limits). The two types of legislation which, in effect, permit employees to "pierce the corporate veil" are (i) employment standards statutes, and (ii) business corporations statutes, such as the CBCA.

In determining their potential exposure for unpaid employee wages, directors must consider both the corporation's jurisdiction of incorporation and the jurisdiction in which the employer carries on business. For example, if the corporation is incorporated in one jurisdiction but carries on business in another jurisdiction where there is no employment standards legislation imposing liability, the directors may, nevertheless, be held liable for amounts owing to the employees if the directors are obligated to pay those amounts under the applicable corporations statute.

B. Are Directors of Not-for-Profit Operations Subject to both Types of Statutes?

Do the obligations that apply to directors of "for-profit" corporations also apply to directors of a "not-for-profit" business? Under most federal and provincial business corporations statutes, the directors of a corporation, including non-profit and charitable corporations, are liable for the payment of the wages of the corporation's employees, up to the limit specified in the corporations statute.[3]

Under the employment standards statutes, directors of not-for-profit operations may not be subject to the obligations imposed under those statutes.[4] This issue is more fully addressed in Chapter 16.

C. What are Corporate Directors Personally Liable For?

Depending on which jurisdiction a corporation is resident or incorporated in, the personal liabilities that are imposed on directors in their capacity as directors will vary across the country. This situation occurs because the obligations of corporate directors are based in statutes that are enacted by each jurisdiction, which vary from province to province. Generally, directors of corporations that are subject to the *Canada Labour Code* or to the employment standards legislation in British Columbia, the three northern territories, Manitoba, or Saskatchewan are personally liable to pay statutory severance to employees of corporations if the employer corporation fails to pay the amounts that are owed. In the other provinces, however, directors do not face this type of personal liability. Yet even in jurisdictions where directors may be personally liable for severance pay owed to employees, there may be no obligation to pay it if the corporation is insolvent or bankrupt.

The following list identifies the various jurisdictions across Canada and whether the applicable employment standards legislation and/or business corporations statute in the jurisdiction imposes personal liability on directors to pay debts that are owed by the corporation to employees. Where there is no specific legislation imposing personal liability on the directors, a

---

[3] In Ontario, directors of not-for-profit corporations remain liable to employees in the same way that directors of "for profit" corporations are. However, in British Columbia, directors of not-for-profit corporations who do not receive more than $500 annually for the appointment are not liable to employees for the wages or other debts owed.

[4] See, for example, Alberta *Employment Standards Code*, R.S.A. 2000, c. E-9, s. 112(1) ("Alta ESC"); British Columbia Reg. 396/95, s. 45, Newfoundland and Labrador *Labour Standards Act*, R.S.N.L. 1990, c. L-2, s. 27.2(1) ("Nfld LSA"); Ontario *Employment Standards Act*, 2000, S.O. 2000, c. 41, s. 80(2) ("Ont ESA").

director cannot be liable. Any obligations imposed on directors to pay the debts of the corporation are all statute based.

JURISDICTION	
Canada[5]	• *Canada Labour Code* — s. 251.18. Directors of a corporation are jointly and severally liable for wages and other amounts to which an employee is entitled under the CLC to a maximum amount equivalent to six (6) months' wages. • Directors are liable for severance pay under the CLC.[6] • *Canada Business Corporations Act* — s. 119. Directors are jointly and severally or solidarily liable to employees of the corporation for all debts not exceeding six (6) months' wages.
Alberta[7]	• *Employment Standards Code* — s. 112. Directors are jointly and severally liable for unpaid wages earned, to a maximum of six (6) months' wages. • For directors, the term "wages" expressly excludes termination pay, overtime pay, holiday pay, and vacation pay. Directors are exempt from liability to pay "wages" under the Alta ESC if the corporation is involved in insolvency proceedings.[8] • The Alberta *Business Corporations Act* employee wage protection provision is similar to the CBCA provision.[9]
British Columbia[10]	• *Employment Standards Act* — s. 96(1). Directors are liable for up to two (2) months' wages that are earned or that should have been paid while they were directors.

[5] *Canada Labour Code*, R.S.C. 1985, c. L-2, s. 251.18 ("CLC"); CBCA, s. 119.

[6] See *Provost v. Canada (Ministre du Travail)* (2000), 258 N.R. 229 (F.C.A.); *Laliberte (Re)*, [1999] F.C.J. No. 501 (F.C.T.D.) (QL), *Laliberte (Re)*, 1999 CarswellNat 2167 (March 10, 1999, F.C.T.D) (eC); *Cote v. Smith* (1998), 157 F.T.R. 299, 45 C.C.E.L. (2d) 311; *Bruys v. Abbott* (1995), 13 B.C.L.R. (3d) 246, 14 C.C.E.L. (2d) 170 (S.C.); and *Senous v. Fontaine* (2003), 250 F.T.R. 194, 2003 F.C.C. 1528. There is no maximum amount or statutory cap of an amount owed to each employee.

[7] Alta ESC, *supra* note 4, s. 112, Alberta *Business Corporations Act*, R.S.A. 2000, c. B-9 ("ABCA").

[8] *Dootjes v. Alberta (Employment Standards)*, 2002 CanLII 45582 (Alta. E.S.U.); and *Global Recycling & Development Inc. v. Alberta (Employment Standards)*, 2001 CanLII 25626 (Alta. E.S.U.), in which both umpires ruled that directors were personally liable for unpaid wages owed by the corporation unless the corporation was involved in insolvency proceedings.

[9] ABCA, *supra* note 7, s. 119.

[10] British Columbia *Employment Standards Act*, R.S.B.C. 1996, c. 113, ss. 96(1) ("BC ESA"), British Columbia *Business Corporations Act*, S.B.C. 2002, c. 57 ("BCBCA").

JURISDICTION	
	• Directors are liable for termination pay under the BC ESA except that directors are exempt from liability to pay statutory termination pay if the corporation is in receivership or is in other proceedings under insolvency legislation.[11] • The British Columbia *Business Corporations Act* does not impose liability on directors for amounts that are owing to employees.
Manitoba[12]	• *Employment Standards Code* — s. 90. Directors are jointly and severally liable for the unpaid wages of an employee that were earned during a period of not more than six (6) months. Directors are also jointly and severally liable for any unpaid vacation allowance earned. • Directors are liable to pay termination pay under the ESC. • The Manitoba *Corporations Act* employee wage protection provision is similar to that of the CBCA.[13]
New Brunswick[14]	• The *Employment Standards Act* does not expressly impose personal liability on directors for employee wage amounts. However, the government authorities can order the directors to pay the outstanding amounts that are owed, along with a fine of up to $1,000 per day for each day the corporation fails to comply with an order to pay the wages. • The New Brunswick *Business Corporations Act* does not impose liability on directors for amounts owing to employees.
Newfoundland and Labrador[15]	• *Labour Standards Act* — ss. 37.1–37.4. Directors are jointly and individually liable for unpaid wages, up to two (2) months' wages in an insolvency or bankruptcy proceeding; or where there are no insolvency proceedings, where an order has been issued against the employer to pay wages (with no cap).

[11] *Re Malet Transport Corp.*, [2004] B.C.E.S.T.D. No. 47 (QL).; and *Citation Industries Ltd. v. British Columbia (Director of Employment Standards)* (1988), 28 B.C.L.R. (2d) 273 (C.A.).

[12] Manitoba *Employment Standards Code*, C.C.S.M. c. E110, ss. 90 and 91 ("Man ESC"); and Manitoba *Corporations Act*, C.C.S.M. c. C225 ("Man CA").

[13] Man CA, *ibid.*, s. 114.

[14] New Brunswick *Employment Standards Act*, S.N.B. 1982, c. E-7.2, ss. 75(3), 65(1)(*c*) ("NB ESA"); New Brunswick *Corporations Act*, R.S.N.B. 1973, c. C-24 ("NBCA").

[15] Nfld LSA, *supra* note 4, ss. 37.1–37.4; Newfoundland and Labrador *Corporations Act*, R.S.N.L. 1990, c. C-36 ("N&LCA").

JURISDICTION	
	• For directors, "wages" do not include termination pay under the LSA. • The Newfoundland and Labrador *Corporations Act* does not impose liability on directors for amounts owing to employees.
Northwest Territories[16]	• *Labour Standards Act* — s. 62. Directors are personally liable for two (2) months' unpaid wages for each employee. • Directors are liable to pay termination pay under the LSA. • The Northwest Territories *Business Corporations Act* employee wage protection provision is similar to the CBCA provision.[17]
Nova Scotia[18]	• *Labour Standards Code* does not impose liability on directors for employee wages or otherwise create offences that are applicable to the directors of a corporation. • The Nova Scotia *Companies Act* does not impose liability on directors for amounts that are owing to employees.
Nunavut[19]	• *Labour Standards Act* — s. 62. Directors are personally liable for two (2) months' unpaid wages for each employee. • Directors are liable to pay termination pay under the LSA. • The Nunavut *Business Corporations Act*'s provision is similar to the CBCA provision.[20]
Ontario[21]	• *Employment Standards Act (2000)* — s. 81. Directors are jointly and severally liable to employees for wages not exceeding six (6) months' wages and vacation pay accrued while they are directors for not more than twelve (12) months.

[16] Northwest Territories *Labour Standards Act*, R.S.N.W.T. 1988, c. L-1 ("NWT LSA"); Northwest Territories *Business Corporations Act*, S.N.W.T. 1996, c. 19 ("NWTBCA").

[17] NWT LSA, *ibid.*, s. 120.

[18] Nova Scotia *Labour Standards Code*, R.S.N.S. 1989, c. 246 ("NS LSC"); Nova Scotia *Companies Act*, R.S.N.S. 1989, c. 81 ("NSCA").

[19] *Labour Standards Act (Nunavut)*, R.S.N.W.T. 1988, c. L-1 ("Nunavut LSA"); Nunavut *Business Corporations Act*, S.N.W.T. 1996, c. 19 ("Nunavut BCA").

[20] Nunavut BCA, *ibid.*, s. 120.

[21] Ont ESA, *supra* note 4, ss. 79–83; Ontario *Business Corporations Act*, R.S.O. 1990, c. B.16 ("OBCA").

JURISDICTION	
	• For directors, the term "wages" excludes termination and severance pay under the Ont ESA. • The Ontario *Business Corporations Act* imposes joint and several liability on directors for all debts not exceeding six (6) months' wages and for vacation pay accrued for not more than twelve (12) months under the ESA or any collective agreement.[22]
Prince Edward Island[23]	• *Employment Standards Act* does not impose liability on directors for employee wages or otherwise create offences that are applicable to directors or officers of a corporation. • The Prince Edward Island *Companies Act* does not impose liability on directors for amounts owing to employees.
Quebec[24]	• *Labour Standards Act* does not impose liability on directors for employee wage amounts. However, once the Labour Standards Commission declares that an employer owes an employee an amount of money pursuant to the legislation and has put the employer in default to pay such an amount, the Que. LSA permits the Commission to exercise the recourse that is available to an employee against the employer and, where the employer is a corporation, against the directors of the employer. • "Wages" under the Que. LSA are defined to include termination pay. Any amounts due to employees also bear interest. • The Quebec *Corporations Act* employee wage protection provision is similar to the CBCA provision.[25]
Saskatchewan[26]	• *Labour Standards Act* — s. 63. Directors are jointly and severally liable to employees for debts for services performed for the corporation while they were directors, up to a maximum of six (6) months' wages.

[22] OBCA, *ibid.*, s. 131.

[23] Prince Edward Island *Employment Standards Act*, R.S.P.E.I. 1988, c. E-6.2 ("PEI ESA"); Prince Edward Island *Companies Act*, R.S.P.E.I. 1988, c. C-14 ("PEICA").

[24] Quebec *Labour Standards Act*, R.S.Q. c. N-1.1 ("Que LSA"); Quebec *Companies Act*, R.S.Q. c. C-38 ("Que CA").

[25] Que CA, *ibid.*, s. 96.

[26] Saskatchewan *Labour Standards Act*, R.S.S. 1978, c. L-1 ("Sask LSA"); Saskatchewan *Business Corporations Act*, R.S.S. 1978, c. B-10 ("SBCA").

JURISDICTION	
	• Directors are liable to pay termination pay under the LSA. • The Saskatchewan *Business Corporations Act* provisions differ from the CBCA provisions. Under the Saskatchewan *Business Corporations Act*, directors are jointly and severally liable in accordance with the provincial employment standards legislation (which has been judicially determined to include wrongful dismissal damages).[27]
Yukon[28]	• *Employment Standards Act* — s. 62. Directors are jointly and severally liable to employees for all debts due for services performed for the corporation while they are directors, up to a total of two (2) months' wages and twelve (12) months' vacation pay for each employee who has not been paid. • Directors are liable to pay termination pay under the Yukon ESA.[29] • Under the Yukon *Business Corporations Act*, directors are jointly and severally liable in accordance with the ESA for all debts that are payable to the employee for services performed for the corporation while the director is a director.[30]

D. Difference Between the Two Methods to Recover Unpaid Wages

As outlined above, in most jurisdictions, directors may be liable to employees for unpaid amounts owed by the corporation under two statutes. The obligations imposed are similar under both statutes. Depending on the specific wording of the statutory section, however, the obligation to pay under the employment standards statutes exists if the amounts owed to the employee are then *payable*, while under the business corporation statutes, the obligation exists if the monies are *earned*. This means that, under a "payable test", directors may not be liable for "wages" such as vacation pay that has accrued but is not yet payable, but under a corporations statute, the

[27] SBCA, *ibid.*, s. 114.

[28] Yukon *Employment Standards Act*, R.S.Y. 2002, c. 72 ("Yukon ESA"); Yukon *Business Corporations Act*, R.S.Y. 2002, c. 20 ("YBCA").

[29] *Benner v. Yukon (Director of Employment Standards)*, [1994] Y.J. No. 172 (S.C.) (QL).

[30] YBCA, *supra* note 28, s. 121.

accrued (but unpaid) vacation pay that is earned would be a directors' liability.[31]

Notwithstanding that there may be a slight variation in the quantum owed to employees under the two statutes, where the employment standards legislation imposes such obligations, it is usually simpler, faster, and more cost-efficient for the employees to proceed under the employment standards legislation, than under the business corporations statutes.

While there has been little judicial consideration as to whether employees may be stopped from proceeding under both statutes if they obtain judgment under one of them, there is at least one decision which suggests that directors may be liable to the same employee under both statutes if the enforcement mechanisms in both are strictly complied with.[32]

E. Who is Primarily Responsible for Payment of the Wages?

The employment standards statutes usually expressly state that the employer bears the primary responsibility to make the payments. However, there is no need to proceed first against an employer and obtain an unsatisfied judgment before proceeding against a director. The enforcement agency can proceed against both of them simultaneously.

There is a similar obligation under the business corporations statutes to seek the payment of unpaid wages from the employer first. If there was any doubt, the Ontario Court of Appeal affirmed the payment priority under the business corporations statutes.[33] An employee can commence a claim against a director only if the corporation is unable (or fails) to satisfy the payment obligations and then, only if the employee follows the strict procedures outlined in the corporations statutes.

F. If the Employer Does Not Pay, Who Pays the Unpaid Wages?

The liability of directors under both types of statutes is "joint and several". This term means that each director is personally liable for the entire amount that is owed to employees, pursuant to the governing statute. Under both types of statutes, the employee is not required to pursue all

[31] *Bell v. British Columbia (Director of Employment Standards)* (1996), 136 D.L.R. (4th) 564, 25 B.C.L.R. (3d) 297 (C.A.).

[32] *Green v. Canada Trust Realty Inc.* (2005), 198 Man. R. (2d) 182 (Q.B.).

[33] *Canadian Automatic Data Processing Services Ltd. v. CEEI Safety & Security Inc.* (2004), 246 D.L.R. (4th) 400 (Ont. C.A.); and also *Canadian Automatic Data Processing Services Ltd. v. Bentley* (2004), 242 D.L.R. (4th) 250, 32 B.C.L.R. (4th) 20 (C.A.).

directors but may target a single director for payment. A director who makes a payment may then seek reimbursement from any other director who is also liable under the legislation.[34]

G. Is There a Limit on the Liability?

Both types of statutes define directors' personal obligations to employees for unpaid amounts, and, except under the CLC, both types of statutes impose a limit on the overall liability imposed.

In *Barrette v. Crabtree Estate*,[35] the Supreme Court of Canada considered the language in the CBCA and stated the following:

> [T]here are two important parameters in connection with the employee's remedy. First, the directors' maximum liability is set at six months' wages. This parameter provides a ceiling which, while establishing a quantitative limit to the liability of the directors, does not in so doing determine the nature of the amounts covered by the action. The nature of the sums which Parliament had in mind must be considered instead from a second angle: regardless of quantum, the amounts claimed must be "debts ... for services performed for the corporation".... In the context of s. 114(1) of the C.B.C.A., the word "wages" refers solely to the quantum of the directors' liability. ...

Therefore, the legislation is clear as to the amount liable. The maximum amount for which a director is liable under a corporation's statute is *an amount equivalent to* six months' wages (and in those cases where vacation pay is identified in the prevailing statute, the additional amount equivalent to twelve months' vacation pay).

Under the employment standards legislation, directors are liable for "*wages*" to the maximum amount identified by the statute (except under the CLC, that amount will be either two months or six months). There is no maximum amount for which a director is liable under the CLC. Under the CLC, if a company owes wages (including statutory severance and termination pay) and fails to pay them, the director is wholly responsible for satisfying the obligation.

---

[34] CBCA, *supra* note 1, s. 119(6). Further, a director who pays an amount in respect of debts that are owed to employees for services performed is "subrogated to" or entitled to stand in the shoes of the employees in enforcing the claim of the employees against the corporation's assets: see CBCA, s. 119(5); and *Bankruptcy and Insolvency Act*, R.S.C. 1985, c. B-3, s. 136(1)(*d*) ("BIA").

[35] [1993] 1 S.C.R. 1027 at 1044-45 ("*Barrette*").

So, while under the business corporations statutes, a director is liable for "*debts* ... for services performed for the corporation", and under the employment standards legislation (except in Saskatchewan), a director is liable for "*wages* owed" by the corporation, practically speaking, the effect on directors is the same if the corporation fails to pay the employee. In such circumstances, the director is personally liable to pay the amounts owed, to the limit specified by the applicable statute.

H. For What Types of Payments are Directors Liable?

Under the business corporations statutes, the case law has interpreted "debts" for which directors may be personally liable to include unpaid wages and vacation pay,[36] commissions,[37] expenses incurred in the course of employment,[38] and monies owed for any kind of quantifiable bonus, such as an incentive plan[39] or stay bonuses.

Under the applicable employment standards statutes, the meaning of "wages" is generally broadly defined to mean any monetary amounts that are owed to employees. Thus, the term can include salary or regular wages, overtime pay, holiday pay, non-discretionary bonuses, shift premiums, commission payments, and even in some jurisdictions, termination pay. (Under the Ont ESA, benefits plan remittances under a collective agreement owed by the employer for benefits were found to not be "debts" that were owed for services rendered.)[40] Note, however, that not all statutes define "wages" identically, so it is necessary to review the specific definition of the applicable statute.

Directors may also be liable to pay interest on outstanding wages for which they are liable under both types of statutes.

---

[36] See *Mills Hughes v. Raynor* (1988), 63 O.R. (2d) 343 (C.A.) ("*Mills Hughes*"); and *Vopni v. Groenewald* (1991), 84 D.L.R. (4th) 366 (Ont. Gen. Div.) ("*Vopni*").

[37] *Masson v. Thompson*, [2000] J.Q. No. 4730 (C.A.) (QL) ("*Masson*"); and *Zavitz v. Brock* (1974), 3 O.R. (2d) 583 (C.A.).

[38] See *Proulx v. Sahelian Goldfields Inc.* (2001), 55 O.R. (3d) 775 (C.A.).

[39] *Maurer v. Frontier Peterbilt Sales Ltd.* (1996), 146 Sask. R. 100, [1996] 8 W.W.R. 193 (Q.B.); and *Masson*, *supra* note 37.

[40] See *International Union of Operating Engineers, Local 793 v. Robert Hume Construction Ltd.*, 2005 CanLII 5192 (O.L.R.B.); see also *Bennett & Wright Group Inc.* (2001), 39 C.B.R. (4th) 149 (OLRB), where the arbitrator concluded that remittances to various funds, including training funds, education funds, employer association funds, and substance abuse funds are not "wages".

I. Is There a Threshold for Liability?

Directors are responsible only for amounts earned or payable (depending on the statutory requirement) while the director was a director. Further, directors are responsible only for outstanding amounts if the demand is brought within the applicable time limits.

J. Are Directors Responsible for all Unpaid Amounts Owed to Employees?

Barrette[41] makes it clear that under the business corporations statutes, directors are not liable for *all* of the debts owed by the corporation to its employees; rather, liability will be imposed only where the debts are for "services performed for the corporation". As noted by the court, "the performance of services by the employee remains the cornerstone of the directors' personal liability for debts assumed by the corporation". Thus, in *Barrette,* the directors were held not liable for the amounts claimed by employees as compensation in lieu of common law notice of termination, as these amounts did not flow from services that were performed for the corporation but rather constituted damages for the failure to provide notice, or compensation in lieu thereof, upon termination of employment. Such damages crystallized only upon a termination.

The decision in *Barrette* reflects the line of case law in Ontario, which holds that statutory termination and severance pay, as well as common law damages for wrongful dismissal, are not "debts ... for services performed for the corporation", but rather claims arising from the termination of employment.[42] In other words, the obligation to pay termination pay, severance pay, or wrongful dismissal damages crystallizes only at the time of termination, not before. As such claims are not "debts for services rendered", the predominant view is that there is no personal liability imposed upon directors to personally pay employees' severance or termination pay, which may be outstanding and owed by the company.

At least until 2006, the courts in Ontario had consistently followed the decision in *Barrette,* so it has been clear that directors of Ontario-regulated companies are not going to be personally liable for (unpaid) severance pay that is owed to employees, at common law or under statute. Recently, however, there have been attempts (discussed below) to alter the *status quo.*

---

[41] *Supra* note 35 at 1049.

[42] See *Mesheau v. Campbell* (1982), 39 O.R. (2d) 702 (C.A.); *Mills Hughes, supra* note 36; *Vopni, supra* note 36; *Jonah v. Quinte Transport (1986) Ltd.* (1994), 5 C.C.E.L. (2d) 73 (Ont. Gen. Div.) ("*Jonah Transport*"); and *St. Pierre v. Supply Chain Management Dialtone Inc.*, 2003 CanLII 10440 (Ont. Sup. Ct. Jus.).

In some employment standards statutes,[43] the legislatures have codified this protection against paying severance pay following the termination of employment by expressly stating in the legislation that directors are not personally liable for termination pay at any time.

In British Columbia, the protection is codified only when the corporation is subject to insolvency proceedings.[44]

For those provinces that do not impose liability on directors, there is no statutory protection required to insulate directors from the obligation to pay severance because the common law holds that an individual (in the absence of a statutory requirement that provides otherwise) cannot be liable for the debts of corporations.

K. Does this Mean that Directors are Never Liable for Severance Pay?

In some circumstances and in some provinces, directors may be liable for severance pay or for wrongful dismissal damages. In such cases, the courts manage to distinguish *Barrette* on the basis that the statute that applies is different from the corporations statute considered by the Supreme Court in *Barrette*, or the facts required to be determined are different from those that the Supreme Court considered.

With respect to different statutes, in *Barrette*, the Supreme Court of Canada considered a corporations statute, not an employment statute. Unlike a corporations statute, some employment standards statutes impose liability upon directors for unpaid severance if the corporation fails to make the payments, even if the corporation is involved in insolvency proceedings.[45]

Alternatively, where courts find that severance is owed as a result of services rendered to a company, to make such a finding, the court has typically characterized the severance payment as a form of "deferred compensation". It seems that such an argument can be made where there is a payment owed upon termination that is based on a written agreement where the quantum is dependent upon length of service with the corporation. Traditionally, this type of interpretation has been prevalent only in Quebec. However, there are current (2006) attempts being made by counsel in other provinces to apply such an interpretation to contract terms in general.

[43] Alta ESC, *supra* note 4, s. 1(1)(*x*); Ont ESA, *supra* note 4, s. 81(3); Nfld LSA, *supra* note 4, s. 37.1.3(3).

[44] BC ESA, *supra* note 10, s. 96(2).

[45] CLC, *supra* note 5, s. 251.18; Man ESC, *supra* note 12, s. 90; Sask LSA, *supra* note 26, s. 63(1.1).

L. When Are Directors Liable for Severance Pay?

Prior to the decision in *Barrette*, appellate courts in Quebec and Saskatchewan had reached a different conclusion than the one reached by the Ontario courts about a director's obligation to pay severance. In those two provinces, the courts had ruled that both statutory and contractual termination and/or severance pay was a director's personal obligation if the company failed to pay such amounts on termination of employment. The courts reasoned that the payments were owed as a result of the employee providing services to the company, and the longer the service, the higher the payment. The two leading decisions[46] in Quebec and Saskatchewan were expressly not overturned by the Supreme Court of Canada in *Barrette*, and they continue to be applied in those provinces. Indeed, based on the concepts contained in those decisions, there have been recent attempts to overturn the effect of *Barrette* and to make directors personally liable for termination and severance pay in Ontario.

In Quebec, unlike in Ontario, the courts have concluded that contractual obligations that arise on termination can create director liability. In *Schwartz v. Scott*,[47] employees of a bankrupt corporation sought to recover from the directors unpaid wages and other benefits, including severance pay, that were payable pursuant to a provision of a collective agreement. The provision in question provided for compensation based on length of service to all employees who left the corporation's employ without cause, whether by retirement, resignation, or dismissal. The Quebec Court of Appeal held that the term provided a guaranteed departure payment that was based on service to the corporation. The union had negotiated the term as a form of deferred compensation and so, the court concluded, it was a debt to the employees for services rendered and it formed part of their remuneration for which the directors were personally liable.

In *Meyers v. Walters Cycle Co.*,[48] the Saskatchewan Court of Appeal also reached the opposite conclusion to that of the Ontario courts about a director's personal liability. The variation in the two provinces is due to different language in the applicable statutes. In *Meyers*, the Saskatchewan Court of Appeal considered the liability of directors for damages for wrongful dismissal under s. 114 of the Saskatchewan *Business Corporations Act*. That statute makes directors personally liable for debts payable to employees for services that were performed for the corporation "in accor-

---

[46] *Meyers v. Walters Cycle Co.* (1990), 71 D.L.R. (4th) 190, [1990] 5 W.W.R. 455 (Sask. C.A.) ("*Meyers*"); and *Schwartz v. Scott*, [1985] C.A. 713 (Que. C.A.) ("*Schwartz v. Scott*").

[47] *Ibid.*, the claim for severance pay was brought pursuant to s. 99 of the *Canada Corporations Act*, R.S.C. 1970, c. C-32, which is similar in substance to s. 119 of the CBCA.

[48] *Supra* note 46.

dance with the *Labour Standards Act*". Noting that pay in lieu of notice had been judicially determined to fall within the statutory definition of "wages" contained in s. 2(*r*) of the *Labour Standards Act*, the court held that damages for wrongful dismissal also fell within that definition, as they are compensation for personal services to which an employee is entitled. As "wages", such amounts were debts for services performed for the corporation for which directors might be held personally liable. Currently, the statute expressly defines the wages for which directors are liable to include termination pay.[49]

Since *Barrette*,[50] the courts in Saskatchewan have regularly held that damages for wrongful dismissal constitute a debt for services performed for which directors may be held liable.[51]

M. What Are the Challenges To Expand Directors' Personal Liability?

The traditional view in Ontario that severance pay and termination pay are not "debts for services rendered" seems to be under attack. At the time of writing, however, it is impossible to gauge if the challenges will ultimately succeed.

In one line of attack, in two class actions commenced against directors of bankrupt companies in Ontario, the plaintiffs have specifically challenged the view that severance pay or wrongful dismissal damages are not "payments for services rendered" for which directors are personally liable.[52] The argument is that decisions that were made by the Supreme Court of Canada following *Barrette* have actually overturned *Barrette* (by inference), so it should no longer be followed. In particular, it is alleged that the Supreme Court of Canada has subsequently held in a wrongful dismissal ruling that payment of monies in lieu of notice is akin to paying wages,[53] the implication of which is that the character of the two types of payments is the same. On this basis, it is argued that the characterization of monies that are paid in

---

[49] Sask LSA, *supra* note 26, s. 63(1.1).

[50] *Supra* note 35.

[51] See *Smith v. General Recorders Ltd.* (1994), 121 Sask. R. 296 (Q.B.); *Parisien v. Sasknative Economic Development Corp.* (1999), 181 Sask. R. 301 (Q.B.); *Neudorf v. Colltekk Services Ltd.*, 2002 SKQB 321; *Warren v. 622718 Saskatchewan Ltd. (c.o.b. Palmx Route Accounting)* (2004), 252 Sask. R. 290, 2004 SKQB 346.

[52] See *Englefield v. Wolf* (2005), 20 C.P.C. (6th) 157 (Ont. Sup. Ct. Jus.), appeal filed, *Englefield v. Wolf* [2006] O.J. No. 1234 (Ont. Sup. Ct. Jus.) (QL) ("*Englefield*"); also *Kanagaratnam v. Li* (2005), 9 C.P.C. (6th) 282 (Ont. Sup. Ct. Jus.).

[53] *Wallace v. United Grain Growers*, [1997] 3 S.C.R. 701 ("*Wallace*"). See also the characterization of severance pay in *Rizzo & Rizzo Shoes Ltd.*, [1998] 1 S.C.R. 27; and *O.N.A. v. Mount Sinai* (2005), 75 O.R. (3d) 245 (C.A.).

lieu of notice as *wages*, which characterization was made in the *Wallace* decision, should prevail over the Ontario line of cases,[54] which characterize the payment of severance as *damages* for the failure to provide reasonable notice. If the amounts paid upon termination are properly characterized as wages for services rendered, then, the argument goes, directors should be personally liable to pay any unpaid amounts that are owed to employees. To date, these arguments have not been successful. However, leave to appeal to the Ontario Court of Appeal has been granted, so the issue remains unsettled.[55]

In the second, unco-ordinated line of attack, the rationale from the *Schwartz v. Scott*[56] case appears.

In a grievance arbitration in Ontario,[57] an arbitrator ordered directors of a corporation to honour a severance provision in a collective agreement and ruled that the directors were responsible to pay the severance owed under that collective agreement to the employees. The employer was bankrupt, and there was no employer representative at the hearing. The directors do not appear to even have received notice of the matter. The rationale articulated in the arbitration decision is that the severance pay was, in effect, deferred compensation, and the quantum was based on length of service with the corporation, so the amount owing was a debt based on "services rendered to the corporation".

Lending support to the suggestion that express, written contractual obligations may be treated differently than obligations that arise at common law, a recent decision issued in British Columbia will be of some interest to those who are keen on developing the argument that contractual entitlements based on service are liabilities of directors. In this decision, a court in British Columbia concluded that severance payments that are owed pursuant to a contractual term in an employment agreement constituted "wages" within the meaning of the British Columbia employment standards legislation.[58] While this case did not address the personal liability of directors, it is of note that in non-insolvency situations in British Columbia, directors are personally liable for up to two months' wages (including termination pay) under the BC ESA. This decision clarifies the view that directors in British Columbia may be liable for contractual obligations as well as for

---

[54] *Supra* note 42.

[55] *Supra* note 52.

[56] *Supra* note 46.

[57] *Northland Superior Supply Co. v. Sheet Workers Int'l Ass'n (Wilson Grievance)*, [2005] O.L.A.A. No. 146 (D. Harris, arbitrator) (QL).

[58] *Colak v. UV Systems Technology Inc.*, 2006 BCSC 1078; also *Fitzgerald v. Waterford Hospital* (1997), 148 Nfld. & P.E.I.R. 271 (C.A.); but see *contra*, *Brown v. Shearer* (1995), 102 Man. R. (2d) 76 (C.A.).

the statutory obligations of the corporation to pay notice or for wrongful dismissal damages upon termination if the corporation fails to make the payments.

It is to be noted that these few cases stand in opposition to the weight of case law holding the contrary position.

N. Are Directors Liable to All Employees?

The answer to this question will depend on the applicable legislation.

In Ontario, directors are liable for the wages of all employees, including the wages that are owed to employees who are *also* directors of the corporation.[59] In the Ont ESA, there is nothing that relieves directors from liability for the unpaid wages of certain groups or types of employees, nor is there language that relieves directors from liability when an employee making the claim is also a director. This position is contrary to the one that was adopted by the enforcement authorities in British Columbia. The Interpretation Guidelines Manual for British Columbia specifies that the policy of the enforcement branch is to *not* permit directors of a corporation to use the wage recovery mechanism under the BC ESA to recover any unpaid wages.

Directors have no obligation to independent contractors.[60]

O. When Will a Director be Required to Pay Under the Business Corporations Statutes?

Under the CBCA and other business corporations statutes, a number of conditions must be satisfied before a director may be held liable for wage-related obligations of the corporation. Further, compliance with these pre-existing conditions must be strictly observed.[61]

The director must have been a director when the services in question were performed,[62] and the director must be sued while he or she is still a director, or within two years of ceasing to be a director.[63]

Practically, a director's liability to pay for services performed will be relevant only where the corporation is insolvent. The CBCA provides that liability will arise only where (a) the corporation has commenced liquidation

---

[59] *Lava Systems Inc. v. MacDonald*, 2000 CanLII 13106 (O.L.R.B.).

[60] *Kornblum v. Dye* (1988), 63 O.R. (2d) 730 (C.A.).

[61] *Stoody v. Kennedy* (2003), 34 C.C.E.L. (3d) 282 (Ont. Sup. Ct. Jus.), (2005), 196 O.A.C. 130 (C.A.) at paras. 45–52 ("*Stoody*").

[62] CBCA, *supra* note 1, s. 119(1).

[63] *Ibid.*, s. 119(3). In Ontario, the relevant limitation period is six months: OBCA, *supra* note 21, s. 131(2)(a).

and dissolution proceedings, has been dissolved, or has made an assignment in bankruptcy, and the claim has been proved within six months of the earlier of the liquidation or dissolution or within six months of the assignment in bankruptcy; or (b) the corporation has been sued for the debt within six months of the debt's due date and execution has been returned unsatisfied in whole or in part.[64] A director will be liable only if, and to the extent that, the employee's claim is not satisfied out of the assets of the corporation but only to a maximum amount that is equivalent to six months wages.[65]

The CBCA provides a defence to a director's liability to employees for services performed: a director is not liable where he or she relies in good faith on the financial statements of the corporation that are represented by an officer or in a written report of the auditor to fairly reflect the financial condition of the corporation, or where he or she relies on a report of a professional, such as an accountant or lawyer.[66] No similar defence is available, however, under the OBCA, ABCA, or BCBCA, or (typically) under federal or provincial employment legislation to an "order to pay" that imposes liability for wage-related obligations.[67] Accordingly, while directors are well advised to require assurances from officers and professionals concerning compliance by the corporation with its wage-related and withholding obligations, the circumstances in which such assurances will provide a defence to an "order to pay" are very narrow.

P. When Will a Director be Required to Pay Under an Employment Standards Statute?

Employment standards statutes typically specify that the employer is primarily liable for the payment of the employee's wages and for vacation pay but that proceedings against the employer need not be exhausted, or indeed even commenced, before an order to pay may be issued against a director.[68] Under the Ont ESA, for example, the enforcement of directors' liability for wage-related obligations is a function of the Employment Standards Branch, and it does not depend, as it does under the business corporations statutes, upon the employee's taking the time-consuming and expensive steps involved in obtaining a civil judgment. An employee's civil remedies against directors are not, however, affected by the Ont ESA.[69]

[64] CBCA, *supra* note 1, s. 119(2). See *Piroth v. Kalinocha* (1985), 43 Sask. R. 166 (Q.B.).

[65] CBCA, *ibid.*, s. 119(4).

[66] *Ibid.*, s. 123(4).

[67] The exception is Newfoundland; see Nfld LSA, *supra* note 4, s. 37.3(7).

[68] Ont ESA, *supra* note 4, s. 81(4).

[69] *Ibid.*, s. 83.

Under the Ont ESA, directors' joint and several liability to employees for wages and vacation pay arises in the following circumstances:[70]

1. where an employer is insolvent and a claim for unpaid wages filed with a court-appointed receiver or with the employer's trustee in bankruptcy has not been paid;
2. where an employment standards officer has made an order that the employer or a director is liable for wages,[71] unless the amount set out in the order has been paid or the employer or director has applied to have it reviewed; or
3. where an adjudicator or a referee appointed under the Act to review an order of an employment standards officer has made, amended, or affirmed an order stating that the employer or the directors are liable for wages, and the amount set out in the order has not been paid.

Similar requirements exist in other jurisdictions.

Although the Ont ESA prohibits a director from contracting out of liability under the Act,[72] it permits corporations to indemnify directors in respect of all costs that were reasonably incurred, provided that the director has acted honestly and in good faith with a view to the best interests of the employer, and, in the case of a proceeding or action enforced by a monetary penalty, the director had reasonable grounds to believe that his or her conduct was lawful.[73]

Q. Related Employer Obligations

Most employment standards statutes across the country authorize the enforcement agency to treat employers carrying on associated or related activities as one employer. Whether or not directors may be jointly and severally liable for the wage-related obligations of the corporation for which they serve as directors, as well as for those of related corporations, varies, depending on the language of the applicable statute.

In the BC ESA,[74] there is an express statutory provision that authorizes courts or tribunals to find that directors of one corporate entity may be

---

[70] *Ibid.*, s. 81.

[71] An order that an employer is liable for wages may be made by an employment standards officer under s. 103, and where such an order is made, an employment standards officer may, by virtue of s. 106, make an order for payment against some or all of the directors.

[72] Ont ESA, *supra* note 4, ss. 81(4) and 82(1).

[73] *Ibid.*, s. 82(2).

[74] *Supra* note 10.

personally liable for the debts owed to employees of a related entity, even though the director may not be appointed to the board of that second entity:

> 95. If the Director considers that businesses, trades or undertakings are carried on by or through more than one corporation, individual, firm, syndicate or association, or any combination of them under common control or direction,
>
> (*a*) the Director may treat the corporations, individuals, firms, syndicates or associations, or any combination of them, as one employer for the purposes of this Act, and
>
> (*b*) if so, they are jointly and separately liable for payment of the amount stated in a determination, a settlement agreement or an order of the tribunal, and this Act applies to the recovery of that amount from any or all of them.
>
> 96. (1) A person who was a director or officer of a corporation at the time wages of an employee of the corporation were earned or should have been paid is personally liable for up to 2 months' unpaid wages for each employee.
>
> (2) Despite subsection (1), a person who was a director or an officer of a corporation is not personally liable for
>
> (*a*) any liability to an employee under section 63, termination pay or money payable in respect of individual or group terminations, if the corporation is in receivership,
>
> (*b*) any liability to an employee for wages, if the corporation is subject to action under section 427 of the *Bank Act* (Canada) or to a proceeding under an insolvency Act,
>
> (*c*) vacation pay that becomes payable after the director or officer ceases to hold office, or
>
> (*d*) money that remains in an employee's time bank after the director or officer ceases to hold office.
>
> (3) This Act applies to the recovery of the unpaid wages from a person liable for them under subsection (1) ...

> (4) In this section, "director or officer of a corporation" includes a director or officer of a corporation, firm, syndicate or association that the Director treats as one employer under section 95 (emphasis added).

The effect of these provisions is that, for corporations subject to the BC ESA, a director's personal liability is significantly expanded. If a corporation becomes bankrupt, related corporations and their respective directors may inherit the bankrupt corporation's obligations to its employees for wages, severance pay, and termination pay. While such inheritance is unlikely, it does not appear to have been determined whether a director of a parent corporation in another province that has a subsidiary in British Columbia also faces expanded personal liability.

Specifically, in *Kelly, Douglas & Co. v. British Columbia (Director of Employment Standards)*,[75] an order to pay wages owing to employees was issued against a corporation. Under the related employer provision of the BC ESA, Kelly, Douglas had been declared related to a second bankrupt corporation that had failed to comply with an order to pay the wages. A director of Kelly, Douglas was found liable to pay the unpaid wages of the bankrupt corporation's employees on the basis that, under the relevant liability provision of the British Columbia statute, he was jointly and severally liable with Kelly, Douglas for the unpaid wages. In *Vencorp Enterprises Corp.*,[76] the court declared that two corporations were related. Directors of both of the related companies were not held responsible for the unpaid wages of the employees of one of the two companies because there was insufficient evidence before the court. Clearly, however, as outlined in the judgment, the court assumed that it had the authority to issue such an order.

In at least one Alberta case,[77] a director of one corporation has been found to be personally liable for wages that were owed to employees of a related employer corporation.

In other provinces where the statute does not expressly state that directors of one corporation may be liable for the unpaid wages owed to employees of a second corporation, the courts have been more circumspect in issuing orders to pay. Clearly, there are rulings stating that more than one corporation is related to a second corporation and that the first group of corporations is liable for the debts owed to employees of the second corpo-

---

[75] (1991), 36 C.C.E.L. 296 (B.C.S.C.).

[76] 1998 CanLII 3943 (B.C.S.C.).

[77] *Land v. Alberta (Umpire under Employment Standards Code)* (1992), 132 A.R. 76 (Q.B.).

ration. Those decisions recognize the fact that an employee can have more than one employer.[78]

Where a "related employer" finding is made, one corporation that is found to be related to a second corporation is liable for the debts of that second "family member". However, the courts in Ontario have not declared that directors are personally liable for the debts that are owed to employees of a related entity in addition to those of the corporation on whose board they sit.[79] To the contrary, in the leading decision, the court stated that it would not extend the liability for termination pay and severance pay to a corporate director of a related entity in the absence of express statutory authorization.[80]

Confirming this approach, the Ontario Court of Appeal recently overturned a lower court finding[81] that two corporations were related and that directors of the solvent (related) corporation were liable to an employee of the insolvent entity, the actual employer, which had failed to pay certain amounts to that employee. In the appeal decision, the court did not address the issue of the "common employer" between the two entities, but it clearly declared that the directors of the solvent entity were not liable for the obligations of the insolvent subsidiary.[82]

R. What about an Oppression Claim Against Directors for Unpaid Wages Owed by a Related Employer?

On rare occasions, courts have made orders against directors personally to pay wages to employees in oppression remedy cases. Generally, such orders are issued to directors of small, closely held corporations (including related corporations) where the director whose conduct was attacked has been the sole controlling owner and its sole directing mind, and where the conduct in question has benefited that person directly.[83]

---

[78] *Kent v. Stop "N" Cash 1000 Inc.*, [2006] O.J. No. 2699 (Ont. Sup. Ct. Jus.) (QL); *Bartholomay v. Sportica Internet Technologies Inc.* (2004), 32 C.C.E.L. (3d) 229, 2004 BCSC 508; *McCulloch v. IPlatform Inc.* (2004), 46 C.C.E.L. (3d) 257 (Ont. Sup. Ct. Jus.); *Vanderpol v. Aspen Trailer Co.* (2002), 100 B.C.L.R. (3d) 381, 2002 BCSC 518; *Downtown Eatery (1993) Ltd. v. Ontario* (2001), 54 O.R. (3d) 161 (C.A.) ("*Downtown Eatery*"); *C.A.W. v. Zettel Metalcraft Ltd.*, 2000 CanLII 6936 (OLRB).

[79] *550551 Ontario Ltd. v. Framingham* (1991), 4 O.R. (3d) 571 (Div. Ct.) ("*Framingham*"); also, *Jonah Transport*, *supra* note 42.

[80] *Framingham*, *ibid.*

[81] *Stoody*, *supra* note 61.

[82] *Ibid.*

[83] *C-L & Associates Inc. c.o.b. Fay-J Packaging v. Airside Equipment Sales* (2003), 174 Man. R. (2d) 150 (Q.B.).

In *Downtown Eatery*,[84] an employee who had been wrongfully dismissed successfully appealed a decision dismissing his claim for an oppression remedy against several individual and corporate respondents. The employee had initially sued his employer, a management company, and he was awarded wrongful dismissal damages following his termination from that company. The individual respondents, who were both directors and functioned as the directing minds of the business of which the management company was a party, restructured the corporate organization prior to trial and, as a result of that reorganization, the management company was left as a non-operating entity. The employee could not enforce his wrongful dismissal award, and he brought an oppression remedy claim. The court held that, although the reorganization was not done with the deliberate intention of harming the employee, the employee had a reasonable expectation that the company's affairs would be conducted with a view to protecting the employee's interests. Therefore, the court held that the reorganization unfairly disregarded the employee's interests and constituted oppressive conduct. The Court of Appeal held that the employee was entitled to recover his judgment from the two directors in view of the way in which those directors had reorganized the business operations.

A claim against a corporate director (as director) for unpaid wages that are owed to an employee of a related company (or of the employee's actual employer, for that matter) will only succeed if the employee can satisfy the tests required to prove that the conduct was oppressive. To succeed, the employee will need to prove that the director benefitted personally from his or her actions.[85]

S. Prosecutions Under Employment Standards Legislation

In all jurisdictions except for Prince Edward Island, the employment standards legislation provides that directors may be prosecuted. Typically, those prosecution sections specify that where a director or officer of the corporation "authorizes, permits or acquiesces in" a contravention of the legislation, the director may be prosecuted (whether or not the corporation has been prosecuted or convicted).

These provisions can affect directors in two ways. First, in provinces where there is no express provision imposing personal liability upon directors for wage-related obligations, directors may still be made personally

---

[84] *Supra* note 78.

[85] *Cain v. Peterson*, [2006] O.J. No. 188 (Ont. Sup. Ct. Jus.) (QL).

liable if a corporation fails to pay the amounts that are owed to its employees.

Thus, in New Brunswick, for example, a director who authorizes or acquiesces in the corporation's non-payment of wages or statutory termination pay or severance pay is guilty of an offence and, upon conviction, that director is liable to a fine of up to $1,000 per day for each day the corporation fails to pay the wages owed.[86] In addition, upon conviction, the court can also order the director to pay the amount owed to the employees.[87]

Second, directors who direct or knowingly permit their corporation to engage in conduct that breaches the governing statute may be personally liable for the failure to comply with it.

Traditionally, government enforcement agencies have not been overly aggressive in prosecuting directors under these provisions. In Ontario, however, there has been increased activity in prosecuting directors for non-payment of amounts owed to employees[88] and for other breaches of the Ont ESA. In one case, a corporate director was sentenced to sixty days in jail for ignoring multiple "orders to pay" wages to employees.[89]

III. Avoiding Liability for Wage Related Claims

Clearly, directors face enormous potential personal liability for the wage-related obligations of the corporation. The obligation to make the payments owed by a corporation generally are "no fault" obligations, and the fact that a director has exercised due care will not prevent a court from

---

[86] NB ESA, *supra* note 14, s. 75(3)(*c*).

[87] *Ibid.*, s. 75(3)(*a*).

[88] *Ontario (Ministry of Labour) v. 3 for 1 Pizza & Wings Inc.*, 2006 CarswellOnt 2502 (C.J.); and *R. v. Lark Manufacturing Inc.* (1992), 42 C.C.E.L. 300 (Ont. Ct. Prov. Div.). The directors' convictions were overturned on appeal but were restored by the Ontario Court of Appeal. The Ontario Ministry of Labour ("MOL") reports the following fines were paid by corporate directors: Coulten Radiator (*Henry Bergmeirer, Director*) pleaded guilty to two charges under the Ont ESA for failing to pay wages to a terminated employee and was fined $3,000 (MOL Press Release, May 26, 2006). Girex Corp. (*Warren Schmidt, Director*) was fined $10,000 for one charge of breaching the ESA by failing to pay wages to eleven employees (MOL Press Release, January 3, 2006). James Bay Wild Fruit (*Michael Poulin, Director*) was fined $6,000 for permitting workers to work in excess of the permitted hours in a week, contrary to the Ont ESA (MOL Press Release, October 18, 2006); see also 920496 Ontario Limited (*Peter Hamidani, Director*). A director was fined $18,000 and ordered to repay outstanding amounts owed to employees (MOL Press Release, March 4, 1999). Added to each fine levied against those directors by the courts is a 25 percent victim fine surcharge, which is imposed pursuant to the *Provincial Offences Act*; see *R. v. Lark Manufacturing*, [1995] O.J. No. 3903 (C.A.).

[89] Glencairn Academy (*and 2 Directors*) was found guilty of fourteen and twelve charges, respectively, for failure to pay wages over a five-year period to fourteen employees. One director was fined $17,000 and sentenced to sixty days in jail; the second director was fined $11,000 for failure to pay wages (MOL Press Release, September 2, 2005).

imposing personal liability under the employment standards statutes nor under most of the business corporations statutes.[90]

Therefore, directors should be aware of their uniquely vulnerable position and take steps to satisfy themselves that the corporation can meet, and is meeting, its statutory obligations to employees. The following additional steps should be taken:

- Potential directors need to consider if they are prepared to spend sufficient time dealing with their duties as a director before they accept an appointment as a director. If they are not, they should not agree to serve as a director or they should resign from their position as a director.

- Directors should understand the requirements (generally) of the applicable legal framework within which the corporation operates. Their knowledge should include a passing familiarity with employment statutes that impose obligations on directors personally (such as the employment standards legislation).

- Directors must take the time to become aware of the corporation's finances and business affairs and to monitor financial risks and other risks within the framework in which the business operates.

- Directors should receive signed statements on a regular basis from senior management, namely the CFO and CEO, attesting to the timely payment of employee wages (including bonus pay, overtime pay, and vacation pay). These certificates should also cover other employee obligations not addressed in this Chapter, such as tax remittances. It is also prudent to have the certificate attest to the absence or existence of regulatory prosecutions, inspections, or appeals (such as employment-related matters, including employment standards, as well as health and safety, workers' compensation, and human rights matters).

- If the corporation enters into written employment agreements that contain termination provisions, directors may wish to require that those provisions expressly state that the payments will not be paid in return for services rendered but rather are paid in lieu of providing notice of termination.

---

[90] As discussed earlier, good faith reliance on financial statements and experts' reports may relieve a director of liability under the CBCA. The director may still be liable, however, pursuant to the employment standards legislation to which the corporation is subject where a due diligence defence is not generally available. A due diligence defence generally only becomes available if the director is prosecuted for a breach of the applicable statute.

- In times of financial uncertainty, directors should request and receive frequent reports and assurances from management concerning the payment of the corporation's wage-related obligations.

- In times of financial uncertainty, directors should consider reducing the period between each pay period in order to limit liability for any unpaid wages. For vacation pay, directors may consider paying the vacation pay accrued for each pay period directly to each employee on each pay date. While payment for each pay period may not be in compliance with the applicable provincial obligations (which generally specifies that payment should be made immediately prior to the vacation time or at the time the vacation is taken), few unions or employees are likely to complain about this practice or to seek double recovery.

- In cases of financial uncertainty, if vacation pay is not paid for each pay period, directors may wish to consider requiring that sufficient funds to pay employees be placed in a segregated trust account.[91]

- In some cases, the mechanism of a unanimous shareholder agreement may be available to relieve a director of liability.[92]

- In cases of financial uncertainty, as a last resort, a director should consider resignation in accordance with the applicable corporate statute.[93] While resignation from the board will not protect directors from liability that has already been incurred, it will prevent the accrual of further obligations. Resignations should be in writing and copies of them should be retained.

- Directors, prudently, must retain their own records of their resignations. Often, corporate records are not updated to reflect board resignations. When the government authorities do a corporate search to determine liability for debts that are owed by the corporation, they

---

[91] In certain circumstances, such a mechanism may be challenged by creditors as a preference or as effecting a change in priorities among the creditors of a corporation: see *Re Westar Mining Ltd.* (1992), 14 C.B.R. (3d) 95 (B.C.S.C.); and *Re Pacific National Lease Holding Corp.* (1992), 72 B.C.L.R. (2d) 368 (C.A.).

[92] Unanimous shareholder agreements, which are discussed in Chapters 2 and 3, are authorized under the various corporate statutes: see CBCA, *supra* note 1, s. 146(5); and OBCA, *supra* note 21, s. 108(5). But see also Ont ESA, *supra* note 4, s. 80(1), which imposes liability on shareholders to the extent that directors are relieved of liability to pay wages under the applicable corporate legislation.

[93] See, for example, CBCA, *supra* note 1, s. 108; and OBCA, *supra* note 21, s. 121. Under these statutes, a written resignation must be sent to the corporation.

rely on the information in the government's records. That information is rebuttable if a director can prove an earlier resignation.[94]

- Directors should insist on Director and Officer Insurance in a sufficient amount (which, in British Columbia, could include amounts sufficient to cover off liabilities owed to employees of any related entities). Alternatively, the business corporations statutes and, generally, the employment standards statutes permit directors to be indemnified. If there is a (solvent) parent corporation, a director may consider obtaining a written guarantee from the parent organization indemnifying the director from liability for wage-related claims or from other liabilities the director may incur.

IV. Regulatory Offences: Occupational Health and Safety

A. How Are Directors Liable for Safety in the Workplace?

Directors face liability under federal and provincial statutes that are designed to ensure the health and safety of employees in the workplace. Under Part II of the CLC, which governs health and safety standards that are applicable to workers who are covered under federal jurisdiction and under similar provisions in most other provinces (but not Ontario and British Columbia), a director or officer who directs, authorizes, assents to, or acquiesces or participates in an offence committed by the corporation is guilty of the offence, whether or not the corporation has been prosecuted or convicted.[95]

In Ontario and British Columbia, the applicable statutes impose personal liability on directors to ensure that the corporation complies with the applicable safety legislation. In Ontario, s. 32 of the *Occupational Health*

---

[94] See *Bagrianski v. Aero Surveys* (2004), 50 C.B.R. (4th) 17 (Ont. Sup. Ct. Jus.); *St. Pierre v. Supply Management Dialtone Inc.*, [2003] O.J. No. 672 (Ont. Sup. Ct. Jus.) (QL); *Michael Alkovic v. Director of Employment Standards*, B.C. EST #RD047/01; *Dynasty Place 2000 v. Caparelli*, 2003 CanLII 46676 (O.L.R.B.); and *Navas v. Blakemore*, 2005 CanLII 1844 (O.L.R.B.).

[95] CLC, *supra* note 5, s. 149(2). See also Manitoba *Workplace Health and Safety Act*, C.C.S.M., c. W210, s. 56; New Brunswick *Occupational Health and Safety Act*, S.N.B. 1983, c. O-0.2, s. 49; Newfoundland and Labrador *Occupational Health and Safety Act*, R.S.N.L. c. O-3, s. 68; Nova Scotia *Occupational Health and Safety Act*, S.N.S. 1996, c. 7, s. 77; Prince Edward Island *Occupational Health and Safety Act*, R.S.P.E.I. 1988, c. O-1.01, s. 43(3); Quebec *Occupational Health and Safety (An Act Respecting)*, R.S.Q. c. S-2.1, s. 241; and Saskatchewan *Occupational Health and Safety Act, 1993*, S.S. 1993, c. O-1.1, s. 60. However, the Northwest Territories *Safety Act*, R.S.N.W.T. 1988, c. S-1, the Nunavut *Safety Act*, R.S.N.W.T. 1988, c. S-1, and the Yukon *Occupational Health and Safety Act*, R.S.Y. 2002, c. 159 do not impose liability on directors. In Alberta, directors may be held liable in certain circumstances; see *Occupational Health and Safety Act*, R.S.A. 2000, c. O-2, ss. 1(*k*), "employer", and 2(1).

and Safety Act[96] ("OHSA") imposes a personal liability on directors to "take all reasonable care to ensure that the corporation complies" with the OHSA and its regulations and with any orders of inspectors or other officials, including the Minister. Failure to comply with the OHSA or with orders made pursuant to the legislation may expose directors and officers to prosecution and, upon conviction, to a fine of up to $25,000 or twelve months' imprisonment, or both.[97] A number of directors who have been convicted under the OHSA have paid fines or, in a few cases, have been incarcerated for breaches of the safety legislation.[98] Typically, the MOL prosecutes directors of businesses who also manage the business because they have greater control over the day-to-day operations of the business, but there are no statutory restrictions on who may be prosecuted.[99]

Under all safety statutes, obligations imposed upon directors for a safe workplace apply to directors of not-for-profit organizations, without distinction to the type of operation conducted.

Steps taken to comply with the provincial health and safety statutes will serve in the event that a director is prosecuted criminally.

B. What Steps Should a Director Take?

In the leading environmental prosecution of *R. v. Bata Industries Limited*,[100] which is equally applicable to safety, the court considered charges against the corporation, the international president and chief executive

---

96 R.S.O. 1990, c. O.1 ("OHSA"); in B.C., see *Workers Compensation Act*, R.S.B.C. 1996, c. 492, s. 121.

97 OHSA, *ibid.*, s. 66(1).

98 In *R. v. Raglan Industries Inc.*, [1994] O.J. No. 3998 (Ont. Ct. Prov. Div.) (QL), for example, a director of a corporate employer was aware of a worker's request for an explosion proof light in an enclosed area but took no steps to ensure that the light was either ordered or installed. Approximately one month following the request, the worker was seriously injured by an explosion in the enclosed area. The director was fined $10,000 and the corporation was fined $55,000. See also *R. v. A.D.M. Steel Inc.*, [1995] O.J. No. 4789 (Ont. Ct. Prov. Div.) (QL), (director convicted and fined $7,500); *R. v. ProShield Corporation and Mandel*, unreported, August 15, 1995 (Ont. Ct. Prov. Div.), Romain J.P. (director convicted and fined $10,000); and *R. v. Normand Fortunat Verville*, unreported, May 14, 1996 (Ont. Ct. Prov. Div.), Quinn J.P. (conviction and fines upheld on appeal); *R. v. Normand Fortunat Verville*, unreported, November 26, 1996 (Ont. Ct. Prov. Div.); *R v. Harvey's and Falca*, unreported, March 25, 1998 (Ont. Ct. Prov. Div) (director convicted and fined $7,000); *R. v. Burns*, unreported, June 13, 2002 (Ont. Ct. Prov. Div.) (director fined $50,000); and *R. v. Graham*, unreported, April 23, 2003 (Ont. Ct. Prov. Div.) (director fined $25,000).

99 Recently, the Ministry of Labour ("MOL") has reported the following convictions of directors in its press releases: A director of Syn-Con Corporation was fined $10,000 where there were no worker injuries but where the MOL identified breaches of the OHSA, such as no joint health and safety committee (May 16, 2006). A director of Premier Pallet Repair Ltd. failed to ensure the company complied with an MOL order to inspect forklifts and was fined $2,500 (April 11, 2006). A director of T.J. Ware Maintenance was fined $2,500 following serious injury to a worker (February 27, 2006).

100 (1992), 9 O.R. (3d) 329 (Ont. Ct. Prov. Div.), rev'd on other grounds (1993), 14 O.R. (3d) 354 (Gen. Div.), rev'd on other grounds (1995), 25 O.R. (3d) 321 (C.A.) ("*Bata*").

officer, and two directors and officers of the corporation. This case provides important guidelines for assessing the due diligence of officers and directors of a corporation under the OHSA.

In *Bata*, the court asked the following questions in determining whether the accused directors and officers had established their defence of due diligence:

- Did the board of directors establish a "system", as outlined in *Sault Ste. Marie*, to ensure compliance with the law and with industry standards?
- Did the directors/officers give instructions for implementing the system?
- Did the directors/officers set up a system to ensure that corporate officers reported back periodically to the board on the operation and effectiveness of the system, and were officers instructed to report on any substantial non-compliance to the board in a timely fashion?
- Did the officers/directors review compliance reports that were provided by officers, consultants, or lawyers? The court suggested that directors can place reasonable reliance on such reports.
- Were the directors aware of industry standards in dealing with the risks faced by their corporation, and did their corporation meet these standards?
- Did the directors react immediately and personally when they became aware that the system had failed?

In Ontario and British Columbia, in order to create the basis for a due diligence defence for officers and members of the boards of directors, it appears that the boards must become involved in the setting of goals, the deciding of responsibility, the allocating of resources, and the buttressing of the necessary support mechanisms if the corporate health and safety policy pronouncement and program are to be reflected in the everyday running of the enterprise. Such direction will, or should, ensure that the workplace is a safer place for workers who are employed by the corporation (or a not-for-profit organization, for that matter), and it should also lay the ground work for a defence of due diligence in the event of a prosecution against an officer or director personally.

Based on the ruling in the *Bata* case, it is clear that directors who are the "directing minds" of the corporation must take steps to ensure that they are kept apprised of major health and safety issues at the workplace. This goal can be accomplished by regular reports to the board or to the environmental, health, and safety committee of the board. It would appear prudent that the person responsible for managing the health and safety affairs at each workplace consider submitting regular periodic reports to senior management and to the board outlining the status of major issues at the workplace and confirming compliance with the governing legislation. The recipients of these reports must understand that it is necessary to consider the information presented and, where appropriate, to issue instructions for remedial action. Failure to act once a director is aware of a problem will limit the potential defence that the directors and officers acted in a diligent fashion. Equally, the failure of directors to take steps to inform themselves of health and safety issues at their workplace will also likely result in directors being unable to prove that they were duly diligent in the performance of their duties as the directing mind of the corporation (or, under the *Criminal Code*, that they were not acting negligently).

Clearly, as a result of the *Bata* decision, the courts of Ontario have indicated that they would like to see written documentation in support of the assertion by directors that they have acted in a duly diligent fashion in directing the operations of the corporation. A paper trail will be critical to establishing a defence of due diligence. The nature and extent of the documentation that will be appropriate will vary in each case and will depend upon the particular corporate culture involved and, perhaps, on other industry standards and practices.

V. Criminal Code Offences for Safety

The 2004 *Criminal Code*[101] amendments will have an effect on corporations, partnerships, not-for-profit operations, and all persons "who direct work" at a workplace.[102] As a result, there must be increased vigilance by directors to ensure that the corporation is compliant with applicable legislation and that appropriate systems are in place to ensure that the organization's employees and other representatives do not act in a fashion that will make the organization a party to a criminal offence.

Corporations can only act through the individuals that represent them. In the past, a criminal conviction would be registered against a corporation only if the "directing mind" of the corporation, acting within his or her authority, was found guilty of criminal behaviour. The amendments to the *Criminal Code* extensively broaden the circle of individuals whose conduct can result in criminal liability for the organization. Importantly, it is no longer only the "directing mind" (directors and most senior executives) of

[101] *Supra* note 2.

[102] *Ibid.*, s. 217.1.

the corporation who will be seen to be acting on behalf of the corporation. Now, "senior officers" (senior employees who establish policies or manage the business of the organization; they include the CEO, CFO, and members of the board) and "representatives" of an organization (directors, officers, partners, employees, *agents, and contractors*) can act in a manner that will make the corporation a party to the criminal offence, even if the "senior officers" or "representatives" are not themselves prosecuted.

Corporations can be convicted under the *Criminal Code* in two ways. First, they can be convicted of criminal negligence if one, or more than one, of the "representatives" act negligently either as an individual or in the aggregate, and if those in authority fail to exercise the appropriate care to prevent the representative(s) from acting in that fashion. Second, corporations can also be convicted where liability is based on recklessness or fraud where a "senior officer", acting with intent to benefit the corporation (at least in part) either (a) commits the offence within the scope of his or her authority, or (b) with criminal intent, and acting within his authority, directs an employee of the corporation to commit an offence, or (c) fails to take reasonable measures to stop a representative from committing an offence that the "senior officer" knows the representative is committing, or is about to commit.

Thus, the *Criminal Code* now covers offences that are based on negligent conduct of all types as well as offences based on recklessness or fraudulent intent. The potential *Criminal Code* prosecutions are *not* limited to violations of safety or environmental requirements at a workplace, although it is these two areas that seem to have attracted the greatest publicity, in part because the amendments also impose a new duty on anyone who directs work to take reasonable measures to protect employee and public safety.

If a corporation is convicted of a breach of the *Criminal Code* for summary offences, the fines range from $25,000 to $100,000 per count. For more serious offences, there is NO maximum fine. Directors can be incarcerated for up to six months and fined $2,000 per count. As well, there are new, creative sentencing options, including the ability of a court to order restitution or to direct the corporation to take specific steps to reduce the chances of a recurrence.

Directors must be cognizant of their new obligations to comply with the *Criminal Code* as well as with the existing obligations under the applicable statutes. Directors and officers have a duty to monitor corporate compliance with laws and with applicable corporate policies and procedures that are designed to ensure compliance with the applicable laws. These amendments to the *Criminal Code* reaffirm the need for prudent directors to ensure that appropriate systems are implemented, monitored, and documented.

A. Steps for Prudent Directors under Regulatory Statutes and Criminal Code

As indicated above, organizations must ensure that they have a system to keep their senior management advised and involved in giving remedial directions with regard to workplace health and safety issues. Now, with the changes to the *Criminal Code*, which apply across the country in all jurisdictions, all directors should take the same type of proactive measures that directors in Ontario and British Columbia are advised to implement as a result of the "personal liability" section in the provincial safety legislation of those provinces.

As with all OHSA due diligence, documentation of the efforts taken will be important. While directors (and perhaps, other senior officers) may delegate, to some extent, their obligations to ensure that the corporation complies with the applicable legislation, it is clear that directors cannot insulate themselves from all responsibility for regulatory matters by delegating away all aspects of compliance to subordinates.

The following list identifies various steps that directors can take to demonstrate compliance with the standard of care that may be reasonably expected in order to provide a safe workplace for employees and others. These steps are generally similar to those that prudent employers should take in any event in order to create a safe workplace and form the basis for a due diligence defence under the OHSA. If they are properly implemented and enforced, these steps should minimize the risks of liability for organizations and individuals alike:

1. Directors should become familiar with the provisions of the applicable health and safety legislation. Someone should be assigned the task of educating the directors about the applicable safety legislation and the new criminal standards.

2. A reporting system should be implemented so that directors receive regular (i.e., semi-annual or annual) reports on health and safety in the workplace and are aware of remedial measures that are necessary to redress noted hazards or potential hazards.

3. The board must allocate adequate resources towards workplace health and safety. Whereas this has always been the case, now it is important that organizations update their safety programs to take the *Criminal Code* obligations into account. This means, at a min-

imum, that sufficient *additional* resources are provided so appropriate programs exist:

(a) to ensure that the public is protected at the workplace;

(b) to train anyone who "directs work"; and

(c) to provide for an adequate contractors' program (given that contractors are "representatives" of the organization whose actions may result in a prosecution against the organization).

4. Directors must understand the components of the safety program developed by the organization to implement the safety policies of the employer. They must also ensure that the program is functioning effectively. A safety program will contain many of the elements described in this list, but there must be an overall confirmation that the various systems have been identified and are in place.

5. Directors should confirm that a system is in place to ensure that steps are taken by corporate officials to comply, on a timely basis, with orders issued by the government officials.

6. Directors should confirm that procedures are in place to allow the identification of hazards before an accident occurs. Such procedures can include regular safety audits or more frequent meetings of the Joint Health and Safety Committee ("JHSC") than are required under health and safety legislation, and they *must* include timely inspections of the workplace by members of the JHSC, as required by the applicable legislation. External audits may also be a useful tool in ensuring that regulatory requirements are complied with and identifying any deficient or missing systems.

7. Directors should confirm that emergency procedures have been developed for use in the event of an accident in the workplace.

8. Directors should confirm that a comprehensive accident/incident investigation procedure exists at the workplace. This will be critical in the event of a workplace accident where parallel investigations under both the *Criminal Code* and health and safety legislation may be commenced.

9. Directors should confirm that there is a process in place to address and respond to a work refusal and that a review is conducted of similar situations in other parts of the organization in order to reduce or eliminate hazards similar to those that gave rise to the work refusal.

10. Directors should confirm that they are advised of the training programs undertaken at the workplace and should satisfy themselves that the training is sufficiently specific to the work performed and is not of too "generic" a nature. Young workers in particular must receive adequate training. All training must be documented. Given that the actions of anyone who "directs work" may lead to a *Criminal Code* prosecution of the organization, it is important that *everyone* who will direct work on behalf of the organization is "competent" to do so within the meaning of the health and safety legislation. Generally, employers are able to demonstrate "competency" through documented training.

11. Directors should ensure that appropriate contractor tendering and contracting procedures are in place and that contractors are made aware of, and appropriately trained for, potential hazards in the workplace that they may encounter while providing their services to the organization. The fact that organizations may be criminally prosecuted for acts or omissions by *contractors*, makes this an important measure.

12. Directors should be familiar with the hazardous materials used in the organization's workplaces, and they should confirm that the organization is acting in compliance with the Workplace Hazardous Materials Information System.

13. In establishing and monitoring health and safety policies and procedures, directors should confirm that, at a minimum, any industry-wide standards are adhered to in the workplace.

14. Directors should ensure that health and safety programs are reviewed by specialists and updated regularly. When the programs are updated, the directors should consider whether they satisfy due diligence requirements. Board members should consider the issue at board meetings. Senior managers should consider the issue at regular management meetings. Both groups should document their discussions.

15. Directors should confirm that employees (including everyone who "directs work") are informed of and understand the legal responsibilities imposed upon them and the organization in respect of workplace health and safety.

16. Where directors become aware that the organization is in contravention of the applicable health and safety legislation or that the systems created to achieve compliance with the applicable health

and safety legislation have failed, the directors should issue directions to immediately rectify the situation.

17. If directions are given, there must be a follow-up system developed so that the director is satisfied that the directions have been complied with and that the problem identified has been addressed.

18. Directors must ensure that the organization properly documents its safety systems and programs. This is a critical component of any defence. Policies must comply with the law and must be in writing. Directives issued by directors for significant safety developments or decisions must be documented. Training must be documented. Even discipline must be documented.

The most important piece of advice for directors of an organization is that they, themselves, must become personally aware of the health and safety issues associated with their organization's different workplaces, and they must actively ensure that their organization complies with the statutory obligations imposed on it by any applicable health and safety legislation.

Proving due diligence or that the appropriate standard of care has been met are questions of fact, and the success of a defence will invariably depend on the reasonableness of the accused's conduct in the context of the offence that is complained of. In the final analysis, whether or not a defence can be proven in any given case will depend on the efforts made by the appropriate persons, as well as on the availability and completeness of records that identify the preventative or remedial measures that have been taken and how they have been implemented.

B. Directors and Workers' Compensation

Recently, a corporate director in Alberta who had not registered as a director under the provincial workers' compensation legislation was found personally liable in a civil suit for the death of a worker.[103] In this case, the director was also president of the company and involved in the day-to-day operations of the business. The court ruled that the director owed a duty of care to workers and that the workers' compensation and health and safety legislation both contemplated that directors would be personally liable in certain circumstances. As a result, the court ruled that there were not sufficient policy reasons to preclude the imposition of tort liability against a corporate director.[104]

---

[103] *Nielsen Estate v. Epton* (2006), 56 Alta. L.R. (4th) 61, 2006 ABQB 21, appeal filed March 22, 2006, (22 March 2006 leave to appeal to Alta. C.A. filed), Edmonton, 0603-0077-AC (Alta. C.A.).

[104] *Ibid.* at paras. 520–599.

Given this recent decision and the potential for the expansion of a director's liability to workers who are injured or killed in a workplace accident, directors should investigate their potential liability under the applicable provincial workers' compensation legislation and should ensure that insurance coverage will extend to claims for workplace deaths.

CHAPTER 10

THE DUTY OF DIRECTORS IN THE PENSION CONTEXT

I. Introduction

Directors of Canadian corporations are paying more attention than ever to the governance of their registered pension plans. The increased focus on governance is, in part, a natural extension of the increased focus placed on corporate governance, following such recent high-profile corporate failures as Enron[1] and WorldCom.[2] Add to this the growth of class actions as a pension litigation vehicle and the increasing attention paid to governance issues by regulatory and non-regulatory industry bodies,[3] and it is no wonder that pension governance is a "hot button" issue.

While the importance of good pension governance is universally recognized, the implementation of an effective pension governance system is complicated by the fact that a corporation, acting through its board of directors ("board"), will usually perform two very distinct roles. Indeed, for the vast majority of company-sponsored private pension plans, the corporation is the (legal) plan's administrator.[4] However, the corporation is also the plan's sponsor.[5] Since these roles involve different obligations, the interests of the corporation can conflict with those of the plan's beneficiaries; consequently, an effective pension governance system must be able to distinguish clearly between the two roles.

---

[1] Enron Corporation was an energy company based in Houston, Texas. Prior to its bankruptcy in late 2001, Enron employed approximately 21,000 people and was one of the world's leading electricity, natural gas, pulp and paper, and communications companies, with claimed revenues of $101 billion in 2000. Enron achieved infamy at the end of 2001 when it was revealed that the company's reported financial condition was sustained mostly by institutionalized, systematic, and creatively planned accounting fraud. Enron's European operations filed for bankruptcy on November 30, 2001, and it sought Chapter 11 protection in the U.S. two days later on December 2, 2001.

[2] At one time, WorldCom was the United States' second-largest long distance phone company. WorldCom grew largely by acquiring other telecommunications companies, most notably MCI Communications. Beginning in 1999 and continuing through to May 2002, the company used fraudulent accounting methods to mask its declining financial condition by painting a false picture of financial growth and profitability to prop up the price of WorldCom's stock. By the end of 2003, it was estimated that the company's total assets had been inflated by around $11 billion. The fraud was a chief factor that led to WorldCom filing for Chapter 11 bankruptcy protection on July 21, 2002.

[3] In its November 1998 report (the Kirby Report), the Senate Committee on Banking, Trade, and Commerce recommended that pension plans in Canada adopt industry best practices with respect to plan governance. The federal pension regulator (i.e., the office of the Superintendent of Financial Institutions) subsequently published a "Guideline for Governance of Federally Regulated Pension Plans". Similarly, the Canadian Association of Pension Supervisory Authorities adopted guidelines (e.g., "Pension Plan Guidelines for Capital Accumulation Plans (Guideline No. 3)") that were designed to assist plan sponsors to put into place a pension governance structure that will allow plan sponsors to deliver on the pension promise.

[4] While the corporation is typically the (legal) administrator of a pension plan, a board of trustees (in the case of a multi-employer pension plan) or a pension committee (particularly in Quebec) can also be the (legal) administrator. The (legal) administrator should be distinguished from those individuals or companies that provide administrative services to the plan (e.g., the plan custodian or record keeper). While these individuals may often be generically referred to as "administrators", they are not the legal administrators of the plan. In this paper, all references to "administrator" will be to the (legal) administrator of a pension plan.

[5] The term "plan sponsor" is not a term that is used in pension legislation. Rather, it is the term that is widely used in the pension industry to denote the person(s) or entity(ies) that established the pension plan and have the ability to amend or terminate the plan. Typically, pension legislation will use the term "employer" when referring to an obligation or right of the corporation in its capacity as plan sponsor rather than in its capacity as plan administrator.

This Chapter examines these two roles in order to assist directors to fulfill their obligations to the corporation and its shareholders, as well as to the beneficiaries of plans, by properly identifying the capacity in which the directors are acting in relation to the pension plan. This Chapter assumes that the pension plan in question is a single-employer pension plan that is registered under the *Income Tax Act* (Canada)[6] ("ITA") and that the appropriate pension benefits standards legislation is from a Canadian common law jurisdiction ("Pension Legislation"). The principles discussed herein generally apply equally to the governance of defined benefit plans and to defined contribution pension plans.

II. Regulatory Framework and Types of Pension Plans

A. Regulatory Framework

The establishment of a pension plan is not mandatory for employers in Canada. Where a corporation chooses to establish a registered pension plan, a variety of statutory and common law obligations and liabilities will arise.

Both the ITA and Pension Legislation govern Canadian registered pension plans. To maintain their tax assisted status, pension plans must be registered with the Canada Revenue Agency ("CRA") under the ITA, and they must comply with the requirements set out in the ITA and its regulations. The provisions of the ITA that relate to registered pension plans are extremely complicated. Although the number of sections outlining the ITA's treatment of registered pension benefits is relatively few, numerous technical notes, newsletters, technical interpretations, and budget speeches dealing with these provisions have been released. As a result, a fair degree of expertise is needed to comply with all aspects of the legislation.

Every jurisdiction in Canada,[7] except the province of Prince Edward Island,[8] has Pension Legislation that establishes minimum funding and administrative requirements for registered pension plans in the relevant jurisdiction. The legislative and regulatory scheme governing Canadian pension plans is administered in each province or jurisdiction by government pension regulators. For example, in Ontario, the *Pension Benefits Act*

[6] R.S.C. 1985, c. 1 (5th Supp.), as amended ("ITA").

[7] Private pension plans for employees who work and reside in the Yukon Territories, Northwest Territories, or Nunavut are subject to the *Pension Benefits Standards Act, 1985*, R.S.C. 1985, c. 32 (2nd Supp.).

[8] Prince Edward Island has passed legislation but it has not been proclaimed into force.

(Ontario) ("PBA") governs pension plans registered in the province, and the provincial regulator is the Financial Services Commission of Ontario ("FSCO").

Pension Legislation across Canada is largely similar to Ontario's, but as each jurisdiction has its own legislation and regulations, a host of minor differences occur between different jurisdictions. As a result, pension plans with members in more than one province can be subject to potentially conflicting laws from more than one province. While a reciprocal agreement between the various jurisdictions provides that a plan should only be registered in the jurisdiction in which the majority of members are employed, such plans must still comply with the Pension Legislation of each province in which plan members are employed.[9]

Corporations that have established a registered pension plan must also consider recent regulatory initiatives that are intended to outline best practices with respect to pension plan governance. Such initiatives include the ACPM/PIAC/OSFI Joint Task Force on Pension Plan Governance and Self-Assessment ("Joint Task Force Guideline"), the Canadian Association of Pension Supervisory Authorities' Guideline No. 4 — Pension Plan Governance Guidelines and Self-Assessment Questionnaire ("CAPSA Governance Guidelines"), and Guideline No. 3 — Guidelines for Capital Accumulation Plans ("CAP Guidelines"). While these and other industry guidelines (collectively, the "Guidelines") do not, by themselves, create any additional legal rights or obligations for any party that is involved with a pension plan, they create the potential for a heightened focus on best practices standards to which the actions of the corporation may be compared. It is likely that such best practices standards would be adopted, or at least considered, by courts in Canada that are assessing the actions of a corporation in its capacity as a plan administrator.

B. Types of Registered Pension Plans

A registered pension plan is an employer-sponsored vehicle designed to provide retirement income to employees on a pre-funded basis through either a policy of insurance or a trust agreement. A pension plan may be non-contributory (totally funded by the employer) or contributory (funded by both required employee and employer contributions), and it may also

[9] In particular, note the current disagreement among the various Canadian pension regulators over whether to apply a "final location" approach (the application of the laws of the jurisdiction where employment terminates to all pensionable service) or a "checkerboarding" approach (the application of the laws of each jurisdiction in which pension credits were earned during plan membership) to the determination of the pension entitlements of employees who have worked in multiple jurisdictions while they were members of a pension plan.

permit employees to make voluntary contributions to provide additional pension benefits.

All registered pension plans can be generally described as one of two basic types of plans (or as a combination of them): defined contribution pension plans or defined benefit pension plans.

Under a defined contribution ("DC") pension plan (also referred to as a "money purchase plan"), the corporation agrees to contribute a specific amount (e.g., 5 percent of each year's salary) towards each employee's retirement benefits. Such plans do not promise to provide the employee with a specific level of benefits; rather, they operate in a similar way to a registered retirement savings plan ("RRSP"). The employee's contributions (if any) and the company's contributions, together with investment yield, accumulate in the employee's plan account until termination of employment (including death or retirement), and they, along with the prevailing interest rate levels at the time the pension is payable, determine the amount of the pension.

Under a defined benefit ("DB") pension plan, the promised benefit is fixed at a defined annual or monthly pension based upon the following: (i) the employee's average salary over each year of his or her working career; (ii) the employee's average salary over the final years of employment (i.e., 2 percent of average salary over the final five years of employment multiplied by years of pensionable service); or (iii) a flat unit credit (i.e., an annual pension equal to $45 for each month of pensionable service). The corporation is responsible for funding the risk in a DB pension plan.

In addition to registered pension plans, corporations may sponsor unregistered supplemental employee retirement plans ("SERPs") that provide supplemental pension accruals to all or to a designated class of registered plan members in excess of the ITA limits that are applicable to the registered plan. Pension Legislation does not regulate SERPs. SERPs may be funded or unfunded. If they are funded (through segregated fund assets or a standby letter of credit), the ITA generally considers them to be retirement compensation arrangements ("RCAs") that are subject to a prescribed tax treatment.

A corporation may also sponsor other types of retirement savings arrangements, such as group registered retirement savings plans ("Group RRSPs") and deferred profit sharing plans ("DPSPs"). While Group RRSPs and DPSPs are not subject to minimum Pension Legislation, they are regulated by the ITA, which, among other things, prescribes the maximum contribution limits that are applicable to such plans.[10]

[10] In addition, because RRSPs and DPSPs are capital accumulation plans, the CAP Guidelines are intended to apply to sponsors and administrators of Group RRSPs and DPSPs.

III. The Corporation's Dual Roles: What Role is the Board Acting in?

A corporation acts through its board. Directors are charged by statute with the fundamental obligation to "manage, or supervise the management of, the business and affairs of the corporation".[11] In other words, the board is the "brain" that controls the corporation and directs its actions.

The board's responsibilities with respect to the governance of a pension plan are somewhat different from the board's responsibilities in other areas of corporate governance. For instance, under corporate governance principles, the board's responsibilities are primarily to the company itself.[12] However, in the context of pension plan governance, the board will, depending on the task at hand, have responsibilities to either the corporation (in its capacity as the plan's sponsor) or to the members and beneficiaries of the corporation's pension plans (in its capacity as the plan's administrator).

A. The Board's Role in Relation to the Company's Role as Plan Sponsor

There is no legal obligation placed on Canadian corporations to establish or "sponsor" a registered pension plan. Accordingly, the decision to establish a pension plan is an action a corporation (acting through its board) makes, taking into consideration its own interests, such as the need to attract and retain employees.

The board has the overall responsibility for the corporation's obligations as pension plan sponsor. As such, the board is responsible for the following: pension plan design[13] (this includes, for example, setting both employer and employee contribution levels under DC pension plans and amending the pension plan to provide for changes to benefits, such as introducing early retirement incentives for plan members); pension plan eligibility (i.e., what classes of employees may participate in the pension

[11] *Canada Business Corporations Act*, R.S.C. 1985, c. C-44, as amended, s. 102(1) ("CBCA").

[12] In carrying out their mandate, directors are subject to two overriding duties, both of which were first developed by the courts at common law and are now codified in the statutes governing all corporations incorporated in Canada, either federally or provincially. As stated in s. 122(1) of the CBCA, the directors are required (i) to act honestly and in good faith with a view to the best interests of the corporation, and (ii) to exercise the care, diligence, and skill that a reasonably prudent person would exercise in comparable circumstances. The Supreme Court of Canada examined these duties in *Peoples v. Wise*, [2004] 3 S.C.R. 461.

[13] Several recent court decisions have considered the issue of whether the plan sponsor is bound by a fiduciary obligation when amending a pension plan. This general trend of the cases to date suggests that an employer is not a fiduciary in the design, amendment, or termination of a plan. See, for example, *Re Imperial Oil Ltd. Retirement Plan (No. 2)* (August 3, 1995), Commission Bulletin Vol. 6, Issue 4 (Fall-Winter '97) p. 68 (Ont. Pension Comm.); and *Association provinciale des retraites d'Hydro-Quebec v. Hydro-Quebec*, 2005 CarswellQue 661 (Que. C.A.).

plan); pension plan changes; merging the pension plan with another plan; splitting the plan; and deciding whether to wind up (i.e., terminate) in whole or in part the pension plan,[14] subject to collective bargaining and regulatory requirements. While the plan is ongoing, the board must also ensure that the minimum funding obligations of a registered pension plan are met (as they are set out in the applicable Pension Legislation).[15]

In the case of a DB pension plan, the board must establish a funding policy (e.g., if a pension plan is in a deficit position, the board decides whether to eliminate the deficit at a faster rate than what is required by the applicable Pension Legislation). The board will select the plan's auditors and may also direct the plan's actuary with respect to the desired accounting and funding valuation assumptions within a range that is acceptable under the applicable standards of the Canadian Institute of Actuaries.[16]

In some cases, Pension Legislation will provide specific examples of actions that can be taken by the corporation in its role as plan sponsor, as opposed to its role as plan administrator. For example, Pension Legislation generally provides that the corporation in its capacity as plan sponsor/employer may take steps to establish a right to surplus under a pension plan and may seek to have the Superintendent consent to the payment of such a surplus out of the pension fund.[17]

Pension Legislation also permits (subject to the terms of the plan) the plan sponsor to use actuarial gains in an ongoing pension plan to reduce its contribution obligations (i.e., to take "contribution holidays"), even where the employees are entitled to surplus funds on the wind up of the plan. A plan sponsor's ability to take contribution holidays is reinforced by the

---

[14] Section 68(1) of the *Pension Benefits Act* (Ontario), R.S.O. 1990, c. P.8 ("PBA") clearly acknowledges that it is the plan's sponsor that may wind up the pension plan in whole or in part. The pension benefits standards legislation in several other jurisdictions, however, suggests that the corporation may terminate a pension plan in its role as plan administrator; see, for example, s. 29(5) of the *Pension Benefits Standards Act, 1985* (Canada), R.S.C. 1985, c. 32 (2nd Supp.) ("PBSA"), s. 50(1) of the *Pension Benefits Standards Act* (British Columbia), R.S.B.C. 1996, c. 352 ("BC PBSA"), and s. 72 of the *Employment Pension Plans Act* (Alberta), R.S.A. 2000, c. E-8 ("EPPA"). While the pension regulator is typically given the power to terminate pension plans in certain specified situations (see, for example, s. 29(2) of the PBSA, s. 69 of the PBA, s. 49 of the BC PBSA, and s. 71 of the EPPA), there is no provision in any Canadian pension statute that allows plan beneficiaries to terminate a pension plan or the associated pension fund.

[15] See, for example, s. 43(3) of the BC PBSA, s. 50(1)(*b*) of the EPPA, and s. 55(2) of the PBA.

[16] The obligations relating to funding policy are one example of the "grey area" between the board's administrative and sponsor duties. For example, while the ability to change plan-funding policy over and above statutory minimum requirements is a sponsor function, once a change has been made or a policy has been introduced, the implementation and enforcement of such a policy would be an administrative function, which would attract fiduciary duties.

[17] See s. 83 of the EPPA and s. 67 of the *Employment Pension Plans Regulation*, Alta. Reg. 35/2000 ("EPPA Regulations").

Supreme Court of Canada's decision in *Schmidt v. Air Products of Canada Ltd.*[18]

When it is fulfilling its responsibility as the plan's sponsor, the corporation is not acting as a fiduciary. The corporation may act in its own interests (i.e., the interests of its shareholder(s)) rather than in the best interests of the plan's members and beneficiaries.[19] For example, the board may decide for fiscal reasons to reduce the future accrual of benefits for members of a DB pension plan. The reduction of future accrual is not likely to be in the best interests of the plan members. However, since the design of the plan is a function of the sponsor, the board may make the decision to reduce future benefit accruals as it is allowed to take its own corporate objectives into consideration.

It should be noted, however, that in some limited circumstances, the corporation's ability to take into account its own interests when it is amending a pension plan may be constrained, notwithstanding the fact that the corporation is wearing its plan sponsor hat. For example, the corporation's ability to act in its own interests can be limited by a collective agreement, the terms of the specific amending power in the plan, and the provisions of the ITA and the applicable Pension Legislation that may impose minimum or maximum standards and limits on the benefits that can be provided. In addition, the Supreme Court of Canada recently suggested that a corporation's ability to amend a federally regulated pension plan would need to be determined with reference to the conflict of interest standard set out in s. 8(10)(*b*) of the PBSA, which states that "where the employer is the administrator pursuant to paragraph 7(1)(*c*), if there is a material conflict of interest between the employer's role as administrator and the employer's role in any other capacity, the employer ... (b) shall act in the best interests of the members of the pension plan".[20]

---

[18] [1994], 2 S.C.R. 611.

[19] Note, however, that there are some limits on the provision of benefits that are imposed by statute. For example, the ITA places maximums on the benefits that can be provided under a registered pension plan, and once the decision to provide benefits has been taken, the pension benefits legislation imposes minimum standards requirements on the benefits to be provided, such as gradual and uniform accrual, eligibility and vesting criteria, form of payment where the member has a spouse, the amount of pension that can be funded by employees, and minimum benefits payable on pre-retirement death.

[20] *Buschau v. Rogers Communications*, [2006] 8 W.W.R. 583 at para. 103 (S.C.C.). This comment was made in response to the suggestion raised by the British Columbia Court of Appeal that the corporation's ability to amend the plan was subject to a duty of "good faith".

B. The Board's Role in Relation to the Company's Role as Plan Administrator

The corporation's role as plan administrator is separate and independent from its role as plan sponsor. Under Pension Legislation, the administrator is charged with the primary responsibility of administering the pension plan in accordance with the relevant Pension Legislation[21] and the plan documents that are filed with the appropriate pension regulator.[22] The administrator's responsibilities are extensive, but they can generally be classified under three broad categories: filing, disclosure, and "other" requirements.

With respect to filing requirements, the corporation, in its capacity as plan administrator, is responsible for ensuring that annual information returns, actuarial valuation reports, and financial statements for a plan are filed in a timely manner. Disclosure requirements include, among other things, ensuring that (i) members receive an annual statement of benefits, (ii) surviving spouses and same-sex partners receive a statement of the benefits that are payable upon the member's death, and (iii) other statements are provided to interested parties, depending on certain prescribed circumstances (i.e., adverse amendments).

The administrator's principal "other" requirement relates to the investment and custody of the pension fund.[23] Pension Legislation typically imposes "fiduciary like" duties on the corporation in its capacity as plan administrator. Specifically, the majority of such statutes require the plan administrator to exercise the care, diligence, and skill in fulfilling its responsibilities that a person of ordinary prudence would exercise in dealing with the property of another person. In the defined benefit context, the corporation will usually employ an institutional trustee to hold the plan's assets, and it will also appoint one or more investment managers to assist it with the investment of the fund.

Board members of the plan's administrator are required to use any special skill that they have by reason of their profession, business, or calling, or any skills that such a person *ought to* possess. Administrators must also avoid conflicts of interest, whether such interests are personal (i.e., relating to personal investments) or belong to the employer (i.e., relating to investments in the interests of the employer). These statutory fiduciary obligations apply to *employees* of the plan administrator who are engaged in plan administra-

---

[21] See, for example, EPPA, ss. 13(1), (2), (3), and (6).

[22] See s. 147.1(7) of the ITA. All registered pension plans in Canada are subject to the ITA, in addition to relevant Pension Legislation.

[23] See, for example, PBA, s. 22(1).

tion functions.[24] In Alberta, the EPPA specifically provides that the plan administrator stands in a fiduciary relationship to plan members.[25]

Based on the nature of the relationship between a pension plan administrator and the plan's members, there is little doubt that an administrator probably also has a common law fiduciary relationship with plan members.[26] This point is significant, as the law imposes a general duty of loyalty upon all fiduciaries. The duty of loyalty encompasses the following: an obligation to act honestly, prudently, diligently, even-handedly, with candor and confidentiality, and strictly in the best interests of plan members. A fiduciary is precluded from making unauthorized profits, from delegating its responsibilities without having the authority to do so, and from placing himself or herself in a position of conflict of interest. In a nutshell, a fiduciary cannot act in his or her own self-interest.

The fact that the corporation (acting through the board) owes fiduciary duties to plan members does not mean that mistakes can never be made. The test is not perfection, and a fiduciary can be wrong without necessarily incurring liability. Rather, the corporation (through the board) cannot, as plan administrator, be negligent, act in breach of its fiduciary duties, or act in bad faith.

It is important to note that the fiduciary duty imposed by statute or common law does not change depending upon whether a pension plan is a DB plan or a DC plan. The plan's administrator owes a fiduciary duty regardless of the type of plan, even though the tasks that the board (directing the company in its role as plan administrator) is required to perform may differ, depending on the context. In this regard, while the same standards apply to DB and DC plans, the nature and scope of potential liability are very different because of the different administrative requirements imposed by the different designs of DC and DB plans.

IV. Delegation of Administrative Functions

While the board is responsible for ensuring that the corporation's registered pension plans are administered in accordance with applicable legislation, plan terms, and all of the other requirements of law, the practical reality is that the full board cannot, and is not expected to, undertake the

[24] See, for example, s. 8(8) of the BC PBSA and s. 22(8) of the PBA.

[25] See EPPA, s. 13(5).

[26] While the nature of the relationship between the corporation (as pension plan administrator) and plan members does not fall within one of the established categories of common law fiduciary relationships, the nature of the relationship is such that it may well meet the common law test for fiduciary duty set out in *Frame v. Smith*, [1987] 2 S.C.R. 99 and reiterated in *Hodgkinson v. Simms*, [1994] 3 S.C.R. 377.

administration of the pension plan and the investment of the pension fund. Indeed, the board may only meet quarterly, whereas pension plans require day-to-day oversight. Fortunately, the administrator has a broad power to delegate its powers and authorities with respect to the administration of a plan and the associated pension fund.[27]

The administrator must personally select any agents to assist it with the plan administration if it is satisfied that such agents are suitable to perform their mandate.[28] Where the agent is a third party service provider, the CAP Guidelines suggest that selection should be based on pre-established criteria that would be used consistently in a selection process. While the CAP Guidelines are directed to DC plans, the stated principles would arguably be equally applicable to DB pension plans. The criteria cited in the CAP Guidelines include the following:[29]

- professional training;
- experience;
- specialization in the type of service to be provided;
- the cost of service;
- understanding of pension legislation and other related rules;
- the consistency of service offered in all geographical areas in which plan members reside; and
- the quality, level, and continuity of services that are offered.

Where the third party service provider is being retained to provide investment education and advice to members of a DC pension plan, the CAP Guidelines suggest that the following factors also be considered:[30]

[27] Many pension statutes contain an express provision permitting the plan administrator to delegate administrative functions to an agent (see, for example, s. 8(7) of the BC PBSA and s. 22(5) of the PBA). However, some Pension Legislation (e.g., the PBSA and the EPPA) does not contain provisions that explicitly authorize a pension plan administrator to employ agents to assist it with its administrative duties. In such cases, it is generally accepted that, as a fiduciary, a pension plan administrator may (and indeed must, in certain circumstances) delegate administrative tasks to others, but it must diligently select and actively supervise those parties. In other words, while an administrator may delegate administrative tasks to others, it must do so prudently, and it cannot absolve itself of its legal responsibilities as the legal administrator of the plan (see, in support of this proposition, *McLellan Properties Ltd. v. Roberge*, [1947] S.C.R. 561 at 566–567, as cited in *Wagner v. Van Cleef*, [1991] O.J. No. 1777 at para. 34 (QL)). Furthermore, the plan administrator must continue to supervise the actions of any delegatee and the delegatee will be subject to the same standard of care (i.e., fiduciary duties) as the administrator.

[28] See, for example, s. 8(7) of the BC PBSA and s. 22(7) of the PBA.

[29] Guideline 2.1.3.

[30] Guideline 3.4.1.

- any real or perceived lack of independence of the service provider relative to other service providers, the corporation, and the plan members;
- any legal requirements that individuals must meet before they can provide investment advice (e.g., registration under applicable securities legislation); and
- any complaints filed against the service provider (whether against an individual or the firm) and any disciplinary actions that were taken.

The administrator must prudently and reasonably supervise all agents[31] to ensure that each agent exercises the care, diligence, and skill that a person of ordinary prudence would exercise in dealing with the property of another person.[32]

The administrator's obligation to supervise and monitor is also reflected in the CAP Guidelines. Specifically, Guideline 6.1 requires the periodic review of all service providers that are retained. When establishing criteria for such a review, the CAP Guidelines suggest that the criteria used to select the service provider should be considered.[33] If the service provider fails the review, the board will need to decide what action to take. In that regard, Guideline 6.1 suggests the following factors be considered by the board:

- the length of time the criteria have not been met;
- any complaints arising from plan members;
- the effect that taking such an action would have on plan members; and
- the availability of alternative service providers.

It is important to remember that a delegate (whether a corporation, individual, or committee) is not the legal administrator of a pension plan and thus, it has no direct authority over the pension plan or the investment of the plan's funds. Rather, the delegate is really an "agent" of the board, and the delegate's authority/mandate extends solely to what it has been delegated, together with any common law or statutory overlay of legal obligations.

---

[31] See, for example, s. 8(7) of the BC PBSA and s. 22(7) of the PBA.

[32] In those cases where the pension statute expressly authorizes the appointment of an agent, the statutes make it clear that the "fiduciary" obligations in the relevant statute apply to agents employed by the administrator. See, for example, s. 8(8) of the BC PBSA and s. 22(8) of the PBA.

[33] Guideline 6.1.

While the board may and should delegate some of its responsibilities for the administration of the pension plan and the pension fund, it cannot absolve itself of its legal responsibilities as the administrator of the pension plan.

V. Avoiding Role Confusion Through Plan Governance

In order to avoid role confusion, a corporation that sponsors a pension plan (regardless of its size) should establish and formalize a governance policy that will clearly identify the board's relevant responsibilities and the capacity in which it undertakes such responsibilities (i.e., as plan sponsor or plan administrator). It would also be advisable for a "pension plan governance manual" to be compiled, bringing together in one location all applicable plan documents, policies, terms of reference, agreements, and other relevant materials.[34]

There is no single correct governance structure for a pension plan in Canada. Similarly, there are no hard and fast rules that dictate which plan governance functions should be performed by any particular individual or committee within a particular corporate structure. Notwithstanding that certain best practices may be developed over time, the ultimate content of the governance structure and the allocation of roles and responsibilities in the structure will depend on the circumstances of the corporation and the pension plan. The key in developing the structure is to understand the factors at play and the reasons why certain industry practices may or may not be appropriate in the context in order to aid the corporation and the board in establishing a "due diligence" defence in the event of conflicts. Regardless of the form of governance structure that is implemented, the board must periodically review the pension governance procedures to assess their effectiveness and the board's performance.[35]

A board will usually delegate to a pension committee, management, and the employees of the corporation's human resources, finance, and legal departments certain tasks that relate to the management or administration of the plan. The board will usually also appoint external service providers, such as investment managers and record-keepers to whom authority will be delegated over certain aspects of the administration of the pension plan or the pension fund.

---

[34] Principle 8 of the CAPSA Governance Guidelines notes that "every pension plan needs documented processes and standards to enable compliance with legislative requirements".

[35] A regular review of plan governance is recommended in Principle 11 of the CAPSA Governance Guidelines.

The delegation of authority from the board to the pension committee would usually be set out in a board resolution. The delegation structure should also be described in the governance policy, together with a detailed description of the functions that are delegated to external service providers or advisors. Indeed, it is critical that all steps taken by the board be documented in the form of resolutions, reports, meeting minutes, written policies, etc. This procedure will assist the corporation in demonstrating that it met (or made every effort to meet) the applicable standard of care in connection with the operation of the pension plan in the event that there is litigation involving the plan or an investigation by a pension regulator.

As the pension committee will be vital to the pension governance system, it is important that care be taken when it is established. Ideally, members will have a variety of backgrounds and skill sets, including business, legal, investment, accounting, actuarial, and human resources skills. Training programs should be put in place to develop core competencies where they are lacking and to constantly update existing knowledge. Where the pension committee does not have all of these skills, outside advisors can and should be retained.

Care should also be taken to ensure that the committee is an effective and manageable size. A pension committee with too few members will likely be overburdened, while a committee with too many members will be ineffective.

The following list describes a possible allocation of responsibilities between the board, the pension committee, and management.

A. Board of Directors

- Will have the authority to terminate and to make significant amendments[36] to the pension plan and to all related funding, investment management, and other documents and agreements.
- Will be responsible for approving the general funding strategy for the pension plan.
- Will be responsible for describing and documenting the roles, responsibilities, and accountability of all participants in the pension plan governance process. Simply put, each delegate must know his or

[36] The adoption of any plan amendments that significantly affect plan liabilities or that reflect changes in the corporation's policy towards pension benefits should be made by the full board. The authority to make less significant amendments should be delegated to the pension committee, while the authority to make any amendments that are required to ensure legal compliance are often delegated to the chief administrative officers. Any plan changes that increase the total funding liabilities of a pension plan by one million dollars or more should be deemed to be a "significant" amendment. However, the board may find it appropriate to consider a lower threshold.

her duties, when the duties must be performed or accomplished, and to whom they should report on the performance of their duties.

- Will be responsible for approving the appointment and replacement of the pension fund auditors, pension fund investment managers, and pension fund custodian/trustee/insurance company.
- Will be responsible for appointing the members of the pension committee,[37] establishing their term of office,[38] and approving the terms of reference governing such a committee.
- Will delegate responsibilities for the overall monitoring of the pension fund and the plan administration to the pension committee, subject to the pension committee's duty to report periodically to the board and make recommendations to the board as appropriate.
- Will delegate to the pension committee the authority to establish and to amend the statement of investment policies and procedures for the pension plan.
- Will be responsible for approving or ratifying any decisions of the committee if it is considered necessary or desirable by the committee or the board.
- Will delegate to management (i.e., the chief executive officer) the power to amend the plan to ensure regulatory compliance as well as the responsibilities listed below in section C.
- Will assign responsibility for the day-to-day plan administration to personnel in the corporation's human resources department or to one or more third party service providers.
- Will establish a monitoring and reporting framework that specifies the major reports and documents that the board, the pension committee, and any other relevant agents and advisors will receive in order to fulfill their responsibilities for the management and administration of the pension plan.
- Will be responsible for reviewing the annual reports prepared in respect of the administration of the pension plan and the pension fund by the pension committee, officers, or employees of the corporation, the auditors to the plan, and any other agents and advisors.

---

[37] When it is establishing a pension committee, the board may want to consider requiring pension committee members to be independent.

[38] The board may wish to stagger the terms of pension committee members and vary their length to provide for continuity in the pension committee.

- Will be responsible for implementing appropriate controls and performance assessment mechanisms to ensure that all persons and entities with operational and oversight responsibilities act in accordance with the terms of the pension plan and any related documents (e.g., trust agreements, statement of investment policies and procedures, etc.) and with the applicable law.[39]

B. Pension Committee

- Will meet often enough to ensure that the pension plan is being well run. Members of the pension committee should be diligent and should attend meetings and devote sufficient time to familiarize themselves with the pension plan and with the various materials contained in the corporation's pension governance manual.
- Will be responsible for the overall monitoring of plan administration and for providing periodic reports, and if appropriate, recommendations, to the board. In this regard, the pension committee should monitor all documents that are required to be filed with the applicable regulatory authorities, such as annual returns, financial statements, actuarial valuations, and cost certificates, as required. While the pension committee is responsible for monitoring these tasks, it is important that it not get drawn into "micro-managing" operational matters that can be better performed by management, the corporation's human resources department, or external advisors and agents.
- Will have authority to establish the statement of investment policies and procedures for the plan and to make amendments to them.
- Will be responsible for the overall monitoring of fund administration, including fund investments, and for providing periodic reports, and if appropriate, recommendations to the board. In this regard, the pension committee should (i) monitor the calculation, remittance, and reconciliation of employee and employer contributions to the plan, (ii) monitor the investment performance of the fund's assets, (iii) monitor compliance with investment restrictions that are required by law and set out in the statement of investment policies and procedures, and (iv) monitor all fund transfers in connection with the pension plan.
- Will make recommendations to the board concerning the corporation's internal pension governance framework and the documents in the pension governance manual.

[39] See, for example, Principles 7 and 8 of the CAPSA Governance Guidelines.

- Will consider amendments to the pension plan and make recommendations in respect thereof to the board.
- Will be responsible for such other specific fund and plan administration matters as the board delegates to the pension committee from time to time.

C. Management

- Will be responsible for providing the pension committee with periodic reports, and where appropriate, recommendations on plan administration issues.
- Will be responsible for reporting and making recommendations to the board and the pension committee, as directed and as appropriate, with respect to all aspects of fund administration.
- Will be responsible for making plan amendments to ensure compliance with regulations and for reporting on any such amendments to the pension committee.
- Will be responsible for monitoring fund administration services and investment performance and for reporting on them to the pension committee and making recommendations, if appropriate, with respect to such matters.
- Will be responsible for other such specific fund administration matters as are from time to time delegated to management by the board or matters which the pension committee may assign to management.

While delegation is permitted and appropriate in various circumstances, the board should have an accompanying system for monitoring and supervising its delegates, both internal and external, to ensure that they are fulfilling their legal duties. In accordance with the CAPSA Governance Guidelines, performance measures for monitoring and evaluating the performance of all parties who have decision-making authority *vis-a-vis* the registered pension plan should be established.[40]

As part of the overall governance process, reporting channels between the various persons involved in the administration of the pension plan and the investment of pension plan assets should be established in order to ensure the effective and timely transmission of relevant and accurate information. In this regard, it is important for the board and/or the pension committee to receive accurate and complete information from any third party service providers that are retained by the board or the committee. In

---

[40] See Principle 4 of the CAPSA Governance Guidelines.

order to receive such information, contracts may require that the third party report to the appropriate person or committee on audit rights and enforcement mechanisms in cases where the third party fails to meet its reporting obligations.

Another key concept in pension governance is the initial and ongoing education of the individuals who are involved in the governance process.[41] Such individuals must ensure that they understand and appreciate both the plan administrator's roles and responsibilities and their own in the management and administration of the pension plan, as well as the legal, regulatory, and financial environment in which the plan operates in order to ensure that the plan administrator's fiduciary role is fulfilled. Different participants in the structure will have different educational needs to fit their roles, and ongoing skills and knowledge assessment should form part of the overall governance procedures.

Finally, as governance best practices constantly evolve, the board should periodically review and assess the effectiveness of its pension governance procedures.[42] The board may wish to seek assistance from outside consultants and legal advisors to assist it with the review and to ensure impartiality.

VI. Addressing Conflicts of Interest through Plan Governance

Pension Legislation prohibits a pension plan administrator from knowingly permitting its interests to conflict with its duties and powers in respect of the pension fund or from receiving any benefit other than a pension benefit, a refund of excess contributions, and reasonable fees and expenses related to the administration of the plan, provided such fees and expenses are permitted by the common law and relate to the administration of the plan.[43] Common law fiduciary duties impose a similar obligation on the plan administrator to avoid any real or perceived conflicts of interest.[44] It should be noted that Pension Legislation usually contains limited exceptions to the statutory conflict-of-interest prohibitions where the pension plan is jointly-governed or a multi-employer pension plan. See, for example, PBA Regulations, ss. 49(1) and (2).

---

[41] See Principle 5 of the CAPSA Governance Guidelines.

[42] See Principle 11 of the CAPSA Governance Guidelines.

[43] See, for example, PBSA, ss. 8(6)–11; BC PBSA, ss. 8(9) and (10); EPPA Reg., s. 54(1); PBA, s. 22(4).

[44] See, for example, *Moffat v. Wetstein* (1996), 135 D.L.R. (4th) 298 (Ont. Gen. Div).

The corporation's dual role as plan sponsor and plan administrator is the source of potentially significant conflicts of interest. Good pension governance involves not only addressing such conflicts of interest but also anticipating their existence.

A written code of conduct and control mechanism for conflicts of interest should be established as part of any governance process, and it should be included in the plan's governance manual.[45] Such a code should anticipate and identify the situations in which conflicts may arise, and it should also set out the necessary response(s) for reporting and otherwise resolving any conflicts that occur. This code of conduct should be made available to each individual who is involved in pension administration, particularly those involved in pension fund investment, and it should be followed as a matter of practice. To ensure that the code of conduct is effective, the board should also establish a review process.[46]

The board must ensure that all conflicts are identified, disclosed, and appropriately addressed. The typical approach in the pension context to dealing with a conflict of interest would be to have the relevant director disclose to the board the nature and extent of his or her interest and to thereafter abstain from the deliberations and decision-making with respect to the matter giving rise to such a conflict.

The board should also maintain a register of any real or perceived conflicts of interest. The register should include a description of each conflict of interest, the director to whom the conflict of interest applied, the date upon which the conflict of interest arose, and the manner in which the conflict of interest was dealt with. (Directors and officers must also comply with the interested director and conflict of interest provisions prescribed under the corporation's governing statute, for example, s. 120 of the CBCA. See also Chapter 2, "The Duties of Directors".)

In the case of a federally regulated pension plan where the corporation has a "material conflict of interest" between its roles as plan sponsor and plan administrator, the corporation must declare this conflict to the plan members, and it must act in the best interests of the plan's members.[47]

---

[45] See, for example, Principle 10 of the CAPSA Governance Guidelines. The CAPSA Governance Guidelines suggest that the code of conduct address both real conflicts and the appearance of conflicts.

[46] See, for example, Principle 10 of the CAPSA Governance Guidelines.

[47] See PBSA, s. 8(10).

VII. Consequences of Breach of Responsibility

What remedies are available when the board fails to fulfil its responsibilities as the plan's administrator?

As a starting point, Pension Legislation typically provides the applicable pension regulator with the power to require an administrator or any other person to take or refrain from taking any action if, on reasonable and probable grounds, the regulator believes that (i) the plan or fund is not being administrated in accordance with Pension Legislation or the terms of the plan; (ii) the plan does not comply with Pension Legislation; or (iii) the administrator or any other person is contravening a requirement of Pension Legislation.[48]

A second way of dealing with a plan administrator who fails to fulfil its responsibilities is the use of the offence provisions of the relevant Pension Legislation. When a corporation is guilty of an offence under Pension Legislation, its directors may be criminally charged under the relevant pension statute if they directed, authorized, assented to, acquiesced in, or participated in the contravention of the relevant statute by the corporation. Depending on the Pension Legislation, a director who is found guilty can be liable for a fine of up to $100,000 for a first offence or to imprisonment for a term not exceeding twelve (12) months, or to both.[49] In many jurisdictions, Pension Legislation specifically provides that a director will be guilty of an offence in such circumstances, whether or not the corporation has been prosecuted or convicted.

Pension Legislation may also subject a director of a corporation to personal liability for the obligations of the corporation to contribute or remit funds to the pension plan where the corporation has been convicted of an offence that is related to the failure to make payment or remit payment.[50] This obligation, if it exists, can be quite substantial.

In addition, directors who fail to fulfill their obligations relating to pension plans may be held liable for the breach of their fiduciary duty of care or under the oppression remedy in the corporation's governing business corporations statute.[51]

---

[48] See, for example, PBSA, s. 11; BC PBSA, s. 71; EPPA, s. 8; PBA, s. 87.

[49] See, for example, PBSA, s. 38 (maximum fine of $100,000 for an individual; jail term of up to twelve months is possible for a person); BC PBSA, s. 72 (maximum penalty is $25,000 for an individual); EPPA, s. 91 (maximum penalty is $100,000 for individual; maximum penalty for a person fraudulently obtaining benefits is $15,000); and PBA, s. 110 (maximum fine is $100,000 for first conviction, $200,000 for subsequent convictions).

[50] See, for example, PBA, s. 110(4).

[51] See, for example, ss. 122 and 241 of the CBCA.

APPENDIX I

Administrators' Duties, Powers, and Statutory Liability under Canadian Pension Legislation

THE PASSAGES SET OUT BELOW ARE SUMMARIES ONLY AND THE READER MUST REFER TO THE SPECIFIC STATUTE FOR A COMPLETE STATEMENT OF THE BOARD'S LEGAL RESPONSIBILITIES AND OF THE STATUTORY CONTEXT IN WHICH THOSE LEGAL RESPONSIBILITIES ARISE.

Jurisdiction	Administrator's Duty	Standard of Care	Power of Delegation	Liability for Offences
Canada (Federal) *Pension Benefits Standards Act, 1985* ("PBSA")	An administrator must administer the plan and fund as trustee for the employer, current and former members, and any other person entitled to benefits or refunds under the plan: s. 8(3).	In plan and fund administration, the administrator must exercise the degree of care that a person of ordinary prudence would use in dealing with the property of another: s. 8(4). An administrator must invest fund assets in accordance with the Regulations and in the manner a reasonable and prudent person would apply in respect to a pension fund investment portfolio: s. 8(4.1). An administrator must employ the particular level of knowledge and skill he or she possesses (or ought to possess) by reason of his or her business or profession in the administration of the plan or fund: s. 8(5).	Not addressed.	Every person who contravenes the PBSA or Regulations (and every employer who fails to remit amounts due to the fund) is guilty of an offence: s. 38(1). An individual who commits an offence is liable to a maximum fine of $100,000 or a maximum 12-month jail term. A corporation is liable to a maximum fine of $500,000: s. 38(1.1).

Jurisdiction	Administrator's Duty	Standard of Care	Power of Delegation	Liability for Offences
Alberta *Employment Pension Plans Act* ("EPPA")	An administrator must administer the plan in accordance with the EPPA and ensure the plan (including its contractual provisions) complies with the EPPA: ss. 6(1) and (2). An administrator must ensure that any funding agreement for the plan does not contain any provisions prohibited by the EPPA: s. 6(6).	An administrator stands in a fiduciary capacity to current and former members and others entitled to benefits: s. 6(5).	Not addressed.	A person who contravenes the EPPA is guilty of an offence and liable to a maximum fine of $100,000: s. 92(1). Where a corporation contravenes an offence provision, any officer, director, or corporate agent who authorized, participated, or acquiesced in the contravention is a party to and guilty of the offence and is separately liable for the penalty provided: s. 92(2).
British Columbia *Pension Benefits Standards Act* ("BC PBSA")	An administrator must administer the plan in accordance with the BC PBSA and Regulations and ensure the plan (including its contractual provisions) complies with the BC PBSA and Regulations: ss. 8(1) and (2).	In administering a plan, the administrator must act honestly, in good faith in the best interest of members, former members, and other persons to whom a fiduciary duty is owed, and must exercise the care, diligence, and skill a person of ordinary prudence would exercise in dealing with the property of another: s. 8(5).	An administrator who employs an agent must be satisfied of such agent's qualification to perform assigned duties and must carry out such supervision of the agent as is prudent and reasonable: s. 8(7).	A person who contravenes the BC PBSA or Regulations commits an offence and is liable to a maximum $25,000 fine. A corporation that commits an offence is liable to a maximum $100,000 fine: ss. 72(1) and (2).

Jurisdiction	Administrator's Duty	Standard of Care	Power of Delegation	Liability for Offences
				Where a corporation commits an offence under the BC PBSA or Regulations, an officer, director, or agent who authorized, acquiesced, or participated in such offence is liable for a maximum $25,000 fine: s. 72(3).
Manitoba *Pension Benefits Act* ("Man PBA")	Not addressed.	In administering the plan (and administering and investing a fund), an administrator must exercise the care, diligence, and skill that a person of ordinary prudence would exercise in dealing with the property of another: s. 28.1(2). An administrator must use all relevant knowledge and skill he or she possesses (or ought to possess) by reason of his or her profession, business or calling in administering a plan (and administering and investing a fund): s. 28.1(3).	An administrator, in administering a plan (and administering and investing a fund), may employ or appoint agent(s) where it is reasonable and prudent to do so in the circumstances: ss. 28.1(6). An administrator must personally select such agent, be satisfied of the agent's suitability to perform the acts assigned, and carry out such supervision of the agent as is prudent and reasonable: s. 28.1(7).	Every person who contravenes the Man PBA or Regulations is guilty of an offence and liable to a minimum $2000 and maximum $100,000 fine: s. 38(1). A person convicted of an offence (in respect of which plan money is lost or owing) shall be ordered to make restitution to the plan in the amount of money lost or owing: s. 38(2). Corporate directors, officers, or agents who participated or acquiesced in an offence are liable to punishment for such offence (whether or not the corporation is convicted): s. 38(3).

Jurisdiction	Administrator's Duty	Standard of Care	Power of Delegation	Liability for Offences
New Brunswick *Pension Benefits Act* ("NB PBA")	An administrator shall ensure that the plan and the fund are administered in accordance with the NB PBA and Regulations: s. 14(1).	In administering and investing the fund, an administrator shall exercise the care, diligence, and skill a person of ordinary prudence would exercise in dealing with the property of another: s. 17(1). In administering a plan (and administering and investing a fund), an administrator must use all relevant knowledge and skill he or she possesses (or ought to possess) by reason of his or her profession, business, or calling: s. 17(2).	In administering a plan (and administering and investing a fund), an administrator may employ agent(s) where it is reasonable and prudent in the circumstances to do so: s. 18(1). An administrator must personally select an agent, be satisfied of the agent's suitability, and carry out such supervision of the agent as is prudent and reasonable: s. 18(2).	A person who violates any provision of the NB PBA or Regulations is guilty of an offence: s. 88.1. In a prosecution under the NB PBA, the act or omission of an employee shall be deemed to be that of the employer unless the person exercising supervisory responsibility over such employee took all reasonable care to avoid such act or omission: s. 89.
Newfoundland and Labrador *Pension Benefits Act* ("Nfld PBA")	An administrator must administer the plan and the fund and file all required documents in accordance with the Nfld PBA: s. 14(2).	An administrator shall administer the plan and the fund as a trustee for the employer, members, former members and other persons beneficially entitled: s. 14(1).	Not addressed.	Every person who contravenes the Nfld PBA or Regulations is guilty of an offence and is liable to a maximum $10,000 fine and/or imprisonment to a maximum of six months: s. 76.

Jurisdiction	Administrator's Duty	Standard of Care	Power of Delegation	Liability for Offences
				Where a corporation is convicted of an offence contrary to the Nfld PBA, each director and each corporate officer, employee, or agent who was wholly or partially responsible for, or acquiesced in, the conduct giving rise to the offence, is guilty of an offence and liable to a maximum $10,000 fine and/or six month's imprisonment: s. 75(2). A person convicted of an offence in relation to a failure to submit or make payments to a fund or insurance company may, in addition to the fine imposed, be ordered to pay any amount not submitted or paid: s. 75(3).
Nova Scotia *Pension Benefits Act, 1987* ("NS PBA")	An administrator must ensure that the plan and the fund are administered in accordance with the NS PBA and Regulations: s. 26(1).	In pension fund administration and investment, an administrator must exercise the care, diligence, and skill that a person of ordinary prudence would exercise in dealing with the property of another: s. 29(1).	An administrator may employ agent(s) for the plan administration and investment, where it is reasonable and prudent in the circumstances to do so: s. 29(4).	Every person who contravenes the NS PBA or Regulations is guilty of an offence and is liable (on 1st offence) to a maximum $10,000 fine: ss. 99 and 100.

Jurisdiction	Administrator's Duty	Standard of Care	Power of Delegation	Liability for Offences
		In administering a plan (and administering and investing a fund), an administrator must use all relevant knowledge and skill that he or she possesses (or ought to possess) by reason of his or her profession, business, or calling: s. 29(2).	An administrator must (i) personally select the agent, (ii) be satisfied of the agent's suitability, and (iii) carry out prudent and reasonable supervision: s. 29(5).	Where a corporation is convicted of an offence, each director, and each corporate officer, employee, or agent wholly or partially responsible for the conduct giving rise to the offence, is guilty of an offence and liable to a maximum $10,000 fine, subject to such person satisfying the court that he or she took all reasonable care to prevent the commission of the offence: s. 100(3). A person so convicted in relation to a failure to submit or make payments to a fund or insurance company may, in addition to the fine imposed, be ordered to pay any amount not submitted or paid: s. 100(4).
Ontario *Pension Benefits Act* ("PBA")	An administrator must ensure that both the plan and the fund are administered in accordance with the PBA and Regulations: s. 19(1).	In administering and investing the fund, an administrator must exercise the care, diligence, and skill that a person of ordinary prudence would exercise in dealing with the property of another: s. 22(1).	An administrator may employ agent(s) for plan administration or pension fund administration and investment where it is reasonable and prudent in the circumstances to do so: s. 22(5).	Every director, officer, official, or agent is guilty of an offence for (i) causing or participating in a contravention of the PBA or Regulations, or (ii) failing to take all reasonable care to prevent a contradiction of the PBA or Regulations: s. 110(2).

Jurisdiction	Administrator's Duty	Standard of Care	Power of Delegation	Liability for Offences
		In administering a plan (and administering and investing a fund), an administrator must use all knowledge and skill he or she possesses (or ought to possess) by reason of his or her profession, business, or calling: s. 22(2).	An administrator must (i) personally select the agent, (ii) be satisfied of the agent's suitability, and (iii) carry out prudent and reasonable supervision: s. 22(7).	Each such person is liable (on 1st offence) to a maximum $100,000 fine: s. 110(3). Each such person may also be ordered to pay any amount that was not submitted or paid to the pension fund or insurer: s. 110(4).
Quebec *Supplemental Pension Plans Act* ("SPPA")	Not addressed.	The pension committee (administrator) shall act in the capacity of a trustee (s. 150) and shall (i) exercise the prudence, diligence, and skill that a reasonable person would exercise in similar circumstances, and (ii) act honestly in good faith in the interest of plan members and beneficiaries: s. 151.	Subject to limitations and prohibitions in the pension plan, a pension committee may delegate all or part of its powers to a third person. Such person may sub-delegate all or part of such delegated powers: s. 152.	Not addressed.

Jurisdiction	Administrator's Duty	Standard of Care	Power of Delegation	Liability for Offences
		In administering the plan, members of a pension committee shall use all relevant knowledge and skill they possess (or ought to possess) by reason of their profession or business: s. 151.	Provided it was authorized to so delegate, a pension committee is only accountable for the care with which it selected and instructed its delegatee: s. 154.	However, unless the directors of a corporate employer (who is a party to a pension plan) have exercised the prudence, diligence, and care that a reasonable person would have exercised in comparable circumstances, such directors shall be solidarily liable for up to six months' contributions that became due but were not paid: s. 52.
Saskatchewan *Pension Benefits Act, 1992* ("Sask PBA")	An administrator shall administer the plan in accordance with the Sask PBA and Regulations and the terms and conditions of the plan: s. 11(1).	The administrator of a plan (i) stands in a fiduciary relationship to members, former members, and beneficiaries of the plan, (ii) holds in trust any fund established or contract arising from the plan, (iii) must act in good faith in the best interests of members, former members, and beneficiaries of the plan, and (iv) must not prefer the interests of one person beneficially entitled over the interests of another person so entitled.	Not addressed.	A person who contravenes the Sask PBA or Regulations is guilty of an offence and liable to a maximum fine of $100,000: s. 70(1).

Jurisdiction	Administrator's Duty	Standard of Care	Power of Delegation	Liability for Offences
				A corporate officer, director, or agent who participates or acquiesces in the commission of an offence is guilty of an offence and liable to the foregoing fine: s. 70(2). An employer who is convicted of an offence shall, in addition to the applicable fine, be ordered to pay all amounts that the employer is found liable to remit: s. 70(3).

CHAPTER 11

REGULATORY LIABILITIES

Scores of federal and provincial statutes impose liability on directors of corporations.[1] Most of these potential liabilities flow from obligations under regulatory statutes that are quite clear. As such, they create few difficulties for careful and well-informed directors. But for other kinds of liabilities, directors must be especially alert to the operation of legal rules that make them liable for the conduct of others, including the corporation. As discussed in Chapter 2, "The Duties of Directors", the most effective armour against liability is the exercise of diligence, including the awareness of direc-

[1] See Appendices I–IV at the end of this Chapter for a summary of directors' and officers' liability under federal, Alberta, British Columbia and Ontario statutes. Note that these summaries include statutes which the majority of corporations will be subject to but should not be viewed as a comprehensive list.

tors' and corporations' legal obligations. This Chapter explains how those obligations expose directors to personal liability.

Directors' regulatory liability takes two main forms: direct liability and indirect liability. Direct liability refers to situations where a statute imposes a specific obligation to do something (such as make a report or keep certain records) or to refrain from doing something (such as discharging an effluent or overloading a vehicle). Persons, including directors, who fail to act accordingly may be liable for an offence under the particular statute.

Indirect liability clauses make directors liable for the corporation's non-compliance with a statute. Directors may be prosecuted along with, or separately from, the corporation for something that the corporation did, or failed to do, in violation of a statute.[2]

It is important for a prudent director to be aware of the following:

- general rules of regulatory liability, which will be discussed below in section I;
- specific directors' obligations set out in general business corporations and securities statutes, such as the *Canada Business Corporations Act* and the Ontario *Securities Act*, and in the statutes that may apply to the particular business activities of the corporation, such as the *Ontario Water Resources Act* or the *Pesticides Act*;[3] and
- the rules under which directors can be made liable for the acts of the corporation, which will be discussed below in sections II and III.

I. General Rules of Regulatory Liability

Before discussing the specific forms of liability to which directors are exposed, the basic rules of liability that apply in the regulatory area should be explained.

In the prosecution of any offence, there are certain ingredients or elements of the offence that the prosecution must prove beyond a reasonable doubt[4] before the defendant can be convicted in a court. If the prosecution cannot prove beyond a reasonable doubt that the defendant breached the law, the defendant will be entitled to an acquittal. Depending

[2] *R. v. Fell* (1981), 34 O.R. (2d) 665; 64 C.C.C. (2d) 456 (C.A.).

[3] R.S.C. 1985, c. C-44 ("CBCA"); R.S.O. 1990, c. S.5 ("OSA"); R.S.O. 1990, c. O.40; R.S.O. 1990, c. P.11.

[4] This standard may be reduced (i.e., to a balance of probabilities) in specific contexts, such as in relation to matters determined by an administrative tribunal. For example, violations of the *Aeronautics Act*, R.S.C. 1985, c. A-2, as amended, prosecuted before the Civil Aviation Tribunal, must be proved on the balance of probabilities.

on the kind of offence, the prosecution may also have to prove that the defendant acted negligently or deliberately violated the law.

The elements of an offence fall into two broad categories:

- those representing the physical aspect of the defendant's conduct; and
- those representing the defendant's blameworthiness, or fault, for the conduct.

The physical element of an offence is the actual conduct that is prohibited by a statute or by regulations. "Conduct" may mean doing something that the law forbids (sometimes called an "act of commission") or failing to do something that the law requires (sometimes called an "act of omission"). In addition, the physical element of the offence may refer to the circumstances under which the conduct took place. The physical elements generally can be determined from the actual wording of the offence. For example, for the offence of bid rigging under the *Competition Act*,[5] the physical element is the submission of a tender that has been arrived at under an agreement or arrangement with other bidders.

The fault element of an offence is often the mental state of the defendant at the point in time when the prohibited conduct (i.e., the physical element) was carried out. There are various kinds of mental states that the law recognizes as blameworthy. They include intention, purposefulness, willfulness, knowledge, and recklessness. These states are subjective states of mind of the defendant. In the example of the offence of bid rigging, the fault element is an intention to enter into an agreement with other bidders. For most regulatory offences, however, proof of the defendant's mental state is not necessary.

Where proof of a particular mental state is not required for a conviction, the prosecution may instead have to prove that the defendant acted negligently; in other words, that the defendant acted in a manner that was unreasonable in the circumstances. Negligence is not considered to be a mental state, since it does not involve the defendant's subjective awareness. Rather, the determination of negligent conduct is an assessment of whether the defendant's conduct met the standard of the reasonable person.[6]

There are three general categories of offences recognized in Canadian law:

- absolute liability offences,

---

[5] R.S.C. 1985, c. C-34, s. 47.

[6] See the discussion of absolute liability and strict liability offences, below.

- strict liability offences, and
- offences requiring proof of fault.

These offences differ in the elements that must be proved in order for the prosecution to succeed.

A. Absolute Liability

An absolute liability offence is an offence for which the prosecution need only prove the physical elements. In other words, the prosecution must simply show that the defendant carried out the conduct that was prohibited by a statute or regulation. It need not prove that the defendant had a blameworthy state of mind or even that the defendant was negligent. The defendant has few available defences to an absolute liability offence. Of course, the defendant can always introduce evidence that the prohibited conduct never took place. If the defendant raises a reasonable doubt about the commission of the conduct, he or she will be entitled to an acquittal.

Absolute liability offences are rare. One example of such an offence is carrying a load in excess of the permissible weight limit, contrary to the Ontario *Highway Traffic Act*.[7] Courts are reluctant to find that an offence is one of absolute liability, since defendants may be convicted even when their conduct may be justified or excusable under the circumstances.[8] Only if the legislation clearly indicates that an offence is one of absolute liability will courts recognize it as such. Where there is any doubt as to whether the legislator intended to create an absolute liability offence, courts will err on the side of caution and treat the offence as one of strict liability (and as such, permit the defendant a defence of due diligence).

B. Strict Liability

As with absolute liability offences, the focus in strict liability offences is on the physical elements of the offence: the actual conduct of the defendant. The prosecution does not have to prove that the defendant had a blameworthy state of mind.

---

[7] R.S.O. 1990, c. H.8, s. 99. Note, however, that the Ontario Court of Appeal in *R. v. Nickel City Transport (Sudbury) Ltd.* (1993), 14 O.R. (3d) 115 was divided on the question as to whether this offence was one of strict liability or absolute liability.

[8] The courts have found that absolute liability offences punishable by imprisonment are contrary to the principles of fundamental justice under s. 7 of the *Charter of Rights and Freedoms*, Part I of the *Constitution Act*, 1982, being Schedule B of the *Canada Act 1982* (U.K.), 1982, c. 11: *Reference Re s. 94(2) of the Motor Vehicle Act (B.C.)*, [1985] 2 S.C.R. 486. In *Nickel City Transport (Sudbury) Ltd., ibid.*, Justice Arbour held that the imposition of a fine for an absolute liability offence also violates the principles of fundamental justice where imprisonment is a possible consequence of nonpayment of the fine. The reasoning underlying these decisions is that a person should not be imprisoned unless there has been a showing of blameworthiness or fault on the person's part.

However, strict liability offences differ significantly from absolute liability offences. The defendant can raise defences that, if supported by sufficient evidence, will result in an acquittal. The most common defence is "due diligence". The defendant will be acquitted if he or she shows that the commission of the offence was the result of a reasonable mistake or that reasonable efforts were taken to avoid the commission of the prohibited conduct.[9] If the defendant raises this defence, the prosecution will have an opportunity to show that the defendant in fact acted negligently; such negligence is just the opposite of due diligence.

Strict liability offences are by far the largest group of offences in federal and provincial statutes. If an offence is not clearly an absolute liability offence or an offence for which proof of fault is required (which is discussed under the next heading), courts are likely to view it as a strict liability offence.

C. Offences Requiring Proof of Fault

In this group of offences are crimes and other offences that involve more than just the failure to comply with legal standards. Most crimes are contained in the *Criminal Code*.[10] However, other federal statutes may also include crimes or they may create offences that specifically require proof of a fault element.[11] Provincial statutes may also create offences that require proof of fault. Some common examples of offences in this category are willfully obstructing an inspector or knowingly making a false statement in a required report.[12]

---

[9] See, for example, the discussion in Chapter 12, "Preparing For and Avoiding Calamity: Some Areas of Practical Concern for Directors", of *R. v. Bata Industries Ltd. et al.* (1992), 9 O.R. (3d) 329 (Ont. Ct. Prov. Div.). See also *R. v. Sault Ste. Marie* (1978), 85 D.L.R. (3d) 161 (S.C.C.); A. Hutchinson, "Sault Ste. Marie, *Mens Rea* and the Halfway House: Public Welfare Offences Get a Home of Their Own" (1979), 17 O.H.L.J. 415.

[10] R.S.C. 1985, c. C-46.

[11] Examples include the provisions in the *Competition Act*, R.S.C. 1985, c. C-34, as amended, ss. 45 and 47, dealing with bid-rigging or price fixing. Penalties include a fine "in the discretion of the court", or imprisonment for up to five years, or both.

[12] For example, Ontario *Business Corporations Act*, R.S.O. 1990, c. B.16 ("OBCA"), s. 256 (misrepresentation or false statements); OSA, s. 122 (misrepresentation, false statements, failure to comply); *Canada Petroleum Resources Act*, R.S.C., 1985, c. 36 (2nd Supp.), s. 19 (failure to carry out instructions of inspector, willful delays or obstruction of inspector). Penalties under the OSA, for example, include fines of up to $1 million or imprisonment for a term of not more than two years, or both.

D. The Burden of Proof

The prosecution's burden of proof is most easily understood as the "flip side" of the presumption of innocence. A person is presumed to be innocent until the contrary is proved; the burden falls on the prosecution to bring forward the proof of guilt.

Exactly what the prosecution has to prove will vary from case to case. The prosecution will have to prove the elements of the offence, as they are set out in the statute or regulation creating it. The prosecution's burden will also vary with the class of offence; that is, whether it is an offence of absolute liability or strict liability or whether proof of fault is required.

For absolute liability offences, the prosecution must prove beyond a reasonable doubt that the defendant engaged in the unlawful conduct (that is, the physical elements of the offence). It will not have to prove that the violator had a blameworthy state of mind or that the defendant was negligent. If the defendant offers evidence showing that the prohibited conduct never took place, the prosecution will have the burden of rebutting or disproving that evidence. At the end of the day, the court will have to be satisfied beyond a reasonable doubt that the defendant contravened the law before the defendant will be convicted.

For strict liability offences, the prosecution will again have to prove beyond a reasonable doubt that the defendant engaged in the unlawful conduct (the physical elements). It does not have to prove that the defendant had a blameworthy state of mind or that the defendant was negligent. As with absolute liability offences, if the defendant disputes the evidence related to the physical elements, the prosecution will have the burden of persuading the court beyond a reasonable doubt that the conduct took place.

If the defendant enters a defence of due diligence in a strict liability case, the defendant then has the burden of proving that defence to the court. The defence does not, however, have to be proved beyond a reasonable doubt. To succeed on the defence, the defendant must offer enough proof to persuade the court that it was more likely than not ("on the balance of probabilities") that the defendant acted with reasonable care in the circumstances. In response to this defence, the prosecution may try to show that the opposite occurred; that is, that the defendant acted negligently. The prosecution does not have to prove negligence beyond a reasonable doubt. Rather, to succeed, it must simply offer sufficient evidence to show that the balance of probabilities is in favour of negligence, not of due diligence.

Crimes or other offences that include a fault requirement in their definition put the heaviest burden of proof on the prosecution. The prosecution must prove both the physical and the fault elements beyond a reasonable doubt. If the defendant merely raises a reasonable doubt about either of these two issues, he or she will be entitled to an acquittal. The same is true for any defences the defendant may enter, such as mistake, necessity, or accident. The defendant does not have to prove a defence to a crime or offence with a fault requirement. If there is sufficient evidence to create a reasonable doubt about the defendant's liability, the result will be an acquittal.[13]

II. Direct Liabilities

There are two kinds of direct liabilities that affect directors. The first one results from failing to comply with statutory obligations or prohibitions that are imposed specifically on directors. Many of these kinds of liabilities are discussed in other Chapters that deal with specific directors' responsibilities. For example, directors are forbidden to engage in "insider trading"; that is, trading in securities on the basis of material information that is not publicly known.[14]

The other form of direct liability arises where statutes impose a general obligation that has a particular significance for directors because of the position they occupy in the corporation. Examples of this form of liability include making a false statement in a prospectus in violation of the Ontario *Securities Act*[15] or failing to provide the federal Minister of the Environment with requested information, contrary to the *Canadian Environmental Protection Act*.[16]

Although there are numerous federal and provincial statutory provisions that set out offences for which directors may be held directly liable, this form of liability should cause them little difficulty if they take steps to make sure that their obligations are met under the particular regulatory statutes that apply to their corporations. In many cases, liability relates to conduct that is clearly improper, such as filing fraudulent or misleading information with a regulatory authority.

In other cases, the liability relates to very specific forms of conduct that the well-informed director can readily carry out or avoid, as the case may be.

---

[13] There are two exceptions to this general rule: the defences of mental disorder and extreme intoxication must be proved by the defendant on the balance of probabilities.

[14] See, e.g., CBCA, ss. 131(4); OSA, s. 76(1); and Chapter 7, "Corporate Finance".

[15] *Supra* note 3, s. 118(1)(*b*).

[16] S.C. 1999, c. 33, s. 273.

Examples include avoiding giving undue preference to a creditor, contrary to the *Insurance Companies Act*,[17] making sure that the conditions of an approval given under the *Environmental Assessment Act*[18] are respected, or refraining from insider trading.[19]

In other words, the risk of direct liability can be readily managed and avoided by efforts to ascertain the conduct that is expected of the director and by putting measures in place to ensure that statutory obligations are met.

In addition, the vast majority of direct liabilities take the form of strict liability offences. As discussed above, this means that, in most cases, directors will have a defence of due diligence available to them. Thus, the standard that is expected of directors in this area, as in others, is a standard of reasonableness. The director is expected to take reasonable steps to prevent the occurrence of conduct that amounts to a violation of a federal or provincial statute. Therefore, directors who adopt appropriate compliance measures will be in a good position to answer a charge in the event that a statutory violation occurs.[20]

III. Indirect Liabilities

Indirect liabilities are liabilities that are imposed on directors for unlawful acts of the corporation. To understand this form of liability, one has to start with an appreciation of how corporations themselves may be found to have committed an offence. Under current Canadian law, corporations are liable for offences committed by their "directing minds".[21] Directing minds include those with decision-making authority in the corporation, such as directors, managers, superintendents, or others to whom authority has been delegated. If a "directing mind" of the corporation commits an offence in the course of his or her duties, the corporation itself may also be prosecuted and convicted of an offence.

Thus, situations where directors may be indirectly liable for an offence that was committed by their corporation may arise when some other "directing mind" (i.e., another director or senior officer) has committed an offence in the course of his or her duties. It should be noted that proposals to broaden corporate liability are made from time to time. Prudent directors

---

[17] S.C. 1991, c. 47, s. 705(2).

[18] R.S.O. 1990, c. E.18, s. 38.

[19] Contrary to the OSA, *supra* note 3, s. 76.

[20] See Chapter 12, "Preparing For and Avoiding Calamity: Some Areas of Practical Concern for Directors".

[21] *R. v. Canadian Dredge and Dock*, [1985] 1 S.C.R. 662.

should keep abreast of these developments because they may expand the basis on which corporations may be held liable for offences. For example, the federal Department of Justice has considered proposals that would alter and expand the basis on which corporations may be held liable for offences. Under discussion are proposals that would impose liability on the corporation in situations where there was collective responsibility on the part of individuals within the firm for the offence or where a corporate culture of non-compliance existed within the firm.[22]

For strict liability and absolute liability offences, the corporation will be liable for the acts of any persons within the corporation, including employees. In the case of strict liability offences, however, the corporation may raise a defence of due diligence by showing that its directing minds made a reasonable mistake of fact in leading to the violation or that they made reasonable efforts to ensure that the violation did not take place.

Directors will be liable for violations that were committed by the corporation if they somehow participate in, or are a party to, those offences. This indirect liability of directors for regulatory offences is governed by general rules of participation in offences provided in the *Criminal Code*[23] and from special rules of liability contained in other statutes. In the former case, directors are treated no differently than other participants in offences. In the latter case, directors and officers (and often agents) receive special attention.

A. Indirect Liability Pursuant to the Criminal Code

In s. 21 of the *Criminal Code* of Canada, the general rule for determining when a person can be held liable as a party to an offence is set out. Subsection 21(1) provides:

> Everyone is a party to an offence who
>
> (*a*) actually commits it;
>
> (*b*) does or omits to do anything for the purpose of aiding any person to commit it;
>
> (*c*) abets any person in committing it.

The provisions of the *Criminal Code* are relevant to regulatory liability, as the *Interpretation Act*[24] provides that the *Criminal Code* applies to all

[22] See Canada, Department of Justice and James W. O'Reilly, *Toward a New General Part of the Criminal Code of Canada — Details on Reform Options* (December 1994), at 26–27.

[23] *Supra* note 10, s. 21.

[24] R.S.C. 1985, c. I-21, s. 34.

federal offences. Provincial offences statutes operate similarly and contain similarrules.[25]

Paragraphs 21(1)(*b*) and (*c*) of the *Criminal Code* are the most relevant for the purposes of directors' liability. These provisions apply to persons whose involvement in the offence is incidental to the activities of the principal perpetrator. The principal could be a corporation or another individual. Thus, these paragraphs apply to conduct on the part of directors and officers that furthers offences committed by the corporation or by any person within the corporation.

Liability as a party does not depend on the prosecution or conviction of the principal. In fact, a person may be convicted even if the principal could not be convicted.[26] This situation might happen when it is impossible to identify the individual within the corporation whose actions resulted in the release of a pollutant or where the actions were diffused among so many employees that it is difficult to establish the point of responsibility.

In essence, a person can be convicted as a party to something even if it turns out that the principal (for example, the corporation) cannot be convicted for that offence. Since the rules of participation in offences provided by the *Criminal Code* operate independently, there is no need for proof of the commission of the offence by the principal. Of course, there must still be evidence that an unlawful act was carried out.

The forms of conduct captured by paragraphs 21(1)(*b*) and (*c*) of the *Criminal Code* are the following:

- the doing of some act for the purpose of assisting another person to carry out the offence;
- the failure to do some act for the purpose of assisting another person to carry out the offence; and
- encouraging (abetting) someone to commit an offence.

These three ways of participating in another's offence require elaboration.

---

[25] See, e.g., s. 77 of the Ontario *Provincial Offences Act*, R.S.O. 1990, c. P.33.

[26] Section 23.1 of the *Criminal Code*, *supra* note 10, provides: "For greater certainty, sections 21 to 23 apply in respect of an accused notwithstanding the fact that the person whom the accused aids or abets, counsels or procures or receives, comforts or assists cannot be convicted of the offence."

Doing an Act

An act whose purpose is to assist in the commission of an offence is covered by s. 21(1)(*b*). Any positive act, including words or gestures, is sufficient to satisfy the physical requirement in this context.

The more difficult aspect of this form of involvement is the fault or blameworthiness element. The act must have been done "for the purpose" of aiding the commission of the offence. The act need not have been effective in order to be culpable. In other words, if a person does something he or she believes will assist in carrying out the offence, the fact that the act was of no help at all is irrelevant. The incompetent abettor may still be liable. At a minimum, however, proof is required that the accused intended to assist the principal in the commission of the offence. Proof may even be required that the very reason for the accused's action was to assist in the offence.[27]

As for directors, they could be held liable as parties to corporate offences under s. 21(1)(*b*) if they carried out an act for the purpose of assisting in the commission of an offence by the corporation. In other words, they would be liable if they assisted one of the other directing minds of the corporation to commit an offence. In addition, in relation to strict and absolute liability offences, they would be liable if they assisted anyone within the corporation in carrying out the offence. It must be shown that what they did was for the purpose of helping to accomplish the unlawful conduct.[28] For example, they would be liable if they purposely assisted one of the other directing minds of the corporation, such as another director or manager, to commit an offence.

For strict liability offences, the accused can be convicted if it is shown that the accused had knowledge of the circumstances constituting the offence and that the accused's actions furthered the commission of the offence.[29] Proof of knowledge of the offence would not be enough on its own to secure a conviction.[30]

---

[27] See E. Colvin, *Principles of Criminal Law*, 2nd ed. (Toronto: Carswell, 1991) at 373.

[28] *R. v. F.W. Woolworth Co. Ltd.* (1974), 3 O.R. (2d) 629 (C.A.).

[29] *Ibid.*; *R. v. Fell*, *supra* note 2.

[30] Compare this, however, to the situation under many regulatory statutes. See section B, "Indirect Liability Pursuant to Regulatory Statutes", and note 43, below.

Failing to Act

Generally speaking, the criminal law (unlike some regulatory statutes) punishes for an omission only where a person is under a duty to act.[31] Thus, more than mere inaction must generally be shown before a person can be convicted either as a principal or as a party to an offence under the rules provided in the *Criminal Code*.

The leading Canadian case on participation by omission is *R. v. Dunlop and Sylvester*.[32] In that case, the Supreme Court of Canada held that persons who stood by during a sexual assault could not be held liable as parties to the offence. The Court stated that a person cannot be convicted unless the person carried out some positive act in furtherance of the offence, or the person's presence amounted to encouragement to commit the offence.

The required fault element for participation by omission is the same as the one for acts. The accused must have failed to do something "for the purpose of aiding any person to commit" the offence.[33] If, for example, the accused had a duty to protect a person from an assault and, for the purposes of assisting in the commission of the assault, failed to come to the victim's aid, that person would be liable.

This theory of participation has implications for the liability of directors and officers for offences that are committed by corporations. Under business corporations statutes, directors and officers are under a general duty to act in the best interest of the corporation.[34] There also appears to be a general duty of directors and officers to ensure that the corporation complies with the law. Thus, in some circumstances, the directors and officers have a duty to take into account interests beyond those of the corporation itself or its shareholders.[35] In fact, they must consider the overall public interest in their decision-making as it relates to compliance with statutory and regulatory standards.[36]

---

[31] For a thorough discussion of secondary liability for omissions see J. Finn, "Culpable Non-Intervention: Reconsidering the Basis for Party Liability by Omission" (1994), 18 Crim. L.J. at 90.

[32] [1979] 2 S.C.R. 881.

[33] An example can be found in *R. v. Nixon* (1990), 57 C.C.C. (3d) 97, at 109–110, where the accused police officer was convicted as a party to an assault committed by another officer. The accused was the senior police officer in charge of the lock-up where the assault occurred and had no active involvement in the assault but was present at it. The British Columbia Court of Appeal held that: "A failure to act in accordance with a duty to act may be an omission to do something for the purpose of aiding or abetting. In some circumstances the presence of an accused will, in itself, be held to have encouraged the commission of the offence. In this situation there will be more than 'mere presence' on the part of the accused and the accused will be liable as a party."

[34] CBCA, s. 122; see Chapter 2, "The Duties of Directors", for further discussion.

[35] *Parke v. Daily News Ltd.* [1962] Ch. 927; see also Chapter 2, "The Duties of Directors".

[36] *Re Standard Trustco Ltd.* (1992), 6 B.L.R. 241 (O.S.C.).

If directors' and officers' duties include the duty to ensure that the corporation does not commit offences, where they fail to take steps to prevent the commission of an offence by the corporation (e.g., by one of its directing minds) and do so for the purpose of furthering that offence, they could be liable pursuant to paragraph 21(1)(*b*) of the *Criminal Code* for the corporation's offence.[37] Furthermore, if directors stand by while an offence is being committed by the corporation, their inaction could amount to encouraging commission of the offence.

Encouraging Commission of an Offence

Actions or omissions short of assisting in the commission of an offence may amount to encouraging the commission of the offence. Even though the *Criminal Code* does not provide an express mental element for this form of participation in offences, courts have held that the specific intent required to prove the aiding of an offence also applies to the abetting of one.[38]

Just as one can assist in the commission of an offence through inaction, one can also encourage the commission of an offence without doing or saying anything. The mere presence of the accused may amount to an encouragement to commit the offence.

In the corporate setting, the failure of directors to admonish those in the corporate structure who violate regulations could amount to encouragement. Directors and officers could be liable if they failed to take steps to ensure compliance with the law and if their purpose in doing so was to encourage non-compliance on the part of others in the firm.

Summary

In summary, the general rules of participation in offences provided in the *Criminal Code* create liability for those who act, or fail to discharge a duty to act, for the purpose of assisting or encouraging the commission of an offence on the part of others. Directors and officers can be held liable for corporate offences under these rules if they purposely assist or encourage the commission of those offences. They could be held liable for inaction if their general duty of care to the corporation can be said to include the duty to prevent the corporation from committing offences.

---

[37] Or pursuant to analogous rules in provincial legislation.

[38] *R. v. Curran* (1977), 38 C.C.C. (2d) 151 (Alta. C.A.), leave to appeal to the Supreme Court of Canada dismissed. The same interpretation would apply to similar provincial rules.

B. Indirect Liability Pursuant to Regulatory Statutes

The most common form of liability clause in Canadian regulatory statutes imposes liability on directors and officers for offences that are committed by their corporations. This is a rule of participation in offences that supplements the rules in the *Criminal Code*. A typical provision is found in the *Canadian Environmental Protection Act, 1999*:[39]

> If a corporation commits an offence under this Act or the regulations any officer, director or agent of the corporation who directed, authorized, assented to, acquiesced in or participated in the commission of the offence is a party to and guilty of the offence, and is liable to the punishment provided for the offence, whether or not the corporation has been prosecuted or convicted.

Both on the surface and in the interpretation given by the courts,[40] this form of directors' liability is broader than the rules of participation in offences that are provided in s. 21 of the *Criminal Code*. Knowledge, rather than intention or purpose, would appear to be the required mental element under these clauses and, in some cases, knowledge may be assumed to exist because of the accused's position or because of other circumstances. Inaction is enough to attract liability.

There has been a great deal of discussion about the importance of directors implementing compliance programs to avoid breaching regulatory requirements and to ensure the availability of a due diligence defence. Generally, this defence is available to the corporation with respect to liability under regulatory statutes and is asserted by the directors themselves. The situation with respect to individual directors is less clear. In many cases, the defence is not available to the directors because the potential liability imposed by the statute does not lend itself to a due diligence defence. A director who authorized or directed the commission of an offence could not, at the same time, argue that he or she took reasonable steps to prevent it.

Due diligence, however, is applicable primarily in relation to acquiescence. Directors should be aware that they may be liable for failing to act in the face of their knowledge of a corporate offence. Their actions may be

---

39 S.C. 1999, c. 33, s. 280.

40 Cases generally hold that directors are liable for mere knowledge of the offence. See, in particular, *R. v. Posner* (1965), 46 C.R. 321 (Ont. S.C.); *R. v. Tri-City Truck Sales Ltd.* (1966), 63 D.L.R. (2d) 507 (B.C.S.C.); *R. v. Vogel*, [1967] 2 O.R. 609 (Co. Ct.); *R. v. Kuhn* (1970), 1 C.C.C. (2d) 132 (B.C. Co. Ct.); *Udell v. M.N.R.*, [1970] Ex. C.R. 176 (Ex. Ct.); *R. v. Rogo Forming Ltd.* (1980), 56 C.C.C. (2d) 31 (Ont. Prov. Ct. J.); *R. v. Wilansky* (1983), 41 Nfld. & P.E.I.R. 29 (Nfld. Dist. Ct.); and *R. v. Swendson* (1987), 78 A.R. 220 (Q.B.).

held to the standard of reasonableness (i.e., that they were duly diligent), and they should act as a reasonably prudent person would to prevent non-compliance. The accused director, therefore, could present evidence that he or she took reasonable steps to prevent the commission or the continuance of an offence of which he or she had knowledge.[41]

Some statutes expressly provide a due diligence defence. For example, s. 283 of the *Canadian Environmental Protection Act, 1999*[42] states: "No person shall be found guilty of an offence ... [except certain offences requiring fault] where the person establishes that the person exercised all due diligence to prevent its commission."

C. A Regulatory Duty of Care

A new form of directors' liability has been enacted in some Ontario statutes to overcome ambiguities in the standard formulation of directors' and officers' liabilities. This new form makes it clear that directors' liability is a form of negligence.[43] An example of this formulation is found in s. 194(1) of the Ontario *Environmental Protection Act*:[44] Every director or officer of a corporation that engages in an activity that may result in the discharge of a contaminant into the natural environment contrary to this Act or the regulations has a duty to take all reasonable care to prevent the corporation from causing or permitting such unlawful discharge.

Similar rules are contained in other provincial, territorial, and federal statutes.[45] Clearly, the standard of conduct that is expected of directors is one of reasonable care. Failure to take appropriate (and probably active) steps to prevent violations of these statutes could result in directors being held liable.

---

[41] This can be seen as either the assertion of a defence of due diligence or as a negation of the Crown's evidence of acquiescence. If it is the former, then the accused must "establish" the defence on the balance of probabilities in order to be acquitted. If it is the latter, the accused must only raise a doubt. Without knowing the elements of proof of acquiescence, it is difficult to state this definitively.

[42] *Supra* note 39.

[43] See the discussion of this issue in J. Swaigen, *Regulatory Offences in Canada: Liability and Defences* (Scarborough: Carswell, 1992), at 152–157.

[44] R.S.O. 1990, c. E.19.

[45] See *Ontario Water Resources Act*, R.S.O. 1990, c. O.40, s. 116; *Occupational Health and Safety Act*, R.S.O. 1990, c. O.1, s. 32; and *Canadian Environmental Protection Act, 1999*, *supra* note 39, s. 280(1).

IV. Effects of Voluntary Codes and Agreements

Companies, industry organizations, and governments are exploring the development and use of voluntary codes and agreements.[46] For companies and industry organizations, a voluntary code can serve a variety of purposes, and it may be general or detailed in scope. Adherence to a code can provide a competitive advantage by providing evidence of quality, adherence to "green" or other accepted standards (e.g., fair labour practices, privacy protection, dispute resolution mechanisms), or service guarantees to customers. Adherence to a code can forestall increased regulation, particularly when it is backed by such mechanisms as independent third-party audits. Certification by a recognized standards certification organization of compliance with management standards, such as the ISO 9000 quality management series or the ISO 14000 series of standards for environmental management systems, will also provide evidence of adherence to standards that are essentially voluntary.[47]

Governments are also interested in the use of voluntary codes by firms and industry organizations. A code of practice can be a strong complement to an existing regulatory system; adherence to a code can ensure compliance with regulatory requirements or even promote "supercompliance" beyond the mandated requirements. Adherence to a code can also result in a company being labelled a "good complier" that requires less enforcement attention. Companies known to be good compliers routinely attract fewer inspections and are more likely to be given warnings rather than be prosecuted when an infraction is detected. In some cases, adherence to a code may underlie a voluntary agreement between a company (or plant) and regulators, with the company getting benefits, such as the faster issuance of permits, reduced inspection, or consultation opportunities.

The practical and likely legal effects of voluntary codes should be recognized by the managers and directors of corporations in industries where codes exist or are being developed. Although these codes may be voluntary, in a practical sense, the continued participation in an industry organization may be contingent on signing on to a code of practice. Contracts may require adherence to a code or to a management standard.

[46] For a discussion of voluntary codes, see Industry Canada, The Office of Consumer Affairs and the Regulatory Affairs Division, Voluntary Codes: A Guide for Their Development, and Industry Canada, A Framework for Evaluating Voluntary Codes, both available on the Industry Canada Website: strategic.ic.gc.ca/volcodes.

[47] The spread of quality management standards is partly due to corporations' attempts to improve their internal processes but also due to the increasing practice of companies to demand that suppliers or other contractors be ISO certified. In some cases, courts have imposed ISO 14000 certification on firms as part of a sentence for environmental non-compliance. For additional information on standards, see the Standards Council of Canada Website: www.scc.ca.

Competitive pressures may also lead a firm to adopt an industry-wide code. Even where a firm does not formally adopt a code, it may find that it must, as a practical matter, adhere to the requirements of its industry code.

The practical effect is strengthened by the courts' increasing tendency to look to codes or standards as evidence of good industry practice that can affect a firm's (or director's) due diligence defence.[48] If the firm, its managers, or its directors deviate from the requirements of a prevalent industry code, explanations will be required.[49] A firm's management systems or internal compliance systems that operate with a lower level of care than those found in the code or in a relevant voluntary management standard may well be found wanting.[50] So, too, a failure to apply known standards, especially in the health and safety area, may attract liability.[51] Directors will then be exposed to the risk of being found wanting themselves in the care they have taken to avoid regulatory offences.

V. Trends in Directors' Regulatory Liability

Under what is called the "responsible corporate officer doctrine", some courts in the United States have held that corporate executives may be found liable for acts of the corporation even if they had no knowledge of the violation and even if the definition of the offence expressly requires fault. This doctrine applies to so-called public welfare statutes or to regulatory statutes that are aimed at protecting the public interest (e.g., health and safety). Liability flows from merely being in an executive position, whether

[48] For example, see *R. v. Domtar,* [1993] O.J. No. 3415 (Ont. Prov. Div.); the judge found that non-compliance with a standard constituted a lack of due diligence; Domtar was acquitted on other grounds. Where alternate standards are available, using the less stringent standard may also attract liability; although not yet specifically applied in Canada see *Dept. of Labour v. Waste Management N.Z. Limited,* [1995] CRN No. 400040511262 (Dist. Ct. Auckland). For a general discussion, see, Kernaghan Webb and Andrew Morrison, "The Law and Voluntary Codes: Examining the 'Tangled Web'", in K. Webb (ed.), *Voluntary Codes: Private Governance, the Public Interest and Innovation* (Ottawa: Carleton University Research Unit for Innovation, Science, and the Environment, 2002). The book is an excellent source of information on voluntary codes in the Canadian context.

[49] Voluntary codes or standards may also be used to establish a standard of care in civil tort actions; the terms of a voluntary code may also establish a duty of care to the general public or to a particular class of individuals. See Webb and Morrison, *ibid.*

[50] Courts may also use standards in sentencing. Several Canadian courts have imposed certification to the ISO 14001 environmental management standard as a term of sentencing: *R. v. Prospect Chemicals* (1996), 19 C.E.L.R. (NS) 178 (Alta. Prov. Ct.); *R. v. Van Waters & Rogers Ltd.* (1998), 220 A.R. (315) (Alta. Prov. Ct.); *R. v. Calgary (City)* (2000), 272 A.R. 161, 35 C.E.L.R. (NS) 253 (Alta. Prov. Ct.); *R. v. Corotec (formerly PCI Inc.) and Zadeh* (1998), (Ont. Prov. Ct. J.) reported in an Environment Canada News Release, "Court Orders Unique Environmental Penalties" (August 20, 1998; archived news releases are available on the Environment Canada Website: www.ec.gc.ca).

[51] Readers may recall the recent dismantling of playgrounds across Canada, following the publication of a new CSA International Standard on Playground Safety. The standard was never intended to apply to existing playgrounds, but school boards and park authorities were concerned that non-complying facilities would attract tort liability. The CSA standard was also adopted as the legal standard in some communities.

that of director or officer, within the organization. If one would expect the person occupying it to be aware of the particular conduct or if the person is in a position to control the conduct, the person may be held liable for the conduct.

This doctrine stems from a series of cases beginning with *United States v. Dotterweich*[52] and extended in *United States v. Park*.[53] The U.S. Supreme Court held that corporate executives who are in a position of responsibility have a duty to seek out and remedy violations and to take measures to ensure that violations do not occur. Due diligence would not be a defence, although defendants could be acquitted if they could prove that they were powerless to prevent the commission of the offence. This doctrine has been applied in prosecutions under environmental statutes, even where the definition of the offence required willfulness or actual knowledge. For example, officers have been convicted of the "willful" discharge of a pollutant where they merely acquiesced in a state of affairs that resulted in the discharge.[54]

Officers in the U.S. have also been convicted of "knowingly" violating the *Resource Conservation and Recovery Act*, even without proof of knowledge, where knowledge could be inferred from the position the defendants occupied in the corporation.[55]

Some U.S. courts have applied the "responsible corporate officer doctrine" to mean that responsibility must be proved, not merely assumed from the status of a particular executive within the corporate structure. Lack of actual knowledge and, in some circumstances, due diligence have both been recognized as valid defences to charges under environmental statutes that clearly require fault or blameworthiness.[56]

Nonetheless, when examining offence-creating provisions in U.S. statutes, directors and their advisors should be wary of taking the legislative language at face value. In relation to corporate executives, at least, the provisions must be read in conjunction with the evolving case law.

Some Canadian courts have been prepared to assume the existence of knowledge on the part of a director in convicting for "acquiescence" in an offence. This approach is akin to adopting the responsible corporate officer doctrine. Given the potential breadth of "acquiescence", there is room for

---

[52] 320 U.S. 277 (1943).

[53] 421 U.S. 658 (1975).

[54] *United States v. Frezzo Bros.*, 602 F.2d 1123 (3rd Cir. 1979), cert. denied, 444 U.S. 1074 (1980).

[55] *United States v. Johnson & Towers*, 741 F.2d 662 (3rd Cir. 1984), cert. denied, 469 U.S. 1208 (1985).

[56] See cases referred to in Block and Voisin, "The Responsible Corporate Officer Doctrine — Can You Go to Jail for What You Don't Know?" (1992), 22 *Environmental Law* 1347, at 1366–1371.

reading into Canadian directors' liability clauses a doctrine along these lines. However, it is unlikely to occur in the Canadian context, since Canadian courts are generally reluctant to impose liability without some evidence of fault or an opportunity to demonstrate due diligence.

VI. Conclusion

The forms of liabilities described in this Chapter expose directors to the risk of being convicted of an offence when they personally breach a statutory or regulatory requirement or when they actually participate in, or acquiesce in, an offence of the corporation. Prudent directors will want to ascertain from corporate counsel and from other knowledgeable advisors precisely what legal requirements apply to them, then take appropriate measures to protect themselves. These measures should ensure that procedures, practices, and policies are put in place that constitute a duly diligent attempt to prevent the commission of an offence.

Directors must also inform themselves about the forms of liability that the corporation may face. Today, these liabilities may stem from non-compliance with relevant and accepted voluntary consensus standards and codes as well as from the more traditional sources of potential liability. Directors may also be liable for the negligent failure to prevent a corporate offence (as they are under some Ontario statutes) or for failing to respond appropriately when it comes to light that the corporation may be in breach of statutory or regulatory requirements. Here again, directors may protect themselves by ensuring that the corporation adopts both reasonable measures to prevent non-compliance and appropriate responses to non-compliance.

APPENDIX I

Common Sources of Directors' Liability Under Federal Statutes (Last Updated June 2006)

THIS IS NOT A COMPREHENSIVE LIST. THE PASSAGES SET OUT BELOW ARE SUMMARIES ONLY, AND THE READER MUST REFER TO THE SPECIFIC STATUTE FOR A COMPLETE STATEMENT OF THE DIRECTOR'S LEGAL RESPONSIBILITIES AND THE STATUTORY CONTEXT IN WHICH THOSE LEGAL RESPONSIBILITIES ARISE.

Federal Statute	Statutory Breach	Liability for Offence	Statutory Defence and Limitation Period
Bankruptcy and Insolvency Act, R.S.C. 1985, c. B-3			No person may commence an action or proceeding against directors that arose before the commencement of bankruptcy proceedings and proceedings related to obligations of the corporation for which directors are liable:[1] [ss. 69.31(1) and (2)]
Bankruptcy and Insolvency Act	Any person privy to non-arm's-length transactions with bankrupt, without adequate consideration, occurring within the 1-year period preceding initial bankruptcy event and bankruptcy, is subject to judgment in favour of trustee: [s. 100]	Liable for difference between the actual consideration given or received and the fair market value: [s. 100]	None[2]

[1] To encourage directors of an insolvent corporation to remain in office during a reorganization, a stay is created in respect of claims against directors. The stay does not apply to actions against a director on a guarantee or actions seeking injunctive relief against a director: [s. 69.31(2)]. See ss. 50(13)–50(15).

[2] "None" means that no defence is built into the statute. A defence may be available at common law.

Federal Statute	Statutory Breach	Liability for Offence	Statutory Defence and Limitation Period
Bankruptcy and Insolvency Act	Director is liable for paying a dividend (other than a stock dividend) or for redeeming or purchasing corporate shares for cancellation, if it occurred within 12 months preceding the bankruptcy and if it is done at a time when the corporation is insolvent: [s. 101(2)]	Liable, jointly and severally, or solidarily, for the amount of the dividend, redemption, or purchase price, plus interest: [s. 101(2)]	Director is not liable if he or she proves the corporation was not insolvent at the time of, or rendered insolvent by, the transaction or the director had reasonable grounds to believe the corporation was not insolvent at the time of, or rendered insolvent by, the transaction: [ss. 101(2) & 101(5)]. In assessing whether the director had reasonable grounds for belief under s. 101(2)(b), the court must consider the statutory "due diligence defence": [s. 101(2.1)][3] Director is not liable if he or she protested against payment: [s. 101(3)]
Bankruptcy and Insolvency Act	Officer or person in direct/indirect control of corporation is liable if he or she failed to perform all of the duties imposed on a bankrupt by s. 158 (see s. 158 for duties): [s. 159]	Punishable as though bankrupt: [s. 159]	None
Bankruptcy and Insolvency Act	Director, officer, agent, mandatory, or a person in direct/indirect control is guilty of an offence if he or she directed, authorized, assented to, acquiesced in, or participated in the commission of the offence under the Act: [s. 204]	Liable to punishment provided for in the offence, whether or not the corporation was prosecuted or convicted; liable to pay for the loss caused to the third party: [ss. 204 and 204.3]	None

[3] Due diligence in s. 101(2.1) states that a director is not liable if the director exercised the care, diligence, and skill that a reasonably prudent person would have exercised in comparable circumstances, including reliance in good faith on (a) the financial statements of the corporation represented to the director by an officer of the corporation or in a written report of the auditor of the corporation to fairly reflect the financial condition of the corporation; or (b) a report of a person whose profession lends credibility to a statement made by the professional person.

Federal Statute	Statutory Breach	Liability for Offence	Statutory Defence and Limitation Period
Canada Business Corporations Act, R.S.C. 1985, c. C-44 ("CBCA")	Director is liable if he or she authorized the issuance of shares under s. 25 for a consideration other than money if the amount received is less than the fair equivalent of money: [ss. 25(3) and 118(1)]	Liable, jointly and severally or solidarily for the difference between the fair equivalent of money and the amount received: [s. 118(1)]	Director is not liable if the director proves that he or she did not reasonably know, and could not reasonably have known, that the share was issued for a lesser consideration: [s. 118(6)]. Action must be commenced within 2 years from the date of the resolution authorizing the action complained of: [s. 118(7)] Director is not liable if the director proves care, diligence, and skill under due defence, set out *supra* note 4: [s. 123(4)][4] or if the director proves that he or she dissented: [s. 123(1)]
Canada Business Corporations Act	Director is liable if he or she authorized (a) purchase, redemption, or other acquisition of shares, contrary to s. 34, 35, or 36; (b) payment of unreasonable commission regarding corporation's shares, contrary to s. 41; (c) payment of dividend, contrary to s. 42; (d) financial assistance, contrary to s. 44; (e) payment of indemnity, contrary to s. 124; or (f) payment to shareholder, contrary to ss. 190 or 241: [s. 118(2)]	Liable, jointly and severally, or solidarily, to restore to the corporation any amounts distributed and not otherwise recovered by the corporation: [s. 118(2)]	Action must be commenced within 2 years from the date of resolution authorizing the action complained of: [s. 118(7)]. Director is not liable if the director proves that he or she exercised care, diligence, and skill under the due diligence defence, set out *supra* note 4: [s. 123(4)] Director is not liable if the director proves that he or she dissented: [s. 123(1)]

[4] Due diligence defence under s. 123(4) states that a director is not liable if the director exercised the care, diligence, and skill that a reasonably prudent person would have exercised in comparable circumstances, including reliance in good faith on (a) financial statements of the corporation represented to the director by an officer of the corporation or in a written report of the auditor of the corporation to fairly reflect the financial condition of the corporation; or (b) a report of a person whose profession lends credibility to a statement made by the professional person.

Federal Statute	Statutory Breach	Liability for Offence	Statutory Defence and Limitation Period
Canada Business Corporations Act	Director is liable to employees of the corporation for wages (if incurred while the director was in office): [s. 119(1)]	Liable, jointly and severally, or solidarily for all debts not exceeding 6 months' wages that are payable to each employee for services performed for the corporation: [s. 119(1)]	Director is not liable unless the corporation (1) sued for debt within 6 months after becoming due and the execution was returned unsatisfied; (2) commenced liquidation and dissolution proceedings or has been dissolved and the claim was proved within 6 months thereof; or (3) made an assignment or was the subject of a receiving order under the *Bankruptcy and Insolvency Act* and the debt was proved within 6 months: [s. 119(2)] Action must be commenced while the director was in office or within 2 years after the director ceases to be a director: [s. 119(3)] Director is not liable if the director proves that he or she exercised care, diligence, and skill under the due diligence defence set out *supra* in note 4: [s. 123(4)]
Canada Business Corporations Act	Directors or officers are liable if in exercising their powers and discharging their duties they failed to (a) act honestly and in good faith with a view to the best interests of the corporation; or (b) exercise the care, diligence, and skill that a reasonably prudent person would exercise in comparable circumstances, and, subject to s. 146(5) (USA), cannot contract out of these duties by provisions in contract, articles, by-laws, or a resolution: [ss. 122(1) and (3)]	Liable for civil liability, which varies depending upon the breach	Director is not liable if he or she establishes good faith reliance on officer or auditor financials or on professional reports: [s. 123(5)][5]

[5] Subsection 123(5) states that a director has complied with his or her duties under s. 122(1) if the director relied in good faith on (a) financial statements of the corporation represented to the director by an officer of the corporation or in a written report of the auditor of the corporation to fairly reflect the financial condition of the corporation; or (b) a report of a person whose profession lends credibility to a statement made by the professional person.

Federal Statute	Statutory Breach	Liability for Offence	Statutory Defence and Limitation Period
Canada Business Corporations Act	Director or officer is liable if he or she failed to comply with Act, regulations, articles, by-laws, and unanimous shareholder agreements (USA), and subject to s. 146(5) (USA), cannot contract out of this duty by provisions in contract, articles, by-laws, or resolution: [ss. 122(2) and (3)]	Liable in accordance with the provision with which they failed to comply	Director is not liable if the director proves that he or she exercised care, diligence, and skill under the due diligence defence, *supra* note 4: [s. 123(4)]
Canada Business Corporations Act	Insider (including a director or an officer) is liable for tipping if he or she discloses to another person (tippee) confidential information regarding the corporation that has not been generally disclosed and that, if generally known, might reasonably be expected to materially affect the value of the corporation's securities: [s. 131(6)]	Liable, jointly and severally, or solidarily (1) to compensate a person with whom the tippee subsequently trades for damages suffered, and (2) to account to corporation for any benefit/advantage received by an insider: [ss. 131(6), (7), (8), and (9)]	Insider is not liable to compensate a person with whom the tippee traded if he or she proves (a) that the insider reasonably believed that information had been generally disclosed; (b) that information was known, or ought reasonably to have been known, by the person with whom the tippee traded; (c) that disclosure of information was necessary in the course of the business of the insider, except if the insider is the offeror in a take-over bid for, or a business combination with, the corporation; or (d) where the insider is an offeror in a take-over bid for or a business combination with the corporation, the disclosure of information was necessary to effect the take-over bid or business combination: [s. 131(6)] Insider is not liable to compensate the corporation if the insider establishes the circumstances described in ss. 131(6)(a), (c), or (d) above: [s. 131(7)]

Federal Statute	Statutory Breach	Liability for Offence	Statutory Defence and Limitation Period
Canada Business Corporations Act	Insider (including a director or an officer) is liable if he or she trades while making use of confidential information that, if generally known, might reasonably be expected to materially affect the value of the security for the insider's own benefit/advantage in a sale or purchase from the shareholder of the corporation or any affiliates: [s. 131(4)]	Liable, jointly and severally, or solidarily (1) to compensate a person with whom the insider traded for damages suffered and, (2) to account to the corporation for any benefit/advantage received by the insider	Insider is not liable to compensate the person with whom the insider traded if he or she proves that (a) the insider reasonably believed that information had been generally disclosed; (b) information was known, or ought reasonably to have been known, by the person with whom the insider traded; or (c) the purchase or sale of the security took place in prescribed circumstances: [s. 131(4)] Insider is not liable to account to the corporation if he or she proves the circumstances described in s. 131(4)(a) above: [s. 131(5)]
Canada Business Corporations Act	Director or officer is liable if he or she knowingly failed to notify the audit committee and the auditor of an error/misstatement in the financial statements reported on by the auditor or former auditor: [s. 171(6)]	Liable to a fine not exceeding $5,000 and/or imprisonment not exceeding 6 months: [s. 171(9)]	None
Canada Business Corporations Act	Director or officer is liable if he or she knowingly failed to prepare/issue revised financial statements and inform shareholders/director: [s. 171(8)]	Liable to a fine not exceeding $5,000 and/or imprisonment not exceeding 6 months: [s. 171(9)]	None

Federal Statute	Statutory Breach	Liability for Offence	Statutory Defence and Limitation Period
Canada Business Corporations Act	Director is guilty of offence if he or she knowingly authorized, permitted, or acquiesced in the corporate transfer of constrained shares where it was not satisfied, on reasonable grounds, that it would assist the corporation or affiliates in receiving licences or permits or maintaining a specific level of Canadian ownership: [s. 32(4)]	Liable to a fine not exceeding $5,000 and/or imprisonment not exceeding 6 months, whether or not the corporation is prosecuted or convicted: [s. 32(4)]	Director is not liable if there was a reasonable cause for transfer: [s. 32(3)]
Canada Business Corporations Act	Director or officer is guilty of an offence if he or she knowingly authorized, permitted, or acquiesced in the corporation failing, without reasonable cause, to issue a proxy while concurrently giving notice of a meeting of shareholders: [ss. 149(1)–(4)]	Liable to a fine not exceeding $5,000 and/or imprisonment not exceeding 6 months, whether or not the corporation is prosecuted or convicted: [s. 149(4)]	None
Canada Business Corporations Act	Director or officer is guilty of an offence if he or she knowingly authorized, permitted, or acquiesced in the failure to send a proxy prior to any solicitation of proxies: [ss. 150(1)–(4)]	Liable to a fine not exceeding $5,000 and/or imprisonment not exceeding 6 months, whether or not the corporation is prosecuted or convicted: [s. 150(4)]	None
Canada Business Corporations Act	Director or officer is guilty of an offence if he or she knowingly authorized, permitted, or acquiesced in the failure of the corporation to comply with the duties of a registrant where the corporation is the registered owner but not the beneficial owner of shares: [ss. 153(1)–(9)]	Liable to a fine not exceeding $5,000 and/or to imprisonment not exceeding 6 months, whether or not the corporation is prosecuted or convicted: [s. 153(9)]	None

Federal Statute	Statutory Breach	Liability for Offence	Statutory Defence and Limitation Period
Canada Business Corporations Act	Director or officer is guilty of an offence if he or she knowingly authorized, permitted, or acquiesced in making a report, return, notice, or other document required under the Act/regulations to be sent to the Director or to another person that (a) contained an untrue statement of material fact, or (b) omitted a material fact: [ss. 250(1) and (2)]	Liable to a fine not exceeding $5,000 and/or imprisonment not exceeding 6 months: [s. 250(2)]	Director or officer is not guilty of an offence if he or she did not know, and in exercise of reasonable diligence could not have known, of an untrue statement or omission: [s. 250(3)]
Canada Cooperative Act, R.S. 1998, c. C-1	Directors and officers are liable for the failure to perform various duties or for offences, similar to those identified under the CBCA, including, but not limited to, those in s. 101(1) (issuance of shares for less than money value); s. 101(3) (redemption of shares contrary to Act, commission contrary to Act, payment of dividend contrary to Act); s. 102(1) (unpaid employee wages for a maximum of 6 months)	Liability varies, according to the circumstances of the case or the penalty imposed by the Act; see the Act for exact provisions.	Director or officer is not liable if various statutory defences or limitation periods apply; see the Act for exact provisions
Canada Corporations Act, R.S.C. 1970, c. C-32	Directors and officers are liable for the failure to perform various duties, or for offences, similar to those identified under the CBCA, including, but not limited to, those in s. 40(2) (transfer of shares to a person without the sufficient means to pay for them); s. 99(1) (unpaid employee wages to a maximum of 6 months); s. 101(2) (issuance of shares for less than money value); s. 204(1) (unpaid wages for clerks, labourers, and apprentices)	Liability varies, according to the circumstances of the case or to the penalty imposed by the Act; see the Act for exact provisions.	Director or officer is not liable if various statutory defences or limitation periods apply; see the Act for exact provisions

Federal Statute	Statutory Breach	Liability for Offence	Statutory Defence and Limitation Period
Canada Labour Code, R.S.C. 1985, c. L-2.	Persons (including directors and officers) are guilty of an offence if they knowingly authorized, permitted, or acquiesced in contravening a direction by a safety officer or if they failed to make accessible to employees the employer's policy concerning safety and health: [s. 148]	Liable to a fine not exceeding $1,000,000 and/or imprisonment not exceeding 2 years: [s. 148]	Director or officer is not liable if the director proves that he or she exercised due care and diligence to avoid a contravention: [s. 148(4)]
Canada Labour Code	Director is liable on the inspector finding that the employer failed to pay wages and other amounts to employees: [ss. 251.1 and 251.18]	Liable, jointly and severally, for wages and other amounts to which the employee is entitled to at the maximum equivalent of 6 months' wages: [s. 251.18]	Director is not liable unless (a) the entitlement arose during the particular director's incumbency; and (b) the recovery of the amount from the corporation is impossible or unlikely: [s. 251.18]
Canada Pension Plan Act, R.S.C. 1985, c. C-8	Director or officer is liable, together with the corporation if the corporation failed to deduct or remit to the Receiver General the amount owing under the Act: [s. 21.1(1)]	Liable, jointly and severally, or solidarily, together with the corporation, to pay the amount and interest or penalties: [s. 21.1(1)][6]	
Canada Pension Plan Act	Director or officer is guilty of an offence if he or she directed, authorized, assented to, acquiesced, or participated in the commission of an offence contrary to the Act: [s. 103(2)]	Liable to punishment provided for the offence, whether or not the corporation is prosecuted or convicted: [s. 103(2)]	None

[6] Subsections 227.1(2) to (7) of the *Income Tax Act* apply in respect of this breach.

Federal Statute	Statutory Breach	Liability for Offence	Statutory Defence and Limitation Period
Canadian Environmental Protection Act, 1999, S.C. 1999, c. C-33.	Director, officer, or agent is guilty of an offence if he or she directed, authorized, assented to, acquiesced, or participated in the commission of the offence by the corporation, or if he or she intentionally or recklessly caused disaster or showed wanton or reckless disregard for lives and safety that could result in prosecution under ss. 203 and 204 of the *Criminal Code*: [ss. 274–280.1] Director or officer is liable if he or she failed to take reasonable care to ensure corporate compliance with the Act: [s. 280(1)]	Liable to fines or imprisonment which vary, depending upon the offence; punishment can be as high as fine of $1,000,000 and/or 3 years imprisonment: [s. 272(2)]	Persons are not guilty, other than those charged under s. 273 (providing false or misleading information if committed knowingly), or under s. 228 (providing false information or obstructing enforcement officer or analyst) or s. 274 (intentionally or recklessly causing disaster or wanton or reckless disregard), where the person exercised due diligence to prevent the commission of the offence: [s. 283] Action must be commenced within 2 years: [ss. 272–280.1]
Competition Act, R.S.C. 1985, c. C-34[7]	Director or officer is liable for the corporation's offence if he or she is in a position to direct or influence the policies of the corporation, such as corporate engagement in deceptive telemarketing practices: [s. 52.1(8)]	Liable for the punishment provided for the offence, whether or not the corporation is prosecuted or convicted: [s. 52.1(8)]	Officer or director is not liable if it is established that he or she exercised due diligence to prevent the commission of the offence: [s. 52.1(8)]
Competition Act	Director or officer is guilty of an offence where he or she directs or influences policies of the corporation in violation of s. 53 (deceptive notice of winning a prize): [s. 53(5)]	Liable for the punishment provided for the offence, whether or not the corporation is prosecuted or convicted: [s. 53(5)]	Officer or director is not liable if it is established that he or she exercised due diligence to prevent the commission of the offence: [s. 53(5)]
Competition Act	Director or officer is guilty of an offence if he or she directed, authorized, assented to, acquiesced in or participated in the corporation's destruction or alteration of a record or another thing required under the Act or for which a warrant has been issued: [s. 65(4)]	Liable for the punishment provided for the offence, whether or not the corporation is prosecuted or convicted: [s. 65(4)]	None

7 The *Competition Act* includes other offences that do not expressly mention directors and officers' liability, but a breach of such an offence could attract liability if a director or an officer is a controlling mind of the corporation.

Federal Statute	Statutory Breach	Liability for Offence	Statutory Defence and Limitation Period
Consumer Packaging and Labelling Act, R.S.C. 1985, c. C-38	Director or officer is guilty of an offence if he or she directed, authorized, assented to, acquiesced in, or participated in the commission of an offence under the Act: [s. 20(3)]	Liable to punishment provided for the offence, whether or not the corporation is prosecuted or convicted: [s. 20(3)]	None
Criminal Code, R.S.C. 1985, c. C-46.	Director or officer is guilty of an offence if he or she made, circulated, or published a prospectus, statement, or account that he or she knew was false with the intent to deceive and defraud: [s. 400(1)]	Liable to imprisonment for up to 10 years: [s. 400(1)]	None
Customs Act, R.S.C. 1985, c. C-1 (2nd Supp.).	Director or officer is guilty of an offence if he or she directed, authorized, assented to, acquiesced in, or participated in the commission of an offence under the Act: [s. 158]	Liable to the punishment provided for the offence, whether or not the corporation is prosecuted or convicted: [s. 158]	None
Employment Insurance Act, S.C. 1996, c. 23	Director or officer is liable if the corporation failed to deduct and remit to the Receiver General the prescribed amount from the employee's remuneration: [s. 83(1)]	Liable, jointly and severally, or solidarily to pay the amount and related interest and penalties: [s. 83(1)]	None
Excise Tax Act, R.S.C. 1985, c. E-15. (Part IX — Goods and Services)	Director is liable if he or she is a director at the time the penalty is imposed for the act or omission under ss. 38 or 39 (false representation, false benefit claims, fraud or deceit): [s. 46(1)]	Liable, jointly and severally, or solidarily for the penalty imposed: [s. 46.1(1)]	Director is not liable unless certain conditions met under s. 46.1(2) or if director establishes due diligence defence under s. 46.1(3)
Excise Tax Act	Director, officer, or agent is guilty of an offence if he or she directed, authorized, assented to, acquiesced in, or participated in the commission of the offence under the Act: [s. 96(3)]	Liable for the punishment provided for the offence, whether or not the corporation is prosecuted or convicted: [s. 96(3)]	None

Federal Statute	Statutory Breach	Liability for Offence	Statutory Defence and Limitation Period
Excise Tax Act	Directors are jointly and severally, or solidarily liable if the corporation fails to remit an amount of net tax as required under the Act: [s. 323(1)]	Liable to pay the amount and any interest on or penalties related to the amount: [s. 323(1)]	Director is not liable unless certain conditions are met under s. 323(2) or if the director establishes a due diligence defence under s. 323(3)
Excise Tax Act	Director, officer, or agent is guilty of an offence if he or she directed, authorized, assented to, acquiesced in, or participated in the commission of an offence under Part IX: [s. 330]	Liable for the punishment provided for the offence, whether or not the corporation is prosecuted or convicted: [s. 330]	None
Export and Import Permits Act, R.S.C. 1985, c. E-19.	Director or officer is guilty of an offence if he or she directed, authorized, assented to, acquiesced in,or participated in the commission of an offence under the Act, for example, the export of goods included in the Export Control List: [s. 20]	Liable for the punishment provided for the offence, whether or not the corporation is prosecuted or convicted: [s. 20]	None
Fisheries Act, R.S.C. 1985, c. F-14.	Director or officer is guilty of an offence if he or she directed, authorized, assented to, acquiesced in, or participated in the commission of an offence by the corporation, for example, carrying on without authorization, any work or undertaking that results in the harmful alteration or destruction of habitat frequented by fish: [s. 78.2.]	Liable to the punishment provided for the offence, whether or not the corporation is prosecuted or convicted: [s. 78.2]	Director or officer is not liable if he or she exercised due diligence or proves that he or she reasonably and honestly believed in the existence of a fact that, if true, would render a person's conduct innocent: [s. 78.6]]
Hazardous Products Act, R.S.C. 1985, c. H-3.	Director or officer is guilty of an offence if he or she directed, authorized, assented to, acquiesced in, or participated in the commission of an offence, for example, advertising, selling, or importing a prohibited product: [s. 28(2)]	Liable to the punishment provided for the offence, whether or not the corporation is prosecuted or convicted: [s. 28(2)]	Action must be commenced within 12 months after subject-matter arose: [s. 28(3)]

Federal Statute	Statutory Breach	Liability for Offence	Statutory Defence and Limitation Period
Income Tax Act, R.S.C. 1985, c. I-1 (5th Supp.)	Director or officer is liable if he or she failed to deduct or withhold amount as required, including unpaid source withholdings of employee payroll deductions (s. 153); 25 percent withholding tax, respecting payments or credits such as dividends, interest, royalties (s. 215): [s. 227.1(1)]	Liable to pay amount required to be deducted or withheld and any interest or penalties relating thereto: [s. 227.1(1)]	Director is not liable unless certain conditions are met: [s. 227.1(2)] or if he or she exercised care, diligence, and skill to prevent failure that a reasonably prudent person would have exercised: [s. 227.1(3)][8]
Income Tax Act	Director or officer is guilty of an offence if he or she directed, authorized, assented to, acquiesced in, or participated in the commission of a corporate offence in failing to file any return, deduct or remit withholdings from employees, and maintain adequate books to allow for inspection: [ss. 238, 239 and 242]	Liable to criminal prosecution under either the *Criminal Code* or s. 242 of the *Income Tax Act*	None
Pension Benefit Standards Act, R.S.C. 1985, c. P-32 (2nd Supp.)	Director or officer is guilty of an offence if he or she directed, authorized, assented to, acquiesced in, or participated in failing to remit all amounts owing: [s. 38(5)]	Liable to the punishment provided for the offence, whether or not the corporation is prosecuted or convicted: [s. 38(5)]	Action must be commenced within 2 years after subject-matter arose: [s. 38(4)]
Proceeds of Crime (Money Laundering) and Terrorist Financing Act, S.C. 2000, c. P-17	Director, officer, agent, or entity is guilty of an offence if he or she directed, authorized, assented to, acquiesced in, or participated in the commission of an offence under the Act: [s. 78].	Liable to the punishment provided for the offence, whether or not the corporation is prosecuted or convicted: [s. 78]	None

[8] IC-89-2, "Director's liability Section 227.1 of the *Income Tax Act*", outlines Revenue Canada's position concerning the application of the due diligence defence. Revenue Canada states that a director may take positive action toward establishing this defence by (a) establishing controls to account for withholdings from employees and remittances; (b) calling upon financial officers of the corporation to report regularly on the continued implementation of these controls; and (c) obtaining regular confirmation that withholdings and remittances have in fact been made during all relevant periods.

Federal Statute	Statutory Breach	Liability for Offence	Statutory Defence and Limitation Period
Transportation of Dangerous Goods Act, 1992, S.C. 1992, c. T-34.	Director or officer is guilty of an offence if he or she directed, authorized, assented to, acquiesced in, or participated in the commission of an offence under the Act, for example, the failure to handle dangerous goods while abiding by prescribed safety requirements: [s. 39]	Liable to the punishment provided for the offence in the Act, whether or not the corporation is prosecuted or convicted: [s. 39]	Director is not liable if it is established that all reasonable measures to comply with the Act were taken: [s. 40]
Winding-up and Restructuring Act, R.S.C. 1985, c. W-11.	Director or officer is liable if the company, within 12 months preceding the commencement of winding-up, paid a dividend in respect of shares of the company (other than a stock dividend) or purchased for cancellation any capital stock of the company, thereby rendering the company insolvent: [s. 102.1]	Liable, jointly and severally, in the amount of the dividend or purchase price that has not been paid to the company: [s. 102.1(2)]	Director is not liable if the director proves that he or she had reasonable grounds to believe that the transaction was occurring at a time when the company was solvent or would not render the company insolvent (the burden of proof is on a director or an officer): [s. 102.1(7)]
Winding-up and Restructuring Act	Director or officer is guilty of an offence if he or she directed, authorized, assented to, acquiesced in, or participated in an attempt to deceive or defraud any person, or to destroy, mutilate, alter, or falsify books, records, or securities of the company being wound up: [s. 141]	Liable to imprisonment not exceeding 2 years: [s. 141]	None

APPENDIX II

Common Sources of Directors' Liability Under Alberta Statutes (Last Updated June 2006)

THIS IS NOT A COMPREHENSIVE LIST. THE PASSAGES SET OUT BELOW ARE SUMMARIES ONLY, AND THE READER MUST REFER TO THE SPECIFIC STATUTE FOR A COMPLETE STATEMENT OF THE DIRECTOR'S LEGAL RESPONSIBILITIES AND THE STATUTORY CONTEXT IN WHICH THOSE LEGAL RESPONSIBILITIES ARISE.

Alberta Statute	Statutory Breach	Liability for Offence	Statutory Defence and Limitation Period
STATUTES AFFECTING MOST DIRECTORS			
Business Corporations Act, R.S.A. 2000, c. B-9	Director is liable if he or she authorized the issuance of shares under s. 27 for consideration other than money if the amount received is less than the fair equivalent of money: [s. 118(1)]	Liable jointly and severally to the corporation for the difference between the amount received and the fair equivalent of money: [s. 118(1)]	Director is not liable if the shares are held pursuant to an escrow agreement required by the Executive Director and surrendered for cancellation pursuant to an agreement: [s. 118(2)] Director is not liable if the director proves that he or she did not know and could not reasonably have known that shares were issued for a consideration less than the fair equivalent of money: [s. 118(7)] Action must commence 2 years from the date of the resolution authorizing the action complained of: [s. 118(9)] Director is not liable if the director established that he or she exercised the care, diligence, and skill that a reasonably prudent person would exercise in comparable circumstances, including good faith reliance on financial statements represented to him/her by an officer or auditor of the corporation or by a professional opinion/report: [s. 123(3)] Director is not liable if the director proves that he or she dissented to the resolution: [s. 123]

Alberta Statute	Statutory Breach	Liability for Offence	Statutory Defence and Limitation Period
Business Corporations Act	Director is liable if he or she authorized (a) the purchase/redemption of the corporation's shares, contrary to ss. 34, 35, or 36; (b) a commission on the sale of the shares, contrary to s. 42; (c) the payment of a dividend, contrary to s. 43; (d) financial assistance, contrary to s. 45; (e) the payment of an indemnity, contrary to s. 124; (f) a payment to a shareholder, contrary to ss. 191 or 242: [s. 118(3)]	Liable, jointly and severally, to restore to the corporation any amounts distributed and not otherwise recovered by the corporation: [s. 118(3)]	Director is not liable under s. 118(3)(d) for authorizing financial assistance if he or she did not know and could not reasonably have known about the authorization given contrary to the Act: [s. 118(8)] Action must be commenced within 2 years from the date of the resolution authorizing the action complained of: [s. 118(9)] Director is not liable if the director proves that he or she exercised the care, diligence, and skill that a reasonably prudent person would exercise in comparable circumstances, including good faith reliance on financial statements represented to him/her by an officer or auditor of the corporation or by a professional opinion/report: [s. 123(3)] Director is not liable if the director proves that he or she dissented to the resolution: [s. 123]
Business Corporations Act	Director is liable if the corporation failed to pay employee wages if they were incurred while the director was in office: [s. 119(1)]	Liable, jointly and severally, to employee for all debts not exceeding 6 months' wages payable for services that were performed for the corporation: [s. 119(1)]	Director is not liable if (1) he or she believed on reasonable grounds that the corporation could pay debts as they become due, or (2) the debts are payable to employees for services that were performed while the property of the corporation was under the control of a receiver, receiver-manager, or liquidator: [s. 119(2)] Director is not liable unless the corporation (1) sued for debt within 6 months after it became due and the execution was returned unsatisfied, (2) commenced liquidation and dissolution proceedings or was dissolved and the claim was proved within 6 months thereof, or (3) was made the subject of an assignment or receiving order under the *Bankruptcy and Insolvency Act* and the debt was proved within 6 months: [s. 199(3)] Action must be commenced within 2 years from the date the director ceased to be a director: [s. 119(4)] Director may not be liable if USA restricts duties: [s. 146]

Alberta Statute	Statutory Breach	Liability for Offence	Statutory Defence and Limitation Period
Business Corporations Act	Director or officer is liable if he or she entered into a material contract/transaction with the corporation without disclosing the director's/officer's interest: [s. 120(1)]	Liable to account to the corporation or to shareholders for any profit realized from the contract/transaction; otherwise, the contract/transaction may be set aside: [s. 120(9)]	Director or officer is not liable if the contract/transaction was approved by directors or shareholders and it was reasonable and fair to the corporation at the time it was approved: [s. 120(8)] Director or officer is not liable if he or she acted honestly and in good faith and the contract/transaction was (a) approved or confirmed by a special resolution at a meeting of the shareholders, (b) disclosed to shareholders in a manner sufficient to indicate its nature before it was approved or confirmed, and (c) reasonable and fair to the corporation when it was approved or confirmed: [s. 120(8.1)]
Business Corporations Act	Director or officer is liable if he or she failed, in exercising his or her powers and discharging his or her duties, to (a) act honestly and in good faith with a view to the best interests of the corporation, and (b) exercise the care, diligence, and skill that a reasonably prudent person would exercise in comparable circumstances: [s. 122(1)] Subject to s. 146(7) (USA), a director cannot contract out of his or her duty under a contract, articles, by-laws, or a resolution: [s. 122(3)]	Civilly liable for the resulting loss which varies, depending upon the breach	Director is not liable if the director established that he or she exercised the care, diligence, and skill that a reasonably prudent person would exercise in comparable circumstances, including good faith reliance on financial statements that were represented to him/her by an officer or auditor of the corporation or by a professional opinion/report: [s. 123(3)]
Business Corporations Act	Director or officer is liable if he or she failed to comply with the Act, regulations, articles, by-laws, and any USA and, subject to s. 146(7) (USA), he or she cannot contract out of his or her duty under a contract, articles, by-laws, or a resolution: [ss. 122(2) and 122(3)]	Liable according to the provision with which he or she failed to comply.	Director is not liable if the director established that he or she exercised the care, diligence, and skill that a reasonably prudent person would exercise in comparable circumstances, including good faith reliance on financial statements that were represented to him/her by an officer or auditor of the corporation or by a professional opinion/report: [s. 123(3)]

Alberta Statute	Statutory Breach	Liability for Offence	Statutory Defence and Limitation Period
Business Corporations Act	Insider (including a director or officer) is liable if he or she makes use of confidential information that, if it was generally known, might reasonably be expected to affect materially the value of a security for an insider's own benefit/advantage in a sale or purchase from a shareholder of the corporation or any of its affiliates: [s. 130(1)]	Liable to compensate a person for any direct loss suffered; and Liable to compensate the corporation for any direct benefit/advantage received or receivable by the insider as a result: [s. 130(1)]	Insider is not liable if he or she proves that information was known or, in the exercise of reasonable diligence, should have been known to the person at the time of the transaction: [s. 130(1)] Action must be commenced within 2 years after the date of the completion of the transaction: [s. 130(2)]
Business Corporations Act	Director or officer is guilty of an offence if he or she knowingly authorizes, permits, or acquiesces in the failure of the corporation to send a proxy form concurrently with a notice of a meeting to a shareholder: [s. 149(5)]	Liable to a fine not exceeding $5,000 and/or imprisonment not exceeding 6 months, whether or not the corporation was prosecuted or convicted: [s. 149(5)]	None[1]
Business Corporations Act	Director or officer is guilty of an offence if he or she knowingly authorized, permitted, or acquiesced in the failure to send a proxy circular prior to any solicitation of proxies: [s. 150(5)]	Liable to a fine not exceeding $5,000 and/or imprisonment not exceeding 6 months, whether or not the corporation was prosecuted or convicted: [s. 150(5)]	None
Business Corporations Act	Director or officer is guilty of an offence if he or she knowingly authorized, permitted, or acquiesced in the failure of the corporation to comply with the duties of a registrant where the corporation is the registered owner but not the beneficial owner of shares: [s. 153(9)]	Liable to a fine not exceeding $5,000 and/or imprisonment not exceeding 6 months, whether or not the corporation was prosecuted or convicted: [s. 153(9)]	None
Business Corporations Act	Director or officer is guilty of an offence if he or she knowingly fails to notify the audit committee and the auditor of any error/misstatement in the financial statements reported on by the auditor or former auditor: [ss. 171(7) and (10)]	Liable to a fine not exceeding $5,000 and/or imprisonment not exceeding 6 months: [s. 171(10)]	None
Business Corporations Act	Director or officer is guilty of an offence if he or she knowingly failed to prepare/issue revised financial statements, and if the distributing corporation filed them with the Executive Director upon the auditor informing the directors of the error or misstatement: [ss. 171(9) and (10)]	Liable to a fine not exceeding $5,000 and/or imprisonment not exceeding 6 months: [s. 171(10)]	None

[1] "None" means that no defence is built into the statute. A defence may be available at common law.

Alberta Statute	Statutory Breach	Liability for Offence	Statutory Defence and Limitation Period
Business Corporations Act	Director or officer is guilty of an offence if he or she knowingly authorized, permitted, or acquiesced in making a report, return, notice, or other document required by the Act or regulations that contains an untrue statement of a material fact or omits to state a fact that is required or necessary to make it not misleading: [ss. 251(1) and (2)]	Liable to a fine not exceeding $5,000 and/or imprisonment not exceeding 6 months, whether or not the corporation was prosecuted or convicted: [s. 251(2)]	Person is not guilty if the untrue statement or omission was unknown to the person, and in exercise of reasonable diligence, it could not have been known to that person: [s. 251(3)] Action must be commenced within 2 years from the time when the subject matter of the complaint arose: [s. 253(2)]
Business Corporations Act	Person is guilty of an offence if, without reasonable cause, he or she contravened a provision of the Act or regulations: [s. 252]	Liable to a fine not exceeding $1,000 and/or to imprisonment not exceeding one month: [s. 252]	None
Alberta Corporate Tax Act, R.S.A. 2000, c. A-15	Director, officer, or agent is guilty of an offence if he or she directed, authorized, assented to, acquiesced in, or participated in the commission of the offence by the corporation: [s. 80]	Liable to the punishment provided for in the particular offence, whether or not the corporation was prosecuted or convicted: [s. 80]	None
Alberta Personal Income Tax Act, R.S.A. 2000, c. A-30	Director and corporation are liable under s. 227.1 of the *Federal Income Tax Act* for the failure to deduct, remit, or pay an amount of tax for the taxation year as required: [s. 77].	Liable, jointly and severally, to pay an amount and interest or penalties relating thereto: [s. 77]	None
Alberta Personal Income Tax Act	Director or officer is guilty of an offence under s. 242 of the *Federal Income Tax Act* if he or she directed, authorized, assented to, acquiesced in, or participated in the commission of the offence by the corporation, including the making of false or deceptive statements in return, disposing of records of account to evade payment of taxes, making of false or deceptive entries or omissions in records of account, and willfully evading compliance with the Act: [s. 83].	Liable to the punishment provided for in the offence, whether or not the corporation was prosecuted or convicted, including the following offences: for tax evasion or attempted tax evasion, a fine of not less than 50 percent and not exceeding 20 percent of the amount of tax that was sought to be evaded and/or imprisonment for not greater than 2 years; for the failure to file a return, a fine of not less than $1,000 and not exceeding $25,000 and/or imprisonment not exceeding 1 year: [s. 83]	None

Alberta Statute	Statutory Breach	Liability for Offence	Statutory Defence and Limitation Period
Climate Change and Emissions Management Act, S.A. 2003, c. C-16.7	Director, officer, or agent is guilty of an offence if he or she directed, authorized, assented to, acquiesced in, or participated in the commission of the offence by the corporation, including failing to properly report the release of specified gas into the environment at or in excess of levels or in circumstances established in or pursuant to regulations (s. 6(1)), or the improper use of the Climate Change and Emissions Management Fund (s. 10(3)): [s. 15]	Liable to the punishment provided for in the offence, whether or not the corporation was prosecuted or convicted: [s. 15]	Action must be commenced within 2 years after the later of (1) the date on which the contravention occurred, and (2) the date on which evidence of the contravention first came to the notice of the Minister to issue the notice of administrative penalty: [s. 13]
Companies Act, R.S.A. 2000, c. C-21	Director and officers are liable if a loan or financial assistance is given to the shareholders or directions for the purchase of shares in the company: [s. 14(1) and (3)]	Liable, jointly and severally, to the company and to any person who was injured for any loss, damage, or costs that the company or person sustained or incurred: [s. 14(3)]	Liability is limited to the amount of the loan made in contravention of s. 14(1) with interest at the rate stipulated in the loan: [s. 14(4)] Director is not liable if he or she proves that the contravention of the section was not the result of misconduct or negligence on part of the director: [s. 14(4)] Action must be commenced within 2 years from the date on which loss, damage, or costs were sustained or incurred: [s. 14(5)]
Companies Act	Director is liable if he or she consented to the resolution authorizing the purchase of company shares where solvency tests were not met: [s. 45(1)]	Liable, jointly and severally, to restore to the company the amount paid and not otherwise recovered: [s. 45(1)]	Action must be commenced within 2 years after the date of the completion of the purchase: [s. 45(5)]
Companies Act	Director is guilty of an offence if he or she authorized, permitted, or acquiesced in the failure to comply with s. 90: [s. 90(4)]	Liable to a fine of not more than $1,000: [s. 90(4)]	None

Alberta Statute	Statutory Breach	Liability for Offence	Statutory Defence and Limitation Period
Companies Act	Director is liable to clerks, labourers, servants, and apprentices for all debts for services that were performed while he or she was a director: [s. 91]	Liable for all debts not exceeding 6 months' wages: [s. 91]	Director is not liable unless (1) the company was sued or a judgment was obtained within 1 year after the debt becomes due, (2) an execution against the company is returned unexecuted, (3) the director is sued within 1 year from the time that he or she ceased to be a director: [s. 91]
Companies Act	Director is guilty of an offence if he or she authorized, permitted, or acquiesced in the failure of the company to file a report required under s. 96 or s. 97 or in the filing of a false or misleading report: [s. 99(1) and (2)]	Liable to a fine of not more than $1,000: [s. 99(1) and (2)]	Director is not guilty of an offence if he or she did not know and with exercise of reasonable diligence could not have known that the report was false or misleading: [s. 99(3)]
Companies Act	Director is guilty of an offence if he or she authorized, permitted, or acquiesced in the failure of the company to send shareholders financial statements and a copy of the auditor's report: [s. 147(3)]	Liable to a fine of not more than $200: [s. 147(3)]	None
Companies Act	Director is guilty of an offence if he or she authorized, permitted, or acquiesced in the failure of the company to send shareholders interim financial statements: [s.148(6)]	Liable to a fine of not more than $1,000: [s. 148(6)]	None
Companies Act	Director is guilty of an offence if he or she authorized, permitted, or acquiesced in the failure of the company to send a form of proxy concurrently or prior to a notice of a meeting of shareholders: [s. 156(2)]	Liable to a fine of not more than $1,000: [s. 156(2)]	None
Companies Act	Director is guilty of an offence if he or she authorized, permitted, or acquiesced in the failure of the company to comply with s. 157(1) relating to the solicitation of proxies: [s. 157(3)] Director is guilty of an offence if he or she authorized, permitted, or acquiesced in the solicitation by a form of proxy that is misleading: [s. 157(4)]	Liable to a fine of not more than $1,000: [s. 157(3) and (4)]	Director is not guilty of an offence if the untruth of the statement was not known to the director and with exercise of reasonable diligence could not have been known: [s. 157(5)]

Alberta Statute	Statutory Breach	Liability for Offence	Statutory Defence and Limitation Period
Companies Act	Director is guilty of an offence if he or she knowingly and willfully authorizes or permits a default in complying with s. 181: [s. 181(3)]	Liable to a fine not exceeding $500: [s. 313(2)]	Action must be commenced within 2 years from the time that the matter arose: [s. 316]
Companies Act	Director is guilty of an offence if he or she knowingly or willfully authorizes or permits any act, default, or refusal by which company is guilty of an offence under the Act: [s. 313(1)]	Liable to a fine not exceeding $500: [s. 313(2)]	Action must be commenced within 2 years from the time the matter arose: [s. 316]
Cooperatives Act, S.A. 2001, c. C-28.1	Director is liable for the failure to act honestly and in good faith with a view to the best interests of the cooperative and for exercising the care, diligence, and skill that a reasonably prudent person would exercise in comparable circumstances: [s. 54(1)]	Civilly liable for the resulting loss, which varies depending on the breach	Action must be commenced within 2 years from the time when the subject-matter arose: [s. 363(2)]
Cooperatives Act	Director is liable if he or she consents to a resolution authorizing the issuance of shares for consideration other than money that is less than the value of money that would otherwise be received: [s. 78(1)]	Liable, jointly and severally, to the cooperative for the amount by which the consideration is less than the money that would have been received: [s. 78(1)]	Director is not liable if he or she did not know or could not reasonably have known that the share was issued for a consideration less in value than the money that would have been received: [s. 78(2)]
Cooperatives Act	Director is liable if he or she consents to a resolution authorizing matters that is set out in s. 78(3): [s. 78(3)]	Liable, jointly and severally, to the cooperative for the amounts distributed or paid and not otherwise recovered by the cooperative: [s. 78(3)]	Director is not liable if the director proves that he or she did not know or could not reasonably have known that the amounts so distributed or paid were paid contrary to the Act: [s. 78(4)]
Cooperatives Act	Director is liable to employees for all debts for services performed while he or she was a director: [s. 79(1)]	Liable, jointly and individually, for all debts not exceeding 6 months' wages: [s. 79(1)]	Director is not liable if he or she believes on reasonable grounds that the cooperative can pay debts as they become due or if debts are under the control of receiver: [s. 78(2)]
Cooperatives Act	Director is guilty of an offence if contravene provisions listed in s. 361(1): [s. 361(1)]	Liable to a fine of not more than $5000 and/or imprisonment of not more than 6 months: [s. 361(3)]	Action must be commenced within 2 years from the date when the subject-matter arose: [s. 363(2)]

Alberta Statute	Statutory Breach	Liability for Offence	Statutory Defence and Limitation Period
Cooperatives Act	Director is guilty of an offence if he or she authorized the act or the omission of a cooperative that constitutes an offence under the Act: [s. 362]	Liable whether or not the cooperative was prosecuted for the offence: [s. 362]	Action must be commenced within 2 years from the date when the subject-matter arose: [s. 363(2)]
Dangerous Goods Transportation and Handling Act, R.S.A. 2000, c. D-4	Director, officer, or agent is guilty of an offence if he or she directed, authorized, assented to, acquiesced in, or participated in the commission of an offence by the corporation under the Act, including obstructing or hindering an inspector from carrying out his or her duties by failing to comply with a reasonable request; knowingly making a false or misleading statement; removing or interfering with anything detained (s. 11); not making a report of occurrence or imminence of the release of dangerous goods in excess of a prescribed quantity or concentration (s. 9); handling, offering, or transporting dangerous goods in breach of safety requirements and documentation (s. 19); and displaying a safety mark that is misleading or in conflict with shipping records (s. 20): [s. 26]	Liable whether or not the corporation has been prosecuted for the offence: [s. 26] Liable if the offence committed, for a first offence to a fine not exceeding $50,000 and/or imprisonment not exceeding 2 years and for a subsequent offence to a fine not exceeding $100,000 and/or imprisonment not exceeding 2 years with a maximum amount of $1,000,000: [ss. 29 and 30] Liable for costs and expenses that were reasonably incurred while taking any measures related to detention or actual or imminent accidental release: [ss. 9, 12, 13, 14, and 15] If the offence is of a continuing nature under s. 30(2), $1,000,000 for the first calendar day, and a prescribed amount for each calendar day after the first one on which the offence was held to have continued: [s. 29(3)]	Director or others are not liable if the director established that he or she took all reasonable measures to comply with the Act: [s. 24] Action must be commenced within 2 years after the day the offence was allegedly committed or, in the case of an offence of a continuing nature, after the day when the last occurrence of the offence alleged happened: [s. 23]
Employment Pension Plans Act, R.S.A. 2000, c. E-8	Director or officer is guilty of an offence if he or she directed, authorized, assented to, acquiesced in, or participated in the commission of an offence under the Act by the corporation, including the failure to meet minimum employer contribution requirements; avoiding compliance by making a false or misleading statement or entry in any records; destroying, altering, mutilating, or disposing of records; or failing to state anything in any records: [s. 92(3)]	Liable to pay a fine not exceeding $100,000, whether or not the corporation was prosecuted or convicted: [s. 92(1)]	Action must be commenced within 2 years from the time the subject matter of the prosecution came to the attention of the Superintendent: [s. 93(1)]

Alberta Statute	Statutory Breach	Liability for Offence	Statutory Defence and Limitation Period
Employment Standards Code, R.S.A. 2000, c. E-9	Director is liable to an employee for unpaid wages: [s. 112(2)]	Liable, jointly and severally, to the employee for unpaid wages earned, not exceeding 6 months: [112(2)]	Director is not liable if he or she was not a director when the unpaid wages were earned: [s. 112] Director is not liable if he or she believed on reasonable grounds that the corporation could pay debts as due, or if the debts were payable to employees for services that were performed while the property of the corporation was under the control of a receiver, receiver-manager, or liquidator, pursuant to ABCA, s. 119 and the *Cooperatives Act*, s. 79: [s. 112] Director is not liable unless the corporation (1) commenced liquidation or dissolution proceedings or dissolved and the claim for the debt was proved within 6 months, or (2) the corporation made an assignment or was subject to a receiving order under the *Bankruptcy and Insolvency Act* and the claim was proved within 6 months, pursuant to ABCA, s. 119 and the *Cooperatives Act*, s. 79: [s. 112]
Employment Standards Code	Director or officer is guilty of an offence if he or she directed, authorized, assented to, permitted, participated in, or acquiesced in the offence by the corporation, including terminating the employment of an employee who has started maternity leave or is entitled to parental leave (s. 52); employing children in contravention of the Act (s. 65); terminating an employee because of garnishment proceedings (s. 124); discrimination (s. 125); failure to pay earnings to an employee or to provide anything to which the employee is entitled under the Act (pay at least minimum wage); failure to pay wages (i.e., overtime); failure to give proper notice of wage reductions; failure to give vacation with pay or sum in lieu (s. 128): [s. 131]	Liable to a fine not exceeding $50,000, whether or not the corporation was prosecuted or convicted: [s. 132(1)]	Action must be commenced within 1 year from the date the alleged offence occurred: [s. 133]

Alberta Statute	Statutory Breach	Liability for Offence	Statutory Defence and Limitation Period
Environmental Protection and Enhancement Act, R.S.A. 2000, c. E-12	Director, officer, or agent is guilty of an offence if he or she directed, authorized, assented to, acquiesced in, or participated in the commission of the offence by the corporation, including knowingly providing false or misleading information (s. 227(a)); failing to provide information (s. 227(c)): knowingly contravening a term or condition of approval, code of practice, various certificates (s. 227(d)); knowingly contravening an enforcement order (s. 227(f)); contravening an enforcement order (s. 227(g)); knowingly contravening an environmental protection order (s. 227(h)); contravening an environmental protection order (s. 227(i)); leasing, transferring, selling, assigning, or otherwise disposing of an approval except in accordance with regulations (s. 75(1)); without approval, releasing or permitting the release of a substance into the environment in an amount or concentration that causes or may cause a significant adverse effect (s. 108(1)); failing to report the release of a substance (s. 110); releasing or permitting the release of a substance in excess of that permitted (s. 109); failing to take reasonable steps to repair, remedy, and confine the effects of the substance released and remove or dispose of the substance in a manner maximizing the protection to human life, health, and the environment (s. 112): [s. 232]	Liable to a punishment provided for in the offence, whether or not the corporation was prosecuted or convicted: [s. 232] Maximum penalty for offences listed in s. 228 is a fine not exceeding $100,000 per day and/or 2 years' imprisonment plus the cost of the loss to property that was damaged (certain offences have lower maximum penalties): [s. 228]	Action must be commenced within 2 years from the later of the date when the offence was committed or evidence of the offence first came to attention of the director: [s. 226]
Fair Trading Act, R.S.A. 2000, c. F-2	Principal, director, manager, employee, or agent is guilty of an offence if he or she authorized the act or omission that constituted the offence or assented to or acquiesced or participated in the act or omission that constituted the offence: [s. 165(1)]	Liable to a fine not exceeding $100,000 or 3 times the amount that was obtained by the defendant as a result of the offence, whichever is greater, and/or imprisonment not exceeding 2 years: [s. 164]	Action must be commenced within 3 years after the commission of the offence: [s. 167]

Alberta Statute	Statutory Breach	Liability for Offence	Statutory Defence and Limitation Period
Gaming and Liquor Act, R.S.A. 2000, c. G-1	Director, officer, employee, or agent is guilty of an offence if he or she directed, authorized, assented to, acquiesced in, or participated in the commission of the offence: [s. 120(1)]	Liable to the penalty provided. For an offence for which no specific penalty has been provided, liable to fine not exceeding $50,000: [s. 117(2)]	
Health Insurance Premiums Act, R.S.A. 2000, c. H-6	Director, officer, or agent is guilty of an offence if he or she directed, authorized, assented to, acquiesced in, or participated in the failure or refusal to remit the amount which the agent is liable to remit: [s. 16(2)]	Liable to a fine, for a first offence not exceeding $500 and in default of payment to imprisonment for not more than 30 days; for a second offence not exceeding $1,000 and in default of payment to imprisonment not exceeding 60 days; and for a third or subsequent offence, imprisonment not exceeding 6 months without the option of a fine: [s. 28(1)]	Action must be commenced within 2 years after the alleged commission of an offence: [s. 28(2)]
Human Rights, Citizenship and Multiculturalism Act, R.S.A. 2000, c H-14	Director, officer, or agent is guilty of an offence if he or she directed, authorized, assented to, acquiesced in, or participated in the contravention of the Act by corporation or employment agency, employers' organization, occupational association, or a trade union that is not a corporation; such offences include hindering, obstructing, or interfering with the Commission in the exercise of its power or carrying out its duty under the Act: [ss. 42(1) and (3)]	Liable to a fine not exceeding $10,000: [s. 41(2)]	
Insurance Act, R.S.A. 2000, c. I-3	Director or officer is guilty of an offence if he or she knowingly authorized, permitted, or acquiesced in the commission of an offence: [s. 785]	Liable to a fine of not more than $200,000: [s. 786(1)]	Action must be commenced within 3 years from the date that the facts became known to the Minister: [s. 787]
Insurance Act	Director is liable if he or she paid incorporation or organization expenses from the capital of the company or from the interest on capital without complying with the requirements of the Act: [s. 359(1)]	Liable, jointly and severally, to shareholders or incorporators of the company for the amount of the expenses: [s. 359(1)]	

Alberta Statute	Statutory Breach	Liability for Offence	Statutory Defence and Limitation Period
Insurance Act	Director is liable if he or she authorized the issuance of shares in contravention of the Act or the issuance of subordinated indebtedness in contravention of the Act for consideration other than money: [s. 360(1)]	Liable, jointly and severally, to the company to make good the amount by which the consideration received is less than the fair equivalent of the money company would have received if the share or subordinated indebtedness had been issued for money: [s. 360(1)]	Director is not liable if he or she relied in good faith on (a) financial statements of the company that were represented to the director, officer or an employee by the officer of the company or in a written report of the auditor of the company to reflect fairly the financial condition of the company, or (b) a report of professional advisor: [s. 364] Action must be commenced within 2 years from the date of the resolution authorizing the act: [s. 362]
Insurance Act	Director is liable if he or she authorized (a) the purchase, redemption, or acquisition of shares, (b) the reduction of share capital, (c) the payment of a dividend in contravention, (d) the payment of an indemnity or a transaction in contravention of the Act: [s. 360(2)]	Liable, jointly and severally, to restore to the company the amounts so distributed or paid and not otherwise recovered by the company and the amounts in relation to the loss suffered by the company: [s. 360(2)]	Director is not liable if he or she relied in good faith on (a) the financial statements of the company that were represented to a director, officer, or employee by an officer of the company or in a written report of the auditor of the company to reflect fairly the financial condition of the company, or (b) a report of a professional advisor: [s. 364] Action must be commenced within 2 years from the date of the resolution authorizing the act: [s. 362]
Insurance Act	Director is liable if he or she failed to pay employee wages: [s. 363(1)]	Liable, jointly and severally, to the employee for all debts not exceeding 6 months' wages that are payable to the employee for services performed for the company while they are directors: [s. 363(1)]	Director is not liable if he or she relied in good faith on (a) the financial statements of the company that were represented to the director, officer, or employee by the officer of the company or in a written report of the auditor of the company to reflect fairly the financial condition of the company, or (b) a report of a professional advisor: [s. 364]

Alberta Statute	Statutory Breach	Liability for Offence	Statutory Defence and Limitation Period
Securities Act, R.S.A. 2000, c. S-4	Director, officer, or a person other than an individual is guilty of an offence if he or she authorized, permitted, or acquiesced in offences including, but not limited to: destroying, concealing, or withholding information, property, or a thing reasonably required for a hearing, review, or investigation (s. 58(4)); trading in a manner the person knows or ought reasonably to know creates or may result in an artificial price or a false or misleading appearance of trading activity (s. 93); failing to comply with a decision of the Commission or Executive Director (s. 93(2)); failing to file a prospectus in respect of a trade (s. 110); filing a prospectus that fails to provide full, true, and plain disclosure of all material facts (s. 113(1)(a)); failing to disclose a material fact or material change (s. 147(2)); failing to provide insider trading reports (s. 182(1)) under the Act: [s. 194(3)]	Liable to a fine of not more than $5,000,000 and/or imprisonment for a term of not more than 5 years whether or not the company was charged or found guilty: [s. 194(3)] If a director or officer profits from trading with knowledge of material information not generally known and likely to impact on share price, he/she is liable to a fine of not less than the profit made by reason of the offence and the amount not exceeding the greater of (1) $5,000,000 and (2) an amount equal to triple the amount of the profit made or the loss avoided by the person or company because of the contravention: [s. 194(4)] Court may order compensation or restitution to the aggrieved person/company and make any other order it considers appropriate: [s. 194(6)]	Director is not liable if he or she proves that the purchaser purchased shares with knowledge of the misrepresentation: [s. 203(4)] Action must be commenced within 6 years from the date of the occurrence of the event giving rise to proceedings (non-civil): [s. 201]
Securities Act	Director is liable for a misrepresentation within a prospectus (s. 203(1)); a misrepresentation within take-over bid circulars (s. 205(1)); trades by persons in a special relationship when the material facts or material changes have not been generally disclosed (s. 207(1)) In Alberta, Bill 25, the *Securities Amendment Act, 2006*, 2d Sess., 26th Leg., Alberta, 2006, creates civil liability for secondary market disclosure under Part 17.01 of the Alberta *Securities Act:* [s. 52]	Liability includes the right of rescission in respect of contracts and damages: [s. 209(1)]	Director is not liable if he or she proves due diligence: [s. 207(2)] Director is not liable if, in respect of insider trading, the purchaser/seller knew or ought reasonably to have known of the material fact/change: [s. 207(4)] Action must be commenced for rescission 180 days from the date of the transaction: [s. 211(a)] Action must be commenced for other causes of action within 180 days from the date when the plaintiff first had knowledge of the facts giving rise to the cause of action or one year from the date of the transaction: [s. 211(b)]

Alberta Statute	Statutory Breach	Liability for Offence	Statutory Defence and Limitation Period
Water Act, R.S.A. 2000, c. W-3	Director, officer, or agent is guilty of an offence if he or she directed, authorized, assented to, acquiesced in, or participated in the commission of the offence, including providing false or misleading information, data, records, reports, or documents pursuant to the requirement under the Act to provide them (s. 142(1)(a)); failing to provide information, data, records, reports, or documents as required under the Act (s. 142(1)(b)); contravening a water management order (s. 142(1)(c)); contravening an enforcement order (s. 142(1)(d)); contravening a term or condition of approval, preliminary certificate, or licence (s. 142(1)(e)): [s. 146]	Liable to the punishment provided for in the offence, whether or not the corporation was prosecuted or convicted: [s. 146]	Action must be commenced within 2 years after the later of the date on which the offence was committed or the date on which the evidence of the offence first came to the attention of the Director: [s. 141]
Workers' Compensation Act, R.S.A. 2000, c. W-15	Director, officer, or agent is guilty of an offence if he or she directed, authorized, assented to, acquiesced in, or participated in the commission of the offence by the corporation: [s. 152.01]	Liable to a fine not exceeding $25,000 and, where an offence is a continuing offence, a further fine not exceeding $10,000 for each day the offence continues and/or imprisonment not exceeding 6 months: [s. 152(2)]	Action must be commenced within 2 years after the subject-matter of the prosecution arose: [s. 152(4)]
ADDITIONAL STATUTES IMPOSING DIRECTOR LIABILITY			
Alberta Treasury Branches Act, R.S.A. 2000, c. A-37	Director liable if he or she consented to a resolution authorizing investment, loan, guarantee, or other transaction that (a) is contrary to regulations and (b) involves payment or distribution of property by ATB: [s. 25(1)]	Liable jointly and severally to restore to ATB any amounts so paid and the value of property so distributed and not otherwise recovered by it: [s. 25(1)]	Director is not liable if he or she did not know and could not reasonably have known that the investment, loan, guarantee, or other transaction was contrary to regulations [s. 25(3)] Director is not liable if he or she relied in good faith on a financial statement or a professional report or opinion: [s. 25(4)] Action must be commenced within 5 years after the happening of the event that gave rise to the cause of action: [s. 25(5)]

Alberta Statute	Statutory Breach	Liability for Offence	Statutory Defence and Limitation Period
Architects Act, R.S.A. 2000, c. A-44	Person, officer, employee, or is agent is guilty of an offence if he or she contravened the Act: [s. 71(1)]	Liable for first offence for a fine not exceeding $2,000, for second offence, for a fine not exceeding $4,000, and for third and subsequent offences to a fine not exceeding $6,000 and/or imprisonment not exceeding 6 months: [s. 71(1)]	Action must be commenced within 2 years after the commission of the alleged offence: [s. 71(2)]
Charitable Fund-raising Act, R.S.A. 2000, c. C-9	Principal, director, manager, employee, or agent is guilty of an offence if he or she authorized, acquiesced, or participated in the contravention, including soliciting by telephone outside of permitted hours (s. 5); failure to maintain accurate financial records (s. 7); soliciting without a license; making representations regarding corporate or individual support without a written consent (s. 37): [s. 55(1)]	Liable to a fine of not less than $1,000 and not exceeding $100,000 or 3 times the amount that the defendant acquired as result of the offence, and/or imprisonment not exceeding 2 years, whether or not the corporation was prosecuted or convicted: [s. 55(2)]	Prosecution must be commenced within 2 years after the commission of the offence: [s. 55(6)]
Credit Union Act, R.S.A. 2000, c. C-32	Directors and officers of credit unions have similar duties and related liabilities and are guilty of similar offences as directors and officers under ABCA. Major liabilities and offences are contained in ss. 73, 74, 142, and 221–223.		
Financial Consumers Act, R.S.A. 2000, c. F-13	Director, officer, employee, or other person is guilty of an offence if he or she directed, authorized, assented to, knowingly acquiesced in, or knowingly participated in the contravention: [s. 43(2)]	Liable to a fine not exceeding $100,000, or 3 times the loss incurred by the consumer as the result of the contravention, whichever is greater: [s. 43(2)]	Action must be commenced within 2 years after the alleged commission of the offence: [s. 41(2)]
Fisheries (Alberta) Act, R.S.A. 2000, c. F-16	Director, officer, or agent is guilty of an offence if he or she directed, authorized, assented to, acquiesced in, or participated in the contravention: [s. 36]	Liable to a fine not exceeding $100,000 and/or imprisonment not exceeding 1 year: [s. 35]	Crown, Minister, or any fishery officer or fishery guardian is not liable for anything done or not done by any of them in good faith while they were exercising powers and performing duties under the Act: [s. 42] Action must be commenced within 2 years after the alleged commission of the offence: [s. 41]

Alberta Statute	Statutory Breach	Liability for Offence	Statutory Defence and Limitation Period
Forest and Prairie Protection Act, R.S.A. 2000, c. F-19	Director, officer, or agent is guilty of an offence if he or she directed, authorized, assented to, acquiesced in, or participated in the contravention: [s. 37.1]	Liable separately to the penalty provided for the offence: [s. 37.1]	Action must be commenced within 2 years after the date on which the evidence of the alleged offence first came to the attention ofthe forest officer: [s. 37.4(1)]
Freehold Mineral Rights Tax Act, R.S.A. 2000, c. F-26	Director or officer is guilty of an offence if he or she directed, authorized, assented to, acquiesced in, or participated in the commission of offences including the failure to keep proper records of place of business in Alberta (s. 7(2)); improper communication of records or information obtained under the Act to someone who is not legally entitled to such material (s. 10(1)): [s. 11(2)]	Liable to a fine not exceeding $5,000: [s. 11(1)]	
Fuel Tax Act, R.S.A. 2000, c. F-28	Director is liable if he or she failed to remit the tax collected by the corporation: [s. 25]	Liable jointly and severally to pay the required tax and the interest or penalties relating to it: [s. 25]	Action must be commenced within 2 years after the director ceased to be a director of the corporation: [s. 25(3)]
Gas Resources Preservation Act, R.S.A. 2000, c. G-4	Director, officer, or agent who directed, authorized, assented to, acquiesced in, or participated in the commission of an offence by the corporation is a party to offences including removing from Alberta without permit, by pipeline or other means, any gas or propane produced in Alberta and owned by a person (s. 18(1)(a)); knowingly removing from Alberta without permit, by pipeline or other means, any gas or propane produced in Alberta and not owned by a person (s. 18(1)(b)); contravening a term or condition of a permit or regulations (ss. 18(2)(a) and (e)): [s. 19(1)]	Liable to a fine not exceeding $100,000 for the first day of the offence and $25,000 for every day thereafter on which the contravention continues: [s. 19(2)]	Action must be commenced within 18 months from the time the subject matter of the prosecution arose: [s. 19(4)]

Alberta Statute	Statutory Breach	Liability for Offence	Statutory Defence and Limitation Period
Loan and Trust Corporations Act, R.S.A. 2000, c. L-20	Director is liable if he or she authorized the issue of shares for consideration other than the money that is less than the fair market value of the money that would have been received: [s. 131(1)]	Liable, jointly and severally, to the corporation to make good the amount by which the consideration received is less than the fair equivalent of the money that the corporation would have received if the share had been issued for money: [s. 131(1)]	Director is not liable if he or she did not know and was not reasonably able to know that the shares issued were issued for a consideration less than the fair equivalent of money that the provincial corporation would have received if the share had been issued for money: [s. 131(3)]
Loan and Trust Corporations Act	Director liable if he or she authorized the following: — an investment, transaction, or guarantee that is contrary to Parts 9, 10, or 11 and involves any payment or distribution of property by the provincial corporation; — a purchase, redemption, or other acquisition of shares, contrary to ss. 63, 64, or 65; — a reduction in the stated capital of the corporation, contrary to s. 67; — the payment of a commission, contrary to s. 71; — the payment of a dividend, contrary to s. 72; — the payment of an indemnity, contrary to s. 135; — a payment to a shareholder, contrary to an order under s. 293; — a payment contrary to s. 25; or — any other payment to a shareholder, director, or officer, the effect of which is to reduce the capital base of the corporation to an amount that is less than that required under this Act: [s. 131(4)]	Liable, jointly and severally, to restore to the corporation amounts so paid and the value of the property so distributed and not otherwise recovered by it: [s. 131(4)]	Director is not liable if he or she did not know and was not reasonably able to know that the investment, transaction, or guarantee was contrary to Parts 9, 10, or 11: [s. 131(5)]
Loan and Trust Corporations Act	Director or officer is guilty of an offence if he or she authorized, permitted, or acquiesced in the commission of an offence by the corporation: [s. 309]	Liable to a fine not exceeding $100,000 for a first offence and not exceeding $200,000 for each subsequent offence: [s. 309]	Action must be commenced within 3 years after the facts on which the action is based first came to the attention of the plaintiff: [s. 310]

Alberta Statute	Statutory Breach	Liability for Offence	Statutory Defence and Limitation Period
Mines and Minerals Act, R.S.A. 2000, c. M-17	Director, officer, or agent is guilty of an offence if he or she directed, authorized, assented to, acquiesced in, or participated in the failure to keep records in accordance with regulations or on any terms and conditions imposed by the Minister: [ss. 47 and 63(4)]	Liable to a fine not exceeding $100,000, whether or not the corporation was prosecuted or convicted: [ss. 63(1) and (4)]	Director is not liable if he or she establishes that the offence was committed without the director's knowledge or consent and that he or she took all reasonable measures to prevent its commission: [s. 63(3)]
Mines and Minerals Act	Director, officer or agent guilty of offence if directed, authorized, assented to, acquiesced in or participated in the failure to provide information when it is requested by the Minister (i.e., operations in which minerals were recovered, costs of such recovery, etc.): [ss. 48 and 63(4)]	Liable to fine not exceeding $100,000, whether or not the corporation prosecuted or convicted [s. 63(1) and (4)]	Director is not liable if he or she establishes that the offence was committed without the director's knowledge or consent and that he or she took all reasonable measures to prevent its commission: [s. 63(3)]
Mines and Minerals Act	Director, officer, or agent is guilty of an offence if he or she directed, authorized, assented to, acquiesced in, or participated in the misuse of confidential information: [ss. 50 and 63(4)]	Liable to a fine not exceeding $100,000, whether or not the corporation was prosecuted or convicted: [s. 63(1) and (4)]	Director is not liable if he or she establishes that the offence was committed without the director's knowledge or consent and he or she that took all reasonable measures to prevent its commission: [s. 63(3)]
Mines and Minerals Act	Director, officer, or agent is guilty of an offence if he or she directed, authorized, assented to, acquiesced in, or participated in the failure to assist or to supply information to the Minister for the purpose of an investigation or inspection: [ss. 52(2) and 63(4)]	Liable to a fine not exceeding $100,000, whether or not the corporation was prosecuted or convicted: [s. 63(1) and (4)]	Director is not liable if he or she establishes that the offence was committed without the director's knowledge or consent and that he or she took all reasonable measures to prevent its commission: [s. 63(3)]
Mines and Minerals Act	Director, officer, or agent is guilty of an offence if he or she directed, authorized, assented to, acquiesced in, or participated in hindering or preventing, or attempting to hinder or prevent, any other person to bid or make an offer in a public tender for agreement by intimidation, combination, unfair management, or otherwise: [ss. 53 and 63(4)]	Liable to a fine not exceeding $100,000, whether or not the corporation was prosecuted or convicted: [s. 63(1) and (4)]	Director is not liable if he or she establishes that the offence was committed without the director's knowledge or consent and that he or she took all reasonable measures to prevent its commission: [s. 63(3)]

Alberta Statute	Statutory Breach	Liability for Offence	Statutory Defence and Limitation Period
Mines and Minerals Act	Director, officer, or agent is guilty of an offence if he or she directed, authorized, assented to, acquiesced in, or participated in winning, working, or recovering a mineral that is the property of the Crown (Alberta) unless he or she is authorized to do so: [ss. 54 and 63(4)]	Liable to a fine not exceeding $100,000, whether or not the corporation was prosecuted or convicted: [s. 63(1) and (4)]	Action must be commenced within 60 months from the date on which the subject-matter of the prosecution arose: [s. 64(5)] Director is not liable if he or she establises that the offence was committed without the director's knowledge or consent and that he or she took all reasonable measures to prevent its commission: [s. 63(3)]
Mines and Minerals Act	Director or officer is guilty of an offence if he or she directed, authorized, assented to, acquiesced in, or participated in the filing or submission by the corporation of a report, return, estimate, or other information or made a statement or answered any question knowing information therein was false or misleading or misrepresented or failed to disclose a material fact: [s. 63(2)]	Liable to a fine equal to the greater of (a) not more than the amount of money equal to the value of the Crown's royalty share of mineral or the amount of money of which the Alberta Crown was deprived by reason of the commission of the offence or (b) to a fine not exceeding $100,000, whether or not the corporation was prosecuted or convicted: [s. 63(2)]	Director is not liable if he or she establishes that the offence was committed without the director's knowledge or consent and that he or she took all reasonable measures to prevent its commission: [s. 63(3)]
Mines and Minerals Act	Director, officer, or agent is guilty of an offence if he or she directed, authorized, assented to, acquiesced in, or participated in the failure to observe and comply with orders and directions of the Minister of Infrastructure: [ss. 63(1) and 79]	Liable to a fine not exceeding $100,000, whether or not the corporation was prosecuted or convicted: [s. 63(4)]	Director is not liable if he or she establishes that the offence was committed without the director's knowledge or consent and that he or she took all reasonable measures to prevent its commission: [s. 63(3)]
Mines and Minerals Act	Director is guilty of an offence if he or she did not co-operate, provide assistance, supply information, or otherwise obstructed an investigation or inspection by the Minister in relation to a program of exploration on land in Alberta, including private land: [ss. 108.3(2) and (3)]	Liable to a fine not exceeding $100,000: [s. 108.3(3)]	

Alberta Statute	Statutory Breach	Liability for Offence	Statutory Defence and Limitation Period
Mines and Minerals Act	Director is guilty of an offence if he or she contravened exploration provisions in the Act or regulations or failed to comply with a condition of the exploration approval, licence, or permit: [s. 112(1)]	Liable to a ministerial order to pay the Crown a penalty not exceeding the maximum penalty prescribed by regulations in relation to that contravention or failure to comply for each day the contravention occurs: [s. 112(1)]	
Natural Gas Marketing Act, R.S.A. 2000, c. N-1	Director, officer, or agent is guilty of an offence if he or she directed, authorized, acquiesced in, assented to, or participated in the commission of an offence by the corporation: [s. 26]	Liable to a fine not exceeding $100,000 or where the contravention occurs and continues for more than 1 day, $25,000 for each day the offence occurs and continues: [s. 26(1)]	Action must be commenced within 3 years from the date on which the subject-matter of the offence arose: [s. 26(3)]
Oil and Gas Conservation Act, R.S.A. 2000, c. O-6	Person is liable if he or she caused any person's failure to comply with the provisions of the Act, regulations, or orders or the directions of the board or terms and conditions under the order of the Lieutenant Governor in Council granting approval or authorization under the Act, which includes committing waste: [s. 108]	Liable to a fine of not less than $50 nor more than $500 and in default of payment to imprisonment not exceeding 6 months. In respect of a continuing offence, directors and officers are liable to a fine of not less than $50 and not exceeding $500 for the first day the offence occurs and not less than $25 nor more than $250 for each day the offence continues thereafter, and in default of payment to imprisonment not exceeding 6 months: [s. 110]	Action must be commenced within 18 months from the time the subject matter of the prosecution arose: [s. 109]
Oil Sands Conservation Act, R.S.A. 2000, c. O-7	Person is guilty of an offence if he or she instructed, ordered, directed, induced, or caused an officer, agent, or employee of the holder of the authorization to breach the Act or personally failed to comply with a provision of the Act or regulations made thereunder, which include committing waste: [s. 24]	Liable to a fine of not less than $50 and not exceeding $1,000 and/or imprisonment not exceeding 6 months: [s. 26(1)(b)]	Action must be commenced within 18 months from the time the subject matter of the proceedings arose: [s. 25]
Real Estate Act, R.S.A. 2000, c. R-5	Director, officer, or agent is guilty of an offence if he or she directed, authorized, acquiesced in, assented to, or participated in the commission of the offence including acting as or dealing as a mortgage broker, real estate broker, or real estate appraiser without the appropriate authorization (s. 17); failing to keep proper trust accounts (s. 25): [s. 81(2)]	Liable for a fine not exceeding $25,000 whether or not the corporation was prosecuted or convicted: [ss. 81(1) and (2)]	Action must be commenced within 3 years after the alleged offence took place: [s. 81(4)]

Alberta Statute	Statutory Breach	Liability for Offence	Statutory Defence and Limitation Period
Residential Tenancies Act, S.A. 2004, c. R-17.1	Director, officer, employee, or agent is guilty of an offence if he or she authorized, assented to, acquiesced in, or participated in the commission of the offence, including failing to comply with notice requirements (s. 18); failing to provide inspection reports (s. 19); entry of premises except in accordance with the Act (s. 23); failing to keep a security deposit in a trust account (s. 44): [s. 60(2)]	Liable to a fine not exceeding $5,000: [s. 60(2)]	Action must be commenced within 3 years after the alleged offence took place: [s. 61]
Tourism Levy Act, R.S.A. 2000, c T-5.5	Director, officer, or agent is guilty of an offence if he or she directed, authorized, assented to, acquiesced in, or participated in the commission of the offence, including wilfully evading payment of tourism levy (s. 35(1)): [s. 37]	Liable (unless penalty is otherwise provided) to a fine for the first offence not exceeding $1,000; fine for the second offence not exceeding $2,500, and fine for a third or subsequent offence not exceeding $5,000, whether or not the corporation was prosecuted: [s. 38]	Action must be commenced within 4 years from the date of the contravention: [s. 39]

APPENDIX III

Common Sources of Directors' Liability Under B.C. Statutes (Last updated June 2006)

THIS IS NOT A COMPREHENSIVE LIST. THE PASSAGES SET OUT BELOW ARE SUMMARIES ONLY, AND THE READER MUST REFER TO THE SPECIFIC STATUTE FOR A COMPLETE STATEMENT OF THE DIRECTOR'S LEGAL RESPONSIBILITIES AND THE STATUTORY CONTEXT IN WHICH THOSE LEGAL RESPONSIBILITIES ARISE.

B.C. Statutes	Statutory Breach	Liability for Offence	Statutory Defence and Limitation Period
STATUTES AFFECTING MOST CORPORATIONS			
Business Corporations Act, S.B.C. 2002, c. B-57 ("BCBCA")	Director or officer is liable if he or she failed, when exercising powers and performing the functions of a director or officer, to (a) act honestly and in good faith with a view to the best interests of the company; (b) exercise the care, diligence, and skill that a reasonably prudent individual would exercise in comparable circumstances; (c) act in accordance with this Act and regulations, and (d) subject to paragraphs (a) to (c), act in accordance with the memorandum and articles of the company: [s. 142(1)]	Civilly liable for resulting loss which varies according to circumstances.	Director is not liable if the director proves that he or she relied in good faith on the financial statements from the officer or auditor, professional report, statement of fact, or record considered reasonable by the court: [s. 157(1)]

B.C. Statutes	Statutory Breach	Liability for Offence	Statutory Defence and Limitation Period
Business Corporations Act	Director or senior officer is liable if he or she entered into a material contract/transaction with the corporation without disclosing interest: [s. 148(1)]	Liable to account to the company for any profit that accrued to the director or senior officer as a result and/or can be prohibited from entering into a contract and/or is liable to any other order that the court considers appropriate: [s. 148(1)]	Director or senior officer is not liable if the contract/transaction is approved by a special resolution under s. 149, after the nature and extent of the disclosable interest had been disclosed to shareholders who are entitled to vote on that resolution: [s. 148(2)(c)] Director or senior officer is not liable, whether or not the contract or transaction is approved under s. 149, if: (1) the company entered into the contract or transaction before the person became a director or senior officer, (2) the disclosable interest is disclosed to directors or shareholders, and (3) the director or senior officer did not participate in, and, in case of a director, did not vote as a director on, any decision or resolution touching on the contract or transaction: [s. 148(2)(d)] Director or senior officer is not liable if the court determines that the contract or transaction is fair and reasonable to the company: [s. 150]
Business Corporations Act	Directors are liable if they authorized the following: (a) act contrary to s. 33(1) as result of which the company has paid compensation to any person; (b) the payment of a commission or allowance of discount, contrary to s. 67; (c) the payment of a dividend, contrary to s. 70(2); (d) the purchase, redemption, or other acquisition of shares, contrary to ss. 78 or 79: [s. 154(1)]	Liable, jointly and severally, to compensate the company, shareholder, or the beneficial owner of shares of the company for losses sustained: [s. 154(2)]	Director is not liable if he or she did not know and could not reasonably have known that the value of the consideration for which the shares were issued was less than the issue price set for the shares: [s. 154(4)] Director is not liable if he or she proves that he or she relied, in good faith, on financial statements from the officer or auditor, a professional report, a statement of fact, or a record considered reasonable by the court under s. 157(1): [s. 157(1)] Director is not liable if the director proves that he or she dissented to the resolution: [s. 154]

B.C. Statutes	Statutory Breach	Liability for Offence	Statutory Defence and Limitation Period
Business Corporations Act	Director is liable if he or she authorized the issue of shares in contravention of ss. 63(2)(b) or 64: [s. 154(2)]	Liable, jointly and severally, to compensate the company, shareholder, or beneficial owner of shares, for any losses, damages, and costs sustained: [s. 154(2)]	Director is not liable if the director proves that he or she did not know and could not reasonably have known that the value of the consideration for which the share was issued was less than the issue price set for the share under s. 63: [s. 154(4)]
Business Corporations Act	Director or officer of the company or extra-provincial company is liable if he or she knowingly permitted the company to fail to display its name or seal, contrary to s. 27(1) or (2): [s. 158(1)]	Liable to indemnify a purchaser or supplier of goods or services or a person holding a security who a suffers loss as a result: [s. 158(1)]	None
Business Corporations Act	Director or officer is liable if he or she issued or authorized the issue of bills of exchange, promissory notes, endorsements, cheques, and money orders used in B.C. signed by it or on its behalf that does not display the name of the company: [s. 158(2)]	Liable to a person holding an instrument for the amount of it, unless it is duly paid by the company: [s. 158(2)]	None
Business Corporations Act	Insider (which includes a director or officer) is liable if he or she made use of specific confidential information for the insider's (or the insider's associates' or affiliates') benefit/advantage, if the information, if it was generally known, might reasonably be expected to materially affect the value of the security: [s. 192(2)]	Liable to compensate a person for any direct loss suffered: [s. 192(3)] Liable to account to the company for any direct benefit/advantage received by the insider (or the insider's associate or affiliate) that is generally known: [s. 192(3)]	Insider not liable to a person if he or she proves (i) information was known or ought reasonably to have been known by that person, or (ii) the insider reasonably believed that the specific confidential information was known to the person who suffered the loss: [s. 192(3)] Insider is not liable to the company if the insider proves that he or she reasonably believed that information was generally known: [s. 192(3)] Action must be commenced 2 years after the discovery of the facts that gave rise to the cause of action: [s. 192(4)]

B.C. Statutes	Statutory Breach	Liability for Offence	Statutory Defence and Limitation Period
Business Corporations Act	Director is guilty of offence if he or she does not ensure that (1) before financial statements are published, they are (a) approved by directors, and (b) signed by 1 or more directors to confirm them; and (2) the financial statements published (a) have attached any auditor's report and (b) do not purport to be audited unless they were audited and auditor's report was made: [ss. 199(1) and 426(1)]	Liable to a fine of not more than $2,000: [s. 428(1)]	Directors are not liable if the shareholders pass a unanimous resolution waiving their duty: [s. 200(1)] Action must be commenced within 3 years of the commission of the offence: [s. 430(1)]
Business Corporations Act	Director or officer is guilty of an offence if he or she failed to communicate to the auditor facts that (a) could reasonably have been determined before the date on which the financial statements were published, and (b) if known before that date, would have required material adjustment to those financial statements: [s. 216(1)]	Liable to a fine of not more than $2,000: [s. 428(1)]	Action must be commenced within 3 years of the commission of the offence: [s. 430(1)]
Business Corporations Act	Director is guilty of an offence if he or she failed to promptly amend the financial statements to reflect facts referred to in s. 216(1) and provide amended financial statements to the auditor: [s. 216(2)]	Liable to a fine of not more than $2,000: [s. 428(1)]	Action must be commenced within 3 years of the commission of the offence: [s. 430(1)]
Business Corporations Act	Director is guilty of an offence if the auditor informed the directors of the error or misstatement in financial statements and the director failed to promptly amend the financial statements and provide amended financial statements to the auditor: [s. 216(4)]	Liable to a fine of not more than $2,000: [s. 428(1)]	Action must be commenced within 3 years of the commission of the offence: [s. 430(1)]
Business Corporations Act	Director is guilty of an offence if he or she failed after the receipt of the amended auditor's report to notify shareholders and provide a statement explaining the effect of the amendment on the financial position and the results of the operations of the company: [s. 216(5)]	Liable to a fine of not more than $2,000: [s. 428(1)]	Action must be commenced within 3 years of the commission of the offence: [s. 430(1)]
Business Corporations Act	Director or officer is guilty of an offence if he or she failed to provide the auditor with access to records and all of the information the auditor requires to make a report: [s. 217]	Liable to a fine of not more than $2,000: [s. 428(1)]	Action must be commenced within 3 years of the commission of the offence: [s. 430(1)]

B.C. Statutes	Statutory Breach	Liability for Offence	Statutory Defence and Limitation Period
Business Corporations Act	Director is guilty of an offence if he or she failed to provide the audit committee with financial statements and the auditor's report in sufficient time to allow the committee to review and report on them as required: [s. 226]	Liable to a fine of not more than $2,000: [s. 428(1)]	Action must be commenced within 3 years of the commission of the offence: [s. 430(1)]
Business Corporations Act	Director or officer is guilty of an offence if he or she failed to provide the auditor with accounting and related records: [s. 251]	Liable to a fine of not more than $2,000: [s. 428(1)]	Action must be commenced within 3 years of the commission of the offence: [s. 430(1)]
Business Corporations Act	Director is guilty of an offence if he or she acted as a director if he or she was not qualified to do so under s. 124 (2): [s. 426(3)]	Liable to a fine not exceeding $2,000: [s. 428(5)]	Action must be commenced within 3 years of the commission of the offence: [s. 430(1)]
Business Corporations Act	Director or officer of a corporation or of a limited liability company is guilty of an offence if he or she knowingly authorized, permitted, or acquiesced in the corporation making a false or misleading statement or omitting a material fact which made the statement false or misleading in the record required or permitted to be made under the Act: [s. 427(1)(a)]	Liable for a fine not exceeding $10,000, whether or not the corporation or limited liability company was prosecuted or convicted: [s. 427(2)]	Director or officer is not liable if he or she did not know, and could not have known with exercise of reasonable diligence, that the statement was false or misleading: [s. 427(3)] Action must be commenced within 3 years of the commission of the offence: [s. 430(1)]
Business Practices and Consumer Protection Act, S.B.C. 2004, c. B-2	Director or officer is guilty of an offence if he or she authorized, permitted, or acquiesced in the commission of various offences under the Act, including a deceptive act or practice; failure to maintain a record of an advertisement; or an unconscionable act or practice: [s. 189(8)]	Liable for a fine not exceeding $10,000 and/or imprisonment not exceeding 12 months: [s. 190]	Action must be commenced within 2 years after the date of the contravention: [s. 170]
Civil Rights Protection Act, R.S.B.C. 1996, c. C-49	Director or officer is guilty of an offence if he or she authorized, permitted, or acquiesced in the commission of a prohibited act, including any conduct or communication interfering with the civil rights of an individual: [s. 2]	Liable for a fine not exceeding $2,000 and/or imprisonment not exceeding 6 months: [ss. 5(1) and (3)]	None
Cooperative Association Act, S.B.C. 1999, c. C-28	Director is liable if the association carries on business without at least three members for more than 6 months: [s. 10(2)]	Liable, jointly and severally, for the payment of the debts of the association that were incurred during that time: [s. 10(2)]	None

B.C. Statutes	Statutory Breach	Liability for Offence	Statutory Defence and Limitation Period
Cooperative Association Act	Director is guilty of an offence if he or she fails to meet the fiduciary duty and duty of care: [s. 84]	Civilly liable in an amount that varies, depending on circumstance	None
Cooperative Association Act	Director is liable to account to the association for any profit that accrues to him or here as a result of the contract/transaction in which the director holds disclosable interest: [s. 89]	Liable to account to the association for part of the profit that the director was not expressly permitted to retain: [s. 89(3)]	Director is not liable if the contract/transaction was approved by the directors of an association or by members of an association by a special resolution: [s. 90]
Cooperative Association Act	Director is guilty of an offence if he or she knowingly authorized, permitted, and acquiesced in the making of misleading statements: [s. 200(2)]	Liable to a fine not exceeding $5,000 and/or imprisonment not exceeding 6 months whether or not the corporation has been prosecuted and convicted: [s. 200(2)]	Director is not liable if he or she did not know that the statement was false or misleading and with the exercise of due diligence, he or she could not have reasonably known that the statement was false or misleading: [s. 200(3)]
Corporation Capital Tax Act, R.S.B.C. 1996, c. C-73	Director or officer is guilty of an offence if he or she directed, authorized, assented to, or acquiesced or participated in the commission of the offence, including making false statements in a return, certificate, statement, or answer (s. 47(2)(a)); destroying records of the financial corporation to evade tax payment (s. 47(2)(b)); making false or deceptive entries in records (s. 47(2)(c)); wilfully evading tax payment (s. 47(2)(d)); conspiring to commit offences the under Act (s. 47(2)(e)): [s. 47(5)]	Liable to a fine of not less than $25 and not exceeding $10,000, plus in an appropriate case, an amount not exceeding double the amount of tax that was sought to be evaded and/or imprisonment not exceeding 2 years: [s. 47(3)]	
Employment Standards Act, R.S.B.C. 1996, c. E-113	Employee, officer, director, or agent is guilty of an offence if he or she authorized, permitted, or acquiesced in the offence by the corporation: [s. 125(2)]	Liable to a penalty provided for in the offence, whether or not the corporation is convicted: [s. 125(3)]	Action must be commenced within 2 years after the facts come to the director's knowledge: [s. 124]
Employment Standards Act	Employee, officer, director, or agent is guilty of an offence if he or she authorized, permitted, or acquiesced in a contravention of the Act by the corporation: [s. 98(2)]	Liable to the penalty provided in the offence: [s. 98]	

B.C. Statutes	Statutory Breach	Liability for Offence	Statutory Defence and Limitation Period
Employment Standards Act	Director or officer is liable if he or she failed to pay the wages of an employee, except termination pay if the corporation is in receivership or is subject to an action under s. 427 of the *Bank Act;* vacation pay that becomes payable after the director ceases to hold office, or money in employee's time bank after the director ceases to hold office: [s. 96(1)]	Liable for up to 2 months' wages for each employee: [s. (96(1)]	
Environmental Assessment Act, S.B.C. 2002, c. E-43	Director or officer is guilty of an offence if he or she authorized, permitted, or acquiesced in the offence of the corporation (for example, failing to obtain an environmental assessment; making a statement that is false or misleading): [s. 41(4)]	Liable for a first offence to a fine not exceeding $100,000 and/or 6 months in prison: [s. 43(b)(i)]; for a subsequent offence, to a fine not exceeding $200,000 and/or 12 months in prison: [s. 43(b)(ii)]	Director is not liable if he or she did not know that the statement was false or misleading and could not have known it was false or misleading in exercising due diligence: [s. 41(3)] Action must be commenced within 3 years after the facts come to the knowledge of the Minister: [s. 46]
Environmental Management Act, S.B.C. 2003, c. E-53	Director or officer is guilty of an offence if he or she authorized, permitted, or acquiesced in the offence of the corporation (for example, the contravention of by-laws imposed to regulate the management of municipal solid waste or recyclable material): [s. 25(3)(p)]	Liable to a fine not exceeding $200,000: [s. 25(3)(p)]	None
Environmental Management Act	Director or officer is guilty of an offence if he or she authorized, permitted, or acquiesced in an offence committed by the corporation (for example, a contravention on provisions including waste disposal, the transportation of hazardous waste, spill prevention, and reporting): [s. 121]	Liability varies, depending on the offence and is applicable whether or not the corporation is convicted: [s. 121]	Action must be commenced within 3 years after the date on which the facts arose or if the Minister completes the certificate, 18 months after the date that the facts on which the information was based came to the knowledge of the Minister: [s. 124]
Freedom of Information and Privacy Act, R.S.B.C. 1996, c. F-165	Director or officer is guilty of an offence if he or she authorized, permitted, or acquiesced in the commission of the offence by the corporation: [s. 74.1(4)]	Liable to a fine of up to $2,000, whether or not the corporation was prosecuted: [ss. 74.1(4) and (5)]	Action must be commenced within 1 year after the event occurred or if the Minister files a certificate, 1 year after the date on which the Minister learned of the act: [s. 74.1(6)]

B.C. Statutes	Statutory Breach	Liability for Offence	Statutory Defence and Limitation Period
Income Tax Act, R.S.B.C. 1996, c. I-215	Director and corporation are liable under s. 227.1 of the *Federal Income Tax Act* for the failure to deduct, remit, or pay an amount of tax for the taxation year as required: [s. 57]	Liable, jointly and severally, to pay the amount and interest or penalties relating thereto: [s. 57]	
Insurance (Captive Company) Act, R.S.B.C. 1996, c. I-227	Director or officer is guilty of an offence if he or she authorized, permitted, or acquiesced in the commission of an offence by the corporation: [s. 12(4)]	Liable to fine of $100,000 or to imprisonment for not exceeding 5 years less a day: [s. 12(6)]	
Medicare Protection Act, R.S.B.C. 1996, c. M-286	Director or officer is liable if he or she failed to remit the premiums required to be paid or collected and remitted by the corporation: [s. 32(6)]	Liable, jointly and severally, to make a payment not exceeding 10 times the amount not paid or collected: [ss. 32(5) and (6)]	
Partnership Act, R.S.B.C. 1996, c. P-348	Director or officer is guilty of an offence if he or she authorized, permitted, or acquiesced in the commission of offences, including making or omitting to make a statement in a registration statement, notice of dissolution, or any other record filed that is false or misleading: [ss. 90.4(1) and (2)]	Liable to a fine not exceeding $2,000: [s. 90.5(b)]	Director is not liable if he or she did not know that the statement was false or misleading and could not have known in it was false or misleading in the exercise of reasonable diligence: [s. 90.4(3)]
Pension Benefits Standards Act, R.S.B.C. 1996, c. P-352	Director or officer is guilty of an offence if he or she authorized, permitted, or acquiesced in the commission of an offence, including contravening Act (s. 72(1)(a)); destroying records (s. 72(1)(b)(i)); making a false or misleading statement (s. 72(1)(b)(ii)); failing to state anything in records (s. 72(1)(b)(iii)): [s. 72(3)]	Liable to a fine not exceeding $25,000: [s. 72(3)]	Action must be commenced within 2 years after the facts come to the attention of the Superintendent: [s. 73(1)]
Safety Standards Act, S.B.C. 2003, c. S-39	Director or officer is guilty of an offence if he or she authorized, permitted, or acquiesced in the commission of the offence by the corporation: [s. 75(1)]	Liable to a fine not exceeding $100,000 and/or 18 months' imprisonment: [s. 78(1)]; for a continuing offence, a fine not exceeding $5,000/day: [s. 78(3)]; whether or not the corporation is prosecuted or convicted: [s. 75(1)]	Director is not liable if the offence was committed without the defendant's knowledge or consent: [s. 75(3)(a)] or if the director exercised due diligence: [s. 75(3)(b)]

B.C. Statutes	Statutory Breach	Liability for Offence	Statutory Defence and Limitation Period
Securities Act, R.S.B.C. 1996, c. S-418	Director is guilty of an offence if he or she authorized, permitted, or acquiesced in the offence of a person other than an individual under s. 155, including, but not limited to, the failure to file records; trading securities without being registered; trading on exchange not recognized by the commission; the failure to file a prospectus; the failure to publish a material change; the failure to file an insider's report; the failure to conform with the requirements for take-over bids; insider trading; making false or misleading statements; concealing or refusing to give information: [s. 155(4)]	Liability varies, depending on the nature of the offence: — a fine not exceeding $3 million and/or 3 years' imprisonment: [s. 155(2)] — for misleading trading activity and acting on generally undisclosed information, a fine of not less than the profit made and not exceeding the greater of $3 million and triple the profit made: [s. 155(5)] — for sharing generally undisclosed information, not less than the profit made and not exceeding the greater of $1 million, triple the profit made, and triple the profit made by the person to whom information was disclosed: [s. 155(6)] — additional remedies include restitution and payment to the commission of the amount obtained as result of the offence: [s. 155.1] — also, the Commission can impose a monetary penalty of no more than $1 million: [s. 162]	Director is not liable if he or she proves reasonable diligence in respect of misleading statements: [s. 50] Director is not liable for insider trading if he or she reasonably believed that information had been generally disclosed: [s. 57] Action must be commenced within 6 years after the date of the event giving rise to proceedings: [s. 159]
Social Service Tax Act, R.S.B.C. 1996, c. S-431	Director is liable if he or she failed to remit taxes: [s. 102.1(1)]	Liable, jointly and severally, with the corporation to pay the amount equal to the taxes that the corporation failed to collect or remit, including penalties and interest: [s. 102.1(1)]	Director is not liable if he or she proves that he or she exercised the care, diligence, and skill that a reasonably prudent person would exercise in comparable circumstances: [s. 102.1(3)] Action must be commenced within 2 years after the date that the person was last a director of the corporation: [s. 115.1(2)]

B.C. Statutes	Statutory Breach	Liability for Offence	Statutory Defence and Limitation Period
Social Service Tax Act	Director or officer is guilty of an offence if he or she authorized, permitted, or acquiesced in the commission of the offence by the corporation: [s. 122]	Liability varies, depending on offence: — not exceeding a fine of $10,000 and/or imprisonment for 2 years plus a fine equal to the tax not collected, including penalties/interest: [s. 123(4)]	Action must be commenced within 6 years after the matter arose, except in cases of fraud, where there is no limitation period: [s. 127]
Society Act, R.S.B.C. 1996, c. S-433	Directors are liable for the failure to perform various duties or for offences similar to those identified under the BCBCA, including, but not limited to, the following: the failure to act honestly and in good faith in the best interests of society and to exercise the care, diligence, and skill of a reasonably prudent person (s. 25(1)); the failure to disclose a contract or transaction in which the director has an interest (ss. 27–29); knowingly participating in or acquiescing in the contravention of an order of the Minister (s. 84(5)); making a statement or omitting a statement of material fact that results in a false or misleading statement (s. 93)	Liability varies according to the circumstances of the case or penalty imposed by the Act; see the Act for the exact provisions.	Director or officer is not liable if various statutory defences or limitation periods apply; see the Act for the exact provisions
Transport of Dangerous Goods Act, R.S.B.C. 1996, c. T-458	Director or officer is guilty of an offence if he or she authorized, permitted, participated in, or acquiesced in the commission of an offence by the corporation whether or not the corporation was prosecuted or convicted: [s. 19]	Liability varies, depending on the offence: — a fine not exceeding $50,000 and/or 2 years' imprisonment (first offence); a fine not exceeding $100,000 and/or 2 years' imprisonment (subsequent offence): [s. 16(2)]; — a fine not exceeding $10,000 and/or 1 year imprisonment: [s. 16(4)]	Director is not liable if the director proves that he or she took all reasonable measures to comply: [s. 17] Action must be commenced within 2 years after the offence was committed: [s. 20]

B.C. Statutes	Statutory Breach	Liability for Offence	Statutory Defence and Limitation Period
Water Act, R.S.B.C. 1996, c. W-483	Employee, officer, director, or agent is guilty of an offence if he or she authorized, permitted, or acquiesced in the commission of the offence by the corporation whether or not the corporation was prosecuted: [s. 97]	Liable in a general offence to a fine not exceeding $200,000 and/or 6 months' imprisonment; for a continuing offence, to a fine not exceeding $200,000/day the offence continues and/or 6 months' imprisonment: [s. 93(4)] Liable in a high penalty offence to a fine not exceeding $1,000,000 and/or 1 year imprisonment; for a continuing offence, not exceeding $1,000,000/day and/or 1 year imprisonment: [s. 94(2)]	Action must be commenced within 2 years after the date the information comes to the knowledge of the Minister: [s. 98]
Water Protection Act, R.S.B.C. 1996, c. W-484	Director or officer is guilty of an offence if he or she authorized, permitted, participated in, or acquiesced in the commission of the offence by the corporation whether or not the corporation was convicted: [s. 17(5)]	Liable to a fine not exceeding $200,000; for a continuing offence, not exceeding $200,000/day the offence continues and/or 12 months' imprisonment: [s. 17(4)]	Action must be commenced within 1 year from the time of the offence: [s. 17(6)]
Workers Compensation Act, R.S.B.C. 1996, c. W-492	Director or officer is guilty of an offence if he or she authorized, permitted, participated in, or acquiesced in the commission of the offence by the corporation: [s. 213(2)]	Liable to a first conviction to a fine not exceeding $583,560.41, and $29,178.04/day if continuing and/or 6 months' imprisonment: [s. 217(a)]. On a subsequent conviction, to a fine not exceeding $1,167,120.80 and $58,356.04/day if continuing and/or 12 months' imprisonment: [s. 217(b)]	Director not liable if he or she proves that he or she exercised due diligence to prevent the commission of the offence: [s. 215] Action must be commenced within 2 years after the last occurrence of the offence: [s. 214]
ADDITIONAL STATUTES IMPOSING DIRECTOR LIABILITY			
Agricultural Produce Grading Act, R.S.B.C. 1996, c. A-11	Director, officer, employee, or agent is guilty of an offence if he or she directed, authorized, assented to, or participated in or knowingly acquiesced in the commission of the offence by the corporation: [s. 11]	Liable to a fine not exceeding $2,000; for a second or subsequent offence, to a fine not exceeding $2,000, and/or imprisonment not exceeding 6 months: [s. 13(1)]	None

B.C. Statutes	Statutory Breach	Liability for Offence	Statutory Defence and Limitation Period
Builder's Lien Act, S.B.C. 1997, c. B-45	Director or officer of a contractor or subcontractor is guilty of an offence if he or she knowingly assented to or acquiesced in the appropriation or conversion of monies held in trust for those who have provided work or supplies or contravenes garnishment provisions under the Act: [s. 11(3)]	Liable to a fine not exceeding $10,000 and/or imprisonment not exceeding 2 years [s. 11(2)]	Not liable if the director retains trust monies that are equal to the amount previously paid or he or she uses trust monies to repay a loan used by a contractor/subcontractor for work or material supplied to it: [s. 11(4)(a) and (b)] Information must be laid within 3 years of the offence occurring: [s. 11(5)]
Credit Union Incorporation Act, R.S.B.C. 1996, c. C-82	Director or officer is guilty of an offence if he or she authorized, permitted, or acquiesced in an offence by a credit union, including acquired equity shares if it would reduce the capital base to a less than adequate amount; declared dividends unless in an amount paid up for the share; knowingly provided false information: [ss. 101(2) and (3)]	Liable on first conviction to fine not exceeding $100,000 and/or imprisonment not exceeding 2 years; each subsequent offence, to a fine not exceeding $200,000 and/or imprisonment not exceeding 2 years: [s. 102(1)] Liable under s. 101(2)(b), (d), and (e) to a fine not exceeding $2,000: [s. 102)(2)]	Action must be commenced within 2 years after the facts came to knowledge of the superintendent or commission, whichever came first: [s. 104]
Drinking Water Protection Act, S.B.C. 2001, c. D-9	Person is liable if he or she authorized, permitted, or acquiesced in the commission of the offence under the Act: [s. 45(4)]	Liable for a fine not exceeding $200,000 and/or imprisonment for not longer than 12 months: [s. 45(2)(a)]; for a fine not exceeding $200,000 for each day the offence is continued and/or for imprisonment not exceeding 12 months: [s. 45(2)(b)]	Action must be commenced within 2 years after the facts come to knowledge of the drinking water officer: [s. 45(6)]
Election Act, R.S.B.C. 1996, c. E-106	Director or officer is guilty of an offence if he or she authorized, permitted, or acquiesced in the offence of the organization [s. 253(2)] (e.g., vote buying, intimidation, corrupt voting, subversion of election by an official, offences in relation to candidates)	Liable for various offences:: — a fine not exceeding $5,000 and/or imprisonment not exceeding 1 year, or — a fine not exceeding $10,000 and/or imprisonment not exceeding 2 years: [s. 255]	Director is not liable if he or she proves that he or she exercised due diligence to prevent the commission of the offence: [s. 254] Action must be commenced within 1 year after the facts come to the knowledge of the Chief electoral officer: [s. 252(2)]

B.C. Statutes	Statutory Breach	Liability for Offence	Statutory Defence and Limitation Period
Employee Investment Act, R.S.B.C. 1996, c. E-112	Director, officer, or shareholder is liable if he or she provided information (a) that person knew or ought to have known was false or misleading, or (b) formed in whole or in part on the basis for which a tax credit certificate was issued under Act: [s. 32(1)]	Liable, jointly and severally, with the person from whom the repayment was due: [s. 32(1)]	
Employee Investment Act	Director or officer is guilty of an offence if he or she authorized, permitted, or acquiesced in a transaction or series of transactions that the person knew or ought to have known would render the corporation incapable of making payment: [s. 32(2)]	Liable, jointly and severally, with the corporation for the amount of repayment: [s. 32(2)]	
Employee Investment Act	Director or officer is guilty of an offence if he or she authorized, permitted, or acquiesced in transactions which resulted in the acquisition of a person's shares by the corporation or an associate or affiliate of the corporation: [s. 32(3)]	Liable, jointly and severally, with a person acquiring a beneficial ownership in shares or an associate of the person holding the beneficial interest in shares: [s. 32(3)]	Action must be commenced within 2 years after coming to the knowledge of the administrator: [s. 43]
Employee Investment Act	Director or officer guilty of offence if he or she authorized, permitted, or acquiesced in the offences, including making a false or misleading statement or omitting to state a material fact; wilfully withholding, destroying, or concealing a record; authorizing, permitting, or acquiescing in respect of a share purchase, transferring or redeeming, contrary to the Act; failing to keep records: [s. 42(2)]	Liable to a fine not exceeding $50,000 and/or to imprisonment not exceeding 1 year: [s. 42(3)]	Director is not liable if he or she did not know that the statement was false or misleading and could not have known so with exercise of reasonable diligence: [s. 42(4)] Action must be commenced within 2 years after coming to the knowledge of the administrator: [s. 43]
Financial Institutions Act, R.S.B.C. 1996, c. F-141	Director or officer is liable if he or she failed to act honestly, in good faith, and in the best interests of the financial institution or to exercise the care, diligence, and skill of a reasonably prudent person: [s. 101(1)]	Civilly liable, which varies, depending on the circumstances	Director may be indemnified if he or she (1) acted honestly and in good faith, and (2) had reasonable grounds for believing that his or her conduct was lawful: [s. 102(1)]

B.C. Statutes	Statutory Breach	Liability for Offence	Statutory Defence and Limitation Period
Financial Institutions Act	Director or officer is guilty of an offence if he or she authorized, permitted, or acquiesced in the offence of a financial institution: [s. 252(5)]	Liability varies, depending on the nature of the offence: [s. 253]: — a fine not exceeding $100,000 and/or imprisonment for 2 years (first conviction) or not exceeding $200,000 and/or 2 years' imprisonment (subsequent conviction); or — a fine not exceeding $2,000. Can also impose an administrative penalty: [s. 253.1]	Action must be commenced within 3 years after the facts on which the proceeding is based came to the knowledge of the superintendent: [s. 255]
Food Products Standards Act, R.S.B.C. 1996, c. F-153	Director or officer is guilty of an offence if he or she authorized, permitted, or acquiesced in the offence including selling/manufacturing food that doesn't comply with the *Food and Drugs Act* (s. 2(2)); not complying with certain requirements set out for B.C. under the *Food and Drugs Act* (s. 4(2)); representing that food complies with certain requirements if it does not (s. 5(2)): [s. 12]	Liable to a fine not exceeding $20,000 and/or 6 months' imprisonment for the contravention of s. 11(3): [s. 11(4)]	
Food Safety Act, S.B.C. 2000, c. F-28	Director or officer is guilty of an offence if he or she authorized, permitted, or acquiesced in the commission of an offence, including the distribution of contaminated food (s. 3); the failure to hold a proper license (s. 4(2); and the failure to comply with license terms (s. 7): [s. 15(5)]	Liable for a first conviction of a fine not exceeding $25,000 for each day the offence continues and/or 6 months' imprisonment: [s. 16(1)(a) and (c)]; for a subsequent conviction, for a fine not exceeding $50,000 each day the offence continues and/or 6 months' imprisonment: [s. 16(1)(b) and (c)]	
Forest and Range Practices Act, S.B.C. 2002, c. F-69	Director or officer is guilty of an offence if he or she authorized, permitted, or acquiesced in the commission of the offence by the corporation: [s. 102]	Liability varies, depending on the nature of the offence: [s. 87] — not exceeding $1,000,000 and/or 3 years' imprisonment; — not exceeding $500,000 and/or imprisonment for 2 years; — not exceeding $100,000 and/or imprisonment for 1 year; — not exceeding $5,000 and/or imprisonment for 6 months; and — for a subsequent offence, double the amount.	Director is not liable if he or she proves that he or she exercised due diligence to prevent the commission of the offence; mistake of fact; or an officially induced error: [s. 101] Action must be commenced within 3 years after the information came to the attention of the official: [s. 86(1)]

B.C. Statutes	Statutory Breach	Liability for Offence	Statutory Defence and Limitation Period
Homeowner Protection Act, S.B.C. 1998, c. H-31	Director or officer is guilty of an offence if he or she authorized, permitted, or acquiesced in the commission of the offence by the corporation: [s. 34(2)]	Liable to a fine not exceeding $25,000 and/or for imprisonment not exceeding 1 year: [s. 34(2)]	
Hotel Room Tax Act, R.S.B.C. 1996, c. H-207	Director or officer is guilty of an offence if he or she authorized, permitted, or acquiesced in the commission of the offence by the corporation, for example, refusing to co-operate with an inspection, failing to provide records, or failing to collect tax imposed by the Act: [s. 35]	Liable to a fine not exceeding $10,000 and/or imprisonment for 2 years: [s. 36(2)] Liable to a fine equal to the amount of tax that should have been collected, plus fine b/w $200 and $1,000 for a first conviction and $500 and $2,000 for a second conviction: [s. 38(3)]	Action must be commenced within 6 years after the complaint arises: [s. 40]
Insurance Premium Tax Act, R.S.B.C. 1996, c. I-232	Director or officer is guilty of an offence if he or she authorized, permitted, or acquiesced in the commission of the offence by the corporation: [s. 33]	Liability varies, depending on the nature of the offence.	Any information in respect of the offence against this Act must be laid within 6 years from the time when the matter of information arose: [s. 36]
International Financial Activity Act, S.B.C. 2004, c. I-49	Director is liable if the corporation failed to pay a recoverable amount: [s. 48(1)]	Liable, jointly and severally, with the corporation to pay the amount due to government: [s. 48(1)]	Director exercised degree of care, diligence, and skill to prevent failure that a reasonably prudent person would in comparable circumstances: [s. 48(3)] Action must be commenced within 5 years after the date the director last ceased to be a director of the corporation: [s. 50(3)] OR 7 years after the date of a determination or assessment of the amount claimed in a proceeding: [s. 50(2)] UNLESS there is wilful default or fraud, in which case there is no limitation period: [s. 50(4)]
International Financial Activity Act	Director or officer is guilty of an offence if he or she authorized, permitted, or acquiesced in the commission of an offence by the corporation: [s. 62(4)]	Liability varies, depending on the nature of offence: — Not exceeding $100,000 and/or 12 months' imprisonment: [s. 63(1)] — Not exceeding $5,000 and/or 12 months' imprisonment: [s. 63(2)] — Additional fine not less than 50 percent and not exceeding 200 percent of the amount the tax refund exceeds the amount of the refund that the person is entitled to: [s. 63(5)]	Action must be commenced within 8 years after the subject matter of the proceeding arose: [s. 64]

B.C. Statutes	Statutory Breach	Liability for Offence	Statutory Defence and Limitation Period
Liquor Control and Licensing Act, R.S.B.C. 1996, c. L-267	Director or officer is guilty of an offence if he or she authorized, permitted, or acquiesced in a contravention of the Act by the corporation: [s. 20(2.4)]	Liable for a monetary penalty — not greater than $50,000 for the unlawful sale of liquor, or — not greater than $25,000 for taking action against a licensee: [s. 20(2.3)]	
Mineral Land Tax Act, R.S.B.C. 1996, c. M-289	Director or officer is guilty of an offence if he or she authorized, permitted, or acquiesced in the commission of an offence including making false statements in a return (s. 20(1)(a)); destroying records in an attempt to evade payment (s. 20(1)(b)); omits to enter material into record book (s. 20(1)(c)): [s. 20(5)]	Liable to a fine not less than $500 and not exceeding $5,000: [s. 20(2)]	Action must be commenced within 12 months after the matter of the offence came to the attention of the administrator: [s. 20(6)]
Mineral Tax Act, R.S.B.C. 1996, c. M-291	Director or officer is guilty of an offence if he or she authorized, permitted, or acquiesced in the commission of the offence by the corporation: [s. 41]	Liability varies, depending on the offence (ss. 39–40): — a fine not less than $25.00 and not exceeding $5,000; — fine not less than $200, not exceeding $10,000 and/or 6 months' imprisonment; or — a fine not less than 25 percent of the tax evaded and/or 2 years' imprisonment	Action must be commenced within 6 years after the offence occurred or 1 year after sufficient evidence came to the attention of the commissioner: [s. 42]
Mines Act, R.S.B.C. 1996, c. M-293	Director or officer is guilty of an offence if he or she authorized, permitted, or acquiesced in the commission of the offence by the corporation: [s. 37(5)]	Liable to a fine not exceeding $100,000 and/or imprisonment not exceeding 1 year: [s. 37(3)]	Action, under s. 10, must be commenced within 1 year after the facts come to the inspector's attention; all other offences: 6 months: [s. 37(3.1)]
Motor Fuel Tax Act, R.S.B.C. 1996, c. M-317	Director or officer is guilty of an offence if he or she authorized, permitted, or acquiesced in the commission of an offence by the corporation: [s. 68]	Liability varies, depending on the offence: — a fine not exceeding $2,000: [s. 64(3)]; or — a fine not exceeding $10,000 and/or 2 years' imprisonment plus a fine in the amount of tax owing: [s. 64(5)]	Action must be commenced within 6 months after the alleged offence was committed: [s. 69]

B.C. Statutes	Statutory Breach	Liability for Offence	Statutory Defence and Limitation Period
Petroleum and Natural Gas Act, R.S.B.C. 1996, c. P-361	Director or officer is guilty of an offence if he or she authorized, permitted, or acquiesced in the commission of the offence by the corporation: [s. 134(3)]	Liable to a fine of not less than $500 and not exceeding $5000: [s. 134(1)]	Director is not liable if he or she did not know that the statement was false and, in exercise of reasonable diligence, could not have known so: [s. 134(5)]
Private Investigators and Security Agencies Act, R.S.B.C. 1996, c. P-374	Director or officer is guilty of an offence if he or she authorized, permitted, or acquiesced in the commission of the offence by the corporation using a security card issued to another person; failing to keep records; making a false statement; obstructing a registrar or inspector: [s. 32(3)]	Liable to a fine not exceeding $5,000 and/or 1 year imprisonment: [s. 32(3)]	Action must be commenced within 1 year after the commission of the offence: [s. 32(4]
Real Estate Development Marketing Act, S.B.C. 2004, c. R-41	Director or officer is guilty of an offence if he or she authorized, permitted, or acquiesced in the commission of an offence by the developer: [s. 39(3)]	Liable to a fine not exceeding $100,000 and/or 2 years' imprisonment for a first conviction: [s. 40(b)(i)]; for a subsequent conviction, a fine not exceeding $200,000 and/or 2 years' imprisonment: [s. 40(b)(ii)]	Action must be commenced within 2 years after the facts arose or if the Superintendent issues a certificate, then 2 years after the facts come to the knowledge of the Superintendent: [s. 41(1)]
Real Estate Services Act, S.B.C. 2004, c. R-42	Director or officer is guilty of an offence if he or she authorized, permitted, or acquiesced in the commission of an offence by the corporation or partnership: [s. 118(3)]	Liable to a first conviction a fine not exceeding $50,000 and/or imprisonment for 2 years: [s. 119(2)(a)]; for a subsequent conviction, a fine not exceeding $100,000 and/or imprisonment for 2 years: [s. 119(2)(b)]	Action must be commenced within 2 years after the facts arose or if the Superintendent issues a certificate, 2 years after the facts come to the knowledge of the Superintendent: [s. 120(1)]
Recall and Initiative Act, R.S.B.C. 1996, c. R-398	Director or officer is guilty of an offence if he or she authorized, permitted, or acquiesced in the commission of the offence, including signature and vote buying offences; intimidation offences; wrongful signing and voting; offences in relation to canvassing for signatures; financing offences; initiative or recall advertising offences; false or misleading information offences; use of information offences: [s. 154(2)]	Liability varies, depending on the nature of the offence: — not exceeding a fine of $10,000 and/or 2 years' imprisonment: [s. 156(6)], or — not exceeding a fine of $5,000 and/or 1 year imprisonment: [s. 160(2)] Liable whether or not the organization was convicted: [s. 154(2)]	Director is not liable if he or she proves that he or she exercised due diligence to prevent the commission of the offence: [s. 155] Action must be commenced within 1 year after the subject matter of the prosecution arises: [s. 165]

B.C. Statutes	Statutory Breach	Liability for Offence	Statutory Defence and Limitation Period
Small Business Venture Capital Act, R.S.B.C. 1996, c. S-429	Director or officer is liable if he or she supplied information that he or she knew or ought to have known was false or misleading and a tax credit certificate is issued on the basis of this information: [s. 26(2)]	Liable to pay the government the amount of tax credit: [s. 26(2)]	
Small Business Venture Capital Act	Director or officer is guilty of an offence if he or she authorized, permitted, or acquiesced in the commission of an offence by the corporation: [s. 35(3)]	Liable to a fine not exceeding $50,000 and/or imprisonment not exceeding 1 year: [s. 35(4)]	Director is not liable if he or she did not know it was misleading or false and could not have known so in exercise of reasonable diligence: [s. 35(5)] Action must be commenced within 2 years after the facts come to the attention of the administrator: [s. 36]
Tobacco Sales Act, R.S.B.C. 1996, c. T-451	Director or officer is guilty of an offence if he or she authorized, permitted, or acquiesced in the commission of the offence by the corporation: [s. 12(2)]	Liable to a first offence a fine not exceeding $2,500 and/or imprisonment not exceeding 3 months: [s. 12(1)(a)]. Liable to a subsequent offence a fine not exceeding $5,000 and/or imprisonment not exceeding 6 months: [s. 12(1)(b)]	Action must be commenced within 12 months after the cause of action arises: [s. 12(5)]
Tobacco Tax Act, R.S.B.C. 1996, c. T-452	Director or officer is guilty of an offence if he or she authorized, permitted, participated in, or acquiesced in the commission of the offence by the corporation: [s. 38]	Liability varies, depending on the offence: [s. 39]	Action must be commenced within 6 years after the complaint arose, except in cases of fraud where no limitation period applies: [s. 42]
Tourism British Columbia Act, S.B.C. 1997, c. T-13	Director is liable if the profit accrued as a result of the corporation entering into a contract where the director had a disclosable interest: [s. 17(1)]	Liable to account for profits: [s. 17(1)]	Director is not liable if his or her interest was disclosed and approved by directors and if the director abstains from voting on the approval of the contract: [s. 17(1)(a)] or the contract was reasonable and fair to the corporation and after full disclosure, was approved by a special resolution of the corporation: [s. 17(1)(b)]
Unclaimed Property Act, S.B.C. 1999, c. U-48	Director or officer is guilty of an offence if he or she authorized, permitted, participated, or acquiesced in the commission of the offence by the corporation: [s. 16(3)]	Liable whether or not the corporation is prosecuted for the offence: [s. 16(4)]	Director is not liable if he or she did not know that the statement was false or misleading and could not have known it was false or misleading in the exercise of reasonable diligence: [s. 16(2)]
Utilities Commission Act, R.S.B.C. 1996, c. U-473	President, vice president, director, managing director, superintendent, and manager is liable if he or she failed to obey an order of the commission made under the Act: [s. 106(1)(e)]	Liable for a fine not greater than $10,000: [s. 106(4)]	Director not liable if he or she took all necessary and proper means to obey the order: [s. 106(2)]

APPENDIX IV

Common Sources of Directors' Liability Under Ontario Statutes (Last updated August 2006)

THIS IS NOT A COMPREHENSIVE LIST. THE PASSAGES SET OUT BELOW ARE SUMMARIES ONLY AND THE READER MUST REFER TO THE SPECIFIC STATUTE FOR A COMPLETE STATEMENT OF THE DIRECTOR'S LEGAL RESPONSIBILITIES AND THE STATUTORY CONTEXT IN WHICH THOSE LEGAL RESPONSIBILITIES ARISE.

Ontario Statutes	Statutory Breach	Liability for Offence	Statutory Defence and Limitation Period
STATUTES AFFECTING MOST DIRECTORS			
Business Corporations Act, R.S.O. 1990, c. B.16	Director is liable if he or she authorized the issuance of shares under s. 23 for consideration, other than money, if the amount received is less than the fair equivalent of money: [s. 130(1)]	Liable, jointly and severally, to the corporation for the difference between the amount received and the fair equivalent of money: [s. 130(1)]	Director is not liable if he or she proves that he or she did not know and could not reasonably have known that the shares were issued for a consideration less than the fair equivalent of money: [s. 130(6)] Director is not liable if he or she established a good faith reliance upon the financial statements that were represented to him/her by an officer or the auditor of the corporation or by professional reports under s. 135(4): [s. 135(4)] Director is not liable if he or she proves that he or she dissented to the resolution: [s. 135]
Business Corporations Act	Director is liable if he or she authorized: (a) financial assistance, contrary to s. 20; (b) the purchase, redemption, or other acquisition of shares, contrary to ss. 30, 31, and 32; (c) a commission, contrary to s. 37; (d) the payment of a dividend, contrary to s. 38; (e) the payment of an indemnity, contrary to s. 136; or (f) a payment to a shareholde,r contrary to s. 185 or s. 248: [s. 130(2)]	Liable, jointly and severally, to the corporation to repay the amounts distributed and not otherwise recovered by the corporation: [s. 130(2)]	Director is not liable if he or she proves that he or she exercised good faith reliance upon the financial statements that were represented to him/her by an officer or the auditor of the corporation or by professional reports under s. 135(4): [s. 135(4)] Director is not liable if he or she proves that he or she dissented to the resolution: [s. 135]

Ontario Statutes	Statutory Breach	Liability for Offence	Statutory Defence and Limitation Period
Business Corporations Act	Director is liable to employees for debts that were incurred while the director was in office: [s. 131(1)]	Liable, jointly and severally, for all debts not exceeding 6 months' wages payable to each employee for services performed and vacation pay accrued not exceeding 12 months under the *Employment Standards Act* or under any collective agreement: [s. 131(1)]	Director is not liable unless the corporation (1) sued and the execution was returned unsatisfied, or (2) goes into liquidation, is ordered wound up, or is made an assignment under the *Bankruptcy and Insolvency Act*, or is subject to a receiving order and the claim isproved: [s. 131(2)] Director is not liable if the shareholders are liable under a USA: [s. 108(5)]
Business Corporations Act	Director or officer is liable if he or she entered into a material contract/transaction with the corporation or has a material interest in any person who is party to a material contract/transaction without disclosing the director's/officer's interest: [s. 132]	Liable to a court order directing the director to account to the corporation or shareholders for any profit realized from the contract/transaction and setting aside the contract/transaction and/or to any other order made by the court: [s. 132 (9)]	Director or officer is not liable if he or she disclosed interest in accordance with the Act and the contract/transaction was reasonable and fair to the corporation at the time it was approved: [s. 132(7)] Director or officer is not liable if he or she acted honestly and in good faith and the contract/transaction was reasonable and fair to the corporation at the time it was approved and (a) the contract/transaction was confirmed or approved by a special resolution of shareholders duly called for that purpose, and (b) the nature and extent of the director's or officer's interest in the contract/transaction was disclosed in reasonable detail in the notice calling a meeting or in an information circular: [s. 132(8)]
Business Corporations Act	Directors or officers are liable if they failed, in exercising their powers and discharging their duties, to (a) act honestly and in good faith with a view to the best interests of the corporation; or (b) exercise the care, diligence, and skill that a reasonably prudent person would exercise in comparable circumstances; [s. 134(1)] Subject to s. 108(5) (USA), a director cannot contract out of his or her duty under a contract, articles, by-laws, or a resolution: [s. 134(3)]	Civilly liable for the resulting loss, which varies depending upon the breach	Director is not liable if he or she proves good faith reliance upon financial statements that were represented to him/her by an officer or the auditor of the corporation or professional reports under s. 135(4): [s. 135(4)]

Ontario Statutes	Statutory Breach	Liability for Offence	Statutory Defence and Limitation Period
Business Corporations Act	Director or officer is liable if he or she did not comply with this Act, regulations, articles, by-laws, and any unanimous shareholder agreement; [s. 134(2)] Subject to s. 108(5) (USA), a director cannot contract out of this duty under a contract, articles, by-laws, or a resolution: [s. 134(3)]	Civilly liable for the resulting loss which varies, depending upon the breach	Director is not liable if he or she proves good faith reliance upon financial statements that were represented to him/her by an officer or the auditor of the corporation or by professional reports under s. 135(4): [s. 135(4)]
Business Corporations Act	Insider (which includes a director or officer) is liable if he or she makes use of confidential information for the insider's benefit/advantage that, if it was generally known, might reasonably be expected to affect materially the value of a security: [s. 138(1), (2) and (5)]	Liable to compensate any person for any direct loss suffered, and Liable to the corporation for any direct benefit/advantage received by an insider: [s. 138 (5)]	Insider is not liable to compensate a person if he or she proves that information was known or in the exercise of reasonable diligence should have been known to that person: [s. 138(5)]
Business Corporations Act	Director or officer is liable if he or she knowingly failed to notify the audit committee and auditor of any error/misstatement in financial statements that were reported on by the auditor or former auditor: [s. 153(2)]		
Business Corporations Act	Director or officer is liable if he or she knowingly failed to prepare/issue revised financial statements, and if the distributing corporation files them with Executive Director, upon the auditor informing the directors of the error or misstatement: [s. 153(4)]		
Business Corporations Act	Director or officer is guilty of an offence if he or she authorized, permitted, or acquiesced in the failure to send a proxy to each shareholder: [ss. 111 and 258(2)]	Liable to a fine of not more than $2,000 and/or imprisonment for a term of not more than one year	Action must be commenced within 2 years of the facts coming to the knowledge of the director [s. 259]
Business Corporations Act	Director or officer is guilty of an offence if he or she authorized, permitted, or acquiesced in the failure to send a proxy circular prior to any solicitation of proxies: [ss. 112(1) and 258(2)]	Liable to a fine of not more than $2,000 and/or imprisonment for a term of not more than one year	Action must be commenced within 2 years of the facts coming to the knowledge of the director [s. 259]

Ontario Statutes	Statutory Breach	Liability for Offence	Statutory Defence and Limitation Period
Business Corporations Act	Person (including a director or officer) is guilty of an offence if he or she made a statement that contained misrepresentations, fails to file any required document, or fails to comply with other requirements made under the Act: [s. 256(2)]	Liable to a fine not exceeding $2,000 and/or imprisonment not exceeding 1 year: [s. 256(2)]	
Business Corporations Act	Director or officer is guilty of an offence if, without reasonable cause, he or she authorized, permitted, or acquiesced in the corporation's transfer of constrained shares where not satisfied, on reasonable grounds, that it will assist cthe orporation or its affiliates in receiving licenses or permits or in maintaining a specified level of Canadian ownership: [ss. 29(5), 258(1)(a) and 258(2)]	Liable to a fine not exceeding $2,000 and/or to imprisonment not exceeding 1 year: [s. 258(2)]	
Business Corporations Act	Director or officer is guilty of offence if, without reasonable cause, he or she authorized, permitted, or acquiesced in the corporation's use of a list of holders of securities in contravention of ss. 52(5) and 146(8): [ss. 52(5), 146 (8), and 258(1)(b) and 258(2)].	Liable to a fine not exceeding $2,000 and/or to imprisonment not exceeding 1 year: [s. 258(2)]	
Business Corporations Act	Director or officer is guilty of an offence if, without reasonable cause, he or she authorized, permitted, or acquiesced in the corporation's failure without reasonable cause to send a prescribed form of proxy to each shareholder of the offering corporation with the notice of a meeting of shareholders: [ss. 111 and 258(1)(c) and 258(2)]	Liable to a fine not exceeding $2,000 and/or to imprisonment not exceeding 1 year: [s. 258(2)]	

Ontario Statutes	Statutory Breach	Liability for Offence	Statutory Defence and Limitation Period
Business Corporations Act	Director or officer is guilty of an offence if, without reasonable cause, he or she authorized, permitted, or acquiesced in the corporation's failure without reasonable cause to send an information circular in connection with a proxy solicitation: [ss. 112(1) and ss. 258(1)(d) and 258(2)]	Liable to a fine not exceeding $2,000 and/or to imprisonment not exceeding 1 year: [s. 258(2)]	
Business Corporations Act	Director or officer is guilty of an offence if, without reasonable cause, he or she authorized, permitted, or acquiesced in the corporation's failure as a proxyholder, without reasonable cause, to comply with the directions of a shareholder who appointed the corporation: [ss. 114(1) and 258(1)(e) and 258(2)]	Liable to a fine not exceeding $2,000 and/or to imprisonment not exceeding 1 year: [s. 258(2)]	
Business Corporations Act	Director or officer is guilty of offence if, without reasonable cause, he or she authorized, permitted, or acquiesced in the corporation's contravention without reasonable cause of section 145: [ss. 145, 258(1)(f), and 258(2)]	Liable to a fine not exceeding $2,000 and/or to imprisonment not exceeding 1 year: [s. 258(2)]	
Business Corporations Act	Director or officer is guilty of an offence if he or she fails, without a reasonable cause, to appoint an auditor: [ss. 149 and 258(1)(g) and 258(2)]	Liable to a fine not exceeding $2,000 and/or to imprisonment not exceeding 1 year: [s. 258(2)]	
Business Corporations Act	Director or officer is guilty of offence if, without reasonable cause, he or she authorized, permitted, or acquiesced in the corporation's failure without reasonable cause to comply with subsection 154 (1): [ss. 154, 258(1)(i), and 258(2)]	Liable to a fine not exceeding $2,000 and/or to imprisonment not exceeding 1 year: [s. 258(2)]	

Ontario Statutes	Statutory Breach	Liability for Offence	Statutory Defence and Limitation Period
Business Corporations Act	Director or officer is guilty of an offence if, without reasonable cause, he or she committed or authorized, permitted, or acquiesced in the corporation's commission of acts which were contrary to, or which failed or neglected to comply with, provisions of this Act or regulations: [ss. 258(1)(j) and 258(2)]	Liable to a fine not exceeding $2,000 and/or to imprisonment not exceeding 1 year: [s. 258(2)]	
Business Corporations Act	Director or officer is guilty of an offence if, without reasonable cause, he or she authorized, permitted, acquiesced or participated in the making of false statements: [ss. 256(2) and (3)]	Liable to a fine not exceeding $2,000 and/or imprisonment not exceeding 1 year: [s. 256(3)]	Director or officer is not liable if he or she did not know, and in exercise of reasonable diligence, could not have known, that a statement was false: [s. 256(4)] Action must be commenced within 2 years after the facts upon which the proceedings are based came to the attention of the Director: [s. 259(1)]
Co-operative Corporations Act, R.S.O. 1990, c. C.35	Director or officer is liable if he or she authorizes or consents to providing financial assistance to any of the co-operative's members, directors, or employees: [s. 17(2)]	Liable, jointly and severally, to the co-operative and its creditors for any actual loss to the co-operative and its creditors with interest at a rate of 6 percent per year: [s. 17(2)]	
Co-operative Corporations Act	Director is liable if he or she consents to a resolution authorizing the acquisition of the co-operative's shares or the repayment of its loans in contravention of the Act: [s. 99(1)]	Liable, jointly and severally, to the extent of the amount paid out: [s. 99(1)]	Director is not liable if he or she carried out the duties of his/her office honestly, in good faith, and in the best interests of the co-operative and exercised the degree of care, diligence, and skill that a reasonably prudent person would exercise in comparable circumstances: [ss. 102 and 108] Director is not liable if he or she proves that he or she dissented to the resolution: [s. 101(1)]
Co-operative Corporations Act	Director is liable if he or she consents to a resolution authorizing the declaration and payment of the dividend in contravention of s. 58: [s. 100(a)]	Liable, jointly and severally, to the co-operative to the extent of the amount of the dividend so declared and paid or such part that renders the co-operative insolvent or diminishes its capital: [s. 100(a)]	Director is not liable if he or she carried out the duties of his/her office honestly, in good faith, and in the best interests of the co-operative and exercised the degree of care, diligence, and skill that a reasonably prudent person would exercise in comparable circumstances: [ss. 102 and 108] Director is not liable if he or she proves that he or she dissented to the resolution: [s. 101(1)]

Ontario Statutes	Statutory Breach	Liability for Offence	Statutory Defence and Limitation Period
Co-operative Corporations Act	Director is liable to employees to whom the *Employers and Employees Act* applies for all debts that become due while he or she is a director: [s. 103(1)]	Liable, jointly and severally, for services performed not exceeding 6 months' wages and for vacation pay accrued not exceeding 12 months under the *Employment Standards Act* or any collective agreement: [s. 103(1)]	Director not liable unless the corporation (1) sued and the execution was returned unsatisfied, or (2) goes into liquidation, is ordered wound up, or made an assignment under the *Bankruptcy and Insolvency Act* or is subject to a receiving order and the claim is proved: [s. 131(2)]
Co-operative Corporations Act	Director is liable if he or she consents to a resolution authorizing the payment of an indemnity contrary to s. 110: [s. 110(8)]	Liable, jointly and severally, to restore to the co-operative any amount so distributed or paid and not otherwise recovered by a co-operative: [s. 110(8)]	
Co-operative Corporations Act	Director or officer is guilty of an offence if he or she authorized, permitted, or acquiesced to the commission of an act contrary to the Act or to the failure to comply with the Act: [s. 176(2)]	Liable to a fine of not more than $5,000 [s. 176(2)]	Action must be commenced within 2 years after the facts upon which the proceeding is based came to the attention of the Superintendent: [s. 177]
Co-operative Corporations Act	Insider (which includes a director or officer) is liable if he or she makes use of confidential information for the insider's benefit/advantage that, if it was generally known, might reasonably be expected to affect materially the value of a security: [s. 111(1)]	Liable to compensate any person for any direct loss suffered, and Liable to the corporation for any direct benefit/advantage received by an insider: [s. 111(1)]	Insider not liable to compensate a person if he or she proves the information was known or in the exercise of reasonable diligence should have been known to that person: [s. 111(1)]
Corporations Act, R.S.O. 1990, c. C.38	Director is liable if he or she authorized, permitted, or acquiesced in the failure of the corporation to file with the Minister a copy of a court order to change the name of the corporation: [s. 13(5)]	Liable to a fine of not more than $200: [s. 13(5)]	
Corporations Act	Director is liable if he or she authorized, permitted, or acquiesced in the failure of the company to comply with the requirement to use "Limited" or "Ltd.", as well as other requirements of s. 21: [s. 21(4)]	Liable to a fine of not more than $200: [s. 21(4)]	
Corporations Act	Director is liable if the consent to registration of the transfer of shares was not fully paid to the person with insufficient means to pay fully: [s. 52(2)]	Liable, jointly and severally, to the company and its creditors in the same manner and to the same extent as the transferor would have been liable if registration had not been made: [s. 52(2)]	Director is not liable if forthwith (if present at the consent), or within 7 days of becoming aware of consent, delivers a written protest to an officer of the company and sends a copy of the protest to the Minister: [s. 52(3)]

Ontario Statutes	Statutory Breach	Liability for Offence	Statutory Defence and Limitation Period
Corporations Act	Director is liable if he or she declares the payment of a dividend or bonus that renders the company insolvent or that diminishes its capital: [s. 62(3)]	Liable, jointly and severally, to the company for the amount of the dividend or bonus or such part that renders the company insolvent or diminishes its capital: [s. 62(3)]	Director is not liable if forthwith (if present at the consent), or within 7 days of becoming aware of the consent, delivers a written protest to an officer of the company and sends a copy of the protest to the Minister: [s. 62(3)]
Corporations Act	Director is guilty of an offence if he or she entered into a contract with the company without disclosing his or her direct or indirect interest and is liable for the profit realized from the contract and the contract is voidable only by reason of the director's interest: [ss. 71(1) and (6)]	Liable to a fine of not more than $200: [s. 71(6)]	Director is not accountable for the profit realized from the contract if he or she disclosed his or her interest and did not vote with respect to the contract: [s. 71(4)] Director is not accountable for the profit realized from the contract if the contract was confirmed by a majority of votes cast at general meeting of shareholders duly called for that purpose and if the director's interest is disclosed in a notice calling the meeting: [s. 71(5)]
Corporations Act	Director is guilty of an offence if he or is required to and fails to file a report under s. 73: [s. 75(1)] Director is guilty of an offence if he or she files a false or misleading report under s. 73: [s. 75(2)]	Liable to a fine of not more than $1,000	Director is not guilty of an offence under s. 75(2) if he or she did not know and in the exercise of due diligence could not have known the report was false or misleading: [s. 75(3)] No prosecution shall be brought under s. 75(1) or (2) without the consent of the Commission: [s. 75(4)]
Corporations Act	Director is liable to employees, apprentices, or other wage earners for all debts due while he or she is a director: [s. 81(1)]	Liable, jointly and severally, for services performed not exceeding six months' wages and for vacation pay accrued not exceeding 12 months under the *Employment Standards Act* or any collective agreement: [s. 81(1)]	Director is not liable unless the corporation (1) sued and the execution was returned unsatisfied, or (2) goes into liquidation, is ordered wound up, or is made an assignment under the *Bankruptcy and Insolvency Act* or is subject to a receiving order and the claim is proved: [s. 81(2)]
Corporations Act	Director is guilty of an offence if he or she fails to send a form of proxy with the notice of meeting [ss. 85(1) and (2)]	Liable to a fine of not more than $1,000 [s. 85(2)]	

Ontario Statutes	Statutory Breach	Liability for Offence	Statutory Defence and Limitation Period
Corporations Act	Director is guilty of an offence if he or she authorized, permitted, or acquiesced in the failure to solicit proxies or in soliciting a proxy with misrepresentations [ss. 86(3) and (4)]	Liable to fine of not more than $1,000 [ss. 86(3) and (4)]	Director is not liable if the misrepresentation was not known or in the exercise of reasonable diligence could not have ben known to the director [s. 86(5)]
Corporations Act	Director is guilty of an offence if he or she authorized, permitted, or acquiesced in the failure of the company to mail financial statements to shareholders: [s. 109(3)]	Liable to a fine of not more than $200: [s. 109(3)]	
Corporations Act	Director is guilty of an offence if he or she authorized, permitted, or acquiesced in the failure of the company to send comparative interim financial statements to shareholders: [s. 110(6)]	Liable to a fine of not more than $1,000: [s. 110(6)]	
Corporations Act	Director is guilty of an offence if he or she commits any act contrary to the Act or does not comply with any provision of the Act: [s. 331]	Liable to a fine of not more than $200: [s. 331]	
Corporations Tax Act, R.S.O. 1990, c. C.40.	Director or officer is guilty of an offence if he or she made, participated in, assented to, or acquiesced in the making of, false, or deceptive statements in a return, certificate, or statement, destroys/hides records of account, makes false entries in records of account, wilfully evades compliance with the Act or the payment of taxes imposed by the Act: [s. 76(4)]	Liable, in addition to any other penalty in the Act, to a fine of not less than the greater of $500 and 50 percent of the tax payable and sought to be evaded and not exceeding the double amount of such tax, and/or imprisonment not exceeding 2 years: [s. 76(5)]	None

Ontario Statutes	Statutory Breach	Liability for Offence	Statutory Defence and Limitation Period
Corporations Tax Act	Director is guilty of an offence if he or she directed, authorized, assented to, acquiesced in, or participated in the commission of an offence contrary to the Act: [s. 96]	Liable to the punishment provided for the offense whether or not the corporation was prosecuted or convicted: [s. 96]	Information in respect of an offence against the Act shall be laid within 6 years of the date when the matter arose: [s. 97]
Dangerous Goods Transportation Act, R.S.O. 1990, c. D.1.	Director or officer is guilty of an offence if he or she directed, authorized, assented to, acquiesced in, or participated in the commission of an offence contrary to the Act, for example, the failure to comply with all applicable safety standards: [s. 7]	Liable for a penalty whether or not the corporation was prosecuted or convicted: [s. 7]	Director is not liable if he or she took all reasonable measures to comply with this Act: [s. 5]
Discriminatory Business Practices Act, R.S.O. 1990, c. D.12.	Director or officer is liable if he or she knowingly furnished false information in an investigation under the Act: [ss. 16(1) and (3)]	Liable to a fine not exceeding $25,000: [s. 16(1)]	Action must be commenced within 2 years after the time when the subject-matter of the proceeding arose: [s. 16(4)] Director or officer is not liable if he or she satisfies the court that he or she did not authorize, permit, or acquiesce in the offence: [s. 16(3)]
Employer Health Tax Act, R.S.O. 1990, c. E.11.	Director or officer is guilty of an offence if he or she directed, authorized, assented to, acquiesced in, or participated in the commission of an offence by the corporation (including evading taxes, destroying or altering secret records or books, non-compliance with the Act, failing to deliver or complete returns, and knowingly or negligently making false statements): [s. 36]	Liable to a fine or, depending on the offence, imprisonment or the percentage of the amount of tax that should have been paid, whether or not the corporation was prosecuted or convicted: [s. 36]	Action must be commenced within 6 years after the date on which the offence was committed: [s. 37]

Ontario Statutes	Statutory Breach	Liability for Offence	Statutory Defence and Limitation Period
Employment Standards Act, 2000	Director is liable for employees' wages if the employer is insolvent, an order is made that the employer is liable for wages, an order is made that the director is liable for wages, or an order is made requiring the director to pay: [s. 81]	Liable, jointly and severally, to employees for wages not exceeding 6 months' wages and vacation pay accrued while he or she was a director, not exceeding 12 months: [s. 81(7)]	Director may be indemnified by the employer if he or she acted honestly and in good faith in the best interests of the employer and had a reasonable belief that his or her conduct was lawful: [s. 82(2)]
Employment Standards Act, 2000, R.S.O. 2000, c. 41	Director is liable if he or she failed to comply with an order of an employment standards officer under ss. 106 or 107: [s. 136(1)]	Liable to a fine not exceeding $50,000: [s. 136(2)]	Action must be commenced within 2 years after the date on which the offence was committed or alleged to have been committed: [s. 139]
Employment Standards Act, 2000	Director is liable if he or she authorized or permitted a contravention of the Act by the corporation or acquiesced in it: [s. 137]	Liable on conviction to a fine or imprisonment provided for in the offence that was committed by the corporation in the Act: [s. 137]	Action must be commenced within 2 years after the date on which the offence was committed or alleged to have been committed: [s. 139]
Environmental Protection Act, R.S.O. 1990, c. E.19.	Director or officer is guilty of an offence if he or she failed to prevent the corporation or failed to take all reasonable care to prevent the corporation from causing or permitting the discharge of a contaminant, fails to notify the Minister of the discharge of a contaminant in contravention of the Act, contravening ss. 27, 40, or 41 in respect of hauled liquid industrial waste or hazardous waste, contravening ss. 93 or 184, failing to install, maintain, operate, replace,or alter any equipment or other thing in contravention of certificate of approval; otherwise contravening an order under the Act: [ss. 194(1) and (2)]	Liable to a penalty provided for in the offence, whether or not the corporation was prosecuted or convicted: [s. 194(3)]	Director is not liable if he or she took all reasonable care to prevent the corporation from contravening the provisions listed in s. 194(1): [s. 194(1)] Action must be commenced within 2 years of: (a) the day on which the offence was committed; and (b) the day on which evidence of the offence first came to the attention of the Director: [s. 195(1)]

Ontario Statutes	Statutory Breach	Liability for Offence	Statutory Defence and Limitation Period
Income Tax Act, R.S.O. 1990, c. 12	Director is liable if he or she failed to deduct or withhold the amount required by s. 153(1) of the Federal *Income Tax Act*: [s. 38(1)]	Liable, jointly and severally, together with the corporation to the amounts outstanding and interest and penalties: [s. 38(1)]	Director will not be liable unless (a) a certificate for the amount of the corporation's liability has been registered in the Superior Court of Justice and the execution for such amount has been returned unsatisfied in whole or in part; (b) the corporation has commenced a liquidation or dissolution proceeding or has been dissolved and the claim for the amount of the corporation's liability has been proved within 6 months after the earlier of the date of the commencement of the proceeding and the date of dissolution; or (c) the corporation has made an assignment or a receiving order has been made against it under the *Bankruptcy and Insolvency Act* (Canada) and a claim for the amount has been proved within 6 months after the date of the assignment or receiving order: [s. 38(2)] Director is not liable if he or she exercised the degree of care, diligence, and skill to prevent the failure that a reasonably prudent person would have exercised in comparable circumstances: [s. 38(3)] Action must be commenced within 2 years after the director last ceased to be a director of that corporation: [s. 38(4)
Income Tax Act	Director is guilty of an offence if he or she directed, authorized, assented to, acquiesced in, or participated in the commission of an offence under the Act [s. 46]	Liable to the punishment provided for the offence whether or not the corporation has been prosecuted or convicted: [s. 46]	

Ontario Statutes	Statutory Breach	Liability for Offence	Statutory Defence and Limitation Period
Insurance Act, R.S.O. 1990, c. I.8.	Director or officer is guilty of an offence if he or she caused, authorized, or participated in making a false or misleading statement or a misrepresentation to an insurer in connection with an entitlement under a contract of insurance; wilfully failed to inform the insurer of a material change in connection with an entitlement to benefit or made false or misleading statements to obtain payment: [s. 447 (4)]	Liable to a fine not exceeding $100,000 for the first offence and not exceeding $200,000 for subsequent offences whether or not the corporation or unincorporated association has been prosecuted or convicted: [s. 447(4)] In addition to any other penalty, the court may order the director to make compensation or restitution in relation thereto: [s. 447(5)]	Action must be commenced within 2 years of the date on which the facts upon which the proceedings are based first came to the knowledge of the Superintendent: [s. 449]
Occupational Health and Safety Act, R.S.O. 1990, c. O-1	Person is guilty of an offence if he or she contravened a provision of this Act or the regulations: [s. 66(1)]	Liable to a fine not exceeding $25,000 and/or imprisonment not exceeding 12 months: [s. 66(1)]	Director is not liable if he or she proves that every reasonable precaution was taken: [s. 66(3)]
Ontario Water Resources Act, R.S.O. 1990, c. O.40.	Director or officer is guilty of an offence if he or she failed to prevent the corporation from causing or permitting the discharge of any material in contravention of this Act or license, permit, or approval under this Act, failing to notify the Ministry of the discharge of any material in contravention of this Act or license or permit, contravening s. 98, contravening an order, direction, notice,or report under this Act other than an order under s. 84 or 106.1: [s. 116(1)]	Liable on conviction to the penalty provided for the offence whether or not the corporation was prosecuted or convicted: [s. 116(3)]	Director or officer is not liable if he or she took all reasonable care to prevent the corporation from committing the offence: [s. 166(1)] Action must be commenced within 2 years after the later of the day on which the offence was committed and the day on which evidence of the offence first came to the attention of the director: [s. 94(1)]
Pension Benefits Act, R.S.O. 1990, c. P.8	Director or officer is guilty of an offence if he or she caused, authorized, permitted, acquiesced, or participated in an offence in contravention of the Act and failed to take reasonable care in circumstances to prevent the corporation from committing an offence under the Act: [s. 110(2)]	Liable to a fine, on first conviction, not exceeding $100,000, and to a fine, on each subsequent conviction, not exceeding $200,000, whether or not the corporation was prosecuted or convicted: [s. 110(3)] May also be ordered to pay any amount that was not submitted or paid to a pension fund or insurer: [s. 110(4)]	Action must be commenced within five years after the date when the offence occurred or is alleged to have occurred: [s. 110(6)]

Ontario Statutes	Statutory Breach	Liability for Offence	Statutory Defence and Limitation Period
Retail Sales Tax Act, R.S.O. 1990, c. R.31.	Director or officer is guilty of an offence if he or she made, or particpated in, assented to, or acquiesced in the making of false or deceptive statements in a return, certificate, statement, or answer, destroyed/altered records of account, made false entries in records of account, wilfully, in any manner, evaded or attempted to evade compliance with the Act or the payment of taxes imposed by this Act: [s. 32(4)]	Liable to one or both of the following penalties, in addition to any penalty otherwise provided by the Act: (1) a fine that is a minimum of $1,000 or 50 percent of the amount of tax that should have been remitted as collected or payable or that was sought to be evaded, whichever is greater, and the maximum of double the amount of tax that should have been remitted as collected or payable or that was sought to be evaded, if the maximum so calculated is greater than $1,000 (2) Imprisonment not exceeding 2 years: [s. 32(4.1)]	Action must be commenced within 6 years of the time when the matter of offence arose: [s. 46]
Retail Sales Tax Act	Director or officer is guilty of an offence if he or she directed, authorized, assented to, acquiesced in, or participated in the commission or omission of an act by the corporation that is an offence under this Act: [s. 42]	Liable to the punishment provided for the offence whether or not the corporation was prosecuted or convicted: [s. 42]	Action must be commenced within 6 years of the time when the matter of offence arose: [s. 46]
Retail Sales Tax Act	Director is liable if the corporation failed to collect or remit the required tax, subject to conditions listed in s. 43(2): [s. 43(1)]	Liable, jointly and severally, together with the corporation to pay outstanding amounts and the interest on such amounts plus a fine of not less than $50 and not exceeding $2,000: [ss. 43(1) and 44(2)]	Director is not liable if he or she exercised the degree of care, diligence, and skill to prevent the failure that a reasonably prudent person would have exercised in comparable circumstances: [s. 43(3)] No assessment of the amount payable by the director of corporation shall be made more than 2 years after the person ceased to be a director of the corporation: [s. 43(5)]

Ontario Statutes	Statutory Breach	Liability for Offence	Statutory Defence and Limitation Period
Securities Act, R.S.O. 1990, c. S.5 ("OSA")	Person (including director or officer) in a special relationship with a reporting issuer is liable (1) if he or she trades in the issuer's securities with knowledge of; (2) informs another of (other than in the necessary course of business), or (3) informs another (other than in the necessary course of business) while proposing a take-over or other reorganization or acquisition of the issuer of, a material fact or a material change regarding the issuer that has not been generally disclosed: [ss. 76(1), (2), and (3)]	Liable to a fine not exceeding $5 million and/or imprisonment not exceeding five years: [s. 122(1)] Person convicted of contravening s. 76(1), (2), or (3) is liable to a minimum fine equal to the profit made or the loss avoided and the maximum fine equal to the greater of (a) $5 million; and (b) the amount equal to triple the amount of the profit made or the loss avoided by the person or company by reason of the contravention: [s. 122(4)]	Person is not liable if he or she proves that the person reasonably believed that a material fact or material change had been generally disclosed: [s. 76(4)] Action must be commenced within 6 years from the date of the occurrence of the last event on which the proceeding is based: [s. 129.1]
Securities Act	Director or officer is guilty of an offence if he or she authorized, permitted, or acquiesced in: (a) making a statement in any material, evidence, or information submitted to the Commission that is misleading or untrue; (b) making a statement in any application, release, prospectus, or financial statement furnished or filed under Ontario securities law that is misleading or untrue; (c) contravening Ontario securities law: [s. 122(3)]	Liable to a fine not exceeding $5 million and/or imprisonment not exceeding 5 years less a day, whether or not a charge is laid or a finding of guilt is made against the company: [s. 122(3)]	Director is not liable if he or she did not know and in exercise of reasonable diligence could not have known that the statement was misleading or untrue or that it omitted a fact that was required to be stated or that was necessary to make a statement not misleading in light of circumstances in which it was made: [s. 122(2)] Action must be commenced within 6 years from the date of the occurrence of the last event on which proceeding is based: [s. 129.1]
Securities Act	Director or officer is liable for a misrepresentation in a prospectus or take-over bid: [ss. 130(1) and 131(1)]	Liable, jointly and severally, for damages limited to the depreciation in value of the security as result of misrepresentation relied upon: [ss. 130(7), 130(8), 131(7) and 131(8)]	Director or officer is not liable if he or she proved (a) that shares were purchased with knowledge of the misrepresentation: [ss. 130(2) and 131(4)] (b) that the misrepresentation was published/sent out without his or her consent or knowledge: [ss. 130(5) and 131(5)] (c) that he or she did not believe that there was a misrepresentation: [ss. 130(3)(c) and 131(5)(c)] Action must be commenced within 180 days after the plaintiff first had knowledge of the facts giving rise to a cause of action or 3 years after the date of the transaction that gave rise to a cause of action: [s. 138]

Ontario Statutes	Statutory Breach	Liability for Offence	Statutory Defence and Limitation Period
Securities Act	Director or officer is liable if he or she authorized, permitted, or acquiesced in the release of a document by the responsible issuer if it contains a misrepresentation: [s. 138.3(1)]	Liable, subject to the limit set out in s. 138.7(1), for the portion of the aggregate amount of damages assessed in favour of plaintiffs that corresponds to his or her responsibility for damages: [s. 138.6(1)] May be liable for the whole amount of damages that were assessed in action if the court determines that the director authorized, permitted, or acquiesced in making the misrepresentation: [s. 138.6(2)] Liable, jointly and severally: [s. 138.6(3)]	Director or officer is not liable for a misrepresentation in a non-core document unless (a) he or she knew at the time that the document was released that the document contained a misrepresentation; (b) at or before the time that the document was released, he or she deliberately avoided acquiring knowledge that the document contained a misrepresentation; or (c) was, through action or the failure to act, guilty of gross misconduct in connection with the release of a document that contained a misrepresentation: [s. 138.4(1)] Director or officer is not liable for a misrepresentation if he or she proved that the plaintiff acquired or disposed of the issuer's security with knowledge that the document contained a misrepresentation: [s. 138.4(5)] Director or officer is not liable for a misrepresentation in a core document if (a) before the release of a document containing a misrepresentation, he or she conducted or caused to be conducted a reasonable investigation; or (b) at the time of the release of the document, the person or company had no reasonable grounds to believe that the document contained a misrepresentation: [s. 138.4(6)] Action must be commenced in case of a misrepresentation in a document within 3 years and within 6 months of a news release disclosing that leave was granted to commence the action: [s. 138.14(a)]

Ontario Statutes	Statutory Breach	Liability for Offence	Statutory Defence and Limitation Period
Securities Act	Director or officer is guilty of an offence if he or she authorized, permitted, or acquiesced in the making of a public oral statement that related to the business or affairs of the responsible issuer and contained a misrepresentation: [s. 138.3(2)]	Liable, jointly and severally: [s. 138.6(3)] Liable subject to the limit set out in s. 138.7(1) for the portion of the aggregate amount of damages that were assessed in favour of the plaintiffs that corresponds to his/her responsibility for damages: [s. 138.6(1)] May be liable for the whole amount of damages that were assessed in action if the court determines that the director authorized, permitted, or acquiesced in making the misrepresentation: [s. 138.6(2)]	Director or officer is not liable for misrepresentation in a public oral statement unless (a) he or she knew that the statement contained a misrepresentation; (b) he or she deliberately avoided acquiring knowledge that the statement contained a misrepresentation; or (c) he or she was, through an action or failure to act, guilty of gross misconduct in connection with the making of a statement: [s. 138.4(1)] Director or officer is not liable for a misrepresentation if he or she proved that the plaintiff acquired or disposed of the issuer's security with knowledge that the public oral statement contained a misrepresentation: [s. 138.4(5)] Director or officer is not liable for a misrepresentation if (a) before the making of a public oral statement containing misrepresentation, he or she conducted or caused to be conducted a reasonable investigation; or (b) at the time of making of a public oral statement, the person or company had no reasonable grounds to believe that the public oral statement contained a misrepresentation: [s. 138.4(6)] Action must be commenced within 3 years of the statement and within 6 months of the news release disclosing that leave was granted to commence an action under s. 138.3 or under comparable legislation in another jurisdiction: [s. 138.14(b)]

Ontario Statutes	Statutory Breach	Liability for Offence	Statutory Defence and Limitation Period
Securities Act	Director or officer is guilty of an offence if he or she authorized, permitted, or acquiesced in the failure of the responsible issuer to make timely disclosure: [s. 138.3(4)]	Liable, subject to a limit set out in s. 138.7(1), for the portion of the aggregate amount of damages assessed in favour of plaintiffs that corresponds to his or her responsibility for damages: [s. 138.6(1)] Liable, jointly and severally: [s. 138.6(3)] May be liable for the whole amount of damages assessed in the action if the court determines the director authorized, permitted, or acquiesced in making the misrepresentation: [s. 138.6(2)]	Director or officer is not liable unless the plaintiff proves that the director or officer (a) knew of the change and that the change was a material change; (b) deliberately avoided acquiring knowledge of the change or that the change was a material change; or (c) was through an action or failure to act, guilty of gross misconduct [s. 138.4(3)] Director or officer is not liable if he or she proves that he or she conducted a reasonable investigation or had no reasonable grounds to believe that the failure to make timely disclosure would ever occur: [s. 138.4(6)(b)] Action must be commenced within 3 years of the date when the disclosure was required to be made and within 6 months of the news release disclosing that leave was granted to commence the action under s. 138.3 or comparable legislation in another jurisdiction: [s. 138.14(c)]
Workplace Safety and Insurance Act, 1997, R.S.O. 1997, c. 16, Sch. A	Director or officer is liable if (a) he or she knowingly made a false statement or representation to the board in connection with any person's claim for benefits under an insurance plan; (b) he or she willfully failed to inform the board of any material change in circumstances in connection with the obligation of the employer within 10 days: [s. 149]	Liable to a fine not exceeding $25,000 and/or imprisonment not exceeding 6 months whether or not the corporation was prosecuted or convicted: [s. 158(1)]	
Workplace Safety and Insurance Act, 1997	Director or officer is guilty of an offence if he or she knowingly authorized, permitted, or acquiesced in the commission of an offence committed by the corporation: [s. 157]	Liable to a fine not exceeding $25,000 and/or imprisonment not exceeding 6 months whether or not the corporation was prosecuted or convicted: [ss. 157 and 158(1)]	Action must be commenced within 2 years after the day on which the most recent act or the omission upon which the prosecution is based comes to the knowledge of the board: [s. 157.1(1)]

Ontario Statutes	Statutory Breach	Liability for Offence	Statutory Defence and Limitation Period
ADDITIONAL STATUTES IMPOSING DIRECTOR LIABILITY			
Auditor General Act, R.S.O. 1990, c. A.35.	Director or officer is liable if he or she obstructed the Auditor General in the performance of a special audit under s. 9.1 or an examination under s. 9.2: [s. 11.2(1)]	Liable to a fine not exceeding $2,000 and/or imprisonment not exceeding 1 year: [s. 11.2(2)]	None
Building Code Act, 1992, S.O. 1992, c. 23.	Director or officer is liable if he or she knowingly concurred in furnishing false information in any application or failed to comply with any order under this Act: [s. 36(2)]	Liable to a fine not exceeding $50,000 for a first offence and $100,000 for subsequent offences: [s. 36(3)]	Action must be commenced within 1 year after the subject matter of the proceeding arose: [s. 36(8)]
Collection Agencies Act, R.S.O. 1990, c. C.14.	Director or officer is liable if he or she knowingly concurred in furnishing false information in any application, failed to comply with an order or direction, or contravened the Act: [s. 28(1)]	Liable, jointly and severally, to a fine not exceeding $50,000 and/or to imprisonment not exceeding 2 years: [s. 28(1)]	Action for furnishing false information must be commenced within 1 year after the facts came to the knowledge of the director: [s. 28(4)] Action for other offences must be commenced within 2 years after the subject matter arose: [s. 28(5)]
Construction Lien Act, R.S.O. 1990, c. C.30.	Director or officer is liable for a breach of trust if he or she assented to, or acquiesced in, conduct that he or she knew or reasonable ought to have known amounts to a breach of trust by the corporation: [s. 13(1)]	Liable, jointly and severally, for the particular breach of trust: [s. 13(3)]	
Mining Act, R.S.O. 1990, c. M-4	Director or officer of the corporation that engaged in the rehabilitation of mining lands project is guilty of an offence if he or she did not ensure that the corporation complied with requirements under Part VII of the Act: [ss. 167(5) and (6)]	Liable to a fine not exceeding $10,000 whether or not the corporation was prosecuted or convicted: [ss. 167(6) and (7)]	Director is not liable if he or she took all reasonable care to ensure that the corporation complied with the requirements under Part VII of the Act: [s. 167(5)] Action must be commenced within 2 years after the later of (a) the day on which the offence was committed; and (b) the day on which the evidence of offence first came to the attention of the Director or the rehabilitation inspector designated: [s. 169(3)]

Ontario Statutes	Statutory Breach	Liability for Offence	Statutory Defence and Limitation Period
Pesticides Act, R.S.O. 1990, c. P.11.	Director or officer is guilty of an offence if he or she failed to prevent the corporation from causing or permitting certain adverse effects contrary to the Act (impairment to the environment; injury to property, plant, or animal; and safety of persons): [ss. 49(1) and (2)]	Liable to a fine and depending on the offence, imprisonment, whether or not the corporation was prosecuted or convicted: [s. 49(4)]	Director or officer is not liable if he or she took reasonable care to prevent the corporation from committing the offence: [s. 49(1)] Action must be commenced within 2 years of the offence: [s. 48]
Real Estate and Business Brokers Act, 2002, R.S.O. 2002, c. 30, Sch. C.	Director or officer of a brokerage is guilty of an offense if he or she failed to prevent the brokerage from committing the following offences: (a) furnishing false information in any application under this Act or in any statement or return required under this Act; (b) failing to comply with an order, other than an order made under s. 21, a direction, or other requirement under this Act; or (c) contravening or failing to comply with any section of this Act or regulations: [s. 40(2)]	Liable to a fine not exceeding $50,000 and/or imprisonment not exceeding 2 years less a day: [s. 40(3)]	Director or officer is not liable if he or she took reasonable care to prevent the brokerage from committing the offence: [s. 40(2)] Action must be commenced within 2 years after the facts upon which the proceeding is based first came to the knowledge of the director: [s. 40(4)]
Smoke-Free Ontario Act, R.S.O. 1994, c. 10	Director is liable if he or she failed to prevent the corporation from contravening the Act: [s. 15(7)]	Liable to a fine not exceeding $100,000 whether or not the corporation was prosecuted or convicted: [ss. 15(9) and 15(10)]	Director is not liable if he or she took all reasonable care to prevent the corporation from contravening the Act: [s. 15(7)]
Tobacco Tax Act, R.S.O. 1990, c. T.10.	Director or officer is guilty of an offence if he or she directed, authorized, assented to, acquiesced in, or participated in the commission of an act that is an offence under this Act: [s. 30]	Liable to the punishment provided for the offence whether or not the corporation was prosecuted or convicted: [s. 30]	None
Tobacco Tax Act	Director is liable if the corporation failed to collect tax or collected tax and failed to remit the tax or failed to pay any interest or penalty related thereto, subject to an exception in s. 30.1(2): [s. 30.1(1)]	Liable, jointly and severally, to pay such amounts: [s. 30.1(1)]	Director is not liable if he or she exercised the degree of care, diligence, and skill to prevent failure that a reasonably prudent person would exercise in comparable circumstances: [s. 30.1(3)] An assessment must be made within 2 years of the director leaving office: [s. 30.1(5)]

CHAPTER 12

PREPARING FOR AND AVOIDING CALAMITY: SOME AREAS OF PRACTICAL CONCERN FOR DIRECTORS

I. Introduction

Imagine that through a phone call or email received late at night, or by reading the morning newspaper, you learn that the corporation that you are a director of has suffered an enormous calamity. A fire has destroyed the building in which its key file storage and computer systems were housed; a competitor has applied to a court for an injunction to restrain your corporation from continuing to market its most important product on the basis of alleged patent or trademark infringement; or the corporation has been ordered to shut down a major manufacturing facility and to undertake a multi-million dollar soil remediation program following the discovery of a chemical leak that occurred many years ago, before your corporation acquired the facility. What will the ensuing days and weeks be like for you and your fellow directors, and for the corporation's management? Will there be chaos or the ordered implementation of a well thought-out contingency and response plan? Will there be second guessing and finger-pointing as to who is responsible for the situation, or will the directors and management be able to confidently say to shareholders and regulatory authorities that they had taken all reasonable steps and precautions to protect the corporation and relevant stakeholders from foreseeable harm?

The focus of the earlier Chapters of this book was on the general duties of directors and on the specific rules and regulations that are applicable under specific legislation, including corporate, securities, and employment legislation. Those Chapters outlined and elaborated upon the principles and rules that all directors should be aware of when carrying out their duties. This Chapter looks at four specific areas of practical concern to directors that relate to the operation of the corporation's business. The common thread between these four areas is that potentially catastrophic consequences can befall a corporation or its directors if these areas are neglected or mishandled. To put it in colloquial terms, this is where the rubber hits the road in terms of good and effective governance in practice, rather than merely in theory.

The four specific areas are:

- Information Technology, Compliance, and Risk Management;
- Intellectual Property Risk Management;
- Environmental, Compliance, and Risk Management; and
- Insolvent Corporations: Some Practical Considerations.

These areas are not the only, or necessarily the most, important ones of practical concern for directors. There are others that may be relevant to particular corporations, such as preparedness for natural disasters, pandemics, or terrorism. Another area of enormous practical importance, which is dealt with as part of Chapter 14, "Internal Investigations", concerns the protection of the corporation from fraudulent activities and from other forms of malfeasance on the part of company employees and third parties. The relative importance of these areas to any given corporation will depend upon the nature of the corporation's business, its size, and the geographic reach of its operations.

Directors do not need to become experts in these fields, nor can they reasonably be expected to understand the details of the corporation's programs, plans, and strategies in order to cope with all of the problems that may arise. They are entitled to rely reasonably on the corporation's employees, who are responsible for looking after these areas of concern, and on expert advisors and consultants, who may be retained by the corporation and its board to assist in the establishment of programs and procedures to protect the corporation from harm. Directors are expected to address the question of what circumstances and events could cause harm to the corporation, and they must satisfy themselves that reasonable steps have been taken to ensure that the risk of such harm is avoided or minimized.

II. Information Technology, Compliance, and Risk Management

A. Introduction

Increasingly, the information technology infrastructure (including data management, electronic records administration, communications, and related financial, customer, and business processing systems) is becoming the nervous system, if not the brain, of almost all companies. Prompt, if not immediate, access to accurate, complete, and reliable information is an essential ingredient of prudent and effective corporate management. The failure or interruption of the communications, data, and business intelligence infrastructure that provides that information to corporate managers can have catastrophic business implications. Therefore, a fundamental and material aspect of any corporate governance program must include programs and activities to assess and ensure the operational integrity of that infrastructure.

In 1994, the Dey Report[1] focused governance attention in Canada on the board of directors' duty to identify and address the principal risks of the company's business and to ensure the implementation of appropriate systems to manage those risks. There can be no doubt that since 1994, the increasing reliance, indeed, the dependence, of companies on their information technology (IT) infrastructure for all aspects of the management, administration, and operation of their businesses places the management of that risk very high on the list of any board's governance considerations. Despite the technologically esoteric nature of an enterprise's IT infrastructure, directors must consider how reliant their company is on that infrastructure, what possible risks may exist (and the possible impact of those risks) and what management and compliance strategies are reasonably necessary to prudently address those risks.

B. Assessing the Risks

The first issue for a director to consider is the nature and extent of the company's reliance on its IT infrastructure. A board should have a reasonable understanding of how the company uses and depends upon its IT infrastructure in the ordinary course of its business. Based on that understanding, the second governance issue to address is the impact that any degree of failure of the IT infrastructure may have on the company. The potential implications of any such IT infrastructure risk may be organized under the following three categories:

1. the risk of harm that may be caused by business interruption, whether it is due to (a) a failure of the company's IT infrastructure, or (b) a failure of the IT infrastructure of the company's strategic trading partner (e.g., suppliers, distributors, telecommunications service providers, or customers);

2. the risks associated with a failure to comply with statutory, regulatory, or contractual obligations to maintain the operation, integrity and security of the company's data, electronic records, and commercial information processing operations; and,

3. the risk of harm that may be caused to others by a failure to anticipate, prepare for, and adequately manage the risks that may be associated with the company's IT infrastructure, including the risks associated with failing to report such circumstances.

[1] Report of the Toronto Stock Exchange Committee on Corporate Governance in Canada. *Where Were the Directors? Guidelines for Improved Corporate Governance in Canada* (the "Dey Report") (Toronto: December 1994).

C. Business Interruption

The more reliance that any enterprise places on its IT infrastructure to manage and perform its day-to-day business operations, the greater the risk that any failure of the IT infrastructure will damage those business operations. Such interruptions can affect the company's supply chain management, electronic records maintenance, revenue generation, and relationships with both suppliers and customers. Moreover, regulated enterprises may also face investigations and remedial action from regulatory bodies in the event that business interruptions are neither avoided nor quickly resolved. Although there are various management strategies that can be relied upon to avoid or mitigate the risk of business interruption resulting from the failure of an IT infrastructure, the following risk management strategies are frequently considered and used by boards:

1. contingency planning and disaster recovery plans that specifically address the failure of the IT infrastructure;

2. third party services for backup and access to alternative IT facilities that may be procured on an "as needed" and "utility provision" basis;

3. parallel IT processing capacity, where co-existing and redundant systems operate in tandem but independently and in segregation from each other (often at a reasonable physical distance from each other);

4. regular and frequent data backup and segregated data (record) storage that is conducted, almost always, at a reasonable physical distance;

5. regular IT infrastructure testing, diagnostics, trouble reporting, and "repair" activities, in conjunction with aggressive ongoing support and maintenance of the IT infrastructure;

6. testing report follow-ups, identification, and elimination of identified possible risks to avoid repeating IT problems that have been corrected (e.g., restructuring to avoid single points of failure, and resolving technology compatibility, interoperability, or connectivity challenges, and even personnel skill and experience deficiencies);

7. adopting policies and practices related to IT enhancement, currency, refreshment, and upgrading, including the adoption of IT integrity and reliability features as they are introduced by new versions and releases; and

8. multiple or triangulated networks and communications systems that may create both channel redundancies and media alternatives (Internet, telephony, cable, wireless, and even satellite).

D. Regulatory Obligations

Your company may also be subject to a wide range of statutory, government policy, regulatory, and industry requirements that directly create corporate governance obligations with respect to the enterprise's IT infrastructure. Some of those IT governance duties arise from the following sources:

(1) **Regulatory Bodies** may have the authority to require corporate records to be maintained to ensure the integrity, reliability, and availability of those records for the purpose of public scrutiny. Such regulatory bodies require accurate, complete, and current information concerning the affairs of the companies they regulate, and almost all regulatory bodies now provide detailed guidelines and requirements concerning the quality of such information that may be stored, processed, and produced electronically, including the following:

- Health industry guidelines and statutory requirements concerning record maintenance standards and confidentiality.[2]
- Ontario Securities Commission (OSC): Section 113 of Part V of the General Regulations,[3] made under the *Securities Act*.[4] The regulations ensure that all electronic records are secured with adequate precautions and with the appropriate means to guard against falsification and to ensure that the electronic records are accessible.
- Stock Exchanges: Stock exchanges require the trading of securities to be conducted with integrity and in a fair and transparent manner. In that regard, the Universal Market Integrity Rules

[2] In Ontario alone, the following statutes have a direct impact on the maintenance of patient records that digitization and electronic processing must take into account: *Cancer Act*, R.S.O. 1990, c. C.1, s. 7 (information to be confidential); *Child and Family Services Act*, R.S.O. 1990, c. C.11, Part VIII, ss. 178–191 (confidentiality of records and access to records); *Health Insurance Act*, R.S.O. 1990, c. H.6, ss. 37-38 (record-keeping and confidential information); *Health Protection and Promotion Act*, R.S.O. 1990, c. H.7, s. 39 (confidentiality of information); *Independent Health Facilities Act*, R.S.O. 1990, c. I.3, s. 37 (confidential information); *Long-Term Care Act, 1994*, S.O. 1994, c. 26, ss. 32–36 (disclosure of personal information); *Mental Health Act*, R.S.O. 1990, c. M.7, s. 35 (personal health information); *Personal Health Information Protection Act, 2004*, S.O. 2004, c. 3, Sch. A, (Part II, practices to protect personal health information, Part IV, collection, use, and disclosure of personal health information, Part V, access to records of personal health information and protection of records); and, *Public Hospital Act*, R.S.O. 1990, c. P.40, s. 14 (records of personal health information).

[3] R.R.O. 1990, Reg. 1015.

[4] R.S.O. 1990, c. S.5.

("UMIR")[5] stipulate a series of audit trail and record retention requirements and instructions.[6] As well, Rule 10.16 of the UMIR specifically addresses the "Gatekeeper Obligations of Directors, Officers and Employees" that are related to the obligations to report any information concerning market activities; these obligations are directly related to the monitoring of electronic transactions and to the maintenance of relevant records.

- Office of the Superintendent of Financial Institutions (OSFI): OSFI published its Guidelines on "Outsourcing of Business Activities, Functions and Processes".[7] OSFI's Policy Statement re: Year 2000 is also instructive (September 25, 1997).
- Canadian Securities Administrators (CSA): The CSA passed new "Investor Confidence" rules that contain requirements similar to those resulting from the *Sarbanes-Oxley* Act in the U.S. These rules include Multilateral Instruments (MI)[8] 52-108 to 52-110. Rule MI 52-109[9] is of the greatest interest from an IT perspective since it creates a responsibility for board members to monitor IT control systems and to ask prudent questions to ensure that the IT systems of the company are properly designed and operating and that there are processes in place to ensure that management's legal requirements are met.

(2) **Tax Records:** The maintenance of commercial records for tax purposes is governed by s. 230 of the *Income Tax Act*[10] and by Regulation 5800,[11] which was passed pursuant to that Act. The Canada Revenue Agency has published two guidelines concerning both the traditional and the electronic maintenance of commercial records. They are entitled, "Books and Records Retention/Destruction", Information Circular No. 78-10RS, and "Books, Records and Other Requirements for Taxpayers Having Foreign Affiliates", Information Circular No. 77-9R. The section of the

---

[5] See http://www.tsx.com/en/trading/rules-regulations/umir.html

[6] See Rules 10.11 and 10.12, including Market Integrity Notice 2003-006, dated March 28, 2003, entitled, "Electronic Audit Trails".

[7] Canada, Office of the Superintendent of Financial Institutions Canada, Guideline No. B-10 (May 2001, revised December 2003), online: <http://www.osfi-bsif.gc.ca/app/DocRepository/1/eng/guidelines/sound/guidelines/b10_e.pdf>.

[8] Available online at Ontario Securities Commission, Category 5: Ongoing Requirements for Issuers and Insiders: <http://www.osc.gov.on.ca/Regulation/Rulemaking/Current/rrn_part5_index.jsp>.

[9] Ontario Securities Commission, MI 52-109, *Certification of Disclosure in Issuers' Annual and Interim Filings*.

[10] R.S.C. 1985, (5th Supp.), c. 1.

[11] Income Tax Regulations, C.R.C., c. 945.

1989 Guidelines entitled, "EDP (Electronic Data Processing) Audit Program", is particularly instructive.

(3) **Customs records**: The *Customs Act*[12] contains various obligations to keep and properly maintain records (s. 40(3)). As well, electronic records must be retained for the amount of time prescribed by the Act (s. 2(1.3), and by the Exporters' and Producers' Records Regulations[13] (s. 2). The Canada Border Services Agency, D17-1-21, *Customs and Excise Memorandum,* (2000) also provides for the maintenance of electronic records (see para. 6).

(4) **Export Controls**: Officers and directors of companies should be aware of the categories of technology and information/records that cannot be exported from Canada without a permit, such as high end and encryption software (information security). The *Export and Import Permits Act*[14] creates the Export Control List, which delineates the items that require a permit before they can be removed from Canada. Of particular importance is the national security nature of that Act; it will be strictly enforced against any person who commits the criminal offence of breaching it. Even an offshore IT outsourcing transaction can invoke the Act if any regulated technology items are to be used by IT service providers outside of Canada.[15]

(5) **Privacy**: The *Personal Information Protection and Electronic Documents Act*[16] restricts access to any information that may identify an individual (see protection of personal information, ss. 5–10, and retention of documents and electronic documents, s. 37). In particular, the Act requires companies to protect personal information with reasonable security; such protection is a direct function of the company's IT infrastructure and of all of the security features that must be implemented to comply with that requirement.

(6) **Electronic Commerce:** It is difficult to imagine a business enterprise that is not engaged in some form of electronic commerce, such as consumer transactions, supply chain management, or advertising. Most jurisdictions around the world, including those across Canada, have enacted legislation that requires the maintenance of electronic records to ensure the reliability and integrity of

---

[12] R.S.C. 1985 (2nd Supp.), c. 1.

[13] S.O.R./97-71.

[14] R.S.C. 1985, c. E-19.

[15] *Export Control List,* SOR/89-202.

[16] S.C. 2000, c. 5.

information concerning electronic transactions.[17] Since e-commerce transactions in Canada represent many billions of dollars of Canada's GDP, the intersection between electronic record integrity for e-commerce purposes and for audit, taxation, and evidence purposes should not escape the purview of any board whose company is engaged in transactional e-commerce.

(7) **Maintenance of Electronic Records as Evidence:** Directors and officers must also consider the extent to which the inability of their company to defend against, or to prosecute, civil claims may be caused by a failure of its IT infrastructure. In order to ensure that their companies can rely on their commercial records as evidence in a court of law or other tribunal, directors must be assured by the company's IT managers that such records are considered "reliable". The *Canada Evidence Act*[18] and most of its provincial counterparts stipulate that the record maintenance system from which information is being introduced as evidence shall not adversely affect the authenticity and integrity of any electronic documents. Obviously, regular testing to ensure document integrity, the ongoing reliability of that information by the company introducing that evidence, reasonable "integrity protection" and security features of the associated "record maintenance system", and reasonable IT infrastructure maintenance and "quality management" procedures will all facilitate a company's ability to rely on its electronic records as evidence in any dispute resolution proceeding.

(8) **Audit Requirements and Financial Management:** The maintenance of any company's financial records and related information is one of the most obvious governance obligations for corporate directors. If, for any reason, those records are compromised or distorted, or as a result of any failure of the IT infrastructure, they fail to accurately reflect the financial affairs of the company, the financial management of the company may be greatly compromised. Canadian GAAP "proposes" that financial records be electronically maintained in accordance with the electronic record guidelines of the Canadian Institute of Chartered Accountants ("CICA"). In 1986, the CICA published those guidelines in a book entitled, *Computer Control Guidelines*. As well, in the early 1990s the EDI Council of Canada published a similar accounting publication that is available directly from the Council. Since that time, companies have become far more dependent on their IT infra-

[17] See, e.g., the *Electronic Commerce Act* (Ontario), S.O. 2000, c. 17.

[18] R.S.C. 1985, c. C-5, ss. 31.1 and 31.8.

structure, and the CICA has provided strong leadership on a broad range of IT governance issues, all of which are directly related to the integrity of financial rewards and to the conduct of an associated audit. The following list includes some examples of that guidance; many (if not all) of these items may attract judicial notice over time concerning the quality and standards of IT supervision, which a director may have to adhere to:

(i) Information Technology Control Guidelines.[19] See Chapter 8 of the Guidelines for application controls (e.g., record storage and management requirements);

(ii) Twenty Questions Directors should ask about IT,[20] which are included at the end of this Chapter (see section II.G.);

(iii) Audit Implications of EDI;[21]

(iv) S.J. Gaston, FCA, *Information Security: Strategies For Successful Management* (Toronto: The Canadian Institute of Chartered Accountants, 1996);

(v) Twenty Questions Directors should ask about Information Technology Outsourcing, 2005;[22]

(vi) *IT Control Assessments in the context of CEO/CFO Certification,* 2004;[23]

(vii) "Independent Advice To Audit Committees On Material Commercial Transactions From IT Outsourcing To Strategic Alliances", presented at the CICA's inaugural Audit Committee Conference;[24] and

(viii) "The Role of IT in Corporate Governance and Control: New Standards and Practices" by Deloitte & Touche (Canada):[25] The IT governance standards published by the CICA have been augmented by many papers written by leading commentators in the accounting profession; this is an example of one of them. Such papers are quickly raising the bar con-

[19] CICA, *Information Technology Control Guidelines,* 3rd ed. (Toronto: CICA, 1997).

[20] CICA, *20 Questions Directors Should Ask About IT* (Toronto: CICA, 2004).

[21] CICA, *Audit Implications of EDI* (Toronto: CICA, 1997).

[22] CICA, *20 Questions Directors Should Ask About IT Outsourcing* (Toronto: CICA, 2005).

[23] CICA, White Paper, *IT Control Assessments in the Context of CEO/CFO Certification* (Toronto: CICA, 2004).

[24] Duncan Card, Partner at Bennett Jones LLP. This paper was presented at the CICA Conference, Toronto Convention Centre, Sept. 19–20, 2005.

[25] October 2004. Presentation available online at <http://www.it-can.ca/files/Hartley.ppt>.

cerning the issue of what directors must understand about the IT infrastructure of their company.

(9) **IT and Governance Professional Associations:** Other prolific sources of IT infrastructure governance and compliance oversight standards are the many industry associations, IT trade organizations, and various professional institutes that have begun to consider both the essential role that IT plays in any business and what the governance role of a director should be in the face of such reliance on IT. Some of the organizations that are specifically considering, researching, and promulgating policy concerning IT governance are

(i) Information Technology Governance Institute (ITGI-US), which has published guidance for IT professionals on how to address CEO/CFO certification from an IT management perspective;

(ii) Public Company Accounting Oversight Board (PCAOB) audit standards,[26] which establishes the importance of IT general controls in program development, program changes, computer operations, and access to programs data;

(iii) Committee of Sponsoring Organizations of the Treadway Commission (COSOTC), which has published an internal control framework and risk assessment methodology for IT that identifies internal control risks that are related to data integrity, system security, system availability, and data confidentiality;

(iv) Institute of Corporate Directors, which is a Canadian organization that frequently considers IT governance issues, including, since the late 1990s, issues related to Year 2000 IT challenges and reporting requirements;[27] and,

(v) Institute of Directors, a U.K.-based organization that has published various papers and articles on a broad range of IT governance and management issues.[28]

---

[26] Subject to SEC approval.

[27] See the paper written and prescribed by Duncan Card and Carol Hansell, "Information Technology Year 2000 Compliance: Corporate Governance Duties and Obligations of Directors" (Institute of Corporate Directors' Annual General Meeting, 1998). See www.icd.ca, generally.

[28] See the following articles published in *Director Magazine* (London, U.K: IOD): "IT Strategy: Get A Return on IT Spending" (May 2006) at 37; "IT Strategy: Supply Chain Management" (March 2006) at 41; and "IT Strategy: Intelligent IT Systems" (April 2006), generally.

(10) **Disclosure Obligations:** In addition to the IT management and governance obligations noted above, directors and officers of companies may have to determine the extent to which any material failure of their company's IT infrastructure should be reported or otherwise disclosed. As a matter of careful IT governance, it is just as important to act prudently and reasonably to correct and report IT infrastructure failures as it is to avoid them altogether. Once an important IT infrastructure failure has occurred, the focus of IT governance switches to the quality and promptness of the response, management, reporting, and resolution of that failure, as well as to the issue of how to avoid its possible recurrence. In particular, directors and officers must consider whether failures of their company's IT infrastructure should be reported to the following parties:

(i) the company's insurers, in anticipation of potential claims or litigation that may arise from such occurrences;

(ii) the company's auditors, concerning the extent to which the electronic manifestation of its financial records may not be in accordance with Canadian GAAP;

(iii) the company's trading partners, concerning the extent to which their commercial transactions and transaction records may be compromised;

(iv) the public through public disclosure (especially in the case of public companies), concerning the extent to which information concerning the company's operations may be compromised and the extent to which the IT failure may pose a material risk to the business or financial affairs of the company; and,

(v) regulators, such as the OSFI, which may promptly require information concerning any material impact on the operations of the company; generally, the threshold of "materiality" will vary on a case-by-case basis.

E. Third Party Harm

The board must be aware of the harm that a company may suffer from a business interruption, the company's breach of legal or regulatory requirements, the company's failure to produce business records that comply with Canadian GAAP, and the company's failure to support its income tax return with reliable records or to even defend itself in court against claims and allegations with reliable records. The board must also be aware that a failure of the company's IT infrastructure may expose others to harm. Suppliers, customers, and other trading partners may look to a company's board and management for evidence that the prudent management of the company's IT infrastructure did not cause or contribute to the harm caused by an IT infrastructure failure.

F. Assessment of IT Infrastructure Governance

In view of the numerous and quickly developing relationships between IT infrastructure and a prudently managed company, directors may wish to consider undertaking a thorough and well-documented review and assessment of the current state of their company's IT infrastructure and related risk management strategies. Such a "due diligence" review may be conducted to address both the quality of the company's IT infrastructure and the company's risk management and response strategies. Such an IT governance assessment may include the following undertakings:

- Ensure that the board is fully informed of the role that IT plays in the business of the company and the extent to which the company depends on the IT infrastructure (or parts of it) for its day-to-day business operations and compliance obligations.
- Undertake a detailed assessment of all of the laws, regulations, government policies, accounting requirements, and other legal requirements that affect the company's IT infrastructure, and conduct a compliance review of the company's current operations, processes, and IT infrastructure.
- Review IT executive management; this procedure may include both an internal review by the corporation's human resources department and an external (independent) review of managers, based on their business and technological skills, their experience, and other related management capabilities.
- Review all IT risk management strategies, including employee screening, contingency planning, security systems, business interruption insurance, testing programs, and maintenance and support practices. Also consider whether or not an external (independent) assessment of those risk management strategies should be conducted.
- Review all medium- and long-term "mission critical" service arrangements with IT infrastructure providers, with regard to the success of those projects (compared to the business plan), incidents of failure, cost escalations, service level performance, "best practices", and

related project management issues. In this regard, external (independent) business and legal advisors are routinely retained to review and assess ("benchmark") the contract terms, business operations, and the performance of technology, as well as to recommend improvements for such arrangements directly to the board of directors. Recently, mid-term re-evaluations have been implemented for such transactions as facility management transactions, shared service arrangements, IT outsourcing transactions, and long-term software development arrangements.

- Obtain reports from the company's senior business executives (such as the CFO, COO, senior HR executive, sales/marketing executives, and compliance executives, all of whom are important constituents of IT management) on their level of satisfaction with IT governance, management, and related issues.
- Ensure that all audit issues associated with the company's IT infrastructure are addressed and resolved in a timely manner and that progress reports are written on them.

G. Twenty Questions the CICA Believes Directors Should Ask About Their Company's IT Infrastructure[29]

(1) Does management have a strategic information systems plan in place that is monitored and updated as required? Does this plan form the basis for the annual plans, annual and long-term budgets and the prioritization of information technology projects?

(2) Have appropriate procedures been established to ensure that the organization is aware of technology trends, periodically assessing them and taking them into consideration when determining how it can better position itself?

(3) Have key performance indicators and drivers of the IT department been determined? Are they monitored from time to time and are they benchmarked against industry standards?

(4) Have relevant indicators been defined and monitored to manage the performance of the organization's third-party service providers?

(5) How has management identified the required technology expertise and how is top talent attracted?

[29] With no editorial revisions, this list of questions is reproduced from the CICA's 2004 publication, *20 Questions Directors Should Ask About IT, supra* note 20, which has been adapted for consideration of a company's IT infrastructure generally. The adapted questions were presented by Duncan Card of Bennett Jones LLP to the Canadian Annual CIO Summit Conference in 2005.

(6) Does management have appropriate procedures to address information technology employee turnover, training and project assignment?

(7) Has the board considered the creation of an IT subcommittee or assigned a board member specific responsibility for the organization's investment in, and use of, information technology?

(8) Has the responsibility for IT corporate governance been assigned to a person in a sufficiently senior management position? How does management communicate their IT policies to personnel?

(9) What procedures are in place to ensure that the company's systems and management are in compliance with Sarbanes-Oxley and/or CSA Investor Confidence rules, as appropriate?

(10) Does management have a plan to periodically conduct risk assessments covering the organization's use of information technology, including internal systems and processes, outsourced services and the use of third-party communications and other services? If it does, are the results of the assessments acted on where appropriate or required?

(11) How does management ensure data integrity, including relevance, completeness, accuracy and timeliness, and its appropriate use within the organization?

(12) What arrangements does the organization have for the regular review and audit of its systems to ensure risks are sufficiently mitigated and controls are in place to support the major processes of the business?

(13) Has the organization assigned someone the responsibility for privacy policy, privacy legislation and compliance therewith?

(14) Has the organization identified the various legislative and regulatory requirements for protecting personal information and developed a policy and procedures for monitoring compliance with them?

(15) If the organization uses e-business to buy or sell products or services, has there been a specific review of the risks and controls over the e-business activities?

(16) Are the organization's e-business activities appropriately protected from external and internal attack by unauthorized persons

or others that, if successful, would result in loss of customer satisfaction or public embarrassment?

(17) Has the organization adopted formal availability policies? Has it implemented effective controls to provide reasonable assurance that systems and data are available in conformity with availability policies?

(18) Does the organization understand the impact of an interruption in service and are there plans in place to deal with potential interruptions? Has a business continuity plan been adopted? If it has been adopted, is it tested regularly and are the results used to improve the plan?

(19) Has management considered and addressed legal implications that pertain to the use of software, hardware, service agreements and copyright laws?

(20) Have policies covering licences, agreements, copyright and acceptable use been formulated and disseminated to all personnel?

III. Intellectual Property Risk Management

The patent litigation between Research In Motion (RIM) and NTP abundantly demonstrated the high stakes in patent infringement and in intellectual property rights in general. NTP, a patent holding company in the United States, successfully sued RIM for infringing on five of its issued U.S. patents.[30] Although RIM vigorously challenged the validity of NTP's patents and initiated re-examination proceedings of the patents in the United States Patent Office, RIM ultimately settled with NTP for over $600 million in March 2006.

The RIM-NTP litigation and the rise in the importance of intellectual property rights in corporate dealings have further changed the environment for directors. This section considers the existing jurisprudence and legal principles regarding the liability of directors and officers, and it provides a framework for managing the risks associated with the infringement of a patent and other intellectual property rights.

As described in Chapter 2, directors, in exercising their powers and discharging their duties, are required to (a) act honestly and in good faith with a view to the best interests of the corporation, and (b) exercise the care, diligence, and skill that a reasonably prudent person would exercise in

[30] US Patent Nos. 5,436,960; 5,625,670; 5,819,172; 6,067,451; and 6,317,592.

comparable circumstances. Courts have provided some guidance as to the nature and extent of these duties.

The leading case in Canada regarding the liability of directors and officers for patent infringement by a corporation is the Federal Court of Appeal decision in *Mentmore Manufacturing Co. v. National Merchandise Manufacturing Co.*[31] More recently, *Mentmore* and the issue of the liability of directors were considered by the Trial Division of the Federal Court in *Halford v. Seed Hawk Inc.*[32]

Mentmore was concerned with an action for patent infringement. The plaintiffs succeeded in their action for the infringement of their Canadian patent for a retractable writing pen. The issue on appeal was whether the defendant officer and director should be held personally liable for the infringement because of his involvement in the manufacture and sale of the infringing pens. While the defendant was not found to be personally liable, the court made it clear that there could be circumstances where personal liability for patent infringement would arise. The court stated:

> I do not think we should go so far as to hold that the director or officer must know or have reason to know that the acts which he directs or procures constitute infringement. That would be to impose a condition of liability that does not exist for patent infringement generally. I note such knowledge has been held in the United States not to be material where the question is the personal liability of directors or officers. See Deller's Walker on Patents, 2nd ed., 1972, vol. 7, pp. 117-118. But in my opinion there must be circumstances from which it is reasonable to conclude that the purpose of the director or officer was not the direction of the manufacturing and selling activity of the company in the ordinary course of his relationship to it but the deliberate, wilful and knowing pursuit of a course of conduct that was likely to constitute infringement or reflected an indifference to the risk of it. The precise formulation of the appropriate test is obviously a difficult one. Room must be left for a broad appreciation of the circumstances of each case to determine whether as a matter of policy they call for personal liability. Opinions might differ as to the appropriateness of the precise language of the learned trial judge in formulating the test which he adopted — "deliberately or recklessly embarked on a scheme,

---

[31] *Mentmore Manufacturing Co. v. National Merchandise Manufacturing Co.* (1978), 22 N.R. 161 (F.C.A.) ("*Mentmore*").

[32] (2004), 246 F.T.R. 1 (F.T.C.), var'd by 2006 F.C.A. 275, 2006 CarswellNat 2397 (eC) ("*Halford*").

> using the company as a vehicle, to secure profit or custom which rightfully belonged to the plaintiffs" — but I am unable to conclude that in its essential emphasis it was wrong. [33]

For personal liability to attach, the test, according to *Mentmore,* requires a director to have caused the company to engage in a deliberate course of conduct with the knowledge of, or in reckless indifference to, the risk of infringement. The court stated that the principle should apply to both the large corporation and to the small, closely held corporation.

Halford was also concerned with an action for patent infringement and with the issue of personal liability for the directors of the defendant corporation. In the action, three officers and directors of the defendant corporation were alleged to have deliberately, willfully, and knowingly directed the corporation to infringe on, and to induce others to infringe on, the patent rights of the plaintiff. In reviewing *Mentmore*, the court in *Halford* made it clear that the issue of the personal liability of a corporation's directors for infringement by the corporation is not an aspect of patent law but rather a particular instance of the broader issue of the liability of directors for acts that were committed by them in connection with the business of the corporation while they occupied the status of directors.[34]

Based on a consideration of *Mentmore*, *Normart Management Ltd. v. West Hill Redevelopment Co.*,[35] and *Montreal Trust Co. of Canada v. ScotiaMcLeod Inc.*,[36] the court in *Halford* restated the test for determining personal liability, ruling that "... corporate directors and officers are personally liable for conduct undertaken in the course of their corporate duties if that conduct is itself tortious or if it serves an interest other than the corporation's".[37] The court concluded:

> In other words, liability attaches when the actions of the director or the officer are either such that the director's own behaviour is tortious, or when the corporation is simply used as a cloak for the personal activities of the director. Both possibilities are consistent with general principles governing the personal liability of director and officer and avoid creating

---

[33] *Mentmore, supra* note 31, at para. 28.

[34] *Halford* trial decision, *supra* note 32 at para. 324.

[35] *Normart Management Ltd. v. West Hill Redevelopment Co.* (1998), 37 O.R. 97 (C.A.) ("*Normart*").

[36] *Montreal Trust Co. of Canada v. ScotiaMcLeod Inc.* (1995), 26 O.R. (3d) 481 (C.A.) ("*Montreal Trust*").

[37] *Halford* trial decision, *supra* note 32, para. 326.

> a type of personal liability of directors which is peculiar to patent infringement.[38]

The court in *Halford* made the following observations concerning *Mentmore* and the test for determining the liability of a director:

(1) the mere fact of exercising control is not sufficient to establish personal liability; and[39]

(2) care should be taken in applying a test based on an analysis of the conduct of the personal defendant in order to determine whether or not her actions can be characterized as "dishonest, deceptive and deliberately reckless behaviour" or as indifference to the obvious consequences of her action. Such a test suggests that the personal liability of directors depends upon the moral quality of their behaviour, but while dishonesty is not commendable, it is not infringement.[40]

The court in *Halford* has reformulated the *Mentmore* test, which focused on the director's knowledge of the patent (i.e., the deliberate, willful, and knowing pursuit of a course of conduct that was likely to constitute infringement or that reflected an indifference to the risk of it) to a test that focuses on the nature of the director's action (i.e., the conduct is itself tortious or it serves an interest other than the corporation's). The Federal Court of Appeal recently affirmed the *Halford* test for the determination of personal liability in patent infringement cases.[41] According to the court:

> The [trial] Judge found that the individual defendants did no more than direct the activities of Seed Hawk Inc. in the ordinary course of their relationship to it. He found no evidence of a deliberate, wilful and knowing pursuit of a course of conduct that was likely to constitute infringment or reflected indifference to the risk of infringement. . . .The [trial] Judge made no error of law or fact in reaching these conclusions.[42]

Following the principles set down in *Mentmore*, officers and directors can avoid liability by (1) not engaging in deliberate acts of infringement, and (2) not being indifferent to the risk of infringement. According to *Halford,* officers and directors can avoid liability by (1) not committing a tortious act

---

[38] *Halford, ibid.* at para. 331.

[39] *Halford, ibid.* at para. 328.

[40] *Halford, ibid.* at para. 332.

[41] *Halford v. Seed Hawk Inc.,* 2006 F.C.A. 275, 2006 CarswellNat 2397 (eC).

[42] *Ibid.* at para. 54.

resulting in patent infringement, and (2) acting in the interests of the corporation. Put another way, directors and officers can take appropriate actions to limit their exposure by acting honestly and in good faith with a view to the best interests of the corporation, and by exercising the care, diligence, and skill that a reasonably prudent person would exercise in comparable circumstances.[43] It seems likely that a court would be hard pressed to find deliberate or willful infringement of a patent in the best interests of the corporation.

Quite apart from the risk of personal liability for directors, patents and other intellectual property rights can be a key corporate asset, and any deficiencies in the intellectual property can be a source of risk to the business of the corporation. So what should directors and officers do?

To minimize the risks that are associated with patent infringement, corporate management needs to develop a comprehensive corporate intellectual property policy that includes a clearance procedure. A clearance procedure involves assessing whether new product developments or activities are likely to infringe on any intellectual property rights of others. A typical patent clearance procedure would include the following steps:

(1) Search in the field of the new product for any patents or pending patent applications by a competitor or other third party that could present an obstacle or block the product's entry into the market.

(2) Determine if there is a potential infringement problem with the blocking patent by assessing the scope of the claims. Consider the validity of the patent, for example, in view of relevant prior art and prior public disclosures.

(3) Pursue a licence under the patent. The cost of licensing should be assessed against the expected return from the commercialization of the product.

(4) If a licence is not commercially feasible, for example, the cost is too high, or a licence is not available, then consider ways to "design around" the blocking patent.

(5) If it is not possible to design around the blocking patent, then terminate the product development to avoid litigation and the potential liability for patent infringement. In the United States, treble damages can be awarded if there is a finding of willful infringement.

---

[43] See Chapter 2 for a further discussion of directors' fiduciary duties and duty of care.

Similar considerations apply to the clearance of trademarks, copyrights, and industrial designs. If the blocking trademark cannot be licensed, then adopt a new mark to avoid confusion. If the existing copyright cannot be licensed, then reverse engineer the work to uncover the underlying idea or concept embodied in the copyright, then independently recreate the work. If the blocking industrial design registration cannot be licensed, create a new industrial design that is distinguishable from the existing design.

Directors should at least ask the following questions with respect to intellectual property issues in the context of entry into a new market or the development of a new product or technology:

(1) What steps has the corporation taken to protect its intellectual property rights and build an intellectual property portfolio?

(2) What opportunities exist for deriving additional revenue from the intellectual property?

(3) What investigations have been undertaken concerning the potential blocking of intellectual property rights (e.g., patents, trademarks, copyright) of a competitor or other third parties?

(4) What course of action has been taken in view of the discovery of any potential blocking intellectual property rights?

The rise in the importance of intellectual property rights to the business of a corporation means that directors need to be aware of intellectual property issues affecting the corporation in terms of competitive advantage and barriers to entry. They also need to be aware of intellectual properties as assets for generating additional revenue or financial opportunities for the corporation. This awareness means that directors should be receiving and reviewing periodic reports on the following:

(1) the status of the intellectual property rights that are being acquired or that are owned by the corporation, and the development and management of the corporation's intellectual property portfolio;

(2) the feasibility of commercially exploiting any intellectual properties owned by the corporation in order to provide additional revenue streams (for example, through a licensing program);

(3) the status of investigations concerning potentially blocking the intellectual property rights of a competitor or other third parties in order to assess potential intellectual property liabilities;

(4) the progress of any intellectual property proceedings launched by the corporation; and

(5) the status of any intellectual property actions against the corporation.

Directors should also consider periodic reviews of the corporate strategy and of the intellectual property policy and procedures and make recommendations as needed.

The stakes are high with patents and intellectual property rights. Directors and officers need to be proactive when they are dealing with intellectual properties.

IV. Environmental, Compliance, and Risk Management

The principal areas of potential liability for corporations and their directors with respect to environmental issues arise under statutes and under the common law.

A. Potential Statutory Liabilities and Obligations

1. Positive Preventative Duty

Twenty years ago, Ontario introduced new groundbreaking statutory obligations for directors (and officers). While the focus of the discussion below is upon Ontario's legislative regime, it is noted that most of the other provinces, and to a certain extent, the federal government, have enacted similar legislation. When this environmental legislation was first introduced in Ontario[44] (through the *Environmental Protection Act*[45] ("EPA") and the *Ontario Water Resources Act*[46] ("OWRA"), directors were required to take all reasonable care to prevent the unlawful discharge of a contaminant into the natural environment, or, under the OWRA, to take all reasonable care to prevent the corporation from causing or permitting such an unlawful discharge.[47] This positive duty was similar to the duty that had been imposed on directors and officers under Ontario's *Occupational Health and Safety Act*.[48] Until changes were made to the EPA and OWRA in 2005, the duty under environmental legislation was restricted to the prevention of discharges or, under the OWRA, causing or permitting such an unlawful dis-

---

[44] Changes to the relevant legislation were made in 2005; they are described in a later section.

[45] *Environmental Protection Act*, R.S.O. 1990, c. E.19 ("EPA").

[46] *Ontario Water Resources Act*, R.S.O. 1990, c. O.40 ("OWRA").

[47] The Ontario Government passed the *Environment Enforcement Statute Law*, S.O. 1986, c. 54, which, among other things, amended the OWRA and the EPA to include provisions regarding duties of directors and officers (now OWRA, s. 116 and EPA, s. 194).

[48] R.S.O. 1990, c. O.1.

charge, whereas under the *Occupational Health and Safety Act*, directors (and officers) had a duty to ensure that a company generally complied with the legislation (i.e., the statute and regulations made thereunder).

Ontario's environmental legislation has imposed, and continues to impose, significant positive duties, and thus, potential liabilities, on directors, although enforcement against directors has been somewhat difficult to predict. The Ministry of the Environment ("MOE") has enforced these provisions where a director has a significant level of control over a company's operations (and the incident in question), such as in the case of smaller and/or privately held companies.

2. R. v. Bata Industries Ltd.

Perhaps one of the most discussed cases in terms of director liability is *R. v. Bata Industries Ltd.* ("*Bata*").[49] In 1989, the Crown laid charges against three directors (who were also officers), alleging that they had breached the duty, under the EPA, to prevent an unlawful discharge into the natural environment. Thomas Bata, the CEO of Bata Industries Ltd., the president of the company, and a director who was on site managing the facility at issue were those who were charged. Many have commented that the case highlighted the obligations of officers, rather than of directors, given that, among other reasons, two of the five directors were not charged.[50]

In *Bata*, Thomas Bata was acquitted, primarily because he satisfied the court that he had taken all reasonable care to prevent the unlawful discharge of contaminants into the natural environment. He did this by implementing an environmental management system, which included a policy and a requirement to have procedures in place to handle hazardous wastes in a lawful manner. The president and the "on-site" director were convicted and each of them fined $12,000. Although the trial judge ordered the company not to pay the fines for the directors, the Court of Appeal overturned the trial judge's order in that regard.

Subsequently, there have been no similar charges brought against directors of such a high profile company, possibly because the shockwaves from this case effectively reached boardrooms across the country, resulting in changes that satisfied regulators. In light of this case, companies that had implemented environmental management systems reviewed and improved

[49] *R. v. Bata Industries Ltd. et al.* (1992), 9 O.R. (3d) 329 (Ont. Ct. J. (Prov. Div.)) ("*Bata*"); fines reduced on appeal (1993), 14 O.R. (3d) 354 (Ont. Gen. Div.) ("*Bata Two*"); probation order preventing indemnification of directors by company removed on appeal (1995), 25 O.R. (3d) 321 (C.A.) ("*Bata Three*"); collectively ("*Bata Cases*").

[50] It is also interesting to note that none of the directors of Bata Industries Ltd. were named in an order that was issued against the company that required investigation, and if necessary, remediation, of the property in issue.

their systems, while companies that had not implemented formal (or informal) systems quickly developed and implemented them. Indeed, it is rare to find a company of any significant size that does not have a formal, written environmental management system that describes the company's policies with respect to environmental protection and the procedures that implement such policies. An environmental management system is usually the cornerstone of how a company manages its operations in compliance with environmental laws, including how it prevents unlawful discharges or spills into the environment. As such, it is also a key tool used by directors to satisfy their statutory obligations.

In *Bata*, the trial judge stated that when the duties imposed on directors (and officers) under the OWRA and the EPA are being considered, guidance can be found in other statutes, such as the (Ontario) *Business Corporations Act*:[51] and the *Canada Business Corporations Act*:[52]

> Directors of corporations receive further statutory guidance in respect to their responsibilities from the Ontario *Business Corporations Act, 1982*, S.O. 1982, c. 4 (now R.S.O. 1990, c. B.16) (OBCA), s. 1(1), [rep. 1982, c. 4, s. 277], and the *Canada Business Corporations Act*, S.C. 1974-75-76, c. 33 (now R.S.C. 1985, c. C-44) (CBCA). **Under corporate law, directors have the duty to manage or supervise the management of the business and affairs of the corporation "in the best interests of the corporation". (OBCA, s. 115(1) and CBCA, s. 117(1)). They must exercise the care, diligence and skill that a reasonably prudent person would exercise in comparable circumstances (BCA, s. 134). Many of their powers may be delegated to the officers, and they must exercise due care in selecting competent officers** (OBCA, s. 133, and CBCA, s. 116). Directors may be absolved from liability if, as part of managing the business of the corporation, they rely in good faith upon the reports of professionals (BCA, s. 135(4) and CBCA, s. 118(4)).[53] [Emphasis added].

Furthermore the court stated that the "reasonable care" described in s. 147 of the EPA and s. 75(1) of the OWRA,[54] is a question of law, but it is a

---

[51] R.S.O. 1990, c. B.16 ("OBCA").

[52] R.S.C. 1985, c. C-44 ("CBCA").

[53] *Bata*, *supra* note 49 at para. 129.

[54] During the 1990 revision of the Statutes of Ontario, these sections were renumbered in the *Environmental Protection Act*, R.S.O. 1990, c. E.19, s. 194(1) and in the *Ontario Water Resources Act*, R.S.O. 1990, c. O.40, s. 116(1), respectively.

question of fact when one is determining whether a specific director (or officer) of a corporation has taken all reasonable care to prevent the corporation from causing or permitting an unlawful discharge.

Once liability has been established and a conviction has been obtained, the principles articulated in *Bata* must be considered when sentencing an offender. In *R v. Varnicolor Chemical Ltd.*,[55] the Ontario Court of Justice sentenced the director and officer of a corporation to an eight-month prison term for continuously violating provisions of the EPA. In issuing this sentence, the court applied the purposes of sentencing: to protect the public, deter and rehabilitate offenders, promote compliance with the law, and express public disapproval of the act. The court stated that, for such offences, general deterrence and protection of the public must be of paramount concern, but it will also consider mitigating factors, such as the lack of any adverse effect and the absence of a criminal record in determining an appropriate sentence.

In applying the above principles, the depth of involvement the accused maintained in the company appeared to be an important aggravating factor. The accused was the only director and officer to take an active part in the operations and actual management of the company, and he was, at all relevant times, the sole directing mind of the company, a role he had held since the company's inception. In addition, he was involved in the negotiations preceding the issuance of the Certificate of Approval by the MOE. The court emphasized his active involvement and in-depth knowledge of the business operations as factors that put him in a unique position to be aware of the procedures of the business and the requirements of the MOE. Furthermore, the court found that it was apparent that the accused had knowledge of the violations. There was some indication of deliberateness or recklessness on the part of the director and officer, but at the very minimum, there was willful blindness. The accused was unco-operative with MOE officials, and he did nothing to rectify the problems or initiate a clean-up of the site.

3. Causing or Permitting a Discharge

In addition to being charged for failing to satisfy the duty to take all reasonable care to prevent an unlawful discharge into the natural environment, or under the OWRA, discharging material of any kind that may impair the quality of the water, in Ontario, a director (or officer) could also be held liable for actually *causing* or *permitting* the discharge of a contaminant into

[55] *R v. Varnicolor Chemical Ltd.* (1992), 9 C.E.L.R. (N.S.) 176 (Ont. Ct. J. (Prov. Div.)).

the natural environment if the discharge caused or may have caused an adverse effect.[56]

The theory behind such a charge is that a director is in a position of sufficient control that he or she can, and should, act to prevent a discharge into the natural environment. By failing to exercise such control, it could be argued that he or she may not have caused the discharge but instead permitted the unlawful discharge to occur.

Typically, one would expect that such a charge would only likely be brought against a director (or officer) of a smaller company, where a director (or officer) would be in a position to actually cause or permit an unlawful discharge into the natural environment, because he or she is directly involved in the activity that resulted in the discharge. Directors (and officers) of larger organizations are less likely to exercise this type of control of the corporation's affairs, and thus, they would not be expected to attract the same liability.

A director could also potentially be charged for failing to report a discharge that occurs out of the normal course of events where the director caused or *permitted* the discharge to occur.[57] Again, as a practical matter, it is unlikely that this charge would be laid against a director of a larger organization, because it would be a rare incident where such a director would be sufficiently involved in a matter that he or she could be seen to have caused, or even *permitted*, the discharge, which are the requirements to trigger a reporting obligation.

4. Contaminated Property

For the most part, Ontario has led the charge in Canada with respect to statutory liability that could be imposed on individuals, such as directors, with respect to contaminated property. This has been done largely through the use of administrative orders, rather than through charges that are laid for offences. Specifically, under s. 17 of the EPA, in certain circumstances where a person causes *or permits* the discharge of a contaminant into the natural environment, so that land, water, property, animal life, plant life, or human health or safety is injured, damaged, or endangered, or is likely to be injured, damaged, or endangered, a Director of the MOE may order such a person to repair the injury or damage, prevent the injury or damage, or where the discharge has damaged or endangered, or is likely to damage or endanger,

---

[56] See EPA, s. 14 and OWRA, s. 30(1).

[57] See EPA, s. 15, OWRA, s. 30(2).

existing water supplies, to provide temporary or permanent alternate water supplies.[58]

Similarly, under s. 18 of the EPA, the MOE has the ability to require a person who owns or owned, or who has or had *management or control* of, an *undertaking* or property to do certain things, such as to conduct investigations and, potentially, remediation, if such actions would be required to prevent or reduce the risk of a discharge of a contaminant into the natural environment from the undertaking or property or to prevent, decrease, or eliminate an adverse effect that may result from the discharge of a contaminant from the undertaking into the natural environment.[59]

5. Management or Control

Subsection 18(1) of the EPA states that an order requiring preventative measures to be taken may be issued to a person who owns or owned or has or had management or control of an undertaking or property. The Environmental Review Tribunal, which decides appeals of orders made by the MOE, has held that "control" includes the formal legal control available to directors (and officers) and also *de facto* control by someone in a position to significantly influence the management of an undertaking.[60]

The Ontario Environmental Appeal Board (now the Environmental Review Tribunal), in *Caltex Petroleum Inc. v. Director, Ministry of Environment and Energy*,[61] considered what "charge, management or control" meant. The Appeal Board held that a lease registered against the title of the land signed by the director of a company demonstrates sufficient management and control of the premises, even if the director was not involved with the day-to-day activities of the premises. In contrast, the Appeal Board held that a director who holds a mortgage on the premises but is not a mortgagee in possession, even though he or she benefits financially from the premises, is not in "charge, management and control" of the undertaking. This was also the ruling in *Canadian National Railway Co. v. Ontario (Director, Environmental Protection Act)*,[62] where a mortgagee not in possession was held not to be a person having "management or control of an undertaking or property", even if it had knowledge of, and a prior connection to, the operations conducted at the site.

---

[58] EPA, s. 17.

[59] OWRA, s. 18.

[60] Dianne Saxe, *Ontario Environmental Protection Act Annotated* (Aurora, Ont.: Canada Law Book, 2006) at p. II–111.

[61] February 17, 1998, Ontario Environmental Appeal Board, File Nos. 00341.A1, 00349.A1, 00350.A1, and 00383.A1 (unreported).

[62] *Canadian National Railway Co. v. Ontario (Director, Environmental Protection Act)* (1991), 80 D.L.R. (4th) 269 (Ont. Gen. Div.), aff'd 87 D.L.R. (4th) 603 (C.A.).

In *Director v. P&L Tire Recycling*[63] the MOE had issued an order under s. 18 of the EPA to four individuals and two companies to clean up a site. A numbered company owned the site, while another company owned the business on the site. The first individual, C, was the director, president, and secretary-treasurer of the numbered company; the next two individuals, P and L, were directors of the business on the site. The last individual, D, was not a director, but he appeared to have management and control of the business on the site, which was sufficient to subject him to the order.

The Board concluded that all four individuals had to comply with the order. The determinative issue was whether the individuals were persons who own or have owned an undertaking on the property that is likely to result in harm if a contaminant is discharged, or if they own or have owned the property, or if they had management or control of either the undertaking or the property at any time. The question of control seemed to be determined by asking if they had taken an active role in the business or if they had a duty or opportunity to take preventive or corrective action but had failed to do so. Another factor was whether the individuals had knowledge of the requisite requirements; with this knowledge, came control.

Unlike the other three individuals, L did not appeal the order, so the Board did not discuss his level of control over the business. P exercised both legal and *de facto* control over the site and business; he was the dominant force who controlled the strategic decisions and financial transactions of the company, and he was intimately involved in most discussions with government officials with regards to the activities on the site. C exercised legal control over the numbered company but played no active role in running the business or site. While C had no *de facto* control, she had full legal control over the site as well as the opportunity to influence the other individuals, D, her husband and P, her son. The Board concluded that while D had no legal control, he had *de facto* control over the site, since he was involved in discussions with government officials, consultants, employees, lawyers, and customers. Furthermore, P would defer to D in the event of any disagreement in the decision-making.

The Board added that before any owner of property could be exempt from complying with an order on compassionate or equitable grounds, the Board would look at the following factors: whether the person made reasonable inquiries before purchasing the property; whether the person exercised due diligence in permitting third parties to occupy and carry on activities on the property; whether the person was actively involved in the activities; the extent of the person's control over the business activities; the extent of the

---

[63] *Director v. P&L Tire Recycling*, [1992] O.E.A.B. No. 21.

person's knowledge; the extent to which the person could foresee possible harm from the activities; the extent to which the person benefitted from the activities; and any other aggravating or extenuating circumstances.

In addition to liability imposed on directors, investors have also attracted liability for contaminated sites (which provides another perspective that may be of interest to directors, particularly because of the introduction of the concept of "fairness" in assigning liability). In *724597 Ontario Inc. (c.o.b. Appletex) v. Ontario (Minister of Environment and Energy)*[64] the Environmental Appeal Board (as it was then known) upheld the MOE's decision and held investors of a bankrupt company liable for the costs of an extensive environmental clean-up. Two issues were considered: whether the MOE had the jurisdiction to impose liability on the individuals (as investors), and the reasonableness of the order. In addressing the first issue, the Board concluded that both individuals, who were investors (but not officers or directors of the corporation) had become sufficiently involved in the financial and operational matters of the company that they had the requisite degree of management, charge, or control necessary to bring them within ss. 18 and 43 of the EPA. Specifically, the Board found that the investors in question retained ultimate control of all significant expenditures of the company through their signing authority. The Board stated that their control encompassed the kind of "formal legal control" that directors and officers have; they also had the *de facto* control that is exercised by other persons who are in a position to significantly influence the actual management of the undertaking. The Board rejected the argument that involvement in the management of a company's financial affairs was not sufficient to constitute management or control because it does not relate directly to the operations causing environmental concerns. The Board concluded that this type and degree of management and control were factors to be taken into account when determining whether the person named in the order should be relieved of liability in whole or in part.

With respect to the second issue in the appeal, in determining the reasonableness of the order, the board considered several mitigating factors, as discussed below.

6. Factors Considered in the Application of S. 18 of the EPA: Fairness!?

The Environmental Review Tribunal has indicated that it is prepared to grant full or partial relief from the liability to comply with an order in the interests of fairness and equity. The key factors that were taken into account

---

[64] *724597 Ontario Inc. (c.o.b. Appletex) v. Ontario (Minister of Environment and Energy)*, [1994] O.E.A.B. No. 17 ("*Appletex*").

in deciding whether to relieve a person from such liability were described in *Appletex*:[65]

(1) whether the person benefitted from participation in the polluting activity or enterprise;

(2) the standard of care that can reasonably be expected of the person, having regard for, among other things, the foreseeability of environmental harm;

(3) the person's degree of influence over the creation of the risk and the extent of his or her contribution to creating the risk;

(4) the steps taken to reduce the risk, with a higher standard imposed when the likelihood of failure becomes obvious. However, the board acknowledged that those who are responsible for a failing business will not have the resources needed to meet all of their responsibilities, so it would be unreasonable to expect investors to deal with every possible environmental contingency. Nonetheless, it is reasonable to expect the person who manages the company's finances or who has control of the company to take reasonable steps against imminent and obvious environmental hazards;

(5) the contributions of others, who are not before the board, towards creating the risks; and

(6) the possibility of unjust enrichment, if there are enough facts present to determine it.

7. Montague v. Ontario (Director, Ministry of the Environment)

Another case that discussed the potential liability that could be attracted by a director was the decision of the Ontario Divisional Court in *Montague v. Ontario (Director, Ministry of the Environment)*.[66] In this case, a company owned a facility that was used to manufacture paints and solvents. The facility was destroyed by a fire. A director of the company was responsible for arranging to clean up the site, which he did by hiring contractors that he personally supervised, at least occasionally. The MOE also occasionally supervised this activity. The company's director was aware that eighty metal drums were present at the site, but he was not aware of what happened to them after the site was cleaned up. The property was sold to an individual who applied successfully to rezone the property from industrial use to residential use. When the new owner attempted to sell the residential

---

65 *Ibid.* at 22–30.

66 *Montague v. Ontario (Director, Ministry of the Environment)* (2004), 6 C.E.L.R. (3d) 95 (Ont. Env. Rev. Trib.), rev'd in part, (2005), 12 C.E.L.R. (3d) 271 (Ont. Div. Ct.) ("*Montague*").

property, an environmental inspection found that eighty drums were buried at the site. Some of the drums still contained hazardous chemicals, and others had apparently leaked their contents into the ground. The MOE issued clean-up orders against the (now defunct) company, the director, and the new landowner to clean up the barrels and the affected soil.

Under s. 17 of the EPA, the Environmental Review Tribunal relieved the individual director of responsibility for the clean-up, but on appeal, the Divisional Court decided otherwise, stating:

> The "permitting" aspect of the offence centers on the defendant's passive lack of interference or, in other words, its failure to prevent an occurrence, which it ought to have foreseen. The fact that Lee [the director] had responsibility for the cleanup of the site, including the 80 drums of waste, yet chose to leave the site unsupervised for two or three days at a time while the cleanup was underway, are factors that should have been considered by the Tribunal in this regard.[67]

With respect to the s. 18 EPA order that was issued against a director, and in particular, considering management or control of an undertaking, the Divisional Court explained,

> While [the director] was not running the company as a whole, he was placed in charge of the cleanup operation which is the undertaking that created the risk of discharge. He hired the subcontractors who did the work, and was therefore in a supervisory position over them and in a position to exert influence in the way the cleanup was conducted.[68]

The court concluded that s. 18 of the EPA could be used as the basis for an order against a director. It indicated that liability under s. 18 flows from having had "management or control of an undertaking or property". As such, it is not necessary that one be acting in one's role as a directing mind of a company to invoke such liability as that defines "management or control" too narrowly.

Montague also involved the disposal of waste, which is an issue that can create many problems for companies and their directors. Where waste has been deposited unlawfully (i.e., without an approval), s. 43 of the EPA enables the MOE to issue an order "... to remove the waste and to restore the site to a condition satisfactory to the [MOE]" against, among others, "a person who otherwise has or had charge and control of the land, building or

[67] *Montague, supra* note 66 at para. 32 [emphasis added].

[68] *Ibid.* at para. 41.

waste". It is not necessary that a person be an owner or have charge and control of the business as a whole in order for that person to be found liable under s. 43. As long as the individual had charge and control of the "waste", jurisdiction lies under this section to make an order against that individual.

B. Director's New Positive Duties

1. Ontario

In 2005, Ontario amended the EPA and the OWRA to impose broader statutory obligations on directors, beyond the positive duty to take all reasonable care to prevent unlawful discharges into the environment. Section 194 of the EPA and s. 116 of the OWRA now provide that a director (and officer) of a corporation has a duty to take all reasonable care to prevent the corporation from discharging or causing or permitting such discharge of contaminants. For example, s. 194 of the Ontario *EPA* states that

> Every director or officer of a corporation has a duty to take all reasonable care to prevent the corporation from,
>
> (*a*) discharging or causing or permitting the discharge of a contaminant, in contravention of,
>
> (i) this Act or the regulations, or
>
> (ii) a certificate of approval, provisional certificate of approval, certificate of property use, licence or permit under this Act;
>
> (*b*) failing to notify the Ministry of a discharge of a contaminant, in contravention of,
>
> (i) this Act or the regulations, or
>
> (ii) a certificate of approval, provisional certificate of approval, certificate of property use, licence or permit under this Act;
>
> (*c*) contravening section 27, 40 or 41 in respect of hauled liquid industrial waste or hazardous waste as designated in the regulations relating to Part V;
>
> (*d*) contravening section 93 or 184;
>
> (*e*) failing to install, maintain, operate, replace or alter any equipment or other thing, in contravention of a certificate of approval, provisional certificate of

approval, certificate of property use, licence or permit under this Act; or

(*f*) contravening an order under this Act, other than an order under section 99.1, 100.1, 150 or 182.1.

The EPA also specifies that if a director is charged in connection with a specific contravention of the corporation, the director has the onus, in the trial of the offence, of proving that he or she carried out the duty in connection with that contravention.[69]

Furthermore, a director is liable to conviction under section 194(3) of the EPA whether or not the company has been prosecuted or convicted.[70]

As a result, the statutory duties imposed on directors in the context of environmental legislation are now more similar to the duties that are imposed under Ontario's *Occupational Health and Safety Act*.

Section 187 of the EPA provides for a fine against an individual of not more than $50,000 for a first time offender and not more than $100,000 and/or imprisonment of not more than one year for a subsequent offender for a contravention of the EPA (including s. 194(2)).

2. Federal

Not to be outdone, the federal government amended the *Canadian Environmental Protection Act, 1999* ("CEPA, 1999") to impose on directors duties that were similar to the duties imposed by Ontario's legislation. Previously, CEPA, 1999 had provided that where a company commits an offence, any officer, director, or agent who directed, authorized, acquiesced in, or participated in the commission of the offence was a party to, and guilty of, the offence and was liable for the punishment provided for the offence, whether or not the company had been prosecuted or convicted.

This provision still applies but new obligations were also imposed on directors (and officers).[71] CEPA, 1999 was amended to incorporate a provision similar to one found in Ontario. Under s. 280.1 of CEPA, 1999, every director or officer of a company now has a duty to take all reasonable care to ensure that the company complies with CEPA, 1999, the regulations made under the Act, and any orders and directions of and prohibitions and requirements imposed by the Minister of Environment, enforcement officers, and review officers.

---

[69] EPA, s. 194(2.1).

[70] OWRA, s. 194(3). See also the *Canadian Environmental Protection Act*, *infra* at s. 280.

[71] *Canadian Environmental Protection Act, 1999*, S.C. 1999, c. 33, s. 280(1) ("CEPA, 1999").

Subsection 272(1) of CEPA, 1999 provides for a fine or imprisonment for any person who contravenes any provision of the Act or its regulations. Subsection 272(2) provides that any person who commits an offence under s. 272(1) may be liable on conviction on indictment to a fine of not more than $1,000,000 or to imprisonment for a term of not more than three years, or to both; and on summary conviction, to a fine of not more than $300,000 or to imprisonment for a term of not more than six months, or to both.

C. Potential Civil Liability under the Common Law

Claims for environmental damage can also be based in tort law (including actions based on negligence), the rule in *Rylands v. Fletcher* (essentially, strict liability with respect to dangerous substances), trespass, and nuisance. In 1999, the Ontario Court of Appeal ruled that directors could be liable in tort for actions that were performed on behalf of the company. In *ADGA Systems International Ltd. v. Valcom Ltd.*,[72] the court held:

> [T]here is no principled basis for protecting the director and employees of Valcom from liability for their alleged conduct on the basis that such conduct was in pursuance of the interests of the corporation. It may be that for policy reasons the law as to the allocation of responsibility for tortious conduct should be adjusted to provide some protection to employees, officers or directors, or all of them, in limited circumstances where, for instance, they are acting in the best interests of the corporation with parties who have voluntarily chosen to accept the ambit of risk of a limited liability company. However, the creation of such a policy should not evolve from the facts of this case where the alleged conduct was intentional and the only relationship between the corporate parties was as competitors.[73]

We are not aware of any case in which this decision has been applied in an environmental law context.

D. Summary and Practical Tips

Directors should take steps to remain current with respect to potential environmental liabilities that may be incurred by themselves and by the company. It is particularly important to be aware of environmental obliga-

[72] *Adga Systems International Ltd. v. Valcom Ltd.* (1999), 43 O.R. (3d) 101 (C.A.).

[73] *Ibid.* at para. 43 [emphasis added].

tions and responsibilities that are imposed by legislation. In Ontario, for example, a director has a positive duty to take reasonable care to prevent the company from unlawfully discharging contaminants into the environment; failing to report statutorily-reportable discharges to the Ministry; breaching laws with respect to hazardous waste; failing to install, maintain, operate, replace, or alter equipment in contravention of an approval; and contravening an order made by the Ministry. It is an offence if the director fails to meet his or her obligations with respect to these matters. There are certain factors that may cause a director to attract liability under environmental legislation, including the following:

- the exercise of a significant level of control over the company's operations, particularly over the incident that resulted in the environmental offence or contamination; it may not be necessary for the control exercised by the director to be directly related to the incident that led to the violation or contamination;
- active involvement in the day-to-day operations of the company — if a director is the "directing mind" of the company, this factor will likely weigh significantly in favour of liability being imposed; the duration of the active involvement may also be an important factor;
- the director's knowledge and awareness not only of the incident in question but also of the requirements or action that could have (and should have) been taken to prevent the incident; and
- the exercise of *de facto* control over the operations of the company. *De facto* control, as well as legal control, can potentially result in exposure to environmental liability.

Directors can mitigate potential exposure to environmental liabilities by exercising reasonable care in fulfilling their duties, including any positive duties that are imposed by statute. The following steps will assist directors in fulfilling their duties:

- Confirm that the company has developed and properly implemented an environmental management system (EMS) that includes the company's policies on environmental protection, as well as specific procedures that implement such policies and protect the environment. The EMS should include the delegation of specific duties, the training of employees, and the steps to be taken to check that the system is working and is continually being improved.
- Confirm that the company has a system in place to ensure that material issues, including the need for, or the lack of, the resources that are required to maintain lawful operations and protect the envi-

ronment, are brought to the attention of management and the board and that appropriate follow-up actions are undertaken to address such issues.

- Confirm that the company has the procedures and training in place to prevent the unlawful discharge or other release of contaminants into the environment and that such procedures and training are being kept current.
- Confirm that the company has procedures in place to ensure that any orders, approvals, permits, or other requirements issued by environmental regulators are followed and that appropriate equipment is installed and maintained to meet the terms of any approval.
- Confirm that the company has specific procedures in place to address the storage, handling, and disposal of wastes.
- Confirm that the company makes lawful and appropriate communications and reports to regulators and that steps will be taken to immediately rectify any activity that has led to a violation or contamination.
- Confirm that the company maintains a written record of the policies, procedures, and actions that are taken to fulfill the lawful requirements that are imposed on the company. Such a record could include a manual that describes the EMS, log books, monthly compliance reports, audits, or other documents that could be relied on by the company and the director to show that reasonable care was taken to comply with lawful requirements and that steps were taken by the directors to prevent violations.

V. Insolvent Corporations: Some Practical Considerations

In ordinary circumstances, the interests of a corporation's various stakeholders are, at least in theory, aligned. The long-term growth of a corporation is seen as beneficial for shareholders, employees, and creditors (particularly, holders of long-term debt) alike. However, if a corporation becomes insolvent or nears insolvency, the interests of these stakeholders often diverge. Employees will want to avoid layoffs and workforce reductions and ensure that their jobs, pensions, and benefits are protected. Creditors will want the corporation to conserve cash and perhaps streamline operations and sell unnecessary assets and even part or all of the business to ensure that the company's debts can be repaid. Shareholders, as the residual beneficiaries of the corporation's assets (if any) that remain after the creditors have been repaid, are interested in trying to ensure that the corporation remains in business and continues to grow in the hope that it will eventually become profitable and provide a positive return on the shareholders' equity.

Faced with such diametrically opposed interests and with the competing demands of various stakeholders, directors are left with a perplexing dilemma as to what should be done when a corporation becomes insolvent. Does the corporation reduce its work-force and streamline its operations in order to conserve cash for the benefit of its creditors? Does the corporation continue to invest in its operations and further leverage its balance sheet to try to grow the business in the hope of becoming profitable and providing a positive return on shareholders' equity over the long term? Does the corporation attempt to sell its business and/or assets or even shut down its operations and seek bankruptcy protection? Which stakeholders' interests should be paramount and how should the directors act in order to protect those interests?

While one would expect that when a corporation becomes insolvent or is on the verge of insolvency, the interests of creditors would precede the interests of shareholders, the Supreme Court of Canada recently affirmed that directors of a corporation do not owe a specific fiduciary duty to creditors, even when that corporation becomes insolvent.[74] In *Peoples*, the Supreme Court held that directors and officers owe their fiduciary duty to the "corporation", whose interests are not to be confused with the interests of creditors or other stakeholders, and that this fiduciary duty does not change when the corporation is "in the nebulous 'vicinity of insolvency'".

While directors do not owe a specific fiduciary duty to creditors or other stakeholders, in *Peoples,* the Supreme Court of Canada left the door open for creditors to sue directors for failing to duly heed creditors' interests by adding that creditors can avail themselves of other means by which to pursue directors, including making a claim under the oppression remedy or a claim that the directors have breached their statutory duty of care under corporate law statutes. Accordingly, directors of corporations that have become insolvent or are on the verge of insolvency must proceed with great caution to minimize the risk that they will be subject to attack by creditors or other stakeholders for failing to adequately regard their interests.

---

[74] *Peoples Department Stores Inc. (Trustee of) v. Wise*, [2004] 3 S.C.R. 461 ("*Peoples*").

A. Directing an Insolvent Company

It is not possible to provide an in-depth discussion here of the myriad of issues and risks that directors of insolvent corporations need to be aware of since each insolvency situation has its own unique set of issues and challenges for directors. However, one thing that virtually all insolvency situations have in common is the need for management to act early in addressing a corporation's insolvency and developing an action plan. Upon becoming aware of a corporation's insolvency (or looming insolvency), directors should act fast to begin considering the options available to the company, with a view to developing and implementing an action plan that is in the best interests of the corporation and that will minimize the amount of harm to creditors and to other stakeholders. Where necessary, directors should retain legal and financial advisors with insolvency expertise to help the board examine strategic options and develop an action plan early in the process.

Typical alternatives that may be considered in respect of an insolvent company include the following: refinancing the company's debt; selling assets or all or part of the business of the company; restructuring the company and/or effecting a compromise with its creditors (either informal or formal); winding down the company and liquidating its assets (either inside or outside of a bankruptcy); or even simply maintaining the status quo (for example, if sufficient resources are available to weather a cyclical downturn). When evaluating alternatives, the role that directors will play throughout the insolvency proceedings should be kept in mind. In an informal arrangement with creditors or in a proposed sale of the company's assets or all or part of its business, directors may continue to play a very active role in the management of the corporation and may bear the responsibility for approving the arrangement or sale. Such a role may result in increased liability for directors, as disgruntled shareholders or other stakeholders look to directors to try to recoup their losses.

In such circumstances, it may make greater sense to seek a formal restructuring under the *Companies' Creditors Arrangement Act* ("CCAA")[75] or Part III of the *Bankruptcy and Insolvency Act* ("BIA")[76] in order to have a court officer, such as a CCAA monitor or a proposal trustee, act as an intermediary who is specifically charged with protecting the interests of creditors and to have the arrangement approved by creditors and the court. In addition to potentially reducing the personal liabilities of directors, both the CCAA and the BIA allow a corporation to obtain a temporary reprieve

[75] *Companies' Creditors Arrangement Act*, R.S.C. 1985, c. C-36, ss. 11(3) and 11(4) ("CCAA").

[76] *Bankruptcy and Insolvency Act*, R.S.C. 1985, c. B-3 ("BIA"), ss. 69 and 69.1.

from the actions of creditors and others in order to give the corporation an opportunity to develop its plan without having to expend precious resources fighting the claims of individual creditors or worrying about creditors seizing assets and disrupting the corporation's business. Such protection from creditors may be available even where a company is not yet insolvent but is facing a looming liquidity crisis.[77]

Another, somewhat less formal option may be to seek the appointment of a receiver, who will take its formal directions and authority from the court. This option may work well, for example, where a sale of the business or assets of the corporation is desired without a formal restructuring. The major actions of a court-appointed receiver (such as the sale of the business or its material assets) can be submitted to the court for approval, thereby reducing the risk that a disgruntled stakeholder will blame the directors and attempt to sue them for any losses that result from those actions.

In some cases, such as situations where a secured creditor appoints a receiver to seize and sell the assets of the corporation or where a creditor successfully petitions the corporation into bankruptcy, directors may retain very little, if any, control over the insolvency process. While the formal role of a director does not change upon a bankruptcy or the appointment of a receiver, practically speaking, directors will have no control over the insolvency process once the assets of the corporation vest in a trustee in bankruptcy or in a receiver, and directors should consider resigning rather than continuing to incur potential liabilities as a ruler with no kingdom (see the discussion below on the resignation of directors).

While trying to formulate an action plan that is in the best interests of the corporation and its stakeholders during a financial crisis is a formidable task in and of itself, directors have the additional burden of dealing with potential personal liabilities that may be amplified in an insolvency environment. Examples of typical personal liabilities that may be faced by directors of insolvent corporations and some practical tips for dealing with such liabilities are discussed below.

B. Personal Liability of Directors

Numerous statutes hold directors personally liable for certain types of obligations of the corporation. Such liability may be particularly worrisome in the context of insolvency, where the corporation does not have the financial means to meet all of its obligations. For example, pursuant to various corporate and employment statutes, directors may be personally

---

[77] *Re Stelco Inc.* (2004), 48 C.B.R. (4th) 299 (Ont. S.C.J.).

liable for unpaid wages and for vacation pay owed to employees.[78] Directors may also incur personal liability for the failure of a corporation to collect, withhold, or remit income tax, Canada Pension Plan contributions, employment insurance, GST, and retail sales tax.[79] Such personal liabilities of directors are typically heightened in insolvency situations where, faced with competing demands by suppliers and other creditors, a corporation may fail to ensure that it has sufficient cash set aside to fund employee payroll and statutory source deductions.

In addition to liabilities for unpaid wages and vacation pay and for the failure to collect, withhold, or remit source deductions, another form of directors' liability that may come to light in an insolvency context is that of liability for environmental offenses. Numerous statutes impose potential personal liability upon directors for failing to prevent a corporation from harming the environment.[80] Environmental contamination may be uncovered in the context of an insolvency situation where, for example, environmental assessments are conducted in connection with the proposed sale of the corporation's assets or operations.

C. Insolvency Liabilities

In addition to liabilities that exist outside of insolvency and that may be heightened in insolvency contexts, there are certain directors' liabilities that may arise specifically in insolvency situations. For example, corporate statutes and the BIA impose personal liability upon directors who authorize the payment of dividends or the repurchase or redemption of shares by a corporation at a time when the corporation is insolvent or where the payment of such dividends or repurchase or redemption of shares renders the corporation insolvent.[81] In addition, the BIA, in an effort to protect the property of a corporation for the benefit of its creditors prior to a bankruptcy, allows trustees in bankruptcy to pursue persons who have been privy to transactions where, in the year preceding bankruptcy, the corporation sold, purchased, leased, hired, supplied, or received property or services for a price conspicuously greater or less than fair market value.[82]

---

[78] See Chapter 9 for a discussion of such liabilities.

[79] *Income Tax Act*, R.S.C. 1986, c. 6, s. 227.1; *Excise Tax Act*, R.S.C. 1985, c. E-15, s. 323(1); *Canada Pension Plan*, R.S.C. 1985, c. C-8, s. 21.1; *Employment Insurance Act*, S.C. 1996, c. 23, s. 83(1); *Income Tax Act* (Ontario), R.S.O. 1990, c. I.2, ss. 38(1) and 46; and the *Retail Sales Tax Act*, R.S.O. 1990, c. R.31, s. 43(1).

[80] See the discussion in section IV of this Chapter.

[81] See, for example, CBCA, *supra* note 52, ss. 34(2), 36(2), 42, and 118(2), OBCA, *supra* note 51, ss. 30(2), 32(2), 38(3), and 130(2), and BIA, *supra* note 76, s. 101.

[82] BIA, *ibid.* at s. 100(2).

In order to help reduce the risks associated with potential personal liability for the repurchase or redemption of shares or the declaration of dividends while a corporation is insolvent or on the verge of insolvency, directors should obtain solvency certificates from the corporation's management (and, if deemed necessary, from external financial advisors) to confirm that the corporation is not insolvent and will not be rendered insolvent by the payment of the proposed dividend or the proposed redemption of shares. In addition, where the authority of the board is sought for the sale of any of the corporation's property (or, for that matter, the purchase of property by the corporation), directors should take the necessary precautions (such as obtaining independent appraisals) to ensure that such property is not being sold or purchased for a price conspicuously less than or greater than fair market value.

In addition to statutory liabilities that arise specifically in the context of insolvency, directors may also face potential common law liability if they participate in or acquiesce in conduct that constitutes fraud. For example, while courts in Canada have generally held that there is no specific duty to refrain from trading while insolvent (i.e., allowing the corporation to procure goods and services at a time when it is insolvent and, therefore, unlikely to be able to pay for those goods or services), directors may be held personally liable if they are found to have participated in a fraud.[83] Accordingly, where it is clear that a corporation is in dire financial circumstances and will not be able to pay for goods or services that are about to be obtained, prudence would suggest that such goods or services not be ordered on credit to avoid allegations by suppliers that the corporation and its directors have perpetrated a fraud.

D. Managing the Risk: Resignation, Indemnities, and Insurance

When faced with the increased risks that may come with an insolvent corporation, a director is faced with a difficult choice: should he or she abandon ship or stay at the helm and try to steer the corporation through the rough waters of insolvency? Generally, resignation will shield directors from liabilities that arise after they resigned but not liabilities that arose prior to their resignation. Accordingly, where events that may give rise to directors' liabilities have already occurred, a director should consider carefully whether it makes more sense to resign or to remain on the board in order to try to deal with those liabilities. If the director decides to resign in order to avoid or limit further liability, the director should ensure that the

[83] *Scotia MacLeod Inc. et al. v. Peoples Jewellers Limited* (1995), 26 O.R. (3d) 481 (C.A.) and *USF Red Star Inc. v. 1220103 Ontario Ltd.*, [2001] O.J. No. 915 (Ont. S.C.J.) (QL).

resignation is delivered to the corporation in writing and that everything that is necessary to make the resignation effective in the applicable jurisdiction on the date it is tendered has been done. The director should retain evidence of the delivery of the resignation (for example, a receipt from the corporation, dated and executed by an authorized officer) in order to clearly establish when he or she resigned.

Certain cases have involved all of the directors resigning from the board of an insolvent, or nearly insolvent, corporation *en masse* in an attempt to limit or reduce potential liability.[84] In the 1995 Manitoba Court of Appeal decision in *Brown v. Shearer*[85] (which involved the resignation of all of the corporation's directors), the court held that there was "nothing in the [CBCA] which limits the right of a director to resign".[86] With no clear statutory prohibition against directors resigning collectively, directors who choose to stay on the board when all others have resigned should ensure that they have adequate protection against personal liability (see the discussion below on indemnities) and Directors' and Officers' Insurance ("D&O Insurance"), since the remaining director(s) will likely be saddled with any directors' liabilities that are incurred from that point onward.

Who is left in charge (and potentially bears the resultant directors' liabilities) in a case where all of the directors have resigned? The CBCA, for example, provides that if *all* of the directors resign, subject to certain exclusions, a person who manages or supervises the management of the business and affairs of the corporation is deemed to be a director.[87] Where there is no one left to manage the corporation, the fiduciary duty of directors may require the remaining director(s) to take reasonable steps to prevent the corporation from being left without proper guidance while it is in a vulnerable state. In such a case, consideration should be given to possibly having the corporation engage in some type of formal restructuring or insolvency process in order to allow a court officer, such as a receiver, trustee, or monitor to be appointed. While such court officers do not take on the formal role of directors, they can help to ensure that the interests of the corporation's stakeholders are safeguarded.

Whether a director intends to resign or to remain on the board, it is important to consider the use of indemnities and insurance to try to mitigate director liabilities. The usual corporate indemnity may be of little use in an insolvency situation, since the corporation is unlikely to have sufficient

[84] See, for example, *Re Westar Mining Ltd.* (1996), 136 D.L.R. (4th) 564, 41 C.B.R. (3d) 145 (B.C. C.A.).

[85] (1995), 102 Man. R. (2d) 76 (C.A.) ("*Brown*").

[86] *Ibid.* at para. 25.

[87] CBCA, *supra* note 52, s. 109(4)

funds to pay under the indemnity if it is called upon. If a director proposes to stay on the board and help guide a corporation while it is insolvent, consideration should be given to other potential sources of indemnification, such as a deep-pocketed parent company or a shareholder.

In addition, in the context of a CCAA restructuring, it may be possible to obtain a court-ordered Directors' and Officers' Charge, which will protect directors and officers from various personal liabilities during the restructuring process by granting the directors and officers a charge on the corporation's property, which may rank ahead of the claims of other creditors of the corporation, including secured creditors. Additionally, it is possible to include in both CCAA and BIA restructuring plans and proposals provisions that provide compromises and releases of directors' liabilities, subject to some exceptions.[88]

Directors, whether they are resigning or staying on board, should also carefully review the corporation's D&O insurance policies to ensure that they provide adequate coverage.[89] Many D&O insurance policies provide coverage on a "claims-made" basis, which means that they only insure against claims made during the policy period and will not cover claims arising after the policy period if the policy expires or is cancelled or replaced, even where the event giving rise to the liability took place during the policy period. In such cases, it is important that directors obtain extended reporting period or "tail" insurance to extend the period of time during which claims may be made to the end of the limitation period for which a director may be sued for the incident. It is also important to check the exclusions in D&O insurance policies to ensure that they do not exclude the types of incidents or liabilities that directors may be most worried about in insolvency situations.

It is during times of financial crisis that a corporation is most in need of strong direction and guidance from its board. Insolvency situations provide directors with unique challenges and problems that will undoubtedly test their metal as leaders of the company. Although potential directors' liabilities may be heightened to some degree in insolvency contexts, they can be dealt with and mitigated to a large extent by careful planning early in the process. By acting early to examine options and obtain any necessary insolvency advice, directors can help to ensure that the interests of the corporation, as well as those of its stakeholders, are protected to the greatest extent possible.

---

[88] CCAA, *supra* note 75, s. 5.1; BIA, *supra* note 76, s. 50(13).

[89] See Chapter 18 for a further discussion of D&O Insurance.

CHAPTER 13

PROTECTING YOURSELF AS A DIRECTOR

I. Introduction

In the previous Chapters, practical areas where directors often run into trouble are discussed. The purpose of this Chapter is to discuss what you, as a director, can do to protect yourself from these trouble areas. This Chapter has two focuses. In Part I, we will evaluate the emerging trend in Canadian securities law to impose liability on directors and officers for misrepresentation in continuous disclosure materials in the secondary market. In Part II, we will provide practical advice for how a person should approach their directorship: what degree of vigilance is necessary, what warning signs should you be aware of, and what steps should you implement to protect yourself personally from litigation as a director?

II. Statutory Civil Liability for Misrepresentations in Continuous Disclosure Materials

A. Introduction

On December 31, 2005, amendments to the Ontario *Securities Act* ("OSA")[1] were proclaimed that provide investors in the secondary market with the right to sue the issuer and other potential defendants, including the directors of the issuer, for a misrepresentation in an issuer's continuous disclosure record or for a failure to make timely disclosure. Manitoba and Alberta recently passed substantially similar amendments to their securities legislation, but neither province has proclaimed them. British Columbia enacted its own liability scheme in 2004, but it too has never been proclaimed. In June and July of 2006, the Government of British Columbia sought public comment on whether to adopt the British Columbia-specific regime or a regime similar to Ontario's.[2] To date, the results of this consultation have not been made public. Common to all of the legislation is a director's potential liability in the secondary markets for misrepresentation and for the failure to make timely disclosure.

B. Potential Parties

1. Potential Plaintiffs

The potential plaintiff in an action under the civil liability regime is anyone who acquires or disposes of an issuer's securities between the time when the disclosure containing the misrepresentation was made and the time when it was publicly corrected, or, in the case of a right of action for failure to make timely disclosure, between the time when the obligation to make timely disclosure arose and the actual disclosure of the material change (called the "disclosure violation period").

The new OSA provisions deem the plaintiff to have relied on the misrepresentation or on the issuer that is making timely disclosure. The deemed reliance feature makes the new civil liability regime particularly

---

[1] *Securities Act*, R.S.O. 1990, c. S.5 ("OSA").

[2] Available online: <http://www.ag.gov.bc.ca/legislation/pdf/SecuritiesConsultation.pdf>.

attractive to class action litigants in that it removes the obstacles of proving individual reliance that exist in common law misrepresentation actions.

2. Potential Defendants

Ontario's secondary market civil liability regime applies to Ontario reporting issuers and to publicly-traded issuers with a "real and substantial connection" to Ontario. The potential defendants vary, depending on whether the action is for a misrepresentation or for a failure to make timely disclosure.

C. Newly Created Statutory Liabilities

1. Misrepresentation

The potential defendants in an action for a misrepresentation in a "document" or a "public oral statement" are

- the issuer;
- each director of the issuer at the time the document containing a misrepresentation was released, or a director who, in the case of a public oral statement, authorized, permitted, or acquiesced in the making of a public oral statement containing a misrepresentation;
- each officer of the issuer who authorized, permitted, or acquiesced in the release of a document or the making of a public oral statement containing a misrepresentation;
- each "influential person" (defined as a control person, promoter, or insider[3]) and each director and officer of an influential person;
- each expert if the document or public oral statement refers to a report of an expert that contains the misrepresentation; and
- the person who made the public oral statement.

A "document" is any written communication, including an electronic communication, that is filed with the Ontario Securities Commission (the "OSC"), any government authority or stock exchange; it also includes any other type of communication that would reasonably be expected to affect the market.[4]

---

[3] OSA, *supra* note 1, s. 1.1(1).

[4] *Ibid.*, s. 138.1.

A "public oral statement" is an oral statement made in circumstances in which a reasonable person would believe that information that is contained in the statement will become generally disclosed.[5]

2. Failure to Make Timely Disclosure

The potential defendants in an action for the failure to make timely disclosure are

- the issuer;
- each director and officer of the issuer who authorized, permitted, or acquiesced in the failure to make timely disclosure; and
- each influential person and each director and officer of an influential person.

A "failure to make timely disclosure" means a failure to disclose a material change in the manner required under the OSA (i.e., issue and file a news release forthwith and a material change report within ten days of the change).

D. Varying Standards of Liability

The burden of proof that a plaintiff must discharge to establish liability varies depending on both the type of action and the type of defendant.

1. Misrepresentation

The burden of proof in an action for misrepresentation depends on whether the misrepresentation is made in (i) a "core document" or (ii) any other document or in a public oral statement. Core documents are a special category of "document", and they are generally defined in the OSA to include the following: mandated disclosure documents such as a prospectus; management's discussion and analysis ("MD&A"); an annual information form; and an information circular.[6] For an officer of a reporting issuer and for the reporting issuer itself, "core document" also includes a material change report.[7]

In an action for misrepresentation in a non-core document or in a public oral statement, the plaintiff has a higher burden of proof in order to establish liability. The plaintiff must prove that the defendant had actual knowledge, deliberately avoided acquiring knowledge, or was guilty of gross

---

[5] *Ibid.*, s. 138.1.

[6] *Ibid.*

[7] *Ibid.*

misconduct.[8] In a core document, a lower burden of proof applies, and the plaintiff need not prove knowledge, avoidance of knowledge, or gross misconduct. However, if the defendant is an expert, the lower burden of proof always applies, regardless of whether the misrepresentation is in a core document or in a non-core document or public oral statement.[9]

2. Failure to Make Timely Disclosure

The burden of proof for the failure to make timely disclosure also varies, depending on the potential defendant. In actions against the issuer and officers of the issuer for the failure to make timely disclosure, the plaintiff need only establish the lower burden of proof. For officers, that burden is the fact that the officer authorized, permitted, or acquiesced in the failure to make timely disclosure.[10] In actions against a director who is not an officer of the issuer, the plaintiff is required to establish the higher burden of proof by proving that the director had actual knowledge, deliberately avoided acquiring knowledge, or was guilty of gross misconduct.[11]

E. Liability Limits[12]

The OSA limits a defendant's liability. However, in order to benefit from the liability limit, the defendant must not have authorized, permitted, acquiesced in, or influenced the making of the misrepresentation or failure to make timely disclosure while knowing it was a misrepresentation or failure to make timely disclosure. The liability limits, if available, are as follows:

- for the issuer, the greater of 5 percent of its market capitalization and $1 million;
- for a director or officer, the greater of $25,000 and 50 percent of the aggregate of the director's or officer's compensation from the issuer and its affiliates for the previous twelve months;
- for an influential person who is not an individual, the greater of $25,000 and 50 percent of the aggregate of the influential person's compensation from the issuer and its affiliates for the previous twelve months;

---

[8] *Ibid.*, s. 138.4(1).

[9] *Ibid.*, s. 138.4(2).

[10] *Ibid.*, s. 138.3(4).

[11] *Ibid.*, s. 138.4(3).

[12] See OSA, *supra* note 1, ss. 138.1 and 138.5–138.7 for damages, proportionate liability, and limitations on damages.

- for an expert, the greater of $1 million and the revenue that the expert and its affiliates earned from the issuer and its affiliates during the preceding twelve months; and

- for a person who makes a public oral statement and who is not an individual covered by one of the other liability limits, the greater of $25,000 and 50 percent of the aggregate of the person's or company's compensation from the issuer or its affiliates.

Another important limitation of liability relates to the limitation period. Under the OSA, secondary market liability extends until three years after the misrepresentation is released, or in the case of a failure to make timely disclosure, three years after the disclosure should have been made or six months after an action has been given leave to proceed by the court. This three-year minimum is longer than a standard limitation period to bring an action in Ontario (which is two years).[13]

F. Defences

The OSA provides a number of defences. The following are the most significant ones:

1. Reasonable Investigation Defence[14]

A defence is available if the defendant conducted a reasonable investigation and had no reasonable grounds to believe that the document or statement contained a misrepresentation or that the failure to make timely disclosure would occur.

The OSA sets out a number of factors that a court is directed to consider in determining whether such an investigation was reasonable. They include the following: the nature of the issuer; the knowledge, experience, and function of the defendant; and, most significantly, the existence and nature of any system to ensure the issuer meets its continuous disclosure obligations and the reasonableness of the reliance that the defendant placed on such a system.

---

[13] *Limitations Act*, S.O. 2002, c. 24 Sch. B, s. 4 ("*Limitations Act* (Ontario)").

[14] OSA, *supra* note 1, ss. 138.4 (6) and (7). Note that the investigation defence only appears to be available to directors and other persons who conducted, or caused to be conducted, a reasonable investigation. So, theoretically, one director cannot rely on the reasonable investigation that was commissioned by one or more other directors.

2. Forward-looking Information[15]

A defendant is not liable for a misrepresentation in forward-looking information if he or she proves that the document or public oral statement contained reasonable, cautionary language that

(i) identified the forward-looking information as such;

(ii) identified material factors that could cause the actual results to differ materially; and

(iii) contained a statement of the material factors or assumptions that were applied in drawing a conclusion or in making a forecast or projection that was set out in the forward-looking information.

The defendant must also prove that the person or company had a reasonable basis for drawing the conclusions or for making the forecasts and projections that were set out in the forward-looking information.

The OSA also provides a safe harbour for forward-looking information provided in the context of public oral statements if a cautionary statement was made that satisfies the requirements of (i) to (iii) above *and* refers to a readily-available document that contains additional information about the material factors that could cause actual results to differ and the assumptions that were applied in drawing a conclusion (such as the MD&A).[16]

3. Expert Report or Opinion[17]

Defendants other than experts have a defence if the misrepresentation in issue is contained in any part of a document or public oral statement that includes, summarizes, or quotes from a report, statement, or opinion made by an expert, provided that the expert gave his or her written consent.

4. Corrective Action[18]

A defendant other than the issuer has a defence if the misrepresentation or failure to make timely disclosure was made without his or her

---

[15] *Ibid.*, s. 138.4 (9).

[16] On June 2, 2006, the OSC published a "Request for Comments — Notice of Proposed Ontario Securities Policy 51-604, *Defence for Misrepresentation in Forward-Looking Information*", (2006) 29 O.S.C. Bull. 4571. The request for comments included the OSC's views on how reporting issuers would meet their disclosure needs for forward-looking information.

[17] OSA, *supra* note 1, s. 138.4(11).

[18] *Ibid.*, s. 138.4(15).

knowledge and, promptly after becoming aware of the misrepresentation or the failure to make timely disclosure, the defendant

(a) notifies the issuer's board of directors; and

(b) if the issuer does not make a correction within two days from the date the defendant notified the board, the defendant promptly notifies the OSC of the misrepresentation or failure to make timely disclosure, unless he or she is prohibited from doing so by law or by professional confidentiality rules.

G. Recommended Action to Minimize Liability

1. Have an Adequate Disclosure Policy

As discussed above, the OSA provides a defence if a reasonable investigation was conducted. One of the factors that the OSA directs courts to consider in determining whether an investigation was reasonable is whether the issuer has a disclosure compliance system in place that is designed to ensure that the issuer meets its continuous disclosure obligations. The issuer's disclosure policy will be very important in establishing that the issuer had such a system in place, and it should reflect the issuer's actual practices and cover matters such as:

- the importance of accurate public disclosure (not just timely disclosure);
- procedures for verifying the accuracy of public disclosure documents before they are released;
- the designation of particular individuals as the only persons who are authorized to make statements on behalf of the issuer;
- procedures for making public oral statements;
- procedures for making materiality determinations;
- procedures for dealing with unintentional misrepresentations or failures to make timely disclosure and any corrective action that is to be taken; and
- procedures for reviewing the content of the issuer's Website both before new content is posted and periodically to ensure that the existing content remains accurate.

2. Review News Releases

Directors should review news releases before they are released whenever possible or immediately after their release.

3. Take Greater Caution When Making Public Oral Statements

Public oral statements made by persons who are speaking on behalf of the issuer will have to be carefully planned. If questions will be taken, some thought should be given to preparing responses for anticipated questions. Impromptu remarks or impromptu responses to questions should be avoided. If forward-looking information will be provided, the appropriate forward-looking information caution should be given so that the safe harbour in the OSA is available.

4. Take Greater Caution When Providing Forward-looking Information

The OSA sets out specific criteria that must be met before the defence (or, in the case of a public oral statement, the safe harbour) for forward-looking information is available. It will not be sufficient to use boilerplate cautionary language. The language must be customized to the particular circumstances, and there must be a reasonable basis for any forecast or projection. It is important that the issuer stays apprised of events and new developments that would have an impact on the material factors and assumptions and that the issuer update its forward-looking information caution accordingly.

5. Establish a Process for Dealing With Alleged Misrepresentations or Failures to Make Timely Disclosure

As discussed above, a defence is available to any defendant other than the issuer who notifies the board of directors of a misrepresentation or failure to make timely disclosure. If the board fails to respond within two business days, the defendant is then required to report the alleged misrepresentation or failure to make timely disclosure to the OSC in order to preserve his or her defence. The board should adopt a process for dealing with such allegations and ensure that it will respond within the prescribed time.

III. When Directors Should Get Worried

A. Introduction

Directors have significant responsibilities, but so do people in many other jobs and roles. There is a big difference between the need to be vigilant and to take your role seriously and the need to be worried about your role.

Most of the time, directors can function exclusively in a vigilant, responsible mode. They should have little need to lie awake at night if they have justified confidence in management; if they receive and scrutinize suitable information; if the board and its committees are suitably staffed, engaged, and focused; and if board and committee meetings are effective.

But so many companies have failed in spectacular fashion in the recent past, and directors have been criticized (and sanctioned, in some cases) for their alleged failures to prevent the crashes. When is this criticism fair? When should directors get worried?

B. General

Directors are not criminal investigators who are responsible for probing beneath apparently supportable assurances to uncover purposeful frauds (although sometimes, directors' efforts and concerns can lead them to involve other experts in investigations of this sort). But directors must develop and operate suitable risk-management strategies to ensure that nothing short of planned criminal behaviour would cause unexpected serious damage. The strategies can be structured and intentional or they can simply require capable directors to be alert to warning signs.

Having a formal risk-management strategy requires the board to continuously manage the risks of the business. These measures would include developing and measuring progress against a plan and annual budget, understanding the business (including the industry and the company's place in it), and being aware of changes (in the macro-environment, market, competitors, and regulation) that could affect the company. The board must also monitor risks relating to the management, including ensuring that the right people (in terms of competence, integrity, and teamwork) are running the business, that succession plans are sound, and that formal risk-management procedures (suitable check processes, a chief risk officer function, suitable internal control processes — now formalized through *Sarbanes-Oxley*[19] 404 audits) are in place. The board must be comfortable that it is receiving the

[19] *Sarbanes-Oxley Act of 2002*, Pub. L. No. 107-204, 116 Stat. 745.

right information in a timely manner; that it is spending adequate meeting time on risk management; that management is candid with the board; and, in general, that it has confidence in management. And finally, the board must be confident that adequate arrangements are in place (suitable advice has been sought, board processes are proper, effective directors' and officers' insurance is in place) to protect the board if things go wrong.

But beyond all of this, there is no substitute for directors who are alert to warning signs that something is wrong. The following list, while not exhaustive, is illustrative of signals that increased vigilance may be in order:

- Corporate governance processes are not being followed.
- Management does not deliver information in a timely manner.
- There are surprises in financial results or in other business results (key customer losses, changes in deals). Particular note should be taken if surprises occur regularly.
- There is an unusually high turnover of employees.
- When the board requests certain information, management is evasive, provides only selective information, or unduly delays providing information.
- Management is unavailable to the board (either it will not respond to the board's enquiries or the management, other than the CEO, is discouraged from contact with the directors).
- The board becomes aware that internal control processes of any sort (from financial compilation to contract signing procedures) are inadequate (the intended purpose of *Sarbanes-Oxley* 404 audits).
- Board members have a sense of discomfort with the corporate culture or with the candour of any employee (on the theory that what is observed anywhere often reflects the leadership culture at the top).
- The board receives express warnings of trouble. Such warnings are far more frequent than one might presume. They come in the form of warnings from advisors (for instance, in auditors' annual reports on issues with management or on financial controls), from members of management (particular board members tend to bond with particular executives, who often share concerns with their "director friend"), or from other directors (directors sometimes consult one another to assess whether a discomfort is warranted).

If even one of these signs appears, it is time for the directors to get out of "business-as-usual" mode. Often if there is any sign of trouble, the trouble is far worse than the sign, and the directors should not lose any time in beginning to investigate the problem(s).

C. Defences

1. Due Diligence

The most important advice for all directors and officers is to exercise due diligence. It is very unlikely that a director or officer will be held liable if appropriate care was taken when he or she made a decision. Such care means ensuring that there is timely, adequate, and appropriate information on which to base a conclusion. For significant decisions (for example, a merger transaction or another company-altering transaction), one board meeting to approve the transaction may not be sufficient; rather, a number of meetings as the transaction develops, with significant input from outside experts (including lawyers and financial advisors), will likely be required. The appropriate reliance on experts can also be a defence to liability in and of itself, in addition to aiding in the establishment of the due diligence defence (though the recent Supreme Court of Canada decision in *Peoples*[20] appears to require the use of outside experts for this defence to be available). An ongoing practice directors and officers should implement is to understand in detail the risks a corporation faces and to ensure that satisfactory preventative measures are in place. Some boards have a "Risks in the Business" item as a standard agenda item at all board meetings. While the focus (in terms of assessing whether or not boards have paid adequate attention) for the past few years has been on accounting and internal control issues, executive compensation and corporate disclosure policies are significant issues that the public is currently sensitive about.

2. Business Judgment Rule

The business judgment rule was recently reaffirmed in *Peoples*. In essence, directors and officers will not be liable for a breach of their duty of care owed to the corporation if they act prudently and on a reasonably informed basis. Perfection is not demanded; rather, a court will examine whether an appropriate degree of prudence and diligence was brought to bear on a decision. *Peoples* also stated that the decision itself must be reasonable in light of the circumstances in which it was made.[21] However, a court is likely to find this requirement was met in a situation where the decision-making process was careful and rigorous.

---

[20] *Peoples Department Stores Inc. (Trustee of) v. Wise*, [2004] 3 S.C.R. 461 ("*Peoples*").

[21] *Ibid.* at para. 67.

D. Practical Steps Directors Should Take

1. Corporate Governance Practices

Both *Peoples* and the recent Delaware decision in *Disney*[22] noted that the establishment of good corporate governance practices can protect directors from liability. Though these two cases do not appear to agree on the weight to be placed on a failure to implement corporate governance developments, the best way to proceed is to establish and follow a good set of corporate governance practices; there are only advantages to using this approach.

2. Establish a Record

In order to establish the due diligence defence, it is important to keep a proper record of deliberations that were made and actions that were taken. Such a record includes the maintenance of a thoughtful collection of board and committee minutes. This does not mean a comprehensive transcript (which will inevitably be unreliable) should be kept; rather, meeting minutes should indicate the major topics of discussion and the important factors that were considered in reaching decisions. Board materials, correspondence, presentations, and similar evidence of the process involved in reaching a decision should also (generally) be maintained.

3. Disclosure Policies and Disclosure Committees

Effective December 31, 2005, directors and officers of public companies face statutory personal liability for misrepresentations in public disclosure and for the failure to make timely disclosure of material events. CEOs and CFOs also currently face potential personal liability for their certifications of the accuracy of their company's public disclosure. The discussion above about due diligence is equally applicable to these liability risks (and, in fact, there is an affirmative statutory due diligence defence to disclosure liability in the legislation). In addition, companies should adopt a disclosure policy to ensure that a process is in place so that material developments are brought to the attention of senior officers and directors in a timely fashion. Companies should also consider the creation of a management disclosure committee that is specifically charged with ensuring that companies comply with their disclosure obligations. These steps will both reduce the likelihood of a disclosure violation occurring and, where a violation has occurred, increase the likelihood that a director or officer can rely on the due diligence defence.

---

[22] *Re Walt Disney Company Derivative Litig.*, 2005 W.L. 20566651 (Del. Ch., Aug. 9, 2005), *Re Walt Disney Company Derivative Litig*, 2006 Del. LEXIS 307 (Del. S.C., June 8, 2006) ("*Disney*").

4. Managing Conflicts

Another key area of risk is conflicts of interest. Where conflicts are at play, due diligence and business judgment may not be enough; a court or a regulator is much more likely to examine the underlying fairness of the transaction to the company. Accordingly, directors and officers must be sure to carefully examine all details and underlying facts before agreeing to a transaction involving or benefitting insiders of the corporation. At a minimum, such transactions must be approved by a committee of independent board members (this is mandated in some cases). Even then, directors must be scrutinizing and challenging, and they should consider obtaining advice from external advisors who are separate from the advisors who are normally retained by the corporation. Enron is one example of a situation where a conflict of interest (in this case, off-balance sheet transactions involving a member of management) was brought to the attention of the board but a number of details that were likely to affect approval of such transactions were not. These details involved compensation to certain investors (including other employees of the corporation, some of whom received huge short-term returns for little or no risk), guarantees provided by the corporation, and the identities of all of the investors (some of whom were spouses or others who had close relationships with management). Conflict situations (including such "routine" ones as executive compensation) require a board to be at its toughest — the risks are otherwise untenable.

5. Record-Keeping

The subject of minutes and record-keeping for boards of directors has had considerable debate over the last few years. Judges have commented on the sparseness of minutes in certain circumstances where the facts are further explored and directors purport to recall matters that were not adequately reflected in the minutes.

A broader issue of record-keeping is inconsistencies. Partial minutes or partial notes that are kept individually by directors can do more harm than good where the notes disagree or conflict and reflect only a portion of a debate and do not adequately illustrate the conclusion and resolution of the matter. Directors can certainly keep notes during the course of a meeting — it will assist them in preparing adequate minutes. However, the general focus of the board should be on ensuring that the minutes reflect the issue raised, the substantive aspect of the discussion, and the questions, along with the resolutions and the reasons for the decision. The very heart of the director's fiduciary duty is to act on an informed and reasonable basis. The minutes should reflect both the information behind and the reason for a director's action. When the minutes have been finalized and approved, it would be appropriate for directors to then dispose of their notes.

A good example of this is directors' minutes for disclosure matters. In the context of civil liability for continuous disclosure documents, an action for the non-disclosure of material information is very difficult to defend where even minutes of board meetings omit important discussions and important reasons. Directors on the witness stand who are faced with a cross-examination that they failed to consider something and who continue to raise matters that are not in the minutes are put in the unenviable position of proving their minutes have serious omissions, creating a stepping-stone to a finding that the public record may also omit important material information.

For this advice, like all advice, there are exceptions. Where a director is in a situation involving the director's loss of confidence in management or in other board members and it appears that conflict or litigation is likely, then the director may wish to keep his or her own notes of discussions with management and/or other directors for the purposes of preparing a record. Where a director is starting to keep his or her own notes in such a fashion, it is likely that independent counsel should also be consulted privately to determine an appropriate course of action for the director.

E. Insurance and Indemnification

Directors and officers must be careful to ensure that appropriate indemnification and insurance is in place. At a minimum, on the indemnification side, directors and officers should have separate indemnification agreements with the corporation to ensure that the maximum amount of indemnification is made available. (The indemnification permitted by the corporate statutes is not always mandatory, and there are a significant number of issues that can arise in accessing indemnification that are not addressed in a typical indemnity agreement, including when indemnity payments will be made, burdens of proof, payment for attending discoveries or regulatory proceedings, etc.) There is often a conflict between the interests of management (in reducing premiums) and those of directors (in obtaining suitable coverage for service that is not highly remunerated in the first place). Insurance applications tend to be prepared by individuals or small groups within management. The application may not be seen by the directors or by many of the officers who are covered by the insurance that is obtained subsequently.

While breadth of coverage may be desirable, it includes a number of risks. First, the number of covered individuals and entities is large and the total insurance pool is potentially shared among the group: a claim and the need to fund defence costs or substantive liability for any group member may (subject to sub-limit or priority of payment arrangements) deplete the insurance, so that it will not be available to others. A misrepresentation in the insurance application by (say) a fraudulent or negligent officer could result in rescission of the policy as against all insureds.

Independent directors may also want to consider obtaining separate independent director liability insurance to ensure that management (who are more likely to have significant insured costs, particularly up front) do not use up all of the available coverage in defence costs or settlements. There is a developing practice of increased director involvement, including independent representation of directors, in such matters.[23]

[23] See Chapter 18 for a more thorough discussion of directors' and officers' indemnification and insurance.

CHAPTER 14

INTERNAL INVESTIGATIONS

I. Introduction

"Fraud and deceit abound these days more than in former times" (Sir Edward Coke, 1602). While high profile scandals such as Enron and Bre-X may give the impression that fraud is on the rise, Sir Edward Coke's 400-year-old observation reminds us that deceitful conduct and fraudulent schemes have always existed. However, the introduction of new and sophisticated financial products and investment vehicles, coupled with an increase in the use of telecommunications and electronic means to send and transfer information and money, have resulted in an increase in the speed and ease with which fraudulent acts can be committed.

The onus on corporate victims of fraud and others to fully investigate and to report potential fraud has been heightened by statutory and regulatory initiatives. Such initiatives are found in federal legislation: the *Proceeds of Crime (Money Laundering) and Terrorist Financing Act*[1] and the estab-

[1] S.C. 2000, c. 17.

lishment of the Financial Transactions and Reports Analysis Centre of Canada ("FINTRAC"). In the United States, the *Sarbanes-Oxley Act*[2] imposes new and significant obligations on directors and audit committees to improve corporate governance and controls. There are also criminal, tax, and securities legislation that address fraud prevention and punishment.[3]

With the November 2005 appointment of David Wilson to the position of Chair of the Ontario Securities Commission, Canadian corporations face a more strict regulatory environment. In his inaugural remarks as Chair, Mr. Wilson promised fair, vigorous, and timely enforcement, stating that, "If we fail to prevent, detect and deter market abuses such as theft, fraud and insider trading, we will send the world a very negative message".[4] "Deterrence is achieved when everyone knows with certainty that the enforcement of regulations will be impartial, swift and uncompromising".[5]

The consequences for being associated with a fraudulent scheme can be severe for a corporation. In addition to the possible criminal, regulatory, and civil consequences, the corporation's reputation will suffer. Loss of reputation can severely inhibit a corporation's ability to operate and, at worst, can put the corporation out of business.[6]

Given this environment, it is important for directors to understand the process, steps, and tools that are required in an internal investigation. Fraud investigation is an expertise. Therefore, regardless of the nature and scale of the fraud, an important first step is retaining counsel that is experienced in fraud investigation and recovery.

This Chapter looks at the instances when an internal investigation is necessary, methods for preventing and discovering fraud, and the process for investigating fraud. It also considers the concepts of privilege and privacy as they relate to internal fraud investigations.

---

[2] *Sarbanes-Oxley Act of 2002*, Pub. L, No. 107–204, 116 Stat. 745, 15 U.S.C. §7201, *et seq.* Among other things, the *Sarbanes-Oxley Act* requires that signing officers "are responsible for establishing and maintaining internal controls" in relation to a corporation's financial reporting (s. 302).

[3] For example, s. 380 of the *Criminal Code*, R.S.C. 1985, c. C-46, provides that anyone who, by deceit, falsehood, or other fraudulent means, defrauds the public or any person of property, money, or any valuable security or service is guilty of an offence. As well, s. 126.1 of the Ontario *Securities Act*, R.S.O. 1990, c. S.5, prohibits fraud or market manipulation. Section 129.2 of that Act imposes liability on directors or officers who authorize, permit, or acquiesce in a corporation's breach of Ontario securities law.

[4] David Wilson, "Setting the Standard" (Lecture presented to the Dialogue With the OSC, 2005, November 17, 2005), online: http://www.osc.gov.on.ca/About/Dialogue/2005/dwo_2005_program.pdf.

[5] *Ibid.*

[6] Mark Williams, "Planning Against Internal and External Threats", *Boardroom Intelligence Series 2005, Part 2, Managing Risks and Resolving Crisis: Planning Against Internal and External Threats* (Montreal: A Financier Worldwide Supplement, 2005) at p. 11.

II. When an Internal Investigation is Necessary

Directors should undertake an internal investigation whenever the corporation is implicated in, or is a victim of, a fraud. Recent legal literature articulates the advantages of conducting internal investigations for corporations that may be subject to significant fines resulting from fraudulent acts that were committed by one of their employees.[7] In fact, it has been argued that the government favours directing its efforts at making corporations police themselves through internal disciplinary procedures in order to better allocate its scarce resources to prosecuting only the corporation.[8]

To defraud means "to deprive a person dishonestly of something which is his or of something to which he is or would or might but for the perpetration of the fraud, be entitled".[9] More generally, fraud is something that is dishonest and morally wrong.[10] Types of fraud include: kickback or secret commission schemes; false invoicing; corporate espionage; payroll fraud; cheque forgery; conversion; theft of corporate opportunity; theft of corporate assets; payments for goods and services not provided; bust outs or bankruptcy fraud; credit card and debit card fraud; employee theft; Internet fraud; telemarketing fraud; and prime bank instrument or high yield investment fraud. The variations of fraudulent schemes are limited only by the ingenuity of the rogues who are perpetrating them.

A common form of fraudulent conduct is the creation of false or misleading financial statements. A number of recent corporate scandals, including Enron, have involved such conduct. The Ontario *Securities Act* contains several provisions regarding misrepresentations to the public. For example, s. 126.2 prohibits a person or company from making a statement that the person or company knows, or ought reasonably to know, is misleading or untrue and significantly affects the market price or value of a

---

[7] See Jennifer A. Quaid, "The Assessment of Corporate Criminal Liability on the Basis of Corporate Identity: An Analysis" (1998) 43 McGill L.J. 67 ("Quaid").

[8] Quaid, *ibid.* see also B. Fisse and J. Braithwaite, *Corporations, Crime and Accountability* (Cambridge: Cambridge University Press, 1993), generally, in which they develop a corporate accountability model which seeks, *inter alia*, to shift the responsibility for investigations of individual responsibility onto the corporation in situations where the complexity of the corporation or the crime involved renders it fruitless for the prosecution to do so. Under their model, three means of enforcement would be employed: imposing sanctions, such as punitive injunctions and adverse publicity orders for the failure to undertake internal disciplinary action against responsible individuals; working with top and middle management to ensure that compliance is taken seriously; and providing courts with the power to impose monitoring and supervisory controls on the corporation (see also note 89 in Quaid, *ibid.*).

[9] *Ontex Resources Ltd. v. Metalore Resources Ltd.* (1990), 75 O.R. (2d) 513 (Gen. Div.).

[10] *Washburn v. Wright* (1914), 31 O.L.R. 138 (C.A.) at 147, cited in *Butera v. Marianos*, [2001] O.J. No. 5211 (S.C.J.) at para. 70.

security. Sections 130, 130.1, and 131 impose liability for misrepresentation in a prospectus, offering memorandum, and circular, respectively.[11]

Sections 138.1 to 138.14 of the Ontario *Securities Act* give shareholders who buy and sell shares on a stock exchange a limited, statutory right to sue the issuing companies, their directors and officers, "influential persons" (including large shareholders, promoters, fund managers, and insiders), and experts.

The total liability of a defendant in an action brought pursuant to ss. 138.3 or 138.4 of the Ontario *Securities Act* is limited. Liability to all plaintiffs, with respect to the same misrepresentation or non-disclosure, is capped at the greater of $1 million or 5 percent of the enterprise's market capitalization. Individuals are capped at the greater of $25,000 or half of that individual's total compensation from the relevant company for the twelve months preceding the violation.[12] These caps do not apply to directors, officers, influential persons, or experts who knowingly authorize, permit, or acquiesce in a continuous disclosure violation. Nor do they apply to common law actions, such as misrepresentation or breach of a fiduciary duty.

A corporation may learn of a fraud allegation through a variety of sources, including the following: an employee complaint or grievance; review of the corporation's accounting or financial documents or records; as part of an investigation by the police, the RCMP, or FINTRAC; the commencement of a civil proceeding; or media reports. As well, unscrupulous competitors may allege that a corporation was involved in a fraud as a means of increasing the competitor's market share. Regardless of how the fraud allegation comes to the corporation's attention, it is necessary for directors to respond swiftly.

Where an employee is the source of information, directors must ensure that there are no threats or retaliation measures taken against that employee. Section 425.1 of the *Criminal Code* precludes an employer from taking disciplinary measures against, demoting, terminating, or otherwise adversely affecting an employee (or threatening to do so):

- with the intent of preventing the employee from providing information relating to a breach of a federal or provincial act or regulation by the corporation or an officer, employee, or director of the corpora-

[11] The other provinces have similar provisions. For example, ss. 131, 132, and 133 of the British Columbia *Securities Act* impose liability for misrepresentations in a prospectus, circular and prescribed disclosure document, respectively. Similarly, ss. 203, 204, and 205 of the Alberta *Securities Act* impose liability for misrepresentations in a prospectus, offering memorandum, and circular, respectively.

[12] Ontario *Securities Act*, *supra* note 3 at s. 138.5.

tion to a person whose duties include the enforcement of federal or provincial law; or

- with the intent of retaliating against the employee because he or she has provided information to a person whose duties include the enforcement of federal or provincial law.

This provision is of limited application. It applies only where the disclosure is made to "a person whose duties include the enforcement of federal or provincial law".[13]

In assessing whistleblower protections laws, however, the Supreme Court of Canada has held that whistleblowers will be accorded protection when they report instances of misconduct or fraud "internally" within the employer's organization as well as "externally" to applicable public authorities.[14] Although the court stressed that whistleblowers were not always required to seek an internal resolution of the alleged misconduct before seeking out the proper authorities (particularly in cases where the employee could reasonably foresee that it is likely that the employer could destroy evidence), the court acknowledged that the failure to "try to resolve the matter internally" was *prima facie* disloyal and considered to be inappropriate conduct where applicable.[15] However, the court limited the applicability of this principle, arguing that it would be anomalous to interpret whistleblower protection laws as requiring recourse to outside agencies as a condition precedent to protection.[16]

Likewise, whistleblowers are accorded protection under the applicable provisions of the *Sarbanes-Oxley Act*.[17] These provisions prohibit employers from retaliating against employees who provide information related to alleged accounting improprieties or who participate in a proceeding related to alleged securities laws violations.

III. The Investigation Process

Once an allegation of fraud has arisen, the board must take reasonable and appropriate steps to investigate the nature and extent of the fraud. A director who turns a blind eye to a fraud allegation could face potential civil and criminal liability. Moreover, conducting an internal investigation enables

---

[13] *Criminal Code*, *supra* note 3.

[14] *Merk v. I.A.B.S.O.I., Local 771*, [2005] 3 S.C.R. 425.

[15] *Ibid.* at para. 25.

[16] *Ibid.*

[17] See *Sarbanes-Oxley Act*, *supra* note 2.

the corporation to learn the facts quickly, and such an investigation will be viewed favourably by the regulators.[18]

A. Preventing and Discovering Fraud

The implementation of measures to prevent fraud is an ongoing process that must evolve (particularly if there is a restructuring in the corporation or organization). Implementing a fraud prevention policy that is actively reviewed and updated will help prevent and detect fraud. The policy should provide a protocol or a response plan once a fraud occurs.

The following measures may be useful in preventing fraud: a well articulated corporate strategy; a strong internal control system that includes the segregation of duties and provides checks and balances; an effective risk management strategy that is ingrained throughout the corporation and reflected in the corporate culture; effective internal reporting; strong management supervision; and education and awareness initiatives.[19]

Certain environmental factors that can be positive motivators in some circumstances can make fraud more likely, such as the following: unrealistic budget pressures; compensation based on individual or unit performance; "boiler room" type office operations; the absence of a corporate code of conduct; weak or no enforcement of a corporate code of conduct; poor accounting records; related party transactions; high management turnover; and an inactive board of directors or audit committee.[20] Efforts should be taken to consider and balance the presence of such factors within the organization.

There are certain "red flags" or indicators of fraud that can assist corporations in detecting fraud. These include the following: changes in expense patterns; lack of invoices to support an expense; generic invoices (without the company's identification or detail); duplicate payments; general ledgers that do not balance; resistance to changes in duties; failure to follow procedures; new venders whose identity and history are unknown; use of position or coercive behaviour to circumvent controls; personal spending

---

[18] Richard Alexander, Michael Trager and Joshua Martin, "Managing Crises by Conducting Internal Investigations", *Boardroom Intelligence Series 2005, Part 2, Managing Risks and Resolving Crisis: Planning Against Internal and External Threats* (Montreal: A Financier Worldwide Supplement, 2005) at p. 17.

[19] Eric T. Young, "The Role of Compliance in Risk Management: How Compliance Can Help Manage Corporate Governance, Operational Risk and Internal Controls" (September 23, 2002). See also Ray Haywood, "Managing Financial Investigations" (Presentation to Aboriginal Financial Management Strategies Forum, Fairmont Chateu Laurier, Ottawa, June 23–24, 2003) at 35. Both online at: <http://www.insightinfo.com/press/brochures/brochure.cfm?product_code=502296>.

[20] The Association of Certified Forensic Investigators of Canada, *The ACIF Fraud Manual,* 2nd ed. (2005) at 6.1.4 ("Fraud Manual"). See also *Re E.A. Manning Ltd.* (1995), 9 C.C.L.S. 231, 18 O.S.C.B. 5317 (O.S.C.).

beyond one's means; dependencies or addictions; and sudden unexpected changes in personal circumstances or in the financial circumstances of the corporation.[21] Corporations should react to "red flags" in a consistent, timely, and appropriate manner.[22]

B. Developing an Action Plan and Investigating Fraud

The ability to quickly assess the situation and to take the appropriate steps is crucial to recovering fraudulently-obtained funds or assets and to successfully respond to fraud. Different considerations arise, depending on the nature and extent of the fraud. However, in any case of fraud, retaining counsel that is experienced in the investigation of fraud and recovery and developing an action plan are important first steps.

Retaining experienced counsel is important for several reasons. First, investigating fraud and recovering assets requires expertise. Experienced counsel is more familiar with the organization's regulatory obligations and is more qualified to conduct an investigation. Second, by retaining counsel to conduct the investigation, certain findings will be protected by solicitor client privilege.[23]

Directors should consider retaining independent counsel to lead an investigation. Although in-house counsel, regular external counsel, and/or advisors may know more about the company and its employees, outside counsel brings greater independence to the task. [24] For example, the Special Committee Report in respect of Enron Corp. determined that an investigation that was conducted by Vinson & Elkins, Enron's regular counsel, was structured with "less skepticism than needed" and that the results of their review were "largely predetermined by the scope and nature of the investigation and the process employed".[25]

In addition to experienced fraud litigation counsel, the effective fraud response team may include the following: public relations consultants; audi-

---

[21] Haywood, *supra* note 19 at 26. See also Fraud Manual, *ibid.*, at 6.1.5.

[22] Haywood, *ibid.* See also Barry Reiter, "Canada: When Directors Should Get Worried", (August/September 2004) *Corporate Governance Review*, online at http://www.mondaq.com/i_article.asp_Q_articleid_E_30373.

[23] *Smith v. Jones*, [1999] 1 S.C.R. 455. See also *R. v. Campbell*, [1999] 1 S.C.R. 565 and *R. v. Murray*, [2000] O.J. No. 685 (S.C.J.).

[24] Michael P. Kenny and William R. Mitchelson, Jr., "Corporate Benefits of Properly Conducted Internal Investigations", 11 Georgia State University Law Review 657 at 665 ("Kenny and Mitchelson").

[25] Cecelia Kempler, "Is Your Investigation Independent"? *Legal Times* (15 November 2004). See also William C. Powers Jr., Raymond S. Troubh and Herbert S. Winoker, "Report of Investigation by the Special Investigative Committee of the Board of Directors of Enron Corp" (1 February 2002), online: http://fl1.findlaw.com/news.findlaw.com/wp/docs/enron/specinv020102rpt1.pdf.

tors and/or forensic accountants; asset investigators; surveillance experts; information technology experts and/or a computer forensics team; and international counsel.

The development of an action plan includes considering the following:

- establishing the goals and priorities for the investigation. Such goals and priorities may include maximizing asset recovery, maintaining a strong public relations record, conforming to regulatory obligations, co-operating with public authorities as much as possible, and assessing liability to third parties;
- conducting a cost-benefit analysis to determine whether commencing certain recovery steps will be worthwhile;
- investigating to determine the quantum of the loss, who is involved, what evidence is available, and how to preserve evidence;
- determining the effect, if any, that civil litigation will have on any ongoing or potential criminal or regulatory proceedings;
- determining if there are potential indemnities to the directors and officers for coverage of legal costs; and
- considering the effect, if any, that the investigation will have on the organization's insurance coverage.

After considering options with counsel, an initial internal investigation is often required. Such an investigation will likely require co-operation from officers and employees. However, it is important to avoid any rapid dissemination of the fact that there has been an allegation or discovery of fraud. To ensure that the investigator's strategy is not compromised, any investigation of fraud should proceed on the basic premise that only those who need to know about it should be informed. The investigator's strategy should include the following:

- securing the evidence and reviewing the "paper" trail; this could include taking steps to preserve paper and electronic documents that relate to the investigation[26] and reviewing the email accounts and computers of the persons who are suspected of being involved in the fraud;
- fully investigating and considering any information that will lead to a full and complete disclosure of the facts;

---

[26] Kenny and Mitchelson, *supra* note 24 at 665.

- without providing notice, conducting interviews of key people that may have information. At the outset of the interview, counsel should advise the employee that they represent the corporation, not the employee, and instruct the employee to not discuss the interview with anyone else, including fellow employees;[27]
- ensuring that any discussions between the employer and employee are performed in a professional and objective manner and advising the employer to be vigilant by identifying defamation and libel risks that may arise as a result of statements made or documents circulated that discuss the investigation;
- identifying the current risk of further losses;
- co-operating with regulators and with law enforcement officials;
- establishing a "litigation file" for use in any subsequent litigation;
- considering privilege and confidentiality issues; and
- maintaining records of the investigation process to help ensure that no steps are missed and that no duplicate steps are taken; the records can also contain information about who is responsible for completing which tasks.[28]

IV. Establishing Privilege

Retaining legal counsel to conduct an internal investigation for the purpose of obtaining legal advice may cloak certain findings with solicitor-client privilege. With a lawyer leading the investigative team, any relevant communications may be protected by privilege.[29]

The solicitor-client privilege is the oldest of the privileges for confidential communication, with roots in the 16th Century. In the past, it was assumed that effectual legal assistance could only be given if clients frankly and candidly disclosed all material facts to their solicitors (the provision of legal assistance being regarded as essential to the effective operation of the legal system). In more modern times, the Supreme Court of Canada has held an elevated privilege to be a "fundamental civil and legal right". A complete statement of the privilege has been given as follows:

> That rule as to the non-production of communications between solicitor and client says that where ... there has been

[27] Kenny and Mitchelson, *ibid.* at 666–667.

[28] Fraud Manual, *supra* note 20 at 7.2.11.

[29] *Grover v. Tolko Manitoba Inc.* (2001), 196 D.L.R. (4th) 716 at paras. 11 to 16 (Man. C.A.).

> no waiver by the client and no suggestion is made of fraud, crime, evasion, or civil wrong on his or her part, the client cannot be compelled and a lawyer will not be allowed without the consent of the client to disclose oral or documentary communications passing between them in professional confidence, whether or not litigation is pending.[30]

A requirement for the creation of privilege is that the communication be made in confidence. The communication need not be expressly made in confidence as long as the circumstances indicate that the party intended to keep it secret. Where legal advice of any kind is sought from a professional legal advisor in his or her capacity as such, communications relating to that purpose, made in confidence by the client, are protected by privilege, unless that privilege is waived.

Solicitor-client privilege does not extend to communications with persons who are not duly qualified legal advisors, even though the advice they might give is legal in nature. For example, the Ontario Superior Court in *CIBC Mellon Trust Co. v. National Trust Co.*[31] ruled that even employees who are subject to confidentiality provisions in their employment agreements would in all likelihood have to provide evidence and testimony.

The party asserting privilege must demonstrate on a balance of probabilities[32] that the communication was created with the dominant purpose of preparing for litigation[33] or to provide legal advice.[34] This hurdle is necessarily easier to overcome if counsel is retained at the outset of the internal investigation.[35]

A. Third-Party Communications

Investigations often require assistance from professionals who are not regularly employed by the corporation. For example, it may be necessary for the corporation to obtain an external forensic auditor to investigate and report on suspicious transactions. In order to avoid the implied waiver exception to privilege for communications that were gathered throughout

[30] *Canada (Director of Investigation & Research) v. Canada Safeway Ltd.*, [1972] 3 W.W.R. 547 at para. 2 (B.C.S.C.).

[31] *CIBC Mellon Trust Co. v. National Trust Co.*, [2000] O.J. No. 3489 at para. 22 (Ont. S.C.) ("*CIBC Melon*").

[32] *McCarthy Tetrault v. Ontario* (1992), 95 D.L.R. (4th) 94 at 101 (Ont. Ct. J. (Prov. Div.)).

[33] *General Accident Assurance Company Co. of Canada v. Chrusz* (1999), 45 O.R. (3d) 321 (C.A.).

[34] *Canada v. Solosky* (1979), 50 C.C.C. (2d) 495 at 510 (S.C.C.) ("*Solosky*").

[35] *Keirouz v. Co-Operators Insurance Assn.* (1983), 39 C.P.C. 164 at paras. 5–7 (Ont. H.C.J.). See also *R. v. CIBC Mellon Trust Co.*, [2000] O.J. No. 4854 at paras. 17–18 (Ont. S.C.).

the course of an investigation, steps must be taken to affirm that the communications were intended to be confidential and were created with a view to contemplated litigation or to providing legal advice. This issue arises as more actors are included in the investigation, including corporate employees and outside experts.

The Ontario Superior Court set out the following test to be applied in determining whether third-party communications are made for the purpose of assisting retained counsel during an investigation in *Prosperine v. Ottawa-Carleton (Regional Municipality)*:[36]

- the communication must be an integral channel of communication between solicitor and client;[37]
- there should be a lack of autonomy on the part of the third party;
- the information that is subject to a claim of privilege should not extend beyond that which is required by the solicitor;[38] and
- a contextual approach is taken; relying upon formalities, such as the signature of legal counsel on the contract between the third party and the client, is not enough.[39]

A client cannot "protect investigative information that it has gathered and that would otherwise be producible, behind the cloak of solicitor-client privilege simply by the expedient of placing control of the claim investigation in the hands of its lawyer".[40]

Courts will require a contextual analysis in almost all cases to determine whether privilege attaches to communications. Each case must be considered in advance and steps taken proactively to establish a true relationship that is protected by privilege.

---

[36] *Prosperine v. Ottawa-Carleton (Regional Municipality)* (2002), 37 C.B.R. (4th) 135 at paras. 22–24 (Ont. S.C.J.) ("*Prosperine*").

[37] See also *Davies v. American Home Assurance Co.* (2002), 60 O.R. (3d) 512 (Div. Ct.) at para. 25 ("*Davies*").

[38] For instance, the court in *Prosperine* found that the consultant was retained to perform work that may have facilitated the client in obtaining legal advice at some later time. The contract did not state that the purpose of retaining the consultant was to facilitate the giving of legal advice but only referred to quantifying financial loss and areas of improvement.

[39] However, the Ontario Superior Court in *Hydro-One Network Services Inc. v. Ontario (Ministry of Labour)*, [2002] O.J. No. 4370 at para. 13 (Ont. Ct. J.), found a report privileged where it was prepared by a non-lawyer employee at the request of in-house counsel to investigate the cause of a workplace accident. The court noted that the report was intended to be kept confidential because it was marked "privileged and confidential", with the cover page of the report stating "[t]his report is prepared for [in-house counsel] for the purpose of providing legal advice".

[40] *Davies, supra* note 37 at para. 25.

B. Disclosure to Regulatory Bodies

Privilege is not absolute. Corporations may be required by law to disclose documents relating to the internal investigation. As well, corporations may choose to co-operate with the authorities and to waive privilege. The recent decision by the United States Court of Appeal for the 10th Circuit in *Re Qwest Communications International*[41] is a good example of this principle, as the court refused to apply the "selective waiver" principle where the same company that was subject to the investigation voluntarily released privileged information to federal agencies.

While protecting privilege is important, reporting misconduct to law enforcement officers should be considered, as it may reduce the company's criminal liability. Section 718.2 of the *Criminal Code* provides that co-operation should be taken into account as a mitigating factor at the time of sentencing.[42] The United States has a more formal approach to granting leniency for companies that co-operate. In deciding whether charges should be filed against a company, prosecutors will consider whether an effective compliance program is in place and whether the company is deemed to have co-operated by waiving privilege. Such co-operation will also be considered as a mitigating factor at sentencing.

A company may be able to co-operate without waiving privilege. For example, a company may agree to identify the witnesses, who can then provide authorities with the relevant information.

V. Privacy Legislation

In investigating fraud allegations, corporations must ensure that they comply with privacy legislation. The *Personal Information Protection and Electronic Documents Act*[43] ("PIPEDA") sets out the ground rules for the collection, use, and disclosure of personal information in the course of commercial activities. The goal of PIPEDA is to balance an individual's right to privacy with an organization's need for personal information for legitimate business purposes.

PIPEDA applies to all personal information collected, used, or disclosed in the course of commercial activities by all private-sector organiza-

---

[41] 2006 U.S. App. LEXIS 14937.

[42] See also *R. v. Laroche* (1983), 6 C.C.C. (3d) 268 (Que. C.A.).

[43] S.C. 2000, c. 5.

tions except in provinces that have enacted legislation that is deemed to be substantially similar to the federal law.[44]

Organizations covered by PIPEDA must obtain an individual's consent when they collect, use, or disclose that individual's personal information. Personal information can only be used for the purposes for which it was collected. If an organization is going to use it for another purpose, consent must be obtained for the subsequent use of the information. There are several exceptions to this rule that may be relevant during a fraud investigation.

Section 7(1)(*b*) allows personal information to be collected, used, or disclosed without consent where obtaining consent would "compromise the availability or the accuracy of the information" regarding a breach of the laws of Canada or the provinces (including the common law[45]).

Section 7(3)(*d*)(i) allows an organization to disclose information to an investigative body[46] or government institution if the organization has reasonable grounds to believe that the information relates to a breach of an agreement or to a contravention of the laws of Canada, a province, or a foreign jurisdiction. Section 7(3)(*h*.2) allows an investigative body to disclose personal information to another private organization. The disclosure must be related to an investigation of a breach of an agreement or a contravention of the law and it must be reasonable. Under this section, the investigative body can disclose the results of its investigation to the organization as needed.

Organizations and investigative bodies that exchange personal information remain responsible for compliance with all other requirements of PIPEDA and are subject to oversight by the Privacy Commissioner. Investigative bodies are still subject to the general requirements that PIPEDA imposes on all organizations. According to the Regulations Specifying Investigative Bodies, investigative bodies are only excused from obtaining consent in exceptional circumstances where obtaining consent is impossible, impractical, or undesirable because it would frustrate the conduct of the investigation.

In *BMG Canada Inc. v. John Doe*,[47] the Federal Court noted that there was no limitation in PIPEDA restricting the ability of the court to order the

---

[44] To date, Alberta, British Columbia, and Quebec are the only provinces with legislation that has been deemed to be substantially similar.

[45] See *Ferenczy v. MCI Medical Clinics et al.* (2004), 70 O.R. (3d) 277 (S.C.J.), where the gathering of video surveillance evidence to defend a personal injury claim was held not to contravene PIPEDA.

[46] The investigative body must be specified in Regulations Specifying Investigative Bodies, SOR 2001-6.

[47] [2004] 3 F.C.R. 241.

production of documents. Section 7(3)(*c*) allows disclosure without consent if it is required to comply with a subpoena or warrant or to comply with the rules of court relating to the production of records. Consequently, directors can disclose personal information without consent in accordance with a subpoena, warrant, or rules of the court.

Innovative Health Group Inc. v. Calgary Health Region[48] dealt with the issue of investigating the improper billing practices of a physiotherapy clinic. The court held that the regional health authority was entitled under ss. 7(3)(*d*)(i) and 7(3)(*i*) to audit certain client files without the client's consent. Section 7(3)(*i*) allows organizations to disclose personal information as "required by law".

VI. Conclusion

Although the aforementioned observations by David Wilson and Sir Edward Coke shed light on fraud's prevalent and persistent character throughout the last four centuries, it is clear that fraud in today's marketplace may take on incredibly complex and intricate forms. Legislatures and courts have responded by putting the onus of preventing and detecting fraudulent schemes not only on applicable regulatory agencies but also on organizations themselves. Indeed, the nature of today's business environment makes it vital for directors and officers to anticipate and adequately respond to cases of fraud by not only conducting internal investigations that protect whistleblower rights but also by retaining experienced counsel that will create the appearance of greater independence. Clearly, the concerns that an organization will encounter during a fraud investigation are significant. These concerns range from understanding the necessary requirements for establishing privilege to knowingly providing the proper information to third parties and regulatory bodies that will properly consider lingering privacy issues. An organization that adopts a thorough and precise internal investigation scheme will be able to better respond to potential problems involving fraud.

---

[48] (2005), 49 Alta. L.R. (4th) (Q.B.).

CHAPTER 15

INCOME TRUSTS AND MUTUAL FUND GOVERNANCE

In recent years, income trusts have become a popular and attractive investment vehicle. An enormous amount of money is now invested in income trusts and much has been written about them. However, the literature tends to focus on the special or unique features of these trusts from an investment value perspective. There is some discussion of corporate governance issues as they might apply to the income trust, but there is virtually nothing on the unique obligations and duties that might arise for, or the potential liability of, directors who are involved with the corporations that administer or manage income trusts or who are similarly involved on a regular basis with such trusts.

I. Nature of Income Trusts

Income trusts offer an investment alternative to the more common share offerings of corporations. From an investor's perspective, there may seem to be little difference between income trusts and shares. The investor purchases a unit (as opposed to a share) in the trust and expects to receive regular payments (distributions on the units) like dividends. The sale offering is made in much the same manner as that for the sale of shares in a publicly-traded corporation. The difference for the investor is the higher anticipated distributions paid by the trust and the potential tax consequences of the same.

The purpose of an income trust, and its attraction to an investor, is that the trust will distribute most of its profits on a regular pre-tax basis. The trust (really the trustee) holds indirectly (through operating corporations or partnerships) interests in operating businesses and flows the bulk of the earnings from these holdings, generally through interest expense on debt owing by the operating entity to the income trust, back to the unitholders.

A typical public income trust structure is depicted graphically below:

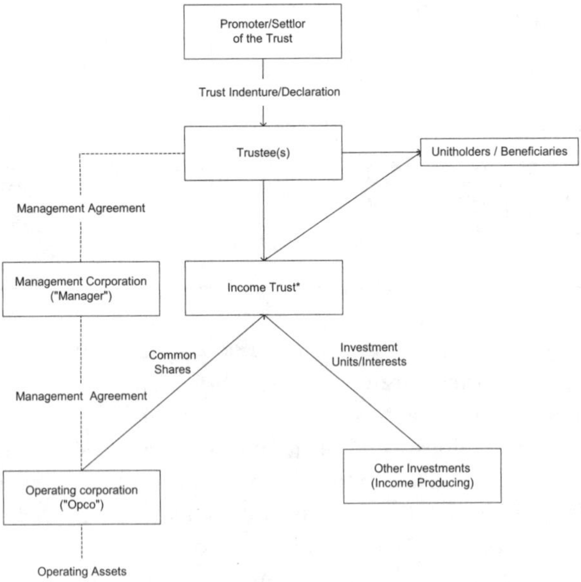

* The Income Trust is not a separate legal entity from the Trustee(s) but is conceptually often shown as distinct.

A properly structured income trust is carefully organized to take advantage of several provisions in the *Income Tax Act*.[1] It must qualify as a "unit trust" and a "mutual fund trust", which in turn, allows the units in it to be "qualified investments" for RRSPs and other tax-exempt plans such RFSPs. Structuring is necessary to ensure that distributions are flowed out to unitholders on an essentially pre-tax basis. Directors must be familiar with the requirements that have to be met to achieve the desired tax status or benefits, and directors must be satisfied that measures are in place to ensure that they are achieved.

A trust is a relationship in which a person (the trustee) holds property for the ultimate benefit of another or others (the beneficiaries) in a manner in which those others have the exclusive entitlement to all benefits from the trust property. Income trusts invariably have a trustee who holds title to the assets concerned (the trust assets) for the benefit of beneficiaries, who are generally referred to as unitholders. Other parties may be involved in the administration and management of the trust but their involvement is not necessary for trust status. The terms "trust", "income trust", and the like are frequently used by lawyers as well as by others as if the trust was a legal person, but there is no separate entity, although the income trust is generally deemed to be an individual taxpayer for tax purposes. A trust is simply the relationship between the trustee, the beneficiaries, and the settlor (the creator) of the trust. The income trust is a trust like any other trust, and it is governed by general principles of trust law, even though it is a business or investment vehicle.

The tendency to refer to such trusts as if they were a separate legal entity, like a corporation, presents the prospect for confusion over the roles of the persons involved with the trust's administration and management. The directors of a corporation that serves as a trustee are not *prima facie*, for example, themselves trustees or treated as trustees (constructive or *de facto*), nor are directors of other corporations involved in the trust. However, such directors need to be familiar with trust principles that concern the operation of the trust and the implications for their own responsibilities and liability, as addressed below.

II. Trust Structure

The governing instrument for the income trust, or for any trust, is the trust indenture or declaration of trust. This instrument creates the trust and establishes the structure for managing and operating it. There must be a trustee or trustees, and often a registered trust company serves as the trustee

[1] R.S.C. 1985 (5th Supp.), c. 1.

of the income trust. This structure is dictated by restrictions that are imposed under the applicable provincial *Trustee Act* if a corporation is to be the trustee.[2] However, the trustee may have a limited role. For this reason among others, the instrument generally limits the liability of the trustee(s) to the unitholders (beneficiaries) of the trust.

The actual day-to-day management of an income trust may not be carried out by the trustee(s). Management may be entrusted to an administrator or manager, and there may be more than one entity involved in addition to the trustee in dealing with the day-to-day operation of the income trust.

Directors of registered trust companies are generally well instructed in the nature of trustee duties, and the companies themselves tend to be conservative in their dealings with trusts and with any parties that have an interest in them. The focus in this Chapter is on the special considerations for the directors of the other corporations that may be involved in the establishment, administration, or management of an income trust. As illustrated above, these individuals may be directors of one or more of the operating entities in which the trust is an investor or even directors of the administrator or manager.

The role of these other corporations has not been the subject of much analysis, either in respect of their duties to the trust and its unitholders or of their potential liability. That persons involved with a trust who are handling, or directing the handling of, trust property might themselves be regarded as trustees, or at least as persons who are subject to a fiduciary duty, should be obvious. The designation is trustee *de son tort*, a *de facto* trustee. There seems to be some doubt in trust law as to what interest in or control over the trust property is necessary in order for a person to be regarded as a trustee *de son tort*. In order to be regarded as a *de facto* trustee, a person would have to have some degree of control over the trust property, but the courts are unlikely to adopt a technical approach to such issues. For example, they may require that person to have title or another legal interest in the trust property in order to impose liability for it. In *Dubai Aluminum Co. v. Salaam*, Lord Millett stated that the position of such *de facto* trustees is that they are trustees in all but name:

> In their relations with the beneficiaries they are treated in every respect as if they had been duly appointed. They are

[2] In Ontario see, generally, the *Trustee Act*, R.S.O. 1990, c. T.23; in Alberta see, generally, the *Trustee Act*, R.S.A. 2000, c. T-8; in British Columbia see, generally, the *Trustee Act*, R.S.B.C. 1996, c. 464.

> true trustees and are fully subject to fiduciary obligations. Their liability is strict ...[3]

The Supreme Court of Canada has suggested that the trustee *de son tort* does not assume personal liability except if he or she commits a breach of trust.[4] This may qualify the above sweeping statement of principle from Lord Millett, but it is not clear as to what extent, if any, it will affect the result in practice.

III. Trust Governance

The obligation of directors to ensure good corporate governance does not change by virtue of the corporation's involvement in an income trust. As addressed in Chapter 1, the directors must ensure that appropriate controls and direction are provided to ensure that the corporation discharges its obligations and duties as required, and to that end, directors need to be mindful of any special or unusual risks or problems that are presented by the particular business activities. The involvement of a corporation in the management and administration of a trust also requires the directors of that corporation to have a reasonable understanding of the operating businesses in which the trust has interests (which may be as diverse as petroleum and natural gas, real estate, and fast food restaurants) and the peculiar constraints or limitations imposed on trusts.

A. Compliance With the Trust Instrument

The governing instrument for the trust is, as noted, the trust indenture or declaration of trust. As an agreement, this instrument is treated much like any other agreement with respect to interpretation (subject to certain limitations addressed below). Strict adherence to the trust instrument is required. While trust agreements and trust statutes typically provide for trustees or other interested parties to seek the advice and directions of a court,[5] trust administration does not have the benefit of the extensive guidance provided to corporations and their directors by modern business corporations statutes and case law. Whatever faults one may find with corporate regimes,

---

[3] *Dubai Aluminum Co. v. Salaam*, [2002] H.L.J. No. 48, [2002] UKHL 48, at para. 138.

[4] *Air Canada v. M. & L. Travel Ltd.*, [1993] 3 S.C.R. 787 at para. 32 ("*M&L Travel*"). See generally the discussion in Waters, D.W.M., Gillin M.R. and Smith, L.D. (ed.), *Waters' Law of Trusts in Canada* (3rd ed.) (Toronto: Thomson Canada Ltd., 2005) at 490–491.

[5] *Trustee Act*, R.S.O. 1990, c. T.23, s. 60(1), states, "A trustee, guardian or personal representative may, without the institution of an action, apply to the Superior Court of Justice for the opinion, advice or direction of the court on any question respecting the management or administration of the trust property or the assets of a ward or a testator or intestate"; similar provisions are found in the *Trustee Act*, R.S.A. 2000, c. T-8, s. 43(1), and the *Trustee Act*, R.S.B.C. 1996, c. 464, s. 86(1).

they and the resulting case law provide considerable guidance as to what the corporation can and cannot do and what consents or approvals of shareholders may be required. There is machinery that allows corporations to engage in a wide variety of complicated corporate arrangements and to deal with shareholder views and interests in a clear fashion, often with the ability to obtain court assistance. All of this guidance provides a freedom and certainty that does not exist in the world of trusts. While business trusts have been around for some time, trust law has to date made little concession to their use as a vehicle for investment and engagement in business. To what extent Canadian courts will adopt or vary trust law in the context of business trusts is largely untested. A business trust is likely still a trust, and it should be subject to fundamental trust principles unless it is altered by legislation.

One significant feature of trust law is that a provision for the amendment of the trust instrument cannot necessarily be taken at face value. This feature was highlighted in a recent Ontario decision, *Kerry (Canada) Inc. v. Ontario (Superintendent of Financial Services)*.[6] As an employer, Kerry Canada had sought to rely upon a power to make unilateral amendments to its employees' pension plan. Any contractual right to amend a trust pension is strictly limited. The power to amend a continuing trust is "subordinated" to trust law principles.[7] These principles, courts have consistently ruled, provide their own set of rules, which apply "in addition to, and in precedence over, the law of contract and rules of construction of contracts".[8]

In order to afford a power to pay certain expenses out of the trust funds that was not provided for in the original trust instrument, there had to be reserved to the employer a power to partially revoke the trust. So in any trust where an amendment is contemplated, where the amendment would result in a payment out of the trust's funds, the parties concerned cannot rely on what seems to be a broad power of amendment but need to consider whether or not the special rules that are applicable to trusts permit such an amendment. In *Kerry*, purported amendments dating back thirty years were held to be invalid, and the employer had to reimburse the pension plan. A *de facto* trustee might also be held responsible for such a breach of trust and, as addressed below, so might a director who benefitted from or assisted in the breach. Equally, trust concepts may influence the interpretation of other provisions in the trust instrument, which may be viewed differently than it would if the same language were found in another form of commercial agreement.

---

6 [2006] O.J. No. 960 (Div. Ct.) ("*Kerry*").

7 *Ibid.* at para. 31.

8 *Ibid.*

In addition to having to strictly adhere to the terms of the trust instrument, trustees owe a fiduciary duty and a duty of care to the beneficiaries in respect of the trust. In order to ensure that a corporation involved with a trust is not involved in any breach of trust or duty of care (to the extent it may be a *de facto* trustee), the directors of the corporation need to be alert to these obligations and to ensure that the corporation complies with any trust obligation it might have imposed on it. The same awareness should apply to the need for directors to take reasonable steps to ensure that the corporation generally meets its contractual obligations (albeit not on a contract by contract basis). However, in trust law, there is the added incentive that the directors can be personally liable to the extent that they participate in a breach of trust.

B. Trustee Fiduciary Duty

The fiduciary duty owed by trustees is somewhat comparable to the fiduciary duty owed by directors to the corporation. The fiduciary duty of a trustee is said to be the highest or most onerous and unforgiving fiduciary duty. As such, it is in legal theory more strict than the director's fiduciary duty to the corporation, although there may be little practical difference given the modern expectations of directors.

There is the potential to confuse the fiduciary duty that the corporation may owe as a trustee with the fiduciary duties that directors of that corporation owe to the corporation. The director's duty is always to the corporation. As part of discharging their duty to the corporation, directors need to be cognizant of the corporation's possible obligations as a fiduciary.

C. Trustee Duty of Care

Trustees also owe a duty of care in respect of the management of the trust property. Again, the trustee is in a similar position to a director, owing both a fiduciary duty and a duty of care. Issues about whether this duty on trustees has been discharged seem to arise most frequently for conventional trusts in respect of how trust funds are invested.

The duty owed by a trustee is said to be that of a reasonable business person who is similarly situated. Those with business or professional skills have a higher standard imposed on them than, say, the standard imposed on a family member who is acting as the trustee of an infant's trust. It has also been suggested that the duty of care is a lower standard than, say, the duty of care owed by directors to their corporation. Much like fiduciary duties, though, in practice, it may be doubtful if there is any significant difference between these different standards, particularly when sophisticated corporations or individuals owe these duties.

One observation that should be noted is that trustees have been thought to be entitled to take a longer-term view in the management of trust property than directors could in respect of a corporation's property. Investors in a corporation are thought to be looking more to short-term gains, whereas a conventional trust has the long-term interests of all beneficiaries to provide for. Whether, or to what extent, the courts will modify that principle where unitholders are the beneficiaries and look upon the income trust units much as they would shares in a publicly-traded corporation, remains to be seen.

IV. Director Liability

The fact that a corporation of which an individual is a director might be a trustee or held to a trustee's duties does not make that individual a trustee. Personal liability can arise for directors, though, where in their decisions or through other actions they participate in a breach of trust, including a breach of fiduciary duty. Directors and other strangers to the trust can be liable for what is known as "knowing assistance", where they facilitate a breach of trust, and for what is known as "knowing receipt", where they obtain trust property improperly. Liability revolves around knowledge, but the authorities are confused about the nature and extent of the knowledge that is required for liability.

A. Knowing Assistance

Liability can be incurred if a stranger to a trust knowingly participates in a breach of trust. More broadly, liability can arise for participation in a breach of any fiduciary duty in relation to property, whether or not there is a formal trust.[9] Consequently, the same principles apply if, in a breach of a fiduciary obligation, an officer or a director misappropriates a company asset, even though that property is not being held in trust for the company.[10]

As for the nature of the relief available, a stranger who is held liable for knowing assistance is subject to a personal obligation to remedy the breach. From *Oosterhoff on Trusts*:

> In most cases, that obligation is quantified by reference to the loss that the beneficiary or trust itself suffered as a result

[9] Oosterhoff, A.H. Chambers R., McInnes, J. and Smith, L., *Oosterhoff on Trusts: Text. Commentary and Materials* (Toronto: Thomson Canada Limited, 2004) at 853.

[10] *Alers-Hankey v. Teixeira* (2000), 75 B.C.L.R. (3d) 232 (C.A.).

> of the defendant's breach. However, if, as a result of participating in the breach, the defendant obtained a benefit, the plaintiff has the option of demanding disgorgement rather than compensation. In that case, the remedial obligation will be quantified by reference to the defendant's gain rather than to the plaintiff's loss.[11]

The possible application of these principles to the directors of a corporation who are involved in the administration or management of a trust will be obvious. What then should the directors be alert to? What sort of knowledge would be required to render a director liable? The degree of knowledge required in order for a stranger to be held liable under the "knowing assistance" form of liability appears to be actual knowledge of the trust's existence and actual knowledge that what is being done is in breach of that trust. Reckless or willful blindness can also suffice in both cases. In terms of knowledge of the underlying breach of trust, the issue is whether the breach of trust was fraudulent and dishonest, not whether the stranger's actions should be characterized as such. It is the trustee's actions that must be examined. It is unnecessary to find that the director or other stranger acted in bad faith or dishonestly.[12] For the director of a corporation who is involved in managing an income trust or its assets, it is the corporation's conduct that is determinative.

If a director or other participating stranger received a benefit as a result of a breach of trust, this situation can ground an inference that the stranger knew of the breach.[13] However, the receipt of a benefit is not a sufficient or a necessary condition for the drawing of such an inference.[14]

The imposition of a constructive trust and the liability of third parties, in particular, directors, for knowing assistance in the breach of trust was considered in *M&L Travel*. It is the leading authority on directors' liability in such matters and warrants a detailed examination for those involved with income trusts or, more broadly, in respect of any trust obligations that a corporation may have.

In this case, Martin and Valiant were the owners, directors, and officers of M&L Travel. Martin and Valiant obtained an operating line of credit to repay Valiant's bank for his investment in the company, and the bank was authorized to withdraw money from the company's account from time to

---

[11] *Oosterhoff on Trusts*, *supra* note 9 at 843–853. And see *Warman Intl Ltd. v. Dwyer* (1995), 128 A.L.R. 201 (Aus. H.C.).

[12] *M&L Travel*, *supra* note 4 at para. 58, citing *Barnes v. Addy* (1874), L.R. 9 Ch. App. 244.

[13] *Groves-Raffin Construction Ltd. v. Canadian Imperial Bank of Commerce* (1975), 64 D.L.R. (3d) 78 (B.C.C.A.).

[14] *M&L Travel*, *supra* note 4 at para. 40.

time to pay for that loan. The company also had an agreement with Air Canada whereby funds collected from ticket sales were the property of Air Canada. M&L Travel was to hold the funds in trust and to remit them, less commission, to Air Canada. The company handled all monies through the company's general operating account. A dispute arose between Martin and Valiant, and the bank withdrew the monies from the account to pay out the operating line. Air Canada then brought an action against Martin and Valiant as well as the company to recover the funds to which it was entitled.

In upholding judgment against Martin and Valiant, knowledge, particularly for Valiant, who did not operate the business, was a key issue. As there was a trust relationship between M&L Travel and Air Canada, strangers to the trust (that is, the two directors) could be held personally liable for a breach of the trust if they knowingly participated in the breach. The court confirmed that a stranger might be liable in two ways for a breach of trust: (i) being in receipt and chargeable with trust property, and (ii) knowingly assisting in a dishonest and fraudulent design on the part of the trustees. Only the latter was applicable here. Actual knowledge as well as recklessness or willful blindness will suffice:

> If the stranger received a benefit as a result of the breach of trust, this may ground an inference that the stranger knew of the breach. The receipt of a benefit will be neither a sufficient nor a necessary condition for the drawing of such an inference.
>
> The reason for excluding constructive knowledge (that is, knowledge of circumstances which would indicate the facts to an honest person, or knowledge of facts which would put an honest person on inquiry) was discussed in *Re Montagu's Settlement Trusts*. Megarry V.C. held that constructive notice was insufficient to bind the stranger's conscience so as to give rise to personal liability. While cases involving recklessness or willful blindness indicate a "want of probity which justifies imposing a constructive trust", Megarry V.C. held that the carelessness involved in constructive knowledge cases will not normally amount to a want of probity, and will therefore be insufficient to bind the stranger's conscience.[15]

Liability for directors does not arise merely by association. What is required is participation in a fraudulent and dishonest breach of trust in order to impose liability on agents or others who are assisting the trustee. It was the trustee's actions in this respect that needed to be examined, not the

[15] *M&L Travel*, *supra* note 4 at paras. 40–41 [footnotes omitted].

knowledge of the stranger to the trust. In *M&L Travel*, as the breach of trust was caused directly by the conduct of the directors, it was held that they had participated in the breach of trust and were personally liable as constructive trustees.

There was no constructive trust *per se* as there was no trust property or its fruit that was held by the directors. The directors were simply treated the same as the actual trustee, M&L Travel, and they were held personally liable.

B. Knowing Receipt

A director or any other recipient of trust property will not be liable to unitholders merely because, at the time he or she receives what is found to be trust property, the existence of the trust attaching to the property was known. The recipient is liable only if the trustee, in fact, committed a breach of trust in making the transfer, and then only if the recipient had notice that the trustee was committing a breach of trust. If the sale was not, in fact, in breach of trust, or if the recipient did not have notice of the breach of trust, the recipient takes the property free and clear of the trust. In *The Law of Trusts*, the practical considerations limiting liability are explained:

> At common law, however, an extraordinary doctrine was widely accepted to the effect that a purchaser of trust property is liable in equity to the beneficiaries for the purchase price, although the trustee had made the sale in the proper exercise of a power of sale and although the purchaser had paid the purchase money to the trustee, unless the money so paid was properly applied by the trustee for the purpose of the trust. As professor Ames has said, "this highly artificial doctrine would seem to be indefensible on any principle:" (Ames, *Cases on Trusts* 269 n (2d) ed. 1893.) Why should the purchaser be responsible for a misapplication of the purchase money by the trustee in which the purchaser did not participate and that he had no reason to anticipate? The effect of the rule is to obstruct the proper administration of trusts by making it difficult for trustees to find persons who are willing to incur the risk attending the purchase of trust property.[16]

The Supreme Court addressed the operation of constructive trusts and knowing receipt in *Citadel General Assurance Co. v. Lloyds Bank of Canada*.[17] Again, as authority on such director liability is limited and con-

---

[16] A.W. Scott and W.F. Fratcher, *The Law of Trusts*, 4th ed., (Boston: Little Brown and Co., 1989), Vol. IV at 237.

[17] [1997] 3 S.C.R. 805 ("*Citadel*").

fusing, some analysis of the decision provides better guidance than a bare statement of principle would. Citadel General had an arrangement with Drive On Guaranteed Vehicle Payment Plan (1982) Limited concerning auto insurance. The premiums were collected by dealers and remitted to Drive On. Drive On paid commissions and settled any current claims, then remitted the balance to Citadel.

Drive On was a subsidiary of International Warranty Company Limited. The companies used one account for all transactions, including the collection of insurance premiums. Drive On and International Warranty also used the same account to cover International Warranty's overdrafts with the bank. In early 1987, Citadel discovered that Drive On had not been depositing the premiums into a trust account; Drive On responded that it would establish one if it was necessary. Later in the year, withdrawals from the account led Drive On to be unable to pay the premiums for July and August to Citadel. An arrangement was made for regular payments, but Drive On and International failed, leaving a substantial balance owing. Citadel therefore made a claim against the bank to which the funds had been remitted claiming the outstanding indebtedness of the companies.

The court ruled that the bank had constructive knowledge of Drive On's breach of trust and would be unjustly enriched if it was held not liable to Citadel as a constructive trustee. The only basis upon which the bank could be liable was as a constructive trustee under the knowing receipt form of liability, which was *M&L Travel.*

Receipt for "knowing receipt" was said to require the stranger, which would include directors, to have received trust property in his or her personal capacity and to have applied it for his or her own use or benefit.

As to knowledge, there were two lines of authority. One line held that the knowledge requirement for knowing assistance and knowing receipt should be the same and that, in particular, constructive knowledge was not appropriate for either one of them. A second line suggested that there is a different standard between the two and that a lower threshold of knowledge was more appropriate in knowing receipt cases. In knowing receipt cases, one is concerned with the receipt of trust property for one's own benefit. The Supreme Court agreed that there should be a lower threshold of knowledge (than for knowing assistance) required of the stranger to the trust. At paragraph 48:

> More is expected of the recipient, who, unlike the accessory, is necessarily enriched at the plaintiff's expense. Because the recipient is held to this higher standard, constructive knowledge (that is, knowledge of facts sufficient to put a rea-

> sonable person on notice or inquiry) will suffice as the basis for restitutionary liability.[18]

It was also held that this lower threshold of knowledge was sufficient to establish the unjust nature of the enrichment, thereby entitling the plaintiff to a restitutionary remedy.[19]

In this case, the bank was aware of the nature of the funds being deposited into, and transferred out of, the account in that it knew that the premiums collected were payable to Citadel. In light of its general knowledge, the daily emptying of the account was (held to be) very suspicious. A reasonable person, it was reasoned, would have inquired as to the possible misapplication of trust funds. The bank therefore should have taken steps, in the form of reasonable inquiries, to determine whether the insurance premiums were being misapplied.

The *Citadel* decision has been criticized as misapplying the concept of unjust enrichment. It has been argued that in an unjust enrichment claim, the knowledge or intent that is important is that of the plaintiff, whether the plaintiff intended to or knew that he or she was parting with the property.[20] However, the Supreme Court has focused on a reasonable man standard.

Gold v. Rosenberg,[21] a companion case to *Citadel*, involved a testamentary trust. Rosenberg, the testator's son, and Gold, the testator's grandson, were executors and equal beneficiaries of the estate. The main estate assets were two real estate companies, Primary and Existing. Gold executed a power of attorney in favour of Rosenberg to allow him to administer the estate. Rosenberg also had a real estate company, Trojan, owned by himself and his wife. The testator, the two estate companies, Rosenberg, and Trojan all banked at the defendant bank, and the accounts were all administered by the bank account manager, Slack. Slack and Rosenberg agreed to use the assets of the two estate companies to refinance Rosenberg's and his personal corporation's indebtedness. Gold, as well as Rosenberg, signed the directors' resolution of Primary that was required for the guarantee of Rosenberg's personal indebtedness. The same law firm represented all parties except for Gold. Gold became suspicious of Rosenberg's management of the estate and revoked his power of attorney. Gold sued Rosenberg, Primary, the bank and the law firm, seeking a declaration that Primary's guarantee was invalid and unenforceable.

---

[18] *Ibid.*

[19] *Ibid.* at para 49.

[20] See David Stevens, "Knowing Assistance and Knowing Receipt in the Supreme Court of Canada" (1998–1999) 14 B.F.L.R. 407.

[21] [1997] 3 S.C.R. 767 ("*Gold*").

Claims against the bank for knowing assistance or knowing receipt were denied by the majority. Knowing receipt was held to be distinguishable by the type of knowledge required and by the fact that receipt was required for knowing receipt. Knowing assistance required proof of (1) a trust, (2) a dishonest and fraudulent breach of that trust, and (3) actual knowledge or willful or reckless blindness by the recipient of the trust property as to the breach of the trust.

The bank was found not liable for knowing receipt on the basis that an honest person in the same circumstances would not have made further inquiries, and even if the bank had investigated further, it would not have discovered anything improper. Furthermore, the bank had not received value at the expense of the trust. Gonthier J., the fourth judge constituting the majority, ruled that the bank had met the standard of reasonableness imposed on a stranger who knowingly receives.

The minority agreed that the bank was not liable for knowing assistance but would have found it liable for knowing receipt. Knowing receipt was said to be a restitutionary claim and the knowledge element was the same as that required in the equitable defence of "*bona fide* purchaser for value without notice". In determining what was required to prove "notice", the minority favoured a "want of probity" test, stating that there was no need for the plaintiff to prove any wrong on the part of the defendant. The "want of probity" test required only that the defendant had failed to make the inquiries that a reasonable person would have made or, having made them, the defendant was put off by an answer that would not have satisfied a reasonable person.

Gold demonstrates that confusion easily arises when assessing a state of facts as a case of knowing receipt or knowing assistance. The Court was divided. The case could well be made in any event that the facts were sufficiently suspicious that even on constructive knowledge, the bank in this case ought to have been liable.

The prudent course for directors is to assume that, where the law is unsettled as to the standard, the more onerous standard will apply. Directors need to be familiar with the trust obligations that the corporation has or may incur and to receive appropriate advice that any features to a transaction that might give rise to an allegation of breach of trust or fiduciary duty are, or will be, properly addressed. Valiant in *M&L Travel* may well have felt ill-informed and therefore innocent of any wrongful intent, but he was nonetheless held liable on what was said to be a higher threshold of knowledge for participating in the corporation's breach of trust. The Supreme

Court found that he ought to have been more probing in carrying out his duties as a director.

V. Conflict Issues

The potential for liability is heightened by the conflicts that can arise for directors who are serving on both the board of the promoter/settlor of the income trust and on the board of a corporation engaged in the management and administration of the trust or trust property (e.g., Opco, in the illustration in this Chapter), or for individuals who are nominated by the promoter to the board of one of these other corporations. Frequently, individuals serve in several roles and there are good practical business reasons for them doing so, not just from a control perspective but because they are familiar with the business generally and with the operation of particular assets that may now be the property of the income trust.

A director in such a position is subject to the same duties as those outlined in Chapter 2, and such a director is no more able to favour interests other than those duties when he or she is involved with a trust. Depending on the structure of the trust, the director may even be a trustee as well. That situation will produce the greatest risk of conflict because of the strict nature of the trustee's fiduciary duty in particular. While a strict approach has been adopted to directors' duties in a number of cases, there is some room for relaxation, such as statutory provisions dealing with material contracts. The trustee's fiduciary duty, on the other hand, is said to be the strictest, as noted above, and there are no comparable provisions for trustees. Individuals in these multiple roles may be faced with frequent conflicts, and they may find that their inability to participate in board of director decisions arises so often that they cannot discharge their duty as directors and therefore, they ought to resign. The corporation is entitled to a director's active involvement on the board, but an individual director will fail in his or her duties if he or she is unable to participate on the board when conflicts arise on more than an occasional basis.

The prospect for conflict should be less likely where individuals serve on the board of the promoter or on the board of a corporation that is engaged in managing the trust or a corporation in which the trust holds the shares, but they will arise from time to time. The conflict will most likely arise in the deliberations of the corporation that is actively managing the trust property or the operating company for the trust. In discharging their duties to the corporation, these directors need to be particularly mindful of the trust structure. Potentially conflicting interests may not be as readily apparent with income trusts as even well-seasoned directors do not have much experience with the trust structure.

As pointed out above, while they are being mindful of their own personal exposure to liability for knowing assistance or knowing receipt, the directors have to be mindful that their duties as directors are owed to the corporation. Those duties require them to be informed of the corporation's obligations, in respect of the income trust or otherwise, but those same duties are not owed to the income trust, trustee(s), or unitholders. Discharge of the corporation's trust obligations should usually be consistent with the discharge of the directors' duties to the corporation, but there could be instances where they are not. From time to time, it may not be in a corporation's best interests to fulfill contractual obligations. How else, for example, could directors justify approving an application for relief under the *Companies' Creditors Arrangement Act*?[22]

In order to address particular conflicts or as a matter of course, the directors of a corporation who are involved with an income trust can and should in many instances appoint an independent committee of the board to address the issue or guide it on an ongoing basis in the area assigned to it. The nature and authority of board committees are addressed in Chapter 6.

There are usually a number, if not a majority, of directors of such corporations that are described in the income trusts' public documents as "unrelated". Any special or even regular committees of the board can be comprised of these individuals; this provides a level of comfort not just to unitholders and prospective investors but also to the other, "related" directors.

Lastly, as with any organization in which there are a number of corporations or other legal entities, special care needs to be taken to assess the insurance coverage that is offered to directors.

Where the directors are covered by a policy of insurance that insures non-directors under the same policy, there is a concern with exclusion of claims involving the non-directors. In addition, exceptions for claims arising out of dishonest or similar actions should be reviewed with potential breach of trust claims in mind.[23]

---

[22] R.S.C. 1985, c. C-36.

[23] See Chapter 18, "Indemnification and Insurance", for a general discussion of this topic.

CHAPTER 16

FURTHER DUTIES OF DIRECTORS WITH RESPECT TO NOT-FOR-PROFIT ORGANIZATIONS

I. Introduction

On the whole, not-for-profit organizations provide a tremendous benefit to the public. Not surprisingly, those who sit on the boards of directors[1] for these organizations are often motivated by a sense of service, community, and altruism.[2] Such boards vary in experience and

[1] For the purposes of this Chapter, "board of directors" refers to the governing body of an organization irrespective of the fact that certain organizations may use different terms for this role. Similarly, "director" refers to a member of the board of directors who is duly elected or appointed and does not include either non-voting *ex officio* directors or honorary directors.

[2] See Appendix I, "Checklist A: Considerations Before Becoming A Director", and "Checklist E: Financial Impact of Serving as a Director".

motivation and include successful, skilled professionals as well as dedicated members with minimal financial, legal, or business experience. Irrespective of background, directors generally forgo remuneration.[3] As volunteers, they are often pressed for time to meet their commitments.

In this context of benevolence, the assumption is often made that these directors are protected from personal liability by their good intentions.[4] On the contrary, the special place in law occupied by the range of not-for-profit organizations often places higher responsibilities on these directors than those in place for the directors of for-profit corporations. Commensurate with these higher responsibilities is the potential for increased personal liability.

This Chapter provides a brief overview of the variety of legal structures available for not-for-profit organizations and details the duties and potential liabilities of directors in respect of not-for-profit corporations,[5] including charities, as they differ from those of for-profit corporations.

The law in respect of not-for-profit corporations is unsettled in certain circumstances. By and large, legislation pertaining to not-for-profit corporations has not been modernized in the same manner as for-profit corporate legislation,[6] and reliance on the common law remains significant. Canadian judicial consideration of some issues is thin or non-existent. To a degree, analogy to for-profit corporate law or trust law principles can assist in filling these gaps but it must be done with caution.

---

[3] In the case of charities, directors may be prohibited from receiving remuneration without prior court approval. See section II.E.2(a) for a more complete discussion of this issue.

[4] See e.g. *R. v. Muskoka Baptist Conference*, 1986 WL 762282 (Ont. Dist. Ct.) at para. 59: "The escape of raw or partially treated sewage into the Muskoka River created a danger of serious harm to many people. The Muskoka Baptist Conference and its managing director cannot excuse carelessness by explaining that it is a nonprofit, religious organization".

[5] For the purposes of this Chapter, "not-for-profit corporation" means those corporations, companies, and societies that are incorporated under the not-for-profit legislation or not-for-profit provisions as set out in Appendix II, Table 1. For a more detailed discussion of the various means of incorporation for not-for-profit organizations, see section II.B.1.

[6] In 2004, the federal government proposed Bill C-21, *An Act Respecting Not-for-profit Corporations and Other Corporations Without Share Capital*, 1st Sess., 38th Parl., to replace Parts II and III of the *Canada Corporations Act*, R.S.C. 1970, c. C-32. The proposed act was intended to modernize the governance of not-for-profit corporations and many of its provisions were modelled on existing modern corporate statutes. This proposed act died on the Order Paper on November 29, 2005, following the dissolution of Parliament for a general election. At the time of publishing, it remains uncertain if the proposed act will be resurrected.

II. Not-For-Profit Organizations: A Structural Overview

A. Not-For-Profit Organizations and Charities Defined

1. Generally

There is no single authoritative definition of not-for-profit organizations and charities. Instead, various statutory and common law definitions apply in different situations. Generally, the classification "not-for-profit organization" includes all charities. Neither not-for-profit organizations nor charities may intend to operate at a profit. Should a profit be made, this profit cannot be distributed to the organization's members or accumulated; instead, it must be used to further the organization's objects. Both not-for-profit organizations and charities must provide a benefit to the public or to an identifiable portion of the public. As the requirements for charities are more restrictive, not all not-for-profit organizations are charities.

There are three sources of definitions for not-for-profit organizations of particular importance: the *Income Tax Act* (Canada),[7] other legislation, and the common law.

2. Definition for Tax Purposes

The definitions of not-for-profit organizations[8] and charities that are found in the *Income Tax Act* are important to many of these organizations as they determine access to certain tax advantages.[9] Not-for-profit organizations are eligible for exemption from paying most types of income tax, while registered charities are ordinarily tax-exempt and able to issue tax receipts for donations.[10]

The *Income Tax Act* defines a non-profit organization as a corporation, club, society, or association other than a charity that is organized and operated exclusively for social welfare, civic improvement, pleasure, recreation, or any other purpose except for profit, which does not distribute or otherwise make available for the personal benefit of a member any of its income, unless its primary function is the promotion of amateur athletics. The Canada Revenue Agency further refines this definition by, for instance,

---

[7] *Income Tax Act*, R.S.C. 1985 (5th Supp.), c. 1 ("Income Tax Act").

[8] The *Income Tax Act*, *ibid.*, uses the term "non-profit".

[9] *Ibid.*, s. 149(1)(l). See also M.N.R., Interpretation Bulletin IT-496R, "*Non-Profit Organizations*" (August 2, 2001) ("IT-496R").

[10] For an overview from the Canada Customs and Revenue Agency of these organizations from a tax perspective, see IT-496R, *ibid.*, and Canada Customs and Revenue Agency, Guide T4063: *Registering a Charity for Income Tax Purposes*.

stating that the prohibition against personal benefit to a member is interpreted to exclude arm's length salaries, wages, fees, honoraria, or reasonable travel reimbursements.[11] Examples of organizations that may qualify as not-for-profit organizations for tax purposes include community associations, social clubs, golf clubs, curling clubs, and residential condominium corporations.

The *Income Tax Act* defines a charity as an organization that is charitable at law and devotes its resources to charitable purposes and activities.[12] The reference to "charitable" requires recourse to the common law for explanation. At common law, to be charitable, an organization's purposes must fit within one of four categories: the relief of poverty, the advancement of education, the advancement of religion, and other purposes beneficial to

---

[11] IT-496R, *supra* note 9 at para. 12.

[12] Section 149.1 (1) of the *Income Tax Act, supra* note 7, defines a charity as either a charitable foundation or a charitable organization. Charitable foundation and charitable organizations are defined in the same section as follows:

> "Charitable foundation" means a corporation or trust that is constituted and operated exclusively for charitable purposes, no part of the income of which is payable to, or is otherwise available for, the personal benefit of any proprietor, member, shareholder, trustee or settlor thereof, and that is not a charitable organization;
>
> "Charitable organization" means an organization, whether or not incorporated,
>
> (*a*) all the resources of which are devoted to charitable activities carried on by the organization itself,
>
> (*b*) no part of the income of which is payable to, or is otherwise available for, the personal benefit of any proprietor, member, shareholder, trustee or settlor thereof,
>
> (*c*) more than 50% of the directors, trustees, officers or like officials of which deal with each other and with each of the other directors, trustees, officers or officials at arm's length, and
>
> (*d*) where it has been designated as a private foundation or public foundation pursuant to subsection (6.3) of this section or s. 110(8.1) or (8.2) of the *Income Tax Act*, Chapter 148 of the Revised Statutes of Canada, 1952, or has applied after February 15, 1984 for registration under paragraph 110(8)(*c*) of that Act or under the definition "registered charity" in s. 248(1), not more than 50% of the capital of which has been contributed or otherwise paid into the organization by one person or members of a group of persons who do not deal with each other at arm's length and, for the purpose of this paragraph, a reference to any person or to members of a group does not include a reference to Her Majesty in right of Canada or a province, a municipality, another registered charity that is not a private foundation, or any club, society or association described in paragraph 149(1)(*l*);

Note that, in addition to meeting the definition of a charity, organizations must comply with the requirements regarding registration in order to become registered charities pursuant to the *Income Tax Act*.

the community in a way that the law regards as charitable.[13] Additionally, the charity must provide an "objectively measurable and socially useful benefit" that is directed to the public or to a sufficiently large section of the public.[14] Examples of charities satisfying this criteria include food banks and soup kitchens, learned societies, educational research institutions making their research available to the public, churches and missionary organizations, organizations providing relief to the victims of natural disasters, nursing and convalescent homes, and environmental protection organizations.

3. Further Statutory Definitions

Definitions found in the enabling statutes for not-for-profit organizations as well as those in other governing statutes are relevant. The definitions found in those statutes under which not-for-profit organizations incorporate must be met for the organization to be constituted under that statute.[15] Not-for-profit organizations may be subject to other legislation as well, based on the scope and definition of the statute.[16] As these assorted statutes do not use a uniform definition for not-for-profit or charitable organizations, care must be taken when determining if a particular statute applies.

4. Common law

As discussed above, the common law definition of charitable organizations continues to infuse meaning into current statutory definitions of "charitable". The common law definition of charitable remains important as the courts retain an inherent jurisdiction in respect of charities. This inherent jurisdiction has been expressed as a supervisory, equitable jurisdiction providing a court with the authority to supervise charities in the absence of

---

[13] These four categories are rooted in the preamble to the *Statute of Charitable Uses*, 1601 (U.K.), 43 Eliz. I, c. 4 and were set out over 100 years ago in England by Lord Macnaghten in *Commissioners for Special Purposes of the Income Tax v. Pemsel*, [1891] A.C. 531 (H.L.) ("*Pemsel*"). Canadian courts have repeatedly reaffirmed the *Pemsel* delineation of the four categories, while at the same time modernizing the content of each category: see, for instance, the recent Supreme Court of Canada decision in *Vancouver Society of Immigrant and Visible Minority Women v. M.N.R.*, [1999] 1 S.C.R. 10 ("*Vancouver Society*").

[14] See *Vancouver* Society, *ibid.* at para. 41; and Canada Customs and Revenue Agency, CPS-024: *Guidelines for Registering a Charity: Meeting the Public Benefit Test*, at s. 3.0.

[15] See Appendix II, "Table 1: Legislation Providing for the Incorporation of Not-for-Profit Organizations".

[16] Ontario's *Charities Accounting Act*, R.S.O. 1990, c. C.10, for example, applies to any organization incorporated for a religious, educational, charitable, or public purpose, regardless of the status of the corporation in respect of the *Income Tax Act*. For a more detailed discussion on statutory duties governing not-for-profit organizations, see section II.F.

express statutory authority.[17] It has been relied on to terminate a benevolent fund and order the distribution of the fund's assets[18] and acknowledged as providing the authority for the court appointment of an interim trustee for a charitable corporation.[19] Similarly, courts often invoke the *cy-près* doctrine to keep a charitable trust from failing.[20]

Both not-for-profit organizations and charities generally use one of the following four legal structures: incorporated organizations, trusts, unincorporated associations, and co-operatives. In addition to these four general categories, organizations may be incorporated for specific purposes pursuant to other enabling legislation.[21] A brief overview of each of these structures is provided in the next section. Note that while information contained in this Chapter may apply to each of these structures, this Chapter primarily addresses the duties and liabilities of directors of corporations, companies, and societies that are incorporated under not-for-profit legislation.

---

[17] See *Roberts v. Yukon Youth Centre Society*, [1993] Y.J. No. 99 (S.C.) at para. 7, see *contra O'Brien v. Whitehorse Christian Bible Fellowship*, [1993] Y.J. No. 80 (S.C.) at para. 33, which held that the exercise of inherent jurisdiction was inappropriate when there were available statutory avenues for the same relief.

[18] See *McCauley v. Fitzsimmons*, [1998] O.J. No. 3690 (C.A.) at para. 34.

[19] See *Trow v. Toronto Humane Society*, [2001] O.J. No. 3640 (S.C.J.) at para. 21, where the court found no improper exercise of the society's powers, but stated: "[t]his Court does have the inherent jurisdiction to direct and control the administration of charities. Such power ought to be exercised where charitable trusts are not being properly administered, where funds are being mismanaged or where the trustees of the funds are breaching their fiduciary obligations".

[20] This doctrine permits the court to modify a charitable trust if the charitable intention is clear, but an aspect of the trust would otherwise make the trust invalid, impractical, or impossible to perform. See for instance, *Canada Trust Co. v. Ontario Human Rights Commission* (1990), 74 O.R. (2d) 481 at 497 (C.A.), where the court, invoking the doctrine in respect of a charitable educational trust that excluded recipients on the grounds of race or religion, held that the trust was valid after the discriminatory restrictions were deleted, "In these circumstances, the trust should not fail. It is appropriate and only reasonable that the court apply the *cy-près* doctrine and invoke its inherent jurisdiction to propound a scheme that will bring the trust into accord with public policy and permit the general charitable intent to advance education or leadership through education to be implemented by those charged with the trust's administration". See also *Lecavalier v. Sussex (Town)*, [2003] NBJ No. 463 (Q.B.) at para. 65.

[21] See, e.g., provincial condominium legislation permitting the incorporation of not-for-profit condominium corporations: *Condominium Property Act*, R.S.A. 1980, c. C-22; provincial legislation providing for the incorporation of regional health authorities: *Regional Health Authorities Act* (Manitoba), C.C.S.M. c. R34 and *Regional Health Authorities Act* (New Brunswick), S.N.B. 2002, c. R-5.05; provincial legislation providing for the incorporation of school boards: *Schools Act, 1997* (Newfoundland), S.N.L. 1997, c. S-12.2 and *Nova Scotia School Boards Association Act*, R.S.N.S. 1989, c. 317; provincial legislation providing for the incorporation of post secondary institutions: *University Foundations Act, 1992* (Ontario), S.O. 1992, c. 22, *University Act* (Prince Edward Island), R.S.P.E.I. 1988, c. U-3; provincial legislation for the incorporation of museums: *An Act Respecting the Montréal Museum of Fine Arts* (Quebec), R.S.Q., c. M-42; or legislation providing for the incorporation of religious institutions: *An Act to Provide for the Continuation of Lutheran Church-Canada, Central District*, S.S. 1997, c. 02.

B. Legal Structures of Not-For-Profit Organizations and Charities

1. Corporations

Each jurisdiction in Canada has at least one statute enabling the creation of not-for-profit corporations.[22] These statutes permit the incorporation of corporations that either do not have share capital or are prohibited from paying dividends to members.[23] Not-for-profit corporations differ from for-profit corporations in that they are composed of members who do not receive a financial benefit from the corporation because of their membership, whereas shareholders of business corporations may receive dividend payments. Furthermore, in some jurisdictions, not-for-profit corporations may only be incorporated for specific permitted objects.[24] These permitted objects are generally quite broad.

Regardless of form, incorporation creates a legal entity, the corporation, which is separate and distinct from its members. As a result, directors of these corporations receive some protection from personal liability.

2. Trusts

A trust is established by a trust document, which must comprise the intention to create a trust, identify the subject matter of the trust, and identify the trust's objects or beneficiary. This structure is more common for charitable organizations than for other not-for-profit organizations. A trust is defined by the division of the legal and beneficial ownership of the trust property. In other words, one party, called the trustee, holds legal title to the property but is legally bound to hold the property for the equitable benefit of another party, called the beneficiary. The trustee owes a fiduciary duty to the beneficiaries of the trust. This is a high standard, both in the content of the duty and the standard to which it must be carried out. Other than the particular circumstance where the duties of directors of charitable corpora-

[22] While less common, not-for-profit corporations may also incorporate under business corporations legislation and restrict objects and prohibit the payment of dividends through constating documents. Note that the scope of this Chapter is directed to directors' liability in respect of corporations, companies, and societies (collectively referred to in this Chapter as "corporations") that are incorporated under specific not-for-profit legislation.

[23] See Appendix II, "Table 1: Legislation Providing for the Incorporation of Not-for-Profit Organizations".

[24] *Ibid.*

tions are akin to the duties of trustees, the duties and liabilities of trustees will not be addressed in this Chapter.[25]

3. Unincorporated Associations

Unincorporated not-for-profit associations, often simply called not-for-profit associations, are the default legal relationship governing people who associate together for a common purpose other than carrying on business with a view to profit.[26] Thus, unless a not-for-profit organization actively adopts another legal structure or contractually agrees to be governed by other rules, it is, with few exceptions, governed by the common law established for not-for-profit associations.[27] Not-for-profit associations can vary in scope from clubs with only the most rudimentary informal arrangements with respect to their organization to organizations that consciously choose this form of legal relationship and establish their creation and governance with formal constating documents. This form of organization may be appropriate for a smaller group of individuals, such as social clubs or hobby groups, who are undertaking low risk activities that do not require the organization to enter into contracts or other legal relationships.

Not-for-profit associations have a myriad of different internal governing structures; those that may be run by all members or those that may delegate authority in any number of ways, including delegating authority to a group of committee members who are functioning as directors.

A not-for-profit association is not a legal entity that is separate from its members, as is the case with a corporation. Instead, it generally has no legal status apart from its members.[28] As a result, the personal assets of all members, particularly those who function like directors, may be at risk for liability in tort or contract.[29]

---

[25] The law pertaining to the liabilities and duties of trustees is complex and distinct from the liabilities and duties of directors of not-for-profit corporations. For a general, leading Canadian authority on trusts, see, D.W.M. Waters, Mark R. Gillen and Lionel D. Smith, *Waters' Law of Trusts in Canada*, 3rd ed. (Toronto: Carswell, 2005).

[26] Note that the law of partnership governs people who associate together for the purpose of carrying on a business with a view to profit, and a general partnership need not be registered.

[27] Robert Flanigan, "Contractual Responsibility in Non-Profit Associations" (1988) 18 Oxford J. Legal Stud. 631 at 632 ("Flanigan, Contractual Liability"). Flanigan details these exceptions, including unions governed by comprehensive statutory regimes, proprietary clubs, and associations with an insufficient amount of organization to qualify even as an association.

[28] See *Alberta Government Telephones v. Canada (Canadian Radio-television and Telecommunications Commission)*, [1989] 2 S.C.R. 225 at para. 183: "[i]t must be kept in mind, however, that the network, as an unincorporated association, is nothing more than the sum of its constituent parts".

[29] For a thorough review of the liabilities of directors of not-for-profit associations in tort and contract, see the following two articles by Robert Flanigan: "The Liability Structure of Nonprofit Associations: Tort and Fiduciary Liability Assignments" (1998) 77 Can. Bar. Rev. 73; and Flanigan, "Contractual Liability", *supra* note 27.

4. Co-operatives

Co-operatives are established pursuant to provincial legislation and can be established either with or without share capital.[30] Co-operatives are vehicles for groups of people working, on a democratic basis, to satisfy common needs, such as access to products or services, sales of products or services, or securing employment. Co-operatives without share capital are similar in nature to not-for-profits in the form of corporations without share capital. In co-operatives structured as not-for-profit organizations, surpluses are applied to common objectives and are not returned to members. Conversely, co-operatives with share capital are more akin to business corporations. Not-for-profit co-operatives in Canada include housing, worker, healthcare, and daycare co-operatives.

C. Ex Officio and Honorary Directors

Ex officio directors are directors by virtue of another office they hold. For instance, the by-laws of the corporation may create an *ex officio* director by providing that the president of the board of directors of a related organization automatically sits as a director. *Ex officio* directors may or may not have voting rights.

Honorary directors may be permitted by an organization's governing documents and may be appointed for many functions, including advisors, fundraisers, benefactors, or sponsors. Honorary directors are generally not permitted to vote but they may have varying levels of involvement at board meetings. The issue of personal liability for an honorary director appears not to have been specifically considered by Canadian courts. Nevertheless, the courts have articulated the principle that a person acting as a director, known as a *de facto* director, may be as liable as a properly appointed director, known as a *de jure* director.[31] Accordingly, an honorary director who is treated as an ordinary director for public purposes may be exposed to the same liability as an ordinary director.[32] Potential liability for honorary

---

[30] See Appendix II, "Table 1: Legislation Providing for the Incorporation of Not-for-Profit Organizations".

[31] See e.g., *Wheeliker v. Canada* (1999), 172 D.L.R. (4th) 708 (F.C.A.) ("*Wheeliker*") at para. 41: "... a failure to recognize the responsibility and liability of persons acting as *de facto* directors amounts to condoning and inviting the performance of acts and omissions by such persons which are detrimental to employees and the public in a trust-like situation".

[32] The Tax Court of Canada in *Bokrika Inc. v. R.*, 2006 G.T.C. 394 (T.C.C. (General Procedure)) considered the personal liability for GST of a son who had taken over the affairs of his late father's corporation. Before finding him liable as a *de facto* director, the court noted that he held himself out as a director, acted as a director, and was relied on by third parties as a director. While this case does not expressly consider honorary directors, the same principles of holding out, ostensible authority, and reliance could result in personal liability for an honorary director who appears for public purposes to have the authority of an ordinary director.

directors may be mitigated by using titles such as benefactor, sponsor, or patron and by ensuring that the honorary director does not have the authority of a director nor is held out to the public as a director.

D. Duties of Directors of Not-for-Profit Corporations

While incorporation generally shields directors from the liability of the corporation, directors remain personally liable for not satisfying the duties that are owed by them as directors to the corporation. The standard of care is the level of competency that a director is required to meet when carrying out these duties.[33]

The duties of directors are found both at common law and in legislation. In general, the common law duties that are applicable to directors and officers of for-profit corporations are applicable to those of not-for-profit corporations.[34] The duties discussed below are duties that are specific to directors of not-for-profit corporations or duties that otherwise warrant particular attention in a not-for-profit context.

1. Duty to Manage

Directors of not-for-profit corporations and charities are, like directors of for-profit corporations, responsible for the management of the corporation.[35] The nature of not-for-profit corporations, however, raises some distinct issues.

First, as directors in the not-for-profit sector are more likely to be volunteers, corporate governance structures in not-for-profit organizations tend to shift more decision-making authority to staff, in particular, to executive directors. Boards of directors should be wary of corporate governance models that restrict the role of the directors to setting the goals of the organization, and they should not delegate to staff all decision-making regarding the manner in which those goals are achieved without the appropriate oversight and reporting mechanisms. It is doubtful if, in practice, this level of delegation would meet the standard of care that is required of directors.

Second, as not-for-profit corporations, by definition, aspire to purposes other than market success, conventional market indicators are often unsuit-

[33] The standard of care is discussed in more detail below in section II.E, "The Standard of Care for Directors".

[34] These duties are discussed in detail in Chapter 2.

[35] This duty is codified for business corporations (see for instance, *Canada Business Corporations Act*, R.S.C. 1985, c. C-44, s. 121), but it applies in respect of other corporations by virtue of the common law. The content of this duty is discussed more extensively in the context of business corporations in Chapter 2.

able as measures of a not-for-profit corporation's success. Effectively managing a not-for-profit organization can require different skills and approaches than those that may be familiar to directors with business experience.[36]

As a result, irrespective of whether affairs are directly managed by a board of directors or whether the board acts in an oversight capacity, the directors must ensure that the administration of the organization's affairs is properly carried out. This oversight requires an effective structure, management of key areas, and the appropriate recourse to external expertise.[37]

(a) Board of Directors and Committee Structure[38]

An appropriate governance structure lays the foundation for successful corporate governance. It is crucial to have the appropriate number and mix of directors, who together possess the skills that are needed by the corporation. An independent nominating process can be crucial to recruiting the diverse talent that is characteristic of a good board. Similarly, a succession plan is vital to a not-for-profit's continuation. Committees, appropriate to the particular not-for-profit organization, such as a risk management committee, an audit committee, a communications committee, a fund development committee, and an investment committee, should be established.

In addition to proper composition, boards and committees must establish effective processes for conducting meetings, record-keeping, the orientation and training of board members, and self-evaluation and review. Internal regulation through constitutions, by-laws, and codes of conduct can promote good governance and institutional continuity. Likewise, documented board philosophies, directors' job descriptions, orientation materials, and the regular review of these materials can promote compliance.

---

[36] Peter H. Harris, Q.C., "Non-Profit and Charitable Organizations" in M. Patricia Richardson, ed., *Directors' and Officers' Duties and Liabilities in Canada* (Canada: Butterworths, 1997) 261 at 266–267.

[37] See Appendix I: "Checklist B: Once Agreeing to Consider Serving"; "Checklist C: Workings of the Board"; "Checklist D: Once Appointed to the Board"; "Checklist G: Board Meetings"; "Checklist H: Professional Opinions"; and "Checklist I: Risk Management". See also The Panel on Accountability and Governance in the Voluntary Sector, *Building on Strength: Improving Governance and Accountability in Canada's Voluntary Sector*, Final Report (Ottawa: February 1999) at 24–30, which organizes effective stewardship by a board of directors into active oversight in eight key areas. This report is available online at: <http://www.vsr-trsb.net>.

[38] See Appendix I: "Checklist C: Workings of the Board"; "Checklist D: Once Appointed to the Board"; "Checklist F: Conflicts of Interest"; "Checklist G: Board Meetings"; and "Checklist I: Risk Management".

(b) Management of Key Areas[39]

Management of key areas includes establishing policies, monitoring compliance, setting goals, and monitoring progress. A not-for-profit corporation is driven by its objects and purposes. Therefore, the directors must ensure that the corporation establishes a mission within its objects, reviews the mission, and monitors the achievement of the mission. In order to effectively supervise the not-for-profit's finances, directors must approve a budget; review financial statements and annual reports; monitor financial transactions; oversee fundraising activities, charitable donations, and charitable receipts; ensure the appropriate stewardship of the property with which the corporation has been entrusted; and be vigilant for signs of misappropriation. Directors are also accountable to manage human resources by ensuring that appropriate employee and volunteer policies, orientation, and training are in place. Finally, the board of directors must manage the external relations of the corporation.

When practicable, directors should rely on objective methods to evaluate compliance with policies and the achievement of goals. Surveying a not-for-profit's target community and stakeholders, for instance, can provide valuable feedback.

(c) Recourse to External Expertise[40]

In order to fulfill the duty to manage, directors may need the assistance of independent third party advisors. Independent financial or compliance audits may be necessary for a board of directors to be duly diligent. Similarly, a board of directors may need to obtain independent legal, financial, or other professional advice in response to an issue outside of the board's capabilities.[41] The challenge of paying for this assistance does not change the requirement to seek external expertise when necessary.

2. Duty to Act Within the Scope of the Corporation's Legal Authority

Modern corporate statutes generally provide "natural person powers" to corporations with share capital. This is not the case for not-for-profit corporations and charities, which instead are bound to restrict their activities to

---

[39] See Appendix I: "Checklist B: Once Agreeing to Consider Serving"; "Checklist D: Once Appointed to the Board"; and "Checklist G: Board Meetings".

[40] See Appendix I: "Checklist H: Professional Opinions"; and "Checklist I: Risk Management".

[41] See section II.F.2 for a more detailed discussion on reasonable reliance on external expertise as a defence against liability.

the scope set out in the corporation's constating documents.[42] An action outside of the scope of legal authority is an *ultra vires* action, whether or not it is conducted in good faith or is ratified by members.[43]

Directors of not-for-profit corporations are personally liable when the corporation pursues *ultra vires* purposes or undertakes *ultra vires* actions as, by definition, the corporation does not have the legal capacity to commit *ultra vires* actions.[44] The directors may be required to personally compensate the corporation for any loss that was suffered as a result of *ultra vires* actions.

Therefore, directors of not-for-profit corporations and charities must ensure that they are familiar with the governing documents and by-laws of the corporation, and they should review these documents before they agree to become directors and at least annually thereafter.[45] Directors should be satisfied that they became a director in accordance with the governing documents of the organization and that the organization's disbursement of funds and other actions fall within the scope of permitted activities.[46] Should an organization wish to expand or to alter its scope, it must first amend its governing documents in accordance with the applicable legislation and its by-laws.

---

[42] This principle is articulated in *Wasauksing First Nation v. Wasausink Lands Inc.*, [2002] 3 C.N.L.R. 287 (Ont. S.C.J.), where at para. 349 the court held that "[a]s a matter of corporate law, [the not-for-profit corporation] must use those assets in a manner consistent with its corporate objects, and its directors have fiduciary obligations to ensure that such is the case. If a corporation applies its assets in a fashion not consistent with its objects there is not a breach of trust; rather, there is an act that is *ultra vires* the corporation, i.e., beyond its powers".

[43] See *Angus v. R. Angus Alberta Ltd.* (1988), 58 Alta. L.R. (2d) 76 at para. 52 (C.A.), where the court applies the principle as stated in *Cullerne v. London & Suburban Gen. Permanent Bldg. Soc.* (1890), 25 Q.B.D. 485 (C.A.): "But if a director acting *ultra vires*, i.e. not only beyond his own power, but also beyond any power the company can confer upon him, parts with money of the company, I fail to see on what principle the fact that he acted *bona fide* and with the approval of a majority of the shareholders can avail him as a defence to an action by the company to compel him to replace the money".

[44] *Ibid.* at para. 47: "Directors owe a duty to the shareholders to act according to law and according to the provisions of the memorandum and articles of association. Misapplication of company funds in breach of that duty in furtherance of an *ultra vires* scheme is treated as a breach of fiduciary duty. The directors are trustees of the money misapplied and their liability for breach of trust is the same as that of any other trustee. They must recoup the loss or compensate the company for it, with interest".

[45] See Hugh M. Kelly, Q.C. and Mark R. Frederick, *Duties and Responsibilities of Directors of Non-Profit Corporations* (Toronto: Canadian Society of Association Executives, 1999) at 10. The Canadian Society of Association Executives recommends, as a best practice, that each directors' meeting include "at least some education" about the operation of the corporation to improve each director's understanding of how the organization's purpose is articulated in action.

[46] See Appendix I: "Checklist A: Considerations Before Becoming A Director"; and "Checklist D: Once Appointed to the Board".

E. The Standard of Care for Directors

1. General

The standard of care is the level of competency a director is required to meet. Whenever a director fails to meet the standard of care, that director may be found liable for damages that result from the breach.

The standard of care for directors of not-for-profit corporations and charities is not uniform, and it differs in some cases from the standard of care applicable to for-profit corporations. Both provincial and federal business corporations legislation have created a statutory objective standard of care, namely, the care, diligence, and skill that a reasonably prudent person would exercise in comparable circumstances.[47] In respect of not-for-profit corporations, only some jurisdictions have adopted similar legislation providing for an objective standard of care.[48] Where a legislated standard of care is provided, directors of not-for-profit organizations and charities will be held to that statutory standard, which, in most cases, is the same standard as that applied to for-profit corporations.[49]

Unless it is modified by statute, the standard of care is that found at common law.[50] The common law subjective standard of care demands not the standard of a reasonably prudent person but instead only requires that a director exercise that level of skill and diligence that can reasonably be expected from a director of his or her knowledge and experience. Arguably, the subjective standard creates a relatively low threshold; the Supreme Court of Canada recently described the common law standard of care as "a reasonably relaxed, subjective standard", as directors were judged according

---

[47] See, for example, *Canada Business Corporations Act*, *supra* note 35, s. 122; *Business Corporations Act*, R.S.A. 2000, c. B-9 at s. 122; *Business Corporations Act*, S.B.C. 2002, c. 57, s. 142; and *Business Corporations Act*, R.S.O. 1990 c. B-16, s. 134.

[48] *Society Act*, R.S.B.C. 1996, c. 433 at s. 25; *Corporations* Act, C.C.S.M. c. C225 at s. 109; *Corporations Act*, R.S.N.L. 1990, c. C-36 at s. 203; and *Non-profit Corporation Act 1995*, S.S. 1995, c. N-4.2 at s. 109.

[49] See, e.g., the Federal Court of Appeal decision in *Wheeliker*, *supra* note 31, where, at para. 46, the court stated: "I agree with counsel for the appellant that the rationale for subsection 227.1(1) [of the *Income Tax Act*] is the ultimate accountability of the directors of a company for the deduction and remittance of employees' taxes and that such accountability cannot depend on whether the company is a profit or not-for-profit company or, I would add, whether the directors are paid or not or whether they are nominal but active or merely passive directors. All directors of all companies are liable for their failure if they do not meet the single standard of care provided for in subsection 227.1(3) of the Act. The flexibility is in the application of the standard since the qualifications, skills and attributes of a director will vary from case to case. So will the circumstances leading to and surrounding the failure to hold and remit the sums due."

[50] The leading case establishing a subjective standard for directors at common law is *Re City Equitable Fire Insurance Co. Ltd.*, [1925] 1 Ch. 407 at 428 (Eng. C.A.), where Romer J. stated, "[a] director need not exhibit in the performance of his duties a greater degree of skill than may reasonably be expected from a person of his knowledge and experience".

to their own personal skills, knowledge, abilities, and capacities.[51] However, in the case of highly skilled or experienced directors, such as lawyers, accountants, or engineers, the standard is raised to the level of their skill and experience.[52] This "professional standard of care" is doubly hazardous to directors who are not aware that the law may demand the same standard of conduct from their voluntary contribution to a board of directors as that demanded of them in their professional practices.

2. The Director as Fiduciary

As with for-profit corporations, directors of not-for-profit corporations and charities are in a fiduciary relationship to the corporation. A fiduciary relationship is characterized by the duties of loyalty, utmost good faith, and the avoidance of conflicts of interest.[53] The same obligations as those set out in Chapter 2 for directors of for-profit corporations also generally apply to

---

[51] *Peoples Department Stores Inc (Trustee of). v. Wise*, [2004] 3 S.C.R. 461 at para. 59.

[52] This point has not been directly considered in Canadian courts in the context of not-for-profit corporations, although the general principle that a subjective standard of care for directors may be "adjusted upward" for professionals has been acknowledged: see *Soper v. Canada*, [1997] F.C.J. No. 881 (F.C.A.) at para. 33.

[53] See *Canadian Aero Service Ltd. v. O'Malley*, [1974] S.C.R. 592 at para. 24 ("*Canadian Aero*"). See also *Austin v. Habitat Development Ltd.*, (1992), 114 N.S.R. (2d) 379 at para. 13 (C.A.), where the court cites with approval Mark Vincent Ellis in *Fiduciary Duties in Canada* (Don Mills, Ont: Richard DeBoo, 1988; 1990 Cumulative Supplement):

> [t]he reposing of trust and confidence, once accepted, impresses the fiduciary with a duty to act in a circumspect manner toward the beneficiary. This duty is aptly described as one of utmost good faith (*uberminae fides*) which itself imports a requirement that the fiduciary act toward the beneficiary with a heightened sense of loyalty and fidelity.
>
> ... the law will strictly enforce this responsibility of faithfulness, loyalty and conformity to the instructions of the beneficiary: An examination of the case law in this court and in the courts of other like jurisdictions on the fiduciary duties ... shows the pervasiveness of a strict ethic in this area of the law. (*Canadian Aero Service Ltd. v. O'Malley* (1973), 40 D.L.R. (3d) 371 at 382 (S.C.C.)) ...
>
> The law requires the fiduciary to act in a manner consistent with the best interests of the beneficiary in all matters related to the undertaking of trust and confidence. As a corollary to the heightened degree of loyalty required, the actions of the fiduciary will be viewed with a strictness unknown to most other areas of law. It is the fact of a departure from adherence to the beneficiary's best interests, rather than an evaluation of the fiduciary's motive in the departure, that constitutes a breach of fiduciary duty. It is in this sense that the absence of malice will not validate a repugnant act.

not-for-profit corporations.[54] However, a higher or different standard may apply in the following circumstances.

(a) Conflicts of Interest

A conflict of interest occurs where a personal interest is sufficiently connected with public or professional duties that it results in a reasonable apprehension that the personal interest may influence the exercise of professional or public responsibilities.[55] Conflicts of interest can arise for directors when they or their friends or family stand to benefit financially from the actions of the board of directors, or when a director serves two or more organizations that may have adverse interests.[56] As conflicts of interest can be both direct and indirect, directors must be vigilant in thinking about and identifying possible personal conflicts of interest.

The common law prohibits directors, as fiduciaries of the corporation, from having a personal interest in any contract or transaction of the corporation. It does not matter if the contract is entered into for the benefit of the corporation and is in good faith; the prohibition against personal interests is almost absolute.[57] The sole exception at common law is a situation where the conflict was fully disclosed and properly approved or ratified at a general

---

[54] Ronald Davis, *Directors' Liability in Canada*, looseleaf (Vancouver: STP, 2005) at §8–9. See also *Ontario (Public Guardian and Trustee) v. National Society for Abused Women and Children*, [2002] O.J. No. 607 (Sup. Ct.) at para. 11, where a breach of fiduciary duty by the directors of a charitable organization is analyzed on the same fiduciary principles as those applied to for-profit breaches. In this case, three directors of a charitable corporation, who had made other egregious breaches of their fiduciary duties, entered into a fundraising contract with a company that employed two of the directors. The court held at para. 11 that this was "a clear conflict of interest and breach of their fiduciary duty as directors of a charitable organization" and ordered that they repay all monies received.

[55] Daphne A. Dukelow and Betsy Nuse, *The Dictionary of Canadian Law*, 2nd ed. (Scarborough, Ontario: Carswell, 1995) at 230.

[56] See, e.g., *Humane Society of Canada for the Protection of Animals & the Environment v. Humane Society of the United States*, 1997 WL 1915388 (Ont. Gen. Div.), at para. 25, where the court held that Irwin, "was a director of the alleged debtor company (HSC) and an agent of the alleged creditor (HSUS). He was fully aware of the dispute over these claims and chose to remove over $1,000,000.00 from the bank account of the corporation of which he was a director to pay on account of the disputed claim. I cannot imagine a more glaring conflict of interest or a more egregious breach of fiduciary duty. It demonstrated an overweening arrogance of a type seldom seen".

[57] This principle is established in the leading House of Lords decision, *Aberdeen Railway v. Blaikie Bros* (1854), [1843–60] All E.R. 249 at 252 (Scot. H.L.), where the court states, "[i]t is a rule of universal application that no one having such duties to discharge shall be allowed to enter into such engagements in which he has or can have a personal interest conflicting or which possibly may conflict with the interests of those whom he is bound to protect".

meeting of the shareholders or members.[58] Otherwise, the director is liable to account for all of the profits made or the benefits received as a result of the self-dealing. This exception has been modified and expanded by safe harbour provisions in modern corporate legislation in the context of for-profit corporations.[59] In the context of not-for-profit corporations, however, the strict common law rule against self-dealing governs.

In the case of charitable organizations operating in Ontario, the law will treat the directors as trustees and will require court approval of conflicts of interest and any remuneration of directors. Other jurisdictions in Canada do not have the same legislation regarding charitable organizations, and it is unclear whether this same principle will be applied elsewhere in Canada.

In Ontario, the *Charities Accounting Act*, which covers any corporation incorporated for a religious, educational, charitable, or public purpose, regardless of the status of the corporation under the *Income Tax Act*, deems the corporations it covers to be trustees.[60] Under trust law, conflicts of interest and remuneration are only permitted if they are approved by the court. Declaration of the conflict, board approval, or member approval is insufficient. Following this principle, the Ontario court held that the directors of the Toronto Humane Society were to be treated as trustees and, therefore, the substantial salary drawn by two of the directors breached their duty to the corporation.[61]

The Ontario courts have similarly held that a director of a charitable foundation breached his duty by using the foundation to transfer his money for personal income tax advantages. As the director breached his duty as a trustee, there was no need to show that the foundation suffered damages before the director was personally liable.[62]

---

[58] See, e.g., *Canadian Aero*, *supra* at note 53 at 608, citing with approval *Regal (Hastings) Ltd. v. Gulliver*, [1942] 1 All E.R. 378 at 389 (H.L.) as follows: "[i]n the result, I am of opinion that the directors standing in a fiduciary relationship to Regal in regard to the exercise of their powers as directors, and having obtained these shares by reason and only by reason of the fact that they were directors of Regal and in the course of the execution of that office, are accountable for the profits which they have made out of them. The equitable rule laid down in *Keech v. Sandford*, *supra*, and *Ex p. James* (1803), 8 Ves. 337 [L.C.], and similar authorities applies . . . in full force. It was contended that these cases were distinguishable by reason of the fact that it was impossible for Regal to get the shares owing to lack of funds, and that the directors in taking the shares were really acting as members of the public. I cannot accept this argument. It was impossible for the *cestui que trust* in *Keech v. Sandford* to obtain the lease, nevertheless the trustee was accountable. The suggestion that the directors were applying simply as members of the public is a travesty of the facts. They could, had they wished, have protected themselves by a resolution (either antecedent or subsequent) of the Regal shareholders in a general meeting. In default of such approval, the liability to account must remain" [emphasis added].

[59] *Business Corporations Act*, R.S.A. 2000, c. B-9, s. 110; *Corporations Act*, R.S.O. 1990, c. C-38, s. 71; and *Business Corporations Act*, R.S.O. 1990, c. B-16, s. 132.

[60] R.S.O. 1990, c. C-10, s. 1(2).

[61] *Re Public Trustee and Toronto Humane Society et al.* (1987), 40 D.L.R. (4th) 111 (Ont. H.C.).

[62] *Re David Feldman Charitable Foundation*, (1987) 58 O.R. (2d) 626 (Ont. Surr. Ct.).

It is unclear whether this doctrine would be applied in other Canadian jurisdictions, as the Ontario courts relied not only on applicable provincial statutes but also on the broad inherent jurisdiction of Canadian courts in charitable matters.[63] This approach was adopted in Yukon, where a director of a charitable organization was found to have breached his fiduciary duties to a society by proposing and supporting board of director resolutions transferring land to him.[64]

While a court may retroactively approve remuneration or a conflict of interest,[65] a preferable practice is to proactively apply to the court to ask permission for them.[66] The remuneration of a director of a charitable organization should likely also be pre-approved by the court, even if the director is acting in two capacities and is receiving remuneration in the non-director capacity (for instance, as the executive director or as legal counsel). The same is true for other transactions that constitute a conflict of interest.[67] This view supports a strong practical argument against having directors of charitable organizations in dual roles unless it is necessary.

Whenever a potential conflict of interest arises, the director must determine if the conflict is one whereby the director may profit at the expense of the corporation or if both parties can benefit from the transaction. Even if a conflict is disclosed and approved, a director is not permitted to profit at the expense of the corporation.[68] If the conflict is one whereby both parties may benefit, such as a transaction with a related business, the director should notify the board of directors in writing, detailing the potential conflict of interest. The conflict must be approved or ratified as discussed above. The written notification and any approval or ratification should be reflected in

---

[63] *Re Royal Society's Charitable Trusts*, [1956] 1 Ch. 87.

[64] *Yukon Youth Centre Society (Receiver of) v. Leonard*, [1994] Y.J. No. 90 (YTSC).

[65] See, e.g., *Faith Haven Bible Training Centre (Re)* (1988), 29 E.T.R. 198 (Ont. Surr. Ct).

[66] As was the case in *Re Harold Fox Education Fund v. Public Trustee* (1989), 69 O.R. (2d) 742 (H.C.J). See Appendix I, "Checklist F: Conflicts of Interest".

[67] See, e.g., *Native People of Thunder Bay Development Corp. v. Pierre*, 1988 CarswellOnt 2745 (Dist. Ct.), aff'd 1989 WL 934347 (Ont. Div. Ct.). In this case, a woman was a tenant of a not-for-profit housing corporation. Later, she obtained a job as a manager of the Indian Friendship Centre, which brought her into contact with a large number of other tenants of this landlord. Their experiences convinced her that the corporation needed to improve its procedure by, for instance, providing written notices of rental increases to the tenants, as required by the *Landlord and Tenant Act* (Ontario). She was elected to the board of directors but had little success effecting change. Finally, out of protest, she stopped paying rent. She did not explain to the board why she was no longer paying rent, even though her name came up on the arrears list at board meetings. The court found that, but for her role as a director, she may well have been entitled to stop paying rent. The court stated at para. 16, "[i]n this case, the tenant was not just a tenant, but was a director of the corporation. As a director of the corporation, she stood in a fiduciary position to the corporation. She owed a duty of loyalty and care. She had surrendered her right to remain quiet when she was aware of a situation which was injurious to the corporation".

[68] See Chapter 2 for a more detailed discussion on conflicts of interest.

the minutes of the next board meeting, and a copy of the notification should be appended to the minutes.[69]

F. Statutory Liabilities

1. Liabilities

The statutory duties applicable to directors of for-profit corporations, which are discussed in Chapter 2, generally also apply to directors of not-for-profit corporations and charities.[70] The purpose of this section is to outline some of the additional statutory liabilities confronting directors of not-for-profit corporations, including charities.

Five provinces have enacted legislation regulating fund-raising activities: Alberta, Saskatchewan, Manitoba, Ontario, and Prince Edward Island.[71] This legislation applies to the solicitation of funds for charitable purposes in each of the legislating jurisdictions. Directors may be personally liable for each breach of the legislation by the corporation.[72] Directors should be familiar with legislation for each jurisdiction in which the corporation solicits funds.

All provincial jurisdictions in Canada have enacted gaming legislation.[73] Not-for-profits raising funds through gaming activities, such as bingos, raffles, pull tickets, or casinos must comply with the applicable gaming legislation. Provincial statutes contain penalty provisions that can be assessed against a director personally for the corporation's failure to comply with them. Directors should ensure that gaming activities are undertaken only if they are satisfied the board is informed about the legislative and procedural requirements and that those activities will be in compliance with the applicable legal requirements.

---

[69] See Appendix I: "Checklist F: Conflicts of Interest"; "Checklist G: Board Meetings"; and "Checklist I: Risk Management".

[70] In *Wheeliker, supra* note 31, it was held that directors of not-for-profit corporations could be personally liable under s. 227.1 of the *Income Tax Act, supra* note 7, for failure to withhold and remit various tax obligations in the same way and to the same standard as directors of for-profit corporations.

[71] See Appendix II, "Table 2: Charitable Fundraising Legislation", for an overview of this legislation, including its scope of application and the penalty provisions in respect of directors' liability. See also Appendix I, "Checklist I: Risk Management".

[72] See Appendix II, "Table 2: Charitable Fundraising Legislation". See also Appendix I, "Checklist I: Risk Management".

[73] See Appendix II, "Table 3: Gaming Legislation". See also Appendix I, "Checklist I: Risk Management".

2. Defences

Due diligence, namely, exercising the care, diligence, and skill of a prudent person, is a defence to the statutory personal liability of a director. Acting in good faith is insufficient to discharge this standard unless it is expressly provided for in the applicable legislation.[74] Due diligence requires that directors aptly oversee the affairs of the corporation, make inquiries if indications of improper conduct appear, and take effective action in response to such conduct.[75] Reliance on professional advisors,[76] officers,[77] or staff will only absolve a director of personal liability if the reliance is reasonable in the circumstances.[78]

---

[74] See *Meadow Lake Swimming Pool Committee Inc. v. R*, [1999] G.S.T.C. 96 (T.C.C. (Informal Procedure)) at paras. 21 and 22, where the court held that the failure of the non-profit corporation to inquire about GST liabilities in respect of payments received from the municipality meant that the directors had not been duly diligent.

[75] See *Callaghan v. Jack*, 2004 BCPC 85 at para. 115 (B.C. Prov. Ct. (Small Claims Div.)), where the court held that the directors of the Society satisfied the standard of care when voluntarily winding up the Society. The directors wound up the Society in accordance with a resolution of the members of the Society in response to a past director who alleged that the Society owed her money. Before ending the Society, the directors made diligent attempts to locate written evidence of such a loan, asked the past director to prove the loan, had the financial statements audited, and sought legal advice.

See also *Parenteau c. R*, 2004 C.C.I. 724 (Procédire Générale) at para. 35, where the directors of a not-for-profit organization were similarly held to satisfy the standard of reasonably cautious directors by taking immediate action to remedy the organization's failure to remit payroll deductions once the failure was uncovered.

Contra, *Wheeliker, supra* note 31, whereby the directors of the not-for-profit corporation failed to meet the standard of care when the corporation failed to remit source deductions. The court held, at para. 49, that the directors had a positive duty to ensure that the remittances were made once they learned of the corporation's financial difficulties.

[76] See *Bathgate v. National Hockey League Pension Society* (1994), 16 O.R. (3d) 761 (C.A.), leave to appeal refused, [1994] 2 S.C.R. (vii), where the court found in favour of the trustee of the Society noting at para. 56 that "[t]he question of entitlement to the surplus funds was complex. We note, however, that actuarial and legal advice was obtained from apparently competent and reliable sources before the decision ... was made".

[77] See *Blair v. Consolidated Enfield Corp.*, [1995] 4 S.C.R. 5 at para. 69, where, when considering the *Business Corporations Act* (Ontario) provision relieving a director of liability if, in good faith, the director relied on professional advice, the court stated:

> I should also mention that s. 135(4) codifies the anterior common law director duties of care, in which a director would be absolved of liability if he or she relied upon the work of an official of the company (in the present appeal, corporate counsel) if such work is properly left to that official and, in the absence of grounds for suspicion, the director is justified in trusting that official to perform the duty: *Re City Equitable Fire Insurance Co.*, [1925] Ch. 407, per Romer J., aff'd [1925] Ch. 500 (C.A.). Consequently, directors will be held liable for the misdeeds of officials of the company only if they have been personally negligent or if they have acted unreasonably in relying on an official whose honesty or competence they have reason to suspect.

[78] See *Wheeliker, supra* note 31 at para. 56, where the court held it was insufficient that the directors relied on an ostensibly qualified manager as they had concerns about his performance. Similarly, a belief that the corporation would later be able to cover the debts did not satisfy the directors' responsibilities (para. 57).

G. Insurance and Indemnification of Directors

Given that directors of not-for-profit corporations can be exposed to personal liability just as directors of for-profit corporations can, they should exercise the same caution in ensuring that the corporation has adequate directors' liability insurance and indemnification provisions.[79] Indemnification provisions are only as meaningful as the resources the corporation has available with which to provide indemnification. With respect to not-for-profit corporations, it is particularly important to evaluate the resources of the corporation when assessing this risk factor.

It is uncertain if, at common law, a charity may purchase directors' and officers' liability insurance without prior court approval.[80] In some jurisdictions, this ambiguity and the concomitant practical inconvenience have been resolved through legislation.[81] The applicable provisions permit the purchase of liability insurance for directors, subject to certain restrictions.[82] For instance, insurance is limited to instances where the director acted honestly and in good faith.[83] In some jurisdictions, the legislation expressly requires the charity to purchase insurance only to the extent that it is reasonably necessary and does not unduly impair the purpose of the organization.[84] This latter restriction is consistent with the general requirement that charities use their resources solely to further their charitable objects. Charities should ensure that directors' liability insurance complies either with the applicable legislated provision or, in the absence of legislation, with the approach at common law.

---

[79] See Appendix I, "Checklist J: Liability Indemnification and Insurance". See also the discussion on directors' insurance in Chapter 2.

[80] See, e.g., Terrance S. Carter, "Advising the Charitable Client: Pro-Active Legal Risk Management Advice" (Paper presented to the Law Society of Upper Canada, Special Lecture Series, 1996 Estates: Planning, Administration and Litigation, November 1996) at 1-36–1-38, where he articulates his understanding of the then position of the Public Guardian and Trustee of Ontario as follows: "since a director of a charity is not entitled to receive any remuneration or benefit from the charity without court approval, and since the placement of directors' and officers' insurance would provide a benefit to a director in the event that a claim was made, then before charitable moneys can be used to purchase director and officer liability insurance, court approval would have to be obtained".

See also Appendix I, "Checklist J: Liability Indemnification and Insurance".

[81] See Appendix II, "Table 4: Insurance and Indemnification Provisions in Respect of Charitable Organizations".

[82] See, e.g., *Society Act*, R.S.B.C. 1996, c. 433 at s. 30(5); *Approved Acts of Executors and Trustees*, O. Reg. 4/01, s. 2(2) ("Approved Acts").

[83] *Ibid.*

[84] See Approved Acts, *supra* note 82.

III. Conclusion

As corporate governance in all sectors continues to fall under public scrutiny, the spectre of personal liability may be sufficient to dampen the enthusiasm of a prospective director of a not-for-profit corporation. However, an understanding of the potential risks, coupled with a commitment to meet the required standards is the key to proactively avoiding liability. Directors who are motivated to better fulfill their responsibilities and to hold their fellow directors and the corporation's staff to account also benefit the organization with their increased vigilance. With due care and attention, the risks associated with directorship can be managed and the benefits more thoroughly enjoyed by directors, the organizations they serve, and their community.

APPENDIX I

Checklists

Checklist A: Considerations Before Becoming a Director

Prior to agreeing to become a Director, the party should consider the following:

1. Why does the party want to become a Director?
2. What does the party hope to achieve as a Director?
3. What knowledge of the not-for-profit does the party have or require to enable him or her to make an informed decision to serve or not to serve?
4. What are the objectives, vision/mission statement, governing documents, and by-laws of the not-for-profit?
5. What is the standing of the not-for-profit in the community?
6. Who is the Chair? Who are the Directors?
7. How well does the Board of Directors work?
8. Is there a set period of service for Directors?
9. If Directors have recently left the Board, other than at the end of the usual service period, why did they leave?
10. If there is a high staff turnover, especially for the position of Executive Director, determine why.

11. What is the tenure and scope of the position of Executive Director?

12. Why does the not-for-profit want the party to be a Director (contacts, expertise, fund-raising, etc.)?

13. How does the party plan to fulfill the expectations of the not-for-profit?

14. Has the party advised other Boards being served of his or her intention to serve on this Board? Are there real or potential conflicts of interest in serving on both or more Boards?

Checklist B: Once Agreeing to Consider Serving

Once the party agrees to consider serving on the Board of Directors, he or she should gather further information on the not-for-profit:

1. Request copies of recent financial statements and critically review them. Have the financial statements been audited?

2. Request copies of all filings that have been done for the not-for-profit.

3. What property does the not-for-profit hold?

4. What are the not-for-profit's current liabilities and assets? What are the not-for-profit's sources of funding?

Checklist C: Workings of the Board

The party should know the following information about the workings of the Board of Directors:

1. What is the rotation of Directors?

2. Are there always new Directors coming on the Board as other Directors are retiring?

3. What is the integration time for new Directors?

4. Is a new Director introduced to the exiting Director(s) for information to be transferred?

5. What is the minimum number of meetings the Board of Directors is required to hold in a year?

6. Over the last two years, have the required number of meetings been held?
7. What is the reporting structure?
8. Is there an Executive Committee, and if so, what is the composition of the Executive Committee and of other committees?
9. What is the role of the Executive Committee vis-à-vis the Board of Directors?
10. What is the role of non-executive committees?
11. How many committees are there? What are the mandates for each of them?
12. What are the scope and duties of committee members?
13. On how many committees is a Director expected to serve?
14. What is the tenure of Directors for all committees?

Checklist D: Once Appointed to the Board

Once appointed to the Board, the party should do the following:

1. Request written confirmation from the Board of Directors that the party's appointment as an incoming Director is valid.
2. Request an organizational chart setting out the positions held in the organization; the names of those holding the positions; and the reporting structure of the Executive Director and other staff.
3. Review the governing documents and by-laws of the not-for-profit at least annually.
4. Ensure that prior to the not-for-profit expanding or altering its scope, the governing documents have been amended in accordance with its by-laws and with the applicable legislation.

Checklist E: Financial Impact of Serving as a Director

The party should be aware of the following:

1. Does the not-for-profit expect financial contributions from its Directors in addition to the free hours and expertise they provide?

2. If money donations are expected, how much is expected, how often, and for what purpose?
3. Are incidental expenses covered? If so, to whom are expenses submitted and within what time frame are they paid?
4. Must the Board preauthorize the expenses of Directors over a specified threshold amount?

Checklist F: Conflicts of Interest

In respect of conflicts of interest ("conflicts") and potential conflicts, the party should consider the following:

1. Is there a mechanism in place to ensure that Directors are reminded on a regular basis to disclose conflicts or potential conflicts? (It is suggested that disclosure documentation be completed by all Directors at least once a year.)
2. What, if any, conflicts currently exist and what possible future conflicts may exist? (The full disclosure of possible and potential conflicts is mandatory.)
3. Have other Directors with a known conflict of interest or a suspected conflict of interest formally disclosed it? Is such disclosure noted in the minutes? If not, why not? Has any known conflict of interest been approved or ratified, and does the affected director have a copy of such?
4. Is court approval required for conflicts of interest and/or remuneration?

Checklist G: Board Meetings

As part of a Director's fiduciary duty to the not-for-profit, it is expected that the Director will attend and participate in meetings, including voting at them. Directors should consider the following:

(a) Frequency of Meetings

1. Is the frequency of meetings sufficient for the Board of Directors to manage the not-for-profit's affairs? In addition, is enough time allotted for the Directors to discuss issues, ask questions, follow up on issues from previous meetings and decisions, hear and consider reports from committees, and actively participate in the meetings?

(b) Notice of Meeting

2. Have the Directors received proper notice of the meeting? Can Directors waive notice of the meeting?

3. Has sufficient time been given between the date of notice and the meeting to allow Directors to prepare for the meeting?

4. Are special meetings required for particular issues?

(c) Agenda

5. Have Directors been invited to place items on the meeting agenda for discussion or consideration?

(d) In Place of Meeting

6. If the Directors are asked to sign a written resolution in place of a meeting, have all of the directors signed it?

(e) Location of Meeting

7. Where is the meeting to be held and is the location for it appropriate?

(f) Preparation for Meeting

8. Have the Directors received, in a timely fashion, pre-meeting documents, such as minutes of previous meetings, briefing notes, draft resolutions, reports, or other information to enable them to prepare thoroughly for the meeting?

9. Have the Directors reviewed the minutes of the previous meeting and notified the Chair, in writing, of their concerns?

10. Have the Directors not in attendance received copies of the minutes of the meeting and had an opportunity to record any dissents?

(g) Attendance at Meeting

11. What quorum of Directors is necessary at meetings?

12. What steps are taken if there is not a quorum?

13. Do the by-laws require the physical presence of Directors at meetings or communication by an appropriate alternate means? (By-laws should provide for attendance by electronic means.)

14. If a Director cannot attend a meeting, is that Director's non-attendance stated in writing?

(h) Voting

15. Have dissenting Directors voiced their dissent? Has their dissent been recorded?

16. Does the Director always vote (unless excluded by reason of conflict of interest or by another prohibition)?

(i) Notice to Board

17. Has the Director sent a letter by registered mail to the Board of the not-for-profit organization if the Chair refused to have noted in the minutes a conflict, a disclosure, a dissent, and the names of Directors who refrained from voting?

(j) Meeting Materials

18. Where are the minutes and other records of the not-for-profit kept? Is the location appropriate? Who has access to these materials and why do they have access?

19. Does the Director maintain a binder of all minutes and important documents? (Such a binder should be retained for at least ten years after his or her departure as a Director.)

Checklist H: Professional Opinions

Has the Director insisted on

1. Written professional opinions from specialists on whose advice the Board is expected to act?

2. Written legal opinions for any important step to be taken by the not-for-profit?

Checklist I: Risk Management

In respect of risk management the Director should ascertain the following:

1. Does the not-for-profit have a risk management committee to advise the Board of potential risks?

2. Is the Executive Director knowledgeable about the necessity and obligation to report on risks to the Board and how often such reports are to be provided? Does the Board take the necessary

action upon the receipt of such a report from the Executive Director?

3. Is the Board aware of legislation regulating fund-raising activities or any other activities carried on by the not-for-profit? Has appropriate professional advice been sought to interpret the legislation, and is such advice followed?

4. Who gives professional advice (legal, insurance, medical, engineering, etc.) to the Board on risk management and mitigation strategies?

5. Do the Directors and staff comply with the duty of confidentiality for all corporate information? Does the not-for-profit have a communications strategy and follow it?

6. Do the Directors always take the appropriate measures to avoid a conflict of interest and note the measures that have been taken?

7. Do the Directors ensure that the not-for-profit has internal controls for cheque writing, other financial transactions, the deduction and remittance of employee taxes and G.S.T., and are reports of the status of each one of them reported to the appropriate committee, with that committee reporting to the Board?

8. Does the not-for-profit have an appropriate investment policy and adhere to it?

9. Does the Board properly delegate the authority to enter into contracts on behalf of the not-for-profit, and is the Board involved in the formulation and execution of all material contracts?

10. Who monitors the issuance of tax receipts and ensures that the value of them is accurate?

11. Are committee chairs required to report to the Board on a regular basis and do they?

12. Who ensures that committee reports go to the Board of Directors and that the Board of Directors gives its approval for the actions taken by all committees?

Checklist J: Liability Indemnification and Insurance

The Director should be aware of the following:

1. Will Directors be indemnified by the organization or by its sister organization, and does the not-for-profit have the funds to do so? If so, for how long?
2. Has the Director requested in writing the verification of indemnification by the not-for-profit and received it? This verification should not be just from the local chapter of the not-for-profit but from the national body if the not-for-profit operates in more than one jurisdiction.
3. Is there insurance in place to protect the Directors? If there isn't, has the Director insisted in writing that the corporation put insurance in place? If there is, what are the terms of the policy? (The Director should obtain a copy of the policy.)
4. Has any required approval for the insurance been obtained?
5. Does the insurance coverage continue to cover the Directors for terms they serve after they leave the Board?
6. Does the Director understand the terms and the duration of the insurance?

APPENDIX II

Tables of Legislation

Please see below for the current dates of the legislation cited in this table.[1]

Table 1: Legislation Providing for the Incorporation of Not-for-Profit Organizations

Canada	*Canada Corporations Act*, R.S.C. 1970, c. C-32	**s. 154(1):** outlines the application process for "corporations without share capital". The purpose of these corporations is described as: "carrying on, without pecuniary gain to its members, objects, to which the legislative authority of the Parliament of Canada extends, of a national, patriotic, religious, philanthropic, charitable, scientific, artistic, social, professional or sporting character, or the like objects".

[1] Canada: *Canada Corporations Act* is current as of March 3, 2006.

Alberta: legislation is current as of July 17, 2006.

British Columbia: legislation is current as of July 26, 2006.

Manitoba: legislation is current as of July 15, 2006.

New Brunswick: legislation is current as of June 21, 2006.

Newfoundland and Labrador: legislation is current as of July 21, 2006.

Northwest Territories: legislation is current as of June 20, 2006.

Nova Scotia: legislation is current as of June 22, 2006.

Nunavut: legislation is current as of May 31, 2006.

Ontario: legislation is current as of July 26, 2006.

Prince Edward Island: legislation is current as of June 14, 2006.

Quebec: legislation is current as of June 1, 2006.

Saskatchewan: The *Co-operatives Act* is current as of June 29, 2006; *The Non-Profit Corporations Act, 1995* is current as of June 21, 2006.

Yukon: legislation is current as of June 15, 2006.

Alberta	*Companies Act,* R.S.A. 2000, c. C-21	**s. 200(1):** To register a charitable organization as a limited company, the association must be formed "for the purpose of promoting art, science, religion, charity or any other useful object", and must also have the intention of applying the profits back into the association. **s. 202(1):** This section adds the purpose of "promoting recreation among its members" to the listed purposes in s. 200(1).
	Business Corporations Act, R.S.A. 2000, c. B-9	**s. 16(1):** "A corporation has the capacity and, subject to this Act, the rights, powers and privileges of a natural person". **s. 17(2):** "A corporation shall not carry on any business or exercise any power that it is restricted by its articles from carrying on or exercising".
	Cooperatives Act, S.A. 2001, c. C-28.1	**s. 3(1):** "Three or more persons who intend to be members of the cooperative may apply to the Director to become incorporated as a cooperative. **(2)** One or more cooperatives, with or without other persons who intend to be members of the cooperative, may apply to the Director to become incorporated as a cooperative. **(3)** A person may not apply to incorporate a cooperative if (a) that person is an individual under 18 years of age, (b) the person (i) has the status of bankrupt, (ii) is a dependent adult under the *Dependent Adults Act,* (iii) is a formal patient under the *Mental Health Act,* or (iv) is the subject of or detained by a warrant of committal or assessment order, or is detained otherwise, under the *Criminal Code*". **s. 388:** "The articles of a non-profit housing cooperative must provide that the primary object of the cooperative is to carry on business as a non-profit continuing housing cooperative or non-profit home ownership cooperative and to provide housing or housing-related facilities to its members together with ancillary services and facilities". **s. 389(1):** "The following restrictions apply to non-profit housing cooperatives: (a) its activities must be carried on without the purpose of gain for its members; . . ."
	Societies Act, R.S.A. 2000, c. S-14	**s. 3(1):** "Five or more persons may become incorporated under this Act for any benevolent, philanthropic, charitable, provident, scientific, artistic, literary, social, educational, agricultural, sporting or other useful purpose, but not for the purpose of carrying on a trade or business".

British Columbia	*Business Corporations Act*, S.B.C. 2002, c. 57	**s. 10(1):** One or more persons may form a company by entering into an incorporation agreement and by filing an incorporation application with the registrar. **s. 12(2)(a):** The articles of a company must set out every restriction on the businesses that may be carried on by the company and on the powers that the company may exercise.
	Society Act, R.S.B.C. 1996, c. 433	**s. 2(1):** A society may be incorporated for any lawful purpose or purposes such as national, patriotic, religious, philanthropic, charitable, provident, scientific, fraternal, benevolent, artistic, educational, social, professional, agricultural, sporting, or other useful purposes, but not for . . . (f) the purpose of carrying on a business, trade, industry, or profession for profit or gain.
	Cooperative Association Act, S.B.C. 1999, c. 28	**s. 8(1):** An association must be organized and operated and must carry on business on a cooperative basis. **s. 10(1):** Any three or more persons, eligible organizations, or both may be incorporated as an association to carry on any lawful business or activity on a cooperative basis. **s. 12(d):** The memorandum must state the purpose of the association.
Manitoba	*Corporations Act*, C.C.S.M., c. C225	**s. 267(1):** For corporations without share capital, there must be prior approval of the minister before filing, and the corporation must "restrict its undertaking to one that is only of a patriotic, religious, philanthropic, charitable, educational, agricultural, scientific, literary, historical, artistic, social, professional, fraternal, sporting or athletic nature or the like".
New Brunswick	*Companies Act*, R.S.N.B. 1973, c. C-13	**s. 18(1):** Application for the incorporation of any charitable, philanthropic, temperance, religious, social, political, literary, educational, athletic, or other like purposes or for the purpose of promoting economic development.
	Co-operative Associations Act, S.N.B. 1978, c. C-22.1	**s. 2:** "The purpose of this Act is to provide for the incorporation, inspection, examination and supervision of associations operated on a co-operative basis".

Newfoundland and Labrador	*Corporations Act*, R.S.N.L. 1990, c. C-36	**Part XXI:** addresses corporations without share capital. s. 420: states that corporations under this Part must "restrict its undertaking to one that is only of a patriotic, religious, philanthropic, charitable, educational, scientific, literary, historical, artistic, social, professional, fraternal, sporting or athletic nature or the like, including development associations".
Northwest Territories	*Societies Act*, R.S.N.W.T. 1988, c. S-11	**s. 2:** Any benevolent, philanthropic, charitable, religious, provident, scientific, artistic, literary, social, educational, sporting, or other useful purpose.
Nova Scotia	*Societies Act*, R.S.N.S. 1989, c. 435	**s. 3(1):** "A society may be incorporated under this Act to promote any benevolent, philanthropic, patriotic, religious, charitable, artistic, literary, educational, social, professional, recreational or sporting or any other useful object, but not for the purpose of carrying on any trade, industry or business".
Nunavut	*Societies Act* (Nunavut), R.S.N.W.T. 1988, c. S-11	**s. 2:** Any benevolent, philanthropic, charitable, religious, provident, scientific, artistic, literary, social, educational, sporting, or other useful purpose.
Ontario	*Corporations Act*, R.S.O. 1990, c. C-38	**s. 118:** "A corporation may be incorporated to which Part V applies or that has objects that are within the jurisdiction of the Province of Ontario". **s. 126(1):** "A corporation ... shall be carried on without the purpose of gain for its members and any profits or other accretions to the corporation shall be used in promoting its objects ..."
	Co-operative Corporations Act, R.S.O. 1990, c. C-35	**s. 4(1)** "A co-operative may be incorporated under this Act for any lawful objects to which the authority of the Legislature extends, except those of a corporation the incorporation of which is provided for in any other Act".
Prince Edward Island	*Companies Act*, R.S.P.E.I. 1988, c. C-14	**s. 89:** "The Minister may by letters patent grant a charter ... for the purpose of carrying on in Prince Edward Island, without pecuniary gain to its members, objects of a patriotic, religious, philanthropic, charitable, scientific, artistic, social, professional or sporting character, or the like".

	Co-operative Associations Act, R.S.P.E.I. 1988, c. C-23	**s. 2:** "Incorporation, inspection, examination and supervision of associations whose primary purpose is to provide service to their members and which belong to the people who use their services, the control of which rests equally with all their members, and the gains from which are distributed among the members in proportion to the use they make of these services".
Quebec	*Companies Act*, R.S.Q., c. C-38	**s. 4(1):** This part applies to every company constituted as a legal person under it.
	Cooperatives Act, R.S.Q., c. C-67.2	**s. 2:** Cooperatives whose objects come under the legislative authority of Quebec may be constituted under this title except for those cooperatives that are constituted to engage in the activities of a trust or savings company, for investment or venture purposes, or for purposes provided for in the Act respecting financial services cooperatives.
Saskatchewan	*Non-profit Corporations Act*, 1995, S.S. 1995, c. N-4.2.	**s. 15(1):** "A corporation has the capacity and, subject to this Act, the rights, powers and privileges of a natural person". **s. 16(2):** "No corporation shall carry on any activities or exercise any power that, by its articles, it is restricted from carrying on or exercising, and no corporation shall exercise any of its powers in a manner contrary to its articles".
	Co-operatives Act, S.S. 1996, c. C-37.3	**s. 3:** "For the purposes of this Act, a body corporate is organized, operated and administered on a co-operative basis where: (a) no member or delegate has more than one vote; (b) no member or delegate is entitled to vote by proxy; (c) its business is carried on primarily for the benefit of its members; (d) its membership is voluntary and available, without any artificial restriction or any unlawful basis of discrimination, to any person who can use its services and is willing to accept the responsibilities of membership; (e) the limit on the interest or dividends on share capital that it pays does not exceed the prescribed rate; and (f) any surplus or saving arising out of its operation is: (i) used to develop its business; (ii) used to provide or improve common services to members; (iii) distributed among members in proportion to their patronage with the co-operative; (iv) used to educate its members, officers or employees or the general public in the principles and techniques of economic and democratic co-operation; or (v) distributed to non-profit, charitable or benevolent organizations".

Yukon	*Societies Act*, R.S.Y. 2002, c. 206	**s. 3:** "Five or more persons may incorporate under this Act for any lawful purpose other than carrying on a trade or business".

Table 2: Charitable Fundraising Legislation

Alberta	*Charitable Fund-raising Act*, R.S.A. 2000, c. C-9	**s. 4(1):** This Act generally applies to all incorporated or unincorporated organizations that solicit funds for charitable purposes from persons in Alberta in excess of $25,000 a year or organizations that involve a fund-raising business. **s. 55(2) and (3):** Directors may be personally liable for any contravention by the corporation if they authorized, assented to, acquiesced to, or participated in the contravention. Penalty provision include fines from $1,000–$100,000 or three times the amount gained in the contravention or jail time.
Manitoba	*Charities Endorsement Act*, C.C.S.M., c. C-60	**s. 2:** This Act requires authorization for all solicitation for charitable purposes other than by religious denominations for themselves or solicitation from the members of the same organization. **s. 4:** Individuals who contravene the Act may be fined $50 and imprisoned for up to ten days, while corporations may be fined $500.
Ontario	*Charities Accounting Act*, R.S.O. 1990, c. C.10	**s. 2:** This Act applies to any corporation incorporated for a religious, educational, charitable, or public purpose. **s. 6:** The Act authorizes any person to complain to the court about how a charitable corporation solicited or used funds. While no specific penalty provisions for the corporation or directors are specified, the court is given the broad authority in s. 10 to make orders as appropriate.
Prince Edward Island	*Charities Act*, R.S.P.E.I. 1988, c. C-4	**s. 1(a):** This Act requires any organization soliciting funds for benevolent, educational, cultural, charitable, or religious purposes to register with the province and obtain authorization. **s. 10:** Persons who contravene the Act may be fined up to $500 and convicted of a summary offence.

Saskatchewan	*Charities Act*, R.S.P.E.I. 1988, c. C-4	**s. 2(b):** This Act applies with respect to any charity registered under the *Income Tax Act* as well as to any professional fund-raising business acting on behalf of the charity. **s. 46:** A first-time contravention of the Act carries a maximum penalty of $10,000 and one year in prison. Directors of corporations are expressly liable if they directed, authorized, assented to, acquiesced in, or participated in the offence.

Table 3: Gaming Legislation

Canada (Federal)	*Criminal Code*, R.S. 1985, c. C-46	**s. 207(1)(b):** Gaming activities are illegal under the *Criminal Code* unless an exception applies. This section permits charitable or religious organizations, provided they have been duly licensed by the federal or a provincial government, to conduct gaming activities wherein the proceeds are used to further the charitable or religious purposes. **s. 207(3):** The penalty for contravening the gaming provisions of the *Criminal Code* may constitute an indictable offence, liable to imprisonment of up to two years.
Alberta	*Gaming and Liquor Act*, R.S.A. 2000, c. G-1	**s. 102(1):** Expressly imposes any duties of the corporation under the Act on the directors of the corporation as well. **s. 120(1):** Directors may be personally liable for any contravention by the corporation if they authorized, assented to, acquiesced to, or participated in the contravention. **s. 117–119:** Penalty provisions range from a maximum of $10,000 and six months imprisonment to $500,000 and one year imprisonment, depending on the type of offence.
British Columbia	*Gaming Control Act*, S.B.C. 2002, c. 14	**s. 97(4):** Directors who authorize, permit, or acquiesce in an offence by the corporation commit the same offence. **s. 98:** Penalties range from a maximum of $5,000 to a maximum of $100,000 and six months imprisonment for a first offence, depending on the type of offence.

Manitoba	*Gaming Control Act*, C.C.S.M., c. G5	**s. 2:** Directors are guilty of offences committed by the corporation if they authorized, permitted, or acquiesced in the commission of those offences. **s. 53(3):** The maximum penalty for an offence is $250,000 on summary conviction.
New Brunswick	*Lotteries Act*, S.N.B. 1976, c. L-13.1	**s. 7:** Authorizes the Lotteries Commission of New Brunswick to conduct and manage lottery schemes, including gaming activities undertaken by charitable organizations. The New Brunswick Department of Public Safety provides the licensing and enforcement of gaming activities on behalf of the Commission.
Newfoundland and Labrador	*Lotteries Act*, S.N.L. 1991, c. 53	**s. 6:** A person contravening the Act may be fined up to $1,000 or imprisoned for up to six months for contravening the Act.
Nova Scotia	Carnival and Charitable Gaming Regulations, N.S. Reg. 39/95; *Gaming Control Act*, S.N.S. 1994-95, c. 4	**s. 20:** These Regulations govern organizations operating for charitable purposes that undertake gaming activities, and they provide a maximum penalty of $3,000 or imprisonment for up to six months.
Ontario	*Gaming Control Act, 1992*, S.O. 1992, c. 24	**s. 46(3):** It is an offence for any director to cause, authorize, permit, or participate or acquiesce in the commission by the corporation of an offence under the Act. **s. 46(4):** The maximum penalty on conviction for an individual is $50,000 and one year of imprisonment.
Prince Edward Island	Gaming Centers Control Regulations, P.E.I. Reg. EC409/05, enabled by *Lotteries Commission Act*, R.S.P.E.I. 1988, c. L-17	**s. 16**: Every person who commits an offence under the Act is liable for a fine of at least $5,000 on summary conviction.
Quebec	*An Act Respecting Lotteries, publicity contests and amusement machines*, R.S.Q., c. L-6; Lottery Schemes Regulation, R.Q. c. L-6, r.8	**s. 121:** The Act provides for a maximum penalty of $7,000 or $50,000 for an individual for a first offence under the Act, the associated regulations, or the rules. **s. 2:** This Regulation governs not-for-profit corporations with charitable purposes that undertake gaming activities.

Saskatchewan	*Alcohol and Gaming Regulation Act*, S.S. 1997, c. A-18.011; Gaming Regulations, 2002, R.R.S., c. A-18.011 Reg. 2	**s. 39.1(1):** The Saskatchewan Gaming and Liquor Authority may assess a penalty of up to $10,000 for contraventions of the Act. Note that the Charitable Gaming and Licensing Branch of the Saskatchewan Gaming and Liquor Authority is responsible for licensing and enforcing charitable gaming activities, which are also regulated under the Gaming Regulations. **s. 5:** Penalties pursuant to the regulation must at least $100, to a maximum of $10,000.

Table 4: Insurance and Indemnification Provisions in Respect of Charitable Organizations

Manitoba	*The Corporations Act*, C.C.S.M., c. C225	**s. 119:** Permits corporations to indemnify and purchase liability insurance for a liability arising out of the honest and good faith conduct of the directors. By virtue of s. 265, this applies to non-share capital corporations as well.
Ontario	*Corporations Act*, R.S.O. 1990, c. C. 38	**s. 80:** Authorizes the indemnification of directors other than for liabilities arising from the willful neglect or default of the directors. By virtue of s. 133, this applies to non-share capital corporations as well.
	Approved Acts of Executors and Trustees, O. Reg. 4/01, enabled under *Charities Accounting Act*, R.S.O. 1990, c. C.10	**s. 2:** Charitable organizations are permitted to indemnify and insure directors for acts or omissions that do not arise from a failure to act honestly and in good faith, provided that the directors considered a list of enumerated factors ensuring that the purchase of the insurance is reasonable and will not impair the charitable purposes.
Saskatchewan	*Non-profit Corporations Act*, 1995, S.S. 1995, c. N-4.2	**s. 111:** This section permits the indemnification of and the purchase of insurance for directors who act honestly and in good faith with a view to the best interests of the corporation. With court approval, the court may indemnify a director in respect of an action by or on behalf of the corporation. A director is entitled to indemnification from the corporation in respect of all costs incurred in defence of an action in which the director is substantially successful and meets the other requirements for indemnification.

Table 5: Number of Directors

Canada	*Canada Corporations Act,* R.S.C. 1970, c. C-32	**ss. 154(1), 155(1)(e):** both of these sections require a minimum of three directors at the time of incorporation.
Alberta	*Companies Act,* R.S.A. 2000, c. C-21	**Schedule, Table A, s. 51:** provides for a minimum of two directors, and a maximum of seven directors.
	Societies Act, R.S.A. 2000, c. S-14	The Act does not list a minimum number of directors.
	Business Corporations Act, R.S.A. 2000, c. B-9	**s. 101(2):** "A corporation shall have one or more directors . . ." **s. 107:** "If the articles provide for cumulative voting, (a) the articles shall require a fixed number and not a minimum and maximum number of directors . . ."
	Cooperatives Act, S.A. 2001, c. C-28.1	**s. 50(1):** A cooperative must have at least three directors or any greater minimum number of directors that is set out in the articles.
British Columbia	*Business Corporations Act,* S.B.C. 2002, c. 57	**s. 120:** A company must have at least one director.
	Society Act, R.S.B.C. 1996, c. 433	**s. 24(4):** A society must have at least three directors.
	Cooperative Association Act, S.B.C. 1999, c. 28	**s. 72(1):** An association must have at least three directors.
Manitoba	*Corporations Act,* C.C.S.M., c. C225	**s. 269(1):** "A corporation shall have not fewer than three directors".
New Brunswick	*Companies Act,* R.S.N.B. 1973, c. C-13	**s. 87(1):** Minimum of three directors.
	Co-operative Associations Act, S.N.B. 1978, c. C-22.1	**s. 31(2):** Minimum of three directors.

Newfoundland and Labrador	*Corporations Act*, R.S.N.L. 1990, c. C-36	**s. 422(1):** Minimum of three directors.
Northwest Territories	*Societies Act*, R.S.N.W.T. 1988, c. S-11	No minimum number of directors.
Nova Scotia	*Societies Act*, R.S.N.S. 1989, c. 435	Although a minimum number of directors is not strictly stated in the Act, **s. 19** provides that the society's annual balance sheet must be signed either by an auditor or "by two directors". This provision implies that a society must have at least two directors.
Nunavut	*Societies Act* (Nunavut), R.S.N.W.T. 1988, c. S-11	No minimum number of directors.
Ontario	*Co-operative Corporations Act*, R.S.O. 1990, c. C-35	**s. 85(2):** "There shall be at least three directors".
	Corporations Act, R.S.O. 1990, c. C-38	**s. 283(2):** "The board of directors of a corporation shall consist of a fixed number of directors not fewer than three".
Prince Edward Island	*Companies Act*, R.S.P.E.I. 1988, c. C-14	Although there is no minimum number of directors for a non-profit corporation (under Part II), s. 89 requires that three or more persons subscribe to the memorandum of agreement as part of the incorporation process. **s. 22:** Provides that the persons named as directors in the letters patent shall be directors until they are replaced.
	Co-operative Associations Act, R.S.P.E.I. 1988, c. C-23	**s. 8:** Minimum of three directors.
Quebec	*Companies Act*, R.S.Q., c. C-38	**s. 83:** "The affairs of the company shall be managed by a board of not less than three directors".
	Cooperatives Act, R.S.Q., c. C-67.2	**s. 80:** The board of directors of a cooperative consists of not fewer than three nor more than fifteen directors. The number of directors is to be determined by the by-law. **s. 61:** If a cooperative has fewer than twenty-five members, they may agree to not elect directors for one year.

Saskatchewan	*Co-operatives Act*, S.S. 1996, c. C-37.3	**s. 7(3):** At least five, unless the number of incorporators or members is less than six, or fewer than five members are eligible to become directors.
	Non-profit Corporations Act, 1995, S.S. 1995, c. N-4.2	**s. 89:** "A membership corporation shall have one or more directors but a charitable corporation or a corporation any of the issued securities of which are or were part of a distribution to the public shall have not fewer than three directors, at least two of whom are not officers or employees of the corporation or its affiliates".
Yukon	*Societies Act*, R.S.Y. 2002, c. 206	A minimum number of directors is not listed under the Act.

Table 6: Qualifications for Directors

Canada	*Canada Corporations Act*, R.S.C. 1970, c. C-32	**s. 155(1):** Directors must be 18 years old and "have power under law to contract".
Alberta	*Companies Act*, R.S.A. 2000, c. C-21	Though there are no listed qualifications for directors, **s. 90(1)** stipulates a residency requirement that 50 percent of the board must be residents of Alberta. **S. 61** states that a director may lose his office if he becomes bankrupt, is found to be of unsound mind, or participates in the profits of any contract of the company.
	Societies Act, R.S.A. 2000, c. S-14	The Act does not list qualifications for directors.
	Business Corporations Act, R.S.A. 2000, c. B-9	**s. 105(1):** A director must be an individual. A director cannot be less than 18 years of age, (i) a "dependant adult" (under the *Dependent Adults Act*), (ii) a patient under the *Mental Health Act*, (iii) subject to an order under the *Mentally Incapacitated Persons Act*, (iv) have been found to be of unsound mind by an Alberta court, or have the status of bankrupt. Additionally, there is a requirement that at least one quarter of directors must be resident Canadians.

	Cooperatives Act, S.A. 2001, c. C-28.1	**s. 52(1):** A person is disqualified from becoming or continuing as a director if that person (a) is not an individual; (b) is under 18 years of age; (c) is an individual who (i) is a dependent adult, as defined in the *Dependent Adults Act* or is the subject of a certificate of incapacity under that Act, (ii) is a formal patient, as defined in the *Mental Health Act*, (iii) is the subject of an order under the *Mentally Incapacitated Persons Act* (R.S.A. 1970, c. 232) appointing a committee of the individual's person or estate or both, or (iv) has been found to be a person of unsound mind by a court elsewhere than in Alberta; (d) has the status of bankrupt. **(2)** A cooperative may provide in its by-laws for additional qualifications or disqualifications. **(3)** Unless Division 2 of Part 18 applies to the cooperative, a majority of the directors must be individuals who are not full-time officers or employees of the cooperative. **(4)** A majority of the directors must be resident in Canada.
British Columbia	*Business Corporations Act*, S.B.C. 2002, c. 57	**s. 124(2):** A person is not qualified to be a director if that person is under the age of 18 years, incapable of managing their own affairs, an undischarged bankrupt, or convicted of a corporate offence or fraud (unless either five years have elapsed since the expiration of the suspension, the imposition of the fine, or the conclusion of a term of imprisonment or probation, or a pardon was granted in respect of the offence).
	Society Act, R.S.B.C. 1996, c. 433	**s. 24(5):** At least one of the directors must be ordinarily resident in British Columbia.
	Cooperative Association Act, S.B.C. 1999, c. 28	**s. 72(1):** "(a) a majority of the directors of the association must be individuals ordinarily resident in Canada, and (b) one of the directors of the association must be an individual ordinarily resident in British Columbia". **s. 72(2):** All directors must be members of the association. **s. 79(2):** Association may provide in its rules for additional qualifications of directors. **s. 79(4):** An individual is not qualified to be a director if he or she is under 18 years of age, has been found by a court to be incapable of managing his or her own affairs, is an undischarged bankrupt, or has been convicted of a corporation-related offence or fraud (unless either that individual has been granted a pardon, or five years have elapsed since the conclusion of a term of imprisonment or probation, or since the period set for a suspension or fine).

Manitoba	*Corporations Act*, C.C.S.M., c. C225	**s. 275(f):** The by-laws may regulate the qualifications of directors. **s. 100(1):** A person is disqualified from being a director if that person is under the age of 18, is not an individual, or has the status of a bankrupt.
New Brunswick	*Co-operative Associations Act*, S.N.B. 1978, c. C-22.1	**s. 31(4):** "The qualifications, power and duties for directors shall be set out in the regulations and by-laws". **N.B. Reg 82–58, s. 32:** "No director shall engage in business that competes with the business of the association".
	Companies Act, R.S.N.B. 1973, c. C-13	**s. 87(1.2):** An individual over the age of 19 who does not have the status of a bankrupt, is of sound mind, and has not been convicted of a corporate or fraud related offence (unless a pardon was granted in respect of the offence, or three years have elapsed since the term of probation, term of imprisonment, fine, or suspension).
Newfoundland and Labrador	*Corporations Act*, R.S.N.L. 1990, c. C-36	**s. 172:** Directors must be individuals over the age of 19 who have not been found to be mentally incompetent by a court and who do not have the status of a bankrupt. **s. 174(1):** At least 25 percent of directors must be residents of Canada.
Northwest Territories	*Societies Act*, R.S.N.W.T. 1988, c. S-11	No qualifications for directors.
Nova Scotia	*Societies Act*, R.S.N.S. 1989, c. 435	**S. 13(2)** requires that the by-laws of a society comply with **Schedule B** of the Act. **Schedule B(4)** states that the appointment, power, and duties for directors shall be set out in the by-laws. There are no specific qualifications listed for directors.
Nunavut	*Societies Act* (Nunavut), R.S.N.W.T. 1988, c. S-11	No qualifications for directors.

Ontario	*Co-operative Corporations Act*, R.S.O. 1990, c. C-35	**s. 85(3):** "A majority of directors on the board of directors of every co-operative shall be resident Canadians". **s. 87:** "No person shall be a director of a co-operative unless he or she is a member thereof or a director, officer, shareholder or member of a corporate member thereof, and, where a director or a corporation of which he or she is an officer, director, shareholder or member ceases to be a member, he or she thereupon ceases to be a director". **s. 89:** "(1) No person under eighteen years of age shall be a director of a co-operative. (2) No undischarged bankrupt or mentally incompetent person shall be a director, and, if a director becomes a bankrupt or a mentally incompetent person, he or she thereupon ceases to be a director". **s. 87:** A director must be a member of the co-operative.
	Corporations Act, R.S.O. 1990, c. C-38	**s. 129(1)(f):** Directors may pass by-laws to regulate the qualifications of directors. **s. 286:** A director must be 18 years of age or older and cannot be an undischarged bankrupt.
Prince Edward Island	*Companies Act*, R.S.P.E.I. 1988, c. C-14	There are no qualifications for directors listed under the Act; however, s. 90(1) states that applicants for letters patent must be 18 years old.
	Co-operative Associations Act, R.S.P.E.I. 1988, c. C-23	**s. 31(4):** "The qualifications, power, and duties for directors shall be set forth in the regulations and by-laws". **P.E.I. Reg EC833/76, s. 29(1)**: Any director or officer shall vacate his or her office if he or she becomes bankrupt. **(2)** No director shall engage in business that competes with the business of the association.
Quebec	*Companies Act*, R.S.Q., c. C-38	**s. 86(1):** No person shall be elected or appointed as a director of a company unless he or she is a shareholder of it. **s. 86(4):** An undischarged bankrupt cannot be elected or appointed as a director, and when any director becomes bankrupt, he or she ceases to be a director.

	Cooperatives Act, R.S.Q., c. C-67.2	**s. 81:** "Every member of the cooperative or representative of a legal person or partnership may be a director". **s. 81.1:** "The by-laws may provide that persons other than members may be eligible as directors". **s. 81.2:** "Minors may be directors of a cooperative whose object concerns them".
Saskatchewan	*Co-operatives Act*, S.S. 1996, c. C-37.3	**s. 72(2):** "Not less than a majority of the directors are to be ordinary residents of Canada". **s. 75:** A person is not eligible to be a director where the person: (a) is less than 18 years of age; (b) is of unsound mind and has been so found by a court in Saskatchewan or elsewhere; (c) is not an individual; (d) is not a member of the co-operative or a duly appointed representative of a member that is a partnership, association, firm, body corporate, or public body; (e) has the status of a bankrupt; or (f) is a member of a prescribed class of persons. **(2)** A co-operative may provide in its by-laws for qualifications of directors that are in addition to those set out in subsection (1).
	Non-profit Corporations Act, 1995, S.S. 1995, c. N-4.2	**s. 92(1):** "The following persons are disqualified from being a director of a corporation: a) anyone who is less than 18 years of age; b) anyone who has been found to be of unsound mind by a court in Canada or elsewhere; c) a person who is not an individual; d) a person who has the status of a bankrupt. **(2)** Unless the articles otherwise provide, a director of a corporation is not required to be a member of the corporation. **(3)** At least one director of a corporation must reside in Saskatchewan. **(4)** At least 25% of the directors of a corporation must be resident Canadians, but if a corporation has fewer than four directors, at least one must be a resident Canadian".
Yukon	*Societies Act*, R.S.Y. 2002, c. 206	There are no qualifications for directors listed under the Act.

Table 7: Appointment of Officers

Canada	*Canada Corporations Act*, R.S.C. 1970, c. C-32	**s. 155(2)(d):** The appointment and removal of officers must be provided for in the by-laws of the corporation.

Alberta	*Companies Act,* R.S.A. 2000, c. C-21	**Schedule, Table A, s. 59:** Requires directors to keep minutes of the appointments of officers.
	Societies Act, R.S.A. 2000, c. S-14	**s. 9(4)(d):** The appointment and removal of officers must be provided for in the by-laws of the corporation. **s. 27:** On request, a society must furnish the Registrar with particulars of its officers and directors.
	Business Corporations Act, R.S.A. 2000, c. B-9	**s. 104(1):** Officers may be appointed by directors at a meeting of directors. **s. 121:** "subject to the articles, the bylaws of any unanimous shareholders agreement, the directors may… appoint as officers individuals of full capacity, specify their duties and delegate to them powers to manage the business and affairs of the corporation" (except for powers listed in s. 115(3)).
	Cooperatives Act, S.A. 2001, c. C-28.1	**s. 93:** "Subject to the articles, the bylaws and any unanimous agreement, the directors may … (c) appoint any individual 18 years of age or older, including a director, to be an officer".
British Columbia	*Business Corporations Act,* S.B.C. 2002, c. 57	**s. 141(1):** Subject to the articles, the directors may appoint officers and may specify their duties. **s. 141(3):** A person who does not meet the qualifications under s. 124 cannot act as an officer of a company.
	Society Act, R.S.B.C. 1996, c. 433	**s. 6(e):** The by-laws of a society incorporated under the Act must contain provisions for the appointment and removal of officers and their duties, powers, and remuneration, if any.
	Cooperative Association Act, S.B.C. 1999, c. 28	No mention.
Manitoba	*Corporations Act,* C.C.S.M., c. C225	**s. 275(h)**: Directors may pass by-laws regulating the appointment, remuneration, functions, duties, and removal of officers.

New Brunswick	*Co-operative Associations Act,* S.N.B. 1978, c. C-22.1	The appointment of officers is not addressed under the Act or the Co-operative Associations Regulations (N.B. Reg. 82-58).
	Companies Act, R.S.N.B. 1973, c. C-13	**s. 96(d):** Directors may appoint and remove officers of the company.
Newfoundland and Labrador	*Corporations Act,* R.S.N.L. 1990, c. C-36	**s. 428(h):** Directors may make by-laws respecting the appointment of officers.
Northwest Territories	*Societies Act,* R.S.N.W.T. 1988, c. S-11	**s. 5(d):** The by-laws of the society shall make provisions for the appointment and removal of officers.
Nova Scotia	*Societies Act,* R.S.N.S. 1989, c. 435	**s. 13(2)**: Requires that the by-laws of a society comply with **Schedule B** of the Act. **Schedule B(4):** "Appointment and removal of directors and other officers ..."
Nunavut	*Societies Act* (Nunavut), R.S.N.W.T. 1988, c. S-11	**s. 5(d):** The by-laws of the society shall make provisions for the appointment and removal of officers.
Ontario	*Co-operative Corporations Act,* R.S.O. 1990, c. C-35.	**s. 105(1):** A co-operative shall have a president and a secretary and such other officers as are provided for by the by-law or by a resolution of the directors.
	Corporations Act, R.S.O. 1990, c. C-38	**s. 129(1)(h):** Directors may pass by-laws to regulate the appointment, remuneration, functions, duties, and removal of officers. **s. 289(2):** Directors shall appoint a secretary and may appoint one or more vice-presidents and other officers.
Prince Edward Island	*Co-operative Associations Act,* R.S.P.E.I. 1988, c. C-23	There is nothing in the Act addressing the appointment of officers; however, under **P.E.I. Reg EC833/76, s. 28(2)**, "The Board of Directors shall meet immediately after the first general meeting of the association, and subsequently immediately after each annual meeting, and shall organize by electing for the current year from their own number a president and vice-president. A secretary or secretary-treasurer shall be appointed and such member may or may not be a director. Notwithstanding the above, the bylaws may provide the time at which the incoming executive officially takes office".
	Companies Act, R.S.P.E.I. 1988, c. C-14	**s. 90(2):** The petition for letters patent must be accompanied by a memorandum setting out the by-laws of the company, which must include, under (d), the appointment of officers.

Quebec	*Cooperatives Act*, R.S.Q., c. C-67.2	**s. 112.1:** Executive officers include the president, vice-president, and secretary. **s. 112.2:** The by-laws may authorize the board of directors to create other executive positions. **s. 114:** The chairman and vice-chairman of the board of directors are the president and vice-president of the cooperative. **s. 116:** "the board of directors shall appoint a secretary, and if necessary, a treasurer".
	Companies Act, R.S.Q., c. C-38	**s. 89(4):** "The directors shall elect from among themselves a president and may also appoint all other officers as they see fit". **s. 91(1)(d):** The directors of a company may make by-laws that provide for the appointment of officers.
Saskatchewan	*Co-operatives Act*, S.S. 1996, c. C-37.3	**s. 94(2)(a)(iii):** Unless the by-laws state otherwise, directors appoint officers.
	Non-profit Corporations Act, 1995, S.S. 1995, c. N-4.2	**s. 108(1):** "Subject to the articles, the bylaws or any unanimous member agreement: a) the directors may designate the offices of the corporation, appoint as officers persons of full capacity, specify their duties and delegate to them any powers that the directors may lawfully delegate . . ."
Yukon	*Societies Act*, R.S.Y. 2002, c. 206	**s. 7(2)(a):** The by-laws shall make provisions for the appointment of members.

Table 8: Role of Directors

Canada	*Canada Corporations Act*, R.S.C. 1970, c. C-32	**s. 155(2)(d):** The powers of directors must be provided for in the by-laws of the corporation.
Alberta	*Companies Act*, R.S.A. 2000, c. C-21	**Schedule, Table A, s. 62:** Directors can be elected or appointed. **Schedule, Table A, s. 55:** Lists the powers of directors which include managing the business of the company and complying with the Act; s. 56 states that directors may also appoint other directors.
	Societies Act, R.S.A. 2000, c. S-14	**s. 9(4)(d):** The duties, powers, and remuneration of directors must be provided for in the by-laws.

	Business Corporations Act, R.S.A. 2000, c. B-9	**s. 101(1):** "Subject to a unanimous shareholders agreement, directors shall manage or supervise the management of the business and affairs of the corporation". **s. 104(1):** Directors have listed powers under this section, which include (a) making by-laws, (c) appointing officers, (d) appointing auditors, (f) making banking arrangements, and (g) transacting any other business.
	Cooperatives Act, S.A. 2001, c. C-28.1	**s. 53**: The directors must manage or supervise the management of the business and affairs of the cooperative, subject to this Act, the regulations and the articles, any unanimous agreement, and the by-laws.
British Columbia	*Business Corporations Act,* S.B.C. 2002, c. 57	**s. 136(1):** The directors of a company must manage, or supervise the management of, the business and affairs of the company.
	Society Act, R.S.B.C. 1996, c. 433	**s. 24(2):** Subject to the by-laws, the directors must manage, or supervise the management of, the affairs of the society and may exercise all of the powers of the society.
	Cooperative Association Act, S.B.C. 1999, c. 28	**s. 76(1):** "The directors must manage or supervise the management of the business of the association and may exercise all the powers of the association".
Manitoba	*Corporations Act,* C.C.S.M., c. C225	**s. 275:** Directors may pass by-laws. **s. 97(1):** The directors shall manage, or supervise the management of, the business and affairs of a corporation.
New Brunswick	*Co-operative Associations Act,* S.N.B. 1978, c. C-22.1	**s. 31(4):** "[D]uties of the directors shall be as set forth in the regulations and by-laws". **N.B. Reg 82-58, s. 33:** "The board of directors shall manage the affairs of the association and implement policies as directed ..." **s. 38:** lists additional duties.

	Companies Act, R.S.N.B. 1973, c. C-13	**s. 96(1):** "The directors may administer the affairs of the company in all things, and make or cause to be made for the company any description of contract that the company may by law enter into, and may make by-laws not contrary to law or to the letters patent of the company or to this Act".
Newfoundland and Labrador	*Corporations Act*, R.S.N.L. 1990, c. C-36	**s. 428:** Directors have power to make by-laws respecting the corporation, including by-laws regarding any affairs of the corporation, that are not contrary to the Act. **s. 167:** Directors have a duty to exercise the powers of the corporation directly (or delegate that power to agents or employees) and to direct the management of the business and affairs of the corporation.
Northwest Territories	*Societies Act*, R.S.N.W.T. 1988, c. S-11	**s. 5(d):** The duties, powers, and remuneration of directors must be provided for in the by-laws.
Nova Scotia	*Societies Act*, R.S.N.S. 1989, c. 435	**s. 16(2):** "The directors of a society may exercise any powers of the society not required by this Act or the by-laws to be exercised by the members of the society at a general meeting". **s. 13(2):** "The by-laws of every society shall contain provisions in respect of the several matters set out in Schedule B". **Schedule B(4):** "Appointment, removal of directors ... and their duties, powers and remuneration".
Nunavut	*Societies Act* (Nunavut), R.S.N.W.T. 1988, c. S-11	**s. 5(d):** The duties, powers, and remuneration of directors must be provided for in the by-laws.
Ontario	*Co-operative Corporations Act*, R.S.O. 1990, c. C-35	**s. 96(1):** The board of directors shall manage or supervise the management of the affairs and business of the co-operative.
	Corporations Act, R.S.O. 1990, c. C-38	**s. 283(1):** "The affairs of every corporation shall be managed by a board of directors howsoever designated".
Prince Edward Island	*Co-operative Associations Act*, R.S.P.E.I. 1988, c. C-23	**s. 31(4):** The "duties, powers and remuneration shall be as set forth in the regulations and by-laws".
	Companies Act, R.S.P.E.I. 1988, c. C-14	**s. 28:** "The directors of a company have full power in all things to administer the affairs of the company, and may make or cause to be made for the company any description of contract which the corporation may by law enter into".

Quebec	*Cooperatives Act*, R.S.Q., c. C-67.2	**s. 89:** "The board of directors has all the powers necessary to manage the affairs of the cooperative". [These powers can be restricted under the by-laws.] **s. 91:** Directors are considered to be mandataries of the cooperative. **s. 90:** Sets out the board of directors' specific powers and duties.
	Companies Act, R.S.Q., c. C-38	**s. 91(1):** "The directors may administer the affairs of the company in all things, and make or cause to be made for it, in its name, any kind of contract which it may lawfully enter into". **s. 91(2):** Directors may make by-laws in relation to "the conduct in all other particulars of the company".
Saskatchewan	*Non-profit Corporations Act, 1995*, S.S. 1995, c. N-4.2	**s. 88:** "Subject to any unanimous member agreement, the directors shall manage the activities and affairs of a corporation".
	Co-operatives Act, S.S. 1996, c. C-37.3	**s. 72(1):** "Unless the articles or bylaws provide otherwise, the board of directors, however designated, shall: (a) exercise the powers of the co-operative directly or indirectly through the employees and agents of the co-operative; and (b) direct the management of the business and affairs of the co-operative".
Yukon	*Societies Act*, R.S.Y. 2002, c. 206	**s. 7(2)(e):** The duties, powers, and remuneration of directors must be provided for in the by-laws.

Table 9: Directors' Liability[2]

Canada	*Canada Corporations Act*, R.S.C., 1970, c. C-32	**s. 93:** Directors may, with the consent of the corporation, be indemnified in suits respecting execution of their office. **s. 99:** Directors are jointly and severally liable for unsatisfied wages for a period not exceeding six months. **s. 157(c):** While s. 93 and s. 99 deal specifically with corporations with share capital, this section applies these provisions to non-profit corporations.

[2] See Appendices I to IV at the end of Chapter 11 for a more comprehensive list of directors' liability under business corporations legislation.

Alberta	*Companies Act*, R.S.A. 2000, c. C-21	**s. 91:** Directors are jointly and severally liable for wages incurred while the director was acting as a director for a period not exceeding six months.
	Societies Act, R.S.A. 2000, c. S-14	**s. 21:** No member of a society is, in the member's individual capacity, liable for a debt or liability of the society.
	Business Corporations Act, R.S.A. 2000, c. B-9	**s. 118:** Directors may be jointly and severally liable for the financial consequences of resolutions. **s. 119(1):** Directors are jointly and severally liable for the wages of employees for a period not exceeding six months.
	Cooperatives Act, S.A. 2001, c. C-28.1	**s. 79:** Directors are jointly and individually liable for the wages of employees for a period not exceeding six months.
British Columbia	*Business Corporations Act*, S.B.C. 2002, c. 57	**s. 154(1):** Subject to s. 157, directors who vote for or consent to a resolution authorizing certain payments or purchases are liable for amounts that are not otherwise recovered. **s. 154(3):** Directors are further liable for any liability imposed under this Act, or under any other enactment, or by any rule of law or equity. **s. 157(1):** A director may be indemnified from liability.
	Society Act, R.S.B.C. 1996, c. 433	**s. 5:** A member of a society is not, in the member's individual capacity, liable for a debt or a liability of the society.
	Cooperative Association Act, S.B.C. 1999, c. 28	**s. 98:** "an association may ... (a) indemnify an eligible party against all eligible penalties to which the eligible party may be liable".
Manitoba	*Corporations Act*, C.C.S.M., c. C225	**s. 143(4):** Where a corporation is guilty of an offence, then whether or not the corporation has been prosecuted or convicted, any director or officer of the corporation who knowingly authorizes, permits, or acquiesces in the failure is also guilty of an offence. **s. 242(2)**: If a director makes or assists in making a report, notice, return, or document required by the Act that either contains an untrue statement of a material fact or omits a material fact is guilty of an offence and liable for summary conviction.

New Brunswick	*Companies Act*, R.S.N.B. 1973, c. C-13	**s. 18(2)(i):** The members of a non-profit company shall not be liable for any debts or obligations of the company.
	Co-operative Associations Act, S.N.B. 1978, c. C-22.1	**s. 60(3):** "Every director or officer of an association who, having knowledge of the facts, moves, seconds, puts or supports by his vote any motion, resolution or proposal which if carried out would constitute an offence against this Act shall be guilty of an offence against this Act . . ."
Newfoundland and Labrador	*Corporations Act*, R.S.N.L. 1990, c. C-36	**s. 193:** Consenting to any resolution that contravenes the Act.
Northwest Territories	*Societies Act*, R.S.N.W.T. 1988, c. S-11	**s. 13:** A member of a society is not liable in his or her individual capacity for any debt or liability of the society.
Nova Scotia	*Societies Act*, R.S.N.S. 1989, c. 435	**s. 30(2):** "A director or officer of a society who knowingly authorizes or permits a contravention or failure to observe any provision of this Act by a society is liable on summary conviction to a penalty of not more than one hundred dollars, whether or not the society has been prosecuted or convicted".
Nunavut	*Societies Act* (Nunavut), R.S.N.W.T. 1988, c. S-11	**s. 13:** A member of a society is not liable in his or her individual capacity for any debt or liability of the society.
Ontario	*Co-operative Corporations Act*, R.S.O. 1990, c. C-35	**s. 99:** "Where a co-operative acquires any of its shares or repays any of its loans in contravention of this Act or the articles, the directors who voted in favour of or consented to the resolution authorizing the acquisition or repayment are jointly and severally liable to the co-operative to the extent of the amount paid out". **s. 103(1):** "The directors of a co-operative are jointly and severally liable to the employees of the co-operative to whom the *Employers and Employees Act* applies for all debts that become due while they are directors for services performed for the co-operative, not exceeding six months wages, and for the vacation pay accrued for not more than twelve months under the *Employment Standards Act* and the regulations thereunder or under any collective agreement made by the co-operative".

	Corporations Act, R.S.O. 1990, c. C-38	**s. 80:** A director may be indemnified in suits respecting the execution of his or her duties, or office. **s. 81:** Directors are jointly and severally liable for the wages of employees for a period not exceeding six months and for vacation pay accrued over a period of not more than twelve months.
Prince Edward Island	*Companies Act,* R.S.P.E.I. 1988, c. C-14	**ss. 53, 54:** Neglecting to keep books for the inspection of the shareholders and creditors at the head office of the company or knowingly making untrue entries in the books (s. 91(1) applies these sections to non-profit companies).
	Co-operative Associations Act, R.S.P.E.I. 1988, c. C-23	There is no explicit mention of director liability in the Act.
Quebec	*Cooperatives Act,* R.S.Q., c. C-67.2	**s. 6:** "The person who performs a deed in the interest of a cooperative before its constitution is bound by that deed unless the contract entered into for the cooperative includes a clause excluding or limiting his liability and a statement to the effect that the cooperative might not be constituted or might not assume its obligations". There is no specific mention of director liability.
	Companies Act, R.S.Q., c. C-38	**s. 96(1):** Directors are "solidarily liable" to employees for wages for a period not exceeding six months.
Saskatchewan	*Co-operatives Act,* S.S. 1996, c. C-37.3	**s. 89:** A director who uses confidential information for his or her own benefit is liable to compensate both the co-operative for any benefit received and anyone who suffered a loss as a result of the transaction. **s. 80:** A director may be liable for any loss suffered by the co-operative as a result of his or her vote in favour of a resolution that contravenes any provisions of the Act.

	Non-profit Corporations Act, 1995, S.S. 1995, c. N-4.2	**s. 105(1):** "Directors of a corporation who vote for or consent to a resolution authorizing the issue of a security ... for a consideration other than money are jointly and severally liable to the corporation to make good any amount by which the consideration received is less than the fair market equivalent of the money that the corporation would have received if the security had been issued for money on the date of the resolution". **105(2):** "Directors of a corporation who vote for or consent to a resolution authorizing any of the following are jointly and severally liable to restore to the corporation any amounts so distributed or paid and not otherwise recovered by the corporation: a) a loan, or guarantee or other financial assistance ... b) a payment to a member, director or officer ... c) a payment of an indemnity ... d) a payment [in relation to the right to dissent, or in respect of an oppression action]." **s. 106:** "Directors of a corporation are jointly and severally liable ... to employees of the corporation for all debts payable to each of those employees for services performed for the corporation while those directors are directors".
Yukon	*Societies Act*, R.S.Y. 2002, c. 206	**s. 12:** A member of a society is not liable in his or her individual capacity for any debt or liability of the society.

CHAPTER 17

ADVISORY BOARDS

Advisory boards have existed as an occasional feature of business organizations for some time.[1] However, a number of factors have combined to make them more common than they were previously. Such factors include the following:

- As we have noted throughout this book, director liability is significant and increasing. Some individuals are willing to serve as advisors but are not willing to take on the risks attendant with being a director.
- A director's role is time-consuming and necessarily comprehensive. An individual who could be helpful to a business might be willing to commit some time to it but not to the extended (and potentially unlimited) time requirements of a director. As well, both the business and the individual may want to focus only on a particular aspect of the business, which an advisory board role permits but a directorship does not.
- The business may only be prepared to provide limited information to an advisory group. Directors require comprehensive information in order to discharge their responsibilities. A variety of businesses, such as small private companies or the subsidiaries of multinational companies, may be unwilling to share significant financial information with intended advisors. Other businesses see their customers (who may be useful advisory board members) as an excellent source of

[1] Barry Reiter, "The Role and Value of an Effective Advisory Board" (September/October 2003) 69 Ivey Business Journal.

advice but they are unwilling to disclose sensitive information to them.

- There are a variety of businesses, ranging from private companies to business trusts, investment funds, and other managed businesses, in which the advice of, and some control by, the manager may be appropriate and acceptable but where the acceptance of a full-fledged directorship could lead to both the unwanted, unlimited liability of the director and to a sharing of control that is unwanted by the business.

Advisory boards have proliferated in a number of contexts. Many businesses have industry advisory councils that provide strategic and/or marketing advice and often provide networking benefits. Many technology companies form customer or user group advisory boards that assist them in understanding customer issues with their products and in developing product direction for the future. Life sciences companies frequently establish scientific advisory boards that assist them with decisions about the direction of research or the status and viability of drug development programs. Private companies establish advisory councils to perform whatever board of director functions the controlling shareholder may wish, in as binding or non-binding a form as may be desired. A variety of businesses (such as private equity funds, business trusts, and the like) form advisory councils to assist them with important investment or business direction decisions and/or to address conflicts between the manager and the investors.

Advisory boards do achieve the limited liability purpose that is often a key consideration behind their formation.[2] This issue is more complicated in the context of business trusts or limited partnerships, where advisory boards may have specific decision-making or veto authority with respect to important proposed business directions. Typical limited partnership legislation provides for limited liability except where a limited partner "takes part in the management" of the partnership.[3] Care must be taken to ensure that the authority given to advisory groups in these circumstances does not give them unlimited liability. However, there are a number of well-established practices that are generally regarded as safe harbours for advisory groups of this sort, and the few cases in which the protection of

[2] *Ibid.* See also Aviv Pichhadze, "Mutual Fund Governance Reforms: A Commentary" (2001) B.F.L.R. 67 at 81; Marcia T. Moffat, "Directors' Dilemma — An Economic Evaluation of Directors' Liability for Environmental Damages and Unpaid Wages" (1996) 54(2) U.T. Fac. L. Rev 293 at paras. 27 and 29.

[3] For example *Limited Partnerships Act*, R.S.O. 1990, c. L16 ("Limited Partnerships Act"); see also *Partnerships Act*, R.S.O. 1990, c. P.5, ss. 44.1–44.4.

limited liability has been lost have involved more active participation by the intended advisors.[4]

Whether an advisory board achieves any other purpose besides the formation or maintenance of limited liability depends on how it is established and operated. Unlike a board of directors, advisory boards have no pre-set rules about responsibilities or processes. A business that is considering a board of advisors must know what it wants out of the board, recruit board members wisely, commit relevant resources to the management of the board, and review the successes and failures of the board on a continuous basis.

An advisory board can be created for almost any purpose, but very different people, processes, and focuses will be required, depending on the board's purpose. Is the advisory board to provide a sounding board for the CEO (who may be unwilling to appear as unconfident before the board of directors)? Is it to provide customers' input on existing products and new product directions? Does it exist to provide scientific or technical advice? Is it intended to be a networking or sales group that will provide introductions and carry the message to potential customers? If there is a lack of clarity on why the board is being established, there will likely be failure in respect of a number of the topics discussed below, and the advisory board will be of limited use.

An advisory board is only as good as the people who are recruited to be on it. Recruiting will obviously be heavily influenced by the intended function of the advisory board. While a board of directors needs to include members who have a variety of skills and interests, most advisory boards will function best if their members have similar interests or skills. As advisory boards are usually intended to be focused on a narrower range of topics than a board might consider, advisory board recruiters should focus on people who share common interests. Such membership is particularly common with scientific, technical, or customer-based advisory boards, whose members choose to serve on a board in order to meet others who have similar interests. Thus, a business that wants scientific and marketing information from advisory board members might consider having two separate advisory boards.

---

[4] *Limited Partnerships Act, ibid.*, s. 13(1); see also *Elevated Construction Ltd. v. Nixon* (1969), [1970] 1 O.R. 650 (Ont. H.C.) (mere fact that limited partners' names were included along with the names of general partners in deed of conveyance of land was not evidence of taking part in the control of the business); *Haughton Graphic (Graphics) Ltd. v. Zivot* (1986), 33 B.L.R. 125 (Ont. H.C.), aff'd (1988), 38 B.L.R., xxxiii (Ont. C.A.), leave to appeal refused (1988), 38 B.L.R., xxxiii (S.C.C.) (evidence suggesting that the limited partnership was completely controlled by limited partners; assumption of control rendering limited partners liable as general partners); *Nordile Holdings Ltd. v. Breckenridge* (1992), 66 B.C.L.R. (2d) 183 (C.A.) (in foreclosure action, the plaintiff was seeking relief as against limited partners; limited partners, minority shareholders, officers and directors of general partner, which managed the limited partnership; limited partners were not taking part in the management of the limited partnership so as to render them personally liable for partnership's debt).

It is also important when recruiting to clarify expectations about the time, travel, and other commitments that may be involved in being an advisory board member. If there is a misalignment between the expectations of the business and those of the recruit, it is unlikely that the recruit will deliver the results that the business had hoped for.

Effective advisory boards require significant resources. Advisory board members join boards for motivations such as the following:

- prestige, camaraderie, and personal networking benefits;
- they are friends with the CEO and want to do a personal favour for him or her;
- the interests of science or technology;
- having the costs that are associated with meetings (which are sometimes held in interesting locations) paid for by the company; this sometimes includes the costs of their spouses attending;
- the opportunity to get to know the business and possibly be retained as consultants for it so that they or the research establishments with which they are associated can obtain a direct financial reward; and
- direct remuneration or financial benefits (through advisory board compensation).

It is important to understand the motivation of those who join an advisory board in order to ensure that the business delivers on its end of the bargain. If a key element of the incentive is the fact that the advisory board meets with the famous or prestigious CEO (or with the CEO who is an alleged friend) or with key scientific or technical people, it is important that the business ensure that these people participate in advisory board meetings when they are scheduled.

If advisory board meetings are intended to be something other than social events, the same issues that arise with respect to a board of directors' effectiveness also exist for advisory boards. Someone or some group must take responsibility for the leadership and management of the advisory board: setting agendas for board meetings, providing material before the meetings, and leading focused and well-run meetings.[5]

The company must deliver on its other commitments as well. Such matters as the company's promises to hold meetings once or twice a year in particular locations or in conjunction with other events cannot be postponed at the last minute when other priorities intervene without the risk that the advisory board will wither away. Lacking the discipline that comes from

[5] See Chapter 4, "Board Meetings".

personal liability and the prescribed duties that are imposed on directors, advisory board members will tend to become detached from their tasks if they are not taken seriously by the business. It is important to not purport to establish an advisory board if the business is not prepared to deliver on such commitments.

Even the best recruiting efforts can produce advisory board members who are less than effective, and what is required of the advisory board may evolve over time. Just as the review and evaluation of boards of directors and individual directors help make boards effective and provide for the succession of individual directors, comparable processes can help to continually improve advisory boards. Because of the delicacy that may be involved in the succession of advisory board members (who may be customers or important scientific or technical colleagues), it may be wise to establish term limits on board members, so that succession may occur naturally over time for members who do not provide the participation that the company anticipated.

Advisory boards are compensated in a great variety of ways. Some boards do not pay their members at all but instead pay meeting expenses; such an arrangement adequately compensates members who are induced to join the board by the networking, travel, or ancillary business opportunities that may be available. Some boards pay meeting fees that are comparable to those that would be paid to a board of directors (say, $500 to $1,500 per meeting) but do not have the annual retainer element. Still others attempt to align the interests of the advisory board with those of the long-term interests of the business by providing equity incentives in the form of stock (restricted or non-restricted), stock options, or other comparable payments.[6] Care must be taken to ensure that the compensation paid does not create issues between an advisory member and his or her employer, does not unduly compromise the independence of an advisory board member who may be looked to for scientific or technical advice, and does not create issues when an advisory board member's compensation is compared to the compensation and workload or the responsibility of a director of the board.

Other delicate issues involve the relationship between an advisory board and a board of directors. The duty of the board of directors to the corporation is not mitigated by the existence of an advisory board. While the advice of such a board may be of interest, the directors retain their ultimate responsibility (which does include the right to rely on experts in certain cases, but only when the directors determine that such reliance is

---

[6] National Instrument 45-106, *Prospectus and Registration Exemptions*, Division 4: "Employee, Executive Officer, Director and Consultant Exemptions", s. 2.24.

appropriate).[7] Caution must be exercised, however, when interpreting the term "profession", as noted by Bruce Welling in *Corporate Law in Canada: The Governing Principles*:[8] "I recommend taking advice on plumbing and electrical matters from plumbers and electricians, not doctors, lawyers or even most judges". However, in *Peoples Department Stores Inc (Trustee of) v. Wise*,[9] the Supreme Court of Canada stated:

> Although Clement did have a bachelor's degree in commerce and 15 years of experience in administration and finance with Wise, this experience does not correspond to the level of professionalism required to allow the directors to rely on his advice as a bar to a suit under the duty of care. The named professional groups in [CBCA] s. 123(4)(*b*) were lawyers, accountants, engineers and appraisers. Clement was not an accountant, was not subject to the regulatory overview of any professional organization and did not carry independent insurance coverage for professional negligence. ... It is noteworthy that the word "profession" is used, not "position". ... Therefore, in our opinion, the Wise brothers cannot successfully invoke the defence provided by s. 123(4)(*b*) of the CBCA but must rely on the other defences raised.

In *Westfair Foods Ltd v. Watt*,[10] it was held that directors could not gain the protection of CBCA, s. 123(4) by getting a lawyer's opinion based on less than the full disclosure of the details of the problem that they faced.

Depending on the purpose of the advisory board, it may or may not be appropriate for the directors to be briefed on a regular basis about advisory board proceedings: while some advisory boards serve, in effect, as direct advisors to the CEO, others operate (in effect) as committees of the board of directors in their areas of expertise, and questions of appropriate communication and liaison must be considered.

Because there is no established regime (like the CBCA for directors) within which they operate, advisory boards require mandates even more than boards of directors do. A sample (edited) mandate, proposed for an advisory board designed to provide advice on market and product direction and primarily comprised of customers and potential customers, is attached at the end of this Chapter as Appendix I.

---

[7] *Canada Business Corporations Act*, R.S.C., 1985, c. C-44, s. 123(4) ("CBCA") describes the type and sources of advice that a director can safely rely on to avoid liability.

[8] 3rd ed. (Queensland, Australia: Scribblers Publishing, 2006) at 330, footnote 113 ("*Welling*").

[9] [2004] 3 S.C.R. 461, 244 D.L.R. (4th) 564 at 593 ("*Peoples*" cited to D.L.R.).

[10] (1989), 48 B.L.R. 43, aff'd (1991), 79 D.L.R. (4th) 48, 5 B.L.R. (2d) 160 (Alta C.A.) ("*Westfair Foods*").

APPENDIX I

Advisory Board Mandate[1]

1. GOALS OF THE ADVISORY BOARD

- Increase value for shareholders
- Generate increased business opportunities for [corporate name]
- Obtain insights into the challenges and solutions in the field of financial risk management
- Develop, nurture and expand networks and contacts to increase [corporate name's] product and market penetration
- Provide feedback to management on [corporate name's] strategic direction, marketing positioning and vision
- Advise management on the effectiveness of market message and [corporate name's] position in various market segments

2. ADVISORY BOARD'S RESPONSIBILITIES

- Influence, guide and focus [corporate name's] strategic product offering direction
- Offer broad industry experience to [corporate name's] decision making processes
- Lend credibility and enhance perception of [corporate name] as a market leader
- Connect [corporate name] to key industry players

[1] Used with permission of Michael Spragge, General Counsel, Algorithmics Incorporated.

3. COMPOSITION

- A maximum of 8 senior executives from the financial risk management community with broad industry experience – not just clients
- Opinion leaders and recognized market innovators
- Must be willing to invest the necessary time and effort
- Must be well-known, respected and authoritative
- Must be closely-knit group, known to each other, to encourage participation
- The members should be from the same market segment as the reason for meeting will be reinforced. Multiple segments and multiple geographies will require separate Advisory Boards.

4. FREQUENCY

- Preferably 2 times a year in person for at least a half day per meeting
- Regularly planned interim telephone conference calls

5. LOCATION

- Meeting place must be centrally located and easily accessible for the majority of the board
- It is recommended that the members be from one general location and that the meetings are held locally

6. TERM

- Members will be appointed for a one year term, renewable at the Board's discretion
- Fixed terms allow the [corporate name] to evaluate members' contributions and provide members with an opportunity to assess the Advisory Board's effectiveness

7. COMPENSATION

- Stock options under [corporate name] stock option plan for independent members
- Travel and related expenses paid

8. ADMINISTRATION

- Must be scheduled well in advance

- Administrator from [corporate name] must coordinate and arrange all the details to make attendance as effortless as possible
- CEO of [corporate name] must attend, organize and run the meetings to his agenda
- Agenda must set specific issues and goals
- Agenda must be developed and circulated well in advance
- Product sponsors from within both [corporate name] and the members' organizations should be encouraged to attend to exchange information and perspectives
- There must be no sales pitch under any circumstance
- Informality, fun, and challenging intellectual discussions are key elements of the program

CHAPTER 18

INDEMNIFICATION AND INSURANCE

As we have demonstrated repeatedly throughout this book, directors' exposure to potential sources of liability is substantial. Directors may attempt to mitigate the risk of liability by performing their duties to the best of their ability, but the responsibility is a collective one and, as some of the worst corporate scandals have demonstrated, there is little that a director can do to thwart purposeful and calculated deception by determined management. The risk to reputations that ensues may, to some extent, be irretrievable, although demonstrated diligence is certainly beneficial. Beyond this, corporate failures, and the interest in holding directors responsible for them, can lead to regulatory exposures and penalties, individual and class civil actions,[1] and even criminal liability.

[1] Recent amendments to the limitation periods in some jurisdictions have also increased the exposure. For instance, s. 4 of the Ontario *Limitations Act, 2002*, being Schedule B to the *Justice Statute Law Amendment Act, 2002*, S.O. 2002, c. 24, states: "Unless this Act provides otherwise, a proceeding shall not be commenced in respect of a claim after the second anniversary of the day on which the claim was discovered". There are special scenarios that extend the limitation period but not beyond the ultimate limitation period set out in s. 15(2): "No proceeding shall be commenced in respect of any claim after the 15th anniversary of the day on which the act or omission on which the claim is based took place". Compare this to the British Columbia *Limitation Act*, R.S.B.C. 1996, c. 266, s. 3 and to the Alberta *Limitations Act*, R.S.A. 2000, c. L-12, s. 3, which share the general limitation period of two years, although neither Act has the ultimate limitation period of fifteen years. In Alberta, the maximum limitation period is ten years after the claim arose unless the claimant knew or ought to have known in the circumstances "(i) that the injury for which the claimant seeks a remedial order had occurred, (ii) that the injury was attributable to conduct of the defendant, and (iii) that the injury, assuming liability on the part of the defendant, warrants bringing a proceeding" (s. 3(1)).

I. Indemnification

When directors' liability is asserted, directors have recourse to at least one, and typically two, sources of financial protection: corporate indemnities and directors' and officers' liability insurance ("D&O insurance"). Corporate statutes generally require corporations to indemnify present and past directors for corporate acts. The *Canadian Business Corporations Act*[2] is typical in providing the following:

> **124.** (1) A corporation may indemnify a director or officer of the corporation, a former director or officer of the corporation or another individual who acts or acted at the corporation's request as a director or officer, or an individual acting in a similar capacity, of another entity, against all costs, charges and expenses, including an amount paid to settle an action or satisfy a judgment, reasonably incurred by the individual in respect of any civil, criminal, administrative, investigative or other proceeding in which the individual is involved because of that association with the corporation or other entity.

Corporate statutes also generally permit corporations to provide additional indemnification to both present and past directors (and to officers) as well as to any person who acts or has acted at the corporation's request as a director or officer of another company of which the corporation was a shareholder or creditor. A corporation may indemnify a director or officer for all costs, charges, and expenses that were reasonably incurred by the director or officer in any criminal, civil, or administrative action. The indemnity may include the legal cost of defending a lawsuit as well as the amount required to pay a judgment or settle a claim. Indemnification is permitted in virtually any circumstance as long as the director acted honestly, in good faith, and with the reasonable belief that the conduct was lawful.[3]

Until recently, corporations typically provided additional indemnification by incorporating the permissive indemnity language into their by-laws. Generally, these by-law indemnities did no more than adopt the language in the permissive statutory indemnity, replacing the permissive language of the statute ("may") with mandatory language (such as "shall"). In an era when claims against directors were rare and indemnification provisions were looked to infrequently, such indemnities were thought to be adequate.

---

[2] *Canada Business Corporations Act*, R.S.C. 1985, c. C-44, s. 124 ("CBCA").

[3] CBCA, s. 124(3).

Times have changed. With the explosion of director liability claims, corporations, directors, and their advisors have focused on indemnity provisions and have often found by-law indemnifications to be inadequate. By-law indemnities that mirror the statutory language do not provide clarity as to their scope with respect to regulatory or criminal liability, and even less so deal with defences of the director in the informal, investigation stage that typically precedes formal charges. These indemnities lack clarity with respect to the amount of expenses that will be reimbursed, the timing of payment, and the burden of proof with respect to director claims for payment. They do not address questions about a director's independent right to counsel, the coverage of directors who sit on subsidiary or community boards at the request of the corporation, or requirements of the corporation to procure and maintain D&O insurance. While these issues are significant to a current director of a financially solvent company, they become even more important for a director who may have limited influence on the way in which the corporation will address indemnity issues, as, for instance, in the case of a former director (particularly one who participated in a hostile takeover defence that was lost) or a director of a corporation in the control of a trustee in bankruptcy. These indemnities also require the director to enforce them (ultimately by litigation that is funded by the director) and since they are set out in the corporate by-laws, they may be amended unilaterally by the corporation (at least to the point where the mandatory indemnification requirements apply).

Accordingly, it has become a much more common practice for directors to request and be protected by contractual indemnities, which are individual agreements between the indemnifying corporation and the individual director. Leadership is required in order for a suitable contractual indemnification program to be introduced and implemented. Such leadership may come from the individual director, general counsel, corporate secretary, corporate governance committee, or chair of the board, or it may emerge through the D&O procurement process (as described below). Conflicts abound in this process. As directors are seeking protection for themselves,[4] there are often issues about the extent to which indemnification will apply to non-independent or management directors (or to management in general), and the general counsel or corporate secretary is often in the unenviable position of being the arbiter in these matters.[5]

[4] Directors are, however, entitled to vote on and to approve indemnification and D&O proposals. CBCA, s. 120(5)(*b*) is typical in providing: "(5) A director required to make a disclosure under subsection (1) shall not vote on any resolution to approve the contract or transaction unless the contract or transaction ... (*b*) is for indemnity or insurance under s. 124".

[5] Barry Reiter, "Counsel in the Crosshairs: Creativity in the Boardroom" *Lexpert* (April 2006).

There are four main limitations to a contractual indemnity provided by a corporation. First, an indemnity is only as good as the corporation providing the indemnity: a director who is entitled to an indemnity from an insolvent corporation ranks as an unsecured creditor. One possible protection for a director is to seek an indemnity from a major shareholder or parent corporation. Second, an indemnity is only permitted by corporate statutes when a director acts honestly and in good faith with a view to the best interests of the corporation. If a director breaches his or her fiduciary duty, or is, objectively, not acting in the best interests of the corporation, the corporation is prohibited by statute from indemnifying the director.[6]

Third, a corporation that is suing a director (in a derivative action, for example) may not indemnify the director for costs without the approval of the court. A recent case indicates that this limitation has been extended beyond the specific case in which a corporation is suing its own director and that the courts have discretion in deciding whether directors with a potential right to indemnification are entitled to payment for ongoing defence costs (rather than awaiting the completion of proceedings). *Manitoba (Securities Commission) v. Crocus Investment Fund*,[7] a factually complex case, laid out important ground rules regarding the discretion the court holds when deciding whether corporations will be allowed to indemnify their directors, the scope of that indemnity, and potential mitigating factors. The following points were made:

- A court should allow for indemnification to be provided on an ongoing basis where the corporation is solvent and where there is an absence of evidence showing that the former directors and officers failed to meet the criteria of having acted honestly and in good faith with a view to the best interests of the corporation and that they had reasonable grounds for believing that their conduct was lawful. If a failure to meet one of these criteria is later proven by evidence, the directors must repay the company.

- A mere allegation of bad faith or dishonesty in respect of a director or officer will not forfeit the right to indemnity since good faith is assumed in the absence of evidence to the contrary.

- The court may, in certain circumstances, impose a cap in respect of the amount of indemnity payments to be made to a director or officer.

---

6 *Catalyst Fund General Partners I Inc. v. Hollinger Inc.* (2006), 79 O.R. (3d) 288 (C.A.).

7 *Manitoba (Securities Commission) v. Crocus Investment Fund* (2006), 18 C.B.R. (5th) 143 (Man. Q.B.).

- The existence or non-existence of any insurance policy or the position of any insurer with respect to coverage is irrelevant to the question of entitlement to indemnification under a corporate by-law.

Finally, a corporation can only indemnify a director for fines in a criminal or administrative proceeding if the director had reasonable grounds for believing that the impugned conduct was lawful, and even then courts have experimented with the idea of prohibiting such indemnities as contrary to public policy. This issue arose in *R. v. Bata Industries Ltd.*,[8] a well-known environmental liability case. The *Bata Cases* involved charges against the company and three of its directors for the improper storage of solvents in barrels outside of a shoe factory. The directors, two of whom were convicted, were charged with failing to exercise reasonable care. The Ontario Court of Justice (Provincial Division) fined the two Bata directors $12,000 each, and the company itself was fined $120,000. As well, the company was ordered to not indemnify the directors for their fines. On appeal, the Ontario Court (General Division) reduced the fines but refused to remove the probation order that prevented Bata from indemnifying the directors for the fines against them. However, the Ontario Court of Appeal, while acknowledging the public policy argument that the punitive effect of a fine may be lost if the director is not forced to pay it, ruled that a probation order was not the correct means by which to prohibit the indemnification of Bata's directors. The Court of Appeal held that the corporate statutes, in this case the Ontario *Business Corporations Act*, contained appropriate limitations with respect to the indemnification of directors. Osborne J.A. stated:

> If Bata is to be prohibited from indemnifying Marchant and Weston, in my view, the prohibition should occur by virtue of s. 136, not by virtue of a probation order under the *Provincial Offences Act*. According to s. 136(1), indemnification is permitted if the directors acted honestly, in good faith and in the reasonable belief that their conduct was lawful. If Marchant and Weston failed to meet these requirements, the probation order is superfluous because Bata is prohibited from indemnifying them under s. 136(1). If they did act honestly, in good faith and in the reasonable belief that their conduct was lawful, the probation order contradicts the legislative scheme of the Ontario *Business Corporations Act*.[9]

---

[8] *R. v. Bata Industries Ltd.* (1992), 9 O.R. (3d) 329 (Prov. Ct.) ("*Bata One*"); fines reduced on appeal (1993), 14 O.R. (3d) 354 (Gen. Div.) ("*Bata Two*"); probation order preventing the indemnification of directors by the company removed on appeal (1995), 25 O.R. (3d) 321 (C.A.) ("*Bata Three*") (collectively, "*Bata Cases*").

[9] *Bata Three*, *ibid.* at para. 26.

A contractual indemnification form can be found at the end of this Chapter as Appendix I.[10]

II. Insurance

Corporate statutes permit corporations to purchase D&O insurance for the benefit of their directors and officers. Section 124(6) of the CBCA is typical:

> (6) A corporation may purchase and maintain insurance for the benefit of an individual referred to in subsection (1) against any liability incurred by the individual
>
> (*a*) in the individual's capacity as a director or officer of the corporation; or
>
> (*b*) in the individual's capacity as a director or officer, or similar capacity, of another entity, if the individual acts or acted in that capacity at the corporation's request.[11]

Until corporate scandals led to significant claims on D&O policies and to results that were sometimes surprising, directors paid little attention to their D&O coverage. If they asked about it at all, it was to inquire about whether the corporation had D&O insurance, what the upper limit of the insurance was, and what the deductible under it was. Directors seemed to assume that D&O insurance was a commodity in respect of which the terms and details of particular policies were both similar and irrelevant.

In much of the litigation that arose out of the biggest corporate scandals, directors learned that there was a great benefit in paying attention to the details of insurance policies. Directors found that their coverage was voided by the fraudulent activities (of which they were completely unaware) of corporate officers. They found that insurance limits could be used up in the defence of these corporate officers so that it was unavailable when the time came for the directors to defend themselves. They found that trustees in bankruptcy could claim the proceeds of insurance as corporate assets and thus deny or delay the claims of directors to the insurance proceeds that were intended to allow the directors to defend themselves in litigation or regulatory proceedings.

"Surprises" of this sort, coupled with increasing director liability and directors' recognition of that increasing liability, have required directors to

---

[10] Used with the permission of Andrea Wood, General Counsel, Alliance Atlantis Communications Inc.

[11] CBCA, *supra* note 2, s. 124(6).

become more familiar with the details of D&O insurance programs. An overview of D&O insurance programs, together with a discussion of some of the most important D&O program features, follows.

A. Key D&O Insurance Terms

An explanation of D&O insurance programs and features must begin with an explanation of simplified definitions of a variety of key D&O insurance terms:

- **Side A Coverage.** A typical director would assume that his or her D&O insurance provides this type of coverage. It represents a direct promise by the insurer to pay the director in respect of a specific loss. Side A coverage is represented schematically in the following diagram:

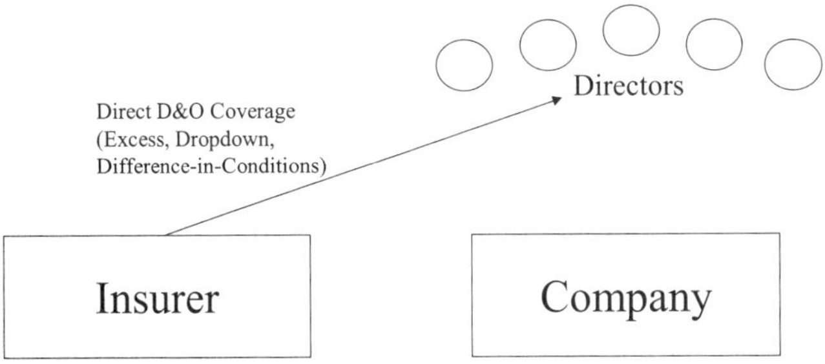

- **Side B Coverage.** Side B coverage represents the promise of the insurer to reimburse the company (typically above a deductible or "retention" amount) in respect of amounts that the company has paid on its statutory, by-law, or contractual indemnities of directors. Side B coverage is shown schematically as follows.

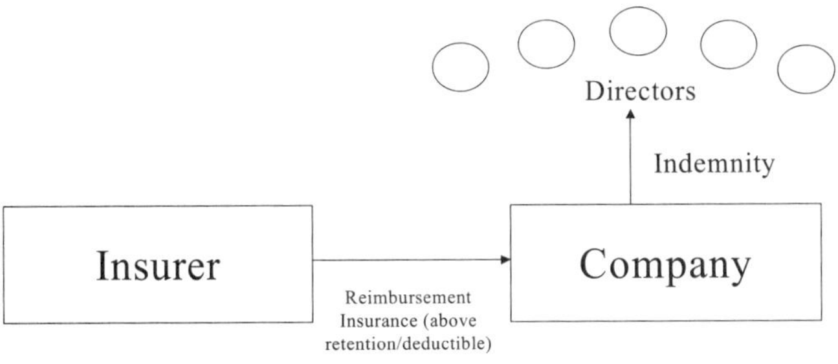

- **Side C Coverage**. Side C coverage is the promise of the insurer to indemnify the company itself in respect of securities claim liability. One might be excused for wondering why Side C coverage is considered to be D&O insurance. Side C coverage became a "throw-in" item at a point some time ago when D&O premiums were very high. At that time, the Side A and Side B coverage that was offered was restricted, and insurers were looking for a way to provide something that might be seen to be attractive to companies without really involving much insurer liability. As a result of the corporate scandals, Side C liability has become meaningful. Since the enactment of Bill 198 in Ontario (and the general relevance of that legislation to issuers in Canada), Side C coverage has increased in importance. Bill 198 (ss. 138.1–138.14 of the *Securities Act*)[12] provides for the unlimited liability of the corporation in many circumstances, and the inclusion of a Side C insured as part of an insurance pool with a Side A insured is, obviously, noteworthy. Side C coverage is represented schematically in the following diagram:

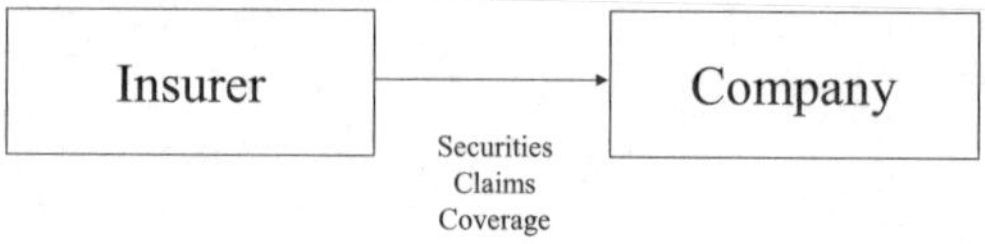

- **Primary Coverage.** Primary coverage refers to the first layer of insurance coverage. Typically, D&O insurance is in a "stack", with the primary insurer carrying the largest amount of coverage and having the most meaningful role in the directors' defence.

- **Excess Coverage.** Excess coverage refers to insurance that is above the primary insurance in the stack. Excess insurance may either "follow form", meaning that it is available simply as an additional amount on the same terms as those on which primary insurance proceeds are available, or it may be "drop-down" or "difference-in-conditions" coverage, meaning that the excess coverage will respond in circumstances in which the primary coverage might not.

- **Claims-Made Basis.** D&O insurance is typically written for a one-year period. It responds to claims that are made during the currency of the policy. Accordingly, if some corporate act occurs in year one but is not discovered and no claim is made until year two, the D&O insurer that is in place in year two will be responsible (if anyone is) for

[12] *Securities Act*, R.S.O. 1990, c. S.5, ss. 138.1–138.14 ("OSA").

responding to the loss rather than the insurer whose insurance was in place in year one (if that insurer is different from the year two insurer).

- **Run-off/Tail/Extended Reporting Period (ERP).** These are terms that refer to insurance that can be procured to deal with the fact that D&O insurance is written on a claims-made basis. For instance, an extended reporting period provides for an extended period of time, after a policy that has otherwise expired, during which a director may report a subsequently discovered claim and have the (now lapsed) policy respond in respect of that claim.
- **Rescission.** Rescission refers to the right of an insurer to declare a policy void on the basis of a misrepresentation in the insurance application. In recent years, the most common application of rescission (or threats of rescission) has been in the context of companies whose financial situation turns out to be significantly different from what was represented in the financial statements that were incorporated as part of the insurance application. Financial differences may arise from innocent acts that require restatements of financial information or from restatements required in consequence of the fraudulent activities of particular corporate officers. In the most extreme case, directors may find themselves without D&O coverage when they need it the most in consequence of the malfeasance (or alleged malfeasance) of corporate officers who set out to deceive them as well as the investing public.[13]
- **In Fact Determination/Final Adjudication.** Several provisions of insuring agreements require determinations that there is or is not coverage for a particular claimant or for a particular type of loss in the particular circumstances. These provisions can be drafted to allow the insurer to make a first instance determination (subject to a claimant's right to sue for a contrary result), to make a factual determination on some basis, or to agree to be bound by a final adjudication reached by a court or in an alternative dispute resolution process. For instance, insurance may be stated to be available to a broad group of insureds but with an ability to cease coverage of a so-called "black hat" (such as an executive within the class of insureds who

---

[13] In *Cutter & Buck, Inc. v. Genesis Ins. Co.*, 144 Fed. Appx. 600 (9th Cir. 2005) ("*Cutter*"), the United States Court of Appeals for the Ninth Circuit upheld a district court decision holding that the insurer's rescission of a corporation's D&O insurance policies was valid. The Ninth Circuit held that the district court had applied Washington law properly in interpreting the severability provision to impute to all directors and officers the misrepresentations knowingly made by the lone officer who had signed the application materials so that the insurer had a right to rescind the insurance policies. Regarding a Canadian corporation, Nortel, the insurer had threatened to rescind the insurance policy against all officers and directors but ultimately backed off and covered the innocent directors, rescinding against the allegedly-malfeasant management only.

perpetrated a purposeful fraud). It is in the interests of "white hats" (innocent insureds) that insurance limits not be "wasted" on black hats, who have (for instance) formally admitted their guilt. On the other hand, it is in the interests of all insureds that insurance proceeds (particularly for ongoing defence costs) be available at least until there is a formal admission or final finding that an insured should not be covered. There are a variety of approaches to the question of when coverage should cease and to the issue of how the determination should be made that an event has occurred that has caused the coverage to cease.

- **Severability.** Severability refers to provisions inserted into D&O coverage to prevent the actions or inactions of some insureds from affecting the insurance rights of other insureds. Carefully drafted severability provisions will ensure that even if the insurance coverage can be voided as against (for instance) executives who purposefully produced false financial information, the coverage cannot be voided as against directors who are unaware of the scheme.

- **Cancellation.** Cancellation refers to the right of the insurer to terminate the insurance policy without cause during the currency of the one-year policy period. Cancellation rights are often found in D&O policies, although many of them require thirty or sixty days' notice by the insurer. However, rights of this sort can be exercised at times that are the most inopportune: they can often be negotiated out of a particular insurance policy.

- **Insured vs. Insured Exclusion.** Most insurance coverage includes provisions that deny coverage when the claim involves one insured suing another (management against the directors, the directors against each other, the directors of the parent suing the directors of a subsidiary, etc.). Provisions of this sort are designed to prevent collusion between insureds, but they can operate in surprising ways from the perspective of those insureds. These exclusions can be modified in some primary coverage and can be restricted or eliminated completely in difference-in-conditions coverage.

- **Major Shareholder Exclusion.** Most insurance programs include provisions denying insurance coverage when the claims involved arise from a suit by a major (25 percent or even 10 percent) shareholder as plaintiff. These exclusions can be modified or eliminated by negotiation, but they can produce surprising results where they have not been addressed.

- **Loss.** This is a key term in most D&O programs, as insurance proceeds are typically available in respect of a "loss" that is suffered by an "insured". It is therefore important to understand what sorts of liabilities qualify as a "loss". For instance, punitive damages or regulatory or criminal penalties will not usually qualify. Similarly, defence costs may or may not qualify as "loss". Many insurance programs today will count as "loss" the costs of the investigation and the defence once a formal regulatory charge has been brought against a director. However, most programs will not cover the costs of informal investigations that are often significant and that continue for lengthy periods before formal charges are brought.

- **Priority of Payment.** Directors do not usually find themselves in trouble on their own. Claims against directors often arise in conjunction with claims against management or when the corporation is in financial difficulty or is insolvent. Accordingly, claims against D&O insurers can be made by the directors themselves, by management (which may include management that has been accused or found guilty of misconduct), and by trustees in bankruptcy (who may be seeking the proceeds of insurance as corporate assets in priority to the claim of directors). Priority issues can be complicated, but they can be addressed to provide clarity in the most likely situations if they are negotiated as part of the insurance procurement process.

With this background, issues regarding the kind of insurance to be obtained and the process for obtaining insurance of that sort can be addressed.

B. Types of Insurance Coverage

As will be apparent from the definitions above, insurance is not a commodity, and it is important for all parties affected by an insurance program to understand the coverage that is sought and ultimately obtained. Typically, insurance programs include Side A and Side B coverage and, in many cases (increasingly so), Side C coverage. Particularly in the context of a (typical) policy that includes a broad definition of "loss" and a broad definition of an "insured person", programs of this sort mean that directors are sharing their insurance limits with all of the other individuals and corporate insureds who might ultimately make a claim on the policy in the case of a corporate failure. This fact has implications for the limit of coverage that might be appropriate (a higher limit, given that people beyond just the directors might be claimants against the policy), but given the massive liabilities that have resulted in the cases of corporate fraud, it is probably likely that almost no limit that could be afforded (in premium cost) will be satisfactory from the directors' perspective.

This issue has been very much on directors' minds in Canada since the passage of Bill 198 in Ontario.[14] Accordingly, directors, corporations, and their advisors are now considering a variety of novel insurance programs to address the issue. At one extreme, corporations that are highly solvent may choose to forego Side C coverage entirely and self-insure in respect of securities claims (thus taking themselves out of the insurance pool that contains directors and the corporation only with respect to reimbursement of indemnity payments made to directors). As well, much innovative use is being made of Side A coverage, particularly Side A difference-in-conditions coverage. Policies that protect directors only eliminate others from the pool and avoid many of the issues that are associated with being lumped in with other insureds. Side A difference-in-conditions policies typically include strong severability language (to reflect the non-involvement of directors in the insurance application itself and in executive malfeasance that may occur subsequently) and eliminate or significantly pare back exclusions, such as the insured vs. insured or major shareholder exclusion that would otherwise apply with respect to typical primary Side A, B, or C coverage.

The various issues highlighted in the definitions above should all be addressed as part of the insurance procurement process. In this regard, it is important to note a long-standing practice in the industry. Insureds and insurers usually deal through insurance brokers in the procurement process. Various coverage plans are discussed and agreed upon in the course of the process and, ultimately, coverage is bound and a premium is paid. However, typically, the actual insurance policy documentation is not provided for weeks or even months after binding. Unfortunately, when claims are ultimately made and occasionally litigated, great attention is paid to the particular words of the policy, and slight variations can have very significant results.[15] It is, therefore, important for the various substantive points to be settled, in language that is provided, reviewed, and fully understood as being the binding insurance contract language before any insurance program is finally accepted.

There are many subsidiary, substantive points that may lead to discussion in the context of the procurement process. Such points range from questions regarding the conditions precedent to the insured bringing a suit on the policy to questions regarding what happens if a claim is brought

---

[14] OSA, *supra* note 12.

[15] In *Cutter, supra* note 13, the severability language was not broad enough to prevent the rescission of the contract against the innocent directors and officers. In the case of *In Re HealthSouth Corp. Ins. Litig.*, 308 F. Supp. (2d) 1253 at 1280 (N.D. Ala. 2004), the district court distinguished *Cutter*, in which the severability provision had provided that misrepresentations made with an actual intent to deceive or that were material would void the policy in its entirety and that material information known to the person who signed the application could be imputed to the other insureds. The court held that the severability language in HealthSouth's policy, by contrast, was effective in providing that the right of each insured to coverage was to be determined separately, so that rescission was permissible only on an individual basis.

against an insured person and an uninsured person or is brought in respect of an insured and uninsured loss (so-called "allocation" issues). Directors will benefit from the involvement of a knowledgeable and experienced insurance broker who is adequately independent and thus able to provide the advice that a variety of interested parties with somewhat differing interests may require. Many boards also seek independent legal advice on the substance of these issues and on the process issues that are discussed below.

The limits of coverage (and sub-limits that may apply with respect to particular types of losses, such as professional liability claims, pollution claims, and employment claims), the deductible amounts that may apply with respect to these claims, and the prices of the various types of coverage are all substantive matters for care and attention. Typically, types of coverage, limits, and deductibles are assessed by "benchmarking" to peers. This benchmarking may involve comparing the insurance programs that are offered against those disclosed in public documentation by companies of a similar size or by companies in the same industry, or it may involve a more sophisticated analysis using proprietary models. Given the complexities of Side A, Side B, and Side C coverage, great care must be taken in understanding what limits will be available to directors in which circumstances. Many issues about the identity of the insurer, including its solvency, its commitment to the sector, the location of its assets, and its reputation in claims settlement are also significant.

C. Insurance Procurement Process

The insurance procurement process used to be the private preserve of a risk or treasury officer or, in a smaller company, the CFO. Recently, directors have become much more interested in and involved in the process. There can be conflicts between the management's goal of keeping directors' insurance costs to a minimum and the directors' goal of ensuring that they are properly protected. The issues regarding inclusion or non-inclusion of particular officers, the definitions of loss, and the fundamental decisions about Side A, Side B, or Side C coverage are all issues in respect of which directors should, and now often do, want to have a voice.

The best process begins with the careful selection of a broker, typically after presentations have been made by several brokers, and with a consultation between management and the relevant board committee to settle the choice. The insurance broker should be selected with care on the basis of expertise, adequate independence, and value for money (brokers are paid on either a commission basis or, increasingly, a retainer with bonus basis). The broker, management, and board committee should then establish a "wish list" of insurance coverage points that they would like to procure in the initial insurance or renewal coverage process. The broker should then work with the insurers and management, involving the board committee as appropriate, to advance the discussions to the point at which a definitive program can be proposed by the broker and supported by management. That program, as it is ultimately supported by the relevant board committee, is then taken to the board for a final decision. Today, the broker is often requested to attend at the board meeting to discuss the process and the substantive elements of the program. There are tradeoffs and conflicts that must be understood by all of the parties affected.

It is also worth noting that a "self-help" protective mechanism, while not yet common, is being adopted and implemented by some companies. Such a mechanism is the creation of a segregated trust fund that is set aside with a trustee (other than the company), typically under the direction of a committee of the board or of certain named directors. The fund exists as a dedicated pool of money available to fund defence costs and awards against directors. The fund may be available generally for these purposes or it may be available only if corporate indemnity or insurance funds are not provided promptly following a request by a director. Funds of this sort (which are often seen in the context of companies at risk of insolvency) may be particularly helpful where a change of control is anticipated (where those with whom directors have been dealing to date may not be the same individuals as those with whom they will be dealing in the future). While there are a variety of complexities and judgments required in establishing this sort of "self-help insurance fund", it is permissible to do so, and it may be beneficial in certain circumstances.

III. Conclusion

Directors' and officers' indemnification insurance deserves careful attention. The nature and form of corporate indemnification should be addressed carefully. D&O insurance coverage is not a commodity but a complex product and service. Inherent conflicts influence the procurement process. Many provisions of a D&O policy can be negotiated, and careful attention should be paid to the ultimate contract terms. Policy wording matters, especially if disputes end in arbitration or litigation proceedings. Partners matter and they should include a quality insurance broker, carefully chosen insurers, and independent, expert legal advisors. It takes time for a process of the sort described above to be implemented. An insurance procurement process should allow enough time to permit the negotiations and deliberations that may be required. Directors may want to consider and implement self-help insurance arrangements in appropriate cases.

APPENDIX I

Indemnification Agreement[1]

THIS INDEMNIFICATION AGREEMENT (the "Agreement") is made as of this ______ day of ____________, 2005, between ALLIANCE ATLANTIS COMMUNICATIONS INC. (the "Corporation") and [Name] (the "Indemnified Party").

RECITALS:

A. The Board of Directors of the Corporation (the "Board") has determined that the Corporation should act to assure the Indemnified Party of reasonable protection through indemnification against certain risks arising out of service to, and activities on behalf of, the Corporation to the extent permitted by law.

NOW THEREFORE the parties agree as follows:

1. **Indemnification.** The Corporation will indemnify and save harmless the Indemnified Party and the heirs and legal representatives of the Indemnified Party to the fullest extent permitted by applicable law:

   1.1 from and against all Expenses (as defined below) sustained or incurred by the Indemnified Party in respect of any civil, criminal, administrative, investigative or other Proceeding (as defined below), whether or not brought by the Corporation, to which the Indemnified Party is made a party by reason of being or having been a director or officer of the Corporation; and

[1] Used by permission of Alliance Atlantis Communications Inc. and its general counsel, Andrea Wood.

1.2 from and against all Expenses sustained or incurred by the Indemnified Party as a result of serving as a director or officer of the Corporation in respect of any act, matter, deed or thing whatsoever made, done, committed, permitted or acquiesced in by the Indemnified Party as a director or officer of the Corporation, whether before or after the effective date of this Agreement and whether or not related to a Proceeding brought by the Corporation.

Subject to applicable law, this indemnity will apply without reduction regardless of whether the Indemnified Party committed any fault or omitted to do anything that the Indemnified Party ought to have done.

"**Expenses**" means all costs, charges, damages, awards, settlements, liabilities, fines, penalties, statutory obligations, professional fees and other expenses of whatever nature or kind, provided that any costs, expenses and professional fees included as Expenses hereunder shall be reasonable.

"**Proceeding**" will include a claim, demand, suit, proceeding, inquiry, hearing, discovery or investigation, of whatever nature or kind, whether anticipated, threatened, pending, commenced, continuing or completed, and any appeal or appeals therefrom.

The indemnities in this Agreement also apply to an Indemnified Party in respect of his or her service at the Corporation's request as (a) an officer or director of another corporation or (b) a similar role with another entity, including a partnership, trust, joint venture or other unincorporated entity.

2. **Presumptions/Knowledge**

2.1 For purposes of any determination hereunder, the Corporation will have the burden of establishing the absence of good faith on the part of the Indemnified Party and/or that the Indemnified Party did not act in the best interests of the Corporation. The termination of any civil, criminal, administrative, investigative or other proceeding by any judgment, order, settlement or conviction shall not, of itself, create a presumption either that the Indemnified Party did not act in good faith and/or in the best interests of the Corporation or that, in the case of a criminal or administrative action or proceeding that is enforced by a monetary penalty, the Indemnified Party did not have reasonable grounds for believing that the Indemnified Party's conduct was lawful.

2.2 The knowledge and/or actions, or failure to act, of any other director, officer, agent or employee of the Corporation or any other entity will not be imputed to the Indemnified Party for purposes of determining the right to indemnification under this Agreement.

2.3 The Corporation will have the burden of establishing that any Expense it wishes to challenge is not reasonable.

3. **Notice by Indemnified Party.** As soon as is practicable, upon the Indemnified Party becoming aware of any Proceeding which may give rise to indemnification under this Agreement (other than a Proceeding commenced by the Corporation), the Indemnified Party will give written notice to the Corporation. Failure to give notice in a timely fashion will not disentitle the Indemnified Party to indemnification.

4. **Investigation by Corporation.** The Corporation may conduct any investigation it considers appropriate of any Proceeding of which it receives notice under s. 3, and will pay all costs of that investigation. The Indemnified Party will, acting reasonably, co-operate fully with the investigation provided that the Indemnified Party will not be required to provide assistance that would materially prejudice his or her defence. The Indemnified Party will, for the period of time that he/she cooperates with the Corporation with respect to an investigation, be compensated by the Corporation at the rate of $2,000 (U.S.) per day (or partial day) plus reasonable out-of-pocket Expenses actually incurred provided that the Indemnified Party will not be entitled to the per diem if he/she is employed as an officer of the Corporation when co-operation is sought.

5. **Payment for Expenses of a Witness.** Notwithstanding any other provision of this Agreement, to the extent that the Indemnified Party is, by reason of the fact that the Indemnified Party is or was a director or officer of the Corporation or of another entity at the Corporation's request, a witness or participant other than as a named party in a Proceeding, the Corporation will pay to the Indemnified Party all out-of-pocket Expenses actually and reasonably incurred by the Indemnified Party or on the Indemnified Party's behalf in connection therewith. The Indemnified Party will also be compensated by the Corporation at the rate of $2,000 (U.S.) per day (or partial day) provided that the Indemnified Party will not be entitled to the per diem if he/she is employed as an officer of the Corporation when co-operation is sought.

6. **Expense Advances.** The Corporation will, upon request by the Indemnified Party, make advances ("Expense Advances") to the Indemnified Party of all amounts for which the Indemnified Party

seeks indemnification under this Agreement before the final disposition of the relevant Proceeding. Expense Advances may include anticipated Expenses. In connection with such requests, the Indemnified Party will provide the Corporation with a written affirmation of the Indemnified Party's good faith belief that the Indemnified Party is legally entitled to indemnification, along with sufficient particulars of the Expenses to be covered by the proposed Expense Advance to enable the Corporation to make an assessment of its reasonableness. The Indemnified Party's entitlement to such Expense Advance will include those Expenses incurred in connection with any Proceeding by the Indemnified Party against the Corporation seeking an adjudication or award pursuant to this Agreement. The Corporation will make payment to the Indemnified Party within 20 days after the Corporation has received the foregoing information from the Indemnified Party. All Expenses for which indemnification is sought must be reasonable and Expense Advances must relate to Expenses anticipated within a reasonable time of the request.

The Indemnified Party will repay to the Corporation all Expense Advances not actually required, and all Expense Advances if and to the extent that it is determined by a court of competent jurisdiction that the Indemnified Party is not entitled to indemnification under this Agreement.

7. **Indemnification Payments.** With the exception of Expense Advances which are governed by s. 6, the Corporation will pay to the Indemnified Party any amounts to which the Indemnified Party is entitled hereunder promptly upon the Indemnified Party providing the Corporation with reasonable details of the claim.

8. **Right to Independent Legal Counsel.** If the Indemnified Party is named as a party or a witness to any Proceeding, the Indemnified Party will be entitled to retain independent legal counsel at the Corporation's expense to act on the Indemnified Party's behalf to provide an initial assessment to the Indemnified Party of the appropriate course of action for the Indemnified Party. The Indemnified Party will be entitled to continued representation by independent counsel at the Corporation's expense beyond the initial assessment unless the parties agree that there is no conflict of interest between the Corporation and the Indemnified Party that necessitates independent representation. A conflict of interest will be deemed to exist if the Indemnified Party reasonably believes that his or her

legal position or reputation could be adversely affected without independent representation.

9. **Settlement.** The parties will act reasonably in pursuing the settlement of any Proceeding. The Corporation may not negotiate or effect a settlement of claims against the Indemnified Party without the consent of the Indemnified Party, acting reasonably. The Indemnified Party may negotiate and effect a settlement without the consent of the Corporation but the Corporation will not be liable for any settlement negotiated without its prior written consent.

10. **Directors' & Officers' Insurance.** The Corporation will ensure that its liabilities under this Agreement are at all times supported by a directors' and officers' liability insurance policy that has been approved by the Board. The Corporation will provide to the Indemnified Party a copy of each policy of insurance providing the coverages contemplated by this section promptly after coverage is obtained, and will promptly notify the Indemnified Party if the insurer cancels, makes material changes to coverage or refuses to renew coverage (or any part of the coverage).

11. **Arbitration.** All disputes, disagreements, controversies or claims arising out of or relating to this Agreement, including, without limitation, with respect to its formation, execution, validity, application, interpretation, performance, breach, termination or enforcement will be determined by arbitration before a single arbitrator under the *Arbitration Act*, 1991 (Ontario).

12. **Tax Adjustment.** Should any payment made pursuant to this Agreement, including the payment of insurance premiums or any payment made by an insurer under an insurance policy, be deemed to constitute a taxable benefit or otherwise be or become subject to any tax or levy, then the Corporation will pay any amount necessary to ensure that the amount received by or on behalf of the Indemnified Party, after the payment of or withholding for tax, fully reimburses the Indemnified Party for the actual cost, expense or liability incurred by or on behalf of the Indemnified Party.

13. **Cost of Living Adjustment.** The $2,000 (U.S.) per diem payable pursuant to ss. 4 and 5 will be adjusted to reflect changes from January 1, 2006 in the All-items Cost of Living Index for Toronto prepared by Statistics Canada or any successor index or government agency.

14. **Governing Law.** This Agreement will be governed by the laws of the Province of Ontario and the federal laws of Canada applicable therein.

15. **Survival.** The obligations of the Corporation under this Agreement, other than s. 10, will continue until the later of (a) 15 years after the Indemnified Party ceases to be a director or officer of the Corporation or any other entity in which he or she serves in a similar capacity at the request of the Corporation and (b) one year after the final termination of all Proceedings with respect to which the Indemnified Party is entitled to claim indemnification hereunder. The obligations of the Corporation under s. 10 of this Agreement will continue for 6 years after the Indemnified Party ceases to be a director or officer of the Corporation or any other entity in which he or she serves in a similar capacity at the request of the Corporation.

IN WITNESS WHEREOF the parties hereto have executed this Agreement.

ALLIANCE ATLANTIS
COMMUNICATIONS INC.

by: ______________________

______________________ l/s
[Name]

____
Witness

____
Witness Name

TABLE OF CASES

SELECTED BIBLIOGRAPHY

Articles

Farrell, Sean and Robert McDermott, "Corporate Governance in Canada" (2004), online: McMillan Binch Mendelsohn LLP <http://www.mbmlex.com/AboutUs.aspx?Section1=AboutUS&Section2=Publication>.

Leon, Jeffery S. & Sarah J. Armstrong, "Business Judgment and Defensive Decision-Making: Directors' and Officers' Duties and Responsibilities after *Peoples*" (2006), online: Fasken Martineau DuMoulin LLP <http://www.fasken.com/WEB/FMDWEBSITEFRENCH.NSF/%20AllDoc/9CEC3B5E302BFD9785257129005CEF56/$File/BUSINESSJUDGMENT.PDF>.

Medland, Christina, "Getting It Right: Proper Compensation Governance Meets Business Objectives and Keeps Directors Out of Trouble" *A Director's Guide to Executive Compensation* 1 (February 2006), online: Torys LLP <http://www.torys.com/publications/pdf/AR2006-6T.pdf>.

Milnes, Robert E., "Directors' and Officers' Duties and Liabilities" (April 2005), online: Gowling Lafleur Henderson LLP <http://www.gowlings.com/resources/PublicationPDFs/MilnesR_DirectorsMemo06.pdf>.

Reiter, Barry J., "A Director's Guide to Corporate Risk Management: Implementing a Comprehensive Strategy" (2004) 11 Corporate Financing No. 2.

Reiter, Barry J., "Building a Great Board of Directors — a Committed and Sustained Process" (2003) *Corporate Governance Journal*, 114.

Reiter, Barry J., "Compensation Concerns" (October 2004), online: CMA Management <http://www.managementmag.com/index.cfm/ci_id/2008/la_id/1>.

Reiter, Barry J., "The Role and Value of an Effective Advisory Board" (September 2003), 68 Ivey Business Journal (Online) No. 1, online: Ivey Business Journal <http://www.iveybusinessjournal.com/view_article.asp?intArticle_ID=440>.

Reiter, Barry J., "The Role of Compensation Committees in Corporate Governance" (2004) *Corporate Governance Journal*, 126.

Reiter, Barry J., "Updating Corporate Governance Processes" *Lexpert* 6 (May 2005) 110.

Reiter, Barry J., "When Directors Should Get Worried" *Torys LLP Corporate Governance Review* (August/September 2004).

Reiter, Barry J. and Aaron Emes, "Corporate Governance: The Audit Committee" *Lexpert* 6:8 (June 2005) 105.

Reiter, Barry J. and Aaron Emes, "Corporate Governance: Managing the Risk" *Lexpert* 7:2 (November 2005) 124.

Reiter, Barry J. and Aaron Emes, "Corporate Governance: The Role of In-House Counsel" *Lexpert* 6:10 (September 2005) 125.

Reiter, Barry J. and Aaron Emes, "Director Compensation: Making Difficult Decisions" *Lexpert* 7:9 (July 2006).

Reiter, Barry J. and Aaron Emes, "Protecting Yourself" *Lexpert* 7:6 (April 2006) 108.

Reiter, Barry J. and Aaron Emes, "Protecting Yourself Using Directors' and Officers' Insurance — Part 1" *Lexpert* 7:7 (May 2006) 98.

Reiter, Barry J. and Aaron Emes, "Protecting Yourself Using Directors' and Officers' Insurance — Part 2" *Lexpert* 7:8 (June 2006) 104.

Reiter, Barry J. and Aaron Emes, "Risky Business" *Lexpert* 7:1 (October 2005) 109.

Reiter, Barry J. and Aaron Emes, "The Compensation Committee" *Lexpert* 6:9 (July/August 2005) 108.

Reiter, Barry J. and Jim Turner, "Board Evaluations: Establishing an Effective Process" *Lexpert* 7:5 (March 2006) 109.

Reiter, Barry J., Jim Turner, and Aaron Emes, "Civil Liability For Continuous Disclosure Violations" *Lexpert* 7:3 (January 2006) 123.

Reiter, Barry J., Jim Turner, and Aaron Emes, "Civil Liability For Continuous Disclosure Violations: Part 2" *Lexpert* 7:4 (February 2006) 108.

Reiter, Barry J. and Nicole Rosenberg, "Meeting the Information Needs of Independent Directors" (January 2003), 67 Ivey Business J. (Online) No. 3, online: Ivey Business Journal <http://www. iveybusinessjournal.com/view_article.asp? intArticle_ID=399#search=%22%22meeting%20the%20information%20needs%20of%20independent%20directors%22%22>.

Books

Daniels, Ronald J. and Morck, Randall, eds., *Corporate Decision-Making in Canada* (Calgary: University of Calgary Press, 1995).

Elliot, Jon F. (Con. Ed.), *Directors' and Officers' Liability in Canada*, looseleaf (North Vancouver, STP Specialty Technical Publishers, n.d.).

Hansell, Carol, *Directors and Officers in Canada — Law and Practice*, looseleaf (Scarborough, Ont: Carswell Publishing, n.d.).

Hansell, Carol, *What Directors Need to Know: Corporate Governance* (Toronto: Carswell, 2003).

Nathan, Hartley, ed., *The Directors Manual*, looseleaf (Don Mills, Ont.: CCH Canadian Ltd., n.d.).

Puri, P. and Larsen, J., ed., *Corporate Governance and Securities Regulation in the 21st Century* (Markham, Ont.: LexisNexis Butterworths, 2004).

Law Firm Publications

Osler, Hoskin & Harcourt LLP, *Corporate Governance in Canada: A Guide to the Responsibilities of Corporate Directors in Canada*, 4th ed. (September 2005), online: Osler, Hoskin & Harcourt LLP <http://www.osler.com/uploadedFiles/Osler_Hoskin_Harcourt_Corporate_Governance_Guide_2005.pdf>.

Stikeman Elliott LLP, *Duties and Liabilities of Canadian Directors and Officers* (N.p.: Stikeman Elliot LLP, 2005).

Stikeman Elliott LLP, *What Canadian Directors & Officers Need to Know* (N.p.: Stikeman Elliott LLP, 2006).

Torys LLP, *Responsibilities of Directors in Canada: A Business Law Guide* (N.p.: Torys LLP, 2005).

Legislative and Regulatory Materials

Canadian Coalition for Good Governance, *Corporate Governance Guidelines for Building High Performance Boards*, Version 1.0 (November 2005), online: Canadian Coalition for Good Governance, <http://www.ccgg.ca/media/files/CCGG%20Guidelines%20v1%20%2D%20November%202005.pdf>.

Institutional Shareholder Services, *ISS 2006 US Proxy Voting Guidelines Summary*, 2005, online: Institutional Shareholder Services, <http://www.issproxy.com/pdf/US2006Summary Guidelines.pdf>.

Multilateral Instrument 52-110, *Audit Committees*.

National Instrument 58-101, *Disclosure of Corporate Governance Policies*.

National Policy 58-201, *Corporate Governance Guidelines*.

New York Stock Exchange Inc., *The New York Stock Exchange Listed Company Manual*, looseleaf (New York, NY: New York Stock Exchange, n.d.).

Ontario Municipal Employees Retirement System, *Proxy Voting Guidelines* (April 2005), online: OMERS, <http://www.omers.com/userfiles/page_attachments/Library/1/pvg_3542832.pdf>.

Ontario Teachers' Pension Plan, *Good Governance is Good Business: Corporate Governance Policies and Proxy Voting Guidelines* (2006) online: Ontario Teachers' Pension Plan, <http://www.otpp.com/web/website.nsf/web/cg_guidelines2006/$FILE/TeachersCorpGovE.pdf>.

Organisation of Economic Co-operation and Development, *Principles of Corporate Governance* (2004), online: OECD, <http://www.oecd.org/document/49/0,2340,en_2649_34813_31530865_1_1_1_1,00.html>.

Toronto Stock Exchange, *The Toronto Stock Exchange Company Manual*, looseleaf (North York, Ont.: CCH Canadian Limited, 1997).

TOPICAL INDEX